Number 289

J.-P. Eckmann, H. Koch
and P. Wittwer

A computer-assisted proof of universality for area-preserving maps

Memoirs
of the American Mathematical Society

Providence · Rhode Island · USA

January 1984 · Volume 47 · Number 289 (first of six numbers) · ISSN 0065-9266

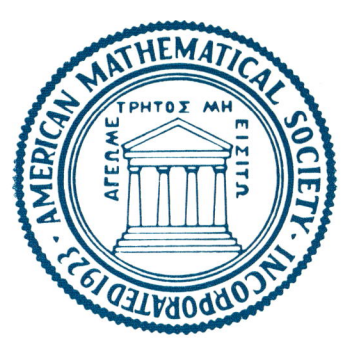

Memoirs of the American Mathematical Society

Number 289

J.-P. Eckmann, H. Koch
and P. Wittwer

A computer-assisted proof of universality for area-preserving maps

Published by the
AMERICAN MATHEMATICAL SOCIETY
Providence, Rhode Island, USA

January 1984 · Volume 47 · Number 289 (first of six numbers)

MEMOIRS of the American Mathematical Society

This journal is designed particularly for long research papers (and groups of cognate papers) in pure and applied mathematics. It includes, in general, longer papers than those in the TRANSACTIONS.

Mathematical papers intended for publication in the Memoirs should be addressed to one of the editors. Subjects, and the editors associated with them, follow:

Ordinary differential equations, partial differential equations and applied mathematics to JOEL A. SMOLLER, Department of Mathematics, University of Michigan, Ann Arbor, MI 48109.

Complex and harmonic analysis to LINDA PREISS ROTHSCHILD, Department of Mathematics, University of California at San Diego, LaJolla, CA 92093

Abstract analysis to WILLIAM B. JOHNSON, Department of Mathematics, Ohio State University, Columbus, OH 43210

Algebra, algebraic geometry and number theory to LANCE W. SMALL, Department of Mathematics, University of California at San Diego, LaJolla, CA 92093

Logic, set theory and general topology to KENNETH KUNEN, Department of Mathematics, University of Wisconsin, Madison, WI 53706

Topology to WALTER D. NEUMANN, Department of Mathematics, University of Maryland, College Park, MD 20742

Global analysis and differential geometry to TILLA KLOTZ MILNOR, Department of Mathematics, University of Maryland, College Park, MD 20742

Probability and statistics to DONALD L. BURKHOLDER, Department of Mathematics, University of Illinois, Urbana, IL 61801

Combinatorics and number theory to RONALD GRAHAM, Mathematical Studies Department, Bell Laboratories, Murray Hill, NJ 07974

All other communications to the editors should be addressed to the Managing Editor, R. O. WELLS, JR., Department of Mathematics, University of Colorado, Boulder, CO 80309

MEMOIRS are printed by photo-offset from camera-ready copy fully prepared by the authors. Prospective authors are encouraged to request booklet giving detailed instructions regarding reproduction copy. Write to Editorial Office, American Mathematical Society, P. O. Box 6248, Providence, Rhode Island 02940. For general instructions, see last page of Memoir.

SUBSCRIPTION INFORMATION. The 1984 subscription begins with Number 289 and consists of six mailings, each containing one or more numbers. Subscription prices for 1984 are $148 list; $74 member. A late charge of 10% of the subscription price will be imposed upon orders received from nonmembers after January 1 of the subscription year. Subscribers outside the United States and India must pay a postage surcharge of $10; subscribers in India must pay a postage surcharge of $15. Each number may be ordered separately; *please specify number* when ordering an individual number. For prices and titles of recently released numbers, refer to the New Publications sections of the NOTICES of the American Mathematical Society.

BACK NUMBER INFORMATION. For back issues see the AMS Catalogue of Publications.

TRANSACTIONS of the American Mathematical Society

This journal consists of shorter tracts which are of the same general character as the papers published in the MEMOIRS. The editorial committee is identical with that for the MEMOIRS so that papers intended for publication in this series should be addressed to one of the editors listed above.

Subscriptions and orders for publications of the American Mathematical Society should be addressed to American Mathematical Society, P. O. Box 1571, Annex Station, Providence, R. I. 02901. *All orders must be accompanied by payment.* Other correspondence should be addressed to P. O. Box 6248, Providence, R. I. 02940.

MEMOIRS of the American Mathematical Society (ISSN 0065-9266) is published bimonthly (each volume consisting usually of more than one number) by the American Mathematical Society at 201 Charles Street, Providence, Rhode Island 02904. Second Class postage paid at Providence, Rhode Island 02940. Postmaster: Send address changes to Memoirs of the American Mathematical Society, American Mathematical Society, P. O. Box 6248, Providence, RI 02940.

TABLE OF CONTENTS

ABSTRACT

We study iterates of area-preserving maps as the simplest examples of conservative dynamical systems. In one-parameter families $\alpha \to \psi_\alpha$ of such maps one observes numerically sequences of period doubling bifurcations : at parameter values α_k elliptic periodic orbits of length 2^k become hyperbolic and give rise to the existence of elliptic periodic orbits of length 2^{k+1}. Apparently, these parameter values α_k accumulate at some finite α_∞, and in addition the limit $\lim_{k\to\infty}(\alpha_{k-1} - \alpha_k)/(\alpha_k - \alpha_{k+1})$ not only exists but is to a large extent independent of the one-parameter family, and equal to $\delta = 8.721...$.

It can be shown that this phenomenon follows from the existence of a fixed point ϕ^* for the non-linear transformation on (some) area-preserving maps

$$N : \psi \to \Lambda_\psi^{-1} \circ\psi\circ\psi\circ\Lambda_\psi ,$$

with Λ_ψ a ψ-dependent coordinate transformation. Furthermore, δ is identified with the (only) unstable eigenvalue of DN at ϕ^*.

The bulk of this paper is devoted to a proof of the existence of a fixed point for the above problem, when formulated in terms of generating functions. This problem will be reduced to showing that a suitable operator M is a contraction on a ball of functions in a Banach space. This ball is centered at a polynomial P. It turns out that, in order to prove that M is a contraction on this ball, the polynomial P has to be chosen of high degree, and the estimates needed to verify the necessary bounds are clearly beyond the computational powers of human beings.

We therefore perform these estimates on a computer. This approach has been put into practice by Lanford [5] in a pioneering paper on a similar, but easier, problem. We document in detail the algorithms needed to prove that M is a contraction. These algorithms take into account the rounding errors of digital computers, and can be applied to other problems in functional analysis as well. The present paper contains the proofs concerning this method, as well as a program printout, showing that estimates on a computer provide proofs of theorems in the sense usually understood by mathematicians.

1980 Mathematics Subject Classification 58F05, 65G99.

Keywords : - Dynamical systems

- Period-doubling universality

- Rigorous error-analysis

Library of Congress Cataloging in Publication Data

Eckmann, Jean Pierre.
A computer-assisted proof of universality for area-preserving maps.

(Memoirs of the American Mathematical Society, ISSN 0065-9266 ; no. 289 (Jan. 1984))
Bibliography: p.
1. Hamiltonian systems--Data processing. 2. Mappings (Mathematics)--Data processing. 3. Errors, Theory of--Data processing. I. Koch, H. (Hans) II. Wittwer, P. (Peter) III. Title. IV. Series: Memoirs of the American Mathematical Society ; no. 289.
QA3.A57 no. 289 [QA614.83] 510s [514'.7] 83-22456
ISBN 0-8218-2289-6

ACKNOWLEDGEMENT

This work has been supported by the Fonds National Suisse and by NSF Grant PHY79-16812. Part of this work has been supported by the IHES, Bûres-sur-Yvette. We wish to thank the Département de la Matière Condensée (Geneva) for placing generously its computer facilities at our disposal.

INTRODUCTION

Consider a topological space M and a continuous mapping T of M into itself. This setup is called a (discrete) dynamical system when the orbits of points of M under iterations of T are studied. Of special interest to our paper is the study of one-parameter families $\alpha \to T_\alpha$ of such dynamical systems, acting on a fixed space M. One much-studied example is the one-parameter family $T_\alpha : M \to M$,

$$T_\alpha(x) = 1 - \alpha x^2$$

which, for $0 \leq \alpha \leq 2$, maps $M = [-1,1] \subset \mathbb{R}$ into itself. In this, and similar examples, what is interesting is not so much the behavior of any particular mapping, but rather the way this behavior changes with α. For the example at hand, one can find values of the parameter for which 0 is a periodic point of period 2^n. Denote the smallest such value by α_n. By investigating numerically a number of one-parameter families, Feigenbaum [8] discovered a striking universality property : The α_n converge to a value α_∞, and for large j, $\alpha_\infty - \alpha_j$ is asymptotic to

$$\text{const.} \cdot \delta_F^{-j} ,$$

where $\delta_F = 4.66920...$ <u>is apparently the same whatever one-parameter family is considered</u>. (Note that, encouragingly, this property of the α_n's is not changed by making a differentiable change of parameter with deriva-

Received by the editor 17 May 1982

tive which does not vanish at α_∞.)

This universality can be understood by a study of the doubling operator. In the case of maps of the interval, this operator, $\mathcal{T}$, is defined for functions f for which $f(1) < 0$, by

$$\mathcal{T}f = \Lambda_f^{-1} \circ f \circ f \circ \Lambda_f ,$$

where $\Lambda_f(x) = f(1)x$. In other terms, the doubling operator is composition, modulo a coordinate transformation. Two important facts about $\mathcal{T}$ are [1,2]: First, $\mathcal{T}$ has a fixed point φ^*, close to the function $1 - 1.4x^2$, and in particular of the same qualitative shape. Second, the fixed point φ^* is hyperbolic, i.e. the spectrum of $D\mathcal{T}$ at φ^* consists of a simple isolated eigenvalue $\delta_F > 1$ and a remainder strictly inside the unit disk (in a suitable Banach space). A theory [1], which we shall partially retrace below, ties up this eigenvalue δ_F with the convergence rate.

Subsequent developments of this theory have included classes of volume-contracting maps on $\mathbb{R}^m$, $m > 1$ [3], with findings similar to those for the one-dimensional dynamical systems. More recently, numerical experiments [4] have indicated that another universal constant δ, $\delta \sim 8.721...$, occurs in the context of area-preserving maps of the plane. The purpose of this paper is to show the existence of a fixed point for a doubling transformation $\mathcal{N}$ in a class of area-preserving maps of the plane, and to study the universality for one-parameter families of certain area-preserving maps near this fixed point.

This existence proof is surprisingly hard, and it has already been hard in the context of maps on an interval [5,6], except for a special limiting case [1]. The reasons for the absence of a really elegant method of proof have not yet been found. In fact, attempts to use the more abstract machinery of index theorems and the like have not been successful. Thus, all existing proofs, (except, in parts, the one of Ref. [6]), as well as the one we are going to present here for the area-preserving case consist essentially of the following steps.

1. Transform the problem into a manageable form by a suitable coordinate transformation in function space.
2. Find a good approximate fixed point.
3. Show that the contraction mapping principle can be applied on a suitable ball around the approximate fixed point.

The numerical experiments seem to indicate that the ball in point 3 can be chosen quite large and that the approximate fixed point need only be very crudely known. The proofs, however, require much more precision, and a very small ball must be chosen. In particular, the approximate fixed point has to be given in the form of a polynomial of high degree, and the estimates become so involved that they can only be done with the help of a computer.

This approach of functional analytical problems is feasible, as has been shown in Lanford's beautiful proof [5] for the case of maps of the interval. Since this approach is somewhat novel on conceptual grounds, we intend to

1. discuss the conceptual problems of computer assisted proofs,
2. document in detail the computer program used for solving the problem at hand.

Obviously, our method has potential applications to many other problems in functional analysis. We have therefore made an effort to do as much of the analysis in a way which is independent of the problem of period-doubling. In particular, Part II and the program corresponding to it are independent of the remainder of the paper.

What do we mean by a computer assisted proof ? In the first place, we wish to stress that in contrast to a sizeable part of the computational mathematics literature, and in particular the jargon of physics, the word proof is here to be understood in its traditional mathematical meaning. A second distinction should be made with respect to some of the numerical mathematics literature, where some of the algorithms use idealized computers, which are supposed to be capable to compute correctly with real numbers. (We do not use any of the devices which use rational arithmetics and which are exorbitant in computer time, and computer memory space.) Rather, we shall show that a suitable ring of functions can be found within which all operations have a counterpart on the computer leading to rigorous bounds. (A trivial statement of this kind is the following : If the supremum of two functions is known, then the pointwise product of the two functions is bounded by the product of their suprema.) Roundoff errors of the computer will be taken into account in devising the algorithms. This will show that rigorous bounds in Banach spaces are possible on a computer, can be documented, and lead to proofs in functional analysis.

We believe that the traditional mathematics education might still leave one or the other of the readers in some state of doubt about the conceptual validity of the principle of computer assisted proofs. We shall show in Part II that the method itself is totally rigorous from a mathematical point of view. If there are any doubts, we think they would be on another level, namely the reliability of the computer itself. We discuss some of these problems and their solution now.

1. Hardware reliability : Usually, computer manufacturers give specifications of machine operations. We have to know what the computer means by the sum, product,... of two "real numbers". It is our feeling that these specifications can be trusted, because deviations would be noticed by many users, and because special attention and long experience of computer manufacturers go into this aspect of computing.
2. Operating system reliability : These are questions of the possible interferences between several users on large computers, leading to incomplete termination of operations, memory allocation and the like. Such errors occur sporadically, and can be eliminated by redoing the calculation several times or changing machines.
3. Software : Programming makes use of some high-level languages (Fortran in our case). These high-level languages sometimes have definitions which are sophisticated or whose implementation is ambiguous, or which may be manufacturer-dependent. We avoid these difficulties by systematically writing a very <u>unsophisticated code</u>, which uses none of the efficient, but possibly incorrectly implemented features.

We are thus convinced that <u>computer-assisted proofs have the same degree of reliability and checkability by fellow mathematicians as any of the more complex and lengthy hand-written proofs in mathematics</u>.

Our paper is written in three parts. In Part I, we consider the problem of period doubling for area-preserving maps of the plane, and give all those parts of the proofs which can be done without a computer. The necessary estimates are given in the form of theorems which have been verified by our program. Part II is a selfcontained exposition of interval arithmetics and of functional analysis on balls in function space. We also discuss rounding. In Part III, we complete the proofs of the estimates needed in Part I by presenting the computer program and its output.

PART I. ANALYSIS OF DOUBLING

I.1. FEIGENBAUM UNIVERSALITY FOR AREA-PRESERVING MAPS

In the following we describe the findings of a numerical study [4] of the one parameter family of maps of the 2-torus into itself :

$$\psi_\alpha(x,y) = \begin{pmatrix} x + y & \mod 1 \\ y + \alpha f(x+y) & \mod 1 \end{pmatrix}$$

with $f(z) = \cos^2 \Pi z$. A detailed analysis has already been given in [7]. The numerical facts are the following : There is a sequence $\alpha_o, \alpha_1, \ldots$ of parameter values, apparently accumulating at some value α_∞, such that for $\alpha \in (\alpha_k, \alpha_{k+1})$, ψ_α has an elliptic periodic orbit of period 2^{k+1}; at α_{k+1} this orbit becomes hyperbolic, but a new elliptic periodic orbit of period 2^{k+2} forms around it, when α passes beyond α_{k+1}. It is observed that

M1) $\displaystyle\lim_{k\to"\infty"} (\alpha_k - \alpha_{k-1})/(\alpha_{k+1} - \alpha_k) = \delta_o = 8.721\ldots$,

and

M2) $\displaystyle\lim_{k\to"\infty"} d_k/d_{k+1} = -1/\lambda_o = 4.018\ldots$,

where d_k is the maximal distance among the differences

$$\psi^{2^k+n}_{\alpha_{k+1}}(x) - \psi^n_{\alpha_{k+1}}(x),\ n = 0,1,\ldots,2^k$$

and x is on the periodic orbit of period 2^{k+1}. More precisely, what is measured in [4] is the following :

MEASUREMENT 1. "Local" measurement. Consider the intervals (α_k, α_{k+1}) described above. To each value $\beta\in(\alpha_k,\alpha_{k+1})$, there is an elliptic periodic orbit of period 2^{k+1}, and each point of this orbit is a fixed point of $\psi^{2^{k+1}}$. We denote by $r_k(\beta)$ the rotation number of this fixed point. The function $r_k(\beta)$ appears to be invertible and we define $\beta_k(r)$ to be its inverse function : $r_k(\beta_k(r)) = r$. Next one fixes r, determines $\beta_k(r)$ and considers the asymptotic ratio ρ_k of the axes of the invariant ellipses (as the radius tends to zero) at a predetermined fixed point z_k of $\psi^{2^{k+1}}_{\beta_k(r)}$. Alternatively, this can be defined as follows : Denote $M_k = D\psi^{2^{k+1}}_{\beta_k(r)}(z_k)$ and define H_k such that $M_k = H_k R(r) H_k^{-1}$, where $R(r)$ is the rotation with rotation number r and H_k is symmetric. Then ρ_k is the ratio of the eigenvalues of H_k.

MEASUREMENT 2. "Global" measurement. For the β_k defined as above, the vectors $t_k = z_k^1 - z_k$ are considered, where z_k is a hyperbolic periodic point of period 2^k and z_k is the farther of the two elliptic periodic points of period 2^{k+1} formed by bifurcation from z_{k-1} when $\alpha = \alpha_k$. Also z_k issued from z_{k-1} when $\alpha = \alpha_k$. The components of t_k are then measured

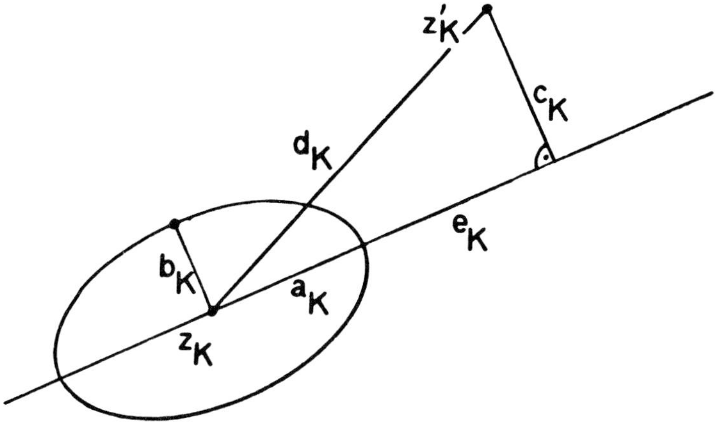

Fig. 1. Geometry of the measurements. An elliptic point z_k and the hyperbolic point z'_k, issued from z_{k-1} at $\alpha = \alpha_k$.

with respect to the axes of the invariant ellipses described in Measurement 1.

Besides M1, M2 one can therefore measure, in addition, cf. the Figure 1 :

M3) Define $\rho_k := b_k/a_k$. Then $\rho_k/\rho_{k+1} \to 4.0726...$,

M4) $c_k/c_{k+1} \to 16.145... = (4.018...)^2$.

It has been shown that phenomena of this kind can be explained under the following circumstances [1, Section 6]. One considers a non-linear map N, acting on a space $\mathcal{E}$ of transformations of $\mathbb{R}^2$ into itself

$$N : \phi \to \Lambda_\phi^{-1} \circ \phi \circ \phi \circ \Lambda_\phi ,$$

with Λ_ϕ a (non-linear) invertible coordinate transformation. It is assumed that N satisfies

1) N has a fixed point ϕ^* in $\mathcal{E}$, $N\phi^* = \phi^*$, and N is twice continuously differentiable.

2) If DN_{ϕ^*} denotes the Frêchet derivative of N at ϕ^*, then this linear operator has an isolated simple eigenvalue not in the unit disk; we shall call it δ. Furthermore, the remainder of the spectrum of DN_{ϕ^*} lies strictly inside the unit disk.

It then follows from invariant manifold theory that N admits a stable manifold W_s of codimension one and a unstable manifold W_u of dimension one. We also give ourselves two further objects :

- A submanifold Σ_o of $\mathcal{E}$ of codimension one which intersects W_u transversally at some point $\psi^* \neq \phi^*$.
- A continuously differentiable parameterized curve $\beta \to \psi_\beta$ in $\mathcal{E}$ which crosses the stable manifold W_s at $\beta = \beta_\infty$ with non-zero transverse velocity. Cf. Fig. 2.

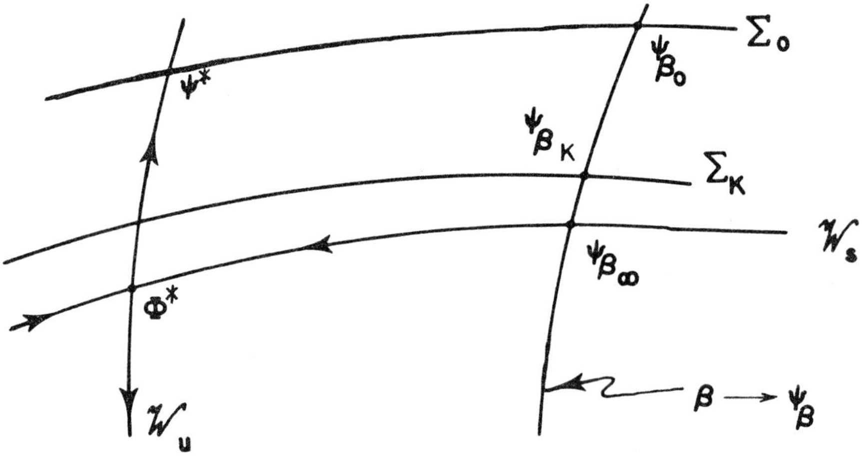

Fig. 2. The fixed point ϕ^* for N and its stable and unstable manifolds.

Here, Σ_k is, for fixed rotation number r, defined as the set of area-preserving maps with an elliptic orbit of period 2^{k+1} and rotation number r at this orbit. Then β_k is defined by the condition $\psi_{\beta_k} \in \Sigma_k$, or equivalently $N^k(\psi_{\beta_k}) \in \Sigma_o$. We assume the necessary regularity and transversality properties which are needed to make Fig. 2 correct near ϕ^* and W_u. Accordingly we only consider one parameter families $\beta \rightarrow \psi_\beta$ of area-preserving maps which cross the stable manifold W_s transversally near ϕ^*. From this set-up one concludes :

a) Every such one-parameter family $\beta \rightarrow \psi_\beta$ passing through W_u near $\phi^* \in \mathcal{E}$ will exhibit a sequence of period doubling bifurcations at α_k (α_k depends on the family), and $(\alpha_k - \alpha_{k-1})/(\alpha_k - \alpha_{k+1}) \rightarrow \delta$, with δ the eigenvalue described before; in particular δ is independent of the family one has chosen.

b) The quantity d_k/d_{k-1} converges to $|\lambda|$, were d_k is the maximal length defined above, and where λ is the eigenvalue with largest modulus of $D\Lambda_{\phi*}$ taken at the fixed point of $\Lambda_{\phi*}$.

For the time being, these statements are conjectures only. In this paper, we prove only part of these conjectures, namely those which seem mainly responsible for the phenomenon. These are the existence and hyperbolicity of the fixed point. We believe that the construction of a surface Σ_o and the verification of its properties would be easier than the problem solved in this paper - and could again be done with a computer - but we have not worked on this problem.

In view of these remarks, we are confronted with the problem of finding a Λ_ϕ and a fixed point for the doubling transformation N, $N\phi = \Lambda_\phi^{-1} \circ \phi \circ \phi \circ \Lambda_\phi$, among the area-preserving maps of the plane. This fixed point should be non-trivial in the sense that $\delta = 8.721...$, $1/\lambda = -4.018...$. It is the solution of this problem, and the development of the necessary tools which occupies the rest of this paper.

I.2. GENERATING FUNCTIONS

We consider area-preserving mappings $(x,y) \to \phi(x,y) = (F(x,y),G(x,y))$ which admit a generating function $H : (x,x') \to H(x,x')$, such that

$$\partial_2 H(F(x,y),x) = -y \quad ,$$

$$\partial_1 H(F(x,y)x) = G(x,y) \ .$$

It is easy to see that, formally, the generating function $\hat{H}$ associated with $\hat{\phi} = \phi \circ \phi$ is

$$\hat{H}(x,x') = H(x,z) + H(z,x') \quad ,$$

where $z = z(x,x')$ is the function which makes this sum stationary,

$$\partial_2 H(x,z) + \partial_1 H(z,x') = 0 \ .$$

A simple change of variables shows that if $N\phi = \Lambda^{-1} \circ \phi \circ \phi \circ \Lambda$, where

$$\Lambda(x,y) = (\lambda x, \mu y) \ ,$$

then the generating function $\tilde{H}$ associated with $N\phi$ is determined by

$$\tilde{H}(x,x') = \frac{1}{\mu}(H(\lambda x, z(x,x')) + H(z(x,x'),\lambda x'))$$

and

$$\partial_2 H(\lambda x, z(x,x')) + \partial_1 H(z(x,x'),\lambda x') = 0 \ .$$

We intend to study the map $H \to \tilde{H}$, or some variant of it, and we shall eventually recover properties of N from it.

We restrict our attention to maps ϕ which, in addition to having a generating function, possess the following symmetry property :

$$T \circ \phi \circ T = \phi^{-1} ,$$

where

$$T(x,y) = (x,-y) .$$

We do not know whether all area-preserving maps of the plane have this property (modulo coordinate changes), but our restriction to such functions eliminates from the beginning many of the symmetries of the composition operator N, see also Refs [4], in particular the paper by Widom and Kadanoff, who, independently, used the generating function approach in their numerical studies. If ϕ is "time-reversal invariant", then H is symmetric in its arguments and we have the equations, for $S = \partial_2 H$ and $\tilde{S} = \partial_2 \tilde{H}$:

$$\begin{aligned} &S(F(x,y),x) = -y \\ &S(x,F(x,y)) = G(x,y) , \end{aligned} \qquad \text{(I.2.1)}$$

$$\partial_1 S(x,x') = \partial_1 S(x',x)$$

and $\tilde{S}(x,x') = \frac{1}{\mu} S(z(x,x'),\lambda x')$,

where $S(\lambda x,z(x,x')) + S(\lambda x',z(x,x')) = 0$.

Thus, we will study the map $S \to \tilde{S}$. We now start to fill in the details of the above definitions.

All functions considered will be analytic on polydisks, i.e. domains of the form $D(\alpha,\tau) \times D(\alpha',\tau') \subset \mathbb{C}^2$, $\tau,\tau' > 0$, where

$$D(\alpha,\tau) = \{z \in \mathbb{C} \mid |z-\alpha| < \tau\} .$$

Given a function f which is analytic on $D(\alpha,\tau) \times D(\alpha',\tau')$, we define its

Taylor coefficients f_{ij} by the equation

$$f(x,x') = \sum_{i,j\geq 0} f_{ij}(x-\alpha)^i \tau^{-i}(x'-\alpha')^j \tau'^{-j} ,$$

and its ℓ_1-norm by

$$\|f\|_1 = \sum_{i,j\geq 0} |f_{ij}| .$$

The space of functions analytic on $D(\alpha,\tau)\times D(\alpha',\tau')$ and continuous on its closure, equipped with the ℓ_1-norm, is a Banach space which we denote $A^c(\alpha,\tau,\alpha',\tau')$. If $\alpha,\alpha'\in\mathbb{R}$, then we define $A(\alpha,\tau,\alpha',\tau')$ to be the subspace of $A^c(\alpha,\tau,\alpha',\tau')$ of functions with real Taylor coefficients, so that $A(\alpha,\tau,\alpha',\tau')$ is a real Banach space. If $\alpha = \alpha'$, $\tau = \tau'$, we abbreviate the notation to $A(\alpha,\tau)$.

For our purposes, we fix, guided by trial and error, the values of the parameters describing domains as follows :

$$\alpha = 0.5,\ \tau = 1.6,\ \tau_t = 2.8,\ \theta = 0.421 .$$

We consider functions S, with the symmetry

$$\partial_1 S(x,x') = \partial_1 S(x',x) ,$$

and the normalizations

$$S(1,0) = 0 , \qquad \text{(I.2.2)}$$

$$\partial_2 S(1,0) = E , \qquad \text{(I.2.3)}$$

which break the dilatation symmetries of the problem. We fix $E = 1/5$. These normalizations will be imposed by requiring S to be in a space A_s :

$$A_s = \{f \in A(\alpha,\tau) \mid \partial_1 f(x,x') = \partial_1 f(x',x) ,$$
$$f(1,0) = 0 , \tag{I.2.4}$$
$$\partial_2 f(1,0) = E\} .$$

This is an affine subspace of $A(\alpha,\tau)$.

We next proceed to describe the action of the operator K. It will be defined on a subset $D_K \subset A_s$, and map it to A_s. A part of our task is to show that D_K is not empty, but for the moment we disregard this problem, and assume all equations described below have solutions.

Given $S \in D_K$, define $\lambda \in \mathbb{R}$ as the solution to the equation

$$S(0,1) + S(\lambda,1) = 0 . \tag{I.2.5}$$

Then define

$$\begin{aligned} T_1(z_1,z_2) &= S(\lambda z_1, 1+z_2) , \\ T_2(z_1,z_2) &= S(\lambda(1+z_1), 1+z_2) . \end{aligned} \tag{I.2.6}$$

Next solve the equation

$$T_1(x,\zeta(x,x')) + T_2(x',\zeta(x,x')) = 0 , \tag{I.2.7}$$

with $\zeta(0,0) = 0$. Set

$$z(x,x') = 1 + \zeta(x,x'-1) . \tag{I.2.8}$$

Define now μ by

$$\mu = \lambda + E^{-1} \partial_1 S(1,0)\, \partial_1 z(1,0) . \tag{I.2.9}$$

Finally, KS is defined by

$$(KS)(x,x') = \mu^{-1} S(z(x,x'),\lambda x') . \qquad (I.2.10)$$

We shall use the notation $\tilde{S}$ for KS.

Before stating the existence theorem, we comment on the defining equations. The equation for ζ, Eq. (I.2.7), when expressed in terms of z, reads

$$S(\lambda x, z(x,x')) + S(\lambda x', z(x,x')) = 0 , \qquad (I.2.11)$$

and z is symmetric, if it exists. The equation (I.2.5) assures the normalization $z(0,1) = z(1,0) = 0$. Now if $S \in \mathcal{D}_K$, then

$$\tilde{S}(1,0) = \mu^{-1} S(z(1,0),0) = \mu^{-1} S(1,0) = 0 .$$

The second normalization condition, $\partial_2 \tilde{S}(1,0) = E$, leads to the equation

$$E = \mu^{-1} \partial_1 S(z(1,0),0)\, \partial_1 z(1,0) + \mu^{-1} \lambda \partial_2 S(1,0) ,$$

which is fulfilled if (I.2.7) and (I.2.9) hold.

THEOREM I.2.1. <u>There is a neighborhood</u> $\mathcal{D}_K \subset A_s$ <u>on which</u> K <u>is defined. There are two intervals</u> I_L <u>and</u> I_M <u>such that for every</u> $S \in \mathcal{D}_K$ <u>the corresponding</u> λ <u>and</u> μ <u>are in</u> I_L <u>and</u> I_M <u>respectively. For every</u> $S \in \mathcal{D}_K$, <u>we have the inclusions</u> $T_i \in A(0,\tau_t,0,\theta)$, $i = 1,2$, $\zeta \in A(0,\tau_t,0,\tau_t)$, <u>and</u> $z \in A(\alpha,\tau,\alpha,\tau)$. <u>The range of</u> z <u>is contained strictly in</u> $D(\alpha,\tau)$.

All these statements are proved by our computer program. It also gives

THEOREM I.2.2. <u>We have the bounds</u>

$$I_L = [-0.24887681, -0.24887376] ,$$

$$I_M = [\ 0.61107811,\ \ 0.61112465] .$$

(See Section II.3.b) for comments on the precise meaning of such numbers.)

The domain $\mathcal{D}_K$ will be described later.

LEMMA I.2.3. K <u>maps</u> $\mathcal{D}_K$ <u>to</u> A_s.

PROOF : We have already verified all conditions except the symmetry of $\partial_1\tilde{S}$. From Eq. (I.2.7), we have

$$\partial_1 T_1(x,\zeta(x,x')) + [\partial_2 T_1(x,\zeta(x,x')) + \partial_2 T_2(x',\zeta(x,x'))]\partial_1\zeta(x,x') = 0 ,$$

i.e. on $D(\alpha,\tau)\times D(\alpha,\tau)$,

$$\lambda\cdot\partial_1 S(\lambda x,z(x,x'))$$
$$+ [\partial_2 S(\lambda x,z(x,x')) + \partial_2 S(\lambda x',z(x,x'))]\partial_1 z(x,x') = 0 .$$

Therefore,

$$\partial_1\tilde{S}(x,x') = \mu^{-1}\partial_1 S(z(x,x'),\lambda x)\partial_1 z(x,x')$$
$$= -\lambda^{-1}\mu^{-1}[\partial_2 S(\lambda x,z(x,x')) + \partial_2 S(\lambda x',z(x,x'))]\partial_1 z(x,x')\partial_1 z(x',x) .$$

This is manifestly a symmetric function and hence $\tilde{S}\in A_s$, as asserted.

Our main result is the

THEOREM I.2.4. <u>The operator</u> K <u>has a fixed point</u> S^* <u>in</u> A_s. <u>It is unique in</u> $\mathcal{D}_K$.

This will be seen as a corollary of the results of the next two sections. We denote λ^*, μ^* the constants associated with S^* through Eqs (I.2.5) and (I.2.9).

I.3. FURTHER REDUCTION OF THE PROBLEM

As we shall see later, the operator K is not a contraction, and Theorem I.2.4 will not be proved by considering K as such. We shall define and analyze in this section a contracting operator M whose action is based on a decomposition of S into a part pointing approximately in the direction which is stretched by DK, and a remainder σ.

Given $S \in A_s$, we recall that $S(1,0) = 0$, $\partial_2 S(1,0) = E = 1/5$. We define now two other S-dependent quantities,

$$B = \partial_2 S(0,1) - E ,$$

$$\text{and} \qquad C = B/2 - S(0,1) . \tag{I.3.1}$$

This allows us to define a projection P :

$$(PS)(x,y) = (C+E)(x-1) + Ey + By^2/2 . \tag{I.3.2}$$

We define $\sigma = (1-P)S$, and $A_\sigma = (1-P)A_s$. Note that by construction,

$$\sigma(1,0) = \partial_2\sigma(1,0) = 0 ,$$

$$\sigma(0,1) = \partial_2\sigma(0,1) = 0 , \tag{I.3.3}$$

$$\text{and} \qquad \partial_1\sigma(x,x') = \partial_1\sigma(x',x) .$$

Intuitively, M is now the operator induced by K on the σ. Given σ in A_σ we define M through the following sequence of steps. Determine first $B(\sigma)$, $C(\sigma)$ in such a way that for

$$S(x,y) = (C(\sigma)+E)(x-1) + Ey + B(\sigma)y^2/2 + \sigma(x,y) , \tag{I.3.4}$$

i.e. $S \in A_s$, one gets

$$P(KS)(x,y) = (C(\sigma) + E)(x - 1) + Ey + B(\sigma)y^2/2 . \tag{I.3.5}$$

In other words, B,C are so chosen that

$$P(KS) = PS .$$

Denote by $H(\sigma)$ the function

$$H(\sigma)(x,y) = (C(\sigma) + E)(x - 1) + Ey + B(\sigma)y^2/2 . \tag{I.3.6}$$

The definition of M is then

$$M\sigma = (1 - P)K(H(\sigma) + \sigma) . \tag{I.3.7}$$

If some σ^* solves $M\sigma^* = \sigma^*$ then the above construction implies that $H(\sigma^*) + \sigma^*$ is a fixed point of K. Similarly, every fixed point S^* of K leads to a $\sigma^* = (1 - P)S^*$ which is a fixed point of M.

REMARK. Our construction may seem mysterious to the reader. The rationale for it stems from the fact that at least numerically, the choice $\sigma \equiv 0$, $S_o = PS_o$, with

$$S_o(x,y) = x - 1 + y/5 + y^2$$

is a relatively good approximate fixed point of K. Unfortunately, we cannot prove that a disk around $\sigma \equiv 0$ is contracted by M into itself, rather we will have to take an initial guess of degree 20.

We now describe an isomorphism between the space A_σ, and a space A_σ^o, whose basis is optimally adapted to our problem. Given $f \in A_\sigma$, we write its

Taylor expansion in the form

$$f(x,x') = \sum_{(i,j)\in I} h_{ij} e_{ij}(x,x') ,$$

where $I = \{(i,j)\in \mathbb{Z}_+^2 \mid (i,j) = (2,1)$ or, $j \geq 2$ and $0 \leq i \leq j+1\}$, and

$$e_{ij}(x,y) = a_{ij} + b_{ij}\left(\frac{x-\alpha}{\tau}\right) + c_{ij}\left(\frac{y-\alpha}{\tau}\right) + d_{ij}\left(\left(\frac{x-\alpha}{\tau}\right)^2 + 2\left(\frac{x-\alpha}{\tau}\right)\left(\frac{y-\alpha}{\tau}\right)\right) + \frac{j+1}{i+j+1}\left(\frac{x-\alpha}{\tau}\right)^i\left(\frac{y-\alpha}{\tau}\right)^j + \frac{i}{i+j+1}\left(\frac{y-\alpha}{\tau}\right)^{i-1}\left(\frac{x-\alpha}{\tau}\right)^{j+1} ,$$

with a_{ij}, b_{ij}, c_{ij} and d_{ij} such that $e_{ij}(x,y)\in A_\sigma$.

The space A_σ^o is the set of sequences

$$\{f_o = \{h_{ij}\}_{ij\in I} \mid h_{ij}\in\mathbb{R}, \sum_{ij\in I} |h_{ij}| < \infty\}.$$

Equipped with the norm $\sum_{ij\in I} |h_{ij}| = \|f_o\|$, the space A_σ^o is a Banach space which is isomorphic to A_σ. We denote this isomorphism by $J_\sigma : A_\sigma \to A_\sigma^o$. Note that J_σ extends naturally to an isomorphism $J_s : A_s \to \mathbb{R}\oplus\mathbb{R}\oplus A_\sigma^o$, defined by $J_s S = B\oplus C\oplus \sigma_o$, where B, C, σ_o are defined by (I.3.1,2). We also define $M_o = J_\sigma M J_\sigma^{-1}$, and $K_o = J_s K J_s^{-1}$, and $B_o = BJ_\sigma^{-1}$, $C_o = CJ_\sigma^{-1}$.

The isomorphisms J_σ and J_σ^{-1} are realized in the subroutines PACK, and UNPACK, respectively, (with a check, in subroutine PROJ whether the element considered is really in A_σ (and not only in A)).

We denote by $\varphi_o \in A_\sigma^o$ a fixed, finite sequence of rational numbers h_{ij}, given in Table 1 page 120, and corresponding to a polynomial $\varphi = J_\sigma^{-1}\varphi_o$, of degree 20. This φ_o is an approximate fixed point of M_o. The polynomial

φ has been produced by a very unsophisticated program which iterates the operator $\mathcal{M}$ a certain number of times (taking as initial choice $\varphi = 0$). The only precaution taken was to carefully correct any deviations from $\mathcal{P}\mathcal{M}^k\varphi = 0$, $k = 1,2,\ldots$. The value of φ_o given corresponds to 28 iterations.

In addition to φ_o we give ourselves a neighborhood $\mathcal{D}^o_{\mathcal{M}}$ of φ_o in A^o_σ as follows :

$$\mathcal{D}^o_{\mathcal{M}} = \{\sigma_o \epsilon A^o_\sigma \mid \|\sigma_o - \varphi_o\| \le 5\cdot 10^{-8}\} .$$

Our first main estimates are described in the following :

THEOREM I.3.1. The operator $\mathcal{M}_o$ is defined on $\mathcal{D}^o_{\mathcal{M}}$ and maps $\mathcal{D}^o_{\mathcal{M}}$ to A^o_σ. The following estimates hold :

1) For every $\sigma_o \epsilon \mathcal{D}^o_{\mathcal{M}}$, one has, with $\sigma = \mathcal{J}_\sigma^{-1}\sigma_o$,

$$\lambda(\sigma)\epsilon I_L , \ \mu(\sigma)\epsilon I_M ,$$

$$B(\sigma)\epsilon I'_B , \ C(\sigma)\epsilon I_C ,$$

where $I'_B = [0.19118611, 0.19118725]$,

$$I_C = [0.82728796, 0.82729138] .$$

2) One has the bound

$$\|\mathcal{M}_o\varphi_o - \varphi_o\| \le 1.3\cdot 10^{-8} = \varepsilon .$$

3) The tangent map $D\mathcal{M}_o$ (at any $\sigma_o \epsilon \mathcal{D}^o_{\mathcal{M}}$) has operator norm bounded by

$$\|D\mathcal{M}_{o,\sigma_o}\| < 0.55 = \rho .$$

Note that $(1-\rho)\cdot 5\cdot 10^{-8} > \varepsilon$. Therefore we can conclude from Theorem I.3.1 :

THEOREM I.3.2. <u>The operator</u> M_o <u>has a unique fixed point</u> σ_o^* <u>in</u> $\mathcal{D}_M^o$.

Define S^* by $S^* = H(J_\sigma^{-1}\sigma_o^*) + J_\sigma^{-1}\sigma_o^*$. Then S^* is a fixed point of K. This proves the existence part of Theorem I.2.4. The uniqueness will follow from the hyperbolicity of K. We define $S_o^* = J_s S^*$ and $\sigma^* = J_\sigma^{-1}\sigma_o^*$.

PROOF OF THEOREM I.3.1 : The proof of Theorem I.3.1, 1)-2) is contained in the part of the program headed by "calculate ℓ-norm of PHIO-PHIONEW". The proof of Theorem I.3.1, 3) is contained in the part headed by "compute tangent map DM". In particular, as will be seen in the general discussion of Part II of this paper, all domain questions are automatically checked by the program. In this section, we give some of the algebra used in computing the action of M_o on a σ_o. We prefer to describe the equations for M rather than those for M_o. Also note that the computer program works with normalized domains (unit disks) so that all functions are brought to this normalized form by a linear coordinate change which we do not describe below.

The first task is to determine $B(\sigma)$, $C(\sigma)$, $\lambda(\sigma)$, $\mu(\sigma)$, given $\sigma\in A_\sigma$. (Because of numerical reasons we do this by viewing $\lambda\in I_L$, $C\in I_C$ as independent variables, and solving explicitly for B and μ.) Guided by Eqs (I.2.1) to (I.2.6), we define

$$w_o = \partial_1\sigma(1,0) \quad ,$$

$$w_1 = \sigma(\lambda,1) \quad , \qquad\qquad (I.3.8)$$

$$w_2 = \sigma(1,\lambda)/\lambda \quad ,$$

$$w_3 = \partial_1\sigma(1,\lambda)\ ,$$

$$w_4 = \partial_2\sigma(1,\lambda)\ , \tag{I.3.8}$$

$$w_5 = \partial_2\sigma(\lambda,1)\ .$$

Next set $c_1 = C + E = C + 1/5$, $c_2 = 2C$. Then B is given by

$$B = c_2 - \lambda c_1 - w_1\ . \tag{I.3.9}$$

Next we want to give expressions for μ, and $\tilde{B}$, $\tilde{C}$, i.e. the values of B, C associated with $\tilde{S} = \mathcal{K}S$. It is useful to introduce

$$\begin{aligned}
g_1 &= -5(c_1 + w_o)^2\ ,\\
g_2 &= 2(B + 1/5) + w_5\ ,\\
q_3 = -g_3 &= B\lambda + w_4\ ,\\
q_4 = 1/g_4 &= 1/(g_1 + g_2)\ ,\\
q_5 = -g_5 &= 2c_1(w_o - w_3) + w_o^2 - w_3^2\ ,\\
q_6 = -g_6 &= w_4 - 2(w_2 + 1/5)\ .
\end{aligned} \tag{I.3.10}$$

With these notations, one finds

$$\mu = \lambda(1 + g_1/g_2)$$

and

$$\tilde{B} = (g_2 q_3 + q_5)q_4\ ,$$

$$\tilde{C} = \frac{1}{2}(g_2 q_6 + q_5)q_4\ . \tag{I.3.11}$$

Recall that $B(\sigma)$ and $C(\sigma)$ are defined by the equations $B(\sigma) = \tilde{B}(\sigma)$,

$C(\sigma) = \tilde{C}(\sigma)$. Taking λ and C as independent variables we solve these equations by looking for a zero of the two functions $F_i = F_i(\lambda, C, \sigma)$, $i = 1,2$:

$$F_1 = Bg_4 + g_2 g_3 + g_5 ,$$
$$F_2 = 2Cg_4 + g_2 g_6 + g_5 , \tag{I.3.12}$$

using Newton's method (see also Section II.1e). This part of the algorithm is done in the subroutine BCLAMU. Now S, λ, μ are determined, and we can solve Eq. (I.2.7) determining z (in subroutine SZ we verify that Eq. (I.2.7) has a solution for every $\lambda \in I_L$, $B \in I'_B$, $C \in I_C$ and $\sigma_o \in \mathcal{D}^o_M$). Now M is defined by

$$(M\sigma)(x,y) = ((1 - P)\tilde{S})(x,y) ,$$

with

$$\tilde{S}(x,y) = \mu^{-1} S(z(x,y), \lambda y) .$$

Note that M <u>is a compact operator</u> since z and λy have a range which is strictly inside $D(\alpha, \tau)$. In fact, our calculations show

$$\text{range } z \subset D(\alpha, 0.45\tau) \text{ and}$$
$$\text{range } \lambda y \subset D(\alpha, 0.64\tau) . \tag{I.3.13}$$

We postpone momentarily the discussion of DM_o and prove first the existence of a nontrivial domain $\mathcal{D}_K$ for K, because the argument is quite similar to the preceding one.

LEMMA I.3.3. <u>For</u> $\sigma_o \in \mathcal{D}^o_M$, $C \in I_C$, $\lambda \in I_L$ <u>we have</u>

$$c_1 + \frac{d}{d\lambda} w_1 \neq 0 .$$

This result is verified by the program.

It follows that there is an interval $I_B \subset I'_B$ such that for $B \in I_B$, $C \in I_C$ and $\sigma_o \in \mathcal{D}^o_M$ the Equation (I.3.9) has a (unique) solution λ, and this solution is in I_L. Note that $B_o(\sigma^*) \in I_B$, so that I_B contains a neighborhood of $B_o(\mathcal{D}^o_M)$.

We show now that K can be defined on $\mathcal{D}_K = J_s^{-1}(I_B \oplus I_C \oplus \mathcal{D}^o_M)$. Namely, given $(B,C,\sigma) \in \mathcal{D}_K$, by the above remarks, Eq. (I.3.9) defines a $\lambda \in I_L$. But our program shows that for every $\lambda \in I_L$ and $C \in I_C$, K is well defined, because we do <u>not</u> use ever that $C = C(\sigma)$ or $B = B(\sigma)$. Hence K is well defined on $\mathcal{D}_K$.

We next describe the essential algebra for the calculation of DM_o. Recall that $\lambda, \nu = \mu^{-1}, B, C$ depend on σ. We denote $\delta\lambda, \delta\nu, \delta B, \delta C$ their functional derivatives with respect to σ. They are obtained by differentiating the equations leading to B, C, λ, ν, used above. These operations are straightforward, if long, and are performed in the subroutine DS. The derivative DM_σ is then given by

$$
\begin{aligned}
&(DM_\sigma h)(x,y) \\
&= \delta\lambda \cdot S_L(x,y) + \delta C \cdot S_C(x,y) + \delta B \cdot S_B(x,y) \\
&+ \delta\nu \cdot S_N(x,y) \\
&+ g(x,y)\{h(\lambda x, z(x,y)) + h(\lambda y, z(x,y))\} \\
&+ \nu h(z(x,y), \lambda y) ,
\end{aligned}
$$

where
$$S_L(x,y) = \nu\partial_2 S(z(x,y),\lambda y)y + g(x,y)[\partial_1 S(\lambda x,z(x,y))x + \partial_1 S(\lambda y,z(x,y))y] ,$$

$$S_C(x,y) = 1 - x - \nu(1 - z(x,y)) - g(x,y)[(1 - \lambda x) + (1 - \lambda y)] ,$$

$$S_B(x,y) = -\frac{1}{2}y^2 + \frac{1}{2}(\lambda y)^2 - 2g(x,y)\frac{1}{2}z(x,y)^2 ,$$

$$S_N(x,y) = S(z(x,y),\lambda y) .$$

These identities are obtained by straightforward application of the chain rule to M, and the identity derived from the equation for z, Eq. (I.2.7) :

$$\delta z(x,y) = -[\partial_2 S(\lambda x,z) + \partial_2 S(\lambda y,z)]^{-1} \cdot\{\partial_1 S(\lambda x,z)x\delta\lambda + \partial_1 S(\lambda y,z)y\delta\lambda + \delta S(\lambda x,z) + \delta S(\lambda y,z)\} ,$$

where $z = z(x,y)$.

The function g is a short-hand notation for

$$g(x,y) = \nu\lambda^{-1}\partial_2 z(x,y) = -\nu\partial_1 S(\lambda y,z)[\partial_2 S(\lambda x,z) + \partial_2 S(\lambda y,z)]^{-1} .$$

Note that the norm of a linear operator on ℓ_1 is the supremum of the ℓ_1 norms of its column vectors, when viewed as a matrix. We shall discuss in Part II more details of the computational aspects of estimating this norm.

I.4. SPECTRAL PROPERTIES

THEOREM I.4.1.

1) The operator K is infinitely differentiable as a map from $\mathcal{D}_K$ to A_s.

2) The operator DK_{S^*} is hyperbolic. Its spectrum is contained in the unit disk apart from a simple eigenvalue δ, which is bounded by

$$8.2 < \delta < 9.2$$

and a simple eigenvalue equal to $1/\lambda^*$.

3) The eigenspace corresponding to the eigenvalue $1/\lambda^*$ is spanned by the function

$$\partial_\varepsilon [P_\varepsilon S^* \circ T_\varepsilon]_{\varepsilon=0} \quad ,$$

where $S^* \circ T_\varepsilon(x,y) = S^*(x+\varepsilon, y+\varepsilon)$, and $P_\varepsilon S^* \circ T_\varepsilon(x,y) = (S^* \circ T_\varepsilon(x+\varepsilon_1 x, y+\varepsilon_1 y)/(1+\varepsilon_2))$ projects $S^* \circ T_\varepsilon$ on A_s.

The equations describing K have been given in Section I.2. To verify that $\partial_\varepsilon [P_\varepsilon S^* \circ T_\varepsilon]_{\varepsilon=0}$ is an eigenvector of the operator DK_{S^*} with eigenvalue $1/\lambda^*$ is a rather lengthy but trivial calculation. This settles point 3) of the theorem. To prove point 2) of the theorem we proceed as follows. We first choose a convenient basis in A_s^o. For $\sigma_o \in A_\sigma^o$, $B \in I_B$, $C \in I_C$, we define

$$\beta = B - B_o(\sigma_o) \quad ,$$

$$\gamma = C - C_o(\sigma_o) \quad .$$

Then K_o maps $I_B \oplus I_C \oplus \mathcal{D}_M^o$ to $A_s^o = \mathbb{R} \oplus \mathbb{R} \oplus A_\sigma^o$:

$$K_o(\beta, \gamma, \sigma_o) = (\tilde{\beta}, \tilde{\gamma}, \tilde{\sigma}_o) \quad ,$$

where

$$\tilde{\beta} = \mathcal{B}(B_o(\sigma_o) + \beta,\ C_o(\sigma_o) + \gamma,\ \sigma_o) - B_o(\sigma_o) \ ,$$

$$\tilde{\gamma} = \mathcal{C}(B_o(\sigma_o) + \beta,\ C_o(\sigma_o) + \gamma,\ \sigma_o) - C_o(\sigma_o) \ ,$$

$$\tilde{\sigma}_o = \Sigma(B_o(\sigma_o) + \beta,\ C_o(\sigma_o) + \gamma,\ \sigma_o) \ .$$

The operator $D\mathcal{K}_{o,S_o^*}$, acting on $I_B \oplus I_C \oplus A_\sigma^o$, can then be represented (see also Section II.2.b) by a 3×3-matrix

$$D\mathcal{K}_{o,S_o^*} = \begin{bmatrix} a_{11} & a_{12} & a_{1\infty} \\ a_{21} & a_{22} & a_{2\infty} \\ a_{\infty 1} & a_{\infty 2} & a_{\infty\infty} \end{bmatrix} .$$

For the matrix elements of $D\mathcal{K}_{o,S_o^*}$ we get (using the notation $B^* = B_o(\sigma_o^*)$, $C^* = C_o(\sigma_o^*)$) :

$$a_{11} = \partial_1 \mathcal{B}(B^*,C^*,\sigma_o^*) - \langle \delta B^*, \partial_1 \Sigma(B^*,C^*,\sigma_o^*)\rangle \ ,$$

$$a_{12} = \partial_2 \mathcal{B}(B^*,C^*,\sigma_o^*) - \langle \delta B^*, \partial_2 \Sigma(B^*,C^*,\sigma_o^*)\rangle \ ,$$

$$a_{1\infty} = \delta B^*(1 - \bullet D\mathcal{M}_{\sigma_o^*}) \ ,$$

$$a_{21} = \partial_1 \mathcal{C}(B^*,C^*,\sigma_o^*) - \langle \delta C^*, \partial_1 \Sigma(B^*,C^*,\sigma_o^*)\rangle \ ,$$

$$a_{22} = \partial_2 \mathcal{C}(B^*,C^*,\sigma_o^*) - \langle \delta C^*, \partial_2 \Sigma(B^*,C^*,\sigma_o^*)\rangle \ ,$$

$$a_{2\infty} = \delta C^*(1 - \bullet D\mathcal{M}_{\sigma_o^*}) \ ,$$

$$a_{\infty 1} = \partial_1 \Sigma(B^*,C^*,\sigma_o^*) \ ,$$

$$a_{\infty 2} = \partial_2 \Sigma(B^*,C^*,\sigma_o^*) \ ,$$

$$a_{\infty\infty\infty} = DM_{o,\sigma_o^*} .$$

We have used the notation δB^* for the 1-form $\partial B^*(\tilde{\sigma}_o)/\partial\tilde{\sigma}_o$ and $<.,.>$ for the action of the dual on A_σ^o. In order to prove the spectral properties we choose, for practical reasons, still another basis in the first two components. Namely we set $(\beta,\gamma) = \underline{S}(p,q)$, where $\underline{S}$ is a two by two matrix:

$$\underline{S}^{-1} = \begin{bmatrix} -0.9923 & 0.9007 \\ -0.1190 & 0.4328 \end{bmatrix} .$$

The elements of DK_{S^*} expressed in this basis will be denoted $b_{11}, b_{12}, \ldots$. We have the following

ESTIMATE I.4.2. <u>One has</u>

$$8.44 < b_{11} < 8.99 , \quad -0.16 < b_{21} < 0.17 ,$$

$$-0.41 < b_{12} < 0.42 , \quad -4.28 < b_{22} < -3.78 .$$

<u>Furthermore</u>

$$\|b_{1\infty}\|_* < 0.186 , \qquad \|b_{\infty 1}\| < 0.654 ,$$

$$\|b_{2\infty}\|_* < 0.111 , \qquad \|b_{\infty 2}\| < 0.272 ,$$

<u>and</u> $\|b_{\infty\infty\infty}\| = \|DM_{o,\sigma_o^*}\| < 0.544.$

These estimates are proved by the computer. In the part of the program headed "compute tangent map DM" the norms of the columns of DM are calculated and to every column the corresponding two elements of $b_{1\infty}, b_{2\infty}$. In the part headed "compute missing parts of tangent map DK" we calculate the columns $b_{\infty 1}, b_{\infty 2}$ and the corresponding elements b_{11}, b_{21} and b_{12}, b_{22}. The norm of

$b_{1\infty}, b_{2\infty}$ is the supremum over the absolute values of the elements, the norm of $a_{\infty\infty}$ the supremum over the norms of the column vectors of DM.

We can now apply Lemma II.1.11 to complete the proof that there is a simple eigenvalue δ,

$$8.2 < \delta < 9.2 ,$$

and a simple eigenvalue α,

$$-4.4 < \alpha < -3.6 ,$$

in the spectrum of DK_{S*}, and that the remainder of the spectrum is strictly contained in the unit disk. For $1/\lambda*$ we have from Theorem I.2.2. the estimate

$$-4.01811 < 1/\lambda* < -4.01805 ,$$

so we identify α to be $1/\lambda*$, since $1/\lambda*$ must be an eigenvalue of DK_{S*}. Point 1) of the theorem follows from the fact that we deal with analytic functions, by the bound on the range of z and of λy, and by Cauchy's theorem.

In order to get the structure needed in function space to prove Feigenbaum universality we should have an operator which has only one eigenvalue larger than one. We therefore construct, as a next step, an operator L which is essentially the same as K but which has no longer the eigenvalue $1/\lambda*$ in its spectrum. We shall then show, that on some family of area-preserving maps which is generated by functions in $\mathcal{D}_L$, the operator which is induced by L acts as a doubling operator.

I.5. CONSTRUCTION OF THE OPERATOR L

The idea in the construction of the operator L is to fix the translations $S(x,x') \to S(x+\varepsilon, x'+\varepsilon)$ (corresponding to a change of coordinates $\phi(x,y) \to \phi(x+\varepsilon,y) - (\varepsilon,0)$), by imposing a third normalization for functions $S \in A_s$, in addition to the normalizations (I.2.2, I.2.3) already used in order to fix dilatations. We shall define a projection $T : \mathcal{D}_K \to \mathcal{D}_L$ such that, for $S \in \mathcal{D}_K$, with $E = 1/5$,

$$\begin{aligned} (TS)(1,0) &= 0 \ , \\ (TS)(0,1) &= 1 \ , \\ E\cdot(\partial_1 TS)(1,0) &= (\partial_2 TS)(1,0)\ \partial_1 S^*(1,0) \ . \end{aligned} \tag{I.5.1}$$

Note that it is the second condition which replaces the condition $\partial_2 S(1,0) = E$, while the third one fixes the translations. Our choice is made in view of the definition of N, given in Section I.6.

In order to define T, we need the following

LEMMA I.5.1. <u>For every</u> $S \in \mathcal{D}_K$ <u>there are unique constants</u> a,b,c <u>such that</u>

$$\begin{aligned} S(a+c,c) &= 0 \\ bS(c,a+c) &= 1 \\ E\cdot\partial_1 S(a+c,c) &= \partial_2 S(a+c,c)\partial_1 S^*(1,0) \ . \end{aligned} \tag{I.5.2}$$

<u>One has the bounds</u>

$$|a+c-1| < 7.38\cdot 10^{-8} \ ,$$

$$|b\cdot S(0,1) - 1| < 1.16\cdot 10^{-5} \ ,$$

$$|c| < 3.79\cdot 10^{-7} .$$

In particular, as a function of the single variable $z \in D(0,1)$,

$$\|(a(\alpha + \rho'\tau\cdot z) + c - \alpha)/\tau\|_1 < 1 ,$$

for all $\rho' \le 0.98$.

The proof follows from the bounds given by the subroutine abc in the program. (Its variables are $a \leftrightarrow a + c - 1$, $b \leftrightarrow bS(0,1) - 1$, $c \leftrightarrow c$.) Note that for $S = S^*$, we have $a = 1$, $b = 1/S(0,1)$, $c = 0$.

Fix now $\rho = 0.98$. By Lemma I.5.1, there is for every $S \in \mathcal{D}_K$, an $S' = \mathcal{T}S$, defined by

$$S'(x,x') = bS(ax + c,\ ax' + c) ,$$

where a,b,c are given as the solutions of (I.5.2). S' is analytic on $D(\alpha,\rho\tau) \times D(\alpha,\rho\tau)$, and it is easy to check that $\mathcal{T}S$ satisfies (I.5.1). Since $\mathcal{K}$ has a fixed point in $\mathcal{D}_K$, and is continuous, there is an open ball $\mathcal{D}'_K \subset \mathcal{D}_K$ for which $\mathcal{K}\mathcal{D}'_K \subset \mathcal{D}_K$. We now define $\mathcal{D}_L = \mathcal{T}\mathcal{D}_K$, $\mathcal{D}'_L = \mathcal{T}\mathcal{D}'_K$.

We shall need in Section I.6 the

LEMMA I.5.2. *For every* $S' \in \mathcal{D}_L$, *one has*

$$\inf_{(x,y)\in D_L} |\mathrm{Re}\ \partial_1 S'(x,y)| > 0.8.$$

We check this on the computer, by using the inequality

$$\inf_{(x,y)\in D_L} |\mathrm{Re}\ \partial_1 S'(x,y)| \ge |\partial_1 S'(0,0)| - \sup_{(x,y)\in D_L} |\partial_1 S'(x,y) - \partial_1 S'(0,0)|.$$

Next we shall show that if $\mathcal{T}S_1 = \mathcal{T}S_2$, then $\mathcal{T}\mathcal{K}S_1 = \mathcal{T}\mathcal{K}S_2$. Therefore we may define L as the operator which renders the diagram

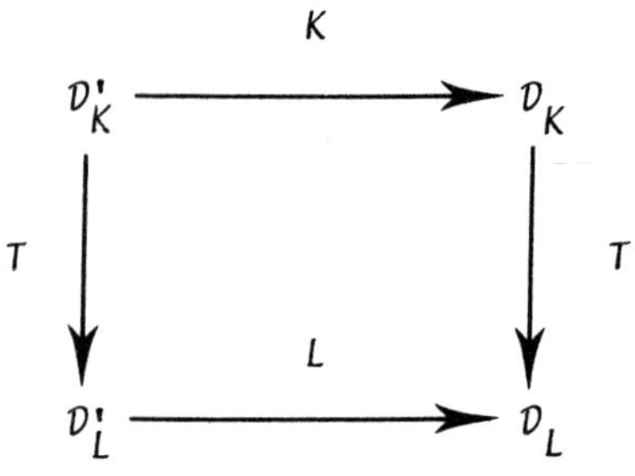

commutative. To prove the existence of L, we consider $s_1, s_2 \in \mathcal{D}'_K$, satisfying $Ts_1 = Ts_2$. This means that

$$b_1 s_1(a_1 x + c_1, a_1 y + c_1) = b_2 s_2(a_2 x + c_2, a_2 y + c_2).$$

On the other hand, by Lemma I.5.1, there are constants $\tilde{a}_i, \tilde{b}_i, \tilde{c}_i$ such that, for $i = 1,2$,

$$TKs_i(x,y) = \tilde{b}_i \mu_i^{-1} s_i(z_i(\tilde{a}_i x + \tilde{c}_i, \tilde{a}_i y + \tilde{c}_i), \lambda_i \tilde{a}_i y + \lambda_i \tilde{c}_i) .$$

If we define $z'_i(x,y) = a_i^{-1} z_i(\tilde{a}_i x + \tilde{c}_i, \tilde{a}_i y + \tilde{c}_i) - a_i^{-1} c_i$ and $a_i \lambda'_i(x) = \lambda_i \tilde{a}_i x + \lambda_i \tilde{c}_i - c_i$, then

$$Ts_i(z'_i, \lambda'_i(x)) + Ts_i(z'_i, \lambda'_i(y)) = 0 .$$

Hence, from $Ts_1 = Ts_2$ and the uniqueness of the solution to the above equation, we find $z'_1 = z'_2$, $\lambda'_1 = \lambda'_2$, and hence $TKs_1 = TKs_2$, as asserted. For the convenience of the reader, we give explicitly the algebra for computing L. Note that we have preferred to work with K in the program because every application of the inverse function theorem tends to worsen the bounds.

Given $S \in \mathcal{D}'_L$, solve the following 5 simultaneous equations in m, ℓ, r, ξ, η,

$$(LS)(1,0) = 0 = m^{-1}S(\xi,r) ,$$

$$(LS)(0,1) = 1 = m^{-1}S(\xi,r+\ell) ,$$

$$S(r,\xi) + S(r+\ell,\xi) = 0 , \quad \text{cf. Eq. (I.2.11)},$$

$$m\cdot(E\partial_1(LS)(\xi,r) - \partial_2(LS)(\xi,r)\ \partial_1(LS)(\xi,r)) = 0$$

$$= E\partial_1 S(\xi,r)\eta - \ell\partial_2 S(\xi,r)\ \partial_1 S^*(1,0) ,$$

and

$$\ell\partial_1 S(\ell+r,\xi) + \partial_2 S(\ell+r,\xi)\eta + \partial_2 S(r,\xi)\eta = 0 .$$

(The equations reflect the normalization conditions.) Now solve the following equation for z :

$$S(\ell x + r, z(x,x')) + S(\ell x' + r, z(x,x')) = 0 \tag{I.5.5}$$

with $z(0,1) = z(1,0) = \xi$. Then define

$$(LS)(x,x') = m^{-1}S(z(x,x'),\ell x' + r) . \tag{I.5.6}$$

The relation to the constants $\lambda,\mu,a,b,\tilde{a}$, and $\tilde{b}$ is established by

$$\ell = \lambda\tilde{a}/a ,$$

$$m = \mu b/\tilde{b} ,$$

$$r = (\lambda\tilde{c} - c)/a .$$

ℓ,m,r will be the effective dilations in x and y respectively, and the translation in x, in the definition of Λ_ϕ.

We can summarize this as

THEOREM I.5.3

1) $\mathcal{L}$ is defined for every $S \in \mathcal{D}'_{\mathcal{L}}$.

2) $\mathcal{L}$ has a unique fixed point $S^*_L \in \mathcal{D}'_{\mathcal{L}}$.

(Of course, $S^*_L = \mathcal{T}S^*$.)

We next describe the spectral properties of $D\mathcal{L}$.

THEOREM I.5.4.

1) The operator $\mathcal{L}$ is infinitely differentiable as a map from $\mathcal{D}'_{\mathcal{L}}$ to $\mathcal{D}_{\mathcal{L}}$.

2) The operator $D\mathcal{L}_{S^*_L}$ is hyperbolic. Its spectrum is contained in the unit disk apart from a simple eigenvalue δ,

$$8.2 < \delta < 9.2 \ .$$

PROOF : The differentiability of $\mathcal{L}$ follows from the differentiability of $\mathcal{K}$, and of the functions $a = a(S), \ldots$. The map $\mathcal{T}$ induces a map Q on suitable subspaces of $\mathcal{A}$, for which

$$D\mathcal{L}_{S^*_L}Q = QD\mathcal{K}_{S^*} \ .$$

By construction, $\mathcal{T}P_\varepsilon S^* \circ T_\varepsilon = \mathcal{O}(\varepsilon^2)$, where T_ε is again translation by ε in both arguments. Therefore Q projects the eigenvector (of $1/\lambda^*$), which is equal to $\partial_\varepsilon [P_\varepsilon S^* \circ T_\varepsilon]_{\varepsilon=0}$ onto zero. It is easy to check that δ remains an isolated eigenvalue of $\mathcal{L}$ and that the remainder of the spectrum of $\mathcal{L}$ is strictly inside the unit disk.

I.6. CONSTRUCTION OF THE DOUBLING OPERATOR

In this section we construct in a first step for every $S \in \mathcal{D}_L$ an area-preserving map ϕ, as indicated in Eqs (I.2.1). Every such ϕ is analytic on some domain $D(S)$, which depends on the S from which ϕ is generated. In a second step we construct a common domain D_ϕ which is contained in every $D(S)$. Next we study the operator $\mathcal{N}$ which is induced by $\mathcal{L}$ and acts on some set $\mathcal{D}'_N$ of area-preserving maps defined on D_ϕ. We show that $\mathcal{N}$ has a fixed point ϕ^* in $\mathcal{D}'_N$ and is a doubling operator on $\mathcal{D}'_N$.

For $S \in \mathcal{D}_L$ set

$$D(S) = \{(x, -S(y,x)) \mid (x,y) \in D_L\} . \tag{I.6.1}$$

Define

$$D_\phi = \bigcup_{z \in D(\alpha, \rho\tau)} \{z\} \times D(c_1(z), c_2) , \tag{I.6.2}$$

where

$$c_1(z) = 4.04 - 1.76z - 7.231z^2 ,$$

$$c_2 = 10.5 .$$

LEMMA I.6.1. <u>One has the inclusion</u>

$$D_\phi \subset \bigcap_{S \in \mathcal{D}_L} D(S) .$$

REMARK I.6.2. <u>The domain</u> D_ϕ <u>contains the five points</u> $(\lambda^*, -\mu^*)$, $(1,-1)$, $(0,0)$, $(1,1)$, (λ^*, μ^*).

PROOF OF LEMMA I.6.1 : We prove the lemma by using the computer, based on the following considerations : Define $P(x,y) = c_1(y) + \alpha\cdot 7.987 - 8.037x$. Our program computes a bound on

$$\sup_{S\in\mathcal{D}_L}\ \sup_{(x,y)\in D_L} |P(x,y) + S(x,y)| = \gamma .$$

Then it is easy to see, that for $x\in D(\alpha,\rho\tau)$ the point (x,y) is in $D(S)$ for every $S\in\mathcal{D}_L$ if y is in a disk, centered at $P(0,x) - 7.987\alpha = c_1(x)$ with radius less than $7.987\tau\rho - \gamma$. We have chosen c_2 less than this constant.

In order to prove later on that the operator N which is induced by L is a doubling operator we shall need to know if a point $(x,-S(y,x))$ lies in D_ϕ or not. Because the estimate used is of the same type as the one for Lemma I.6.1, we give it already at this point.

LEMMA I.6.3. <u>For every</u> $S\in\mathcal{D}_L$ <u>the points</u>

$$(x,y) = (x,-S(x',x))$$

<u>are in</u> D_ϕ <u>if</u> $x\in D(\alpha,\rho\tau)$ <u>and</u> $x'\in D(\alpha,\eta)$, <u>where</u> $\eta = 1.1$.

PROOF : We have to show that for every $x\in D(\alpha,\rho\tau)$

$$\sup_{S\in\mathcal{D}_L}\ \sup_{y\in D(\alpha,\eta)} |c_1(x) + S(y,x)| < c_2 .$$

This we verify again on the computer.

This lemma provides an alternate proof of Remark I.6.2, which follows from the identities

$$(\lambda^*,-\mu^*) = (\lambda^*,-S_L^*(1,\lambda^*)) \quad ,$$

$$(1,-1) = (1,-S_L^*(0,1)) \quad ,$$

$$(0,0) = (0,-S_L^*(1,0)) \quad ,$$

$$(1,1) = (1,-S_L^*(\lambda^*,1)) \quad ,$$

$$(\lambda^*,\mu^*) = (\lambda^*,-S_L^*(z^*(\lambda^*,1),\lambda^*)) \ .$$

That $z^*(\lambda^*,1)$ lies in $D(\alpha,\eta)$ is proved by the bound on the range of z^*.

We define now on D_ϕ a set $\mathcal{D}_N$ of area-preserving functions as follows. For every $S\in\mathcal{D}_L$ and every $(x,y)\in D_\phi$ there exists by the construction of D_ϕ a point $(x,\tilde{y})\in D_L$ for which

$$(x,y) = (x,-S(\tilde{y},x)) \ .$$

This $\tilde{y}$ is unique because $|\mathrm{Re}\ \partial_1 S(z_1,z_2)| > 0$ for all $S\in\mathcal{D}_L$ and for all $(z_1,z_2)\in D_L$ as we have proved in Lemma I.5.2. We can therefore define for every $(x,y)\in D_\phi$:

$$F(x,y) = \tilde{y} \ .$$

Note that by construction $\tilde{y}\in D(\alpha,\rho\tau)$.

The function F solves the equation

$$S(F(x,y),x) = -y \quad \text{on} \quad D_\phi \ ,$$

and F is analytic on D_ϕ.

Next we define on D_ϕ

$$G(x,y) = S(x,F(x,y)) .$$

Finally, we define our main object of interest,

$$\phi : D_\phi \to \mathbb{C}^2 ,$$

by

$$\phi(x,y) = (F(x,y),G(x,y)) .$$

The set of ϕ's we get by varying S in $\mathcal{D}_L$ we call $\mathcal{D}_N$, and $\mathcal{D}'_N \subset \mathcal{D}_N$ is the set of ϕ's we get by varying S in $\mathcal{D}'_L \subset \mathcal{D}_L$.

The operator which associates to a $S \in \mathcal{D}_L$ a $\phi \in \mathcal{D}_N$ we call I. Note that I is one-to-one. We now have the

THEOREM I.6.4. Every $\phi \in \mathcal{D}_N$ has the following properties

1) ϕ is "time-reversal-invariant" : $\phi \circ T \circ \phi = T$ on $D_\phi \cap T \circ \phi D_\phi$, where $T(z_1,z_2) = (z_1,-z_2)$.
2) ϕ is area-preserving on D_ϕ, $\det D\phi = 1$.
3) $\phi = (F,G)$ is normalized :

$$F(0,0) = 1 ,$$

$$G(0,0) = 1 ,$$

$$\partial_1 F(0,0) = -E/\partial_1 S^*(1,0) .$$

PROOF : Point 3) follows from the normalization condition for functions $S \in \mathcal{D}_L$. In particular this shows, that the probably somewhat mysterious normalizations I.5.1 have served to fix $\phi(0,0) = (1,1)$ and to hold the first component of $D\phi$ fixed, and thus equal to $\partial_1 F^*(0,0)$, where $\phi^* = (F^*,G^*)$ is associated to S^*_L.

Recall that

$$S(F(x,y),x) = -y \quad \text{on} \quad D_\phi$$

and

$$F(x,-S(y,x)) = y \quad \text{at least on} \quad D(\alpha,\rho\tau)\times D(\alpha,\eta)\ , \text{ by} \quad \text{Lemma I.6.3.}$$

For $x\epsilon D(\alpha,\eta)$, $\tilde{y}\epsilon F(x,D(\alpha,\rho\tau))$ we have :

$$x = F(\tilde{y},-S(x,\tilde{y})) = F(F(x,y),-S(x,F(x,y)))$$

$$= F(F(x,y),-G(x,y)), \quad \text{for some} \quad y\epsilon D(\alpha,\rho\tau)\ ,$$

and

$$-y = S(F(x,y),x) = S(F(x,y),F(F(x,y),-G(x,y)))$$

$$= G(F(x,y),-G(x,y))\ .$$

By analytic continuation the proposition follows. Note that the symmetry of $\partial_1 S$ has not been used here.

Point 2) of the theorem follows from the fact that we restrict ourselves to functions S for which $\partial_1 S$ is symmetric. From the definition of F and G we have

$$\partial_1 S(F(x,y),x)\partial_2 F(x,y) = -1\ , \quad \text{when} \quad (x,y)\epsilon D_\phi\ .$$

Similarly,

$$\partial_1 G(x,y) = \partial_1 S(x,F(x,y)) + \partial_2 S(x,F(x,y))\partial_1 F(x,y)$$

$$= \partial_1 S(F(x,y),x) + \partial_2 S(x,F(x,y))\partial_1 F(x,y)$$

$$\partial_2 G(x,y) = \partial_2 S(x,F(x,y))\partial_2 F(x,y)\ .$$

We have used the symmetry of $\partial_1 S$ in the second equation. From this we find

$\partial_1 F \partial_2 G - \partial_2 F \partial_1 G = 1$. This completes the proof of Theorem I.6.4.

We are now prepared to define the doubling operator. Recall that $\mathcal{D}'_N$ is the set of ϕ's in $\mathcal{D}_N$ which are generated by a S in $\mathcal{D}'_L$. For $\phi \in \mathcal{D}'_N$ we define the doubling operator N by

$$\begin{array}{ccc} \mathcal{D}'_L & \xrightarrow{\;L\;} & \mathcal{D}_L \\ \Big\downarrow I & & \Big\downarrow I \\ \mathcal{D}'_N & \xrightarrow{\;N\;} & \mathcal{D}_N \end{array}$$

THEOREM I.6.5.

1) N is defined as a map $\mathcal{D}'_N \to \mathcal{D}_N$.

2) N takes the form

$$N\phi = \Lambda_\phi^{-1} \circ \phi \circ \phi \circ \Lambda_\phi ,$$

on D_ϕ, where

$$\Lambda_\phi(z_1, z_2) = (\lambda(\phi) z_1 + c(\phi), \mu(\phi) z_2) .$$

The functions $\lambda(\phi), \mu(\phi)$, and $c(\phi)$ are determined from the normalization conditions for $N\phi$.

(They will be given below.)

3) N has a fixed-point ϕ^* in $\mathcal{D}'_N$ and we have

$$\lambda(\phi^*) = \lambda^* ,$$

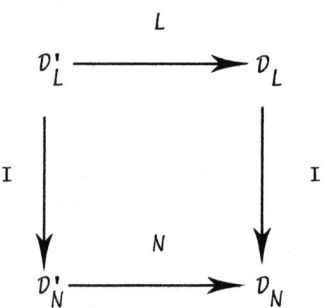

$$\mu(\phi^*) = \mu^* ,$$

$$c(\phi^*) = 0 .$$

REMARK. In fact, the map I is <u>onto</u> a local neighborhood of ϕ^* in the submanifold of all area-preserving, time-reversible maps, which are analytic on D_ϕ.

PROOF : Point 1) follows from the fact that $I : \mathcal{D}_L \to \mathcal{D}_N$ is one-to-one onto. Point 2) is proved by explicit calculation. Recall that

$$S(F(x,y),x) = -y \qquad \text{on } D_\phi ,$$

$$G(x,y) = S(x,F(x,y)) \qquad \text{on } D_\phi ,$$

$$S(\ell x + r, z(x,y)) + S(\ell y + r, z(x,y)) = 0 \qquad \text{on } D_L ,$$

$$m\tilde{S}(x,y) = S(z(x,y), \ell y + r) \qquad \text{on } D_L .$$

It is easy to see that $\lambda(\phi), \mu(\phi)$ and $c(\phi)$ are trivially related to the corresponding quantities of the map L by

$$\lambda(\phi) = \ell ,$$

$$\mu(\phi) = m ,$$

$$c(\phi) = r .$$

We now first show that $\Lambda_\phi D_\phi \subset D_\phi$.

Let $(x,y) \in D_\phi$, then by definition of D_ϕ we have

$$(x,y) = (x, -\tilde{S}(\tilde{y},x)) ,$$

and therefore

$$\Lambda_\phi(x,y) = (\ell x+r,my) = (\ell x+r,-m\tilde{S}(\tilde{y},x)) = (\ell x+r,-S(\tilde{\tilde{y}},\ell x+r)) ,$$

because $\tilde{\tilde{y}} = z(\tilde{y},x)$ implies

$$m\tilde{S}(\tilde{y},x) = S(z(\tilde{y},x),\ell x+r) = S(\tilde{\tilde{y}},\ell x+r) .$$

Next we show $\tilde{\tilde{y}}\in D(\alpha,\eta)$. This follows from the bound for $z(x,y)$ given in Eqs (I.3.13), and the bounds for ℓ,m,r, calculated with Eqs (I.5.3), and bounds for a,b,c,λ,μ, given in Lemma I.5.1 and Theorem I.2.2. From this we conclude, using Lemma I.6.3, that $\Lambda_\phi(x,y)\in D_\phi$.

Next we show that $\phi\circ\Lambda_\phi D_\phi \subset D_\phi$. We have on D_ϕ :

$$S(z(x,\tilde{F}(x,y)),\ell x+r) = m\tilde{S}(\tilde{F}(x,y),x) = -my ,$$

and

$$S(F(\ell x+r,my),\ell x+r) = -my .$$

Because the solution is unique, we conclude

$$z(x,\tilde{F}(x,y)) = F(\ell x+r,my) \quad \text{on} \quad D_\phi . \tag{I.6.3}$$

Furthermore, again on D_ϕ, we have

$$S(\ell x+r,z(x,\tilde{F}(x,y))) + S(\ell\tilde{F}(x,y)+r,z(x,\tilde{F}(x,y))) = 0 .$$

Thus we conclude that for $(x,y)\in D_\phi$,

$$\begin{aligned}\phi\circ\Lambda_\phi(x,y) &= (F(\ell x+r,my),G(\ell x+r,my))\\ &= (F(\ell x+r,my),S(\ell x+r,F(\ell x+r,my)))\\ &= (F(\ell x+r,my),-S(\ell\tilde{F}(x,y)+r,F(\ell x+r,my)) .\end{aligned}$$

This is by Lemma I.6.3 again a point in D_ϕ, because $\ell\tilde{F}(x,y)+r\in D(\alpha,\eta)$.

This follows from the fact that $\tilde{F}$ maps into $D(\alpha,\rho\tau)$ and from the estimates for ℓ and r.

Now $\phi\circ\phi\circ\Lambda_\phi$ is defined on D_ϕ, and we have for $(x,y)\in D_\phi$:

$$F(F(\ell x+r,my),G(\ell x+r,my))$$

$$= F(F(\ell x+r,my),-S(\ell\tilde{F}(x,y)+r,F(\ell x+r,my)))$$

$$= \ell\tilde{F}(x,y)+r\ ,$$

and with this equation and (I.6.3) we get

$$G(F(\ell x+r,my),G(\ell x+r,my))$$

$$= S(z(x,\tilde{F}(x,y)),\ell\tilde{F}(x,y)+r)$$

$$= m\tilde{S}(x,\tilde{F}(x,y)) = m\tilde{G}(x,y)\ .$$

This settles point 2) of the theorem. That the function ϕ^* which is induced by S^*_L is a fixed point of $\mathcal{N}$ and that $\lambda(\phi^*) = \lambda^*$, $\mu'(\phi^*) = \mu^*$, and $c(\phi^*) = 0$ is clear.

This completes the proof of Theorem I.6.5.

PART II. FUNCTIONAL ANALYSIS ON THE COMPUTER

II.1. INTERVAL AND NEIGHBORHOOD ARITHMETICS

In this section, we will first discuss the arithmetics of intervals, a well-known subject [9,10]. Then we shall do an analogous discussion for the arithmetics of balls of functions in a certain space of analytic functions. In the Section II.3, we shall show that all the operations described here are algorithmically implementable in such a way that they lead to rigorous bounds, which can be performed on a computer.

DEFINITION II.1.1. By the word <u>interval</u>, we always mean a finite, closed interval of $\mathbb{R}$. We denote intervals by $[a,b]$, $a,b \in \mathbb{R}$, $a \le b$. The set of intervals will be denoted $\mathcal{J}$.

The arithmetic operations on intervals are defined in such a way that the result of pointwise operations lies in the resulting interval.

We list the operations

addition :

$$[a,b] +_i [a',b'] =: [a+a', b+b']$$

unary minus :

$$-_i [a,b] =: [-b,-a]$$

inverse :

$$1 \div_i [a,b] =: \begin{cases} [1/b, 1/a] & \text{if } a > 0 \text{ or } b < 0 \\ \text{undefined otherwise.} \end{cases}$$

multiplication :

$$[a,b] *_i [a',b'] =: [\min(aa',ab',ba',bb'), \max(aa',ab',ba',bb')] ,$$

absolute value :

$$\mathrm{abs}_i[a,b] =: \begin{cases} [0,\max(|a|,|b|)] & \text{if } ab \le 0 \\ [\min(|a|,|b|),\max(|a|,|b|)] & \text{otherwise,} \end{cases}$$

absolute value (real) :

$$\mathrm{abs}_{ir}[a,b] =: \max(|a|,|b|) .$$

Thus, e.g. if $x\in[a,b]$, $x'\in[a',b']$ then

$$xx'\in[a,b] *_i [a',b'] .$$

REMARK II.1.2. The multiplication $*_i$ is, in general, not distributive. In fact, for $u,u',u''\in J$ one has

$$(u +_i u') *_i u'' \subset (u *_i u'') +_i (u' *_i u'') ,$$

with a <u>strict</u> inclusion in some cases where $u,u'\not\ni 0$, but $u +_i u'\ni 0$. In some of our estimates we have taken this inequality into account, and have on purpose recalculated a product.

Estimates analogous to the case of intervals are possible for operations on sets of functions, and we want to derive these now. Note that we want to give prescriptions of how to form the image set under these operations in such a way that they lead to algorithmically implementable operations.

We start by defining the class of "balls" we admit in our function space. Several choices are possible, but the choice presented here is a carefully balanced compromise between computational efficiency and quality of estimation.

We shall consider functions in two variables, and we leave to the reader the details of extension to more variables or the reduction to one variable. So let D denote the unit polydisk $D = \{x,y \in \mathbb{C}^2 \mid |x| < 1, |y| < 1\}$ and denote by $\mathcal{A}^c$ the set of analytic functions on D, continuous and bounded on $\bar{D}$ and of finite ℓ_1 norm. The ℓ_1 norm of a function is defined by

$$|f|_1 = \sum_{i,j\geq 0} |f_{ij}| ,$$

where $f(x,y) = \sum_{i,j\geq 0} f_{ij} x^i y^j$.

We let $\mathcal{A} \subset \mathcal{A}^c$ be the set of functions with real Taylor coefficients. Equipped with the ℓ_1-norm, $\mathcal{A}$ is a real Banach space. The restriction to real coefficients is for convenience only, and it is sufficient for our purposes. The generalization to arbitrary coefficients is straightforward.

DEFINITION II.1.3. Fix $N \in \mathbb{Z}^+$, and let $v_{ij} \in \mathcal{J}$, $i+j \leq N$, $v_G, v_H \in \mathbb{R}^+$. The set $v = \{v_{ij}, i+j \leq N, v_G, v_H\}$ defines the following subset $\mathcal{A}(v)$ of $\mathcal{A}$, called the ball associated with the boundary v. We denote $\mathcal{B}$ the set of all boundaries. The definition is

$$\mathcal{A}(v) = \{f \in \mathcal{A} \mid \exists\, f_{ij} \in v_{ij},\ 0 \leq i+j \leq N,\ f_G \in \mathcal{A},\ f_H \in \mathcal{A}$$

such that

$$f(x,y) = \sum_{0\leq i+j\leq N} f_{ij} x^i y^j + f_G(x,y) + f_H(x,y)$$

and

$$|f_G|_1 \le v_G \text{ , } |f_H|_1 \le v_H \text{ ,}$$

and for all $(x,y)\in\bar{\mathcal{D}}$,

$$\lim_{s\to 0} f_H(sx,sy)s^{-N-1} \text{ is finite}\} \text{ .}$$

In words, $A(v)$ is the set of those functions f of A which can be written as

$$f = f_P + f_H + f_G \text{ ,}$$

where f_P is a polynomial of degree N whose coefficients lie in the v_{ij},

f_H is a function of high order in A, with norm $\le v_H$,

f_G is a general function in A, with norm $\le v_G$.

We denote $A_{>N}$ the set of high-order functions

$$A_{>N} = \{f\in A | \lim_{s\to 0} f(sx,sy)s^{-N-1} \text{ is finite for all } (x,y)\in\bar{\mathcal{D}}\} \text{ .}$$

Note that $A(v)$ is a closed, convex set in A.

We now discuss several operations on $\mathcal{B}$, in the order of increasing complexity.

a) Linear operations

Multiplication by a real number

Let $s\in\mathcal{J}$, $v\in\mathcal{B}$. Then we define

$$s *_{ia} A(v) = \{f | f = x\cdot g;\ x\in s,\ g\in A(v)\} \text{ .}$$

It is then easy to see that

$$s *_{ia} A(v) \subset A(s *_{ib} v) \text{ ,}$$

where $*_{ib} : \mathcal{J} \times \mathcal{B} \to \mathcal{B}$ is defined by

$$s *_{ib} v = \{s *_i v_{ij} , \text{abs}_{ir}(s)\cdot v_G , \text{abs}_{ir}(s)\cdot v_H\} .$$

Sums

For $v, v' \in \mathcal{B}$, we define

$$A(v) +_a A(v') = \{f | f = g + g', g \in A(v), g' \in A(v')\} .$$

Then we have

$$A(v) +_a A(v') \subset A(v +_b v') ,$$

where $+_b : \mathcal{B} \times \mathcal{B} \to \mathcal{B}$ is defined by

$$v +_b v' = \{v_{ij} +_i v'_{ij} , v_G + v'_G , v_H + v'_H\} .$$

Norms

We define $\text{norm}_b : \mathcal{B} \to \mathcal{J}$ by

$$\text{norm}_b(v) = [\inf_{f \in A(v)} |f|_1 , \sup_{f \in A(v)} |f|_1] .$$

Note that

$$\text{norm}_b(v) \subset \sum_{mn} {}_i \, \text{abs}_i v_{mn} +_i [0, v_H] +_i [-v_G, v_G] .$$

We shall use this bound in the program. It will be convenient to make use of another function $\text{norm}_{br} : \mathcal{B} \to \mathbb{R}^+$,. defined by $\text{norm}_{br}(v) = \sup_{f \in A(v)} |f|_1$, with a bound similar to the one for norm_b.

b) Multiplication

This is the first estimate which is not totally obvious. Given two vectors, v, v' we define

$$A(v) *_a A(v') = \{f | f = g\cdot g' \ , \ g\in A(v), \ g'\in A(v')\} \ ,$$

i.e. the pointwise multiplication of functions in A. It is easy to see from the Taylor expansion that the following inequality is true

$$|g\cdot g'|_1 \le |g|_1 |g'|_1 \ . \tag{II.1.1}$$

We shall decompose the product $g\cdot g'$ as follows :

$$[\sum_{i+j\le N} g_{ij} x^i y^j + g_G(x,y) + g_H(x,y)]$$

$$\cdot[\sum_{i+j\le N} g'_{ij} x^i y^j + g'_G(x,y) + g'_H(x,y)]$$

$$= \sum_{i+j\le N} h_{ij} x^i y^j + h'_G(x,y) + h'_H(x,y) \ ,$$

where

$$h_{ij} = \sum_{\substack{k+\ell\le i \\ m+n\le j \\ k+m\le N,\, \ell+n\le N}} g_{km} g'_{\ell n} \ , \tag{II.1.2}$$

$$h_G(x,y) = g_G(x,y)\cdot(g' - g'_G - g'_H)(x,y)$$

$$+ g'_G(x,y)(g - g_G - g_H)(x,y)$$

$$+ g_G(x,y) g'_G(x,y) \ , \tag{II.1.3}$$

$$h_H(x,y) = \sum_{k+\ell+m+n>N} g_{km} g'_{\ell n} x^{k+\ell} y^{m+n}$$

$$+ g_H(x,y) g'_G(x,y) + g'_H(x,y) g_G(x,y)$$

$$+ g_H(x,y) g'_H(x,y) \ . \tag{II.1.4}$$

Thus h_H contains all high order terms. Using the inequality (II.1.1), it is easy to derive an adequate definition of $*_b$ for the inclusion

$$A(v) *_a A(v') \subset A(v *_b v') ,$$

by defining in parallel to (II.1.2,4) :

$$(v *_b v')_{ij} = \sum_{\substack{k+\ell\le i\\ m+n\le j\\ k+m\le N,\ \ell+n\le N}} v_{km} *_i v'_{\ell n}$$

$$\begin{aligned}(v *_b v')_G &= v_G \cdot \sum_{i+j\le N} \mathrm{abs}_{ir}(v'_{ij}) \\ &+ v'_G \cdot \sum_{i+j\le N} \mathrm{abs}_{ir}(v_{ij}) \\ &+ v_G \cdot v'_G\end{aligned}$$

and analogously for $(v *_b v')_H$.

c) Composition

Given $f,g,g' \epsilon A$ we want to bound the composite function

$$h = f\circ(g\oplus g'),\ h(x,y) = f(g(x,y),g'(x,y))$$

in terms of bounds on its constituents. The following bound is useful.

LEMMA II.1.4. *If* $f,g,g' \epsilon A$, $|g|_1 \le 1$, $|g'|_1 \le 1$, *then*

$$h\epsilon A, \ \text{and}\ \ |h|_1 \le |f|_1 .$$

If, in addition, $f\epsilon A_{>N}$ *(i.e.* f *of order* $>N$), *then*

$$|h|_1 \le |f|_1 \max(|g|_1, |g'|_1)^{N+1} .$$

PROOF : This follows at once from the inequality (II.1.1) combined with

$$h = \Sigma f_{ij} g^i g'^j .$$

Given the above bound, we can now *define a bound* $\mathrm{comp}_b : B \times B \times B \to B$, *such* that

$$\{f\circ(g\oplus g') \mid f\in A(v),\ g\in A(w),\ g'\in A(w')\} \subset A(\mathrm{comp}_b(v,w,w')) \ , \qquad \text{(II.1.5)}$$

provided $\mathrm{norm}_{br}(w) \le 1$, $\mathrm{norm}_{br}(w') \le 1$.

Since composition is linear in the first argument, it suffices to consider separately the cases $v = \{v_{ij}\}$, $v = \{v_G\}$, $v = \{v_H\}$, i.e. a "polynomial", a general "function", and a high order "function". In the case of a polynomial, we define

$$\mathrm{comp}_b(v,w,w') = \Sigma_b v_{ij} *_{ib} \underbrace{w *_b \cdots *_b w}_{i} *_b \underbrace{w' *_b \cdots *_b w'}_{j} \ .$$

This clearly leads to the desired bound (II.1.5) in view of the results of the earlier subsections.

In the case of a general function, $v = \{v_G\}$, we define

$$[\mathrm{comp}_b(v,w,w')]_{ij} = [0,0] \ ,$$

$$[\mathrm{comp}_b(v,w,w')]_G = v_G \ ,$$

$$[\mathrm{comp}_b(v,w,w')]_H = 0 \ .$$

This leads to the desired bound by the Lemma II.1.4, and by the assumption $\mathrm{norm}_{br} w \le 1$, $\mathrm{norm}_{br} w' \le 1$.

Finally, in the case of a high order function, $v = \{v_H\}$, we want to use the second part of the lemma, sacrificing some of the bounds for computational efficiency. We base the construction of comp_b on the following

LEMMA II.1.5. Assume $f\in A_{>N}$, $g,g'\in A$, $|g|_1$, $|g'|_1 \le 1$. Then

$f\circ(g\oplus g') = h_G + h_H$ with $h_G \in A$, $h_H \in A_{>N}$ and

$$|h_G|_1 \le |f|_1 \max_{i+j=N+1} (|g|_1^i |g'|_1^j - |g|_1^{*i} |g'|_1^{*j}) ,$$

$$|h_H|_1 \le |f|_1 \max(|g|_1^*, |g'|_1^*)^{N+1} ,$$

where $|g|_1^* = |g - g(0,0)|_1$.

Postponing the proof, we are led to the definition : If $v = \{v_H\}$, then

$$[\mathrm{comp}_b(v,w,w')]_{ij} = [0,0] ,$$

$$[\mathrm{comp}_b(v,w,w')]_G$$

$$= v_H \cdot \max_{m+n=N+1} (\mathrm{norm}_{br}^m(w) \cdot \mathrm{norm}_{br}^n(w') - \inf\{\hat{w}^{*_i m} *_i \hat{w}'^{*_i n}\}) ,$$

$$[\mathrm{comp}_b(v,w,w')]_H = v_H(\sup\{\hat{w} \cup \hat{w}'\})^{N+1} ,$$

where the interval $\hat{w}$ is defined by

$$\hat{w} = \sum_{i+j>0} \mathrm{abs}_i(w_{ij}) +_i [0,w_H] +_i [-w_G,w_G] ,$$

i.e. $\hat{w} = \mathrm{norm}_i(w$ with w_{oo} set to $[0,0])$, which provides a lower bound on $|f|_1^*$, $f \in A(w)$.

We leave to the reader the verification that these bounds are a consequence of the lemma.

PROOF OF THE LEMMA : Consider a term for fixed i,j,

$$X = f_{ij}(\alpha+\beta)^i(\alpha'+\beta')^j ,$$

where $\alpha = g(0,0)$ and $\alpha + \beta = g$, and similarly for g'. Recall that

$i + j > N$. If $i \le N + 1$, we decompose X as follows :

$$X = f_{ij}\beta^i\beta'^{N+1-i}(\alpha' + \beta')^{j-N-1+i}$$

$$+ f_{ij}(\alpha' + \beta')^{j-N-1+i}((\alpha + \beta)^i(\alpha' + \beta')^{N+1-i} - \beta^i\beta'^{N+1-i}) ,$$

and we consider the first term as a contribution to h_H, the second as a contribution to h_G. The bound on the first term is

$$|f_{ij}||\beta|_1^i|\beta'|_1^{N+1-i}$$

and the bound on the second term is

$$f_{ij} \;(|\alpha + \beta|_1^i|\alpha' + \beta'|_1^{N+1-i} - |\beta|_1^i|\beta'|_1^{N+1-i}) ,$$

since the ℓ_1 norm is additive in the coefficients of the Taylor expansion of a function. (Cf. also Hille [11] for a general discussion of properties of the ℓ_1 norm.)

If $i > N + 1$ then we decompose X as

$$X = f_{ij}\beta^{N+1}(\alpha + \beta)^{i-N-1}(\alpha' + \beta')^j$$

$$+ f_{ij}((\alpha + \beta)^{N+1} - \beta^{N+1})(\alpha + \beta)^{i-N-1}(\alpha' + \beta')^j ,$$

leading to the bounds

$$|f_{ij}||\beta|_1^{N+1} ,$$

and $|f_{ij}|(|\alpha + \beta|_1^{N+1} - |\beta|_1^{N+1})$.

Summing over i,j, we obtain the bound of the lemma.

REMARK II.1.6. The preceding discussion leads with obvious simplifications to an algorithm

$$\text{value}_b : \mathcal{B} \times \mathcal{J} \times \mathcal{J} \to \mathcal{J} ,$$

corresponding to evaluation of a function :

$$\{f(x,x') \in \mathbb{R} \mid f \in A(v),\ x \in u,\ x' \in u'\} \subset \text{value}_b(v,u,u') .$$

d) Derivative and composition

Here, we wish to describe operations of the form $\partial_1 f \circ (g \oplus g')$, where the range of g, g' is strictly inside the unit disk.

We define $\text{dx comp}_b : \mathcal{B} \times \mathcal{B} \times \mathcal{B} \to \mathcal{B}$ in such a way that for all w, w' with $\text{norm}_{br}(w) < 1$, $\text{norm}_{br}(w') \le 1$, we have

$$\{h \mid h = \partial_1 f \circ (g \oplus g') \mid f \in A(v),\ g \in A(w),\ g' \in A(w')\} \subset A(\text{dx comp}_b(v,w,w')) .$$

The modifications for $\text{dx value}_b : \mathcal{B} \times \mathcal{J} \times \mathcal{J} \to \mathcal{J}$ are similar to the ones leading from comp_b to value_b, and are left to the reader.

The construction of dx comp_b again uses the linearity of composition. If the function is a polynomial, $v = \{v_{ij}\}$, then, obviously

$$\text{dx comp}_b(v,w,w') = \text{comp}_b(\hat{v},w,w') ,$$

$$\text{where} \qquad \hat{v}_{k\ell} = \begin{cases} [k,k] *_i v_{k+1,\ell} & \text{if } k+\ell < N \\ [0,0] & \text{if } k+\ell = N \end{cases}$$

$$\hat{v}_G = \hat{v}_H = 0 .$$

If the function is general, $v = \{v_G\}$, then

$$\text{dx}\,\text{comp}_b(v,w,w')_{k\ell} = [0,0]\ ,$$

$$\text{dx}\,\text{comp}_b(v,w,w')_G = v_G \cdot \sup_{k>0} k(\text{norm}_{br}\ w)^{k-1}\ ,$$

$$\text{dx}\,\text{comp}_b(v,w,w')_H = 0\ .$$

Finally, if $v = \{v_H\}$, then we have the bound

$$\text{dx}\,\text{comp}_b(v,w,w')_{k\ell} = 0$$

$$\text{dx}\,\text{comp}_b(v,w,w')_G = v_H \sup_{k+\ell>N} k(\text{norm}_{br}\ w)^{k-1}(\text{norm}_{br}\ w')^{\ell}$$

$$\text{dx}\,\text{comp}_b(v,w,w')_H = 0\ .$$

These definitions follow from the equality

$$\partial_1 f\circ(g \oplus g') = \sum_{k,\ell} f_{k\ell} k g^{k-1} g'^{\ell}\ ,$$

and Lemma II.1.5.

REMARK II.1.7. The expressions $\sup_{k>0} k(\text{norm}_{br}\ w)^{k-1}$ and $\sup_{k+\ell>N} k(\text{norm}_{br}\ w)^{k-1}(\text{norm}_{br}\ w')^{\ell}$ are computable with a finite amount of effort since the suprema are attained for $k < k_o$, $\ell < \ell_o$, where k_o, ℓ_o are finite numbers depending only on $\text{norm}_{br}(w)$, $\text{norm}_{br}(w')$.

e) Roots of functions

In this subsection, we consider equations of the form $f(x) = 0$ with $x \in \mathbb{R}^2$ and $f \in A(v)$. The problem is to find a rectangle $u \in \mathcal{J}^2$ such that every $f \in A(v)$ has a root $x \in u$. The extension to more variables is straightforward. Our analysis is a variant of the standard Newton method.

Given $v \in \mathcal{B}$ and $u_o \in \mathcal{J}^2$, we define

$$e = \{f(x) \in \mathbb{R}^2 \mid f \in A(v),\ x \in u_o\} .$$

This e measures the quality of approximation of the approximate "root" u_o. Given now $t \in J^2$, we define

$$A_{ij} = A_{ij}(v,t) = \{(Df_x)_{ij} \mid f \in A(v),\ x \in t\}, \quad i,j = 1,2 ,$$

in other words, each matrix element of Df varies in a set $A_{ij} \in J$, when f varies in $A(v)$ and the point of evaluation varies in t. Denote by A the matrix $\{A_{ij}\}$ and by A^{-1} the matrix of intervals

$$A^{-1} = \bigcup_{a_{ij} \in A_{ij}} [a]^{-1}_{ij}$$

In the case of $\mathbb{R}^2$, A^{-1} is easily computed : Let $d = 1 \div_i (A_{11} *_i A_{22} -_i A_{12} *_i A_{21})$. Then

$$A^{-1}_{11} = d *_i A_{22} \quad , A^{-1}_{22} = d *_i A_{11} \quad ,$$

$$A^{-1}_{12} = -_i d *_i A_{12} \, , A^{-1}_{21} = -_i d *_i A_{21} \, .$$

Thus the inverse of every matrix in A is contained in A^{-1}. Note that, in general, $(A^{-1})^{-1} \supsetneq A$.

THEOREM II.1.8. <u>With the above notations, assume</u>

$$u_o +_i A^{-1} *_i e \subset \text{interior of } t .$$

<u>Then every</u> f <u>in</u> $A(v)$ <u>has a unique zero in</u> t.

REMARK II.1.9. One can improve the bounds by iteratively replacing t by $t' = u_o +_i A^{-1} *_i e$ and recalculating $A = A(v,t')$ and A^{-1} for the smaller set t'.

PROOF : Fix an $f\in A(v)$. For every $x_o \in u_o$ and $y \in t -_i [x_o, x_o]$ we define

$$y' = -\left[\int_0^1 Df_{x_o+\tau y}\, d\tau\right]^{-1} f(x_o) \ . \tag{II.1.6}$$

By assumption, $(Df_{x_o+\tau y})_{ij} \in A_{ij}$ for all $x_o \in u_o$, all $y \in t -_i [x_o, x_o]$ and all $\tau\in[0,1]$. Hence,

$$\left[\int_0^1 Df_{x_o+\tau y}\, dy\right]^{-1}_{ij} \in (A^{-1})_{ij} \ .$$

The assumption of the theorem implies that $y' + x_o \in$ interior of t. Thus the map $x_o + y \to x_o + y'$, defined by Eq. (II.1.6), maps t strictly into itself. Hence it has a fixed point y^* and then

$$y^* = -\left[\int_0^1 Df_{x_o+\tau y^*}\, d\tau\right]^{-1} f(x_o)$$

or, equivalently

$$y^* \int_0^1 Df_{x_o+\tau y^*}\, d\tau + f(x_o) = 0$$

i.e. $f(x_o + y^*) = 0$, as asserted. The invertibility of A implies the unicity of the fixed point.

f) <u>The Implicit Function</u>

Given $v\in \mathcal{B}$, we want to discuss the solutions g of the equations

$$f(g(x),x) = 0 \ ,$$

when f varies in $A(v)$ and $f(0,0)=0$. The function g will then vary in a set $A'(v')$, where

$$v' \in \mathcal{B}' = \{v \mid v_i \ , \ i \le N, \ v_G \ , \ v_H\}$$

and

$$A'(v') = \{g : \mathbb{C} \to \mathbb{C} \mid g(x) = \sum_{i\le N} g_i x^i + g_G(x) + g_H(x)$$

and $g_i \in v_i \in J$, $|g_G|_1' \le v_G$, $|g_H|_1' \le v_H$ and

$\lim_{x\to 0} g_H(x)x^{-N-1}$ is bounded$\}$, with $|\cdot|_1'$ the ℓ_1-norm on functions in 1 variable. Thus A' is the analog of A for the case of one variable.

Assume v is given and $v_{oo} = [0,0]$, $v_{10} \not\ni 0$. Assume first $v_G = v_H = 0$. Given N, there is, for every $f \in A(v)$ a unique polynomial $g_{P,f}$ of degree N such that $f(g_{P,f}(x),x)$ is $O(x^{N+1})$. Define

$$E = \bigcup_{f\in A(v)} f(g_{P,f}(x),x)$$

and

$$e = \sup_{h\in E} |h|_1' .$$

Next we define, for $\rho < 1$,

$$d_\rho = \inf_{f\in A(v)} (|\partial_1 f(0,0)| - |\partial_1 f\circ(\rho.\oplus 1.) - \partial_1 f(0,0)|_1) ,$$

where $h\circ(\rho.\oplus 1.)(x,y) = h(\rho x,y)$. Note that d_ρ is a lower bound for $|\partial_1 f(\rho x,y)|$.

<u>REMARK</u> II.1.10. Bounds on d_ρ and e and $|g_{P,f}|_1'$ can be constructively given for the set $\{f|f\in A(v)\}$. Namely, $g_{P,f}$ can be arithmetically constructed from f (using interval arithmetics). The number d_ρ is bounded below by

$$d_\rho \ge \inf\{\mathrm{abs}_i(v_{10})\} - \mathrm{norm}_{br}(\mathrm{dx\,comp}_b(\hat{v},\text{"}\rho x\text{"},\text{"}y\text{"})) ,$$

where $\hat{v}$ equals v with v_{10} replaced by zero, "ρx", "y" represent the boundaries of the functions ρx and y.

Let $g = \sup_{f\in A(v)} |g_{P,f}|_1'$. If $g + e/d_\rho < \rho$ then there is, for every

$x\in D_1$ and every $f\in A(v)$, a unique $h_f(x)$ such that $|h_f(x)| < e/d_\rho$ and and $f(g_{P,f}(x) + h_f(x),x) = 0$. In addition, $h_f(x)$ is analytic by the implicit function theorem. To bound the ℓ_1-norm of h, consider the map T_f :

$$T_f(h)(x) = -[\int_0^1 \partial_1 f(g_{P,f}(x) + \tau h(x),x)d\tau]^{-1} f(g_{P,f}(x),x) .$$

Under the above conditions, T_f maps the ball $\{h | |h|_1' \le e/d_\rho\}$ strictly into itself. On the other hand, if we set $h_o = 0$ then $T_f^n(h_o)$ produces the correct h_f up to and including order $N + n$. Thus $\lim_{n\to\infty} T_f^n(h_o)$ converges to a fixed point h_f of T_f, which is the solution to $f(g_{P,f}(x) + h_f(x),x) = 0$, and $|h_f|_1' \le e/d_\rho$.

In the case when v_G or v_H are not zero, one considers first the polynomial part as before. The quantities e,d_ρ are defined as above, but the sets $A(v)$ are now larger. The argument then goes through as before. Note that if $f = f_P + f_H$, i.e. if the f_G term is zero, then h_f is higher order only.

II.2. SPECTRAL THEORY

In this section we present some of the considerations which are more specifically necessary for our problem :

a) Showing that the derivative of a map $A \to A$ is a contraction

This is needed as the main ingredient of Theorem I.3.1. In the case at hand, the tangent map in question has an explicit algebraic definition, i.e. there are a certain number of equations to be solved to determine a matrix element. Thus, for every $f \in A$, and reasonable S, say, $DK_S f$ is well defined. Note that the norm of a linear operator on ℓ_1 is the supremum of the norms of its column vectors.

We now split $A = A_P \oplus A_{>N}$, where A_P are polynomials of degree $\leq N$. Then, for all $S \in A(v)$ for some v, we can certainly estimate the matrix elements, and hence the ℓ_1 norm of $DK_S|_{A_P}$. Since DK_S is well defined, algorithmically, on all of A, the algorithms described before will be able to deal with $f \in A_{>N}$ exactly as with $f \in A_P$. Namely, every $f \in A_{>N}$ with $|f|_1 \leq 1$ is contained in $A(v_1)$ with $v_1 = \{v_H\}$, $v_H = 1$. Thus, in the case of $A_{>N}$ it suffices to check that $\{DK_S f \mid f \in A(v_1), S \in A(v)\} \subset A(v')$ for some v' with $\mathrm{norm}_{br}(v') < 1$. This is a finite problem.

A trivial example of this phenomenon is the following. Assume $DK_S f(x,y) = f(\rho x, \rho y) - f(0,0)$ with $0 < \rho < 1$. Clearly we see immediately that this operator is a contraction. But suppose we may only use the algorithms described above. Then application of comp_b in the case of the high-order part also shows that we are in the presence of a contraction on an infinite dimensional space, with a finite amount of computation. The point of our method is that this principle remains valid for very complex operators N. [We need degree $N \sim 20$ for the bound on the high-order term to become sufficiently small. The operation comp_b, in that case needs about $0.9 \cdot 10^7$ multiplications, and $1.6 \cdot 10^8$ additions.]

b) Checking spectral properties of a linear map $A \to A$

In order to discuss the spectral properties of DK, we develop some general machinery. Let X be a Banach space $X = \mathbb{R} \oplus \mathbb{R} \oplus X'$ with the norm of $(u,v,w) \in X$ defined by

$$|(u,v,w)| = |u| + |v| + |w|_{X'} , \quad \text{where}$$

$|\ |_{X'}$ is the norm on X'. A linear operator $A : X \to X$ can then be viewed as a 3×3 "matrix"

$$\begin{bmatrix} A_{11} & A_{12} & A_{13} \\ A_{21} & A_{22} & A_{23} \\ A_{31} & A_{32} & A_{33} \end{bmatrix} ,$$

in an obvious fashion. Denote by

$$B_{13} = |A_{13}|_{X'*} , \ B_{23} = |A_{23}|_{X'*} ,$$

$$B_{31} = |A_{31}|_{X'} , \ B_{32} = |A_{32}|_{X'} , \ B_{33} = |A_{33}|_{X' \to X'} ,$$

$$B_{12} = |A_{12}| , \ B_{21} = |A_{21}| .$$

Our first result is the following

LEMMA II.2.1. For $\lambda \in \mathbb{R}$, $A - \lambda$ is invertible if, in the sense of interval arithmetics, the matrix

$$M_\lambda = \begin{pmatrix} [A_{11}-\lambda, A_{11}-\lambda] & [-B_{12}, B_{12}] & [-B_{13}, B_{13}] \\ [-B_{21}, B_{21}] & [A_{22}-\lambda, A_{22}-\lambda] & [-B_{23}, B_{23}] \\ [-B_{31}, B_{31}] & [-B_{32}, B_{32}] & [-B_{33}-\lambda, B_{33}-\lambda] \end{pmatrix}$$

has non-zero determinant.

PROOF : Denote by $D_\lambda = 1/\mathrm{abs}_{ir}$ (determinant M_λ). We shall show that if $(u,v,w)\in X$ has norm 1 then $A(u,v,w)$ has norm at least $\mathcal{O}(D_\lambda)$, proving the assertion.

Let us consider the first component of $A(u,v,w)$. It is equal to

$$(A_{11}-\lambda)u + A_{12}v + A_{13}w$$

$$= (A_{11}-\lambda)u + A_{12}v + x\cdot|w|_{X'} \quad \text{with} \quad x\in[-B_{13},B_{13}].$$

A similar formula holds for the second component. For the third component, we have

$$A_{31}u + A_{32}v + (A_{33}-\lambda)w = t \ ,$$

where the norm of t is

$$|t|_{X'} = |x_1u + x_2v + (x_3-\lambda)|w|_{X'}| , \quad \text{with} \quad x_i\in[-B_{3i},B_{3i}],\ i = 1,2,3 \ .$$

Under the assumptions of the lemma, every vector $(U,V,W)\in\mathbb{R}^3$ is mapped by every matrix X in M_λ onto a vector whose norm is at least

$$(|U| + |V| + |W|)/(|(X-\lambda)^{-1}|_{\mathbb{R}^3\to\mathbb{R}^3}) \geq \text{const } D_\lambda(|U| + |V| + |W|) \ ,$$

where the constant depends only on the numbers A_{ij}, B_{ij} and is positive.

Given $(u,v,w)\in X$, we apply this last observation to the vector $U = u$, $V = v$, $W = |w|_{X'}$ and obtain the result, since $|U| + |V| + |W| = |(u,v,w)|_X$.

For the remainder of this section, we deviate slightly from the principle of discussing only general problems, and restrict out attention now to a subproblem more specifically designed for Part I.

In fact, in the subroutine SPECTRUM, we verify, for the case at hand i.e. $M \sim DK$, that the determinant of M_λ is negative for $\lambda \in [-50,-4.4]$, positive for $\lambda \in [-3.6,-0.83]$, again negative for $\lambda \in [+0.85,8.2]$ and finally positive for $\lambda \in [9.2,50]$. These inequalities are checked as follows: Each of the four intervals is cut into several smaller intervals. For every one of them, one then calculates $\det M_L$, where the interval L replaces the number λ. It is then checked whether the resulting interval does lie on the expected side of zero.

Note that the diagonal matrix elements of M are about 8.5, -4.1 and $[-.55,.55]$, cf. Estimate I.4.2. Hence, for the central values of the off-diagonal elements (i.e. the value 0) the matrix M has 1 eigenvalue near 8.5 and another near -4.1, and they are both simple. Therefore the same is true for the operator A', which is defined by

$$A' = \begin{pmatrix} A_{11} & 0 & 0 \\ 0 & A_{22} & 0 \\ 0 & 0 & A_{33} \end{pmatrix} .$$

The remainder of the spectrum of M and of A' is strictly inside a disk of radius 0.55.

We want to use perturbation theory (see e.g. [12]), and therefore we would like to bound the resolvent in the complex plane. Clearly, our operator A has norm <49, and hence the resolvent $(A-\lambda)^{-1}$ is bounded on a circle of radius, say 49 (i.e. less than 50) around the origin. The same is of course true for $(M-\lambda)^{-1}$, for all possible choices of the individual matrix elements. Hence A has no spectrum outside this disk. Next, consider e.g. the "eigenvalue" near 8.5, and consider the contour γ shown below. Cf. Fig.3

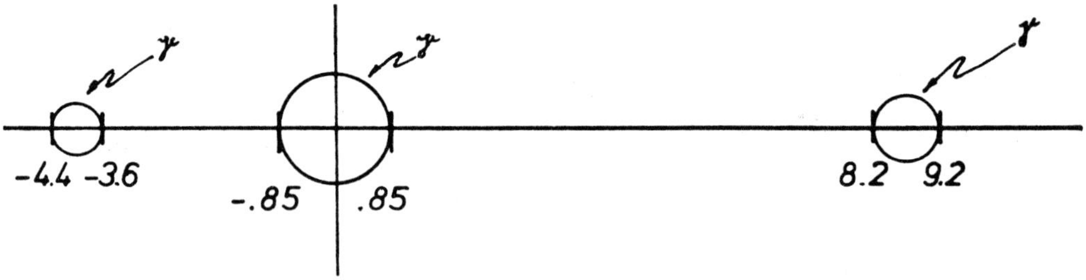

Fig.3. Contour γ.

We claim the bounds given before suffice to show that the resolvent is not singular on γ. This follows at once from the fact that $\lambda - B_{11}$, $\lambda - B_{22}$, $\lambda - B_{33}$ are the only terms forming the determinant M_λ which have a definite sign. Hence our estimate really said that

$$\inf \left| \prod_{i=1}^{3} (\lambda - B_{ii}) \right| - \left| \text{other terms of determinant} \right| > 0$$

and this clearly extends to contours of the shape of γ. Thus the resolvent is regular on γ. Viewing A as a perturbation of A', we conclude :

LEMMA II.2.2. A has a simple eigenvalue near 8.5 and near -4.1. If A is real then these two eigenvalues are real. Thus Theorem I.4.1 is proven (since $A = DK$ is real.)

II.3. INTERVAL AND NEIGHBORHOOD ARITHMETICS ON A COMPUTER

The aim of this section is to discuss and to document how the analysis of the preceding section can be carried over to a digital computer, yielding rigorous bounds.

It might seem, after the careful algorithmic discussion of the preceding section that this is an obvious task. But this is not quite so, because computers fail at the most trivial level : They cannot do calculations with real numbers but only with some rational numbers which can be internally represented in the memory of the computer. We call such numbers representable numbers, or reps for short. Thus the task of this section is to define the sort of operation of the average computer, and to show that it is possible to systematically correct roundoff errors in such a way that rigorous bounds on intervals and boundaries of neighborhoods are possible. This then proves, together with the last section, that RIGOROUS FUNCTIONAL ANALYTICAL ESTIMATES ARE POSSIBLE ON A COMPUTER.

a) Rounding

We assume that integer operations on indices, counting loops, and the like are performed without any rounding errors on the computer, and we do not discuss this matter any further. Let us consider next real numbers. As we have just said, the computer can only represent a finite subset of $\mathbb{R}$, called the representable numbers, or reps. We denote the set of reps by $\mathcal{R}$, and we enumerate now a set of requirements a computer must fulfill in order for our method to work. These requirements (or very simple variants thereof) seem to be satisfied on most modern computers.

R1) R contains zero and one.

R2) If $x \in R$, then $-x \in R$.

R3) There is a smallest positive number, x_o, in R.

The arithmetic operations should then satisfy :

R4) If $x \in R$, the computer correctly finds $-x \in R$.

R5) For any pair $x, y \in R$, the computer can correctly decide whether $x = y$, $x > y$, or $x < y$.

R6) Given $x \in R$, and defining $R_e = R \cup$ "undefined", it is possible to define operations up, down : $R \to R_e$ by

$$\mathrm{up}(x) = \begin{cases} \inf\{y \in R \mid y > x\} & \text{if this set is not empty} \\ \text{undefined otherwise}, & \end{cases}$$

$$\mathrm{down}(x) = \begin{cases} \sup\{y \in R \mid y < x\} & \text{if this set is not empty} \\ \text{undefined otherwise}. & \end{cases}$$

R7) Given $x, y \in R$, the computer can perform their approximate product, denoted $x *_c y$, yielding a result $z \in R_e$ (undefined only if the product is too large or too negative). The precision of the result is such that

$$\mathrm{down}(x *_c y) \le xy \le \mathrm{up}(x *_c y) .$$

Mutatis mutandis, the same requirements are made for the operation of taking inverses, denoted $1 \div_c x$.

$\mathcal{R}8$) We require for the computer addition

$$\mathrm{down}(x +_c y) \le x + y \le \mathrm{up}(x +_c y) .$$

In short, the computer is required to perform the arithmetic operations to as many places as is possible, with a minimal rounding error, among the numbers it can represent.

It is straightforward, if tedious, to implement the operations up, down : $\mathcal{R} \to \mathcal{R}_e$ in practice. We give below the Fortran code for up on a Univac 1100. Down is realized as

$$\mathrm{down}(x) = -_c\, \mathrm{up}(-_c\, x) .$$

REMARK II.3.1. As for most algorithms, we give now an introduction to the program, followed by a listing.

On a Univac 1100, with the ASCII compiler, double real numbers consist of two integer words of 36 bits each, which we number from 1 to 72 from left to right. If all 72 bits are 0, the number is interpreted as $0 \in \mathbb{R}$. All positive reps have a 0 bit in position 1 and a 1 bit in position 13. The number 1/2 is in $\mathcal{R}$ and is represented as

200040000000 , 000000000000

in octal notation. In fact, the rules are as follows. Bits 2 to 12 represent the exponent and bits 13 to 72 the mantissa. View bits 2 to 12 as the binary representation of a non-negative integer, n, and bits 13 to 72 as the fractional part $x\epsilon[1/2,1)$ of a binary number. Then the number represented by the 72 bits is

$$x2^{n-2^{10}} .$$

Thus, 1/2 is represented as $0.5 \times 2^{2^{10}-2^{10}}$. The smallest positive rep is

000040000000 , 000000000000

$= 0.5 \cdot 2^{-2^{10}} \sim 0.278 \cdot 10^{-308}$

and the largest positive rep is

677777777777 , 777777777777

$= (1 - 2^{-60}) \cdot 2^{(2^{11}-1)-2^{10}} \sim 0.899 \cdot 10^{+308}$.

All negative numbers x are represented as the two's complement of -x.

Essentially, up consists in adding 1 to bit 72, with the 72 bits viewed as a single huge integer. The only programming precaution, which may be necessary on other computer models as well is the following. The integer addition of the Univac 1100 does not correctly operate on the numbers 777777777777 and 777777777776 when they are viewed as positive integers, because, internally, the first is considered to be 0 and the second to be -1, and therefore the first never occurs as the result of an integer operation. We handle these special cases by operating directly on bits.

The program listing follows. BITS(K,L,M) gets or puts M bits, starting from bit L in a simple integer word of 36 bits whose name is K.

```
      REAL FUNCTION rUP*8(r)
      IMPLICIT REAL*8(r)
      DIMENSION LL(2)
      EQUIVALENCE (rRES,LL(1),K),(LL(2),L)
      DATA L351/O377777777777/
      rRES=r
C..IF LOW PART OF MANTISSA IS,0,777777777776,OR 777777777777
C  THEN EXCEPTIONAL HANDLING
      IF(BITS(L,1,35).EQ.L351)GOTO 3
      IF(L)2,1,2
C..LOW PART ZERO.CHECK IF R IS ZERO
    1 CONTINUE
      IF(rRES.NE.0.D+00)GOTO 2
C..R IS ZERO. UP IS SMALLEST POSITIVE NUMBER
      BITS(K,13,1)=1
      rUP=rRES
      RETURN
C..GENERIC CASE, ADD ONE TO LOWER PART OF MANTISSA
    2 CONTINUE
      L=L+1
      rUP=rRES
      RETURN
C..LOWER PART OF MANTISSA IS 777777777776 OR 777777777777
    3 CONTINUE
      IF(BITS(L,36,1).EQ.1)GOTO 4
C..CASE OF 777777777776, CHANGED TO 777777777777
      BITS(L,36,1)=1
      rUP=rRES
      RETURN
C..CASE OF 777777777777
    4 CONTINUE
      L=0
      KSAVE=BITS(K,13,1)
      BITS(K,13,1)=1
      K=K+1
C..CHECK CASE OF OVERFLOW OR UNDERFLOW
      IF(BITS(K,1,1).EQ.KSAVE)GOTO 5
C..RESTORE BIT 13
      BITS(K,13,1)=KSAVE
      rUP=rRES
      RETURN
C..DISTINGUISH OVERFLOW UNDERFLOW
    5 CONTINUE
      IF(KSAVE.EQ.0)GOTO 6
C..OVERFLOW
      WRITE(9,*)'OVERFLOW IN UP'
      rUP=R
      RETURN
C..UNDERFLOW,RESULT IS ZERO
    6 CONTINUE
      L=0
      K=0
      rUP=rRES
      RETURN
      END
```

```
REAL FUNCTION rDOWN*8(r)
IMPLICIT REAL*8(r)
rDOWN=-rUP(-r)
RETURN
END
```

It will be convenient to define upward-rounded operations $R \times R \to R$:

$$x +_u y = \mathrm{up}(x +_c y) ,$$

$$x -_u y = \mathrm{up}(x +_c (-_c y)) ,$$

$$x *_u y = \mathrm{up}(x *_c y) ,$$

$$1 \div_u y = \mathrm{up}(1 \div_c y) .$$

These operations are not programmed as subroutines, but are written explicitly whenever they are used.

b) Input-Output

Computers accept input and produce output generally in decimal notation. This poses a conceptual problem which is, e.g. illustrated by the number 1/3 on a machine with binary internal representation. Thus, if we "give" the number 1/3 to the machine, it will actually compute with another number, near to, but not equal to, one third. We discuss now how this problem is solved in principle. In the case of input, it is not the input itself for which certain facts hold, but the effective internal representation of this input. For the output, it is not the numbers printed on the sheet of paper, but the content of the corresponding memory registers (which represent a diadic rational). One could use as output the list of bits in this register, and this would be a totally rigorous way of representing reps in output.

Such a method is possible, but of course terribly cumbersome. Since output of numbers is for information only, we have chosen to perform dec-imal output. Thus, when we say that the output has produced a number x, we mean the following : The memory register has contained a rep y, and y differs from x at most by one unit in the last figure shown. When we say that, e.g. we work with $\tau = 1.6$, then we mean that the rep τ' which represents τ has been generated by the subroutine sCONST and differs from τ at most by one part in 2^{+59} : $\mathrm{up}(\tau') \geq \tau$, $\mathrm{down}(\tau') \leq \tau$.

All this being said, we henceforth do not readress this problem.

c) Scalars

A scalar is the rep-version of an interval. That is, the set $\mathcal{S}$ of scalars is defined by $\mathcal{S} = \mathcal{J} \cap (R \oplus R)$. For convenience, every scalar on the computer is represented by a double precision complex number, the real part playing the role of the lower boundary and the imaginary part the role of the upper boundary. One can decompose a scalar into its reps by the computer supplied operations

```
R = X          ,
R = DIMAG(X)   ,
```

where X is type COMPLEX * 16 ,
R is type REAL * 8 .

Conversely, X = DCMPLX(R1,R2) makes a scalar from two reps. Instead of the operations $\cdot_i$, we have now operations $\cdot_s$, which are similar, but include the necessary - and in fact obvious - provisions for rounding. It should suffice to consider the programs given here.

Addition. $+_i$, $+_s$, sSUM

```
      COMPLEX FUNCTION sSUM*16(sA,sB)
      IMPLICIT COMPLEX*16(s)
      IMPLICIT REAL*8(r)
      rDA=sA
      rDB=sB
      IF(rDA.EQ.0.D+00.OR.rDB.EQ.0.D+00)GOTO 1
      rD=rDOWN(rDA+rDB)
      GOTO 11
    1 CONTINUE
      rD=rDA+rDB
   11 CONTINUE
      rUA=DIMAG(sA)
      rUB=DIMAG(sB)
      IF(rUA.EQ.0.D+00.OR.rUB.EQ.0.D+00)GOTO 2
      rU=rUP(rUA+rUB)
      GOTO 21
    2 CONTINUE
      rU=rUA+rUB
   21 CONTINUE
      sSUM=DCMPLX(rD,rU)
      RETURN
      END
```

The different conditional statements have the purpose of making $0 \in R$ a neutral element for addition. This is not strictly necessary.

Unary minus and subtraction. $-_i$, $-_s$, sNEG, sDIFF

```
      COMPLEX FUNCTION sNEG*16(s)
      IMPLICIT COMPLEX*16(s)
      IMPLICIT REAL*8(r)
      rD=s
      rU=DIMAG(s)
      sNEG=DCMPLX(-rU,-rD)
      RETURN
      END

      COMPLEX FUNCTION sDIFF*16(sA,sB)
      IMPLICIT COMPLEX*16(s)
      IMPLICIT REAL*8(r)
      sDIFF=sSUM(sA,sNEG(sB))
      RETURN
      END
```

Multiplication. $*_i$, $*_s$, sPROD

```
      COMPLEX FUNCTION sPROD*16(sA,sB)
      IMPLICIT COMPLEX*16(s)
      IMPLICIT REAL*8(r)
      COMMON /CONST/sZER,sONE,sUNIT
      IF(sA.EQ.sZER.OR.sB.EQ.sZER)GOTO 1
      rDA=sA
      rUA=DIMAG(sA)
      rDB=sB
      rUB=DIMAG(sB)
      rP1=rDA*rDB
      rP2=rDA*rUB
      rP3=rUA*rDB
      rP4=rUA*rUB
      sPROD=DCMPLX(rDOWN(DMIN1(rP1,rP2,rP3,rP4)),
     *             rUP  (DMAX1(rP1,rP2,rP3,rP4)))
      RETURN
    1 CONTINUE
      sPROD=sZER
      RETURN
      END
```

DMIN 1 and DMAX 1 are provided by the computer to determine min and max.

Inverse, division. $\div_i$, $\div_s$, sINV, sQUOT

```
      COMPLEX FUNCTION sINV*16(s)
      IMPLICIT COMPLEX*16(s)
      IMPLICIT REAL*8(r)
      rD=s
      rU=DIMAG(s)
      IF(rD.GT.0.D+00.OR.rU.LT.0.D+00)GOTO 1
      WRITE(9,*)'ERROR IN sINV'
      STOP
    1 CONTINUE
      sINV=DCMPLX(rDOWN(1.D+00/rU),rUP(1.D+00/rD))
      RETURN
      END
```

```
      COMPLEX FUNCTION sQUOT*16(sA,sB)
      IMPLICIT COMPLEX*16(s)
      IMPLICIT REAL*8(r)
      sQUOT=sPROD(sA,sINV(sB))
      RETURN
      END
```

Absolute value. abs_i, abs_{ir}, abs_s, abs_{sr}, sABS, rABS

```
      COMPLEX FUNCTION sABS*16(s)
      IMPLICIT COMPLEX*16(s)
      IMPLICIT REAL*8(r)
      rD=s
      rU=DIMAG(s)
      IF(rD.GE.0.D+00.OR.rU.LE.0.D+00)GOTO 1
      sABS=DCMPLX(0.D+00,DMAX1(DABS(rD),DABS(rU)))
      RETURN
    1 CONTINUE
      rA=DABS(rD)
      rB=DABS(rU)
      sABS=DCMPLX(DMIN1(rA,rB),DMAX1(rA,rB))
      RETURN
      END
```

```
      REAL FUNCTION rABS*8(s)
      IMPLICIT COMPLEX*16(s)
      IMPLICIT REAL*8(r)
      rD=s
      rABS=DMAX1(DABS(rD),DIMAG(s))
      RETURN
      END
```

The function DABS is furnished by the computer. It takes the absolute value of a rep.

Powers.

These functions are needed in various derivative routines to estimate the norms. We give here only the version which rounds upwards. See the main listing for other variants.

```
      REAL FUNCTION rPOWER*8(rR1,K)
C..COMPUTES rR1**K, ASSUMING rR1>=0 AND GIVES UPPER BOUND
      IMPLICIT COMPLEX*16(s)
      IMPLICIT REAL*8(r)
      r=rR1
      IF(r.EQ.0.D+00)GOTO 1
      N=K
      rRES=1.D+00
    3 CONTINUE
      IF(N.EQ.0)GOTO 4
      NN=N/2
      IF(NN*2.EQ.N)GOTO 2
      rRES=rUP(rRES*r)
      N=N-1
      GOTO 3
    2 CONTINUE
      r=rUP(r*r)
      N=NN
      GOTO 3
    1 CONTINUE
      rRES=0.D+00
      IF(K.EQ.0)rRES=1.D+00
    4 CONTINUE
      rPOWER=rRES
      RETURN
      END
```

Thus rPOWER produces a rep which is not smaller than $R1^k$ where R1 is a non-negative rep.

d) Vectors

On the computer, a boundary $b \in \mathcal{B}$ is replaced by an object we call a vector, and we replace the operations $\cdot_b$ by $\cdot_v$. A vector is an aggregate, called "data-structure" in some programming languages.

We define a vector v associated to a boundary $b \in \mathcal{B}$ to be the collection of $(N+1)(N+2)/2$ scalars v_{ij} each containing the interval b_{ij}, $i + j \le N$ and two reps v_G and v_H, being upper bounds on the real numbers b_G and b_H. Since all operations on reps and on scalars give rigorous bounds, on reals and on intervals, the same will be possible now for vectors relative to boundaries.

The programmer is of course free on how to represent a vector in his program. We have chosen the following device, adapted to the structure of the Fortran language; below, we also give an example of how we would have implemented vectors in Pascal.

Thus, a vector is represented by a 1-dimensional array of double complex numbers. If the degree we consider is N, then the elements 1 to $(N+1)(N+2)/2 =: NN$ of this array contain the scalars $v_{00}, v_{10}, \ldots v_{N0}, v_{01}, \ldots v_{N-1,1}, \ldots, v_{0N}$ in this order. The next element, whose index is always called NH, contains the scalar formed by $[-_c v_H, v_H]$ and the element NG (the next one) contains $[-_c v_G, v_G]$.

With these definitions in mind, it is now easy to see that the discussion of the preceding section on boundaries carries over to the case of vectors, and is hence programmable on a computer. We give a list of correspondences. The listing of the subroutines will be given at the end of the paper as part of the whole program.

Implementation of vectors in Pascal.

```
TYPE  SCALAR =RECORD L,R :REAL
              END;
      POLYNOM=ARRAY[1..NN]OF SCALAR;
      VECTOR =RECORD P :POLYNOM;
                     G :REAL;
                     H :REAL
              END;
```

List of correspondences

Operation	for boundaries	for vectors
definition of constants	-	INI
ℓ_1-norm	norm_b	sL1NORM
addition	$+_b$	FADD
subtraction	$-_b$	FMINUS
scalar multiplication	$*_{ib}$	FsMULT
scalar multiplication and addition	$(v +_b i *_{ib} v' \to v)$	FsMPYAD
multiplication	$*_b$	FMULT
multiplication and addition	$(v +_b v' *_b v'' \to v)$	FMULTAD
composition	comp_b	FCOMP
derivative of polynomial		DERX, DERY
derivative and composition	$\mathrm{dx\,comp}_b$, $\mathrm{dy\,comp}_b$	FDXCOMP, FDYCOMP
evaluation		FVALUE
derivative and evaluation		sDXVALUE, ...

PART III. PROOFS

III.1. COMPUTER PROGRAM

```
      IMPLICIT COMPLEX*16(A-H,O-Z)
      REAL*8 rIN,rRHO,rBETA,rEPS,rALPHA,rTAU,rUP,rDOWN
      COMPLEX*16 LA,LAINV,MU,NU
      DIMENSION vT1(233),vT2(233),vT3(233)
      DIMENSION vPHIO(128),vSIG(233),vS(233)
      DIMENSION vZ(233),vLAY(233),vSNEW(233)
      DIMENSION vDSIGO(128),vDSIG(233),vDYZ(233),vLAX(233)
      DIMENSION vDSIGNEU(233)
      DIMENSION vG(233),vSB(233),vSC(233),vSL(233),vSN(233)
      DIMENSION vDPS(233),vDQS(233)
      COMMON /DEG/N,N1,N2,N3,NN,NH,NG,NC
      COMMON /AUX/vAUX1(233),vAUX2(233),vAUX3(233),vAUX4(233)
      COMMON /CONST/sZER,sONE,sUNIT,sTWO,sHALF,sFIVE,sFIFTH,sTEN
      COMMON /TEST/ITEST
      COMMON /BCRES/B,C,LA,LAINV,MU,NU,TAUINV,TAU2INV,
     *             DF1L,DF2L,DF1C,DF2C,
     *             C1,C2,X0,X1,XL,
     *             G1,G2,G3,G4,G5,G6,
     *             W0,W1,W2,W3,W4,W5,
     *             DLW1,DLW2,DLW3,DLW4,DLW5,
     *             DCG1,DLG2,DCG2,DLMU,DCMU,DLB,DCB
      COMMON /SPEK/DPP ,DQP ,DSPN,
     *             DPQ ,DQQ ,DSQN,
     *             DPSN,DQSN,DSSN

C..ACTIVATE EXPONENT OVERFLOW TEST
      CALL OVFSET(5)

C..INPUT
      READ(18,*)N
C..INITIALIZE PARAMETERS FOR SUBROUTINES TO DEGREE N
      CALL INITIALIZE(N)
      WRITE(6,*)'DEGREE FOR PHI-PHIO   =',N
      READ(18,*)NTANG
      WRITE(6,*)'DEGREE FOR TANGENT MAP=',NTANG
      READ(18,*)rALPHA
      ALPHA=sONE*rALPHA
      READ(18,*)rTAU
      TAU=sONE*rTAU
      WRITE(6,*)'PARAMETERS OF DOMAIN:'
      WRITE(6,*)'CENTER ALPHA=',rALPHA
      WRITE(6,*)'RADIUS TAU  =',rTAU
      DO  1 I=1,NC-1
      READ(18,*)rIN
      vPHIO(I)=sONE*rIN
    1 CONTINUE
      vPHIO(NC)=sZER
      READ(18,*)rBETA
```

```
C..PRODUCE A CORRECTLY NORMALIZED vPHIO
C  MANIPULATE COEFFICIENTS ONLY. TURN TEST OF DOMAINS OFF
      ITEST=0
      CALL UNPACK(vPHIO,sZER,sONE,vSIG)
      vSIG(NG)=sZER
      vSIG(NH)=sZER
      CALL FLINX(vT1,ALPHA,TAU)
      CALL FLINY(vT2,ALPHA,TAU)
      CALL FCOMP(vSIG,vT1,vT2,vT3)
      CALL PACK(vT3,ALPHA,TAU,vPHIO,DUMMY)
      vPHIO(NC)=sZER
      ITEST=1
C..WE DEFINE THE BINARY CONTENT OF vPHIO TO BE THE
C  INPUT VECTOR REPRESENTING PHIO


C  CALCULATE L-NORM OF vPHIO-vPHIONEW
C  ====================================

      CALL UNPACK(vPHIO,ALPHA,TAU,vSIG)
C..DETERMINE B,C,LA,MU, AND OTHER VARIABLES OF /BCRES/
      CALL BCLAMU(vSIG,ALPHA,TAU)
C..DETERMINE vS
      CALL SIGS(B,C,vSIG,ALPHA,TAU,vS)
C..DETERMINE vZ
      D=sSUM(sPROD(sPROD(sTWO,sSUM(sFIFTH,B)),TAU),sDYVALUE(vSIG,XL,X1))
      CALL SZ(vS,ALPHA,TAU,LA,D,vZ,vDYZ)
C..PRODUCE vLAY
      CALL FLINY(vLAY,sPROD((sDIFF(LA,sONE)),sQUOT(ALPHA,TAU)),LA)
C..DETERMINE vSNEW
      CALL FCOMP(vS,vZ,vLAY,vSN)
      CALL FsMULT(vSN,NU,vSNEW)
C..CALCULATE EPSILON
      CALL FEQU(vSNEW,vT1)
      CALL FMINUS(vS,vT1)
      CALL PACK(vT1,ALPHA,TAU,vT2,EPS)
      WRITE(6,*)'L-NORM(PHIO-PHIONEW)',EPS
      rEPS=DIMAG(EPS)

C  COMPUTE TANGENT MAP DM
C  ======================

C..REDUCE POLYNOMIAL PART OF vSIG TO DEGREE NTANG
C  SUM DISCARDED COEFFICIENTS INTO BOUND OF HIGH ORDER TERM
      CALL UNPACK(vPHIO,ALPHA,TAU,vSIG)
      CALL CHANGE(vSIG,N,NTANG)
C..A NEIGHBORHOOD OF vPHIO IS INTRODUCED.
      WRITE(6,*)'DERIVATIVE IS CALCULATED ON'
      WRITE(6,*)'A NEIGHBORHOOD OF vPHIO WITH RADIUS'
      WRITE(6,*)'BETA=',rBETA
      svPHIOG=sUNIT*rBETA
```

```
C..COMPUTE A NEIGHBORHOOD OF vSIG CONTAINING IMAGE OF
C  ABOVE BALL AROUND vPHIO
      AA=sZER
      BB=sZER
      CC=sZER
      DD=sZER
      EE=sZER
      DO  4 I=1,NC
      CALL FZERO(vT1)
      vT1(I)=svPHIOG
      CALL UNPACK(vT1,ALPHA,TAU,vT2)
      AA=sMAX(AA,sABS(vT2( 1)))
      BB=sMAX(BB,sABS(vT2( 2)))
      CC=sMAX(CC,sABS(vT2(N2)))
      DD=sMAX(DD,sABS(vT2( 3)))
      EE=sMAX(EE,sABS(vT2(N3)))
    4 CONTINUE
      vSIG(NG)=svPHIOG
      vSIG( 1)=sSUM(vSIG( 1),sPROD(sUNIT,AA))
      vSIG( 2)=sSUM(vSIG( 2),sPROD(sUNIT,BB))
      vSIG(N2)=sSUM(vSIG(N2),sPROD(sUNIT,CC))
      vSIG( 3)=sSUM(vSIG( 3),sPROD(sUNIT,DD))
      vSIG(N3)=sSUM(vSIG(N3),sPROD(sUNIT,EE))
C..DETERMINE B,C,LA,MU, AND OTHER VARIABLES OF /BCRES/
      CALL BCLAMU(vSIG,ALPHA,TAU)
C..PRINT DERIVATIVE FOR INFORMATION
C..DETERMINE vS
      CALL SIGS(B,C,vSIG,ALPHA,TAU,vS)
C..DETERMINE vZ AND vDYZ
      D=sSUM(sPROD(sPROD(sTWO,sSUM(sFIFTH,B)),TAU),sDYVALUE(vSIG,XL,X1))
      CALL SZ(vS,ALPHA,TAU,LA,D,vZ,vDYZ)
C..PRODUCE vLAX,vLAY
      CALL FLINX(vLAX,sPROD((sDIFF(LA,sONE)),sQUOT(ALPHA,TAU)),LA)
      CALL FLINY(vLAY,sPROD((sDIFF(LA,sONE)),sQUOT(ALPHA,TAU)),LA)
C..OUTPUT RADII FOR INFORMATION
      OUT=sL1NORM(vZ)
      WRITE(6,*)'RADIUS Z   =',OUT
      OUT=sL1NORM(vLAY)
      WRITE(6,*)'RADIUS LA  =',OUT
C..DETERMINE vSNEW
      CALL FCOMP(vS,vZ,vLAY,vSN)
      CALL FsMULT(vSN,NU,vSNEW)
C..DETERMINE MISSING DERIVATIVES
C..vG
      CALL FsMULT(vDYZ,sPROD(NU,LAINV),vG)
C..vSL
      CALL FDXCOMP(vS,vLAX,vZ,vT1)
      CALL FLINX(vT3,sQUOT(ALPHA,TAU),sONE)
      CALL FMULT(vT3,vT1,vT1)
      CALL FDXCOMP(vS,vLAY,vZ,vT2)
      CALL FLINY(vT3,sQUOT(ALPHA,TAU),sONE)
      CALL FMULTAD(vT3,vT2,vT1)
      CALL FMULT(vT1,vG,vSL)
      CALL FDYCOMP(vS,vZ,vLAY,vT1)
      CALL FMULT(vT3,vT1,vT1)
      CALL FsMPYAD(vT1,NU,vSL)
```

```
C..vSC
      CALL FsMULT(vZ,sPROD(NU,TAU),vSC)
      vSC(1)=sSUM(vSC(1),sPROD(sDIFF(sONE,NU),sDIFF(sONE,ALPHA)))
      vSC(2)=sDIFF(vSC(2),TAU)
      CALL FZERO(vT1)
      vT1(1 )=sSUM(sTWO,sPROD(LA,sPROD(sTWO,sNEG(ALPHA))))
      vT1(2 )=sPROD(sNEG(LA),TAU)
      vT1(N2)=vT1(2)
      CALL FMULT(vT1,vG,vT1)
      CALL FMINUS(vT1,vSC)
C..vSB
      CALL FsMULT(vZ,TAU,vT3)
      vT3(1)=sSUM(vT3(1),ALPHA)
      CALL FMULT(vT3,vT3,vT1)
      CALL FMULT(vG,vT1,vSB)
      sFAC=sPROD(sHALF,sDIFF(sPROD(NU,sPROD(LA,LA)),sONE))
      vSB(   1)=sSUM(vSB(   1),sPROD(sFAC,sPROD(ALPHA,ALPHA)))
      vSB(  N2)=sSUM(vSB(  N2),sPROD(sTWO,sPROD(sFAC,sPROD(ALPHA,TAU))))
      vSB(N+N2)=sSUM(vSB(N+N2),sPROD(sFAC,sPROD(TAU,TAU)))
C..vSN
C     vSN=MU*vSNEW

C..CHOICE OF BASIS IN FIRST TWO VARIABLES OF DK
      S11=sONE*(-0.9923D+00)
      S12=sONE*( 0.9007D+00)
      S21=sONE*(-0.1190D+00)
      S22=sONE*( 0.4328D+00)
      DETS=sDIFF(sPROD(S11,S22),sPROD(S12,S21))
      SI11=sQUOT(S22,DETS)
      SI12=sNEG(sQUOT(S12,DETS))
      SI21=sNEG(sQUOT(S21,DETS))
      SI22=sQUOT(S11,DETS)

C..CALCULATION OF DM, LOOP OVER VECTOR OF vDSIGMA´S
      DSSN=sZER
      DSPN=sZER
      DSQN=sZER
C..PRODUCE A BASIS VECTOR
      DO 9 JNC=1,NC
      DO 5 I=1,NC
      vDSIGO(I)=sZER
    5 CONTINUE
      vDSIGO(JNC)=sONE
      IF(JNC.EQ.NC)vDSIGO(JNC)=sUNIT
      CALL UNPACK(vDSIGO,ALPHA,TAU,vDSIG)
C..START COMPUTING IMAGE OF BASIS VECTOR
      CALL FCOMP(vDSIG,vZ,vLAY,vT1)
      CALL FsMULT(vT1,NU,vDSIGNEW)
      CALL FCOMP(vDSIG,vLAX,vZ,vT1)
      CALL FCOMP(vDSIG,vLAY,vZ,vT2)
      CALL FADD(vT2,vT1)
      CALL FMULTAD(vG,vT1,vDSIGNEW)
C..PARTIAL DERIVATIVE OF B,C W.R. TO SIGMA
C  DERIVATIVE OF LAMDA,MU W.R. TO SIGMA (ON SUBMANIFOLD
C  (SIG,BSTAR(SIG),CSTAR(SIG) )
      CALL DS(vDSIG,DB,DC,DL,DNU)
```

```
C..COMPLETE COMPUTING IMAGE OF BASIS VECTOR
      CALL FsMPYAD(vSB,DB ,vDSIGNEW)
      CALL FsMPYAD(vSC,DC ,vDSIGNEW)
      CALL FsMPYAD(vSL,DL ,vDSIGNEW)
      CALL FsMPYAD(vSN,DNU,vDSIGNEW)
      CALL PACK(vDSIGNEW,ALPHA,TAU,vDSIGO,sLNORM)
      DSSN=sMAX(sLNORM,DSSN)
      rRHO=DIMAG(DSSN)

C..FUNCTIONAL DERIVATIVE OF P,Q W.R. TO vDSIG
C  THIS IS A PREPARATORY CALCULATION FOR THE TANGENT MAP
C  OF K AND IS CALCULATED AT THIS POINT FOR PROGRAMMING
C  CONVENIENCE
      CALL DS(vDSIGNEW,DSNEWB,DSNEWC,DUMMY,DUMMY)
      DSP =sDIFF(DB,DSNEWB)
      DSQ =sDIFF(DC,DSNEWC)
      XP  =sSUM(sPROD(SI11,DSP),sPROD(SI12,DSQ))
      XQ  =sSUM(sPROD(SI21,DSP),sPROD(SI22,DSQ))
      DSPN=sMAX(DSPN,sABS(XP))
      DSQN=sMAX(DSQN,sABS(XQ))
    9 CONTINUE

C..MATRIX DM IS GENERATED
      WRITE(6,*)'RADIUS OF NEIGHBORHOOD =',rBETA
      WRITE(6,*)'NORM OF MATRIX DM      =',DSSN
      WRITE(6,*)'NORM OF PHIO-PHIONEW   =',EPS
      WRITE(6,*)' '
      IF(rEPS.LT.rDOWN((rDOWN(1.D+00)-rUP(rRHO))*rBETA))
     * WRITE(6,*)'CONTRACTION ON BALL'
      WRITE(6,*)' '
      WRITE(6,*)' '


C  COMPUTE MISSING PARTS OF TANGENT MAP DK
C  ======================================

C..PREPARATIONS
      CALL FLINX(vT1,sDIFF(sONE,ALPHA),sNEG(TAU))
      CALL FLINY(vT2,sNEG(sPROD(sPROD(sHALF,ALPHA),ALPHA)),
     *      sNEG(sPROD(ALPHA,TAU)))
      vT2(N1+N1)=sNEG(sPROD(sPROD(sHALF,TAU),TAU))


C  DETERMINE MATRIX D(BNEW,CNEW)/D(B,C)
C  -------------------------------------
C..PREPARATORY CALCULATIONS
C  DEFINE SOME NEW VARIABLES
      Q3=sNEG(G3)
      Q4=sINV(G4)
      Q5=sNEG(G5)
      Q6=sNEG(G6)
C..PARTIAL DERIVATIVE OF LAMDA W.R. TO B,C
      DBL=sINV(DLB)
      DCL=sPROD(sDIFF(LA,sTWO),DBL)
```

```
C..PARTIAL DERIVATIVE OF BNEW,CNEW W.R. TO B
      DBW2=sPROD(DLW2,DBL)
      DBW3=sPROD(DLW3,DBL)
      DBW4=sPROD(DLW4,DBL)
      DBW5=sPROD(DLW5,DBL)
      DBG2=sSUM(sTWO,DBW5)
      DBQ3=sSUM(sSUM(LA,sPROD(B,DBL)),DBW4)
      DBQ4=sNEG(sPROD(sPROD(DBG2,Q4),Q4))
      DBQ5=sNEG(sPROD(sPROD(sTWO,sSUM(C1,W3)),DBW3))
      DBQ6=sDIFF(DBW4,sPROD(sTWO,DBW2))
      DBBNEW=sSUM(sPROD(sSUM(sSUM(sPROD(DBQ3,G2),sPROD(Q3,DBG2)),DBQ5),
     *       Q4),sPROD(sSUM(sPROD(Q3,G2),Q5),DBQ4))
      DBCNEW=sPROD(sHALF,sSUM(sPROD(sSUM(sSUM(sPROD(DBQ6,G2),sPROD(
     *       Q6,DBG2)),DBQ5),Q4),sPROD(sSUM(sPROD(Q6,G2),Q5),DBQ4)))
C..PARTIAL DERIVATIVE OF BNEW,CNEW W.R. TO C
      DCW2=sPROD(DLW2,DCL)
      DCW3=sPROD(DLW3,DCL)
      DCW4=sPROD(DLW4,DCL)
      DCW5=sPROD(DLW5,DCL)
      DCG1=sNEG(sPROD(sTEN,sSUM(C1,W0)))
      DCG2=DCW5
      DCQ3=sSUM(DCW4,sPROD(B,DCL))
      DCQ4=sNEG(sPROD(sPROD(sSUM(DCG2,DCG1),Q4),Q4))
      DCQ5=sPROD(sTWO,sDIFF(sDIFF(W0,W3),sPROD(sSUM(C1,W3),DCW3)))
      DCQ6=sDIFF(DCW4,sPROD(sTWO,DCW2))
      DCBNEW=sSUM(sPROD(sSUM(sSUM(sPROD(DCQ3,G2),sPROD(Q3,DCG2)),DCQ5),
     *       Q4),sPROD(sSUM(sPROD(Q3,G2),Q5),DCQ4))
      DCCNEW=sPROD(sHALF,sSUM(sPROD(sSUM(sSUM(sPROD(DCQ6,G2),sPROD(
     *       Q6,DCG2)),DCQ5),Q4),sPROD(sSUM(sPROD(Q6,G2),Q5),DCQ4)))
C..CALCULATE DERIVATIVES OF NU W.R. TO B AND C
      OPG1G2=sSUM(sONE,sQUOT(G1,G2))
      DBMU=sDIFF(sPROD(OPG1G2,DBL),sQUOT(sPROD(sPROD(LA,G1),DBG2),
     *     sPROD(G2,G2)))
      DCMU=sSUM(sPROD(OPG1G2,DCL),sPROD(LA,
     *     sDIFF(sQUOT(DCG1,G2),sQUOT(sPROD(DCG2,G1),sPROD(G2,G2)))))
      DBNU=sNEG(sQUOT(DBMU,sPROD(MU,MU)))
      DCNU=sNEG(sQUOT(DCMU,sPROD(MU,MU)))
C..DERIVATIVE OF OPERATOR K W.R. TO P. RESULTS ARE ELEMENTS
C  DPP,DPQ, AND VECTOR vDPS
      CALL FEQU(vSB,vDPS)
      CALL FsMPYAD(vT1,DBCNEW,vDPS)
      CALL FsMPYAD(vT2,sDIFF(DBBNEW,sONE),vDPS)
      CALL FsMPYAD(vSL,DBL,vDPS)
      CALL FsMPYAD(vSN,DBNU,vDPS)
      CALL DS(vDPS,DPSB,DPSC,DUMMY,DUMMY)

      DPP=sDIFF(DBBNEW,DPSB)
      DPQ=sDIFF(DBCNEW,DPSC)

C..DERIVATIVE OF OPERATOR K W.R. TO Q. RESULTS ARE ELEMENTS
C  DQP,DQQ, AND VECTOR vDQS
      CALL FEQU(vSC,vDQS)
      CALL FsMPYAD(vT1,sDIFF(DCCNEW,sONE),vDQS)
      CALL FsMPYAD(vT2,DCBNEW,vDQS)
      CALL FsMPYAD(vSL,DCL,vDQS)
      CALL FsMPYAD(vSN,DCNU,vDQS)
      CALL DS(vDQS,DQSB,DQSC,DUMMY,DUMMY)
```

```
      DQP=sDIFF(DCBNEW,DQSB)
      DQQ=sDIFF(DCCNEW,DQSC)

C..BASIS TRANSFORMATION IN FIRST TWO ELEMENTS
      X11=sSUM(sPROD(S11 ,DPP),sPROD(S21 ,DQP))
      X21=sSUM(sPROD(S11 ,DPQ),sPROD(S21 ,DQQ))
      X12=sSUM(sPROD(S12 ,DPP),sPROD(S22 ,DQP))
      X22=sSUM(sPROD(S12 ,DPQ),sPROD(S22 ,DQQ))
      DPP=sSUM(sPROD(SI11,X11),sPROD(SI12,X21))
      DQP=sSUM(sPROD(SI11,X12),sPROD(SI12,X22))
      DPQ=sSUM(sPROD(SI21,X11),sPROD(SI22,X21))
      DQQ=sSUM(sPROD(SI21,X12),sPROD(SI22,X22))
      CALL FsMULT (vDPS,S11,vT1)
      CALL FsMPYAD(vDQS,S21,vT1)
      CALL FsMULT (vDQS,S22,vDQS)
      CALL FsMPYAD(vDPS,S12,vDQS)
      CALL FEQU   (vT1,vDPS)

      CALL PACK(vDPS,ALPHA,TAU,vT3,DPSN)
      CALL PACK(vDQS,ALPHA,TAU,vT3,DQSN)

      WRITE(6,*)'DPP =',DPP
      WRITE(6,*)'DQP =',DQP
      WRITE(6,*)'DSPN=',DSPN
      WRITE(6,*)'DPQ =',DPQ
      WRITE(6,*)'DQQ =',DQQ
      WRITE(6,*)'DSQN=',DSQN
      WRITE(6,*)'DPSN=',DPSN
      WRITE(6,*)'DQSN=',DQSN
      WRITE(6,*)'NORM=',DSSN

C..CHECK SPECTRUM
      CALL SPECTRUM
C
C..MAIN ESTIMATES DONE.
C..MISCELLANEOUS FURTHER ESTIMATES
C
      WRITE(6,*)' '
C..PROOF OF LEMMA 1.3.3.
      WRITE(6,*)'BOUND FOR LEMMA 1.3.3.'
      WRITE(6,*)'C1+DW1/DLAMDA =',DLB
C..PROOF LEMMA 1.5.1.,1.6.1. AND 1.6.4.
      CALL abc(vS,ALPHA,TAU)
C..PROOF OF LEMMA 1.5.2.
      WRITE(6,*)'BOUND FOR LEMMA 1.5.2.'
      CALL DXS(vS,ALPHA,TAU)

      END
```

```
      SUBROUTINE INITIALIZE(K)
      IMPLICIT COMPLEX*16(s)
      COMMON /DEG/N,N1,N2,N3,NN,NH,NG,NC
      COMMON /CONST/sZER,sONE,sUNIT,sTWO,sHALF,sFIVE,sFIFTH,sTEN
      CALL INI(K)
      KK=N/2
      IF(N.EQ.2*KK)NC=(N*N+6*N+4)/4
      IF(N.NE.2*KK)NC=(N*N+6*N+5)/4
      NC=NC-3
      sTWO  =(2.D+00,2.D+00)
      sFIVE =(5.D+00,5.D+00)
      sFIFTH=sINV(sFIVE)
      sTEN  =(10.D+00,10.D+00)
      sHALF =(.5D+00,.5D+00)
      RETURN
      END
```

```
      SUBROUTINE CHANGE(vSIG,NIN,NOUT)
C..INPUT IS vSIG OF DEGREE NIN, OUTPUT IS DEGREE NOUT<NIN
C  ALL HIGH ORDER COEFFICIENTS ARE ADDED TO vSIG(NH)
C  SYSTEM IS INITIALIZED TO DEGREE NOUT
      IMPLICIT COMPLEX*16(A-H,O-Z)
      DIMENSION vSIG(1)
      COMMON /DEG/N,N1,N2,N3,NN,NH,NG,NC
      COMMON /CONST/sZER,sONE,sUNIT,sTWO,sHALF,sFIVE,sFIFTH,sTEN
      COMMON /AUX/vAUX1(233)
      KIN =1
      KOUT=1
      SNH=sZER
      DO 1 I=1,NOUT+1
      DO 2 J=1,NOUT+2-I
      vAUX1(KOUT)=vSIG(KIN)
      KOUT=KOUT+1
      KIN =KIN+1
    2 CONTINUE
      DO 3 J=NOUT+3-I,NIN+2-I
      SNH=sSUM(SNH,sABS(vSIG(KIN)))
      KIN=KIN+1
    3 CONTINUE
    1 CONTINUE
      DO 4 I=NOUT+2,NIN+1
      DO 5 J=1,NIN+2-I
      SNH=sSUM(SNH,sABS(vSIG(KIN)))
      KIN=KIN+1
    5 CONTINUE
    4 CONTINUE
      SNH=sSUM(SNH,vSIG(NH))
      SNG=vSIG(NG)
      CALL INITIALIZE(NOUT)
      CALL FEQU(vAUX1,vSIG)
      vSIG(NH)=sUNIT*DIMAG(SNH)
      vSIG(NG)=SNG
      RETURN
      END
```

```
      SUBROUTINE abc(vS,ALPHA,TAU)
      IMPLICIT COMPLEX*16(A-H,O-Q,S-Z)
      IMPLICIT REAL*8(r)
      COMPLEX*16 LA,LAINV,MU,NU
      DIMENSION vS(1)
      COMMON /DEG/N,N1,N2,N3,NN,NH,NG,NC
      COMMON /AUX/vAUX1(233),vAUX2(233),vAUX3(233),vAUX4(233)
      COMMON /CONST/sZER,sONE,sUNIT,sTWO,sHALF,sFIVE,sFIFTH,sTEN
      COMMON /TEST/ITEST
      COMMON /BCRES/B,C,LA,LAINV,MU,NU,TAUINV,TAU2INV,
     *              DF1L,DF2L,DF1C,DF2C,
     *              C1,C2,X0,X1,XL,
     *              G1,G2,G3,G4,G5,G6,
     *              W0,W1,W2,W3,W4,W5,
     *              DLW1,DLW2,DLW3,DLW4,DLW5,
     *              DCG1,DLG2,DCG2,DLMU,DCMU,DLB,DCB
      rA=1.D-5
      rB=5.D-5
      rC=1.D-5
      sRHO=sCONST(.98D+00)
      sA=sUNIT*rA
      sB=sUNIT*rB
      sC=sUNIT*rC
      S01=sDIFF(sPROD(B,sHALF),C)
      XI=sPROD(sDXVALUE(vS,X1,X0),TAUINV)
      A=sDIFF(sPROD(sHALF,B),C)
      U =sPROD(XI,sFIVE)
C..CENTRAL VALUES
C     ERRF1=sZER
      ERRF2=sDIFF(XI,XI)
C..SOLVE FOR A,C
      sA1=sPROD(sDIFF(sSUM(sONE,sA),ALPHA),TAUINV)
      sC1=sPROD(sDIFF(sC,ALPHA),TAUINV)
      A11=sPROD(sDXVALUE(vS,sA1,sC1),TAUINV)
      A12=sPROD(sDYVALUE(vS,sA1,sC1),TAUINV)
      A21=sPROD(TAU2INV,
     *    sDIFF(sDXYVALUE(vS,sC1,sA1),sPROD(U,sDXYVALUE(vS,sA1,sC1))))
      A22=sPROD(TAU2INV,
     *    sDIFF(sDXYVALUE(vS,sA1,sC1),sPROD(U,sDYYVALUE(vS,sA1,sC1))))
      DET=sDIFF(sPROD(A11,A22),sPROD(A12,A21))
      DET=sINV(DET)
      sANEW=sNEG(sPROD(sPROD(DET,A12),ERRF2))
      sCNEW=     sPROD(sPROD(DET,A11),ERRF2)
      IF(rABS(sANEW).LE.rA)GOTO 1
      WRITE(6,*)'a INCOMPATIBLE IN abc',rA,sANEW
    1 CONTINUE
      IF(rABS(sCNEW).LE.rC)GOTO 2
      WRITE(6,*)'c INCOMPATIBLE IN abc',rC,sCNEW
    2 CONTINUE
      sA=sANEW
      sC=sCNEW
C..DETERMINE NOW b WITH THESE CHOICES OF a,c
      ERR=sDIFF(S01,S01)
      sB1=sPROD(sDIFF(sSUM(sONE,sB),ALPHA),TAUINV)
      sC1=sPROD(sDIFF(sC,ALPHA),TAUINV)
      sBNEW=sQUOT(ERR,
     *      sSUM(sVALUE(vS,sC1,sB1),
     *      sPROD(sPROD(sB1,sDYVALUE(vS,sC1,sB1)),TAUINV)))
```

```
      IF(rABS(sBNEW).LE.rB)GOTO 3
      WRITE(6,*)'b INCOMPATIBLE IN abc',rB,sBNEW
    3 CONTINUE
      WRITE(6,*)'BOUNDS FOR LEMMA 1.5.1.'
      WRITE(6,*)'a=',sANEW
      WRITE(6,*)'b=',sBNEW
      WRITE(6,*)'c=',sCNEW
C..LEMMA 1.6.1.
C..CREATE POLYNOMIAL P(X,Y)
      sP00=sCONST(8.03706798D+00)
      sP10=sCONST(-7.98701149D+00)
      sP01=sCONST(-1.75613835D+00)
      sP02=sCONST(-7.231102258D+00)
      CALL FZERO(vAUX3)
      vAUX3( 1)=sP00
      vAUX3( 2)=sP10
      vAUX3(N2)=sP01
      vAUX3(N2+N)=sP02
C..CHANGE ARGUMENTS TO UNIT DISC
      ITEST=0
      CALL FLINX(vAUX1,ALPHA,sPROD(sRHO,TAU))
      CALL FLINY(VAUX2,ALPHA,sPROD(sRHO,TAU))
      CALL FCOMP(vAUX3,vAUX1,vAUX2,vAUX4)
      ITEST=1
C..CALCULATE MAXIMAL DEVIATION FROM -S(Y,X)
      CX=sPROD(sDIFF(sSUM(sONE,sANEW),sCNEW),sRHO)
      CC=sPROD(TAUINV,sSUM(sPROD(sDIFF(sANEW,sCNEW),
     *   ALPHA),sCNEW))
      CALL FLINX(vAUX1,CC,CX)
      CALL FLINY(vAUX2,CC,CX)
      CALL FCOMP(vS,vAUX1,vAUX2,vAUX3)
      CALL FsMPYAD(vAUX3,sPROD(sINV(A),sSUM(sONE,sBNEW)),vAUX4)
      rC2=sDIFF(sPROD(sPROD(sABS(sP10),TAU),sRHO),sL1NORM(vAUX4))
      WRITE(6,*)'BOUND FOR LEMMA 1.6.1.'
      WRITE(6,*)'C2 MUST BE LESS THAN ',rC2
C..LEMMA 1.6.4.
C..CREATE FUNCTION C(Y)
      CALL FZERO(vAUX3)
      vAUX3( 1)=sSUM(sP00,sPROD(ALPHA,sP10))
      vAUX3(N2)=sP01
      vAUX3(N2+N)=sP02
C..CHANGE ARGUMENTS TO UNIT DISC
      ITEST=0
      CALL FZERO(vAUX1)
      CALL FLINY(vAUX2,ALPHA,sPROD(sRHO,TAU))
      CALL FCOMP(vAUX3,vAUX1,vAUX2,vAUX4)
      ITEST=1
C..CALCULATE MAXIMAL DEVIATION FROM -S(X,Y)
      ETA=sCONST(1.1D+00)
      CC=sPROD(TAUINV,sSUM(sPROD(sDIFF(sANEW,sCNEW),
     *   ALPHA),sCNEW))
      CY=sPROD(sDIFF(sSUM(sONE,sANEW),sCNEW),sRHO)
      CX=sPROD(sPROD(CY,ETA),TAUINV)
      CALL FLINX(vAUX1,CC,CX)
      CALL FLINY(vAUX2,CC,CY)
      CALL FCOMP(vS,vAUX1,vAUX2,vAUX3)
      CALL FsMPYAD(vAUX3,sPROD(sINV(A),sSUM(sONE,sBNEW)),vAUX4)
```

```
      r164=DIMAG(sL1NORM(vAUX4))
      WRITE(6,*)'BOUND FOR LEMMA 1.6.4'
      WRITE(6,*)'BOUND IS ',r164
      RETURN
      END




      SUBROUTINE SPECTRUM
      IMPLICIT COMPLEX*16(A-H,O-Z)
      REAL*8 rL,rR,rX
      DIMENSION rX(26)
      DATA (rX(I),I=1,26) /-50.D0,-10.D0,-5.D0,-4.5D0,-4.4D0,
     * -3.6D0,-3.5D0,-3.D0,-2.D0,-1.1D0,-1.D0,-.9D0,-.85D0,-.83D0,
     * .85D0,.86D0,.9D0,1.D0,3.D0,7.D0,8.D0,8.2D0,
     * 9.2D0,9.5D0,10.D0,50.D0/
C..CHECK INVERTIBILITY OF DK-rX(I)
      IS=0
      DO 1 I=1,4
      CALL DETVAL(rX(I),rX(I+1),rL,rR)
      IF(rR.LT.0.D+00)GOTO 1
      WRITE(6,*)'SIGN OF DETERMINANT NOT AS EXPECTED',I
      IS=1
    1 CONTINUE
      DO 2 I=6,13
      CALL DETVAL(rX(I),rX(I+1),rL,rR)
      IF(rL.GT.0.D+00)GOTO 2
      WRITE(6,*)'SIGN OF DETERMINANT NOT AS EXPECTED',I
      IS=1
    2 CONTINUE
      DO 3 I=15,21
      CALL DETVAL(rX(I),rX(I+1),rL,rR)
      IF(rR.LT.0.D+00)GOTO 3
      WRITE(6,*)'SIGN OF DETERMINANT NOT AS EXPECTED',I
      IS=1
    3 CONTINUE
      DO 4 I=23,25
      CALL DETVAL(rX(I),rX(I+1),rL,rR)
      IF(rL.GT.0.D+00)GOTO 4
      WRITE(6,*)'SIGN OF DETERMINANT NOT AS EXPECTED',I
      IS=1
    4 CONTINUE
      IF(IS.EQ.0)WRITE(6,*)'DETERMINANT CHANGES SIGN AS EXPECTED'
      RETURN
      END
```

```
      SUBROUTINE DETVAL(rR1,rR2,rL,rR)
      IMPLICIT COMPLEX*16(A-H,O-Z)
      REAL*8 rR1,rR2,rL,rR,rUP,rDOWN
      COMMON /CONST/sZER,sONE,sUNIT,sTWO,sHALF,sFIVE,sFIFTH,sTEN
      COMMON /SPEK/A1,A2,A3,
     *            B1,B2,B3,
     *            C1,C2,C3
      DX =DCMPLX(rDOWN(rR1),rUP(rR2))
      A11=sDIFF(DX,A1)
      A12=sPROD(sUNIT,sABS(A2))
      A13=sPROD(sUNIT,A3)
      A21=sPROD(sUNIT,sABS(B1))
      A22=sDIFF(DX,B2)
      A23=sPROD(sUNIT,B3)
      A31=sPROD(sUNIT,C1)
      A32=sPROD(sUNIT,C2)
      A33=sDIFF(DX,sPROD(sUNIT,C3))
      SDET=sSUM(sSUM(sPROD(A33,sDIFF(sPROD(A11,A22),sPROD(A12,A21)))
     *     ,sPROD(A32,sDIFF(sPROD(A13,A21),sPROD(A11,A23))))
     *     ,sPROD(A31,sDIFF(sPROD(A12,A23),sPROD(A22,A13))))
      rL=SDET
      rR=DIMAG(SDET)
      RETURN
      END
```

```
      SUBROUTINE DXS(vS,ALPHA,TAU)
      IMPLICIT COMPLEX*16(A-H,O-Z)
      REAL*8 rRHO
      LOGICAL logZERO
      DIMENSION vS(1)
      COMMON /DEG/N,N1,N2,N3,NN,NH,NG,NC
      COMMON /CONST/sZER,sONE,sUNIT,sTWO,sHALF,sFIVE,sFIFTH,sTEN
      COMMON /AUX/vAUX1(233),vAUX2(233),vAUX3(233),vAUX4(233)
      rRHO=.98D+00
      CALL FZERO(vAUX3)
      CALL FZERO(vAUX4)
      vAUX3(2)=sONE*rRHO
      vAUX4(N2)=sONE*rRHO
      CALL FDXCOMP(vS,vAUX3,vAUX4,vAUX2)
      S=sABS(vAUX2(1))
      vAUX2(1)=sZER
      S=sDIFF(S,sL1NORM(vAUX2))
      IF(logZERO(S))GOTO 1
      rRHO=sQUOT(S,TAU)
      WRITE(6,*)'BOUND FOR DXS IS',rRHO
      RETURN
    1 CONTINUE
      WRITE(6,*)'BOUND ON DXS NOT OK.'
      RETURN
      END
```

```
      SUBROUTINE SIGS(B,C,vSIG,ALPHA,TAU,vS)
      IMPLICIT COMPLEX*16(A-H,O-Z)
      DIMENSION vSIG(1),vS(1)
      COMMON /DEG/N,N1,N2,N3,NN,NH,NG,NC
      COMMON /CONST/sZER,sONE,sUNIT,sTWO,sHALF,sFIVE,sFIFTH,sTEN
      CALL FEQU(vSIG,vS)
          svS1=sPROD(sSUM(C,sFIFTH),sDIFF(ALPHA,sONE))
      vS( 1)=sSUM(sSUM(sSUM(vSIG(1),svS1),sPROD(ALPHA,sFIFTH)),
     *       sPROD(B,sPROD(sPROD(sHALF,ALPHA),ALPHA)))
      vS( 2)=sSUM(vSIG(2),sPROD(sSUM(C,sFIFTH),TAU))
      vS(N2)=sSUM(sSUM(vSIG(N2),sPROD(sFIFTH,TAU)),
     *       sPROD(B,sPROD(ALPHA,TAU)))
      vS(N+N2)=sSUM(vSIG(N+N2),sPROD(B,sPROD(sPROD(TAU,TAU),sHALF)))
      RETURN
      END
```

```
      SUBROUTINE PROJ(v,ALPHA,TAU,P10,P01,PY10,PY01)
      IMPLICIT COMPLEX*16(A-H,O-Z)
      DIMENSION v(1)
      COMMON /CONST/sZER,sONE,sUNIT,sTWO,sHALF,sFIVE,sFIFTH,sTEN
      X0  =sNEG (sQUOT(ALPHA,TAU))
      X1  =sQUOT(sDIFF(sONE,ALPHA),TAU)
      P10 =sVALUE(v,X1,X0)
      P01 =sVALUE(v,X0,X1)
      PY10=sPROD(sDYVALUE(v,X1,X0),sINV(TAU))
      PY01=sPROD(sDYVALUE(v,X0,X1),sINV(TAU))
      RETURN
      END
```

```
      SUBROUTINE PACK(vB,ALPHA,TAU,vA,sLNORM)
      IMPLICIT COMPLEX*16(A-H,O-Z)
      LOGICAL logZERO
      DIMENSION vA(1),vB(1)
      DIMENSION P(4)
      COMMON /DEG/N,N1,N2,N3,NN,NH,NG,NC
C..CHECK PROPER NORMALIZATION
      CALL PROJ(vB,ALPHA,TAU,P(1),P(2),P(3),P(4))
      DO 7 I=1,4
      IF(logZERO(P(I)))GOTO 7
      WRITE(6,*)'ERROR IN PACK',I,P(I)
    7 CONTINUE
      IP=1
      K =N2+N
      KD=N-1
      DO 1 I=3,N1
      vA(IP)=vB(K)
      K =K+KD
      KD=KD-1
      IP=IP+1
    1 CONTINUE
      IJ=N3/2
      K =2
      KD=N2
      DO 2 J=2,IJ
      KK =K
      KKD=KD-1
      KH =K
      LS =J-1
      LE =N2-J
      DO 3 L=LS,LE
      IF(L.LT.3.AND.J.EQ.2)GOTO 4
      vA(IP)=sSUM(vB(KK),vB(KH))
      IF(KH.EQ.KK)vA(IP)=vB(KH)
      IP=IP+1
    4 CONTINUE
      KK =KK+KKD
      KKD=KKD-1
      KH =KH+1
    3 CONTINUE
      K =K+KD
      KD=KD-1
    2 CONTINUE
      vA(NC)=vB(NH)
C..COMPUTE L-NORM OF vA
      sLNORM=vB(NG)
      DO 5 I=1,NC
      sLNORM=sSUM(sLNORM,sABS(vA(I)))
    5 CONTINUE
      sLNORM=sABS(sLNORM)
      RETURN
      END
```

```
      SUBROUTINE UNPACK(vA,ALPHA,TAU,vB)
      IMPLICIT COMPLEX*16(A-H,O-Z)
      DIMENSION vA(1),vB(1)
      COMMON /DEG/N,N1,N2,N3,NN,NH,NG,NC
      COMMON /CONST/sZER,sONE,sUNIT,sTWO,sHALF,sFIVE,sFIFTH,sTEN
C..FILL IN vB
      CALL FZERO(vB)
      vB(NH)=vA(NC)
      IP=1
      K =N2+N
      KD=N-1
      DO 1 I=3,N1
      vB(K)=vA(IP)
      K =K+KD
      KD=KD-1
      IP=IP+1
    1 CONTINUE
      IJ=N3/2
      K =2
      KD=N2
      DO 2 J=2,IJ
      KK =K
      KKD=KD-1
      KH =K
      A2 =sICONST(J-1)
      LS =J-1
      LE =N2-J
      DO 3 L=LS,LE
      IF(L.LT.3.AND.J.EQ.2)GOTO 4
      A1=sICONST(L)
      vB(KK)=sPROD(vA(IP),sINV(sSUM(sONE,sQUOT(A2,A1))))
      vB(KH)=sPROD(vB(KK),sQUOT(A2,A1))
      IF(KH.EQ.KK)vB(KH)=vA(IP)
      IP=IP+1
    4 CONTINUE
      KK =KK+KKD
      KKD=KKD-1
      KH =KH+1
    3 CONTINUE
      K =K+KD
      KD=KD-1
    2 CONTINUE
      CALL PROJ(vB,ALPHA,TAU,P10,P01,DP10,DP01)
      X1=sQUOT(sDIFF(sONE,ALPHA),TAU)
      X0=sNEG(sQUOT(ALPHA,TAU))
      DD=sPROD(sDIFF(DP01,DP10),sPROD(sPROD(TAU,TAU),sHALF))
      CC=sNEG(sSUM(sPROD(TAU,DP10),sPROD(sPROD(DD,X1),sTWO)))
      BB=sSUM(sSUM(sPROD(sDIFF(P01,P10),TAU),
     *   sPROD(sNEG(DD),sSUM(X1,X0))),CC)
      AA=sSUM(sSUM(P10,sPROD(BB,X1)),sPROD(CC,X0))
      AA=sNEG(sSUM(AA,sPROD(DD,sPROD(X1,sSUM(sPROD(sTWO,X0),X1)))))
      vB(1) =sSUM(vB(1),AA)
      vB(2) =sSUM(vB(2),BB)
      vB(N2)=sSUM(vB(N2),CC)
      vB(3) =sSUM(vB(3),DD)
      vB(N3)=sSUM(vB(N3),sPROD(DD,sTWO))
      RETURN
      END
```

```
      SUBROUTINE BCLAMU(vSIG,ALPHA,TAU)
C..THIS SUBROUTINE USES vSIG,ALPHA,TAU AS ARGUMENTS.
C  IT FURNISHES ALL VARIABLES OF /BCRES/
C  AS RESULTS.
      IMPLICIT COMPLEX*16(A-H,O-Z)
      REAL*8 rUP,rDOWN
      REAL*8 rLA0,rERRLA,rUPL,rUPLN,rDNL,rDNLN
      REAL*8 rC0 ,rERRC ,rUPC,rUPCN,rDNC,rDNCN
      COMPLEX*16 LA,LAINV,MU,NU,LANEW,LA0
      LOGICAL logZERO
      DIMENSION vSIG(1)
      COMMON /CONST/sZER,sONE,sUNIT,sTWO,sHALF,sFIVE,sFIFTH,sTEN
      COMMON /BCRES/B,C,LA,LAINV,MU,NU,TAUINV,TAU2INV,
     *              DF1L,DF2L,DF1C,DF2C,
     *              C1,C2,X0,X1,XL,
     *              G1,G2,G3,G4,G5,G6,
     *              W0,W1,W2,W3,W4,W5,
     *              DLW1,DLW2,DLW3,DLW4,DLW5,
     *              DCG1,DLG2,DCG2,DLMU,DCMU,DLB,DCB
C..THE FOLLOWING DATA ARE BEING USED BY THE SUBROUTINE
      rLA0 =-.24887528871852299 1D+000
      rC0  = .82728967264867222 2D+000
      rERRLA=.01D+00
      rERRC =.01D+00

C  PART 1: COMPUTE PRECISION OF APPROXIMATION OF CENTRAL VALUES
C  ------------------------------------------------------------
      I=0
      TAUINV =sINV(TAU)
      TAU2INV=sPROD(TAUINV,TAUINV)
      LA =sONE*rLA0
      C  =sONE*rC0
      LA0=LA
      C0 =C
      rUPL=rUP(rLA0+rERRLA)
      rDNL=rDOWN(rLA0-rERRLA)
      rUPC=rUP(rC0+rERRC)
      rDNC=rDOWN(rC0-rERRC)
      GOTO 2

C  PART 2: DETERMINE NEIGHBORHOODS FOR LAMDA AND C
C  -----------------------------------------------
    1 CONTINUE
      I=1
      LA=DCMPLX(rDNL,rUPL)
      C =DCMPLX(rDNC,rUPC)
C..COMMON PIECE FOR BOTH PARTS
    2 CONTINUE
      LAINV=sINV(LA)
      X0=sNEG  (sQUOT(ALPHA,TAU))
      X1=sQUOT (sDIFF(sONE,ALPHA),TAU)
      XL=sSUM  (sPROD(LA,TAUINV),X0)
      W0=sPROD (sDXVALUE(vSIG,X1,X0),TAUINV)
      W1=sVALUE(vSIG,XL,X1)
      W2=sPROD (sVALUE(vSIG,X1,XL),LAINV)
      W3=sPROD (sDXVALUE(vSIG,X1,XL),TAUINV)
```

```
      W4=sPROD (sDYVALUE(vSIG,X1,XL),TAUINV)
      W5=sPROD (sDYVALUE(vSIG,XL,X1),TAUINV)
      C1=sSUM (sFIFTH,C)
      C2=sPROD(sTWO,C)
      B =sDIFF(C2,sSUM(sPROD(LA,C1),W1))
      G1=sNEG (sPROD(sPROD(sFIVE,sSUM(C1,W0)),sSUM(C1,W0)))
      G2=sSUM (sPROD(sTWO,sSUM(sFIFTH,B)),W5)
      G3=sNEG (sSUM(sPROD(LA,B),W4))
      G4=sSUM (G1,G2)
      G5=sPROD(sTWO,sPROD(C1,sDIFF(W3,W0)))
      G5=sDIFF(sSUM(G5,sPROD(W3,W3)),sPROD(W0,W0))
      G6=sDIFF(sPROD(sTWO,sSUM(sFIFTH,W2)),W4)
      IF(I.EQ.1)GOTO 3
C..CONTINUATION OF PART 1
      ERRF1=sSUM(sSUM(sPROD(G4,B ),sPROD(G3,G2)),G5)
      ERRF2=sSUM(sSUM(sPROD(G4,C2),sPROD(G6,G2)),G5)
      GOTO 1
C..CONTINUATION OF PART 2
    3 CONTINUE
C..PARTIAL DERIVATIVES W.R. TO LAMDA
      DLW1=W3
      DLW2=sPROD(LAINV,sDIFF(W4,W2))
      DLW3=sPROD(sDXYVALUE(vSIG,X1,XL),TAU2INV)
      DLW4=sPROD(sDYYVALUE(vSIG,X1,XL),TAU2INV)
      DLW5=sPROD(sDXYVALUE(vSIG,XL,X1),TAU2INV)
      DLB =sNEG(sSUM(C1,DLW1))
      DLG2=sSUM(sPROD(sTWO,DLB),DLW5)
      DLG3=sNEG(sSUM(sSUM(B,sPROD(LA,DLB)),DLW4))
      DLG4=DLG2
      DLG5=sPROD(sTWO,sPROD(C1,DLW3))
      DLG5=sSUM(DLG5,sPROD(sTWO,sPROD(DLW3,W3)))
      DLG6=sDIFF(sPROD(sTWO,DLW2),DLW4)
C..PARTIAL DERIVATIVES W.R. TO C
      DCC1=sONE
      DCC2=sTWO
      DCB =sDIFF(DCC2,sPROD(LA,DCC1))
      DCG1=sNEG(sPROD(sTEN,sSUM(C1,W0)))
      DCG2=sPROD(sTWO,DCB)
      DCG3=sNEG(sPROD(LA,DCB))
      DCG4=sSUM(DCG1,DCG2)
      DCG5=sPROD(sTWO,sPROD(DCC1,sDIFF(W3,W0)))
C..MATRIX  D(F1,F2)/D(LAMDA,C)
      DLF1=sSUM(sSUM(sPROD(DLG4,B),sPROD(G4,DLB)),sPROD(DLG3,G2))
      DLF1=sSUM(sSUM(DLF1,sPROD(G3,DLG2)),DLG5)
      DLF2=sSUM(sPROD(DLG4,C2),sPROD(DLG6,G2))
      DLF2=sSUM(sSUM(DLF2,sPROD(G6,DLG2)),DLG5)
      DCF1=sSUM(sSUM(sPROD(DCG4,B),sPROD(G4,DCB)),sPROD(DCG3,G2))
      DCF1=sSUM(sSUM(DCF1,sPROD(G3,DCG2)),DCG5)
      DCF2=sSUM(sPROD(DCG4,C2),sPROD(G4,DCC2))
      DCF2=sSUM(sSUM(DCF2,sPROD(G6,DCG2)),DCG5)
C..INVERT
      DET=sDIFF(sPROD(DLF1,DCF2),sPROD(DLF2,DCF1))
      IF(.NOT.logZERO(DET))GOTO 4
      WRITE(6,*)'ERROR IN DLAMDA-DC,DET=',DET
      STOP
    4 CONTINUE
```

```
      DET =sINV(DET)
      DF1L=sPROD(DET,DCF2)
      DF2C=sPROD(DET,DLF1)
      DF2L=sNEG(sPROD(DET,DCF1))
      DF1C=sNEG(sPROD(DET,DLF2))
C..CHECK COMPATIBILITY OF NEW BOUNDS WITH ORIGINAL BOUNDS
C  TAKE ACTION IF IMPROVEMENT IS SIGNIFICANT
      LANEW=sDIFF(LA0,sSUM(sPROD(DF1L,ERRF1),sPROD(DF2L,ERRF2)))
      rUPLN=DIMAG(LANEW)
      rDNLN=LANEW
      IF(rUPLN.LE.rUPL.AND.rDNLN.GE.rDNL)GOTO 5
      WRITE(6,*)'ERROR OF LAMDA INCOMPATIBLE'
    5 CONTINUE
      IMPROVE=0
      IF(ABS(rUPLN/rUPL-1.D+00).GT.1.D-18)IMPROVE=1
      IF(ABS(rDNLN/rDNL-1.D+00).GT.1.D-18)IMPROVE=1
      CNEW=sDIFF(C0,sSUM(sPROD(DF1C,ERRF1),sPROD(DF2C,ERRF2)))
      rUPCN=DIMAG(CNEW)
      rDNCN=CNEW
      IF(rUPCN.LE.rUPC.AND.rDNCN.GE.rDNC)GOTO 6
      WRITE(6,*)'ERROR OF C INCOMPATIBLE'
    6 CONTINUE
      IF(ABS(rUPCN/rUPC-1.D+00).GT.1.D-18)IMPROVE=1
      IF(ABS(rDNCN/rDNC-1.D+00).GT.1.D-18)IMPROVE=1
      IF(IMPROVE.EQ.0)GOTO 7
C..IMPROVEMENT SIGNIFICANT. REPLACE LAMDA AND C BY NEW VALUES
      rUPL=rUPLN
      rDNL=rDNLN
      rUPC=rUPCN
      rDNC=rDNCN
      GOTO 1
    7 CONTINUE
C..CHECK IF INITIAL CHOICE COMPATIBLE
      IF(rUPL.GE.rLA0.AND.rDNL.LE.rLA0)GOTO 8
      WRITE(6,*)'INITIAL LAMDA INCOMPATIBLE'
    8 CONTINUE
      IF(rUPC.GE.rC0.AND.rDNC.LE.rC0)GOTO 9
      WRITE(6,*)'INITIAL C INCOMPATIBLE'
    9 CONTINUE
C..CHOICE OF LA,C IS NOW DEFINITIVE
C..COMPUTE MU
      OPG1G2=sSUM(sONE,sQUOT(G1,G2))
      MU=SPROD(LA,OPG1G2)
      DLMU=sDIFF(OPG1G2,sQUOT(sPROD(sPROD(LA,G1),DLG2),sPROD(G2,G2)))
      DCMU=sPROD(LA,sDIFF(sQUOT(DCG1,G2),
     *     sQUOT(sPROD(DCG2,G1),sPROD(G2,G2))))
      NU=sINV(MU)
      WRITE(6,*)'B =',B
      WRITE(6,*)'C =',C
      WRITE(6,*)'LA=',LA
      WRITE(6,*)'MU=',MU
      RETURN
      END
```

```
      SUBROUTINE SZ(vS,ALPHA,TAU,LA,D,vZ,vDYZ)
C..COMPUTES vZ FROM vS
C..USES vAUX1,2,3,4
      IMPLICIT COMPLEX*16(A-H,O-Z)
      REAL*8 rTAUT,rTHETA,rOUT
      COMPLEX*16 LA
      LOGICAL logLT,logGE,logZERO
      DIMENSION vS(1),vZ(1),vDYZ(1)
      DIMENSION vT1(233),vT2(233),vZETA(233)
      COMMON /DEG/N,N1,N2,N3,NN,NH,NG,NC
      COMMON /AUX/vAUX1(233),vAUX2(233),vAUX3(233),vAUX4(233)
      COMMON /CONST/sZER,sONE,sUNIT,sTWO,sHALF,sFIVE,sFIFTH,sTEN
      s1PEPS=sONE*1.001D+00
C..COMPUTE T
      rTAUT =2.800D+00
      rTHETA=0.421D+00
      WRITE(6,*)'TAUT                  =',rTAUT
      WRITE(6,*)'INITIAL CHOICE FOR THETA=',rTHETA
      TAUT =sONE*rTAUT
      THETA=sONE*rTHETA
    8 CONTINUE
C..QUOT= 1/D3T(0,0,0)
      QUOT=sNEG(sINV(sPROD(D,sQUOT(THETA,TAU))))
      CALL FLINY(vAUX1,sQUOT(sDIFF(sONE,ALPHA),TAU),sQUOT(THETA,TAU))
      B1=sPROD(s1PEPS,sQUOT(sABS(vAUX1(N2)),sDIFF(sONE,sABS(vAUX1(1)))))
      vAUX1(N2)=sPROD(vAUX1(N2),sINV(B1))
      CALL FLINX(vAUX2,sNEG(sQUOT(ALPHA,TAU)),sPROD(LA,sQUOT(TAUT,TAU)))
      B2=sPROD(s1PEPS,sQUOT(sABS(vAUX2(2)),sDIFF(sONE,sABS(vAUX2(1)))))
      vAUX2(2)=sPROD(vAUX2(2),sINV(B2))
      CALL FCOMP(vS,vAUX2,vAUX1,vT1)
      CALL FLINY(vAUX3,sZER,B1)
      CALL FLINX(vAUX4,sZER,B2)
      CALL FCOMP(vT1,vAUX4,vAUX3,vAUX2)
      CALL FEQU(vAUX2,vT1)
C..vT1(NG) HAS NO CONSTANT TERM
      vT1(NG)=sPROD(vT1(NG),sMAX(B1,B2))
      CALL FLINX(vAUX2,sPROD(sDIFF(LA,ALPHA),sINV(TAU)),
     *     sPROD(LA,sQUOT(TAUT,TAU)))
      B2=sPROD(s1PEPS,sQUOT(sABS(vAUX2(2)),sDIFF(sONE,sABS(vAUX2(1)))))
      vAUX2(2)=sPROD(vAUX2(2),sINV(B2))
      CALL FCOMP(vS,vAUX2,vAUX1,vT2)
      CALL FLINX(vAUX4,sZER,B2)
      CALL FCOMP(vT2,vAUX4,vAUX3,vAUX2)
      CALL FEQU(vAUX2,vT2)
C..vT2(NG) HAS NO CONSTANT TERM
      vT2(NG)=sPROD(vT2(NG),sMAX(B1,B2))
C..HERE BEGIN CALCULATIONS
      CALL FZERO(vZETA)
      vZETA(2) =sPROD(vT1(2),QUOT)
      vZETA(N2)=sPROD(vT2(2),QUOT)
      CALL FLINX(vAUX1,sZER,sONE)
      CALL FLINY(vAUX3,sZER,sONE)
      KS =N2+N
      KDS=N-1
      DO 1 I=3,N1
      K =KS
      KD=KDS
```

```
      CALL FCOMP(vT1,vAUX1,vZETA,vAUX2)
      CALL FCOMP(vT2,vAUX3,vZETA,vAUX4)
      DO 2 J=1,I
      vZETA(K)=sPROD(sSUM(vAUX2(K),vAUX4(K)),QUOT)
      K =K-KD
      KD=KD+1
    2 CONTINUE
      KS =KS+KDS
      KDS=KDS-1
    1 CONTINUE
C..AT THIS POINT vZETA IS CORRECT TO ORDER N (INCLUDED)
C  CHECK INVERTIBILITY AND OPTIMIZE BOUNDS
      CALL FLINY(vAUX1,sQUOT(sDIFF(sONE,ALPHA),TAU),sQUOT(THETA,TAU))
      CALL FLINX(vAUX2,sNEG(sQUOT(ALPHA,TAU)),sPROD(LA,sQUOT(TAUT,TAU)))
      CALL FDYCOMP(vS,vAUX2,vAUX1,vAUX3)
      vAUX2(1)=sSUM(vAUX2(1),sPROD(LA,sINV(TAU)))
      CALL FDYCOMP(vS,vAUX2,vAUX1,vAUX4)
      FF=sSUM(vAUX3(1),vAUX4(1))
      IF(.NOT.logZERO(FF))GOTO 9
      WRITE(6,*)'ERROR IN SZ,D3T NOT INVERTIBLE'
    9 CONTINUE
      ERR=sABS(FF)
      vAUX3(1)=sZER
      vAUX4(1)=sZER
      ERR=sDIFF(sDIFF(ERR,sL1NORM(vAUX3)),sL1NORM(vAUX4))
      IF(logGE(ERR,sCONST(.01D+00)))GOTO 3
      WRITE(6,*)'ERROR IN SZ,D3T NOT INVERTIBLE, ERR=',ERR
    3 CONTINUE
      WRITE(6,*)'ABS(D3T)   >=',ERR
      ERR=sINV(sPROD(ERR,sQUOT(THETA,TAU)))
      CALL FLINX(vAUX1,sZER,sONE)
      CALL FLINY(vAUX3,sZER,sONE)
      CALL FCOMP(vT1,vAUX1,vZETA,vAUX2)
      CALL FCOMP(vT2,vAUX3,vZETA,vAUX4)
      vZETA(NG)=sPROD(sSUM(vAUX2(NG),vAUX4(NG)),ERR)
      vZETA(NH) =sPROD(sSUM(vAUX2(NH) ,vAUX4(NH) ),ERR)
C..NOW vZETA IS PRODUCED, CHECK ITS RANGE
      ERR=sL1NORM(vZETA)
      rOUT=DIMAG(ERR)
      WRITE(6,*)'RANGE OF ZETA=',rOUT
      IF(logLT(ERR,sONE))GOTO 4
      WRITE(6,*)'ERROR IN SZ, RANGE OF ZETA TOO LARGE'
    4 CONTINUE
      CONST=sCONST(.95D+00)
      IF(logGE(ERR,CONST))GOTO 5
C..RANGE CAN BE REDUCED
      THETA=sPROD(THETA,ERR)
      rOUT=DIMAG(THETA)
      WRITE(6,*)'THETA REDUCED TO',rOUT
      GOTO 8
    5 CONTINUE
C..TRANSFORM vZETA TO vZ
      CALL FLINX(vAUX1,sQUOT(ALPHA,TAUT),sQUOT(TAU,TAUT))
      CALL FLINY(vAUX2,sQUOT(sDIFF(ALPHA,sONE),TAUT),sQUOT(TAU,TAUT))
      CALL FDYCOMP(vZETA,vAUX1,vAUX2,vDYZ)
      CALL FsMULT(vDYZ,sQUOT(THETA,TAUT),vDYZ)
```

```
C..vZETA(NG) HAS NO CONSTANT TERM
      ZETAG=vZETA(NG)
      vZETA(NG)=sZER
      CALL FCOMP(vZETA,vAUX1,vAUX2,vAUX3)
      B1=sL1NORM(vAUX1)
      B2=sL1NORM(vAUX2)
      vAUX3(NG)=sSUM(vAUX3(NG),sPROD(ZETAG,sMAX(B1,B2)))
      CALL FsMULT(vAUX3,sQUOT(THETA,TAU),vZ)
      vZ(1)=sSUM(vZ(1),sQUOT(sDIFF(sONE,ALPHA),TAU))
      RETURN
      END
```

```
      SUBROUTINE DS(vDSIG,DB,DC,DL,DNU)
C..DERIVATIVE OF BSTAR,CSTAR W.R. TO SIGMA
C  PARTIAL DERIVATIVE OF LAMDA, MU W.R. TO SIGMA
      IMPLICIT COMPLEX*16(A-H,O-Z)
      COMPLEX*16 LA,LAINV,MU,NU
      DIMENSION vDSIG(1)
      COMMON /CONST/sZER,sONE,sUNIT,sTWO,sHALF,sFIVE,sFIFTH,sTEN
      COMMON /BCRES/B,C,LA,LAINV,MU,NU,TAUINV,TAU2INV,
     *              DF1L,DF2L,DF1C,DF2C,
     *              C1,C2,X0,X1,XL,
     *              G1,G2,G3,G4,G5,G6,
     *              W0,W1,W2,W3,W4,W5,
     *              DLW1,DLW2,DLW3,DLW4,DLW5,
     *              DCG1,DLG2,DCG2,DLMU,DCMU,DLB,DCB
      DW0 =sPROD(sDXVALUE(vDSIG,X1,X0),TAUINV)
      DW1 =sVALUE(vDSIG,XL,X1)
      DW2 =sPROD(sVALUE  (vDSIG,X1,XL),LAINV)
      DW3 =sPROD(sDXVALUE(vDSIG,X1,XL),TAUINV)
      DW4 =sPROD(sDYVALUE(vDSIG,X1,XL),TAUINV)
      DW5 =sPROD(sDYVALUE(vDSIG,XL,X1),TAUINV)
      DSB =sNEG(DW1)
      DSG1=sPROD(sTEN,sNEG(sPROD(sSUM(C1,W0),DW0)))
      DSG2=sSUM(sPROD(sTWO,DSB),DW5)
      DSG3=sNEG(sSUM(sPROD(LA,DSB),DW4))
      DSG4=sSUM(DSG1,DSG2)
      DSG5=sPROD(sTWO,sPROD(C1,sDIFF(DW3,DW0)))
      DSG5=sSUM(DSG5,sPROD(sTWO,sDIFF(sPROD(DW3,W3),sPROD(DW0,W0))))
      DSG6=sDIFF(sPROD(sTWO,DW2),DW4)
      DSMU=sDIFF(sPROD(DSG1,G2),sPROD(G1,DSG2))
      DSMU=sPROD(DSMU,sINV(sPROD(G2,G2)))
      DSMU=sPROD(LA,DSMU)
      DSF1=sSUM(sSUM(sPROD(DSG4,B),sPROD(G4,DSB)),sPROD(DSG3,G2))
      DSF1=sSUM(sSUM(DSF1,sPROD(G3,DSG2)),DSG5)
      DSF2=sSUM(sPROD(DSG4,C2),sPROD(DSG6,G2))
      DSF2=sSUM(sSUM(DSF2,sPROD(G6,DSG2)),DSG5)
      DL  =sNEG(sSUM(sPROD(DF1L,DSF1),sPROD(DF2L,DSF2)))
      DC  =sNEG(sSUM(sPROD(DF1C,DSF1),sPROD(DF2C,DSF2)))
      DB  =sSUM(sSUM(sPROD(DLB,DL),sPROD(DCB,DC)),DSB)
      DMU =sSUM(sSUM(sPROD(DLMU,DL),sPROD(DCMU,DC)),DSMU)
      DNU=sNEG(sPROD(DMU,sPROD(NU,NU)))
      RETURN
      END
```

```
C  ****************************************************
C  ARITHMETIC OPERATIONS WITH ERROR ANALYSIS
C  ALL FUNCTIONS ARE ASSUMED TO BE DEFINED ON UNIT DISC
C  ****************************************************


C  INITIALIZATION
C  ==============

      SUBROUTINE INI(K)
      IMPLICIT COMPLEX*16(v,s)
      COMMON /DEG/N,N1,N2,N3,NN,NH,NG
      COMMON /CONST/sZER,sONE,sUNIT
      COMMON /TEST/ITEST
      ITEST=1
      N =K
      N1=N+1
      N2=N1+1
      N3=N2+1
      NN=N1*N2/2
      NH=NN+1
      NG=NH+1
C..ALL EXPLICITLY GIVEN CONSTANTS ARE OF TYPE REPS
      sZER  =(0.D+00,0.D+00)
      sONE  =(1.D+00,1.D+00)
      sUNIT =(-1.D+00,1.D+00)
      RETURN
      END
C  OPERATIONS ACTING ON VECTORS
C  ============================

C  1) MAKE VECTORS REPRESENTING LINEAR FUNCTIONS
C  ---------------------------------------------
      SUBROUTINE FLINX(v,sC,sX)
C..VECTOR v = sC+X*sX
      IMPLICIT COMPLEX*16(v,s)
      DIMENSION v(1)
      CALL FZERO(v)
      v(1)=sC
      v(2)=sX
      RETURN
      END


      SUBROUTINE FLINY(v,sC,sY)
C..VECTOR v = sC+Y*sY
      IMPLICIT COMPLEX*16(v,s)
      COMMON /DEG/N,N1,N2,N3,NN,NH,NG
      DIMENSION v(1)
      CALL FZERO(v)
      v(1) =sC
      v(N2)=sY
      RETURN
      END
```

```
C  2) L1-NORM
C  ----------
      COMPLEX FUNCTION sL1NORM*16(v)
      IMPLICIT COMPLEX*16(v,s)
      DIMENSION v(1)
      COMMON /DEG/N,N1,N2,N3,NN,NH,NG
      sS=v(NG)
      DO 1 I=1,NH
      sS=sSUM(sS,sABS(v(I)))
    1 CONTINUE
      sL1NORM=sABS(sS)
      RETURN
      END


C  3) BASIC ARITHMETIC OPERATIONS
C  ------------------------------
      SUBROUTINE FZERO(v)
      IMPLICIT COMPLEX*16(v,s)
      DIMENSION v(1)
      COMMON /DEG/N,N1,N2,N3,NN,NH,NG
      COMMON /CONST/sZER,sONE,sUNIT
      DO 1 I=1,NG
      v(I)=sZER
    1 CONTINUE
      RETURN
      END


      SUBROUTINE FEQU(v,vRES)
      IMPLICIT COMPLEX*16(v,s)
      DIMENSION v(1),vRES(1)
      COMMON /DEG/N,N1,N2,N3,NN,NH,NG
      DO 1 I=1,NG
      vRES(I)=v(I)
    1 CONTINUE
      RETURN
      END


      SUBROUTINE FsMULT(v,s,vRES)
      IMPLICIT COMPLEX*16(v,s)
      DIMENSION v(1),vRES(1)
      COMMON /DEG/N,N1,N2,N3,NN,NH,NG
      DO 1 I=1,NN
      vRES(I)=sPROD(s,v(I))
    1 CONTINUE
      vRES(NH)=sPROD(v(NH),sABS(s))
      vRES(NG)=sPROD(v(NG),sABS(s))
      RETURN
      END
```

```
      SUBROUTINE FsMPYAD(v,s,vRES)
C..vRES=vRES+C*v
      IMPLICIT COMPLEX*16(v,s)
      DIMENSION v(1),vRES(1)
      COMMON /DEG/N,N1,N2,N3,NN,NH,NG
      DO 1 I=1,NN
      vRES(I)=sSUM(vRES(I),sPROD(s,v(I)))
    1 CONTINUE
      vRES(NH)=sSUM(vRES(NH),sPROD(v(NH),sABS(s)))
      vRES(NG)=sSUM(vRES(NG),sPROD(v(NG),sABS(s)))
      RETURN
      END


      SUBROUTINE FADD(v,vSUM)
      IMPLICIT COMPLEX*16(v,s)
      DIMENSION v(1),vSUM(1)
      COMMON /DEG/N,N1,N2,N3,NN,NH,NG
      DO 1 I=1,NG
      vSUM(I)=sSUM(vSUM(I),v(I))
    1 CONTINUE
      RETURN
      END


      SUBROUTINE FMINUS(v,vDIFF)
C..vDIFF=vDIFF-v
      IMPLICIT COMPLEX*16(v,s)
      DIMENSION v(1),vDIFF(1)
      COMMON /DEG/N,N1,N2,N3,NN,NH,NG
      DO 1 I=1,NN
      vDIFF(I)=sDIFF(vDIFF(I),v(I))
    1 CONTINUE
      vDIFF(NH)=sSUM(vDIFF(NH),v(NH))
      vDIFF(NG)=sSUM(vDIFF(NG),v(NG))
      RETURN
      END


      SUBROUTINE FMULT(vA,vB,vPROD)
      IMPLICIT COMPLEX*16(v,s)
      IMPLICIT REAL*8(r)
      DIMENSION vA(1),vB(1),vPROD(1)
      DIMENSION vC(233)
      DIMENSION rA(20),rB(20)
      COMMON /DEG/N,N1,N2,N3,NN,NH,NG
      COMMON /CONST/sZER,sONE,sUNIT
      IND=0
      GOTO 99
      ENTRY FMULTAD(vA,vB,vPROD)
      IND=1
   99 CONTINUE
      CALL FZERO(vC)
      IA  =0
      IRA =-1
      IRDA=N1
```

```
      DO 1 NXA=1,N1
      LYA =N2-NXA
      DO 2 NYA=1,LYA
      IA  =IA+1
      IF(vA(IA).EQ.sZER)GOTO 2
      IR  =IRA+NYA
      IRD =IRDA
      IB  =0
      IBD =N1
      LXB =LYA+1-NYA
      DO 3 NXB=1,LXB
      LYB =LXB+1-NXB
      DO 4 NYB=1,LYB
      IF(vB(IB+NYB).EQ.sZER)GOTO 4
      vC(IR+NYB)=sSUM(vC(IR+NYB),sPROD(vA(IA),vB(IB+NYB)))
    4 CONTINUE
      IR  =IR+IRD
      IRD =IRD-1
      IB  =IB+IBD
      IBD =IBD-1
    3 CONTINUE
    2 CONTINUE
      IRA =IRA+IRDA
      IRDA=IRDA-1
    1 CONTINUE
C..COMPUTE BOUNDS
      rASUM=rABS(vA(1))
      rBSUM=rABS(vB(1))
      DO 5 I=2,N1
      rA(I-1)=0.D+00
      rB(I-1)=0.D+00
      K =I
      KD=N
      DO 6 J=1,I
      rA(I-1)=rUP(rA(I-1)+rABS(vA(K)))
      rB(I-1)=rUP(rB(I-1)+rABS(vB(K)))
      K =K+KD
      KD=KD-1
    6 CONTINUE
      rASUM=rUP(rASUM+rA(I-1))
      rBSUM=rUP(rBSUM+rB(I-1))
    5 CONTINUE
      rREST1=DIMAG(vB(NH))
      rREST =rUP(rABS(vA(1))*rREST1)
      DO 7 I=1,N
      rREST1=rUP(rREST1+rB(N1-I))
      rREST =rUP(rREST+rUP(rREST1*rA(I)))
    7 CONTINUE
      vC(NH)=sUNIT*rUP(rREST+rUP(rUP(rREST1+rABS(vB(1)))*DIMAG(vA(NH))))
      vC(NH)=sSUM(sSUM(vC(NH),sPROD(vA(NH),vB(NG))),
     *       sPROD(vA(NG),vB(NH)))
      vC(NG)=sSUM(sPROD(vA(NG),sONE*rBSUM),sPROD(vB(NG),sONE*rASUM))
      vC(NG)=sSUM(vC(NG),sPROD(vA(NG),vB(NG)))
      IF(IND.EQ.0)CALL FEQU(vC,vPROD)
      IF(IND.EQ.1)CALL FADD(vC,vPROD)
      RETURN
      END
```

```
      SUBROUTINE FCOMP(vA,vX,vY,vB)
C..vB MUST BE DIFFERENT FROM vA
C..vB=vA(vX,vY)
      IMPLICIT COMPLEX*16(v,s)
      IMPLICIT REAL*8(r)
      LOGICAL logLE
      DIMENSION vA(1),vX(1),vY(1),vB(1)
      DIMENSION vC(233)
      COMMON /DEG/N,N1,N2,N3,NN,NH,NG
      COMMON /CONST/sZER,sONE,sUNIT
      COMMON /TEST/ITEST
      sX    =vX(1)
      vX(1) =sZER
      sXL1H=sL1NORM(vX)
      vX(1) =sX
      sXL1 =sSUM(sABS(vX(1)),sXL1H)
      sY    =vY(1)
      vY(1) =sZER
      sYL1H=sL1NORM(vY)
      vY(1) =sY
      sYL1 =sSUM(sABS(vY(1)),sYL1H)
      IF(ITEST.EQ.0)GOTO 7
C..CHECK RANGE OF vX,vY
      IF(logLE(sXL1,sONE))GOTO 6
      WRITE(6,*)'ERROR IN FCOMP,NORM vX>1',sXL1
    6 CONTINUE
      IF(logLE(sYL1,sONE))GOTO 7
      WRITE(6,*)'ERROR IN FCOMP,NORM vY>1',sYL1
    7 CONTINUE
      CALL FsMULT(vY,vA(NN),vB)
      L=NN-1
      DO 1 I=2,N1
      DO 2 J=1,I
      IF(J.EQ.1)GOTO 3
      CALL FMULT(vX,vC,vC)
      vC(1)=sSUM(vC(1),vA(L))
      GOTO 4
    3 CONTINUE
      CALL FZERO(vC)
      vC(1)=vA(L)
    4 CONTINUE
      L=L-1
    2 CONTINUE
      CALL FADD(vC,vB)
      IF(I.EQ.N1)GOTO 5
      CALL FMULT(vY,vB,vB)
    1 CONTINUE
    5 CONTINUE
      rH=sXL1H
      sXL1H=sONE*rH
      rH=sYL1H
      sYL1H=sONE*rH
      sSUP =sPOWER(sMAX(sXL1H,sYL1H),N1)
      sSUP1=sZER
      DO 8 I=0,N1
```

```
      sSUP1=sMAX(sSUP1,
     *     sDIFF(sPROD(sPOWER(sXL1,I),sPOWER(sYL1,N1-I)),
     *     sPROD(sPOWER(sXL1H,I),sPOWER(sYL1H,N1-I))))
    8 CONTINUE
      vB(NH)=sSUM(vB(NH),sPROD(vA(NH),sSUP))
      vB(NG)=sSUM(sSUM(vB(NG),vA(NG)),sPROD(vA(NH),sSUP1))
      RETURN
      END


C   4) BASIC DERIVATIVE ROUTINES
C   ----------------------------
      SUBROUTINE DERX(vF,vDF)
      IMPLICIT COMPLEX*16(v,s)
      DIMENSION vF(1),vDF(1)
      COMMON /CONST/sZER,sONE,sUNIT
      COMMON /DEG/N,N1,N2,N3,NN,NH,NG
      KDF=1
      KF =2
      DO 1 I=1,N
      DO 2 J=1,N1-I
      vDF(KDF)=sPROD(sICONST(J),vF(KF))
      KDF=KF
      KF =KF+1
    2 CONTINUE
      vDF(KDF)=sZER
      KDF=KF
      KF =KF+1
    1 CONTINUE
      vDF(KDF)=sZER
      vDF(NH) =sZER
      vDF(NG) =sZER
      RETURN
      END


      SUBROUTINE DERY(vF,vDF)
      IMPLICIT COMPLEX*16(v,s)
      DIMENSION vF(1),vDF(1)
      COMMON /DEG/N,N1,N2,N3,NN,NH,NG
      COMMON /CONST/sZER,sONE,sUNIT
      KDF=1
      KF =N2
      DO 1 I=1,N
      DO 2 J=1,N1-I
      vDF(KDF)=sPROD(sICONST(I),vF(KF))
      KDF=KDF+1
      KF =KF +1
    2 CONTINUE
      vDF(KDF)=sZER
      KDF=KDF+1
    1 CONTINUE
      vDF(KDF)=sZER
      vDF(NH) =sZER
      vDF(NG) =sZER
      RETURN
      END
```

```
C  5) OPERATIONS YIELDING SCALARS
C  ------------------------------
      COMPLEX FUNCTION sVALUE*16(v,sX,sY)
      IMPLICIT COMPLEX*16(v,s)
      LOGICAL logLE
      DIMENSION v(1)
      COMMON /DEG/N,N1,N2,N3,NN,NH,NG
      COMMON /CONST/sZER,sONE,sUNIT
      COMMON /TEST/ITEST
C..CHECK ARGUMENTS
      IF(ITEST.EQ.0)GOTO 3
      IF(logLE(sMAX(sABS(sX),sABS(sY)),sONE))GOTO 3
      WRITE(6,*)'ERROR IN VALUE'
    3 CONTINUE
      sZ=sZER
      K=NN
      sZT=v(K)
      DO 1 I=1,N
      sZ =sSUM(sPROD(sZ,sY),sZT)
      K  =K-1
      sZT=v(K)
      DO 2 J=1,I
      K=K-1
      sZT=sSUM(sPROD(sX,sZT),v(K))
    2 CONTINUE
    1 CONTINUE
      sVALUE=sSUM(sSUM(sSUM(sPROD(sZ,sY),sZT),sPROD(
     *       v(NH),sPOWER(sMAX(sABS(sX),sABS(sY)),N1))),v(NG))
      RETURN
      END


      COMPLEX FUNCTION sDXVALUE*16(v,sX,sY)
C..USES vAUX1
      IMPLICIT COMPLEX*16(v,s)
      LOGICAL logLE
      DIMENSION v(1)
      COMMON /DEG/N,N1,N2,N3,NN,NH,NG
      COMMON /AUX/vAUX1(233)
      sTAUX=sABS(sX)
      s99=sCONST(.99D+00)
      IF(logLE(sTAUX,s99))GOTO 1
      WRITE(6,*)'ERROR IN sDXVALUE,sTAUX=',sTAUX
    1 CONTINUE
      CALL DERX(v,vAUX1)
      sTAUY=sABS(sY)
      CALL SBOUND(sTAUX,1,sTAUY,0,sFAC,sFAC1)
      sDXVALUE=sSUM(sSUM(sVALUE(vAUX1,sX,sY),sPROD(v(NH),sFAC)),
     *         sPROD(v(NG),sFAC1))
      RETURN
      END
```

```
      COMPLEX FUNCTION sDYVALUE*16(v,sX,sY)
      IMPLICIT COMPLEX*16(v,s)
      LOGICAL logLE
      DIMENSION v(1)
      DIMENSION vDY(233)
      COMMON /DEG/N,N1,N2,N3,NN,NH,NG
      COMMON /TEST/ITEST
      sTAUY=sABS(sY)
      IF(ITEST.EQ.0)GOTO 2
      s99=sCONST(.99D+00)
      IF(logLE(sTAUY,s99))GOTO 1
      WRITE(6,*)'ERROR IN sDYVALUE,sTAUY=',sTAUY
    1 CONTINUE
      CALL DERY(v,vDY)
      sTAUX=sABS(sX)
      CALL SBOUND(sTAUY,1,sTAUX,0,sFAC,sFAC1)
      sDYVALUE=sSUM(sSUM(sVALUE(vDY,sX,sY),sPROD(v(NH),sFAC)),
     *         sPROD(v(NG),sFAC1))
      RETURN
    2 CONTINUE
      CALL DERY(v,vDY)
      sDYVALUE=sVALUE(vDY,sX,sY)
      RETURN
      END


      COMPLEX FUNCTION sDXYVALUE*16(v,sX,sY)
C..USES vAUX1,2
      IMPLICIT COMPLEX*16(v,s)
      LOGICAL logLE
      DIMENSION v(1)
      COMMON /DEG/N,N1,N2,N3,NN,NH,NG
      COMMON /AUX/vAUX1(233),vAUX2(233)
      sTAUX=sABS(sX)
      s99=sCONST(.99D+00)
      IF(logLE(sTAUX,s99))GOTO 1
      WRITE(6,*)'ERROR IN sDXYVALUE,sTAUX=',sTAUX
    1 CONTINUE
      CALL DERX(v,vAUX1)
      sTAUY=sABS(sY)
      s99=sCONST(.99D+00)
      IF(logLE(sTAUY,s99))GOTO 2
      WRITE(6,*)'ERROR IN sDXYVALUE,sTAUY=',sTAUY
    2 CONTINUE
      CALL DERY(vAUX1,vAUX2)
      CALL SBOUND(sTAUX,1,sTAUY,1,sFAC,sFAC1)
      sDXYVALUE=sSUM(sSUM(sVALUE(vAUX2,sX,sY),sPROD(v(NH),sFAC)),
     *          sPROD(v(NG),sFAC1))
      RETURN
      END
```

```
      COMPLEX FUNCTION sDYYVALUE*16(v,sX,sY)
C..USES vAUX1,2
      IMPLICIT COMPLEX*16(v,s)
      LOGICAL logLE
      DIMENSION v(1)
      COMMON /DEG/N,N1,N2,N3,NN,NH,NG
      COMMON /AUX/vAUX1(233),vAUX2(233)
      sTAUY=sABS(sY)
      s99=sCONST(.99D+00)
      IF(logLE(sTAUY,s99))GOTO 1
      WRITE(6,*)'ERROR IN sDYYVALUE,sTAUY=',sTAUY
    1 CONTINUE
      CALL DERY(v,vAUX1)
      CALL DERY(vAUX1,vAUX2)
      sTAUX=sABS(sX)
      CALL SBOUND(sTAUY,2,sTAUX,0,sFAC,sFAC1)
      sDYYVALUE=sSUM(sSUM(sVALUE(vAUX2,sX,sY),sPROD(v(NH),sFAC)),
     *           sPROD(v(NG),sFAC1))
      RETURN
      END


C  6) DIFFERENTIATE AND COMPOSE VECTORS
C  ------------------------------------
      SUBROUTINE FDXCOMP(vA,vX,vY,vB)
      IMPLICIT COMPLEX*16(v,s)
      LOGICAL logLE
      DIMENSION vA(1),vX(1),vY(1),vB(1)
      DIMENSION vC(233)
      COMMON /DEG/N,N1,N2,N3,NN,NH,NG
      sTAU=sL1NORM(vX)
      sTAU2=sL1NORM(vY)
      s99=sCONST(.99D+00)
      IF(logLE(sTAU,s99))GOTO 4
      WRITE(6,*)'ERROR IN DXCOMP,sTAU=',sTAU
    4 CONTINUE
      CALL DERX(vA,vC)
      GOTO 3
      ENTRY FDYCOMP(vA,vX,vY,vB)
      sTAU =sL1NORM(vY)
      sTAU2=sL1NORM(vX)
      s99  =sCONST(.99D+00)
      IF(logLE(sTAU,s99))GOTO 2
      WRITE(6,*)'ERROR IN DYCOMP,sTAU=',sTAU
    2 CONTINUE
      CALL DERY(vA,vC)
    3 CONTINUE
      CALL FCOMP(vC,vX,vY,vB)
      CALL SBOUND(sTAU,1,sTAU2,0,sFAC,sFAC1)
      vB(NG)=sSUM(sSUM(vB(NG),sPROD(vA(NH),sFAC)),sPROD(vA(NG),sFAC1))
      RETURN
      END
```

```
C  7) THE FOLLOWING ROUTINE DOES AUXILIARY CALCULATIONS
C  ----------------------------------------------------
C  FOR THE DERIVATIVE AND COMPOSITION ROUTINES
C  ----------------------------------------
      SUBROUTINE SBOUND(sRHO1,I1,sRHO2,I2,sFAC,sFAC1)
C..THIS SUBROUTINE COMPUTES THE L1-NORMS OF
C  (DX**I1*DY**I2 F)(RHO1*X,RHO2*Y)
C  sFAC1 IS THE RESULT FOR F WITH L1-NORM EQUAL TO 1
C  sFAC  IS THE RESULT FOR F OF DEGREE >= N+1 WITH L1-NORM EQUAL TO 1
C  ADMISSIBLE CHOICES (I1,I2)=(1,0),(2,0),(1,1)
      IMPLICIT COMPLEX*16(v,s)
      IMPLICIT REAL*8(r)
      COMMON /DEG/N,N1,N2,N3,NN,NH,NG
      rRHO1=DIMAG(sRHO1)
      rRHO2=DIMAG(sRHO2)
      IF(I1.EQ.1)M1=-1.D+00/LOG(rRHO1+1.D-7)+1
      IF(I2.EQ.1)M2=-1.D+00/LOG(rRHO2+1.D-7)+1
      IF(I1.NE.2)GOTO 1
      rRHOA=LOG(rRHO1+1.D-7)
C..NEXT LINE IS UPPER BOUND
      M1=.5D+00*(-3-2/rRHOA+SQRT((3+2/rRHOA)*(3+2/rRHOA)-8-12/rRHOA))+2
    1 CONTINUE
      IF(I2.EQ.0)M2=1
      M1=MAX(M1,N1)
      M2=MAX(M2,N1)
      rFAC1=0.D+00
      rFAC=0.D+00
      IF(I1.EQ.1.AND.I2.EQ.0)GOTO 10
      IF(I1.EQ.1.AND.I2.EQ.1)GOTO 20
      IF(I1.EQ.2.AND.I2.EQ.0)GOTO 30
      WRITE(6,*)'WRONG ARGUMENTS IN SBOUND'
      STOP
   10 CONTINUE
      DO 11 I=1,M1
      rR=rUP(rPOWER(rRHO1,I-1)*I)
      rFAC1=DMAX1(rR,rFAC1)
   11 CONTINUE
      DO 12 I=1,M1
      rR=rUP(rUP(rPOWER(rRHO1,I-1)*I)*rPOWER(rRHO2,MAX(0,N1-I)))
      rFAC=DMAX1(rR,rFAC)
   12 CONTINUE
      GOTO 40
   20 CONTINUE
      DO 21 I=1,M1
      rR=rUP(rPOWER(rRHO1,I-1)*I)
      rFAC1=DMAX1(rR,rFAC1)
   21 CONTINUE
      DO 22 I=1,M2
      rR=rUP(rPOWER(rRHO2,I-1)*I)
      rFAC=DMAX1(rR,rFAC)
   22 CONTINUE
      rFAC1=rUP(rFAC1*rFAC)
      rFAC=0.D+00
      DO 23 I=1,M1
      II=MAX(1,N1-I)
```

```
      DO 24 J=II,M2
      rR=rUP(rUP(rUP(rPOWER(rRHO1,I-1)*I)*rPOWER(rRHO2,J-1))*J)
      rFAC=DMAX1(rR,rFAC)
   24 CONTINUE
   23 CONTINUE
      GOTO 40
   30 CONTINUE
      DO 31 I=1,M1
      rR=rUP(rPOWER(rRHO1,I-1)*(I*(I+1)))
      rFAC1=DMAX1(rR,rFAC1)
   31 CONTINUE
      DO 32 J=1,M1
      rR=rUP(rUP(rPOWER(rRHO1,J-1)*(J*(J+1)))*rPOWER(rRHO2,MAX(0,N-J)))
      rFAC=DMAX1(rR,rFAC)
   32 CONTINUE
   40 CONTINUE
      sFAC =DCMPLX(0.D+00,rFAC)
      sFAC1=DCMPLX(0.D+00,rFAC1)
      RETURN
      END

C  ROUTINES ACTING ON SCALARS
C  ==========================

C  1) ROUNDING,CREATION OF CONSTANTS,OUTPUT
C  ----------------------------------------
      REAL FUNCTION rUP*8(r)
      IMPLICIT REAL*8(r)
      DIMENSION LL(2)
      EQUIVALENCE (rRES,LL(1),K),(LL(2),L)
      DATA L351/0377777777777/
      rRES=r
C..IF LOW PART OF MANTISSA IS,0,777777777776,OR 777777777777
C  THEN EXCEPTIONAL HANDLING
      IF(BITS(L,1,35).EQ.L351)GOTO 3
      IF(L)2,1,2
C..LOW PART ZERO.CHECK IF R IS ZERO
    1 CONTINUE
      IF(rRES.NE.0.D+00)GOTO 2
C..R IS ZERO. UP IS SMALLEST POSITIVE NUMBER
      BITS(K,13,1)=1
      rUP=rRES
      RETURN
C..GENERIC CASE, ADD ONE TO LOWER PART OF MANTISSA
    2 CONTINUE
      L=L+1
      rUP=rRES
      RETURN
C..LOWER PART OF MANTISSA IS 777777777776 OR 777777777777
    3 CONTINUE
      IF(BITS(L,36,1).EQ.1)GOTO 4
C..CASE OF 777777777776, CHANGED TO 777777777777
      BITS(L,36,1)=1
      rUP=rRES
      RETURN
```

```
C..CASE OF 777777777777
    4 CONTINUE
      L=0
      KSAVE=BITS(K,13,1)
      BITS(K,13,1)=1
      K=K+1
C..CHECK CASE OF OVERFLOW OR UNDERFLOW
      IF(BITS(K,1,1).EQ.KSAVE)GOTO 5
C..RESTORE BIT 13
      BITS(K,13,1)=KSAVE
      rUP=rRES
      RETURN
C..DISTINGUISH OVERFLOW UNDERFLOW
    5 CONTINUE
      IF(KSAVE.EQ.0)GOTO 6
C..OVERFLOW
      WRITE(6,*)'OVERFLOW IN UP'
      rUP=R
      RETURN
C..UNDERFLOW,RESULT IS ZERO
    6 CONTINUE
      L=0
      K=0
      rUP=rRES
      RETURN
      END


      REAL FUNCTION rDOWN*8(r)
      IMPLICIT REAL*8(r)
      rDOWN=-rUP(-r)
      RETURN
      END


      COMPLEX FUNCTION sCONST*16(r)
      IMPLICIT COMPLEX*16(s)
      IMPLICIT REAL*8(r)
      sCONST=DCMPLX(r,r)
      RETURN
      END


      COMPLEX FUNCTION sICONST*16(I)
      IMPLICIT COMPLEX*16(s)
      IMPLICIT REAL*8(r)
      r=I
      sICONST=DCMPLX(r,r)
      RETURN
      END
```

```
C  2) BASIC ARITHMETIC OPERATIONS
C  ------------------------------
      COMPLEX FUNCTION sSUM*16(sA,sB)
      IMPLICIT COMPLEX*16(s)
      IMPLICIT REAL*8(r)
      rDA=sA
      rDB=sB
      IF(rDA.EQ.0.D+00.OR.rDB.EQ.0.D+00)GOTO 1
      rD=rDOWN(rDA+rDB)
      GOTO 11
    1 CONTINUE
      rD=rDA+rDB
   11 CONTINUE
      rUA=DIMAG(sA)
      rUB=DIMAG(sB)
      IF(rUA.EQ.0.D+00.OR.rUB.EQ.0.D+00)GOTO 2
      rU=rUP(rUA+rUB)
      GOTO 21
    2 CONTINUE
      rU=rUA+rUB
   21 CONTINUE
      sSUM=DCMPLX(rD,rU)
      RETURN
      END


      COMPLEX FUNCTION sNEG*16(s)
      IMPLICIT COMPLEX*16(s)
      IMPLICIT REAL*8(r)
      rD=s
      rU=DIMAG(s)
      sNEG=DCMPLX(-rU,-rD)
      RETURN
      END


      COMPLEX FUNCTION sDIFF*16(sA,sB)
      IMPLICIT COMPLEX*16(s)
      IMPLICIT REAL*8(r)
      sDIFF=sSUM(sA,sNEG(sB))
      RETURN
      END


      COMPLEX FUNCTION sPROD*16(sA,sB)
      IMPLICIT COMPLEX*16(s)
      IMPLICIT REAL*8(r)
      COMMON /CONST/sZER,sONE,sUNIT
      IF(sA.EQ.sZER.OR.sB.EQ.sZER)GOTO 1
      rDA=sA
      rUA=DIMAG(sA)
      rDB=sB
      rUB=DIMAG(sB)
      rP1=rDA*rDB
      rP2=rDA*rUB
      rP3=rUA*rDB
      rP4=rUA*rUB
```

```
      sPROD=DCMPLX(rDOWN(DMIN1(rP1,rP2,rP3,rP4)),
     *             rUP  (DMAX1(rP1,rP2,rP3,rP4)))
      RETURN
    1 CONTINUE
      sPROD=sZER
      RETURN
      END


      COMPLEX FUNCTION sINV*16(s)
      IMPLICIT COMPLEX*16(s)
      IMPLICIT REAL*8(r)
      rD=s
      rU=DIMAG(s)
      IF(rD.GT.0.D+00.OR.rU.LT.0.D+00)GOTO 1
      WRITE(6,*)'ERROR IN sINV'
      STOP
    1 CONTINUE
      sINV=DCMPLX(rDOWN(1.D+00/rU),rUP(1.D+00/rD))
      RETURN
      END


      COMPLEX FUNCTION sQUOT*16(sA,sB)
      IMPLICIT COMPLEX*16(s)
      IMPLICIT REAL*8(r)
      sQUOT=sPROD(sA,sINV(sB))
      RETURN
      END


      REAL FUNCTION rPOWER*8(rR1,K)
C..COMPUTES rR1**K, ASSUMING rR1>=0 AND GIVES UPPER BOUND
      IMPLICIT COMPLEX*16(s)
      IMPLICIT REAL*8(r)
      r=rR1
      IF(r.EQ.0.D+00)GOTO 1
      N=K
      rRES=1.D+00
    3 CONTINUE
      IF(N.EQ.0)GOTO 4
      NN=N/2
      IF(NN*2.EQ.N)GOTO 2
      rRES=rUP(rRES*r)
      N=N-1
      GOTO 3
    2 CONTINUE
      r=rUP(r*r)
      N=NN
      GOTO 3
    1 CONTINUE
      rRES=0.D+00
      IF(K.EQ.0)rRES=1.D+00
    4 CONTINUE
      rPOWER=rRES
      RETURN
      END
```

```
      REAL FUNCTION rPOWD*8(rR1,K)
C..COMPUTES rR1**K, ASSUMING rR1>=0 AND GIVES LOWER BOUND
      IMPLICIT COMPLEX*16(s)
      IMPLICIT REAL*8(r)
      r=rR1
      IF(r.EQ.0.D+00)GOTO 1
      N=K
      rRES=1.D+00
    3 CONTINUE
      IF(N.EQ.0)GOTO 4
      NN=N/2
      IF(NN*2.EQ.N)GOTO 2
      rRES=rDOWN(rRES*r)
      N=N-1
      GOTO 3
    2 CONTINUE
      r=rDOWN(r*r)
      N=NN
      GOTO 3
    1 CONTINUE
      rRES=0.D+00
      IF(K.EQ.0)rRES=1.D+00
    4 CONTINUE
      rPOWD=rRES
      RETURN
      END

      COMPLEX FUNCTION sPOWER*16(s,K)
C..COMPUTES s**K
      IMPLICIT COMPLEX*16(s)
      IMPLICIT REAL*8(r)
      rU=DIMAG(s)
      rU=rPOWER(rU,K)
      rD=s
      rD=rPOWD(rD,K)
      sPOWER=DCMPLX(rD,rU)
      RETURN
      END
```

```
C  3) RELATIONAL OPERATORS
C  -----------------------
C..SECOND ARGUMENT CONSIDERED TO BE INTERVAL OF LENGTH ZERO
      LOGICAL FUNCTION logLT(s1,s2)
      IMPLICIT COMPLEX*16(s)
      IMPLICIT REAL*8(r)
      logLT=.FALSE.
      r=DIMAG(sDIFF(s1,s2))
      IF(r.LT.0.D+00)logLT=.TRUE.
      RETURN
      END


      LOGICAL FUNCTION logGE(s1,s2)
      IMPLICIT COMPLEX*16(s)
      IMPLICIT REAL*8(r)
      logGE=.FALSE.
      r=sDIFF(s1,s2)
      IF(r.GE.0.D+00)logGE=.TRUE.
      RETURN
      END


      LOGICAL FUNCTION logLE(s1,s2)
      IMPLICIT COMPLEX*16(s)
      IMPLICIT REAL*8(r)
      logLE=.FALSE.
      IF(DIMAG(s1).LE.DIMAG(s2))logLE=.TRUE.
      RETURN
      END


      LOGICAL FUNCTION logZERO(s)
      IMPLICIT COMPLEX*16(s)
      IMPLICIT REAL*8(r)
      logZERO=.TRUE.
      r=s
      IF(r.GT.0.D+00.OR.DIMAG(s).LT.0.D+00)logZERO=.FALSE.
      RETURN
      END
```

```
C  4) MAX,ABS
C  ----------
      COMPLEX FUNCTION sMAX*16(sA,sB)
      IMPLICIT COMPLEX*16(s)
      sMAX=sA
      IF(DIMAG(sB).GT.DIMAG(sA))sMAX=sB
      RETURN
      END

      COMPLEX FUNCTION sABS*16(s)
      IMPLICIT COMPLEX*16(s)
      IMPLICIT REAL*8(r)
      rD=s
      rU=DIMAG(s)
      IF(rD.GE.0.D+00.OR.rU.LE.0.D+00)GOTO 1
      sABS=DCMPLX(0.D+00,DMAX1(DABS(rD),DABS(rU)))
      RETURN
    1 CONTINUE
      rA=DABS(rD)
      rB=DABS(rU)
      sABS=DCMPLX(DMIN1(rA,rB),DMAX1(rA,rB))
      RETURN
      END

      REAL FUNCTION rABS*8(s)
      IMPLICIT COMPLEX*16(s)
      IMPLICIT REAL*8(r)
      rD=s
      rABS=DMAX1(DABS(rD),DIMAG(s))
      RETURN
      END
```

III.2. PROGRAM OUTPUT

```
DEGREE FOR PHI-PHIO   =           20
DEGREE FOR TANGENT MAP=           15
PARAMETERS OF DOMAIN:
CENTER ALPHA=  .500000000000000000+000
RADIUS TAU  =  .160000000000000000+001
B = ( .191186676638215463+001, .191186676638215533+001)
C = ( .827289672648672113+000, .827289672648672317+000)
LA= (-.248875288718523089+000,-.248875288718522890+000)
MU= ( .611101382123083292-001, .611101382123086210-001)
TAUT                      =  .280000000000000000+001
INITIAL CHOICE FOR THETA=  .421000000000000000+000
ABS(D3T)   >= ( .413737713779843370+001, .413737713779843869+001)
RANGE OF ZETA=  .992835064763068123+000
L-NORM(PHIO-PHIONEW) ( .000000000000000000     , .120349037785755569-007)
DERIVATIVE IS CALCULATED ON
A NEIGHBORHOOD OF vPHIO WITH RADIUS
BETA=  .500000000000000000-007
B = ( .191186106093445286+001, .191187247183607148+001)
C = ( .827287954074444574+000, .827291381223115377+000)
LA= (-.248876814320826866+000,-.248873763116424482+000)
MU= ( .611078112368347591-001, .611124652236404781-001)
TAUT                      =  .280000000000000000+001
INITIAL CHOICE FOR THETA=  .421000000000000000+000
ABS(D3T)   >= ( .413734947800133924+001, .413740479760518201+001)
RANGE OF ZETA=  .992872357442342530+000
RADIUS Z    = ( .446608317748037738+000, .446620374104967609+000)
RADIUS LA   = ( .639146814090307129+000, .639150818796085264+000)
RADIUS OF NEIGHBORHOOD =  .500000000000000000-007
NORM OF MATRIX DM      = ( .542961257814249109+000, .543747241494526944+000)
NORM OF PHIO-PHIONEW   = ( .000000000000000000     , .120349037785755569-007)

CONTRACTION ON BALL

DPP = ( .844585420507045498+001, .898721229210163473+001)
DQP = (-.406732443959458477+000, .417653155319029197+000)
DSPN= ( .000000000000000000     , .185624898687465281+001)
DPQ = (-.154585334949933817+000, .169013676308452841+000)
DQQ = (-.427287708308878208+001,-.378001730155202048+001)
DSQN= ( .000000000000000000     , .110742307416589058+001)
DPSN= ( .645320139679006722+000, .653267443741918952+000)
DQSN= ( .259711765991506833+000, .271665611253069431+000)
NORM= ( .542961257814249109+000, .543747241494526944+000)
DETERMINANT CHANGES SIGN AS EXPECTED

BOUND FOR LEMMA 1.3.3.
C1+DW1/DLAMDA = (-.104034764005069663+001,-.104034380236834370+001)
BOUNDS FOR LEMMA 1.5.1.
a= (-.737163830239187437-007, .737163830239187437-007)
b= (-.115711102525403419-004, .115711102525403419-004)
c= (-.378615860317750098-006, .378615860317750098-006)
BOUND FOR LEMMA 1.6.1.
C2 MUST BE LESS THAN   .105949471895549860+002
BOUND FOR LEMMA 1.6.4
BOUND IS   .977298505704838593+001
BOUND FOR LEMMA 1.5.2.
BOUND FOR DXS IS  .802891946821145562+000
```

Table 1 : coefficients of the packed vector φ_o used as input.

1:	-.302218250463128873-001
2:	.154830664195353367-002
3:	-.129578370556081318-003
4:	.108523586647550293-004
5:	-.987372844807154123-006
6:	.935463250541952263-007
7:	-.915390414245415699-008
8:	.917640087941869132-009
9:	-.937621886025294370-010
10:	.972897515408567785-011
11:	-.102231566401946393-011
12:	.108518062717437766-012
13:	-.115942535488959455-013
14:	.123599515512696595-014
15:	-.128585000700047043-015
16:	.124514720295842190-016
17:	-.103253974956103418-017
18:	.639459674649833898-019
19:	-.221947015573720828-020
20:	.791742899101695183-002
21:	-.741859716302175834-003
22:	.750979401365909050-004
23:	-.789543633541830282-005
24:	.851409854814131693-006
25:	-.934137538514596987-007
26:	.103792560799945019-007
27:	-.116433094642290927-008
28:	.131593518407010228-009
29:	-.149612482867518388-010
30:	.170853124534413310-011
31:	-.195425608391321948-012
32:	.222107065134780887-013
33:	-.245419372762764689-014
34:	.251247438081158377-015
35:	-.218208096671618356-016
36:	.138215493093105955-017
37:	-.463194073132168188-019
38:	.626224565328406937-002
39:	-.160675645442736537-002
40:	.204716420599186307-003
41:	-.259467491588060176-004
42:	.327320570884602615-005
43:	-.411205831371326772-006
44:	.514710323846259959-007
45:	-.642219993765179074-008
46:	.799081151329943560-009
47:	-.991748882180860719-010
48:	.122762272148014029-010
49:	-.151302549229142636-011
50:	.184369284522256626-012
51:	-.217535815466223768-013
52:	.237023192465046574-014
53:	-.218477801082521684-015
54:	.146481789444569259-016
55:	-.518208022232986191-018
56:	.140548932455512415-003
57:	-.452915480150940848-004
58:	.693100354025415795-005
59:	-.102351969771038658-005
60:	.147227644402519850-006
61:	-.207537155249882862-007
62:	.287876987339816273-008
63:	-.394077781101782018-009
64:	.533343923174530136-010
65:	-.713501356833401317-011
66:	.938041898760630842-012
67:	-.118823208969553820-012
68:	.138435550860119163-013
69:	-.135977095938542519-014
70:	.968451999492137331-016
71:	-.362824768103934656-017
72:	.441568418143338155-005
73:	-.158606941711927689-005
74:	.268805158807486310-006
75:	-.436322206017262056-007
76:	.684939719910452141-008
77:	-.104682361536778030-008
78:	.156466072603692124-009
79:	-.229122650076956052-010
80:	.327324070519198133-011
81:	-.447853420756558709-012
82:	.560831487210665231-013
83:	-.589667813699498405-014
84:	.447886551807202722-015
85:	-.178324075195023030-016
86:	.163586969339542905-006
87:	-.626359250225299106-007
88:	.113343750494654797-007
89:	-.196244073310274145-008
90:	.327794308704771235-009
91:	-.530586837100769928-010
92:	.830439595632213275-011
93:	-.123581485933800022-011
94:	.167324109563134508-012
95:	-.189271473107272035-013
96:	.153993821616953699-014
97:	-.654120828619607172-016
98:	.668653115380598254-008
99:	-.267045827599544460-008
100:	.505616944454200397-009
101:	-.915162759778108392-010
102:	.158429307720013615-010
103:	-.258483170627742805-011
104:	.380947666251526417-012
105:	-.466259898814247500-013
106:	.408365445469242406-014
107:	-.185866559520685867-015
108:	.291630529962384718-009
109:	-.119702801334653713-009
110:	.231810283391865535-010

```
111:   -.418527993466551614-011
112:    .676636874219246717-012
113:   -.901977627407920390-013
114:    .855168134438476962-014
115:   -.419102891528817993-015
116:    .131439002736733006-010
117:   -.531059160446456976-011
118:    .950426601207490573-012
119:   -.139035251649604742-012
120:    .143615663695012141-013
121:   -.762065976759714626-015
122:    .531784274011477496-012
123:   -.172266563961423343-012
124:    .195312992445814170-013
125:   -.112927963043820731-014
126:    .108133294048250410-013
127:   -.137259515463036950-014
```

REFERENCES

1. Collet P., Eckmann J.-P. and Lanford O., 1980, Commun. Math. Phys. 76, 211.

2. Collet P. and Eckmann J.-P., 1980, Iterated maps on the interval as dynamical systems, Progress in Physics (Birkhäuser Basel), Vol. 1.

3. Collet P., Eckmann J.-P. and Koch H., 1981, J. Stat. Phys. 25, 1.

4a) Benettin G., Cercignani C., Galgani L. and Giorgilli A., 1980, Lettere al Nuovo Cimento 29, 163-166.

4b) Bountis T., Physica 3D, 577 (1981).

4c) Greene J.M., MacKay R.S., Vivaldi F. and Feigenbaum M., Physica 3D, 468-486, 1981.

4d) Widom M., Kadanoff L.P., Physica D, to appear.

4e) Helleman R.H.G., 1980, in "Fundamental problems in statistical mechanics", Ed. by E.G.D. Cohen (North-Holland, Amsterdam, p. 165).

4f) Eckmann J.-P., Koch H., Wittwer P., Phys. Rev. A/R, 26,720 (1982).

5. Lanford O., 1981, Bull.A.M.S.(New Series)6,427 (1982).

6. Campanino M., Epstein H. and Ruelle D., 1981, Commun. Math. Phys. 79, 261-302; 1982, Topology 21, 125-129.

7. Collet P., Eckmann J.-P. and Koch H., 1980, Physica 3D, 457-467 (1981).

8. Feigenbaum M.J., 1978, J. Stat. Phys. 19, 25; 1979a, J. Stat. Phys. 21, 669; 1979b, Phys. Lett. A74, 375; 1980, Commun. Math. Phys. 77, 65.

9. Fundamentals of numerical computation, Computing Supplementum 2, Springer-Verlag 1980, and references therein.

10. Moore R.E., Interval analysis, Prentice-hall, Series in automatic computation 1966, and Methods and applications of interval analysis, SIAM, Philadelphia 1979.

11. Hille E., Ordinary differential equations in the complex domain, J. Wiley, New York 1976.

12. Kato T., Perturbation theory for linear operators, in : Die Grundlehren der mathematischen Wissenschaften in Einzeldarstellung, Band 132.

J.-P. Eckmann and P. Wittwer
Département de Physique Théorique
Université de Genève
1211 Genève 4, Switzerland

H. Koch
Harvard University
The Physics Laboratories
Cambridge, Mass. (USA)

General instructions to authors for
PREPARING REPRODUCTION COPY FOR MEMOIRS

For more detailed instructions send for AMS booklet, "A Guide for Authors of Memoirs." Write to Editorial Offices, American Mathematical Society, P. O. Box 6248, Providence, R. I. 02940.

MEMOIRS are printed by photo-offset from camera copy fully prepared by the author. This means that, except for a reduction in size of 20 to 30%, the finished book will look exactly like the copy submitted. Thus the author will want to use a good quality typewriter with a new, medium-inked black ribbon, and submit clean copy on the appropriate model paper.

Model Paper, provided at no cost by the AMS, is paper marked with blue lines that confine the copy to the appropriate size. Author should specify, when ordering, whether typewriter to be used has PICA-size (10 characters to the inch) or ELITE-size type (12 characters to the inch).

Line Spacing – For best appearance, and economy, a typewriter equipped with a half-space ratchet – 12 notches to the inch – should be used. (This may be purchased and attached at small cost.) Three notches make the desired spacing, which is equivalent to 1-1/2 ordinary single spaces. Where copy has a great many subscripts and superscripts, however, double spacing should be used.

Special Characters may be filled in carefully freehand, using dense black ink, or INSTANT ("rub-on") LETTERING may be used. AMS has a sheet of several hundred most-used symbols and letters which may be purchased for $5.

Diagrams may be drawn in black ink either directly on the model sheet, or on a separate sheet and pasted with rubber cement into spaces left for them in the text. Ballpoint pen is *not* acceptable.

Page Headings (Running Heads) should be centered, in CAPITAL LETTERS (preferably), at the top of the page – just above the blue line and touching it.

LEFT-hand, EVEN-numbered pages should be headed with the AUTHOR'S NAME;

RIGHT-hand, ODD-numbered pages should be headed with the TITLE of the paper (in shortened form if necessary).

Exceptions: PAGE 1 and any other page that carries a display title require NO RUNNING HEADS.

Page Numbers should be at the top of the page, on the same line with the running heads.

LEFT-hand, EVEN numbers – flush with left margin;

RIGHT-hand, ODD numbers – flush with right margin.

Exceptions: PAGE 1 and any other page that carries a display title should have page number, centered below the text, on blue line provided.

FRONT MATTER PAGES should be numbered with Roman numerals (lower case), positioned below text in same manner as described above.

MEMOIRS FORMAT

It is suggested that the material be arranged in pages as indicated below.
Note: Starred items (*) are requirements of publication.

Front Matter (first pages in book, preceding main body of text).

Page i – *Title, *Author's name.

Page iii – Table of contents.

Page iv – *Abstract (at least 1 sentence and at most 300 words).

*1980 Mathematics Subject Classifications represent the primary and secondary subjects of the paper. For the classification scheme, see Annual Subject Indexes of MATHEMATICAL REVIEWS beginning in December 1978.

Key words and phrases, if desired. (A list which covers the content of the paper adequately enough to be useful for an information retrieval system.)

Page v, etc. – Preface, introduction, or any other matter not belonging in body of text.

Page 1 – Chapter Title (dropped 1 inch from top line, and centered).

Beginning of Text.

Footnotes: *Received by the editor date.
Support information – grants, credits, etc.

Last Page (at bottom) – Author's affiliation.

ABCDEFGHIJ–AMS–8987654

Number 290

Baruch Solel

Irreducible triangular algebras

Memoirs
of the American Mathematical Society

Providence · Rhode Island · USA

January 1984 · Volume 47 · Number 290 (second of six numbers) · ISSN 0065-9266

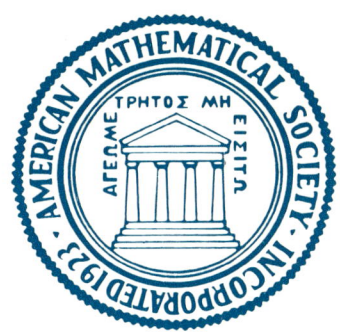

Memoirs of the American Mathematical Society
Number 290

Baruch Solel

Irreducible triangular algebras

Published by the
AMERICAN MATHEMATICAL SOCIETY
Providence, Rhode Island, USA

January 1984 · Volume 47 · Number 290 (second of six numbers)

MEMOIRS of the American Mathematical Society

This journal is designed particularly for long research papers (and groups of cognate papers) in pure and applied mathematics. It includes, in general, longer papers than those in the TRANSACTIONS.

Mathematical papers intended for publication in the Memoirs should be addressed to one of the editors. Subjects, and the editors associated with them, follow:

MEMOIRS are printed by photo-offset from camera-ready copy fully prepared by the authors. Prospective authors are encouraged to request booklet giving detailed instructions regarding reproduction copy. Write to Editorial Office, American Mathematical Society, P. O. Box 6248, Providence, Rhode Island 02940. For general instructions, see last page of Memoir.

SUBSCRIPTION INFORMATION. The 1984 subscription begins with Number 289 and consists of six mailings, each containing one or more numbers. Subscription prices for 1984 are $148 list; $74 member. A late charge of 10% of the subscription price will be imposed upon orders received from nonmembers after January 1 of the subscription year. Subscribers outside the United States and India must pay a postage surcharge of $10; subscribers in India must pay a postage surcharge of $15. Each number may be ordered separately; *please specify number* when ordering an individual number. For prices and titles of recently released numbers, refer to the New Publications sections of the NOTICES of the American Mathematical Society.

BACK NUMBER INFORMATION. For back issues see the AMS Catalogue of Publications.

TRANSACTIONS of the American Mathematical Society

This journal consists of shorter tracts which are of the same general character as the papers published in the MEMOIRS. The editorial committee is identical with that for the MEMOIRS so that papers intended for publication in this series should be addressed to one of the editors listed above.

Subscriptions and orders for publications of the American Mathematical Society should be addressed to American Mathematical Society, P. O. Box 1571, Annex Station, Providence, R. I. 02901. *All orders must be accompanied by payment.* Other correspondence should be addressed to P. O. Box 6248, Providence, R. I. 02940.

MEMOIRS of the American Mathematical Society (ISSN 0065-9266) is published bimonthly (each volume consisting usually of more than one number) by the American Mathematical Society at 201 Charles Street, Providence, Rhode Island 02904. Second Class postage paid at Providence, Rhode Island 02940. Postmaster: Send address changes to Memoirs of the American Mathematical Society, American Mathematical Society, P. O. Box 6248, Providence, RI 02940.

TABLE OF CONTENTS

ABSTRACT

This memoir is devoted to the study of the structure of irreducible triangular algebras generated by a maximal abelian algebra and an ordered semigroup of unitary operators acting on the maximal abelian algebra.

1980 Mathematics Subject Classification. Primary 47D25, Secondary 46L99, 47A35.

Key words and pharases : Triangular algebra, irreducible algebra, action of a unitary group, Arveson's expectation, automorphism, derivation.

Library of Congress Cataloging in Publication Data

Solel, Baruch, 1952-
Irreducible triangular algebras.

(Memoirs of the American Mathematical Society, ISSN 0065-9266 ; no. 290)
"Volume 47, number 290 (second of six numbers)"
Bibliography: p.
1. Triangular operator algebras. 2. Operator algebras.
3. Ergodic theory. I. Title. II. Series.
QA3.A57 no. 290 [QA326] 510s [512'.55] 83-22524
ISBN 0-8218-2290-X

INTRODUCTION

This memoir is devoted to the study of the structure of irreducible triangular algebras generated by a maximal abelian algebra $\mathcal{a}$ and an ordered semigroup G of unitary operators acting on $\mathcal{a}$. In its basic mathematical aspects, this investigation follows two paths. Along the first, and most primitive, it is a further development of the structure theory of a subclass of non-self-adjoint operator algebras - the irreducible triangular algebras. Along the second, it is an exploration of some parts of non-commutative ergodic theory - with emphasis on non-self adjoint features of this theory.

We elaborate somewhat on both these aspects of our investigation. The theory of triangular operator algebras was initiated by Kadison and Singer in a paper [33] which appeared in 1960. With H a complex Hilbert space and B(H) the algebra of all bounded operators on it, a subalgebra $\mathcal{g}$ of B(H) such that $\mathcal{g} \cap \mathcal{g}^*$ is maximal abelian in B(H) is said to be triangular and $\mathcal{g}\cap\mathcal{g}^*$ is said to be its diagonal. An application of Zorn's lemma permits us to conclude that $\mathcal{g}$ is contained in a maximal triangular algebra $\mathcal{g}_0$ (and, necessarily, $\mathcal{g} \cap \mathcal{g}^* = \mathcal{g}_0 \cap \mathcal{g}_0^*$). The projection E is said to be a hull (in $\mathcal{g}$) when E is invariant under each T in $\mathcal{g}$ - that is ETE=TE for each T in $\mathcal{g}$ (the range of E is stable under each T in $\mathcal{g}$). Such a projection, E, is invariant under the self-adjoint algebra $\mathcal{g}\cap\mathcal{g}^*$, hence commutes with $\mathcal{g} \cap \mathcal{g}^*$ - and, hence, lies in (the maximal abelian) $\mathcal{g} \cap \mathcal{g}^*$.

If H is finite dimensional, an (ordered) orthonormal basis $e_1,\ldots,e_n$ for H can be chosen so that $\mathcal{g} \cap \mathcal{g}^*$ appears as the algebra of all diagonal matrices relative to this basis and $\mathcal{g}$ appears as the algebra of (upper) triangular matrices relative to this (ordered) basis. Again, if H is infinite dimensional and $\mathcal{g} \cap \mathcal{g}^*$ is generated by its minimal (that is, one-dimensional) projections (we say that $\mathcal{g} \cap \mathcal{g}^*$ is totally-atomic, in this case),

Received by the editors June 8, 1982.

we can choose an orthonormal basis and an ordering on it such that g appears
as the algebra of all bounded operators whose matrices are upper triangular
relative to the basis in that ordering. (see [33, Theorem 3.2.1].) For
a finite basis the (total) ordering is not essential - there is only one total
ordering - up to order isomorphism. In the infinite-dimensional case the
(total) ordering is essential (the basis might be ordered as the rationals, or
as the integers, with a first or last element or without, among other possibilities); and it is shown in [33, Theorem 3.2.1] that two maximal triangular
algebras with totally-atomic diagonals are unitarily equivalent if and only if
their sets of minimal projections are order isomorphic.

For the more general triangular algebra g , it is still the case that
the set of hulls is totally ordered (by the usual projection ordering). (See
[33, Lemma 2.3.3].) But it need not be true that there are very many hulls.
The (abelian) von Neumann subalgebra C of $g \cap g^*$, generated by the hulls,
is called the core of g . In the case of a totally-atomic diagonal, $C = g \cap g^*$.
The maximal triangular algebras for which the core coincides with the diagonal
are called hyperreducible by Kadison and Singer; and this class is the one
analyzed in detail in [33]. The diagonal need not be totally atomic if the
algebra is hyperreducilbe. In fact there is one whose diagonal contains no
minimal projections (and only one, up to unitary equivalence, in the case of
separable Hilbert space -see [33, Theorem 3.3.1].) The opposite extreme is
the case where C consists of scalar multiples of the identity operator I .
Such algebras are called irreducible in [33], and examples are given (based
on [33, Theorem 2.2.1]) to show that the class of such algebras is not empty.

An orthonormal basis in a Hilbert space gives rise to a totally-atomic
maximal abelian algebra and such an albegra corresponds to an (essentially
unique) orthornormal basis. It is natural to regard the general maximal
abelian algebra as a generalized orthonormal basis. In the same way, a maximal
triangular algebra with totally-atomic diagonal corresponds to an ordered
orthonormal basis; and a general hyperreducible maximal triangular algebra

with totally-atomic diagonal corresponds to an ordered orthonormal basis; and a general hyperreducible maximal triangular algebra should be viewed as a generalized, oredered orthonormal basis.

Part of the motivation for the study of the maximal triangular algebras lies in their role in formalizing the concept of a generalized ordered orthonormal basis. Another part of the motivation lies in the general attempt to put arbitrary bounded operators on a Hilbert space in "triangular form" and, more broadly, to reduce certain algebras of operators to triangular form. For this purpose, the hyperreducible algebras provide the most satisfactory "triangularization".

The irreducible triangular algebras appear as a byproduct of the studies related to the first two motivating aspects of the total investigation. In some sense, they provide the key to the third motivating aspect. As noted in the introduction to [33], Kadison and Singer expect the (maximal) triangular algebras to serve in the theory of non-self-adjoint operator algebras in something resembling the position that the von-Neumann algebras fill in the self-adjoint theory. Carrying this correspondence further, we would associate the hyeperreducible algebras with the abelian von Neumann algebras. (The core of a triangular algebra would correspond to the center of the von Neumann algebra.) The irreducible maximal triangular algebras would be associated with the factors (in the theory of von Neumann algebras). As a consequence, we might expect the problems associated with the irreducible triangular algebras to be the most intractable. This turned out to be the case. The questions concerning this class of triangular algebras posed in [33] remain open. (See [33, Qestions 2.4.4, 2.4.5, 2.4.6].)

We extend the construction of Kadison and Singer [33, Theorem 2.2.1, Example 2.2.2] to include (free, ergodic) actions of ordered semigroups G of unitary operators on a maximal abelian algebra $\mathcal{a}$. We prove the extended version of [33, Theorem 2.2.1], the key point of which establishes the "$\mathcal{a}$-independence of G" and of $\bar{G}$, the group generated by G. (See Proposition

1.2 and Corollary 1.3.) That construction provides us with the class of irreducible triangular algebras whose detailed analysis is the subject of this treatise. The measure-theoretic constructs and results needed for this construction and the specific examples are contained in Chapter I. Along the lines of the structure theory of the irreducible triangular algebras our examples provide us with instances of such algebras that are not isomorphic. (See Corollary 3.24 and Example 3.25.) This is another step in the direction of answering Question 2.4.6 of [33]: Are there two (or more) irreducible maximal triangular algebras on separable Hilbert space which are not algebraically isomorphic. The first such step was taken by Arveson and Josephson in [7, Theorem 4.1] where they distinguish such (norm-closed) algebras in terms of conjugacy classes of ergodic measure preserving transformations. Our techniques allow us to decide when the acting semigroup is singly generated. Although the fundamental difficulty remains of describing the operators in some irreducible maximal triangular algebra (in manner susceptible to computational application), these maximal algebras are reached, in the final stage, by an application of Zorn's Lemma; it seems well worthwhile to bypass this difficulty and study explicitly constructed classes of irreducible triangular algebras.

The second path we follow, that of non-commutative (non-self-adjoint) ergodic theory, relates to the fact that the class of examples we study arises from constructions in ergodic theory.
The origin of operator algebra considerations in ergodic theory is, of course, the "group-measure space" construction of Murray and von Neumann [41, pp. 192-209] with which they produced their first examples of type II factors. In two papers, basic to this development [12,13], Dye carries the study of groups of measure-preserving transformations further, introducing several constructs and techniques that are key aspects of the theory. In particular, a variant and elaboration of his "F-analysis" is developed in the second section of our Chapter II. Combining it with estimates (Theorem 2.14 and Lemma 2.15), this

analysis allows us to detect (normalizing) unitary operators in the algebra generated by the (ordered) semigroup and the maximal abelian algebra on which it acts (as distinguished from its various closures - cf. Theorem 2.16 and Corollary 2.17) by their action on the maximal abelian algebra.

In an important sense, from the ergodic-theoretic viewpoint, our study is a direct descendant of the work of Arveson in this area [3,7]. One of the vital tools in our investigation is the "Arveson expectation". (Lemma 2.1 through 2.9 are a recapitulation of Arveson's results related to this expectation.) With regard to the relation between [3,7] and the results of this study, we note that Arveson's emphasis is on relating the algebraic structure of the (norm-closed) algebra (and C*-algebra) generated by the action of a single transformation (a discussion of more general groups appears in [3, Section 2]) to the (measure) conjugacy class of the transformation; while our emphasis is on passing from these algebras, generated by ordered semigroups, to the structure of the semigroups (and associated groups). Samples of results of this nature are to be found in Proposition 2.27, Corollary 2.28, Theorem 2.29 and Proposition 2.30.

In connection with the general subject of triangular operator algebras, important work following [33] is to be found in Arveson [1], Erdos [14], Hopenwasser [31], Rosental [46] and Schue [48].
Ringrose extended the study of the hyperreducible algebras to "nest algebras" [44] and these were further developed by Christensen [9], Deddens [10], Erdos [15,16,17,18,19], Fall, Arveson and Muhly [20],Gilfeather and Larson [23,24, 25], Larson [36], Longstaff [37], Lance [34,35], Ringrose [43,45] and Arveson [6].
The reflexive algebras were introduced and studied by Halmos [26] and further studied by Arveson [4], Hopenwasser [30,32], and Longstaff [38,39,40].

We acknowledge with gratitude several conversations with Professor Effros at the earliest stage of our interest in this erea of operator-ergodic theory.

Our thanks are due to Professor Kadison for crystallizing the specific topic of this thesis, for his patient guidance of our research and for his careful reading of the thesis and many helpful suggestions.
Professor Arveson kindly filled in for us the details of an arguement alluded to in [2] which enabled us to include Example 4.25. We are grateful for this help. Our scientific debts to the work of Arveson [3.7] , Dye [12,13] and Kadison-Singer [33] will be apparent to any reader familiar with those papers.

We described, briefly, some of the major points in the four chapters that follow.

In Chapter I we prove that if G is an ordered semigroup of unitary operators acting freely and ergodically on a maximal abelian algebra $\mathcal{a}$ then the algebra $\mathcal{g}$, generated by $\mathcal{a}$ and G, is an irreducible triangular algebra. The study of this algebra will be taken up in the following chapters.
Several examples are presented, among them is the algebra generated by the multiplication algebra on $L^2(\mathbb{T})$ ($\mathbb{T}$ is the unit circle) and the unitary operator associated with an irrational rotation (this example appeared in [33]).

For another example we construct an ordered semigroup T of real numbers, dense in $\mathbb{R}$, and show that the semigroup of the unitary operators on $L^2(\mathbb{R})$ associated with translations of $\mathbb{R}$ by members of T generates, with the multiplication algebra on $L^2(\mathbb{R})$, an irreducible triangular algebra.

Chapter II studies the structure of an irreducible triangular algebra generated by a maximal abelian algebra $\mathcal{g}$ and a semigroup G of unitary operators acting freely and ergodically on $\mathcal{a}$.

We present the Arveson's expectation from the C*-algebra $\mathcal{B}(\mathcal{a},G)$ generated by $\mathcal{g}$ onto $\mathcal{a}$ (see [3]) and some of its properties.
We note that if the group $\bar{G}$, generated by G, is amenable the expectation is faithful (Proposition 2.7). Under a condition (that holds for a semigroup

of unitary operators arising from measure preserving transformations on a finite measure space) the converse is also true.

We discuss unitary operators acting on $\mathcal{a}$ and define, for such an operator W, a projection F(W) in $\mathcal{a}$ indicating, roughly, the part of the Hilbert space H on which W acts "locally" as an operator in $\bar{G}$. This definition is inspired by Dye's analysis of groups of measure preserving automorphisms (see [12]) and so is the following result (see Theorem 2.16): If W is a unitary operator acting on $\mathcal{a}$ then $F(W)=I$ if and only if $W = \Sigma_{U\in\bar{G}} VP_U U$ where the sum is understood in the sense of strong-operator convergence, $\{P_U\}$, $\{U^*P_U U\}$ are orthogonal families of projections in each with sum I, and V is a unitary operator in $\mathcal{a}$.
We use this analysis and some estimates (Theorem 2.14 and Lemma 2.15) to prove (Corollary 2.17) that each unitary operator in $\mathcal{B}(\mathcal{a},G)$, acting on $\mathcal{a}$, is actually in $\mathcal{g}+\mathcal{g}^*$.

Next, we investigate the relationship between the order properties of G and the structure of $\mathcal{g}$. For example, we find (Theorem 2.29) that if G_1 and G_2 are two ordered semigroups acting freely and ergodically on the abelian algebra $\mathcal{a}$ and generating the same irreducible triangular algebra $\mathcal{g}$ then G_1 is generated by a single operator if and only if G_2 is generated by a single operator. Moreover, if G_1 is generated by U and G_2 by V then $UV^*\in\mathcal{a}$

In Chapter III we define a homomorphism from the irreducible triangular algebra $\mathcal{g}$ into B(K), for some Hilbert space K, to be a linear multiplicative map whose restriction to $\mathcal{a}$ is self adjoint.

For a homomorphism that maps $\mathcal{a}$ onto a maximal abelian algebra we find conditions that are equivalent to the homomorphism being an isomorphism (Proposition 3.50). For example, we show that if the homomorphism maps each unitary operator in G into an invertible operator and if its restriction to $\mathcal{a}$ ia an isomorphism, then the homomorphism is an isomorphism.

We discuss the possibility of extending an automorphism on $\mathcal{g}$, that maps $\mathcal{a}$ onto itself, to a *-automorphism on $\mathcal{g}+\mathcal{g}^*$ and, furthermore, to a

-automorphism on $\mathcal{B}(\mathcal{a},G)$ (the C-algebra generated by $\mathcal{g}$).
We see (Corollary 3.14) that if Ψ is an automorphism of $\mathcal{g}$ that maps $\mathcal{a}$ onto itself and $\mathcal{B}(\mathcal{a},G)$ has a faithful G-invariant state g such that $g(AU) = 0$ for each A in $\mathcal{a}$ and U in $G\setminus\{I\}$, then Ψ extends to a *-automorphism of $\mathcal{B}(\mathcal{a},G)$ if and only if $\Psi(U)$ is a unitary operator for each U in G.

Using a result of E. Størmer ([49]) we see (Corollary 3.18) that for each isometry Ψ from $\mathcal{B}(\mathcal{a},G)$ onto itself that leaves fixed each operator in $\mathcal{a}$, either $\Psi(U)U^* \in \mathcal{a}$ for each U in G or $U\Psi(U) \in \mathcal{a}$ for each U in G. (A related result was obtained in [29] for a semigroup G generated by a single unitary operator arising from a measure preserving transformaiton).

Next, we utilize what we know about homomorphisms of $\mathcal{g}$ to show that some properties of $\mathcal{g}$, related to the ordering on G (as discussed in Chapter II), are preserved by a homomorphism. We prove (Corollary 3.24) that if the algebra $\mathcal{g}_1$, generated by $\mathcal{a}_1$ and G_1 is isomorphic to the algebra $\mathcal{g}_2$, generated by $\mathcal{a}_2$ and G_2, and if the isomorphism Ψ maps $\mathcal{a}_1$ onto $\mathcal{a}_2$ then G_1 is generated by a single unitary operator if and only if G_2 is generated by a single unitary operator. We also show (Corollary 3.22) that if Ψ can be extended to a *-isomorphism of $\mathcal{B}(\mathcal{a}_1,G_1)$ onto $\mathcal{B}(\mathcal{a}_2,G_2)$ and if G_1 and G_2 are unitary semigroups arising from semigroups of measure preserving transformations of a finite measure space, then G_1 is amenable if and only if G_2 is amenable.

Chapter IV deals with the group of *-automorphisms of $\mathcal{B}(\mathcal{a},G)$ leaving fixed each operator in $\mathcal{a}$ (to be denoted by $Aut(\mathcal{B},\mathcal{a})$) and the skew adjoint (not necessarily bounded) derivations on $\mathcal{g} + \mathcal{g}^*$ vanishing on $\mathcal{a}$ (denoted by $D(\mathcal{g} + \mathcal{g}^*,\mathcal{a})$).
In this analysis we use the theory of spectrum and spectral spaces associated with an action of a group on a C*-algebra introduced by Arveson in [5].

We define a map $E: D(\mathcal{g} + \mathcal{g}^*,\mathcal{a}) \to Aut(\mathcal{B},\mathcal{a})$ such that $E(\delta)(T) = (\exp(i\delta))(T)$ for T in $\mathcal{g} + \mathcal{g}^*$.

For a *-automorphism Ψ in $\mathrm{Aut}(\mathcal{B},\mathcal{a})$ we show the equivalence of the following conditions (see Lemma 4.15 and Proposition 4.15):

(1) Ψ is implemented by a unitary operator in $\mathcal{a}$.

(2) Ψ is $E(\delta)$ for some bounded derivation δ in $D(g + g^*,\mathcal{a})$.

(3) Ψ lies in the connected component of the identity in Aut $(\mathcal{B},\mathcal{a})$ (the topology on $\mathrm{Aut}(\mathcal{B},\mathcal{a})$ being the norm topology).

For a derivation δ in $D(g + g^*,\mathcal{a})$ we prove the equivalence of the following conditions (see Lemma 4.12 and Theorem 4.20):

(1) δ is bounded.

(2) Then is an operator D in $\mathcal{a}$ such that

$$\delta(T)=DT-TD \qquad \text{for } T \text{ in } g+g^*.$$

(3) $\mathrm{Sup}\ \{||\delta(U)|| : U \in G\} < \infty$.

CHAPTER I: INTRODUCING THE MODEL AND SOME EXAMPLES

In this chapter we describe the structure basic to the remaining work. The irreducible triangular algebras to be studied are introduced and some examples are given

We will deal with the action of a semigroup of unitary operators on a maximal abelian von Neumann algebra.

For this we define an ordered (unitary) semigroup to be a semigroup G such that: (1) $G \cup G^{-1}$ is a group, to be denoted by $\bar{G}$.

(2) $G \cap G^{-1} = \{I\}$ where I is the unit element.

(3) For any $W \in \bar{G}$, $WGW^{-1} = G$.

When such G is given it defines an ordering on $\bar{G}$. For U and V in $\bar{G}$ we write $U > V$ if $UV^{-1} \in G$. With U, V and W in $\bar{G}$, we have:

(i) $U > V$ implies $WU > WV$ and $UW > VW$.

(ii) $U > V$ if and only if V^*U is in G (because $V^*U=U^*(UV^*)U$).

Henceforth X will denote a locally compact Hausdorff space and m a σ-finite regular Borel measure on X. Let H be the Hilbert space $L^2(X,m)$ and $B(H)$ be the algebra of all bounded linear operators acting on H.

For any function f in $L^\infty(X,m)$ define the operator L_f in $B(H)$ by $L_f g=fg$ (multiplication by f). The algebra $\mathcal{A} = \{L_f : f \text{ is in } L^\infty(X,m)\}$ is a maximal abelian algebra in $B(H)$. Any unitary operator U that satisfies: $U^* \mathcal{A} U=\mathcal{A}$ is said to <u>act</u> on $\mathcal{A}$, the <u>action</u> being $A \to U^*AU$.

We say that U acts freely on $\mathcal{A}$ if for any non zero projection Q in $\mathcal{A}$, there is a non zero projection E in $\mathcal{A}$ such that $E \leq Q$ and $EU^*EU=0$.

We say that the semigroup G acts freely on $\mathcal{A}$ when each U in G, other then I, acts freely.

Lemma 1.1.: Let W be a unitary operator in $B(H)$ acting on $\mathcal{A}$, then there exists a unique projection F in $\mathcal{A}$ such that:

(1) For any non zero projection Q in $\mathcal{A}$, $Q \leq F$, $QW^*QW \neq 0$ and F is maximal with this property.

(2) F is a maximal projection in $\mathcal{A}$ such that $FW=WF \in \mathcal{A}$. Also, for each subprojection E of F in $\mathcal{A}$ $EW=WE$.

(3) For each non zero projection Q in $\mathcal{A}$, $Q \leq I-F$, there is a non zero subprojection E of Q in $\mathcal{A}$ such that $EW^*EW=0$. The projection F is minimal with this property.

Proof: If W acts freely on $\mathcal{A}$ then $F=0$ clearly satisfies (1) and (3). It also satisfies (2) because if there is a non zero projection F in $\mathcal{A}$ such that $FW=WF \in \mathcal{A}$, then there is a non zero subprojection E of F such that $EW^*EW=0$ (by the free action).
But $EW=EFW=E(FW)=FWE=WFE=WE$ hence $0=EW^*EW=EW^*WE=E$. We assumed that E is a non zero projection and this contradiction proves (2).

If W does not act freely there is a non zero projection F_1 in $\mathcal{A}$ such that for any non zero subprojection Q of F_1 in $\mathcal{A}$ $QW^*QW \neq 0$.
Let $\{F_a\}_{a\in\Lambda}$ be a maximal orthogonal family of projections with this property and set $F=\sum_{a\in\Lambda}F_a$. If Q is a non zero subprojection of F in $\mathcal{A}$ then $QF_a \neq 0$ for some a and $QF_aW^*QF_aW \leq QW^*QW$, so that $QW^*QW \neq 0$. If F_0 has the property that for each non zero subprojection Q of F_0 in $\mathcal{A}$, $QW^*QW \neq 0$, then each non zero subprojection of F_0 has this property.
Now F_0-F_0F is a subprojection of F_o orthogonal to each projection $F_a (a\in\Lambda)$. By maximality of this family, $F_0-F_0F=0$. Thus $F_0 \leq F$, and F satisfies (1). We see, too, that this F satisfies (3), for, again, by maximality of $\{F_a\}_{a\in\Lambda}$, each non zero subprojection Q of $I-F$ in $\mathcal{A}$ has a non zero subprojection E in $\mathcal{A}$ such that $EW^*EW=0$.
Moreover, if F' is a proper subprojection of F in $\mathcal{A}$ then $F-F'$ is a non zero subprojection Q of F (and of $I-F'$) so that each non zero subprojection of E of Q in $\mathcal{A}$ satisfies: $EW^*EW \neq 0$ (from the properties

of F). Thus F' does not satisfy the property of (3), and F is minimal with this property.

To prove that F satisfies (2), we show, first, that for any non zero subprojection Q of F in $\mathcal{a}$, there is a non zero subprojection E of Q in $\mathcal{a}$ such that $EW=WE\in\mathcal{a}$. Let E be QW^*QW. If E' is a non zero subprojection of E in $\mathcal{a}$ and $W^*E'W \not\leq E'$, then $0\neq W^*E'W(I-E')$ $(=E_1) \leq I-E'$ and $0\neq WE_1W^*$ $(=E_2) \leq E'$. But then $E_2W^*E_2W=E_2E_1=0$, contradicting the property of (1) for F (as $0\neq E_2 \leq E \leq Q \leq F$). Thus $W^*E'W \leq E'$. If $W^*E'W < E'$ then $E' < WE'W^*$. Let E_0 be $E'-W^*E'W$ so that $E_0\neq 0$ and $0\neq WE_0W^*=WE'W^*-E' \leq WE'W^* \leq WEW^*=WQW^*Q \leq Q$. Hence $0\neq WE_0W^* \leq Q-E'$, and $W^*E_0WE_0=W^*(E_0WE_0W^*)W \leq W^*E'(Q-E')W=0$. But this contradicts the property of (1) for F. Thus $W^*E'W=E'$. It follows that WE restricted to E(H) commutes with $\mathcal{a}E$. But $\mathcal{a}E$ is maximal abelian on E(H), so the $WE \in \mathcal{a}E$. Hence $WE\in\mathcal{a}$ which establishes our claim.
If $\{E_a\}_{a \Lambda}$ is a maximal orthogonal family of subprojections of F in $\mathcal{a}$ commuting with W and such that $WE_a\in\mathcal{a}$, then $F = \sum E_a$ (for otherwise, by what we have just established, $F-\sum E_a$ contains a non zero subprojection E_0 in $\mathcal{a}$ such that $E_0W=WE_0\in\mathcal{a}$ contradicting the maximality of $\{E_a\}_{a\in\Lambda}$). Thus $FW=WF\in\mathcal{a}$.

Finally, we show that F, as constructed, is maximal with the property that $FW=WF\in\mathcal{a}$.
Suppose that $F'\in\mathcal{a}$ and $F'W=WF'\in\mathcal{a}$. As noted above, $QW=WQ \in\mathcal{a}$ for each subprojection Q of F' in $\mathcal{a}$. In particular, this holds for each non zero subprojection Q of F'-FF'. Thus $QW^*QW=Q^2=Q\neq 0$. By maximality of $\{F_a\}_{a\in\Lambda}$, F'-FF' must be 0. It follows that $F' \leq F$, and (2) is established for F. ###

From now on G will always be a semigroup of unitary operators in B(H) and $\mathcal{g}$ (or $\mathcal{a}$ (G)) will be the algebra (not necessarily closed or self adjoint) generated by $\mathcal{a}$ and G.
We will assume that $G \cap \mathcal{a} = \{I\}$.

Note that if G is an ordered semigroup and U,V are in G and are different from I (the unit element) then also $UV \neq I$.

The following proposition extends a result of R.V.Kadison and I.M.Singer in [33, Theorem 2.2.1].

Proposition 1.2.: If G is an ordered semigroup of unitary operators each of which, other the I, acts freely on $\mathcal{a}$ then the algebra $\mathcal{g}$ is triangular.

Proof: Let T be a self adjoint operator in $\mathcal{g}$.

Then $T=A_0+A_1U_1+\ldots+A_nU_n=T^*=A_0^*+U_1^*A_1^*+ \ldots +U_n^*A_n^*$

$$=A_0^*+B_1U_1^*+ \ldots +B_nU_n^*,$$

where $A_0, \ldots, A_n, B_1, \ldots, B_n \in \mathcal{a}$, $U_j \neq U_k$ $(j\neq k)$ and $I < U_1 < U_2 < \ldots < U_n$; and

$$0=B_n+B_{n-1}U_{n-1}^*U_n+ \ldots +B_1U_1^*U_n+(A_0^*-A_0)U_n-A_1U_1U_n-\ldots-A_nU_n^2 . \qquad (*)$$

Note that

$$I < U_{n-1}^*U_n < \ldots < U_1^*U_n < U_n < U_1U_n < \ldots < U_{n-1}U_n < U_n^2.$$

We refer to an equation of the form:

$0=C_0+C_1V_1+C_2V_2+ \ldots +C_mV_m$, where $C_0,\ldots,C_m \in \mathcal{a}$ and $I < V_1 < \ldots < V_m$, $V_j \neq V_k$ $(j\neq k)$, as a dependence relation (for G over $\mathcal{a}$) of length m; so that $(*)$ is such a relation of length at least 1 unless $T=A_0$ $(=A_0^*)$ and $n=0$.

Let $0=A_0+A_1U_1+\ldots+A_nU_n$ be a dependence relation of minimal length and let E be the range projection of A_n. We prove that E is 0 (as a consequence of the free action of U_n on $\mathcal{a}$), whence $A_n=0$ and the only dependence relation is $0 = 0$. It will follow from this that $T=A_0$ and $\mathcal{g}$ is triangular.

Suppose $F \in \mathcal{a}$ and $F \leq E$. Let Q be $U_nFU_n^*$. We show that $Q \leq F$. If this is not the case, then $M=Q-QF$ is a non zero projection smaller than Q and $0 < U_n^*MU_n (=N) \leq F \leq E$. Hence $NA_n \neq 0$ and, $0=NA_0+NA_1U_1+\ldots+NA_nU_n$, is another dependence relation (for G over $\mathcal{a}$). Now $NA_0 \neq 0$, by minimality of n (for otherwise, $0=NA_1+NA_2U_2U_1^*, +\ldots+NA_nU_nU_1^*$ is a "smaller" dependence relation).

But $0=N(A_0+A_1U_1+\dots+A_{n-1}U_{n-1}+A_nU_n)N=NA_0+B_1U_1+\dots+B_{n-1}U_{n-1}+NA_nMU_n$, and $NA_nM=FNA_nM=MFNA_n=0$ (as $MF=0$). Hence $Q \leq F$; and $Q=QF=UFU_n^*F$.
If $E\neq 0$ and F is chosen as a non zero subprojection of E in $\mathfrak{a}$, then $0\neq U_n^*QU_n=FU_n^*FU_n$, which contradicts the free action of U_n on $\mathfrak{a}$. Thus $E=0$. ###

In fact we have proved that if $A_0+A_1U_1+\dots+A_nU_n=0$ where $A_i\in\mathfrak{a}$, $U_i \in G\setminus\{I\}$, and $U_i\neq U_j$ when $i\neq j$ then $A_i=0$ for all i. We derive from this the following:

<u>Corollary 1.3.</u>: If G acts freely on and $0=\sum_{k=1}^{m} B_kV_k+\sum_{j=0}^{n} A_jU_j$, where $B_k,A_j\in\mathfrak{a}$, $I < U_0 < \dots < U_n$, $U_i \in G$, $U_i\neq U_j$ when $j\neq i$, $V_k^* \in G\setminus\{I\}$, $V_1^* < V_2^* < \dots < V_m^*$, and $V_k\neq V_i$ when $k\neq i$ then $B_k=A_j=0$ for all k and j.

<u>Proof</u>: From our hypothesis, we have
$0=\sum_{k=1}^{m} B_kV_kV_m^*+ \sum_{j=0}^{n} A_jU_jV_m^*$, $V_kV_m^*$, $U_jV_m^* \in G$, $V_kV^*_m\neq U_jV_m^*$ for all k and j, $V_kV_m^*\neq V_iV_m^*$ when $k\neq 1$, $U_jV_m^*\neq U_iV_m^*$ when $i\neq j$.
Thus we are in the situation of Proposition 1.2 and can conclude (from its proof) that $B_k=A_j=0$ for all k and j. ###

We refer to the property described in this Corollary as <u>$\mathfrak{a}$-independence of</u> $\bar{G}$.

<u>Definition</u>: We say that G acts ergodically on $\mathfrak{a}$ (or that G is ergodic) if for each non zero projection P in $\mathfrak{a}$, $I =\vee\{U^*PU:U \in G\}$.

<u>Lemma 1.4.</u>: For a (unitary) semigroup acting on $\mathfrak{a}$ the following are equivalent:

(1) G is ergodic.

(2) $G^{-1}(=G^*)$ is ergodic.

(3) For every projection $Q \in \mathfrak{a}$: $QUQ=UQ$ for all U in G implies $Q=0$ or $Q=I$.

<u>Proof</u>:

(1) implies (2): For a projection P in $\mathfrak{a}$ let $Q = \vee\{UPU^* : U \in G\}$ then

$VQV^* \leq Q$ for all V in G. Therefore $I-Q \geq V^*(I-Q)V$ for all V in G,

hence $I-Q \geq \bigvee \{V^*(I-Q)V : V \in G\}$. If $Q \neq I$ then, by (1), $I-Q \geq I$ hence

$Q=0$ and so $P=0$.

Therefore, for $P \neq 0$, $Q=I$ which proves (2).

(2) implies (3) : We assume $QUQ=UQ$ for all U in G. For all U in G

$QUQU^*=UQU^*$ hence $Q \leq UQU^*$, but this, by (2), implies that $Q=0$ or $0=I$.

(3) implies (1): For a non zero projection P in a let $Q = \bigvee \{U^*PU : U \in G\}$.

then $V^*QV \leq Q$ for all V in G, hence $V^*(I-Q)V=I-V^*QV \geq I-Q$ so

$V^*(I-Q)V(I-Q)=I-Q$ and $(I-Q)V(I-Q)=V(I-Q)$. This, by (3), shows that $Q=0$ or

$Q=I$ but, since $Q \geq P \neq 0$, $Q=I$.   # ##

Definition: An algebra g of operators on a Hilbert space H is called

irreducible if $\text{Lat} g = \{0,I\}$ where $\text{Lat} g = \{P \in B(H) : PTP=TP$ for every T in

$g\}$.

Corollary 1.5.: Let G be an ordered semigroup acting freely and ergodically

on a. Then g is an irreducible triangular algebra.

Proof: g is triangular by Proposition 1.2, and is irreducible by (3) of

Lemma 1.4.   ###

Lemma 1.6.: Let G be an abelian ordered semigroup that acts ergodically on

a . Then g is an irreducible triangular algebra.

Proof: What we have to prove is that G acts freely on a.

If U is in $G \setminus \{I\}$ but does not act freely, then, by (2) of Lemma 1.1,

there exists a non zero projection E in a such that $EU=UE$ and EU is

in a.

Since U is not in a, and a is maximal abelian, there is a projection F

in a such that $U^*FU \neq F$ and we can assume $(I-F)U^*FU \neq 0$ (if $U^*FU < F$ take

$FU^*(I-F)U$ instead). Let Q be $(I-F)U^*FU$ then $QU^*QU=0$. For V in G

let Q_V be V^*QV. Then

$$Q_V U^* Q_V U = V^* QVU^* V^* QVU = V^*(QU^*QU)V=0.$$

Since $I=\bigvee\{Q_V : V \in G\}$, there exists V in G such that $Q_V E\neq 0$. Now $U^*Q_V U Q_V = Q_V U^* Q_V U = 0$; so that

$$Q_V U E Q_V E U = U(U^* Q_V U E Q_V E)U = U(U^* Q_V U Q_V E)U = 0.$$

Using the fact that $EU=UE$ and EU is in $\mathcal{a}$ we see that $Q_V EU=0$ thus $Q_V E=0$, and this contradiction completes the proof. ###

Let $\mathcal{a}$ be as before and let G be the semigroup generated by a single unitary operator U acting on $\mathcal{a}$. Then G acts ergodically if and only if, for every projection P in $\mathcal{a}$ such that $PU^nP=U^nP$, for all n, $P=0$ or $P=I$.

For ergodicity it is equivalent to assume that $PUP=UP$ implies $P=0$ or $P=I$, since $PUP=UP$ implies

$PU^nP=PU^{n-1}UP=PU^{n-1}PUP= \dots =PUPUP\dots UP=UPUP\dots UP=U^2PUP\dots P=U^3P\dots P=\dots=U^nP.$

We can, therefore, conclude (see [33, Theorem 2.2.1]):

Lemma 1.7.: If U is a unitary operator acting ergodically on an infinite dimensional maximal abelian algebra $\mathcal{a}$, then $\mathcal{g}$ (the algebra generated by U and $\mathcal{a}$) is an irreducible triangular algebra.

Proof: As noted above, the semigroup G, generated by U, acts ergodically on $\mathcal{a}$. We can, therefore, apply Lemma 1.6 provided G is an ordered semigroup.

For this we have to show that $G \cap G^*=\{I\}$.

If this is not so, there are positive integers m and p such that $U^m=U^{-p}$; so that $U^{m+p}=I$.

Let n be the least positive integer such that $U^n=I$. We note the (easy) fact that a finite group $\{U^j : j=1,2,\dots,n\}$ cannot act ergodically on the infinite-dimensional maximal abelian algebra $\mathcal{a}$.

If we assume that U does act ergodically on $\mathcal{a}$ and E is a non zero projection in $\mathcal{a}$, then

$$I=\bigvee_{j=1}^{n} U^{*j}EU^j \leq U^*EU+ \dots +U^{*n}EU^n.$$

If E is a minimal projection in $\mathcal{a}$, then I is the union of n minimal

projections - contradicting the fact that $\mathcal{A}$ is infinite dimensional.
Since $\mathcal{A}$ has no minimal projections, if x_0 is a unit vector in H, there is a projection E in $\mathcal{A}$ such that $<Ex_j,x_j> < \frac{1}{n}$ $(j=1,\ldots,n)$ where $x_j=U^j x_0$.
But then

$$1= < x_0,x_0> \leq \sum_{j=1}^{n} <Ex_j,x_j> <1$$

- a contradiction ###

Examples of irreducible triangular algebras

Example 1.8.: (See [33, Example 2.2.2]) Let $X = \mathbb{T}$ (the unit circle) and m be the Haar measure on $\mathbb{T}$.

Let U be the unitary operator on $H=L^2(X,m)$ induced by an irrational translation (i.e. $Uf(e^{2\pi it})=f(e^{2\pi i(t-s)})$ where s is a real irrational number). For f in $L^\infty(X,m)$, L_f is in $\mathcal{A}$ and $U^*L_fU=L_{f\circ\tau^{-1}}$ where τ is the transformation $\tau(e^{2\pi it})=e^{2\pi i(t-s)}$ on X, hence $U^*\mathcal{A}\ U=\mathcal{A}$.

To prove that U acts ergodically notice that each projection P in $\mathcal{A}$ can be written as L_f where f is the characteristic function of a set E in X.

The condition $PUP=UP$ (or $U^*PUP=P$) yields $fg=f$ where $g(=f\circ\tau^{-1}=Uf)$ is the characteristic function of $\tau(E)$. This, using the fact that $m(E)=m(\tau(E)) < \infty$, implies that $f=g$. Hence $Uf=f$.

The function f has an expansion, $f=\sum_{n=-\infty}^{\infty}a_ne_n$, where $\{e_n\}_{n=-\infty}^{\infty}$ is the orthonormal basis of $L^2(X,m)$, $e_n(e^{it})=e^{nit}$. But $Uf=\sum_{n=-\infty}^{\infty}c^na_ne_n=f=\sum_{n=-\infty}^{\infty}a_ne_n$, where $c=e^{-2\pi is}$; so that, for each integer n, $c^na_n=a_n$. By choice of s, $c^n=1$ only when $n=0$. Thus $f=a_0$, P is 0 or I, and U acts ergodically on $\mathcal{A}$. By Lemma 1.7 the algebra generated by U and $\mathcal{A}$ is an irreducible triangular algebra.

Example 1.9.: Let X be $\mathbb{R}$ (the set of all real numbers) and m be Lebesgue measure on $\mathbb{R}$.

Fix a negative irrational number u and define the set T in $\mathbb{R}$: $T= \{au-r : a > 0,\ a\in\mathbb{Q},\ r\geq 0,\ r\in\mathbb{Q}\} \cup \{bu+r: r,b\in\mathbb{Q},\ b\geq 0,\ r\geq 0\}$.

Let G be the semigroup of translations by t in T, i.e. U in G is of the form $Uf(s)=f(s-t)$ for some t in T, where $f \in L^2(X,m)$.

We claim that G satisfies the conditions of Lemma 1.6:

1) G is clearly a semigroup.

2) G is an ordered semigroup because $T \cap (-T)=\{0\}$ and $T \cup (-T)=u\mathbb{Q}+\mathbb{Q}$.

3) $U^*\mathcal{A}\ U=\mathcal{A}$, for if U in G is the operator corresponding to t in T

and f is in $L^\infty(X,m)$, then $U^*L_fU=L_{f_{-t}}$ where $f_t(s)=f(s-t)$.

4) The action of G is ergodic. This fact will be proved for a more general case in Proposition 1.10 below, and is omitted here.

This shows that the algebra $\mathcal{G}$ generated by G and $\mathcal{A}$ is irreducible and triangular.

The following Proposition generalizes Examples 1.8 and 1.9.

Proposition 1.10.: Let N be a locally compact group with a left invariant Haar measure m. Let T be an ordered semigroup of N which is dense in N. For each x in N define the unitary operator U_x on $L^2(N,m)$ by a left translation: $(U_xf)(y)=f(x^{-1}y)$. Denote by G the semigroup of the unitary operators U_x for x in T. Then the algebra generated by G and the multiplication algebra $\mathcal{A}$ is irreducible triangular.

Proof : We will show that G satisfies the conditions of Corollary 1.5.

Let A be the operator in $\mathcal{A}$ corresponding to multiplication by a function g(in $L^\infty(N,m)$). Then

$(U^*_xAU_xf)(y)=(AU_xf)(xy)=g(xy)(U_xf)(xy)=g(xy)f(y)=g_x(y)f(y)$ where $g_x(y)=g(xy)$.

Thus $U^*_xAU_x=A_x$, where A_x corresponds to multiplication by g_x; and $U^*_x\,\mathcal{A}\,U_x=\mathcal{A}$ for each x in N.

We show, next, that each $U_x(x\neq e)$ acts freely on $\mathcal{A}$.

Suppose the contrary. Then, from (2) of Lemma 1.1, there is a non zero projection E in $\mathcal{A}$ such that $FU_x=U_xF\in\mathcal{A}$ for each subprojection F of E in $\mathcal{A}$. Let Y be a Borel set in N corresponding to E (i.e. E is multiplication by the characteristic function of Y).

Since $E\neq 0$, $m(Y)>0$; and there is a compact subset K of Y such that $m(K)>0$ (by regularity of m). As $x\neq e$, we can choose a symmetric open neighbourhood V of e such that $x\notin V^2$. Then $Vy\cap x^{-1}Vy=\emptyset$ for each y in N. Now $\{Vy : y\in K\}$ is an open covering of K from which we can select a finite subcovering.

Thus $m(Vy\cap K)>0$ for some y in K. Let F be the projection corresponding to multiplication by the characteristic function of $Vy \cap K$ $(=Z)$; so that F is a non zero subprojection of E in $\mathcal{a}$, and $U_x^*FU_x=F$. But $U_x^*FU_x$ is the projection corresponding to multiplication by the characteristic function of $x^{-1}Z$ and

$Z \cap x^{-1}Z \subseteq Vy \cap x^{-1}Vy=\emptyset$. Thus $FU_x^*FU_x=F^2=F=0$

a contradiction. Hence U_x acts freely on $\mathcal{a}$.

To prove the ergodicity of G we, first, show that, for a non zero projection $P \in \mathcal{a}$, $I = \bigvee\{U_x^*PU_x \; ; \; x \in N\}$. For this, let Q be $\bigvee\{U_x^*PU_x; \; x \in N\}$ and let Y be a set of positive measure such that Q is the projection corresponding to multiplication by the characteristic function of Y.

Define a measure on the Borel sets of N by

$$m_1(Z)=m(Z \cap Y).$$

Since $m_1(xZ)=m(xZ \cap Y)=m(Z \cap x^{-1}Y)=m(Z \cap Y)+m(Z \cap (x^{-1}Y \setminus Y))$

$-m(Z \cap (Y \setminus x^{-1}Y))=m(Z \cap Y)=m_1(Z)$ (as $m(Y \setminus x^{-1}Y)=m(x^{-1}Y \setminus Y)=0$,

it follows that $m_1(xZ)=m_1(Z)$.

Thus m_1 is a left Haar measure provided $m_1(U) > 0$ for every non empty open set U in N. This condition is equivalent to the assertion that m_1 is not identically zero (see [27, p. 252]). Indeed, if $m_1(U)=0$ for some non empty open set U, and if C is any compact set then the class $\{xU : x \in C\}$ is an open covering of C. Since C is compact, there exists a finite subset $\{x_1,\ldots,x_n\}$ of C such that $C \subseteq \bigcup_{i=1}^n x_iU$, and the left invariance of m_1 implies $m_1(C) \leq \sum_{i=1}^n m_1(x_iU)=n\, m_1(U)$.

It follows that $m(C)=0$ for every compact set C contained in Y, and this, by regularity, implies that $m(Y)=0$. This contradicts our assumption and completes the proof that m_1 is a left Haar measure on N.

Therefore $m_1=cm$, for some constant c, and since m_1 vanishes on the complement of Y, so does m. This proves that $Q=I$.

We will now show that for a non zero projection P in $\mathcal{a}$,

$I = \bigvee\{U_x^*PU_x : x \in G\}$.

For this, let Q be $I-\bigvee\{U_x^*PU_x : x \in G\}$.

Choose any f in $L^2(N,m)$ such that $Qf=f$. It is known that the map $x \to U_x f$, from N to $L^2(N,m)$, is continuous.
Thus the map $x \to ||U_x^* P U_x f||^2 = \langle U_x^* P U_x f, f\rangle = \langle PU_x f, U_x f\rangle$ is continuous.
Since $P_x Q=0$ for each x in G, $U_x^* P U_x f=0$. As G is dense in N, the continuity implies that $U_x^* P U_x f=0$ for each x in N. This is possible only if $f=0$ (since $I = \vee\{U_x^* P U_x \; ; \; x \in N\}$).
Consequently $Q=0$ and the action is ergodic.

The conditions of Corollary 1.5 are satisfied; and by that corollary the algebra generated by G and the multiplication algebra is irreducible triangular. ###

The last proposition enables us to present an example of an irreducible triangular algebra where the semigroup G is non abelian.

Example 1.11.: Let N be the group of $2x2$ matrices of the form: $\begin{pmatrix} a & b \\ 0 & 1 \end{pmatrix}$ where a and b are real numbers and $a > 0$. For x in N we denote by $a(x)$ and $b(x)$ the numbers such that $x = \begin{pmatrix} a(x) & b(x) \\ 0 & 1 \end{pmatrix}$.

As $\begin{pmatrix} a & b \\ 0 & 1 \end{pmatrix} \begin{pmatrix} c & d \\ 0 & 1 \end{pmatrix} = \begin{pmatrix} ac & ad+b \\ 0 & 1 \end{pmatrix} \in N$

and $\begin{pmatrix} a & b \\ 0 & 1 \end{pmatrix}^{-1} = \begin{pmatrix} a^{-1} & -ba^{-1} \\ 0 & 1 \end{pmatrix} \in N$;

N is a group. We denote the unit element by e. We can identify N, as a set, with a subset of $\mathbb{R}^2$ and the topology on N is induced from $\mathbb{R}^2$ i.e. $x_n \to x$ if and only if $a(x_n) \to a(x)$ and $b(x_n) \to b(x)$. With this topology, N is a locally compact group.
Let M_1 be any dense, ordered, subsemigroup of the additive group of all the real numbers (e.g. the semigroup T of Example 1.9).
Let M denote the multiplicative semigroup $\exp(M_1)$, hence $M \cap M^{-1} = \{1\}$.
Let G be the set of all elements x in N for which either $a(x) \in M \setminus \{1\}$ or $a(x)=1$ and $b(x) \geq 0$.

It is easy to verify that G is a semigroup. In fact, an ordered semigroup. This can be seen as follows:

1) If x is in $G \cap G^{-1}$ then $a(x) \in M \cap M^{-1}=\{1\}$ and therefore $b(x) \geq 0$. But $b(x^{-1})=-b(x)a(x)^{-1} \leq 0$ hence x^{-1} is in G only if $b(x)=0$, and then $x=e$.

2) $G \cup G^{-1}$ is the set of the elements x in N such that $a(x) \in M \cup M^{-1}$ and $b(x)$ is a real number. Since $M \cup M^{-1}$ is a multiplicative group, $G \cup G^{-1}$ is a group.

3) For every x in $G \cup G^{-1}$ and y in G,

$$x = \begin{pmatrix} a & b \\ 0 & 1 \end{pmatrix}, \quad x^{-1} = \begin{pmatrix} a^{-1} & -ba^{-1} \\ 0 & 1 \end{pmatrix}, \quad y = \begin{pmatrix} c & d \\ 0 & 1 \end{pmatrix}$$

and $x^{-1}yx = \begin{pmatrix} c & (cb+d-b)a^{-1} \\ 0 & 1 \end{pmatrix}$

if $c \neq 1$ then $x^{-1}yx$ is in G, and if $c=1$ then $d \geq 0$ and $(cb+d-b)a^{-1}=da^{-1} \geq 0$. Hence $x^{-1}yx$ is in G in any case.

This shows that G is an ordered semigroup and clearly G is dense in N, therefore, by Proposition 1.10, the algebra generated by the semigroup of unitary operators associated with G, and the multiplication algebra on $L^2(N,m)$ is an irreducible triangular algebra.

Example 1.12. : Let U be a unitary operator on H acting ergodically on $\mathcal{a}$. Let H_2 be $H \oplus H$. Each operator in $B(H_2)$ can be written as a 2x2 matrix with entries in $B(H)$.

Let V in $B(H_2)$ be the operator $\begin{pmatrix} 0 & U \\ I & 0 \end{pmatrix}$ and then:

$$V^2 = \begin{pmatrix} U & 0 \\ 0 & U \end{pmatrix} \qquad V^3 = \begin{pmatrix} 0 & U^2 \\ U & 0 \end{pmatrix} \qquad \text{etc.}$$

$\mathcal{a}_2 = \{ \begin{pmatrix} A_1 & 0 \\ 0 & A_2 \end{pmatrix} : A_i$ for $i=1,2\}$ is a maximal abelian algebra.

Since $V^* \begin{pmatrix} A_1 & 0 \\ 0 & A_2 \end{pmatrix} V = \begin{pmatrix} A_2 & 0 \\ 0 & U^*A_1U \end{pmatrix}$ is in $\mathcal{a}_2$, $V^* \mathcal{a}_2 V = \mathcal{a}_2$.

Each projection P in $\mathcal{a}_2$ has the form $\begin{pmatrix} P_1 & 0 \\ 0 & P_2 \end{pmatrix}$,

and $PVP=VP$ when $\begin{pmatrix} 0 & UP_2 \\ P_1 & 0 \end{pmatrix} = \begin{pmatrix} 0 & P_1UP_2 \\ P_2P_1 & 0 \end{pmatrix}$ (P_i are projections in $\mathcal{a}$).
Thus $PVP=VP$ if and only if $P_1 \leq P_2$ and $P_1UP_2=UP_2$ (hence also $P_2UP_2=UP_2$).
Since U acts ergodically we get $P_2=0$ or $P_2=I$.

If $P_2=0$ then, since $P_1 \leq P_2$, $P_1=0$ hence $P=0$.

If $P_2=I$ then, since $P_1UP_2=UP_2$, $P_1=1$; and $P=I$.

Therefore V acts ergodically on a_2 and the algebra generated by a_2 and V is triangular and irreducible. This example is different from Example 1.8 because V^2 is not ergodic, while in Example 1.8 any power of the generator is also ergodic.

Example 1.13.: Let U be a unitary operator on H acting ergodically on a. Define $K = \sum_{i=1} \oplus H_i$ and $H^{(n)} = \sum_{i=1}^{2n-1} \oplus H_i$ where $H=H_i$ $(H^{(k+1)}=H^{(k)}\oplus H^{(k)})$. Let E_i and F_i be the projections from K onto H_i and $H^{(i)}$ respectively, and let $\bar{a}$ the maximal abelian algebra of all operators A in $B(K)$ such that for any positive integer n $E_nA=AE_n$ and E_nAE_n is in a.
We define algebras g_n by induction. Let g_1 be g (the algebra generated by U and a on H).
Let g_2 on $H^{(2)}$ $(=H\oplus H)$ be generated by $a\oplus a$ and the operator represented by the matrix $\begin{pmatrix} 0 & U \\ I & 0 \end{pmatrix}$. Then

g_2 is irreducible triangular (Example 1.12) and $g_1 = E_1g_2E_1 = E_2g_2E_2$.
Assume that g_k is defined and let g_{k+1} on $H^{(k+1)}$ be generated by the algebra $a_k\oplus a_k$ $(a_k = g_k \cap g_k^*)$, and the operator U_{k+1} represented by the matrix $\begin{pmatrix} 0 & U_k \\ I & 0 \end{pmatrix}$ where U_k is the generator of g_k.
Define $\bar{g}$ (on $B(K)$) to be the algebra generated by $\cup_{n=1}^{\infty} g_n$ and $\bar{a}$, where we identify g_n with $F_ng_nF_n \subseteq B(K)$. With T_n in g_n and A in $\bar{a}$, $T_nA=T_nF_nA=T_nF_nAF_n \in g_n$. Similarly $AT_n \in g_n$; so that each operator in $\bar{g}$ has the form $A+T_n$ with A in $\bar{a}$ and T_n in g_n for some n. If $A+T_n$ is self adjoint, so is $F_m(A+T_n)F_m$. Now $F_m(A+T_n)F_m \in g_m$ so that $F_m(A+T_n)F_m$ is in $a_m (\subseteq \bar{a})$, for all m.
Since $F_m \uparrow I$, $A+T_n \in \bar{a}$ and $\bar{g}$ is triangular.

If P is a non zero projection in $\bar{a}$ invariant under $\bar{g}$, then, since $F_n \uparrow I$, F_nP is a non zero projection for some n (and, hence, for all larger n). Now F_nP is in g_n and invariant under g_n. Since g_n is irreducible,

$F_n P = F_n$; and $F_n \leq P$. Now $F_n P \leq F_m P$ if $m \geq n$; whence $F_m \leq P$ if $m \geq n$, and $P=I$. Thus $\bar{g}$ is irreducible.

Therefore $\bar{g}$ is an irreducible triangular algebra but is not described by Corollary 1.5 because no operator in $\bar{g}$ is acting freely on α.

CHAPTER II: THE STRUCTURE OF THE IRREDUCIBLE TRIANGULAR ALGEBRAS

In this chapter we will study the structure and properties of the algebra $\mathcal{g}$ generated by a semigroup G of unitary operators and a maximal abelian algebra $\mathcal{a}$, where and G satisfy the conditions of Corollary 1.5. By that corollary the algebra is irreducible and triangular.

We will deal also with the algebra $\mathcal{g}+\mathcal{g}^*$ which is the self adjoint algebra generated by $\mathcal{g}$, and the algebra $\mathcal{B}(\mathcal{a}, G)$ which is the closure of $\mathcal{g}+\mathcal{g}^*$ in the norm topology. The algebra $\mathcal{B}(\mathcal{a}, G)$ is a C*-algebra and, when it does not cause any confusion, we will denote it by $\mathcal{B}(\mathcal{g})$ or just $\mathcal{B}$.

The map Φ.

The following results, from Lemma 2.1 to Lemma 2.9, are Arveson's and appeared in [3].

Recall (Corollary 1.3) that if $A_0+A_1U_1+\ldots+A_nU_n=0$ for $U_i \in \bar{G}\setminus\{I\}$, $A_i \in \mathcal{a}$, and $U_i \neq U_j$ for $i \neq j$, then $A_i=0$ for all i.

This enables us to define a map Φ from $\mathcal{g}+\mathcal{g}^*$ onto $\mathcal{a}$ by:

$\Phi(A_0+A_1U_1+\ldots+A_nU_n)=A_0$ $\quad A_i \in \mathcal{a}$, $U_i \in \bar{G}\setminus\{I\}$. Clearly Φ is linear and onto .

Lemma 2.1:

(1) $\Phi \circ \Phi = \Phi$ and $\Phi(I)=I$.

(2) $\Phi(AT)=A\Phi(T)$, $\Phi(TA)=\Phi(T)A$ for $A \in \mathcal{a}$, $T \in \mathcal{g}+\mathcal{g}^*$.

(3) $\Phi(T^*)=\Phi(T)^*$ for $T \in \mathcal{g}+\mathcal{g}^*$.

(4) $\Phi(U)=0$ for U in $\bar{G}\setminus\{I\}$.

(5) $0 \leqslant \Phi(T)^*\Phi(T) \leqslant \Phi(T^*T)$ for $T \in \mathcal{g}+\mathcal{g}^*$.

Proof: (1)-(4) are clear from the definition. To prove (5), let T be $A_0+A_1U_1+\ldots+A_nU_n$ with $A_i \in \mathcal{a}$, $U_i \in \bar{G}$. $T^*=A_0^*+U_1^*A_1^*+\ldots+U_n^*A^*$ and $T^*T=A_0^*A_0+U_1^*A_1^*A_1U_1+\ldots+U_n^*A_n^*A_nU_n+S$ where $\Phi(S)=0$. Therefore:

$\Phi(T^*T)=A_0^*A_0+U_1^*A_1^*A_1U_1+\ldots+U_n^*A_n^*A_nU_n \geq A_0^*A_0=\Phi(T)^*\Phi(T) \geq 0.$ ###

Lemma 2.2. : For any non zero projection P in $\mathcal{a}$, there exists a state ρ of $\mathcal{B}(\mathcal{a},G)$ such that $\rho(P)=1$ and $\rho(\mathcal{a}U)=0$ for each $U\in\bar{G}\setminus\{I\}$.

Proof: Fix a non zero projeciton P in $\mathcal{a}$. Let Γ be the collection of all finite subsets of G. For any $F\in\Gamma$, let K_F be the set of all states ρ of $\mathcal{B}(\mathcal{a},G)$ such that $\rho(P)=1$ and $\rho(\mathcal{a}U)=0$ for every U in F. Each K_F is a weak* closed, hence compact, subset of the state space of $\mathcal{B}(\mathcal{a},G)$ and $F_1\subseteq F_2$ implies $K_{F_1}\supseteq K_{F_2}$.

By free action, there exists, for each F in Γ, a non zero projection Q_F in $\mathcal{a}$ such that $Q_F\leq P$ and $U^*Q_FUQ_F=0$ for U in F. Choose any unit vector f in the range of Q_F and let: $\rho_F(T)=\langle Tf,f\rangle$ for $T\in\mathcal{B}(\mathcal{a},G)$. Clearly $\rho_F(P)=1$ and one has $\rho_F(Q_FTQ_F)=\rho_F(T)$ $T\in\mathcal{B}(\mathcal{a},G)$. If $A\in\mathcal{a}$ and $U\in F$: $\rho_F(AU)=\rho_F(Q_FAUQ_F)=\rho_F(Q_FUQ_FU^*AU)=0$.

Thus $\rho_F\in K_F$ and this shows that the K_F's are non empty and have the finite intersection property. Hence $\cap\{K_F : F\in\Gamma\}\neq\emptyset$, and any state in the intersection has all the required properties. ###

Proposition 2.3.: $||\Phi(T)||\leq||T||$ for $T\in g+g^*$.

Proof: Let T be in $g+g^*$, and suppose that $||\Phi(T)||>||T||$. Since $\Phi(T)\in\mathcal{a}$, there is a unitary operator $W\in\mathcal{a}$ such that $\Phi(T)W\geq 0$. Now $||\Phi(T)W||=||\Phi(T)||\geq||T||+\varepsilon$, for sufficiently small $\varepsilon>0$. So by spectral theory there exists a non zero projection $P\in\mathcal{a}$ such that $\Phi(T)WP\geq(||T||+\frac{1}{2}\varepsilon)P$. Now choose ρ as in Lemma 2.2 : $\rho(P)=1$, $\rho(\mathcal{a}U)=0$ $U\in\bar{G}\setminus\{I\}$. By the definition of Φ, it follows that $\Phi(S)=\rho\circ\Phi(S)$ for $S\in g+g^*$. Hence

$\rho(TWP)=\rho\circ\Phi(TWP)=\rho(\Phi(T)WP)\geq(||T||+\frac{1}{2}\varepsilon)\rho(P)=||T||+\frac{1}{2}\varepsilon.$

But this is impossible, since: $|\rho(TWP)|\leq||TWP||\leq||T||$ and this contradiction completes the proof. ###

We can now extend Φ to $\mathcal{B}(\mathcal{a},G)$ and Lemma 2.1 is still valid for the extension which we denote, again, by Φ.

For the next result we will need the concept of amenable group.

Definition: A (discrete) group N is said to be amenable if there exists a finitely additive probability measure on the field of all subsets of N such that $\mu(xE) = \mu(E)$ for all $X \in N$, $E \subseteq N$.
When such a μ exists, it is called a (left invariant) mean.
Examples of amenable groups are the solvable and the locally finite groups.
In particular any commutative group is amenable. An example of a non amenable group is the free group on $n \geq 2$ generators.

Let $C_{00}(N)$ be the set of complex valued functions on N having a finite support, and let $x \to 1_x$ be the left regular representation of N in $1^2(N)$ (i.e. $1_x g(y)=g(x^{-1}y)$, $g \in 1^2(N)$).
For any $f \in C_{00}(N)$, we can form the operator $T = \sum_x f(x)1_x$ on $1^2(N)$; f is said to be of positive type if $T \geq 0$.
We state the following lemma:

Lemma 2.4.: The following are equivalent, for any discrete group N:

(1) N is amenable.

(2) For any finite set $F \subseteq N$ and $\varepsilon > 0$, there is a finite subset $E \subseteq N$ such that $\left| \frac{|xE \cap E|}{|E|} - 1 \right| \leq \varepsilon$, for all $x \in F$ ($|\cdot|$ denotes "number of elements in").

(3) If $f \in C_{00}(N)$ is of positive type, then $\sum f(x) \geq 0$.

(4) For any finite subset F of N and $\varepsilon > 0$, there exists a unit vector $g \in 1^2(N)$ such that for all $x \in F$ $|< 1_x g,g> -1| \leq \varepsilon$.

The equivalence of (1) and (2) was proved by Følner [21], and the rest of the proof can be found in [3, Lemma 2.2].

We shall now construct another C^*-algebra C and a faithful positive map $w:C \to \mathcal{a}$. We then define a $*$-homomorphism Π_0 of a dense $*$-subalgebra of C into $\mathcal{B}(\mathcal{a},G)$ such that $\Phi \circ \Pi_0=w$ and we shall analize the extensions of Π_0 to C.

Let us form the space $H \otimes l^2(\bar{G})$. For $A,B \in \mathcal{A}$ and $U,V \in \bar{G}$, $(AU \otimes 1_U)(BV \otimes 1_V)=AUBV \otimes 1_{UV}=AUBU^*UV \otimes 1_{UV}$ and $(AU \otimes 1_U)^*=U^*A^*UU^* \otimes 1_{U^*}$. Thus $C_0=\{\sum_{U\in F} A_U U \otimes 1_U : F \subseteq \bar{G}$ is finite$\}$ forms a $*$-algebra with identity. Let C be the norm closure of C_0 in $B(H \otimes l^2(\bar{G}))$.
Let g_0 in $l^2(\bar{G})$ be defined by $g_0(I)=1$, $g_0(U)=0$ for $U \neq I$.

Lemma 2.5.: There exists a faithful positive linear map $w:C \to \mathcal{A}$ such that $\langle w(C)f,g\rangle=\langle C(f \otimes g_0), g \otimes g_0\rangle$ for any $f,g \in H$. One has $w(\sum_{U\in F} A_U U \otimes 1_U) = A_I$ for any finite subset F of $\bar{G}$.

Proof: For any $C\in C$ define a bilinear form on $H \times H$ by: $[f,g] = \langle C(f \otimes g_0),g \otimes g_0\rangle$. Then $\|[f,g]\| \leq \|C\| \|f\| \|g\|$, hence there is an operator $w(C)$ in H such that $[f,g] = \langle w(C)f,g\rangle$, $w(I \otimes 1_I)=I$, w is positive linear and $\|w\|= 1$.

$\langle\sum_U A_U U \otimes 1_U(f \otimes g_0), g \otimes g_0\rangle = \sum_U \langle A_U Uf,g\rangle \langle 1_U g_0,g_0\rangle = \langle A_I f,g\rangle$. Thus

$w(\sum_U A_U U \otimes 1_U)=A_I$.

Let r_U denote the right regular representation $(r_U g(V) = g(VU))$ then $C(f \otimes r_U g_0)=C(I \otimes r_U)f \otimes g_0 = (I \otimes r_U)C(f \otimes g_0)$ (*).

To see that w is faithful note that $w(C^*C)=0$ implies that $C(f \otimes g_0)=0$ and, by (*), $C(f \otimes r_U g_0)=0$.

Since the set of vectors of the form $f \otimes r_U g_0$ generates $H \otimes l^2(\bar{G})$ $C=0$

###

We now claim that $\sum_U A_U U \otimes 1_U=0$ implies $A_U=0$ for all $U \in \bar{G}$. To see this fix V in $\bar{G}$,

$$\sum_U VA_U V^*VU \otimes 1_{VU}=(V \otimes 1_V) \sum_U A_U U \otimes 1_U=0.$$

Hence $VA_{V^*}V^*=w(\sum_U VA_U V^*VU \otimes 1_{VU})=0$ and so $A_{V^*}=0$.

We can now define $\Pi_0:C_0 \to \mathcal{B}(\mathcal{A},G)$ by $\Pi_0(\sum_U A_U U \otimes 1_U)= \sum_U A_U U$. Π_0 is a $*$-homomorphism of C_0 onto a dense $*$-subalgebra of $\mathcal{B}$, and by the definition of w,Φ, $\Phi \circ \Pi_0=w$ on C_0.

Lemma 2.6.: Π_0 is bounded if and only if Φ is faithful.

Proof:

1) Suppose Π_0 is bounded, then we can extend it to a map $\Pi: C \to B$ such that $\Phi \circ \Pi = w$. $\Pi(C)$ is closed and containing $\Pi_0(C_0)$, which is dense in B, hence $\Pi(C)=B$.

If A is in B, $A \geq 0$, and $\Phi(A)=0$ then $A=\Pi(C)$ for some $C \in C$, $C \geq 0$, and $w(C)=\Phi(\Pi(C))=\Phi(A)=0$. Since w is faithful, this cannot happen and thus Φ is faithful.

2) Suppose Φ is faithful. Let T be in C_0, $||T|| \leq 1$, and $H=T^*T$ then $0 \leq H \leq I$. Consider the C^*-algebra generated by I and $\Pi_0(H)$. We can identify this algebra with the algebra $C(X)$ where X is the pure state space. Let the function f correspond to $\Pi_0(H)$. If $\Pi_0(H) \not\leq I$ then there is $r > 1$ such that $\omega = \{x \in X: f(x) > r\}$ is non empty.

Let g in $C(X)$ be such that: $0 \leq g \leq 1$, g is 1 at some point of ω and g is 0 on $X \setminus \omega$ (if $X \neq \omega$). Since $g(x) \neq 0$ implies $f(x) \geq r$ we have $gf^n \geq r^n g$ for any n. Let A be the operator corresponding to the function g. Then $A \neq 0$, $0 \leq A \leq I$, $A\Pi_0(H) = \Pi_0(H)A$, $A \in B$, and $A\,\Pi_0(H^n)=A\,\Pi_0(H)^n \geq r^n A$ for any n.

Since Φ is faithful $\Phi(A) \neq 0$, hence there is a state ρ_1 of B such that $\rho_1(\Phi(A)) \neq 0$. Let $\rho = \rho_1 \circ \Phi$ then ρ is a state, $\rho \circ \Phi = \rho$ and $\rho(A) \neq 0$.

$$\rho(A\,\Pi_0(H^n))^2 \leq \rho(A^2)\,\rho(\Pi_0(H^n)^2) \leq \rho(I)\,\rho(\Pi_0(H^n)^2) = \rho(\Pi_0(H^{2n})) =$$
$$= \rho \circ \Phi(\Pi_0(H^{2n})) = \rho \circ w(H^{2n}).$$

But $H^{2n} \leq I$ and $w(H^{2n}) \leq w(I)=I$ so $\rho \circ w(H^{2n}) \leq \rho(I)=1$ thus $\rho(A\,\Pi_0(H^n)) \leq 1$.

Since $r^n A \leq A\,\Pi_0(H^n)$ and $r^n\rho(A) \leq \rho(A\,\Pi_0(H^n)) \leq 1$ for any n, we get $\rho(A)=0$ which is a contradiction. Therefore $\Pi_0(H) \leq 1$ and $||\Pi_0(T)||^2 = ||\Pi_0(T)^*\ \Pi_0(T)|| = ||\Pi_0(T^*T)|| \leq 1$.

So $||\Pi_0(T)|| \leq 1$ hence Π_0 is bounded. ###

Proposition 2.7.: If $\bar{G}$ is amenable then Φ is faithful.

Proof: For $T = \sum_U A_U U \otimes 1_U$ in C_0 we will show:

$||\sum_U A_U U|| \leq ||T||$, hence $||\pi_0|| \leq 1$.

Fix $\varepsilon > 0$ and let F be a finite subset of $\bar{G}$ such that $A_U=0$ for $U \notin F$. By part (4) of Lemma 2.4 there exists $g \in l^2(\bar{G})$ such that $||g||=1$ and $|<1_U g,g> -1| \leq \varepsilon$ for each U in F. For each pair of unit vectors f and h in H one has: $<T(f \otimes g), h \otimes g> = \sum_U <A_U Uf \otimes 1_U g, h \otimes g> = \sum_U <A_U Uf,h><1_U g,g>$. Therefore:

$$| <T(f \otimes g), h \otimes g> - <\sum_U A_U Uf,h>| \leq \sum_U |<A_U Uf,h>|\,| <1_U g,g>-1| \leq \varepsilon \sum_U ||A_U U||.$$

Since $| <T(f \otimes g),h \otimes g> | \leq ||T||$, we get:

$| <\sum_U A_U Uf,h> | \leq ||T||+ \varepsilon \sum_U ||A_U U||$. Since ε is arbitrary, we have: $| <\sum_U A_U Uf,h> | \leq ||T||$. Taking the supremum of the left hand side over all pairs of unit vectors completes the proof. ###

The converse of the last proposition is true under the following condition : If $\sum_U a_U U$ is a positive operator in $g+g^*$ and a_U are scalars then $\sum_U a_U \geq 0$. We denote this condition by (+).

Note that if each U in $\bar{G}$ comes from a measure preserving transformation on X (i.e. $(Uf)(x)=f(\varphi^{-1}(x))$ where $m \circ \varphi^{-1}=m$), and $m(X) < \infty$, then (+) is satisfied. To see this, let f_0 be the constant function 1 on X and, for $T \in \mathcal{B}$, let $g(T)$ be $<Tf_0,f_0>$. Thus g is a positive linear function and $g(\sum_U a_U U)=m(X)(\sum_U a_U)$.

The proof of the following proposition is different from the one given by Arveson.

Let m be the C*¯algebra generated by the operators U in $\bar{G}$.

<u>Proposition 2.8.:</u> Assuming condition (+), if Φ is faithful $\bar{G}$ is amenable.

<u>Proof:</u> Let ρ_1 be a faithful state on $\mathcal{a}$, and let $\rho= \rho_1 \circ \Phi$ then ρ is faithful state on $\mathcal{B}$ and $\rho(U)=0$ for each U in $\bar{G}$ different from I. Consider now the C*¯algebra $\mathcal{L} \subseteq B(l^2(\bar{G}))$ generated by the operators $\{1_U : U \in \bar{G}\}$. Let g_0 be the characteristic function of I, i.e. $g_0(I)=1$, $g_0(U)=0$ for $U \neq I$. Define a linear functional w on $\mathcal{L}$ by $w(T)=<Tg_0,g_0>$;

then $w(I)=1$ and $w(1_U)=0$ for $U\neq I$. w is a state on $\mathcal{L}$ and is faithful because $Tg_0=0$ implies $Tr_U g_0 = r_U T g_0 = 0$ (where $r_U f(V)=f(VU)$) and the set $\{r_U g_0 : U \in \bar{G}\}$ is total in $l^2(\bar{G})$.

Since $\bar{G}$ is $\mathcal{A}$-independent we can define a $*$-homomorphism φ from a dense $*$-subalgebra m_0 of m (namely finite linear combinations of elements of $\bar{G}$) onto a dense $*$-subalgebra of $\mathcal{L}$ by $\varphi(U)=1_U$ and by linearity.

Now, ρ and w are both faithful states and $w \circ \varphi = \rho|_{m_0}$. Therefore, by [7, Proposition 2.5], we can extend φ to a $*$-isomorphism from m onto $\tilde{\mathcal{L}}$. Condition (+) now implies (3) of Lemma 2.4 and hence $\bar{G}$ is amenable. ###

Lemma 2.9.: Let $\mathcal{D}(g)$ be the norm closed algebra generated by g.

(1) Φ is multiplicative on $\mathcal{D}(g)$.

(2) If Φ is faithful, $\mathcal{D}(g) \cap \mathcal{D}(g)^* = \mathcal{A}$. Thus $\mathcal{D}(g)$ is triangular.

Proof: For (1) it is enough (from Proposition 2.3) to show that Φ is multiplicative on g and, in fact, it suffices to show: $\Phi(AUBV) = \Phi(AU)\,\Phi(BV)$ (*) for A,B in $\mathcal{A}$ and U,V in G. But if either U or V is different from I then both sides of (*) are 0, and if $U=V=I$ then both sides of (*) are AB.

To prove (2) it is enough to prove that any self adjoint operator T in $\mathcal{D}(g)$ is in $\mathcal{A}$. If T is self adjoint then $\Phi(T)$ is also self adjoint and $(T-\Phi(T))^2$ is positive.

But $\Phi((T-\Phi(T))^2) = \Phi(T^2) - \Phi(T)^2$ and this, by (1), equals 0. Since we assumed that Φ is faithful $T = \Phi(T)$. ###

Lemma 2.10.: If Φ is faithful and T is in $\mathcal{B}$ such that $\Phi(TU)=0$ for each $U \in \bar{G}$, then $T=0$.

Proof: Let A be in $\mathcal{A}$ and U in $\bar{G}$, then $\Phi(TAU)=\Phi(TUU^*AU)=\Phi(TU)U^*AU=0$. Therefore $\Phi(TS)=0$ for any $S \in g+g^*$ and by continuity of Φ, $\Phi(TS)=0$ for any S in $\mathcal{B}$. By setting $S=T^*$ we see that $\Phi(TT^*)=0$ hence $T=0$. ###

Unitary operators acting on $\mathcal{a}$.

Lemma 2.11. : Let V in $g+g^*$ be unitary operator such that $V^* \mathcal{a} V=\mathcal{a}$, then V has the form $V = \sum_{i=1}^n A_i U_i$ where $A_i \in \mathcal{a}$, $U_i \in \bar{G}$ and:

(1) $A_i=F_iV'$ where F_i are projections in $\mathcal{a}$ and V' is a unitary operator in $\mathcal{a}$.

(2) $\{F_i\}$ and $\{U_i^*F_iU_i\}$ are two orthogonal families of projections in $\mathcal{a}$.

(3) $A_iA_j=A_iA_j^*=0$ for $i\neq j$, and $A_iA_i^*=F_i$.

(4) $\sum_{i=1}^n F_i = \sum_{i=1}^n U_i^*F_iU_i=I$.

Proof: Fix $j \leq n$; let W be VU_j^* $(=\sum_{i=1}^n A_iU_iU_j^*)$ and let F_j be the projection defined in Lemma 1.1 (i.e. F_j is the maximal projection in $\mathcal{a}$ such that $F_jW=WF_j$ and $F_jW \in \mathcal{a}$). For every $Q \leq I-F_j$ there exists a projection $E \leq Q$ in $\mathcal{a}$ such that $EW^*EW=0$. Let $\{E_a\}_{a\in\Lambda}$ be a maximal orthogonal family of subprojections of Q with this property, then $\sum_{a\in\Lambda}E_a=Q$. In fact, if $Q_1=Q-\sum_{a\in\Lambda}E_a$ then there is a non zero projection $E_1 \leq Q_1$ such that $E_1W^*E_1W=0$. Now $\Phi(W)E_a=E_a$ $\Phi(W)E_a=E_a$ $\Phi(WE_a)=E_a$ $\Phi(WE_aW^*W)=E_aWE_aW^*\Phi(W)=0$, so that $\Phi(W)Q=0$ for each subprojeciton Q of $I-F_j$ in $\mathcal{a}$.

Therefore $A_j(I-F_j) = \Phi(W)(I-F_j)=0$ and $A_j=A_jF_j$. As $F_jW \in \mathcal{a}$ and $F_jW = \sum_{i=1}^n F_jA_iU_iU_j^*$, we have $F_jA_j = F_jW$ and $F_jA_i = 0$ for $i\neq j$ (by the $\mathcal{a}$-independence of $\bar{G}$). Since $A_j = F_jA_j = F_jW$; $A_j^*A_j = A_jA_j^* = F_jWW^*F_j = F_j$ and $F_jF_i = F_jA_iA_i^* = 0$. Thus $\{F_j\}_{j=1}^n$ is an orthogonal family of projections in $\mathcal{a}$ and $A_iA_j = A_iA_j^* = 0$ $i\neq j$, $A_iA_i^* = F_i$ Let $F = \sum_{i=1}^n F_i$ then $(I-F)V=0$ hence $I-F = 0$ so $\sum_{i=1}^n F_i = I$. Note that A_i is $F_iVU_i^*$. Let V' be $\sum_{i=1}^n A_i$. Then $A_i = F_iV'$, and $V'V'^* = V'^*V' = \sum_{i,j=1}^n A_i^*A_j =$
$= \sum_{i,j=1}^n (F_iVU_i^*)^*F_jVU_j^* = \sum_{i=1}^n U_iV^*F_iVU_i^* = \sum_{i=1}^n V^*F_iV = V^*(\sum_{i=1}^n F_i)V = I$, from which (1) follows. Now

$$I = V^*V = \sum_{i=1}^n U_i^*A_i^*A_iU_i = \sum_{i=1}^n U_i^*F_iU_i;$$ which establishes (2) and (4)

###

Lemma 2.12.: Let V be a unitary operator in $g+g^*$ such that $V^* \mathcal{a} V = \mathcal{a}$, then V acts freely on $\mathcal{a}$ if and only if $\Phi(V) = 0$.

Proof.: Let j in the proof of Lemma 2.11 be such that $U_j = I$ and then $\Phi(V) = F_j V'$ where F_j is the projection associated with V by Lemma 1.1. Since V acts freely if and only if $F_j = 0$ then it acts freely if and only if $\Phi(V) = 0$. ###

We will now generalize this description to other unitary operators acting on $\mathcal{A}$ (not necessarily in $\mathcal{G}+\mathcal{G}^*$).
For this let $V(\mathcal{A})$ be the set of operators in $B(H)$ that are unitary and satisfy $V^* \mathcal{A} V = \mathcal{A}$.
Let W be in $V(\mathcal{A})$ and U in $V(\mathcal{A}) \cap (\mathcal{G}+\mathcal{G}^*)$. Define $F(W,U)$ to be the projection in $\mathcal{A}$ given by Lemma 1.1 applied to the operator WU^*, i.e. $F(W,U)$ is the maximal projection F in $\mathcal{A}$ such that $FWU^* = WU^*F \in \mathcal{A}$. Let $F(W)$ be $\vee\{F(W,U) : U \in \bar{G}\}$.

Lemma 2.13.: For $W \in V(\mathcal{A})$ and $U,V \in \bar{G}$, $U \neq V$, we have:

(1) $F(W,U)F(W,V) = 0$.

(2) $V^*F(W,V)VU^*F(W,U)U = 0$

(3) $F(W) = \bigvee\{F(W,U) : U \in V(\mathcal{A}) \cap (\mathcal{G}+\mathcal{G}^*)\}$.

Proof:

(1) Let $Q = F(W,V)F(W,U)$ then QWU^*, $QWV^* \in \mathcal{A}$ hence $QW \in \mathcal{A}U \cap \mathcal{A}V$. So $QW = 0$ (by the $\mathcal{A}$-independence of $\bar{G}$).

(2) Let $Q = V^*F(W,V)VU^*F(W,U)U$. Then $VQV^* \leq F(W,V)$ and $UQU^* \leq F(W,U)$. Hence WU^*UQU^* and WV^*VQV^* are in $\mathcal{A}$.

(3) Let T be a unitary operator in $V(\mathcal{A}) \cap (\mathcal{G}+\mathcal{G}^*)$ then $T = \sum_{i=1}^n V'F_iU_i$, where $U_i \in \bar{G}$, V' is a unitary operator in $\mathcal{A}$, and $\{F_i\}$ is an orthogonal family of projections in $\mathcal{A}$ with sum I. By definition, $F(W,T) \in \mathcal{A}$ and $WT^*F(W,T)$ $(= \sum_{i=1}^n WU_iF_iV'^*F(W,T)) \in \mathcal{A}$. Hence $WT^*F(W,T)F_i (= WU_i^*F_iV'^*F(W,T)) \in \mathcal{A}$ for each i; and $WU_i^*F_iF(W,T) \in \mathcal{A}$. Thus $F_iF(W,T) \leq F(W,U_i) \leq F(W)$, and $\sum_{i=1}^n F_iF(W,T) = F(W,T) \leq F(W)$, which establishes (3). ###

We will now prove that

$V(\mathcal{a}) \cap (g+g^*) = V(\mathcal{a}) \cap \mathcal{B}(\mathcal{a},G)$. In fact we will prove the following:

Theorem 2.14.: Let W be an operator in $V(\mathcal{a})$ and $T \in g+g^*$ such that $||W-T||<1/3$. Then if $T = \sum_{i=1}^n A_iU_i$, where $A_i \in \mathcal{a}$ and $U_i \in \bar{G}$, we have $\vee\{F(W,U_i): i \leqslant n\} = I$. In particular this holds for any $W \in V(\mathcal{a}) \cap \mathcal{B}(\mathcal{a},G)$.

Proof: Let E be $I - \vee\{F(W,U_i) : i \leqslant n\}$ and assume $E \neq 0$. $E \leqslant I-F(W,U_1)$ hence, by Lemma 1.1, there is a projection E_1 in $\mathcal{a}$, $0 \neq E_1 \leqslant E$, such that $E_1U_1W^*E_1 = 0$.
$E_1 \leqslant I-F(W,U_2)$ hence, by the same lemma, there is a projection $E_2 \leqslant E_1$, $E_2 \neq 0$, and $E_2U_2W^*E_2 = 0$. Repeating the use of Lemma 1.1 n times we get a non zero projection Q such that $QU_iW^*Q = 0$ for any $i \leqslant n$, hence $QTW^*Q = 0$.
We have $2/3 < ||QW||-||QW-QT|| \leqslant ||QT|| \leqslant ||T|| \leqslant ||W|| + ||W-T|| < 4/3$.
and also $||QTW^*Q-QTT^*Q|| \leqslant ||TW^*-TT^*|| \leqslant ||T||\ ||W^*-T^*|| < 4/3\cdot 1/3 = 4/9$.
Since $QTW^*Q = 0$, $||QTT^*Q|| < 4/9$ (*). But $||QT|| > 2/3$ thus $||QTT^*Q|| = ||QT||^2 > (2/3)^2=4/9$ and this contradicts (*). ###

The theorem shows that the distance between two distinct operators in $\bar{G}$ is at least 1/3 but, in **fact**, more than this is true as seen in the following lemma.

Lemma 2.15.: Let W,V be in $V(\mathcal{a}) \cap (g+g^*)$ and assume that there is an operator U in $\bar{G}$ such that $F(W,U) \neq 0$ and $F(V,U) = 0$. Then $||W-V||\geqslant\sqrt{2}$.

Proof: Note that $V^*W \in V(\mathcal{a}) \cap (g+g^*)$ and that $V^*W \notin \mathcal{a}$; for otherwise V and W have the same action on $\mathcal{a}$, as do WU^* and VU^*. But, by hypothesis, VU^* acts freely on $\mathcal{a}$ while WU^* does not. Thus, we can express V^*W in the form described in Lemma 2.11 as $A_0 + \sum_{i=1}^n A_iU_i$ where $A_1U_1 \neq 0$ and $U_i \neq U_j$ if $i\neq j$. We have $(V^*W-I)(V^*W-I)^* = \sum_{i,j=1}^n A_iU_iU_j^*A_j^* - \sum_{i=1}^n A_iU_i - \sum_{i=1}^n U_i^*A_i^* + (I-A_0)(I-A_0^*)$.
From Lemma 2.11, $\sum_{i=0}^n A_iA_i^* = I$, $A_0 = F_0V' = V'F_0$, and $A_1 = F_1V'$ where F_0 and F_1 are mutually orthogonal projections in $\mathcal{a}$. Since $A_1U_1 \neq 0$; $F_1 \neq 0$

and $A_0+A_0^*$ annihilates some unit vector. Thus

$$2 \leq ||2I-A_0A_0^*||=||\sum_{i=1}^n A_iA_i^*+(I-A_0)(I-A_0^*)||=||\Phi((V^*W-I)(V^*W-I)^*)||$$

$$\leq ||(V^*W-I)(V^*W-I)||=||V^*W-I||^2=||W-V||^2, \qquad \text{since } ||\Phi||=1. \qquad \#\#\#$$

Distinct elements W,V of $\bar{G}$ satisfy the hypothesis of the preceding lemma; for we may use W as U. In this case, $F(W,W) = I$ and $F(V,W) = 0$.

The next theorem describes those operators in $V(\alpha)$ that satisfy $F(W) = I$.

Theorem 2.16.: The conditions, $W \in V(\alpha)$, $\Lambda \subseteq \bar{G}$, and $\vee\{F(W,U) : U \in \Lambda\} = I$ hold if and only if $W = \sum_{U\in\Lambda} VP_UU$ where this sum is understood in the sense of strong-operator convergence if Λ is infinite, V is a unitary operator in α, and $\{P_U\}$, $\{U^*P_UU\}$ are orthogonal families of projections in α each with sum I. Moreover, if $W \in V(\alpha)$ and $\vee\{F(W,U) : U \in \Lambda\} = I$, the representation of W as $\sum_{U\in\Lambda} VP_UU$, where V is a unitary operator in α, and $\{P_U\}$, $\{U^*P_UU\}$ are orthogonal families of projections in α each with sum I, is unique, $P_U = F(W,U)$ and $V = W(\sum_{U\in\Lambda} P_UU)^*$.

Proof: a) assume, first, that $W \in V(\alpha)$ and $\vee\{F(W,U) : U \in \Lambda\} = I$. If U_1 and U_2 are distinct elements of $\bar{G}$ and $F = F(W,U_2)$ then $WU_1^*F = FWU_1^* \in \alpha$ and $WU_2^*F = FWU_2^* \in \alpha$. Thus $(FWU_2^*)^*(WU_1^*F) = U_2U_1^*F = FU_2U_1^* \in \alpha$. But $U_2U_1^*$ $(\in\bar{G}\setminus\{I\})$ acts freely on α; so that $F = 0$. It follows that $\{F(W,U) : U \in \Lambda\}$ is an orthogonal family of projections in α. Since H is separable, $F(W,U) = 0$ for all but a conutable number of U in $\bar{G}$. Enumerate the U in Λ for which $F(W,U) \neq 0$ as $U_1,U_2,\ldots$, let Q_n be $F(W,U_n)$ and P_n be W^*Q_nW. By definition of $F(W,U_n)$ (see Lemma 1.1), $Q_nWU_n^* = WU_n^*Q_n \in \alpha$; so that $U_nW^*Q_n \in \alpha$ and, if $A \in \alpha$, $Q_nA = (Q_nWU_n^*)A(U_nW^*Q_n) = U_nW^*Q_nAWU_n$. Hence $U_n^*Q_nU_n = W^*Q_nAW$. In particular, with I in place of A, $U_n^*Q_nU_n = P_n$ and $U_nP_n = Q_nU_n$.

Since $\{Q_n\}$ is an orthogonal family; $\{U_nP_nU_n^*\}$ and $\{P_n\}$ $(=\{W^*Q_nW\}=\{U_n^*Q_nU_n\})$ are orthogonal families. By assumption $\sum Q_n = I$, so that $\sum P_n = \sum W^*Q_nW = I$. Now U_nP_n is a partial isometry with initial projection $P_n(=(U_nP_n)^*U_nP_n)$

and final projection $Q_n (=U_nP_n(U_nP_n)^*)$ so that $\sum U_nP_n$ is strong-operator convergent to a unitary operator T, and $T^*Q_nAT = P_nU_n^*Q_nAU_nP_n = W^*Q_nAWP_n$ $= W^*Q_nAQ_nW = W^*Q_nAW$ for each n and each A in $\mathcal{a}$. Summing over n, we have $T^*AT = W^*AW$. Thus $WT^*A = AWT^*$ for each A in $\mathcal{a}$; so that WT^* is a unitary operator V in $\mathcal{a}$.

Hence $W = VT = \sum VU_nP = \sum VQ_nU_n$. Letting P_{U_n} be Q_n for $n=1,2,\ldots$ and P_U be 0 when $F(W,U) = 0$, we arrive at the stated representation of W.

b) Suppose, now, that $W = \sum_{U\in\Lambda} VP_UU$, where V is a unitary operator in $\mathcal{a}$ and $\{P_U\}$, $\{U^*P_UU\}$ are orthogonal families of projections in $\mathcal{a}$ with sum I. Then P_UU is a partial isometry with initial projection U^*P_UU $(=Q_U)$ and final projection P_U; so that $\sum_U P_UU$ is a unitary operator T with adjoint $\sum_U U^*P_U$. With A in $\mathcal{a}$, $T^*AP_UT = U^*AP_UU = U^*AUU^*P_UU \in \mathcal{a}Q_U$.

Thus $T^*AT = \sum_{U\in\Lambda} T^*AP_UT = \sum_{U\in\Lambda} U^*AUQ_U \in \mathcal{a}$. But $W = VT$, with V a unitary operator in $\mathcal{a}$; so that W (and T) are in $V(\mathcal{a})$ and $W^*AW = T^*AT$ for each A in $\mathcal{a}$.

Since $P_UW = VP_UU$, we have $P_UWU^* = VP_U \in \mathcal{a}$. In addition $W = \sum_{U\in\Lambda} VUU^*P_UU$; so that $WU^*P_UU = VUU^*P_UU = VP_UU$, and $WU^*P_U = VP_U = P_UWU^*$. Thus $P_U \leq F(W,U)$. Now $\{F(W,U) : U \in \Lambda\}$ is an orthogonal family (as noted at the beginning of this proof); and $\sum P_U = I$. Thus $P_U = F(W,U)$ for all U and $\bigvee\{F(W,U) : U \in \Lambda\} = I$. Hence $W \in V(\mathcal{a})$ and the representation of W is unique. ###

Recall that $\mathcal{D}(\mathcal{g})$ is the norm closure of $\mathcal{g}$.

<u>Corollary 2.17.:</u> If $W \in \mathcal{B}(\mathcal{a},G)$ [resp. $\mathcal{D}(\mathcal{g})$] is a unitary operator in $V(\mathcal{a})$, then $W \in \mathcal{g}+\mathcal{g}^*$ [resp. $\mathcal{g}$].

<u>Proof:</u> This result follows from Theorems 2.14 and 2.16, applied to a finite set of $\bar{G}$ (or G). ###

<u>Corollary 2.18.:</u> Let G_1 and G_2 (acting on $\mathcal{a}$) give rise to the triangular algebras $\mathcal{g}_1$, $\mathcal{g}_2$ respectively and to the C*-algebras $\mathcal{B}_1$, $\mathcal{B}_2$ (and $\mathcal{D}(\mathcal{g}_1)$,

$\mathcal{D}(g_2)$) respectively. Then $\mathcal{B}_1 = \mathcal{B}_2$ (or $\mathcal{D}(g_1) = \mathcal{D}(g_2)$) implies $g_1 + g_1^* = g_2 + g_2^*$ (or $g_1 = g_2$)

Proof: Since

$G_1 \subseteq V(\mathcal{a}) \cap \mathcal{B}_1 = V(\mathcal{a}) \cap \mathcal{B}_2 = V(\mathcal{a}) \cap (g_2 + g_2^*)$, we have $g_1 + g_1^* \subseteq g_2 + g_2^*$. Equality follows from symmetry. Similarly, if $\mathcal{D}(g_1) = \mathcal{D}(g_2)$ then

$G_1 \subseteq V(\mathcal{a}) \cap \mathcal{D}(g_1) = V(\mathcal{a}) \cap \mathcal{D}(g_2) = V(\mathcal{a}) \cap g_2$; and $g_1 = g_2$. ###

We will show that the operators in $V(\mathcal{a})$ that satisfy $F(W) = I$ form a group. For this we will need the following lemma.

Lemma 2.19.: For W_1, W_2 in $V(\mathcal{a})$ and U_1, U_2 in $\bar{G}$, $(U_1F(W_2,U_2)U_1^*)F(W_1,U_1) \leq F(W_1W_2,U_1U_2)$.

Proof: Writing A for $W_2U_2^*F(W_2,U_2)$ we have

$W_1W_2U_2^*U_1^*\ (U_1F(W_2,U_2)U_1^*)F(W_1,U_1) = W_1(W_2U_2^*F(W_2,U_2))\ \ U_1^*F(W_1,U_1)$

$= W_1U_1^*U_1AU_1^*F(W_1,U_1)$.

But $W_1U_1^*U_1AU_1^*F(W_1,U_1) = W_1U_1^*F(W_1,U_1)U_1AU_1^* \in \mathcal{a}$ and

$W_1U_1^*F(W_1,U_1)U_1AU_1^* = F(W_1,U_1)W_1U_1^*U_1W_2U_2^*F(W_2,U_2)U_1^* =$

$F(W_1,U_1)W_1U_1^*U_1F(W_2,U_2)W_2U_2^*U_1^* =$

$U_1F(W_2,U_2)U_1^*F(W_1,U_1)W_1U_1^*U_1W_2U_2^*U_1^* =$

$(U_1F(W(W_2,U_2)U_1^*)F(W_1,U_1)W_1W_2U_2^*U_1^*$. This, by the definition of $F(W_1W_2U_1U_2)$, completes the proof. ###

Proposition 2.20.: The set of the operators W in $V(\mathcal{a})$ such that $F(W) = I$ is a group.

Proof:

a) Let W_1, W_2 be in $V(\mathcal{a})$ and $F(W_1) = F(W_2) = I$. By the previous lemma $(U_1F(W_2,U_2)U_1^*)F(W_1,U_1) \leq F(W_1W_2,U_1U_2)$ for $U_1,U_2 \in \bar{G}$ and

$\bigvee\{(U_1F(W_2,U_2)U_1^*)F(W_1,U_1) : U_1,U_2 \in \bar{G}\} = \bigvee\{U_1F(W_2)U_1^*F(W_1,U_1) : U_1 \in \bar{G}\} =$

$\bigvee\{F(W_1,U_1) : U_1 \in \bar{G}\} = F(W_1) = I$. Therefore

$F(W_1W_2,U_1U_2) = I$, and $F(W_1W_2) = I$.

b) We prove that

$F(W^*,U^*) = U^*F(W,U)U = W^*F(W,U)W$ (*) when $W \in V(\mathcal{a})$ and $U \in \bar{G}$.

The last equality of (*) is a consequence of the proof of Theorem 2.16. (In the notation of that proof, $U_n^* A_n U_n = P_n = W^* Q_n W$.) Thus

$W^*UU^*F(W,U)U = W^*F(W,U)WW^*U = U^*F(W,U)UW^*U = U^*(WU^*F(W,U))^*U \in \mathcal{a}$; and

$$U^*F(W,U)U \leq F(W^*,U^*).$$

This same inequality, with W and U replaced by W^* and U^*, yields

$$UF(W^*,U^*)U^* \leq F(W,U) \quad ;$$

and (*) follows. From (*), we have $F(W^*) = W^*F(W)W$.

Thus $F(W^*) = I$ if $F(W) = I$.

Induced algebras

We will prove in Proposition 2.22, that when $\mathcal{g}$ is an irreducible triangular algebra as constructed, from an ordered semigruop G acting freely and ergodically on a maximal abelian algebra $\mathcal{a}$ in $B(H)$, then $P\,\mathcal{g}\,P$, for a projection P in $\mathcal{a}$, is also an irreducible triangular algebra. The algebra $P\,\mathcal{g}\,P$ will said to be the algebra induced by $\mathcal{g}$ on $P(H)$.

Lemma 2.21.: With E a projection in $\mathcal{a}$, let $\mathcal{g}_1$ be the algebra generated by $\mathcal{a}$ and the operators EUE for $U \in G$. Then: Lat $\mathcal{g}_1 = \{P \in \mathcal{a}: EP=0 \text{ or } EP=E\}$

Proof: If for P in $\mathcal{a}$, $EP=0$ then $EUEP=0=PEUEP$ and if $E=EP$ then $EUEP=EUE=PEUEP$. Hence $P \in$ Lat $\mathcal{g}_1$. If P is in Lat $\mathcal{g}_1$ then P is in $\mathcal{a}$. Moreover, P satisfies $EUEP=PEUEP$; so that $(I-P)EUEPU^*=0$.

But if $EP \neq 0$, then by ergodicity, $\vee\{UEPU^*;\ U \in G\} = I$; and $(I-P)E=0$.

###

Proposition 2.22. : Let $\mathcal{a}$ and G generate the irreducible triangular algebra $\mathcal{g}$. Then $E\,\mathcal{g}\,E (= \{ETE: T \in \mathcal{g}\})$ is an irreducible triangular algebra, for each projection E in $\mathcal{a}$.

Proof: Let E be a projection in $\mathcal{a}$.

$E\,\mathcal{g}\,E \cap (E\,\mathcal{g}\,E)^* = \mathcal{a}E$ hence, on $E(H)$, $E\,\mathcal{g}\,E$ is a triangular algebra.

Let P be a projection in $\mathcal{a}E$. If $P \in \text{Lat}(E\,\mathcal{g}\,E)$ then, considering P as a projection in $\mathcal{a}$, $P \in$ Lat $\mathcal{g}_1$ (in the notation of the preceding lemma).

Therefore $EP=0$ or $E=EP$. Since $P \in \mathcal{a}E$, $P=0$ or $P=E$. Hence $E\,\mathcal{g}\,E$ is irreducible. ###

An extension of the order on $\bar{G}$

We have ordered $\bar{G}$ by : $U > V$ if $UV^* \in G$. We shall now extend this order to a larger group of operators in $\mathcal{g} + \mathcal{g}^*$.

Let $M(\mathcal{g})$ (or just M) be the group of all operators of the form AU where A in $\mathcal{a}$ is invertible and $U \in V(\mathcal{a}) \cap (\mathcal{g} + \mathcal{g}^*)$.

Let $N(\mathcal{g})$ (or simply N) be $M(\mathcal{g}) \cap \mathcal{g}$. Note that $N(\mathcal{g})$ is a semigroup.

For T,S in $M(\mathcal{g})$, we will say that T is larger than $S(T > S)$ if there is R in $N(\mathcal{g})$ (equivalently, in $\mathcal{g}$) such that $T=SR$.

The following lemma describes some of the basic properties of this ordering.

Lemma 2.23.: The relation $>$ on $M(\mathcal{g})$ has the following properties:

(1) $T > S$ if and only if S^*T is in $\mathcal{g}$;

(2) it is transitive;

(3) $T > S$ and $S < T$ implies $S \in T\mathcal{a}$;

(4) it is an extension of the order on $\bar{G}$.

Proof:

(1) $T > S$ if and only if $S^{-1}T \in \mathcal{g}$. But $S^{-1}T=(S^*S)^{-1}S^*T$ and, from the definition of $M(\mathcal{g})$, $(S^*S)^{-1}$ is in $\mathcal{a}$. Thus $S^{-1}T \in \mathcal{g}$ if and only if $S^*T \in \mathcal{g}$.

(2) If $T_1=T_2R_1$ and $T_2=T_3R_2$ then $T_1=T_3R_2R_1$. Since $N(\mathcal{g})$ is a semigroup, the order is transitive.

(3) $T=SR$ and $S=TL$ imply $I=LR$. So $L=R^{-1}=(R^*R)^{-1}R^* \in \mathcal{g}^*$, hence $L \in \mathcal{g} \cap \mathcal{g}^* = \mathcal{a}$, and $S \in T\mathcal{a}$.

(4) Let U,V be in $\bar{G}$. Then $U > V$ with respect to the order on $\bar{G}$ if and only if $V^*U \in G$. On the other hand, U is greater than V with respect to the order on M if and only if $V^*U \in N(\mathcal{g})$. Since $N(\mathcal{g}) \cap \bar{G}=G$ (by the

$\mathcal{a}$- independence of $\bar{G}$), the two orderings coincide on $\bar{G}$.

###

Remark: The reason for extending the order from $\bar{G}$ to $M(g)$ is that the set $M(g)$ is defined in terms of $\mathcal{a}$ and g and is independent of G.

We will say that $T \in N(g)$ is a smallest element in $N(g)$ if : $\Phi(T)=0$ and for any $S \in N(g)$ such that $\Phi(S)=0$, $S > T$.
If T_1, T_2 are both smallest elements in $N(g)$ then $T_1 > T_2 > T_1$ hence $T_2=T_1A$ where A is in $\mathcal{a}$. This shows that the smallest element in $N(g)$ is essentially unique.

Lemma 2.24.: If G has a minimal element V (i.e. $V < U$ for every U in G, $U\neq I$) then BV is smallest in $N(g)$ for each invertible B in $\mathcal{a}$. Conversely, if T is smallest in $N(g)$ then $T=AU$ where $A \in \mathcal{a}$, and U is minimal in G.

Proof:

a) Let V be minimal in G, and let T be in $N(g)$ such that $\Phi(T)=0$. $T= \sum_{i=1}^{n} A_iU_i$ where A_i in $\mathcal{a}$ and $U_i \in G$, $U_i\neq I$. Therefore $B^{-1}V^*T \in g$, because $V^*U_i \in G$ for all i. Hence $T > BV$.

b) Let $T = \sum_{i=1}^{n} A_iU_i$ be smallest in $N(g)$ and assume that U_1 is the smallest among the U_i's. Since $U_1^*T \in g$; $T > U_1$. But T is smallest. Thus $T=AU_1$, $A \in \mathcal{a}$. If $U \in G\setminus\{I\}$ and $U_1 > U$ then $T > U$ (in $N(g)$) so that $U=CT=CAU_1$ for some C in $\mathcal{a}$. By $\mathcal{a}$-independence of G, $U=U_1$; and U_1 is minimal in G.

###

It is also natural to define $T \in N(g)$ to be minimal if $S < T$ for S in $N(g)$, implies that $S \in \mathcal{a}$ or $S \in \mathcal{a}T$.

Lemma 2.25.:

(1) If T is smallest in $N(g)$ and T acts ergodically on $\mathcal{a}$ then T is minimal.

(2) If T is smallest in $N(g)$ and S in $N(g)$ satisfies $S < T$, then

$S=A+BT$ where $A,B \in \mathcal{a}$.

(3) If T is minimal in $N(g)$ and $\Phi(T)=0$, then T is smallest.

Proof:

(2) Let T be smallest in $N(g)$ and S in $N(g)$ satisfy $S < T$. From the previous lemma $T=AU$, where U is minimal in G. Let $S=A_0+A_1U_1+\ldots+A_nU_n$ then $S^*T=(A_0^*+U_1^*A_1^*+\ldots+U_n^*A_n^*)AU\in g$. By the $\mathcal{a}$-independence of $\bar{G}$, $U_i^*U \in G$ for $i=1,2,\ldots,n$.

Hence, for each $i \leq n$, $U > U_i$. Since U is minimal in G, $U_i=I$ or $U_i=U$ and $S=A_0+A_1U$.

(1) Let T be a smallest element in $N(g)$ that acts ergodically on $\mathcal{a}$. We know that $T=AU$ where U is minimal in G, and, by (2), to prove minimality we should show that $D+BU \in N(g)$ $(D,B \in \mathcal{a})$ implies $D=0$ or $B=0$.

Suppose $S=D+BU \in N(g)$. Then, by Lemma 2.11, $S=C(F+EU)$ where $C \in \mathcal{a}$ and F,E are projections in $\mathcal{a}$ satisfying: $FE=0$, $F+E=I$, and $F+U^*EU=I$. Hence $E=I-F=U^*EU$. Ergodicity of T (and thus of U) implies that $E=0$ or $E=I$.

(3) Let T be minimal in $N(g)$ satisfying $\Phi(T)=0$. We can write $T = \sum_{i=1}^n A_iU_i$. Let U_1 be the smallest among the U_i's. Since $U_1^*U_i \in G$ for each i, $U_1^*T \in g$. Thus $T > U_1$ and, by minimality of T, $T \in \mathcal{a}U_1$ and U_1 is minimal in G. By the previous lemma T is smallest in $N(g)$.

###

The following definitions are based on the terminology of [8,Chapter XIII].

Definitions:

(1) G is integrally closed if, for U and V in G, $U^n < V$ for $n=1,2,\ldots$ implies $U=I$.

(2) G is complete if any bounded subset of $\bar{G}$ has a l.u.b. and a g.l.b.

(3) G satisfies the (DCC) condition if every non empty subset of G contains a minimal member.

Lemma 2.26.: If G has a minimal element U, then the following are equivalent:

(1) $G = \{U^n: n=0,1,2,\ldots\}$.

(2) G is integrally closed.

(3) G is complete.

(4) G satisfies the (DCC) condition.

Proof: We will prove (3) implies (2), (2) implies (1), and (4) implies (1). As (1) clearly **implies** (3) and (4), this will complete the proof. (3) implies (2): This part of the lemma is true also if G does not have a minimal element, and is proved in [8, Chapter XIII, p.291, Lemma 5]. Let W,V in G be such that $W^n \leq V$ for all $n \geq 1$.
By completness, the set $\{W^n : n=1,2,\ldots\}$ has a l.u.b. W_0. W_0W is therefore the l.u.b. of the set $\{W^{n+1} : n=1,2,\ldots\}$ and, since the latter set is contained in the former, $W_0W < W_0$. But $W_0W > W_0$ implies $W=I$.
(2) implies (1) : Let V be an element of G different from I. Since G is integrally closed, there exists n such that $V < U^n$. Let m be the minimal positive integer satisfying this,then $U^{m-1} < V < U^m$ and $U^{m-1} \neq V$. Hence $U > VU^{-m+1} > I$, $VU^{-m+1} \neq I$, and by minimality of U this implies $V=U^m$.
(4) implies (1) : Let V be an element of G different from I, and consider the set of all operators in G of the form VU^{-n}, where n is a positive integer. Since $U < V$, this set contains VU^{-1} and is nonempty.
Since G satisfies the (DCC) condition, this set has a minimal member, say VU^{-m}. We get $U^m < V < U^{m+1}$, $U^{m+1} \neq V$, and, as before, this implies $V=U^m$.

###

Proposition 2.27.: G is integrally closed if and only if for any $S,T \in N(\mathcal{g})$ such that $\Phi(S)=0$ there exists $n \geq 1$ such that $S^n > T$.

Proof.: With U and V in place of S and T the given condition implies at once that G is integrally closed.
Suppose, now, that $S,T \in N(\mathcal{g})$ and that $\Phi(S)=0$. We can write $S = A_1U_1+\ldots+A_nU_n$ and $T = B_0+B_1V_1+\ldots+B_mV_m$ where $A_i,B_j \in \mathcal{a}$ and $U_i,V_j \in G\setminus\{I\}$. Assume that U_1 is the smallest among the U_i's and V_m is the greatest among the V_j's. By the assumption that G is integrally closed,

there is a positive integer k such that $U_1^k > V_m$. S^k is a sum of terms each of the form CW where $C \in \mathcal{a}$ and W, in G, is greater than U_1^k, thus $S^k > U_1^k$. By choice of V_m, $T^*V_m \in \mathcal{g}$ and from Lemma 2.23 (1) $V_m > T$. Since $U_1^k > V_m > T$, we get $S^k > T$. ###

If $G = \{U^n : n = 0,1,2,\ldots\}$, for some operator U, we say that G is <u>singly generated</u>.

<u>Corollary 2.28.</u> : $\mathcal{g}$ is generated by a singly generated semigroup if and only if $\mathcal{g}$ satisfies the following two conditions:

(1) $N(\mathcal{g})$ has a smallest element.

(2) For any S,T in $N(\mathcal{g})$ such that $\Phi(S) = 0$ there exists $n \geq 1$ such that $S^n > T$.

<u>Proof:</u> By Lemma 2.24, (1) is equivalent to the existence of a minimal element in G. By proposition 2.27, (2) is equivalent to the property: G is integrally closed. Lemma 2.26 completes the proof. ###

<u>Remark</u>: Conditions (1) and (2) of the previous corollary are independent of the choice of G. They depend only on $\mathcal{g}$ and $\mathcal{a}$.
To see this it should be recalled that for S in $M(\mathcal{g})$, $\Phi(S) = 0$ if and only if S acts freely on $\mathcal{a}$ (Lemma 2.12).

<u>Theorem 2.29.</u>: Let G_1 and G_2 be two ordered semigroups acting freely and ergodically on the maximal abelian algebra $\mathcal{a}$ and generating the same irreducible triangular algebra $\mathcal{g}$.
If G_1 is singly generated, with generator U, then G_2 is also singly generated and its generator is in $\mathcal{a}U$.

<u>Proof:</u> The fact that G_2 is also singly generated is a result of Corollary 2.28. Let V be the generator of G_2, then V and U are both smallest elements in $N(\mathcal{g})$, hence, by Lemma 2.24, $V \in \mathcal{a}U$. ###

<u>Proposition 2.30</u>: If $\mathcal{g}$ is generated by the semigroup G and satisfies conditions (2) of Corollary 2.28, then G is abelian.

Proof: By Proposition 2.27 G is integrally closed. By [8, Theorem 12, Chapter XIII] this implies that G is isomorphic to a subsemigroup of the non negative real numbers (under addition), hence abelian. ###

CHAPTER III: THE HOMOMORPHISMS OF $\mathcal{G}$

In this chapter we deal, once again, with the triangular algebra $\mathcal{G}$ generated by a maximal abelian algebra $\mathcal{a}$, acting on a separable Hilbert space H, and an ordered semigroup of unitary operators. We will study the linear multiplicative maps from $\mathcal{G}$ (or $\mathcal{G} + \mathcal{G}^*$) into the algebra B(K) of all bounded operators on some Hilbert space K, whose restriction to $\mathcal{a}$ is self adjoint. In particular we will deal with such automorphisms of $\mathcal{G}$.

Definitions:

(1) $\Psi: \mathcal{G} \longrightarrow B(K)$ is a homomorphism if it is multiplicative, linear, and $\Psi(A^*)=\Psi(A^*)$ for $A \in \mathcal{a}$.

(2) A homomorphism Ψ is a bounded homomorphism if

$$\operatorname{Sup}\{||\Psi(T)||: ||T|| \leq 1\} < \infty.$$

(3) A $*$-homomorphism is a homomorphism Ψ which satisfies $\Psi(U)^* = \Psi(U)^{-1}$ for each U in G.

(4) Isomorphisms and $*$-isomorphisms are one-to-one homomorphisms and $*$-homomorphisms respectively.

Proposition 3.1.: Let $\Psi: \mathcal{G} \longrightarrow B(K)$ be a homomorphism, then Ψ can be extended to a $*$-homomorphism of $\mathcal{G}+\mathcal{G}^*$ if and only if Ψ is a $*$-homomorphism If Ψ is a bounded $*$-homomorphism then it can be extended to $\mathcal{B}(\mathcal{a},G)$.

Proof: It is clear that, if Ψ can be extended to a $*$-homomorphism Ψ' on $\mathcal{G}+\mathcal{G}^*$ then, Ψ is a $*$-homomorphism on $\mathcal{G}$.

For the converse, suppose that $\Psi(U)$ is a unitary operator for each U in G. Each operator T in $\mathcal{G}+\mathcal{G}^*$ can be expressed in only one way (by $\mathcal{a}$- independence of $\bar{G}$) in the form $A_0+A_1U_1+\dots+A_nU_n$, where $A_j \in \mathcal{a}$ and $U_j \in \bar{G}$. Define $\Psi'(T)$ to be $\Psi(A_0)+\Psi(A_1)\Psi'(U_1)+\dots+\Psi(A_n)\Psi'(U_n)$, where $\Psi'(U_j) = \Psi(U_j)$ if $U_j \in G$ and $\Psi'(U_j) = \Psi(U_j^*)^{-1}$ if $U_j^* \in G$. We have that

Ψ' is well defined and linear on $\mathcal{g}+\mathcal{g}^*$.

To see that Ψ' is multiplicative, it will suffice to show that $\Psi'(AUBV) = \Psi(A)\Psi'(U)\ \Psi(B)\Psi'(V)$ when $A,B \in \mathcal{a}$ and $U,V \in \bar{G}$. Suppose, for example, that $U \notin G$, $V \in G$, and $UV \in G$. Then $U^* \in G$ and

$\Psi'(V) = \Psi(V) = \Psi(U^*UV) = \Psi(U^*)\Psi(UV)$; so that

$\Psi'(UV) = \Psi(UV) = \Psi(U^*)^{-1}\ \Psi(V) = \Psi'(U)\Psi'(V)$.

We also have, $\Psi(BU^*) = \Psi(U^*UBU^*) = \Psi(U^*)\ \Psi(UBU^*)$; so that

$\Psi'(U)\Psi'(B)\Psi'(U^*) = \Psi(U^*)^{-1}\Psi(B)\Psi(U^*) = \Psi(U^*)^{-1}\Psi(BU^*) = \Psi(UBU^*)$. Thus

$$\Psi'(AUBV) = \Psi'(AUBU^*UV) = \Psi(A)\Psi(UBU^*)\Psi'(UV) = \Psi(A)\Psi'(U)\Psi(B)\ \Psi'(U^*)\ \Psi'(U)\ \Psi'(V) =$$
$$\Psi(A)\ \Psi'(U)\ \Psi(B)\ \Psi'(V).$$

The other cases for U,V, and UV, are handled by similar computations. Thus Ψ' is a $*$-homomorphism of $\mathcal{g}+\mathcal{g}^*$ that extends Ψ.

For the last assertion of this proposition, note that, with T in $\mathcal{g}+\mathcal{g}^*$ $TU \in \mathcal{g}$ for a suitable U in $\bar{G}$. If $||T||(=||TU||) \leq 1$ then $||\Psi'(T)|| = ||\Psi'(T)\Psi'(U)|| = ||\Psi'(TU)|| = ||\Psi(TU)|| \leq ||\Psi||$. Thus $||\Psi'|| = ||\Psi||$ and, in particular, Ψ' is bounded when Ψ is . ###

We will mostly deal with homomorphisms satisfying $\Psi(\mathcal{a}) = \Psi(\mathcal{a})'$ (i.e.the image of Ψ is maximal abelian).

Proposition 3.2.: Each homomorphism $\Psi : \mathcal{g} \longrightarrow B(K)$ whose restriction to $\mathcal{a}$ is weak operator continuous and for which $\Psi(\mathcal{a}) = \Psi(\mathcal{a})'$ has the form $\Psi=\Psi_2 \cdot \Psi_1$ where:

a) Ψ_1 is a homomorphism from $\mathcal{g}$ into the algebra $F\mathcal{g}F$ (with F some projeciton in $\mathcal{a}$) satisfying: $\Psi_1(A)=AF$ for A in $\mathcal{a}$ and $\Psi_1(U)=F\varphi(U)UF$ for U in G, where φ maps G into $\mathcal{a}F$.

b) $\Psi_2 : F\mathcal{g}F \longrightarrow B(K)$ is implemented by a unitary transformation $W:K \longrightarrow F(H)$ i.e. $\Psi_2(T)=W^*TW$.

Proof: Since $\Psi|\mathcal{a}$ is weak operator continuous, its kernel has the form $\mathcal{a}(I-F)$ for some projection F in $\mathcal{a}$, and $\Psi|\mathcal{a}F$ is a $*$-isomorphism onto $\Psi(\mathcal{a})$. Since $\mathcal{a}F$ is maximal abelian on $F(H)$ and $\Psi(\mathcal{a})$ is maximal abelian (by assumption); $\Psi|\mathcal{A}F$ is implemented by a unitary transformation $W:K \longrightarrow F(H)$ (i.e. $\Psi(AF) = W^*AFW$ for A in $\mathcal{A}$).

Consider $\Psi_1:\mathcal{G} \longrightarrow B(F(H))$ defined by $\Psi_1(S)=W\Psi(S)W^*$ (so that $\Psi_1(A)=AF$ for A in $\mathcal{A}$). If $A \in \mathcal{A}$ and $U \in G$, then $\Psi_1(A)\Psi_1(U) = \Psi_1(U)\Psi_1(U^*AU)$ so that $AF\Psi_1(U) = \Psi_1(U)U^*AUF$. But $\Psi_1(U) = F\Psi_1(U)F$.

Hence $AF\Psi_1(U)U^* = F\Psi_1(U)U^*A$ so that $F\Psi_1(U)U^* \in \mathcal{A}' = \mathcal{A}$.

Let $\varphi(U)$ be $F\Psi_1(U)U^*$. Then $F\Psi_1(U) = F\varphi(U)U$ and $F\Psi_1(U) = F\varphi(U)UF$.

Hence $\Psi_1(U) = F\varphi(U)UF \in F\mathcal{G}F$. ###

Proposition 3.3.: Let F be a projection in $\mathcal{A}$, $F \neq I$, and let $\Psi:\mathcal{G} \longrightarrow F\mathcal{G}F$ be a homomorphism such that $\Psi(A) = AF$ for A in $\mathcal{A}$ and $\Psi(U) = F\varphi(U)UF$ for U in G where $\varphi(U)$ is in $\mathcal{A}F$.

Then there exists some U in G such that $\varphi(U)$ has a non zero null space in $F(H)$. Thus if Ψ satisfies the conditions of Proposition 3.2 and its restriction to $\mathcal{A}$ is not an isomorphism then there is some U in G such that $\Psi(U)$ has a non zero null space.

Proof: As G acts ergodically on $\mathcal{A}$, there is a V in G such that $Q=FV^*(I-F)V\neq 0$. Since $VQV^* \leq I-F$, $FVQV^*=0$ and $FVA=0$. As G acts ergodically on $\mathcal{A}$, and $VQV^*\neq 0$ there is some W in G such that $FWVQV^*W^*\neq 0$ hence $FWVQ\neq 0$. If $\varphi(WV)$ annihilates no vector in $F(H)$ then $0 \neq \varphi(WV)FWVQ = \varphi(WV)FWVFQ = \varphi(WV)Q = \varphi(W)\ \varphi(V)Q = \Psi(W)\ \varphi(V)FVFQ = 0$ (since $FVQ=0$) - a contradiction. Therefore $\varphi(WV)$ annihilates some non zero vector in $F(H)$. With WV for U, the first assertion follows.

The last assertion follows from the fact that $F\neq I$ if $\Psi|\mathcal{A}$ is not an isomorphism and $\Psi(U) = \varphi(U)UF = \varphi(U)FUF$. ###

Our interest is, primarily, in the case where F (above) is I. The next definition refers to this case.

Definition: Let $W:K \longrightarrow H$ be a unitary transformation and let φ be a map from G (resp. $\bar{G}$) into $\mathcal{A}$.

A homomorphism Ψ from $\mathcal{G}$ (resp. $\mathcal{G}+\mathcal{G}^*$) into $B(K)$ will be said to be implemented by (W,φ) if the following hold:

For $A \in \mathfrak{a}$, $\quad \Psi(A) = W^*AW$.

For $U \in \bar{G}$, $\quad (U) = W^*\varphi(U)UW$.

If Ψ is a homomorphism on $\mathfrak{g}+\mathfrak{g}^*$ (resp. $\mathfrak{g}$) implemented by (W,φ) then for all U,V in $\bar{G}$ (resp. G) $\varphi(UV) = W\Psi(UV)W^*V^*U^* = W\Psi(U)\Psi(V)W^*V^*U^* =$

$W\Psi(U)W^*U^*UW\Psi(V)W^*V^*U^*$. Hence

$$\varphi(UV) = \varphi(U)U\varphi(V)U^* \qquad (*).$$

Conversly, if (*) holds, for all U,V in $\bar{G}$ (resp. G), and $W:K \longrightarrow H$ is a unitary transformation, then there is a homomorphism Ψ from $\mathfrak{g}+\mathfrak{g}^*$ (resp. $\mathfrak{g}$) into $B(K)$ which is implemented by (W,φ).

In fact, each operator T in $\mathfrak{g}+\mathfrak{g}^*$ (resp. $\mathfrak{g}$) can be expressed in only one way (by $\mathfrak{a}$-independence of $\bar{G}$) in the form $A_0+A_1U_1+\ldots+A_nU_n$, where $A_i \in \mathfrak{a}$ and $U_i \in \bar{G}$ (resp. G). Define $\Psi(T)$ to be $W^*(A_0+A_1\varphi(U_1)U_1+\ldots+A_n\varphi(U_n)U_n)W$.

We have that Ψ is well defined and linear on $\mathfrak{g}+\mathfrak{g}^*$ (resp. $\mathfrak{g}$).

To see that Ψ is multiplicative, it will suffice to show that $\Psi(AUBV) = \Psi(AU)\Psi(BV)$ when $A,B \in \mathfrak{a}$ and $U,V \in \bar{G}$ (resp. G) But $\Psi(AUBV) = \Psi(AUBU^*UV) = W^*AUBU^*\ (UV)UVW = W^*AUBU^*\ (U)U\ (V)U^*UVW =$

$$W^*A\varphi(U)UBU^*U\varphi(V)VW = W^*A\varphi(U)UWW^*B\varphi(V)VW$$

Thus $\Psi(AUBV) = \Psi(AU)\Psi(BV)$.

Hence Ψ is a homomorphism and is implemented by (W,φ).

We will now turn to the case where Ψ is an isomorphism.

<u>Lemma 3.4:</u> Let Ψ be a homomorphism of $\mathfrak{g}$ satisfying $\Psi(\mathfrak{a}) = \Psi(\mathfrak{a})'$ and such that $\Psi|\mathfrak{a}$ is an isomorphism, then Ψ is implemented by (W,φ) for some W and φ.

<u>Proof:</u> Apply Proposition 3.2 in the case where $F=I$. ###

<u>Proposition 3.5:</u> Let Ψ be a homomorphism of $\mathfrak{g}$ into $B(K)$ satisfying $\Psi(\mathfrak{a}) = \Psi(\mathfrak{a})'$ then the following are equivalent:

(1) Ψ is an isomorphism.

(2) Ψ is implemented by some (W,φ) where $\varphi(U)$ is invertible for each U in G.

(3) $\Psi|\mathcal{a}$ is weak operator continuous and $\Psi(U)$ is invertible for any U in G.

(4) $\Psi|\mathcal{a}$ is a *-isomorphism and $\Psi(U)$ is invertible for each U in G.

Proof:

(1) implies (2): Assume that Ψ is an isomorphism. By Lemma 3.4, Ψ is implemented by some (W,φ). If, for some U in G, $\varphi(U)$ is not invertible, then there exists a non zero projection F in $\mathcal{a}$ such that $\varphi(U)F=0$. In this case: $\Psi(FU) = W^*FWW^*\varphi(U)UW = W^*F\varphi(U)UW = 0$ contradicting the assumption that Ψ is an isomorphism.

(2) implies (1): Assume that (2) holds and that for some $A_i \in \mathcal{a}$ and $U_i \in G$, $\Psi(A_0+A_1U_1+\ldots+A_nU_n) = 0$. Then $0 = W^*(A_0+A_1\varphi(U_1)U_1+\ldots+A_n\varphi(U_n)U_n)W$. Thus $0 = A_0+A_1\varphi(U_1)U_1+\ldots+A_n\varphi(U_n)U_n$ and so $A_i = 0$ for each i.

(2) implies (3): Since $\Psi|\mathcal{a}$ is implemented by a unitary operator, and $\Psi(U) = W^*\varphi(U)UW$; $\Psi|\mathcal{a}$ is weak operator continuous and $\Psi(U)$ is invertible.

(3) implies (4): Assuming $\Psi|\mathcal{a}$ is weak operator continuous, we can apply Proposition 3.2. If $\Psi|\mathcal{a}$ is not an isomorphism then $F\neq I$, hence, by Proposition 3.3, there is a U in G such that $\Psi(U)$ is not invertible contradicting the assumption of (3).

(4) implies (2) : This is the assertion of Lemma 3.4. ###

In Proposition 3.5 we assumed that the image of $\Psi|\mathcal{a}$ is a maximal abelian algebra. If we assume only that the commutant of the image is of type $I_m(m \leq \infty)$ we get the following:

Proposition 3.6.: Let $\Psi:\mathcal{g} \longrightarrow B(K)$ be an isomorphism such that $\Psi(\mathcal{a})'$ is of type $I_m(m \leq \infty)$, then Ψ is unitarily equivalent to a homomorphism τ of the following form:

$\tau:\mathcal{g} \longrightarrow B(H\otimes K_m)$ (where $\dim K_m=m$) and $\tau(A)=A\otimes I_m$ for A in $\mathcal{a}$,

$\tau(U) = C(U)(U\otimes I_m)$ for U in G, where $C(U)$ is in $\mathcal{a}\otimes B(K_m)$ and I_m is the identity operator on K_m.

Proof: Define $w: \mathcal{g} \longrightarrow \mathcal{g}\otimes I_m$ by $w(S) = S\otimes I_m$ for S in $\mathcal{g}$. Then $w(\mathcal{a})' = (\mathcal{a}\otimes I_m)' = \mathcal{a}\otimes B(K_m)$ is a type I_m von Neumann algebra. The map $\Psi\cdot w^{-1}$ is a $*$-isomorphism from $w(\mathcal{a})$ onto $\Psi(\mathcal{a})$, two algebras of type I_1 with commutants of type I_m. Hence $\Psi\cdot w^{-1}$, restricted to $\mathcal{a}\otimes I_m$, is implemented by a unitary transformation $V: K \longrightarrow H\otimes K_m$.

With U in G and A in $\mathcal{a}$, $\Psi(A)\Psi(U) = \Psi(U)\Psi(U^*AU)$; so that $V^*(A\otimes I_m)V\Psi(U) = \Psi(U)V^*(U^*AU\otimes I_m)V$.

Hence $(A\otimes I_m)V\Psi(U)V^*(U^*\otimes I_m) = V\Psi(U)V^*(U^*\otimes I_m)(A\otimes I_m)$. Let $C(U)$ be $V\Psi(U)V^*(U^*\otimes I_m)$ then $C(U) \in (\mathcal{a}\otimes I_m)' = \mathcal{a}\otimes B(K_m)$ and $\Psi(U) = V^*C(U)(U\otimes I_m)V$. By choice of V, $\Psi(A) = V^*(A\otimes I_m)V$ for A in $\mathcal{a}$. Thus defining $\tau(S)$ to be $V\Psi(S)V^*$, completes the proof. ###

Corollary 3.7: If $\Psi: \mathcal{g} \longrightarrow B(K)$ is a homomorphism such that $\Psi(\mathcal{g})\cap\Psi(\mathcal{g})^*$ is abelian and $\Psi(\mathcal{a}) = \Psi(\mathcal{a})'$, then conditions (1)-(4) of Proposition 3.5 are equivalent, and if any one of them is fulfilled, $\Psi(\mathcal{g})$ is an irreducible triangular algebra unitarily equivalent to $\mathcal{g}$.

Proof: Since $\Psi(\mathcal{a})$ is maximal abelian and contained in the abelian algebra $\Psi(\mathcal{g})\cap\Psi(\mathcal{g})^*$; $\Psi(\mathcal{g})\cap\Psi(\mathcal{g})^* = \Psi(\mathcal{a})$, and $\Psi(\mathcal{g})$ is triangular. From Proposition 3.5, Ψ is implemented by some (W,φ). As $\varphi(U)$ is invertible for each U in G and $W^*AW = \Psi(A)$ for each A in $\mathcal{a}$; $W^*UW = \Psi(\varphi(U)^{-1}U)$. Thus the mapping, $T \longrightarrow W^*TW$, of into $B(K)$ maps $\mathcal{g}$ in $\Psi(\mathcal{g})$. Now $\Psi(A)\Psi(U) = W^*A\varphi(U)UW$ when $A \in \mathcal{a}$ and $U \in G$; so that the mapping, $T \longrightarrow W^*TW$, carries $\mathcal{g}$ onto $\Psi(\mathcal{g})$. It follows that $\Psi(\mathcal{g})$ is an irreducible triangular algebra unitary equivalent to $\mathcal{g}$. ###

Corollary 3.8.: (1) Any $*$-homomorphism $\Psi: \mathcal{g} \longrightarrow B(K)$ that maps $\mathcal{a}$ onto a maximal abelian algebra is a $*$-isomorphism if and only if $\Psi|\mathcal{a}$ is an isomorphism.

(2) Any automorphism of $\mathcal{g}$ (i.e. isomorphism from $\mathcal{g}$ onto itself) that maps

$\mathcal{A}$ onto iteself is implemented by some (W,φ) where φ is a map form G into $\mathcal{A}$, $\varphi(U)$ is invertible for each U in G, and W is in $V(\mathcal{A})$.

Proof: (1) By the definition of a *-homomorphism, $\Psi(U)$ is a unitary operator for each U in G. Thus Ψ is a *-isomorphism by the equivalence of conditions (1) and (4) of Proposition 3.5.

For (2) apply the equivalence of conditions (1) and (2) of Proposition 3.5 for the case where $\Psi(\mathcal{A}) = \mathcal{A}$. As $W^*\mathcal{A}W = \Psi(\mathcal{A}) = \mathcal{A}$, $W \in V(\mathcal{A})$.

###

Proposition 3.9.: Let $\mathcal{g}_i$ (i=1,2) be irreducible triangular algebras generated by $\mathcal{A}_i$ and G_i and $\mathcal{B}_i$ the C*-algebras they generate. Let $\Psi:\mathcal{B}_1 \longrightarrow \mathcal{B}_2$ be a *-homomorphism satisfying $\Psi(\mathcal{A}_1) = \mathcal{A}_2$. Then $\Psi(\mathcal{g}_1+\mathcal{g}_1^*) \subseteq \mathcal{g}_2 + \mathcal{g}_2^*$.

Proof: Let U be a unitary operator in $\bar{G}_1$. Then $\Psi(U)$ is unitary in $\mathcal{B}_2$ and $\Psi(U)^*\Psi(A)\Psi(U) = \Psi(U^*AU) \in \Psi(\mathcal{A}_1)$ for A in $\mathcal{A}_1$.
Hence $\Psi(U)$ is in $V(\mathcal{A}_2)\cap\mathcal{B}_2$, and by Corollary 2.17, $\Psi(U)$ is in $\mathcal{g}_2+\mathcal{g}_2^*$. So $\Psi(\bar{G}_1) \subseteq \mathcal{g}_2+\mathcal{g}_2^*$, and by assumption $\Psi(\mathcal{A}_1) \subseteq \mathcal{g}_2+\mathcal{g}_2^*$. Hence $\Psi_1(\mathcal{g}_1+\mathcal{g}_1^*) \subseteq \mathcal{g}_2+\mathcal{g}_2^*$.

###

States and representations. The GNS construction.

Definitions:

(1) $f : \mathcal{g} \longrightarrow \mathbb{C}$ is a state on $\mathcal{g}$ if f is linear, $f|\mathcal{A}$ is a state on $\mathcal{A}$, and $||f|| \leq 1$.

(2) By a representation of $\mathcal{g}$ on the Hilbert space K we mean a bounded homomorphism from $\mathcal{g}$ into B(K).

We will construct a representation from a given state, using the GNS construction, and establish the uniqueness of a cyclic representation that gives rise to a given state.

Remark: Any state of $\mathcal{g}$ has a unique extension to a state of $\mathcal{B}(\mathcal{A},G)$. In fact, if f is a state of $\mathcal{g}$ it has an extension g of norm 1 to B(H) (from the Hahn-Banach Theorem). Since $I \in \mathcal{A}$ and $f|\mathcal{A}$ is a state of

$\mathcal{a}$, $f(I)=1=g(I)$. Thus g is a state of $B(H)$ and the restriction of g to $\mathcal{B}(\mathcal{a},G)$ is the unique extension of f to a state of $\mathcal{B}(\mathcal{a}, G)$

Proposition 3.10.: To any state g of $\mathcal{B}(\mathcal{a},G)$ we can associate two representations, a representation Π of $\mathcal{B}(\mathcal{a},G)$ on a Hilbert space K, and a representation Π' of $\mathcal{g}$ on a Hilbert space K', and vectors $\xi\in K$, $\xi'\in K'$ such that : (1) $\langle\Pi(T)\xi,\xi\rangle=g(T)$ $\quad T \in \mathcal{B}(\mathcal{a},G)$.

$$\langle\Pi'(T)\xi', \xi'\rangle=g(T)\rangle , \qquad T\in \mathcal{g}.$$

(2) $K=[\Pi(\mathcal{B}(\mathcal{a},G))\xi]$, $K'=[\Pi'(\mathcal{g})\xi']$ where $[M]$ denotes the closed linear subspace generated by M. (3) There is a unique isometric linear mapping τ of K' into K such that, for each T in $\mathcal{g}$, $\Pi(T)\cdot\tau=\tau\cdot\Pi'(T)$ and $\tau(\xi')=\xi$.
(4) For each U in G, $\Pi'(U)$ is an isometry.

Proof: Let Π, ξ, and K be the representation, the cyclic vector and the Hilbert space obtained by the GNS construction applied to the state g of $\mathcal{B}(\mathcal{a},G)$.

Let N be $\{T \in \mathcal{g} : g(T^*T)=0\}$. Then N is a left ideal in $\mathcal{g}$. Let K_0 be the linear space $\mathcal{g}/N$ equipped with the inner product $\langle S+N,T+N\rangle=g(T^*S)$; and let K' denote the completion of K_0. Then K' is a Hilbert space.

Define a map $\tau':K_0 \longrightarrow K$ by $\tau'(T+N)=T+N_1$ where $N_1 = \{T \in \mathcal{B}(\mathcal{a},G) : g(T^*T) = 0\}$. τ' is certainly an isometry and can be extended to an isometry map, τ, from K' into K. Since $\langle TS+N,TS+N\rangle=g(S^*T^*TS) \leq ||T||^2 \langle S+N,S+N\rangle$; (*) we can define an operator $\Pi'(T)$ on K_0 by $\Pi'(T)(S+N)=TS+N$ and extend it to a bounded operator on K'.

Clearly, $T \longrightarrow \Pi'(T)$ is a representation of $\mathcal{g}$ (by (*) $||\Pi'(T)|| \leq ||T||$).

Let ξ' be the vector $I+N$ in K_0 and, since ξ is $I+N_1$, $\tau(\xi')=\xi$. Now $g(T)=g(IT)= \langle T+N,I+N\rangle = \langle\Pi'(T)\xi', \xi'\rangle$ for $T \in \mathcal{g}$ so this proves (1).

For (2), note that $K' =[\Pi'(\mathcal{g})\xi']$ since K' is the completion of K_0 ($=\{\Pi'(T)\xi' : T \in \mathcal{g}\}$).

Condition (3) follows from:

$\Pi(T)\tau(S+N) = \Pi(T)(S+N_1) = TS+N_1 = \tau(TS+N) = \tau(\Pi'(T)(S+N))$ for T,S in $\mathcal{g}$. Condition (4) is a consequence of (3) and the fact that $\Pi(U)$ is a unitary operator for each U in G. ###

Proposition 3.11.: Let Π be a representation of $\mathcal{g}$ on K_1 such that :

(1) there is a unit vector $\eta \in K_1$ for which $K_1 = [\Pi(\mathcal{g})\eta]$.

(2) For each U in G, $\Pi(U)$ is an isometry.

Let g be the state on $\mathcal{g}$ defined by $g(T) = \langle\Pi(T)\eta,\eta\rangle$ and let Π' be the representation of $\mathcal{g}$ associated with g. Then Π and Π' are unitarily equivalent.

Proof: a) If we were dealing with a self adjoint algebra instead of $\mathcal{g}$, we would have an equality of the form, $g(T^*T)=||\Pi(T)\eta||^2$, directly from our assumptions. We must obtain the corresponding information, in the present case, by other means.

In the first place, as noted earlier, g has a unique extension to a state of $\mathcal{B}(a,G)$. We denote by g, again, this state extension (so that $g(T^*T)$ refers to the value of this extension at T^*T, for T in $\mathcal{g}$).

Let T be $\sum_i U_iA_i$ where A_i in a and U_i in G, and assume that for any i, $U_i^*U_{i+1}$ is in G. Since $\Pi(U_i)$ is an isometry, we have $||\Pi(U_iA_i)\eta||^2=||\Pi(A_i)\eta||^2=g(A_i^*A_i)$ for each i; so that

$$\begin{aligned}\langle\Pi(T)\eta,\ \Pi(T)\eta\rangle &= \textstyle\sum_{i,j}\langle\Pi(U_iA_i)\eta,\ \Pi(U_jA_j)\eta\rangle\\ &= \textstyle\sum_i||\Pi(U_iA_i)\eta||^2+2\sum_{i>j}\mathrm{Re}\langle\Pi(U_iA_i)\eta,\ \Pi(U_jA_j)\eta\rangle\\ &= \textstyle\sum_i g(A_iA_i)+2\sum_{i>j}\mathrm{RE}\langle\Pi(U_iA_i)\eta,\ \Pi(U_jA_j)\eta\rangle.\end{aligned}$$

For $i > j$, $U_j^*U_i \in G$, hence $\langle\Pi(U_iA_i)\eta\ ,\ \Pi(U_jA_j)\eta\rangle$

$$\begin{aligned}&= \langle\Pi(U_j)\Pi(U_j^*U_iA_i)\eta,\ \Pi(U_j)\Pi(A_j)\eta\rangle =\\ &= \langle\Pi(U_j^*U_iA_i)\eta,\ \Pi(A_j)\eta\rangle = g(A_j^*U_j^*U_iA_i).\end{aligned}$$

So $\langle\Pi(T)\eta,\ \Pi(T)\eta\rangle = \sum_i g(A_i^*A_i)+2\sum_{i>j}\mathrm{Re}\ g(A_j^*U_j^*U_iA_i) = g(T^*T)$.

b) Define an operator $V:K' \longrightarrow K_1$ by $V\Pi'(T)\xi' = \Pi(T)\eta$, where K' is the representation space of Π', and $g(T) = \langle\Pi'(T)\xi',\xi'\rangle$. Then V is well defined and isometric on a dense subspace of K' with range dense in K_1 since $||\Pi'(T)\xi'||^2=g(T^*T) = ||\Pi(T)\eta||^2$. Thus V can be extended to a unitary transformation of K' onto K_1 and $V\xi'=\eta$. We have $V\Pi'(T)V^*\Pi(S)\eta = V\Pi'(T)\Pi'(S)\xi' = \Pi(TS)\eta = \Pi(T)\,\Pi(S)\eta$; so that

$$V\Pi'(T)^*V = \Pi(T).$$

###

Definition: A state g of $\mathcal{B}(\mathcal{a},G)$ will be called G-invariant if for each T in $\mathcal{B}(\mathcal{a},G)$ and each U in G $g(U^*TU) = g(T)$.

Note that if g is a state and $g(U^*T^*TU) = g(T^*T)$ for each T in $\mathcal{g} + \mathcal{g}^*$ and each U in G, then g is G-invariant. In fact, since $\mathcal{B}(\mathcal{a},G)$ is the norm closure of $\mathcal{g} + \mathcal{g}^*$ and g is norm continuous; the equality, $g(U^*T^*TU) = g(T^*T)$, is valid for each T in $\mathcal{B}(\mathcal{a},G)$. But each positive operator in $\mathcal{B}(\mathcal{a},G)$ has the form T^*T for some T in $\mathcal{B}(\mathcal{a},G)$; and each operator in $\mathcal{B}(\mathcal{a},G)$ is a linear combination of at most four positive operators in $\mathcal{B}(\mathcal{a},G)$. Thus $g(U^*TU) = g(T)$ for each T in $\mathcal{B}(\mathcal{a},G)$ and each U in G.

Proposition 3.12.: Let g be a faithful G-invariant state of $\mathcal{B}(\mathcal{a},G)$ and let Π' be the representation of $\mathcal{g}$ associated with g. Then Π' is an isometry. i.e. $||\Pi'(T)|| = ||T||$.

Proof: Fix $\varepsilon > 0$. Let Π be the representation of $\mathcal{B}(\mathcal{a},G)$ associated with g, then $||\Pi(T)|| = ||T||$. Thus there is a unit vector x in K (the space on which Π acts) such that $||\Pi(T)x|| > ||T|| - \varepsilon$. With the notation of Proposition 3.10, there is an R in $\mathcal{g}+\mathcal{g}^*$ satisfying $g(R^*R) = 1$ and $||\Pi(T)(R+N_1)|| > ||T|| - \varepsilon$. Hence $(||T|| - \varepsilon)^2 < ||\Pi(TR)(I+N_1)||^2 = g(R^*T^*TR) = g(U^*R^*T^*TRU)$ for each U in G. Choose U such that $(S=)\ RU \in \mathcal{g}$. Then, with T in $\mathcal{g}$, $||\Pi'(T)(S+N||^2 = ||\Pi'(TS)(I+N)||^2 = ||\Pi'(TRU)(I+N)||^2$

$$= g(U^*R^*T^*TUR).$$

Thus $||\Pi'(T)(S+N)|| > ||T|| - \varepsilon$. Since ε is an arbitrary positive number and $g(S^*S) = g(U^*R^*RU) = g(R^*R) = 1$, we have that $||\Pi'(T)|| = ||T||$.

###

<u>Boundedness of isomorphisms</u>

Let g_1, g_2 be two irreducible triangular algebras generated by a_1, G_1 and a_2, G_2 respectively, and let Ψ be an isomorphism from g_1 onto g_2. We know that such a map is implemented by some (W,φ). In what follows we will find conditions for Ψ to be bounded. For this purpose we may assume that $W=I$.

<u>Theorem 3.13.:</u> If Ψ is an automorphism of g implemented by (I,φ) and g is a faithful state of $\mathcal{B}(\mathit{a},G)$ satisfying, for A in a and U in $G\setminus\{I\}$:

(1) $\mathrm{g}(AU) = 0$

(2) $\mathrm{g}(U^*A^*AU) = \mathrm{g}(A^*A)$;

and there are positive constants N and M such that for each U in G $NI \leq |\varphi(U)| \leq MI$ then Ψ is bounded.

<u>Proof:</u> We note, first, that g is $\bar{G}$-invariant on $\mathcal{B}(\mathit{a},G)$. Since g is G-invariant on the positive elements of a and such elements generate a (linearly); $\mathrm{g}(U^*AU) = \mathrm{g}(A)$ for each A in a and U in G. If $V \in \bar{G}\setminus G$ then $V^* \in G$ so that

$$\mathrm{g}(A) = \mathrm{g}(VV^*AVV^*) = \mathrm{g}(V^*AV)$$

and $$\mathrm{g}(AV) = \overline{\mathrm{g}(V^*A^*)} = \overline{(V^*A^*VV^*)} = 0,$$

when $A \in \mathit{a}$ (from (1), as $V^*A^*V \in \mathit{a}$). Thus, if $T \in \mathit{g}+\mathit{g}^*$, $T = A_0+\sum_{j=1}^{n} A_jU_j$ where $A_j \in \mathit{a}$ and $U_j \in \bar{G}\setminus\{I\}$, and with U in $\bar{G}$, $\mathrm{g}(U^*TU)=\mathrm{g}(U^*A_0U+\sum_{j=1}^{n} U^*A_jUU^*U_jU)=\mathrm{g}(U^*A_0U)=\mathrm{g}(A_0)=\mathrm{g}(T)$. By norm continuity of g on $\mathcal{B}(\mathit{a},G)$ it follows, now, that g is $\bar{G}$-invariant on $\mathcal{B}(\mathit{a},G)$.

Let Π', K', and ξ' be the representation, the space, and the cyclic vector correspond to g. Define an operator V_0 on $\Pi'(\mathit{g})\xi'$ by: $V_0\Pi'(T)\xi' = \Pi'(\Psi(T))\xi'$, where $T \in \mathit{g}$. Then $||\Pi'(\Psi(T))\xi'||^2=\mathrm{g}(\Psi(T)^*\Psi(T))$ and $||\Pi'(T)\xi'||^2 = \mathrm{g}(T^*T)$.

Let T be $\sum AU_U$. Then, using the facts that $\mathrm{g}(AU)=0$ for $U\neq I$ and $\Psi(A)=A$ for each A in a (recall that $W=I$ here) we have: $\mathrm{g}(T^*T) = \mathrm{g}(\sum U^*A_U^*A_UU) = \sum \mathrm{g}(A_U^*A_U)$ and $\mathrm{g}(\Psi(T)^*\Psi(T))=\mathrm{g}(\sum U^*\varphi(U)^*A_U^*A_U\varphi(U)U) = \sum \mathrm{g}(A_U^*|\varphi(U)|^2A_U)$.

By assumption (3): $N^2 g(T^*T) \leq g(\Psi(T)^*\Psi(T)) \leq M^2 g(T^*T)$. Thus $||V_0|| \leq M$ and V_0 can be extended to operator V on K' such that $||V|| \leq M$.
Since Ψ is an automorphism of $\mathcal{g}$ and $[\Pi'(\mathcal{g})\xi'] = K'$, V_0 has dense range; so that V has a bounded inverse and $||V^{-1}|| \leq N^{-1}$. As $V\xi' = \xi'$, we have

$$V\Pi'(T)V^{-1} \Pi'(S) \xi' = V\Pi'(T)\Pi'(\Psi^{-1}(S)) \xi' = V\Pi'(T\Psi^{-1}(S))\xi'$$

$$= \Pi'(\Psi(T)S)\xi' = \Pi'(\Psi(T)) \Pi'(S)\xi'$$ for T and S in $\mathcal{g}$. Thus $V\Pi'(T)V^{-1} = \Pi'(\Psi(T))$; and $||V\Pi'(T)V^{-1}|| \leq ||V|| \, ||\Pi'(T)|| \, ||V^{-1}|| \leq N^{-1}M||T||$ hence $||\Pi'(\Psi(T))|| \leq N^{-1}M||T||$.
By Proposition 3.12, Π' is an isometry; so that $||\Psi(T)|| \leq N^{-1}M||T||$, and Ψ is bounded. ###

Remark: If $\bar{G}$ is amenable, g' is a faithful G-invariant state of $\mathcal{a}$, and g is $g'\cdot\Phi$, where Φ is the Arveson expectation of $\mathcal{B}(\mathcal{a},G)$ on $\mathcal{a}$ then g is a faithful $\bar{G}$-invariant state of $\mathcal{B}(\mathcal{a},G)$ (from the preceding theorem and the properties of Φ - see Lemma 2.1 and Proposition 2.7) for:

$$g(U^*AU) = g'(\Phi(U^*AU)) = g'(U^*AU) = g'(A) \; ; \text{ and } \; g(AU) = g'(\Phi(AU)) = g'(0) = 0,$$

for each A in $\mathcal{a}$ and U in $G\setminus\{I\}$. Thus g satisfies conditions (1) and (2) of the preceding theorem.

Corollary 3.14: If Ψ is an automorphism of $\mathcal{g}$ implemented by (I,φ) and $\mathcal{B}(\mathcal{a},G)$ has a faithful G-invariant state g such that $g(AU) = 0$ for each A in $\mathcal{a}$ and U in G then Ψ extends to a *-automorphism of $\mathcal{B}(\mathcal{a},G)$ if and only if $\varphi(U)$ is a unitary operator for each U in G.

Proof: If Ψ extends to a *-automorphism of $\mathcal{B}(\mathcal{a},G)$ then, of course, $\Psi(U)$ is unitary for each U in G. Now $\Psi(U) = \varphi(U)U$; so that $\varphi(U) = \Psi(U)U^*$, and $\varphi(U)$ is unitary for each U in G.

If $\varphi(U)$ is unitary for each U in G then condition (3) of the preceding theorem is satisfied (with 1 for N and M). From our assumptions, conditions (1) and (2) are also satisfied; and Ψ extends to a *-homomorphism on $\mathcal{B}(\mathcal{a},G)$. Since $\Psi(\mathcal{g}) = \mathcal{g}$; we have $\Psi(\mathcal{g}^*) = \mathcal{g}^*$ and Ψ maps $\mathcal{B}(\mathcal{a},G)$. onto $\mathcal{B}(\mathcal{a},G)$ (where we denote by Ψ, again, the extension of Ψ

to $\mathcal{B}(\mathcal{a},G)$.

The automophism Ψ^{-1} of g is implemented by (I,φ^*), where $\varphi^*(U) = \varphi(U)^*$; for $\Psi(U) = \varphi(U)U$ so that $U = \varphi(U)\Psi^{-1}(U)$ and $\Psi^{-1}(U) = \varphi(U) = \varphi(U)^*$. But $\varphi(U)^*$ is a unitary operator, for each U in G; so that, from what we have proved, to this point, Ψ^{-1} extends to a *-homomorphism (that we denote by Ψ^{-1}, again) of $\mathcal{B}(\mathcal{a},G)$ onto itself. Now $\Psi^{-1}\cdot\Psi$ is the identity transformation on g and, hence, on $g+g^*$. By (norm) continuity $\Psi^{-1}\cdot\Psi$ is the identity on $\mathcal{B}(\mathcal{a},G)$; and Ψ is a *-automorphism of $\mathcal{B}(\mathcal{a},G)$. ###

Isometries and anti-isomorphisms

A map $\Psi: g \longrightarrow B(K)$ is said to be an anti-isomorphism if it is linear one-to-one and self adjoint on $\mathcal{a}$, and satisfies: $\Psi(TS)=\Psi(S)\Psi(T)$ $T,S \in g$. An anti-isomorphism Ψ will be said to be implemented by (W,φ) (where W is in $V(\mathcal{a})$ and φ is a map from G to $\mathcal{a}$) if for A in $\mathcal{a}$, $\Psi(A)=W^*AW$ and, for U in G, $\Psi(U) = W^*U^*\varphi(U)W$.

Proposition 3.15.: Let $\Psi: g \longrightarrow g^*$ be an anti-isomorphism implemented by (I,φ). Assume that the conditions of Theorem 3.13 are fulfilled then Ψ is bounded.

Proof: With T in g^*, let $\tau(T)$ be T^* and let Ψ_1 be $\tau\cdot\Psi$. Then Ψ_1 is multiplicative and conjugate-linear. If $A \in \mathcal{a}$, $U \in G$ then $\Psi_1(A) = A^*$, and $\Psi_1(U) = \varphi(U)^*U$.

The proof of Theorem 3.13 now applies to Ψ_1 with minor changes. In the present case, the operator V_0 is conjugate-linear; and $g(\Psi(T)^*\,\Psi(T)) = g(\sum U^*\varphi(U)A_U A_U^*\varphi(U)^*U) = \sum g(A_U A_U^*|\varphi(U)|^2)$. As in Theorem 3.13, we conclude that $V\Pi'(T)V^{-1} = \Pi'(\Psi_1(T))$; so that $||\Psi_1(T)|| = ||\Pi'(\Psi_1(T))|| \leq N^{-1}M||T||$. ###

Proposition 3.16.: The mapping Ψ defined by: $\Psi(AU) = U^*A$, for A in $\mathcal{a}$, U in G, is an anti-isomorphism of g onto g^*. If conditions (1), (2) of Theorem 3.13 are satisfied, then Ψ can be extended to a *-anti-isomorphism on $\mathcal{B}(\mathcal{a},G)$.

Proof.: From $\mathcal{a}$-invariance of G,Ψ is well defined (and linear). If $A,B\in\mathcal{a}$ and $U,V\in G$ then $\Psi(AU(BV)) = \Psi(AUBU^*UV) = V^*U^*AUBU^* = (V^*BU^*AUU^* = (V^*B)(U^*A)$

$$= \Psi(BV)\ \Psi(AU)\ .$$

By linearity, then, Ψ is an anti-isomorphism. Since Ψ satisfies the conditions of Proposition 3.15 (where $\varphi(U) = I$ for each U in G), Ψ is bounded (and $||\Psi|| = 1$).

Let $\Psi_0(S_1+S_2^*)$ be $\Psi(S_1) + \Psi(S_2)^*$, when $S_1,S_2\in g$. Then Ψ_0 is a $*$-anti-automorphism of $g+g^*$. Note, too, that, with $\sum A_jU_j$ the (unique) representation of T in $g+g^*$ where $A_j\in\mathcal{a}$ and $\{U_j\}$ are distinct elements of $\bar{G}$, we have

$$\Psi_0(\Psi_0(T)) = \Psi_0(\sum U_j^*A_j) = \sum A_jU_j = T.$$

Moreover, we can choose U in G such that $TU\in g$. Then

$$\Psi(TU) = \Psi_0(TU) = \Psi_0(U)\ \Psi_0(T) = \Psi(U)\ \Psi_0(T) = U^*\Psi_0(T)\quad ;$$

so that

$$||\Psi_0(T)|| = ||\Psi(TU)|| \leq ||TU|| = ||T||.$$

Hence $||T|| = ||\Psi_0(\Psi_0(T))|| \leq ||\Psi_0(T)||$, and Ψ_0 is an isometry on $g+g^*$. It follows that Ψ_0 (and, hence, Ψ) extends to a $*$-anti-automorphism of $\mathcal{B}(\mathcal{a},G)$. ###

In [49, Theorem 6.4] E. Størmer proved the following: Let m and R be two unital C*-algebras and let $\Psi:m \longrightarrow R$ be a linear map satisfying:

(1) $\Psi(I) = I$.

(2) Ψ is positive.

(3) For any positive B in R, $\Psi^{-1}(B)$ contains a positive operator.

(4) $m_*\cap\mathrm{Ker}\,\Psi$ is linearily generated by the positive elements, where $m_*=\{A\in m:\ A=A^*\}$

(5) Ψ is surjective.

Then, for any irreducible representation Π of R, the map $\Pi\cdot\Psi$ is a $*$-homomorphism or a $*$-anti-homomorphism.

Let $\mathcal{B}(\mathcal{a}_1,G_1)$ and $\mathcal{B}(\mathcal{a}_2,G_2)$ be the C*-algebras generated by the irreducible triangular algebras $\mathcal{g}_1$ and $\mathcal{g}_2$ respectively. Application of the result mentioned above gives:

Corollary 3.17.: Let Ψ be a linear isometry from $\mathcal{B}(\mathcal{a}_1,G_1)$ onto $\mathcal{B}(\mathcal{a}_2,G_2)$ which maps I into I. Then Ψ is either a *-isomorphism or a *-anti-isomorphism.

Proof.: Apply the result of Størmer to the identity representation. The conditions are satisfied because any isometry between C*-algebras is positive.

###

Similarily to what we showed for an isomorphism in Proposition 3.5 we can show that if Ψ is a *-anti-isomorphism from $\mathcal{g}+\mathcal{g}^*$ onto itself, mapping $\mathcal{a}$ onto $\mathcal{a}$, then it is implemented by some (W,φ). Also, we can prove Proposition 3.9 for a *-anti-isomorphism. Hence a *-anti-isomorphism on $\mathcal{B}(\mathcal{a},G)$ that maps $\mathcal{a}$ onto itself can be reduced to a *-anti-isomorphism on $\mathcal{g}+\mathcal{g}^*$. All this immediately implies the following:

Corollary 3.18.: Let Ψ be an isometry from $\mathcal{B}(\mathcal{a},G)$ onto itself that maps $\mathcal{a}$ onto $\mathcal{a}$ and I into I. Then there are a unitary operator $W \in V(\mathcal{a})$ and a map φ from G into $\mathcal{a}$ such that $\Psi(A) = W^*AW$ for A in $\mathcal{a}$, and for each U in G, $\Psi(U) = W^*\varphi(U)UW$ or $\Psi(U) = W^*U^*\varphi(U)W$. ###

The order is preserved by isomorphisms

In chapter II we defined an ordering on the group $M(\mathcal{g})$, with $N(\mathcal{g})$ its positive cone. We will see that an isomorphism preserves this ordering. Let $\mathcal{g}_1$, $\mathcal{g}_2$ be irreducible triangular algebras generated by $\mathcal{a}_1$, G_1 and $\mathcal{a}_2,G_2$ respectively. Throughout this section, Ψ will be an isomorphism from $\mathcal{g}_1$ onto $\mathcal{g}_2$ implemented by (W,φ).

We will denote by Φ_1 and Φ_2 the Arveson expectations onto $\mathcal{a}_1$ and $\mathcal{a}_2$ respectively.

Proposition 3.19.: The isomorphism Ψ maps $N(\mathcal{g}_1)$ onto $N(\mathcal{g}_2)$. If Ψ can be extended to a $*$-isomorphism from $\mathcal{G}_1+\mathcal{G}_1^*$ onto $\mathcal{G}_2+\mathcal{G}_2^*$ then this extension maps $M(\mathcal{G}_1)$ onto $M(\mathcal{G}_2)$.

Proof.: An element in $N(\mathcal{G}_1)$ has the form AV, where A is invertible in $\mathcal{a}_1$, $V \in V(\mathcal{a}_1) \cap \mathcal{G}_1$, and (from Lemma 2.11) we can write $V = \sum F_iU_i$ where U_i are in G_1, and F_i are projections in $\mathcal{a}_1$ with sum I. Since $F_iF_j = 0$, $i \neq j$, $F_iV = F_iU_i$ and: $\Psi(AV)=W^*A(\sum\varphi(U_i)F_iU_i)W=W^*A(\sum\varphi(U_i)F_i)VW=BW^*VW$, where $B=W^*A(\sum\varphi(U_i)F_i)W$. Moreover, B is an invertible element of $\mathcal{a}_2$ because A and $\varphi(U_i)$ are invertible (cf. Proposition 3.5) and $\sum F_i = I$.

Since $\Psi|\mathcal{a}$ is adjoint preserving, $\Psi(\mathcal{a}_1) \subseteq \mathcal{a}_2$. By definition of "implementation", $W^*\mathcal{G}_1W = \mathcal{G}_2$, so that $W\mathcal{a}_2W^* \subseteq \mathcal{G}_1$ and, as $W\mathcal{a}_2W^*$ is self adjoint, $W\mathcal{a}_2W^* \subseteq \mathcal{a}_1$. Thus $\Psi(\mathcal{a}_1) = W^*\mathcal{a}_1W = \mathcal{a}_2$.

For any C in $\mathcal{a}_2$, WCW^* is in $\mathcal{a}_1$, hence V^*WCW^*V is in $\mathcal{a}_1$ and $W^*V^*WCW^*VW$ is in $\mathcal{a}_2$, hence W^*VW is in $V(\mathcal{a}_2) \cap \mathcal{G}_2$. Thus Ψ maps $N(\mathcal{G}_1)$ into $N(\mathcal{G}_2)$. Now Ψ^{-1} is an isomorphism of $\mathcal{G}_2$ onto $\mathcal{G}_1$; and we have just noted that Ψ restricted to $\mathcal{a}_1$ is a $*$-isomorphism of $\mathcal{a}_1$ onto $\mathcal{a}_2$ so that Ψ^{-1} restricted to $\mathcal{a}_2$ is a $*$-isomorphism of $\mathcal{a}_2$ onto $\mathcal{a}_1$. From Proposition 3.2, Ψ^{-1} is implemented by (W^*,φ'); and, by what we have proved, Ψ^{-1} maps $N(\mathcal{G}_2)$ into $N(\mathcal{G}_1)$. Hence Ψ maps $N(\mathcal{G}_1)$ onto $N(\mathcal{G}_2)$.

For the second assertion of this proposition, note that if Ψ extends to a $*$-isomorphism Ψ' of $\mathcal{G}_1+\mathcal{G}_1^*$ onto $\mathcal{G}_2+\mathcal{G}_2^*$ and $U \in V(\mathcal{a}_1) \cap (\mathcal{G}_1+\mathcal{G}_1^*)$ then $\Psi(U) \in V(\mathcal{a}_2) \cap (\mathcal{G}_2+\mathcal{G}_2^*)$; for each operator in $\mathcal{a}_2$ has the form, $\Psi(A)$, with A in $\mathcal{a}_1$, and

$$\Psi(U)^*\Psi(A)\Psi(U) = \Psi(U^*AU) \in \mathcal{a}_2.$$

Thus, with AU in $M(\mathcal{G}_1)$, $\Psi(AU) \in M(\mathcal{G}_2)$. It follows (applying the same considerations to Ψ^{-1}) that Ψ maps $M(\mathcal{G}_1)$ onto $M(\mathcal{G}_2)$. ###

In connection with the preceding proposition, recall (from Proposition 3.1) that Ψ extends to a $*$-isomorphism of $\mathcal{G}_1+\mathcal{G}_1^*$ if and only if $\Psi(U)$ is unitary for each U in G_1. As a consequence, we have:

Corollary 3.20.: If Ψ is an isomorphism of $\mathcal{G}_1$ onto $\mathcal{G}_2$ and S,T in

$N(\mathcal{g}_1)$ satisfy $S > T$ then $\Psi(S) > \Psi(T)$.

If Ψ is an isomorphism (not necessarily *-) of $\mathcal{g}_1+\mathcal{g}_1^*$ onto $\mathcal{g}_2+\mathcal{g}_2^*$ that maps $\mathcal{g}_1$ onto $\mathcal{g}_2$ and S,T in $M(\mathcal{g}_1)$ satisfy $S > T$ then $\Psi(S) > \Psi(T)$.

Lemma 3.21.: For any T in $\mathcal{g}_1$ $\Phi_2 \cdot \Psi(T) = \Psi \cdot \Phi_1(T)$. If Ψ can be extended to a *-isomorphism of $\mathcal{g}_1+\mathcal{g}_1^*$ then the equality holds for any T in $\mathcal{g}_1+\mathcal{g}_1^*$ and if it can be further extended to a *-isomorphism of $\mathcal{B}(\mathcal{a},G)$ then it will hold for any T in $\mathcal{B}(\mathcal{a},G)$.

Proof: It is enough to prove the statement concerning $\mathcal{g}_1$. The statements about $\mathcal{g}_1+\mathcal{g}_1^*$ and $\mathcal{B}(\mathcal{a},G)$ will follow from self-adjointness and norm continuity of $\Phi_2 \cdot \Psi$ and $\Psi \cdot \Phi_1$.

Let $T = \sum A_i U_i$, where $A_i \in \mathcal{a}$, $U_i \in G_1$, and $U_0 = I$. Then $\Psi(T) = W^*(\sum A_i \varphi(U_i) U_i)W = \sum W^* A_i \varphi(U_i) W(W^* U_i W)$. If $\Phi_2(W^*U_iW) \neq 0$ there is a non zero projection P in $\mathcal{a}_2$ such that $E\Phi_2(W^*U_iW) = 0$ for each non zero subprojection E of P in $\mathcal{a}_2$. But then $0 \neq E\Phi_2(W^*U_iW) = E\Phi_2(W^*U_iW)E = \Phi_2(EW^*U_iWE) = \Phi_2(W^*WEW^*U_iWEW^*W)$, for such subprojection E. In particular $0 \neq FU_iF$ for each subprojection $F(=WEW^*)$, in $\mathcal{a}_1$, of Q $(=WPW^*)$. Hence $0 \neq FU_iFU_i^*$ for each such F - contradicting the assumption that U_i acts freely on $\mathcal{a}_1$. Thus $\Phi_2(W^*U_iW) = 0$ for each i; and $\Phi_2(\Psi(T)) = W^*A_0W$.
On the other hand, $\Phi_1(T) = A_0$; so that

$$\Psi(\Phi_1)(T)) = W^*A_0W = \Phi_2(\Psi(T)).$$ ###

Corollary 3.22.: If the isomorphism Ψ of $\mathcal{g}_1$ onto $\mathcal{g}_2$ extends to a *-isomorphism of $\mathcal{B}(\mathcal{a}_1,G_1)$ onto $\mathcal{B}(\mathcal{a}_2,G_2)$ then Φ_2 is faithful if and only if Φ_1 is faithful. If, in addition, G_1 and G_2 are unitary semigroups arising from measure preserving transformations of a finite measure space, then G_1 is amenable if and only if G_2 is amenable.

Proof: Since $\Phi_2 \cdot \Psi' = \Psi' \cdot \Phi_1$, where Ψ' is the extension of Ψ to a *-isomorphism of $\mathcal{B}(\mathcal{a}_1,G_1)$ onto $\mathcal{B}(\mathcal{a}_2,G_2)$, from the preceding lemma; Φ_2 is faithful if and only if Φ_1 is faithful. From Proposition 2.7, the discussion following it, and Proposition 2.8, with G_1 and G_2 semigroups of measure preserving transformations, G_1 is amenable if and only if Φ_1 is faithful and G_2 is amenable if and only if Φ_2 is faithful. Thus, in this case, G_1 is amenable if and only if G_2 is amenable. ###

Corollary 3.23.: If Ψ is an isomorphism and $N(\mathcal{G}_1)$ has a smallest element T, then $\Psi(T)$ is a smallest element in $N(\mathcal{G}_2)$. If R is another smallest element in $N(\mathcal{G}_2)$ then $\Psi(T)$ is in $\mathcal{A}_2R$.

Proof: By Lemma 3.21 we see that $\Phi_1(T) = 0$, for T in $\mathcal{G}_1$, if and only if $\Phi_2(\Psi(T)) = 0$. This, with Proposition 3.19, Corollary 3.20, and the definition of a smallest element, completes the proof. ###

Similarily we can get, from the results of Chapter II:

Corollary 3.24.: If Ψ is an isomorphism:

(1) G_1 is integrally closed if and only if G_2 is.

(2) G_1 has a minimal element if and only if G_2 has one.

(3) G_1 is singly generated if and only if G_2 is.

Proof:

(1) is a result of Proposition 2.27 and the fact that the isomorphism is multiplicative and order preserving.

(2) is a result of Lemma 2.24 and Corollary 3.23.

(3) is a result of Corollary 3.21, Proposition 2.27, and Corollary 2.28.

###

From the preceding we learn that an algebra generated by a singly generated semigroup cannot be isomorphic to an algebra whose semigourp is not singly generated. This gives us many examples of non isomorphic irreducible triangular algebras.

In the following example we will construct two non isomorphic irreducible triangular algebras. The semigroups that generate them are each generated by two operators and the two algebras generate the same self adjoint algebra.

Example 3.25.: Let H be the Hilbert space $L^2(\mathbb{T})$, and $\mathcal{a}$ be the maximal abelian algebra of multiplication by functions in $L^\infty(\mathbb{T})$. Let r and s be two real irrational numbers satisfying $(\mathbb{Z}r + \mathbb{Z}s) \cap \mathbb{Z} = \{0\}$ (e.g. $r=\sqrt{2}$, $s=\sqrt{3}$).

Let U and V be the following operators:

$$Uf(e^{2\pi it}) = f(e^{2\pi i(t-r)})$$

$$Vf(e^{2\pi it}) = f(e^{2\pi i(t-s)}).$$

Define two semigroups:

$G_1 = \{V^kU^n : k,n \in \mathbb{Z}, k > 0 \text{ or } k=0 \text{ and } n \geq 0\}$.

$G_2 = \{V^kU^n : k,n \in \mathbb{Z}, n+k\sqrt{2} \geq 0\}$.

For each pair (k,n) in $\mathbb{Z}\times\mathbb{Z}\setminus\{(0,0)\}$, the operator V^kU^n corresponds to the translation by $ks+nr$; this number is irrational (as $(\mathbb{Z}s+\mathbb{Z}r)\cap\mathbb{Z}=\{0\}$) hence V^kU^n acts freely and ergodically on $\mathcal{a}$ (see Example 1.8). Thus G_1 and G_2 each acts freely and ergodically on $\mathcal{a}$.

Since $G_1^* \cup G_1 = \{V^kU^n: (k,n) \in \mathbb{Z}\times\mathbb{Z}\}$ and U commutes with V, $G_1^* \cup G_1$ $(=\bar{G}_1)$ is a group homomorphic to the additive group $\mathbb{Z}\times\mathbb{Z}$ via the homomorphism $\tau(k,n) = V^kU^n$.

As $(\mathbb{Z}r+\mathbb{Z}s) \cap \mathbb{Z} = \{0\}$, $V^kU^n = I$ only if $n=k=0$. Hence τ is an isomorphism.

Define the lexicographic ordering on $\mathbb{Z}\times\mathbb{Z}$ by: $(k,n) \geq (1,m)$ if $k > 1$ or $k=1$ and $n \geq m$.

The positive cone of this ordering is the set p of all pairs (k,n) such that $k > 0$ or $k = 0$ and $n \geq 0$. From the definition of G_1, τ maps p onto G_1. Since $p\cap(-p) = \{(0,0)\}$, $G_1 \cap G_1^{-1} = \{I\}$, hence G_1 is an ordered semigroup, order-isomorphic to p. The pair $(0,1)$ is minimal in $p\setminus\{(0,0)\}$ hence U $(=\tau(0,1))$ is a minimal element in G_1.

Thus G_1 is an ordered semigroup, with a minimal element, that acts freely and ergodically on $\mathcal{a}$. It gives rise to an irreducible triangular algebra $\mathcal{g}_1$ (by Corollary 1.5).

For G_2, let Λ be the set $\mathbb{Z}+\sqrt{2}\mathbb{Z}$ $(\subseteq \mathbb{R})$ and define a map $\eta:\Lambda \longrightarrow G_2 \cup G_2^{-1}(=\bar{G}_2)$ by $\eta(n+k\sqrt{2}) = V^kU^n$. As $\mathbb{Z}\cap\mathbb{Z}\sqrt{2} = \{0\}$, η is well defined and is a homomorphism from Λ (an additive group) onto $\bar{G}_2$.
If $n+k\sqrt{2} \neq 0$ then $(n,k) \neq (0,0)$, hence $V^kU^n \neq I$; so that η is an isomorphism.
If we let Λ have the ordering induced from $\mathbb{R}$ then, by the definition of G_2, η preserves the ordering and maps the set of non negative numbers in Λ (to be denoted by Λ_+) onto G_2. Since $\Lambda_+\cap(-\Lambda_+) = \{0\}$, $G_2 \cap G_2^{-1} = \{I\}$; so that G_2 is an ordered semigroup. To see that G_2 has no minimal element, let $\{r_k\}$ be a sequence of rational numbers such that $r_k \longrightarrow \sqrt{2}$ and $r_k > \sqrt{2}$ for each k. For each k, let m_k, n_k be positive integers such that $r_k = m_k/n_k$, then $m_k/n_k - \sqrt{2} \longrightarrow 0$ and $m_k/n_k - \sqrt{2} > 0$, hence $m_k - n_k\sqrt{2} \longrightarrow 0$ and $m_k - n_k\sqrt{2} \in \Lambda_+\setminus\{0\}$.
Thus $\Lambda_+\setminus\{0\}$ has no minimal number, hence G_2 has no minimal element.
The semigroup G_2 acts freely and ergodically on $\mathcal{a}$ and gives rise to an irreducible triangular algebra $\mathcal{g}_2$.

Since G_1 has a minimal element and G_2 has no such element, Corollary 3.24 implies that $\mathcal{g}_1$ is not isomorphic to $\mathcal{g}_2$.

CHAPTER IV: AUTOMORPHISMS AND DERIVATIONS

In this chapter we will study groups of *-automorphisms on $\mathcal{B}(\mathcal{a},G)$ (where $\mathcal{a}$ is a maximal abelian algebra and G is a semigroup of unitary operators acting freely and ergodically on $\mathcal{a}$) that map $\mathcal{a}$ onto itself, and their relationship to derivations of $\mathcal{B}(\mathcal{a},G)$ (or $\mathcal{g}+\mathcal{g}^*$) that vanish on $\mathcal{a}$.

We will use the notions of spectrum and spectral spaces, and the theory introduced by Arveson in [5].

Let $\mathrm{Aut}(\mathcal{B},\mathcal{a})$ denote the group of *-automorphisms Ψ on $\mathcal{B}(\mathcal{a},G)$ satisfying $\Psi(A) = A$ for each A in $\mathcal{a}$. By Corollary 3.8 (2) every Ψ in $\mathrm{Aut}(\mathcal{B},\mathcal{a})$ is implemented by some (W,φ'). Since $A = \Psi(A) = W^*AW$, $W \in \mathcal{a}' = \mathcal{a}$ and $\Psi(U)$ $(=W^*\varphi'(U)UW = W^*\varphi'(U)UWU^*)U)$ is in $\mathcal{a}U$ for each U in $\bar{G}$. Letting $\varphi(U)$ be $W^*\varphi'(U)UWU^*$ we conclude that Ψ is implemented by (I,φ).

Throughout the chapter Λ will denote a locally compact abelian group with a Haar measure m. We denote by $L^1(\Lambda)$ the (classes of) m-integrable functions on Λ. With the norm $||f||_1 = \int_\Lambda |f(t)\, dm(t)$ the space $L^1(\Lambda)$ is a Banach space.

Let $M(\Lambda)$ denote the Banach space of all complex finite regular Borel measures on Λ with the total variation as the norm. For each f in $L^1(\Lambda)$ the measure $f(t)dm(t)$ is in $M(\Lambda)$ and its total variation equals $||f||_1$.

For a Banach space X let $X^\#$ be the dual space; i.e. the space of all linear bounded functionals on X. With the norm $||g|| = \mathrm{Sup}\,\{|g(x)|$: $x \in X$, $||x|| \leq 1\}$ $X^\#$ is a Banach space.

The following result is a special case of Proposition 1.2 of [5] and will be stated here without a proof.

Proposition 4.1.: Let X be a Banach space and let β be a map from the group Λ into X such that $\mathrm{Sup}\{||\beta(t)|| : t \in \Lambda\} < \infty$. Assume that for each

g in $X^{\#}$ the map $t \longrightarrow g(\beta(t))$ is continuous, then, for each μ in $M(\Lambda)$, there is a vector x in X such that for every g in $X^{\#}$ $g(x) = \int_{\Lambda} g(\beta(t))d\mu(t)$.

We will employ the usual notation for this integral:

$$x = \int_{\Lambda} \beta(t)d\mu(t).$$

The vector x, above, is unique with this property since the functionals in $X^{\#}$ separate vectors in X.

Let α be a homomorphism from Λ into $\mathrm{Aut}(\mathcal{B},\mathcal{a})$ such that for every T in $\mathcal{B}(\mathcal{a},G)$ the map $t \longrightarrow \alpha_t(T)$ is norm-continuous. As noted above, for every t in Λ, α_t is implemented by (I,φ_t) for some map φ_t from $\bar{G}$ into $\mathcal{a}$.

If U is in $\bar{G}$ and t,s are in Λ then

$$\varphi_{t+s}(U) = \alpha_{t+s}(U)U^* = \alpha_t(\alpha_s(U))U^* = \alpha_t(\varphi_s(U)U)U^* = \alpha_t(\varphi_s(U))\ \alpha_t(U)U^*$$
$$= \varphi_s(U)\ \varphi_t(U).$$

Thus the map $t \longrightarrow \varphi_t(U)$ is a homomorphism for each U in $\bar{G}$. we will denote this homomorphism by φ_U.

Corollary 4.2.:

(1) For every μ in $M(\Lambda)$ and T in $\mathcal{B}(\mathcal{a},G)$ there is a unique bounded operator $\alpha_\mu(T)$ in $\mathcal{B}(\mathcal{a},G)$ such that for each g in $\mathcal{B}(\mathcal{a},G)^{\#}$

$$g(\alpha_\mu(T)) = \int_{\Lambda} g(\alpha_t(T))d\mu(t).$$

(2) For every μ in $M(\Lambda)$ and U in $\bar{G}$ there is a unique bounded operator $\varphi_\mu(U)$ in $\mathcal{a}$ such that for each g in $\mathcal{a}^{\#}$

$$g(\varphi_\mu(U)) = \int_{\Lambda} g(\varphi_t(U))d\mu(t).$$

Proof: For (1) apply Proposition 4.1 with $\mathcal{B}(\mathcal{a},G)$ in place of X and $\alpha_t(T)$ in place of $\beta(t)$. For (2) apply the same proposition with $\mathcal{a}$ in place of X and φ_U in place of β (since $\varphi_U(t) = \alpha_t(U)U^*$; φ_U is norm-continuous). ###

We will write $\alpha_\mu(T) = \int_{\Lambda}\alpha_t(T)d\mu(t)$

and $\varphi_\mu(U) = \int_{\Lambda} \varphi_t(U)d\mu(t)$.

We will write $\hat{\Lambda}$ for the dual group of Λ ; i.e. $\hat{\Lambda}$ is the group of all characters of Λ.

Equipped with the topology of uniform convergence on compact subsets of Λ, the dual group $\hat{\Lambda}$ is a locally compact abelian group.

For f in $L^1(\Lambda)$ we write

$\hat{f}(\tau) = \int_\Lambda \tau(t)f(t)dm(t)$ for $\tau \in \hat{\Lambda}$ (Fourier transform).

Let $K(\Lambda)$ denote the dense ideal of $L^1(\Lambda)$ consisting of the functions f whose Fourier transform has a compact support (in $\hat{\Lambda}$). We will write Supp f for the support of $\hat{f}$ (in $\hat{\Lambda}$).

By the w-topology on $\mathcal{B}(\mathcal{a},G)$ we mean the weak topology induced by the dual of $\mathcal{B}(\mathcal{a},G)$ i.e. T_n tend to T in this topology if and only if $g(T_n)$ tend to $g(T)$ for each linear bounded functional g on $\mathcal{B}(\mathcal{a},G)$.

Let Ω be an open set in $\hat{\Lambda}$. Denote by $K(\Lambda,\Omega)$ the set of functions f in $K(\Lambda)$ such that the support of $\hat{f}$ is contained in Ω, and define $R^\alpha(\Omega)$ to be the w-closed (equivalently norm-closed) linear space spanned by the set of all operators of the form $\alpha_f(T)$ for T in $\mathcal{B}(\mathcal{a},G)$ and f in $K(\Lambda,\Omega)$.

Lemma 4.3.: For every μ in $M(\Lambda)$, U in $\bar{G}$, and A in $\mathcal{a}$

$\alpha_\mu(AU) = A\varphi_\mu(U)U$.

Proof.: Fix U in $\bar{G}$, A in $\mathcal{a}$, and μ in $M(\Lambda)$. For g in $\mathcal{B}^\#$:

$g(\alpha_\mu(AU)) = \int_\Lambda g(\alpha_t(AU))d\mu(t) = \int_\Lambda g(A\varphi_t(U)U)d\mu(t)$.

Let g_0, in the dual of $\mathcal{a}$, be defined by $g_0(B) = g(BAU)$. As g is linear, g_0 is linear and $|g_0(B)| = |g(BAU)| \leq ||g||\ ||B||\ ||A||$; so that g_0 is in $\mathcal{a}^\#$.

By the definition of $\varphi_\mu(U)$ we now have:

$g(\alpha_\mu(AU)) = \int_\Lambda g_0(\varphi_t(U))d\mu(t) = g_0(\varphi_\mu(U)) = g(A\ \varphi_\mu(U)U)$.

Since this holds for each g in the dual of $\mathcal{B}(\mathcal{a},G)$ we obtain

$\alpha_\mu(AU) = A\varphi_\mu(U)U$. ###

Lemma 4.4.: For each open subset Ω of $\hat{\Lambda}$, $R^\alpha(\Omega)$ is the w-closed linear space spanned by the operators of the form $A\alpha_f(U)U$ where f is in $K(\Lambda,\Omega)$. A in $\mathcal{a}$, and U is in $\bar{G}$.

Proof.: Since $\alpha_f(AU) = A\varphi_f(U)U$, the operators of this form are in $R^{\alpha}(\Lambda)$, for f in $K(\Lambda,\Omega)$, A in $\mathcal{a}$ and U in $\bar{G}$. Denote the w-closed linear space they span by R'. Hence $R' \subseteq R^{\alpha}(\Lambda)$ and it will suffice to prove that $R^{\alpha}(\Lambda) \subseteq R'$.

Any T in $g+g^*$ can be expressed as $\sum_{i=1}^{n} A_i U_i$ where A_1 are in $\mathcal{a}$ and U_i are in $\bar{G}$. Thus $\alpha_f(T) = \sum_{i=1}^{n} A_i \varphi_f(U_i) U_i$ hence $\alpha_f(T)$ is in R'. Let T be in $\mathcal{B}(\mathcal{a},G)$. Then there are operators T_n in $g+g^*$ tending in norm to T. Now,, $\alpha_f(T)$ is an element of $\mathcal{B}(\mathcal{a},G)$ such that

$g(\alpha_f(T)) = \int_{\Lambda} g(\alpha_t(T)) f(t) dm(t)$ for each g in $\mathcal{B}(\mathcal{a},G)^{\#}$. If $||g|| \leq 1$ then $|g(\alpha_f(T))| = |\int_{\Lambda} g(\alpha_t(T)) f(t) dm(t)| \leq \int_{\Lambda} |g(\alpha_t(T))| |f(t)| dm(t) \leq$

$||T||\ ||f||_1$.

Since this holds for each g in the unit ball of $\mathcal{B}^{\#}$,

$$||\alpha_f(T)|| \leq ||T||\ ||f||_1.$$

From the defining property of α_μ, for μ in $M(\Lambda)$, α_μ is a linear mapping of $\mathcal{B}(\mathcal{a},G)$ into itself. The preceding inequality tells us that

$||\alpha_f|| \leq ||f||_1$. Hence $\alpha_f(T_n)$ tends to $\alpha_f(T)$ in norm and therefore also in the w-topology. Thus, for each T in $\mathcal{B}(\mathcal{a},G)$ and each f in $K(\Lambda,\Omega)$, $\alpha_f(T)$ is in R'. Since those operators span $R^{\alpha}(\Omega)$, $R^{\alpha}(\Omega)$ is contained in R'. ###

For a closed subset Z of $\hat{\Lambda}$ we define $M^{\alpha}(Z)$ to be the set of all operators T in $\mathcal{B}(\mathcal{a},G)$ such that $\alpha_f(T) = 0$ for each f in $K(\Lambda,\hat{\Lambda}\setminus Z)$.

Let T in $g+g^*$ be $\sum A_U U$, then T is in $M^{\alpha}(Z)$ if and only if $\sum \varphi_f(U) A_U U = 0$ for all f in $K(\Lambda,\hat{\Lambda}\setminus Z)$, Hence T is in $M^{\alpha}(Z)$ if and only if for every f in $K(\Lambda,\hat{\Lambda}\setminus Z)$ $\varphi_f(U)A_U = 0$. We, therefore, conclude:

Lemma 4.5: $M^{\alpha}(Z) = \mathcal{B}(\mathcal{a},G)$ if and only if for each f in $K(\Lambda,\hat{\Lambda}\setminus Z)$ and each U in $\bar{G}$, $\varphi_f(U) = 0$.

Proof: If $M^{\alpha}(Z) = \mathcal{B}(\mathcal{a},G)$ then, for each f in $K(\Lambda,\hat{\Lambda}\setminus Z)$ and each $T(=\sum A_U U)$

in $\mathcal{g}+\mathcal{g}^*$, $\varphi_f(U)A_U = 0$. Hence $\varphi_f(U) = 0$ for each U in G.

For the other direction, note that $M^\alpha(Z)$ is closed in the norm topology hence it will suffice to show that each T in $\mathcal{g}+\mathcal{g}^*$ is in $M^\alpha(Z)$. The discussion preceding this lemma completes the proof. ###

The <u>spectrum</u> of α is defined as the smallest closee set Z in Λ such that $M^\alpha(Z) = \mathcal{B}(\mathcal{a},G)$ and is denoted by $sp(\alpha)$. For the spectrum of an operator T we will use the notation $\sigma(T)$.

Let Λ be $\mathbb{R}$ and fix U in $\bar{G}$, then $t \longrightarrow \varphi_t(U)$ is a norm continuous one parameter unitary group. Hence there is a self adjoint operator $C(U)$ in $\mathcal{a}$ such that $\varphi_t(U) = \exp(itC(U))$ by [11, Theorem VII, 1.2]).

<u>Theorem 4.6.:</u> Let $t \longrightarrow \alpha_t$ be a homomorphism from $\mathbb{R}$ into $\mathrm{Aut}(\mathcal{B},\mathcal{a})$ implemented by (I,φ_t), such that for each T in $\mathcal{B}(\mathcal{a},G)$ the map $t \longrightarrow \alpha_t(T)$ is norm continuous. For U in $\bar{G}$, let $C(U)$ be the operator in $\mathcal{a}$ such that $\exp(itC(U)) = \varphi_t(U)$, then $sp(\alpha) = \overline{\cup_{U \in \bar{G}} \sigma(C(U))}$ where $\bar{Y}$ denotes the closure of the set Y.

<u>Proof.</u>: a) Fix U in $\bar{G}$. If t' is in $\sigma(C(U))$ but not in $sp(\alpha)$ then there is f in $K(\mathbb{R})$ with $\hat{f}(t)=1$ and $\mathrm{Supp}\ f \subseteq \mathbb{R} \setminus sp(\alpha)$. Since $M^\alpha(sp(\alpha))$ is $\mathcal{B}(\mathcal{a},G)$, Lemma 4.5 implies that $\varphi_f(U)=0$; hence $0=\varphi_f(U)=\int \varphi_t(U)f(t)dm(t)=\int_{\mathbb{R}} \exp(it\ (C(U)))f(t)dm(t)$. Let τ be a pure state of $\mathcal{a}$ and let s be $\tau(C(U))$ then:

$$0 = \tau(\varphi_f(U)) = \int_{\mathbb{R}} \exp(it\ \tau(C(U)))f(t)dm(t)$$
$$= \int_{\mathbb{R}} \exp(its)f(t)dm(t) = \hat{f}(s).$$

But, since t' is in $\sigma(C(U))$, $t' = \tau(C(U))$ for some pure state τ, therefore $\hat{f}(t') = 0$. This contradicts the choice of t' and the contradiction proves that $\sigma(C(U))$ is contained in $sp(\alpha)$.

Since U is an arbitrary member of $\bar{G}$ and since $sp(\alpha)$ is closed, $\overline{\cup_{U \in \bar{G}} \sigma(C(U))} \subseteq sp(\alpha)$.

b) Let f be in $K(\mathbb{R})$ with $\mathrm{Supp}\ \hat{f}$ contained in $\overline{\cup_{U \in \bar{G}} \sigma(C(U))}$, then for each U in $\bar{G}$. $\mathrm{Supp}\ \hat{f} \subseteq \mathbb{R} \setminus \overline{\sigma(C(U))}$.

Fix U in $\bar{G}$, then for each pure state τ of $\mathcal{a}$ $\tau(\varphi_f(U)) = \hat{f}(\tau(C(U))) = 0$, thus $\varphi_f(U) = 0$.

Since this holds for each U in $\bar{G}$, it implies, by Lemma 4.5, that $M^{\alpha}(\overline{\cup_{U \in \bar{G}} \sigma(C(U))}) = \mathcal{B}(\mathcal{a},G)$. Hence $sp(\alpha) \subseteq \overline{\cup_{U \in \bar{G}} \sigma(C(U))}$ and the proof is complete. ###

Proposition 4.7.: Let α_1 be a *-automorphism in $Aut(\mathcal{B},\mathcal{a})$ and let α be the homomorphism from $\mathbb{Z}$ into $Aut(\mathcal{B},\mathcal{a})$ that maps n into α_1^n. If α_1 is implemented by (I,φ) then $sp(\alpha) = \overline{\cup_{U \in \bar{G}} \sigma(\varphi(U))}$.

Proof: The proof is similar to the proof of the preceding theorem.

a) If t is in $\mathbb{T} \setminus sp(\alpha)$ there is some f in $K(\mathbb{Z})$ with $\hat{f}(t) = 1$ and $Supp\ \hat{f} \subseteq \mathbb{T} \setminus sp(\alpha)$. By Lemma 4.5, applied to $Z = sp(\alpha)$, $\varphi_f(U) = 0$ hence $0 = \varphi_f(U) = \sum_{n=-\infty}^{\infty} \varphi_n(U) f(n)$.

Since $n \longrightarrow \varphi_n(U)$ is a homomorphism (see the discussion preceding Corollary 4.2) and $\varphi(U) = \varphi_1(U)$, $\varphi_n(U) = \varphi(U)^n$ for each n in $\mathbb{Z}$ and each U in $\bar{G}$. Let τ be a pure state of $\mathcal{a}$, and let s be $\tau(\varphi(U))$, then

$$0 = \tau(\varphi_f(U)) = \sum \tau(\varphi(U))^n f(n) = \sum s^n f(n) = f(s).$$

But, if t is in the spectrum of $\varphi(U)$ $(\subseteq \mathbb{T})$, t equals $\tau(\varphi(U))$ for some pure state τ of $\mathcal{a}$; and $\hat{f}(t) = 0$. This contradicts the choice of f and proves that, for each U in $\bar{G}$, $\sigma(\varphi(U)) \subseteq sp(\alpha)$.

Since $sp(\alpha)$ is closed, $\overline{\cup_{U \in \bar{G}} \sigma(\varphi(U))} \subseteq sp(\alpha)$.

b) Let f be in $K(\mathbb{Z})$ with Supp $\hat{f}$ contained in $\mathbb{T} \setminus \overline{\cup_{U \in \bar{G}} \sigma(\varphi(U))}$, then for each U in $\bar{G}$ $Supp\ \hat{f} \subseteq \mathbb{T} \setminus \sigma(\varphi(U))$. For such f in $K(\mathbb{Z})$, U in $\bar{G}$, and a pure state τ of $\mathcal{a}$ $\tau(\varphi_f(U)) = \hat{f}(\tau(\varphi(U))) = 0$, thus $\varphi_f(U) = 0$. This, by Lemma 4.5, implies that $M^{\alpha}(\overline{\cup_{U \in \bar{G}} \sigma(\varphi(U))})$ is $\mathcal{B}(\mathcal{a},G)$ hence $sp(\alpha) \subseteq \overline{\cup_{U \in \bar{G}} \sigma(\varphi(U))}$.. This completes the proof. ###

We now state, without proof, two general results (Corollary 8.1.11 and Theorem 8.1.12 from [42]).

Corollary 4.8.: Let β be an invertible isometry on a Banach space X, and consider the representation $n \longrightarrow \beta^n$ of $\mathbb{Z}$ on X. The spectrum of this representation is equal to the spectrum of β as an operator on X.

Theorem 4.9.: The following conditions are equivalent:

(1) $sp(\alpha)$ is compact.

(2) The representation α is uniformly continuous, i.e. $||id-\alpha_t|| \longrightarrow 0$ as $t \longrightarrow 0$, when id is the identity automorphism.

We can apply Corollary 4.8 to a *-automorphism Ψ in $Aut(\mathcal{B},\mathcal{a})$ and use Proposition 4.7 to conclude:

Corollary 4.10.: Let Ψ, in $Aut(\mathcal{B},\mathcal{a})$, be implemented by (I,φ), then the spectrum of Ψ as an operator on $\mathcal{B}(\mathcal{a},G)$ is $\overline{\cup_{U \in \bar{G}} \sigma(\varphi(U))}$. ###

Remark: Let $t \longrightarrow \alpha_t$ be a homomorphism from $\mathbb{R}$ into $Aut(\mathcal{B},\mathcal{a})$, implemented by (I,φ_t), where $\varphi_t(U) = \exp(itC(U))$ for every U in $\bar{G}$, and $C(U)$ are operators in $\mathcal{a}$ satisfying $\mathrm{Sup}_{U \in \bar{G}}||C(U)|| < \infty$. Then, by Theorems 4.6 and 4.9, the homomorphism $t \longrightarrow \alpha_t$ is uniformly continuous.

By Theorem VII.1.2 of [11] there is a bounded operator η on $\mathcal{B}(\mathcal{a},G)$ satisfying $\exp(it\,\eta) = \alpha_t$, and $\eta = \lim_{t \to 0} \frac{1}{t}(\alpha_t - id)$, where the limit is in the norm topology.

Derivations.

Let us denote by $D(g+g^*,\mathcal{a})$ the set of all skew adjoint derivations on $g+g^*$ vanishing on $\mathcal{a}$. i.e. a map δ from $g+g^*$ into $g+g^*$ is in $D(g+g^*,\mathcal{a})$ if:

(1) δ is linear.

(2) $\delta(TS) = T\,\delta(S) + \delta(T)S$ for T and S in $g+g^*$.

(3) $\delta(A) = 0$ for A in $\mathcal{a}$.

(4) $\delta(T^*) = -\delta(T)^*$ for T in $g+g^*$.

Lemma 4.11.: Let δ be in $D(g+g^*,\mathcal{a})$. Then there is a map C from $\bar{G}$ into $\mathcal{a}$

such that for each U and V in $\bar{G}$: (1) $\delta(U) = C(U)U$.

(2) $C(U)$ is self adjoint.

(3) $C(UV) = C(U)+UC(V)U^*$

We will say that δ is implemented by the map C. Conversely, if $C:\bar{G} \longrightarrow \mathcal{A}$ satisfies (2),(3) and $C(I) = 0$, then the map δ defined by $\delta(T) = \delta(\sum A_U U) = \sum A_U C(U)U$ (for $T = \sum A_U U$ in $\mathcal{G}+\mathcal{G}^*$) is in $D(\mathcal{G}+\mathcal{G}^*,\mathcal{A})$.

<u>Proof:</u> Let A be in $\mathcal{A}$ and U in $\bar{G}$, then

$0 = \delta(U^*AU) = \delta(U^*)AU+U^* \delta(AU) = \delta(U^*)AU+U^* \delta(A)U+U^*A \delta(U)$.

For $A = I$ we get $0 = \delta(U^*)U+U^* \delta(U)$; so that

$$\delta(U^*) + -U^* \delta(U)U^* \qquad (*).$$

Hence $0 = -U^* \delta(U)U^*AU+U^*A \delta(U)$ and $\delta(U)U^*AU = A \delta(U)$.

Thus $\delta(U)U^*$ commutes with each operator A in $\mathcal{A}$, hence $\delta(U)U^*$ is in $\mathcal{A}$ and we denote it by $C(U)$.

We have $\delta(U) = C(U)U$ and , since δ is skew adjoint, $\delta(U^*) = -\delta(U)^* = -(C(U)U)^* = - U^*C(U)^*$; thus $C(U^*)U^* = -U^*C(U)^*$.

Using $(*)$ we get : $C(U^*)U^* = \delta(U^*) = -U^* \delta(U)U^* = -U^*C(U)$. Hence $U^*C(U) = U^*C(U)^*$ and $C(U) = C(U)^*$, which proves (2).

Part (3) results from:

$C(UV)UV = \delta(UV) = \delta(U)V+U \delta(V) = C(U)UV+UC(V)V$.

To prove the last statement of the lemma it is enough, by linearity of the map δ, to prove that for each A,B in $\mathcal{A}$ and U,V in $\bar{G}$,

$\delta(AUBV) = \delta(AU)BV+AU \delta(BV)$ and $\delta((AU)^*) = -\delta(AU)^*$.

In fact, $\delta(AUBV) = \delta(AUBU^*UV) = AUBU^*C(UV)UV = AUBU^*C(U)UV + AUBU^*UC(V)U^*UV= AC(U)UBV + AUBC(V)V = \delta(AU)BV + AU \delta(BV)$.

Since $0 = C(I) = C(U^*) + U^*C(U)U$ $C(U^*) = -U^*C(U)U$;

hence $\delta((AU)^*) =\delta(U^*A^*UU^*) = U^*A^*UC(U^*)U^* =C(U^*)U^*A^* = U^*C(U)A^* =$

$= - (AC(U)U)^* = - \delta(AU)^*$. ###

The preceding lemma applies also to every skew adjoint derivation δ of $\mathcal{B}(\mathcal{A},G)$ that vanishes on $\mathcal{A}$. Thus every such derivation maps $\mathcal{G}+\mathcal{G}^*$ into $\mathcal{G}+\mathcal{G}^*$ and, hence, is an extension of a derivation in $D(\mathcal{G}+\mathcal{G}^*,\mathcal{A})$. We denote by $D(\mathcal{B},\mathcal{a})$ the set of all skew adjoint derivations on $\mathcal{B}(\mathcal{a},G)$ that vanish on $\mathcal{a}$. Every such derivation is bounded (since every derivation of a C*-algebra is bounded, by [47, Lemma 4.1.3]), and, as noted above, is an extension of a (bounded) derivation in $D(g+g^*,\mathcal{a})$.

On the other hand, if δ, in $D(g+g^*,\mathcal{a})$, is bounded then it can be extended, in a unique way, to a map δ' from $\mathcal{B}(\mathcal{a},G)$ into itself. Since δ is a skew adjoint derivation and $g+g^*$ is dense in $\mathcal{B}(\mathcal{a},G)$, δ' is a skew adjoint derivation on $\mathcal{B}(\mathcal{a},G)$ by continuity. Thus δ is in $D(\mathcal{B},\mathcal{a})$.

Therefore there is one-to-one correspondence between $D(\mathcal{B},\mathcal{a})$ and the set of all bonded derivations in $D(g+g^*,\mathcal{a})$. We will sometimes refer to the latter set as $D(\mathcal{B},\mathcal{a})$.

Definition: A derivation δ in $D(g+g^*,\mathcal{a})$ will be called inner if there is an operator D in $B(H)$ such that $\delta(T) = DT-TD$ for each T in $g+g^*$. In this case we write $\delta = ad(D)$.

Lemma 4.12.:

(1) δ, in $D(g+g^*,\mathcal{a})$, is inner (i.e. $\delta = ad(D)$), then D is in $\mathcal{a}$ and we can choose D such that $D = D^*$.

(2) The set of all inner derivations in $D(g+g^*,\mathcal{a})$ is $D(\mathcal{B},\mathcal{a})$.

Proof:

(1) Let δ be $ad(D)$. For each A in $\mathcal{a}$, $\delta(A) = 0$ hence $DA = AD$; so that $D \in \mathcal{a}' = \mathcal{a}$.

Let D_1 be $\frac{1}{2}(D+D^*)$, then D_1 is self adjoint and, to complete the proof of part (1), it will suffice to show that $ad(D_1)$ equals $ad(D)$ $(=\delta)$.

In fact, if T is in $g+g^*$ then $DT - TD = \delta(T) = -\delta(T^*)^* = -(DT^* - T^*D)^* = -TD^* + D^*T$ hence $ad(D_1)(T) = D_1T - DT_1 = \frac{1}{2}(DT+D^*T-TD-TD^*) = DT - TD = ad(D)(T)$.

(2) If δ is inner then, clearly, it is bounded. Let δ be a bounded derivation and extend it to a derivation on $\mathcal{B}(\mathcal{a},G)$.

It is known (see [47, Corollary 4.17]) that for a derivation δ on a C*-algebra $\mathcal{C}$, there is an element A in the weak-operator closure of $\mathcal{C}$ satisfying $\delta = \mathrm{ad}(A)$. The application of this result to the algebra $\mathcal{B}(\mathcal{a},G)$ completes the proof. ###

If A is in $\mathcal{a}$ we let exp(A) be the sum of the norm convergent series $\sum_{n=0}^{\infty} \frac{1}{n!} A^n$.

For δ in $D(b,\mathcal{a})$ we can define $\exp(i\delta)$ by the series $\sum_{n=0}^{\infty} \frac{1}{n!}(i\delta)^n$. Since δ is bounded, the series is convergent and defines a linear bounded operator on $\mathcal{B}(\mathcal{a},G)$.

For δ in $D(g+g^*),\mathcal{a})$, A in $\mathcal{a}$, and U in $\bar{G}$, $\delta(AU) = C(U)AU$ for some C(U) in $\mathcal{a}$ (see Lemma 4.11); hence δ is bounded on $\mathcal{a}U$ (a Banach space) and $\exp(i\delta)$ is defined on $\mathcal{a}U$ by $(\exp(i\delta))(AU) = \sum_{n=0}^{\infty} \frac{1}{n!}(i\delta)^n(AU)$. Hence

$$(\exp(i\delta))(AU) = (\exp(iC(U)))AU.$$

We can, therefore, define $\exp(i\delta)$ on $g+g^*$ by:

$$(\exp(i\delta))(A_0+A_1U_1+\ldots+A_nU_n) = A_0+(\exp(iC(U_1)))A_1U_1+\ldots+(\exp(iC(U_n)))A_nU_n.$$

Lemma 4.13.: Let A and B be operators in $\mathcal{a}$, and U in $\bar{G}$. Then:

(1) $\exp(A+B) = (\exp A)(\exp B)$

(2) $\exp(U^*AU) = U^*(\exp A)U$.

If $\delta = \mathrm{ad}(D)$ for some D in $\mathcal{a}$, and T is in $\mathcal{B}(\mathcal{a},G)$, then

(3) $(\exp(i\delta))(T) = (\exp(iD))T(\exp(-iD))$.

Proof: (1) The algebra $\mathcal{a}$ is *-isomorphic to the algebra $C(X)$ of the continuous functions on some compact Hausdorff space X. For every f and g in $C(X)$ $\exp(f+g) = (\exp f)(\exp g)$ since equality holds pointwise on X. Hence (1) foloows.

(2) If φ is a *-representation of a C*-algebra $\mathcal{C}$ and A is a self adjoint (or normal) element in $\mathcal{C}$ then for each continuous funciton f defined on the spectrum of A, $\varphi(f(A)) = f(\varphi(A))$. In the present case, let $\varphi(A)$ be U^*AU (a *-representation of the algebra $\mathcal{a}$) and f be $t \longrightarrow \exp(t)$;

hence $\exp(U^*AU) = U^*(\exp A)U$.

(3) Since $\exp(i\delta)$ is bounded and linear, it will suffice to prove the assertion for $T = AU$ where A is in $\mathcal{A}$ and U is in $\bar{G}$. As noted above, $(\exp(i\delta))(AU) = (\exp(iC(U)))AU$ where δ is implemented by the map C from $\bar{G}$ into $\mathcal{A}$. For $\delta = ad(D)$ we have $\delta(U) = DU - UD = (D-UDU^*)U$; so that $C(U) = D-UDU^*$. Therefore

$$\begin{aligned}(\exp(i\delta))(AU) &= (\exp(iD))(\exp(-iUDU^*))AU \\ &= (\exp(iD))U(\exp(-iD))U^*AU \\ &= (\exp(iD))AU(\exp(-iD)).\end{aligned}$$ ###

Since we will use the conclusion of Theorem 3.13, we will assume, throughout the rest of this chapter, that conditions (1) and (2) of that theorem are satisfied; i.e. there is a faithful state g of $\mathcal{B}(\mathcal{A},G)$ satisfying, for A in $\mathcal{A}$ and U in $G\setminus\{I\}$: (1) $g(AU) = 0$ and (2) $g(U^*A^*AU) = g(A^*A)$.

Lemma 4.14.: For every δ in $D(\mathcal{G}+\mathcal{G}^*,\mathcal{A})$ the map $T \longrightarrow \exp(i\delta)(T)$, from $\mathcal{G}+\mathcal{G}^*$ into itself, can be extended, in only one way, to a $*$-automorphism in $\mathrm{Aut}(\mathcal{B},\mathcal{A})$. We denote the extension, again, by $\exp(i\delta)$ and write E for the map, so obtained, from $D(\mathcal{G}+\mathcal{G}^*,\mathcal{A})$ into $\mathrm{Aut}(\mathcal{B},\mathcal{A})$; i.e. $E(\delta) = \exp(i\delta)$. For bounded derivation δ, this extension coincides with the sum of the convergent series $\sum_{n=0}^{\infty} \frac{1}{n!}(i\delta)^n$.

Proof: We have defined $\exp(i\delta)$ on $\mathcal{G}+\mathcal{G}^*$ by $(\exp(i\delta))(A_0+A_1U_1+\ldots+A_nU_n) = A_0 + (\exp(iC)(U_1)))A_1U_1 +\ldots+(\exp(iC(U_n)))A_nU_n$ where δ is implemented by the map $U \longrightarrow C(U)$, A_i are in $\mathcal{A}$, and U_i in $\bar{G}$. We will now fix δ and write Ψ for the map $T \longrightarrow \exp(i\delta)(T)$.

We, first, show that Ψ is multiplicative. For this, note that $C(UV) = C(U) + UC(V)U^*$ for U and V in $\bar{G}$ (see Lemma 4.11). Hence, for A,B in $\mathcal{A}$ and U, V in $\bar{G}$, : $\Psi(AUBV) = \Psi(AUBU^*UV) = AUBU^*(\exp(iC(UV)))UV = AUBU^*(\exp(iC(U)))U(\exp(iC(V)))U^*UV = \Psi(AU)\Psi(BV)$. By linearity of Ψ, this shows that Ψ is a homomorphism and, since $\Psi(U) = \exp(iC(U)))U$ is a unitary operator, Ψ is a $*$-homomorphism.

Let Ψ' be the map $T \longrightarrow \exp(-i\delta)(T)$, then, $\Psi'(AU) = (\exp(-iC(U)))AU$; so that $\Psi'(\Psi(AU)) = \Psi(\Psi'(AU)) = AU$ for $A \in \mathcal{A}$, $U \in \bar{G}$. Hence, by linearity $\Psi' = \Psi^{-1}$; so that Ψ is a $*$-automorphism on $\mathcal{G}+\mathcal{G}^*$.

Using Corollary 3.14 (where Ψ is implemented by $\Psi(U) = \exp(iC(U))$) we can extend Ψ, in a unique way, to a $*$-automorphism in $\mathrm{Aut}(\mathcal{B},\mathcal{A})$.

If δ is in $D(\mathcal{B},\mathcal{A})$, let Ψ be defined as above and let Ψ' be the sum of the convergent series $\sum_{n=0}^{\infty} \frac{1}{n!} (i\delta)^n$. Then, for A in $\mathcal{A}$ and U in $\bar{G}$, $\Psi'(AU) = \sum_{n=0}^{\infty} \frac{1}{n!}(i\delta)^n(AU) = (\exp(iC(U)))AU = \Psi(U)$. Since both Ψ and Ψ' are linear and continuous, $\Psi = \Psi'$. ###

<u>Lemma 4.15.:</u> A $*$-automorphism Ψ on $\mathcal{B}(\mathcal{A},G)$ is in $E(D(\mathcal{B},\mathcal{A}))$ if and only if Ψ is implemented by some unitary operator V in $\mathcal{A}$.

<u>Proof:</u> a) Let Ψ be $E(\delta)$ for some δ in $D(\mathcal{B},\mathcal{A})$. By Lemma 4.12, $\delta = \mathrm{ad}(D)$ for some self adjoint operator D in $\mathcal{A}$. Let V be the operator $\exp(iD)$ then, by Lemma 4.13 (3), Ψ is implemented by V.

b) Assume now that Ψ is implemented by V i.e. $\Psi(T) = VTV^*$ for T in $\mathcal{B}(\mathcal{A},G)$. There is a self adjoint operator D in $\mathcal{A}$ such that $\exp(iD) = V$. Let δ be $\mathrm{ad}(D)$. Then by Lemma 4.13 (3), $\Psi = E(\delta)$. ###

<u>Lemma 4.16.:</u> Let Ψ be in $\mathrm{Aut}(\mathcal{B},\mathcal{A})$ such that either $||\mathrm{id} - \Psi|| < 2$, or $\nu(\mathrm{id} - \Psi) < \sqrt{3}$, then Ψ is in $E(D(\mathcal{B},\mathcal{A}))$. Here, id is the identity automorphism of $\mathcal{B}(\mathcal{A},G)$ and $\nu(T)$ is the spectral radius of T.

<u>Proof:</u> This is Theorem 8.7.7 of [42]. ###

<u>Corollary 4.17.:</u> Let $\mathcal{G}_1$ and $\mathcal{G}_2$ be irreducible triangular algebras generated by $\mathcal{A}_1,G_1$ and $\mathcal{A}_2,G_2$ respectively, and assume that $\mathcal{G}_1$ satisfies conditions (1) and (2) of Theorem 3.13. Let Ψ and Ψ' be $*$-isomorphisms from $\mathcal{G}_1$ onto $\mathcal{G}_2$ such that Ψ is implemented by a unitary transformation W and $||\Psi - \Psi'|| < 2$. Then Ψ' is implemented by a unitary transformation. In particular, the set $E(D(\mathcal{B},\mathcal{A}))$ (in $\mathrm{Aut}(\mathcal{B},\mathcal{A})$) is open.

<u>Proof.:</u> Since Ψ is implemented by a unitary operator, Ψ is an isometry;

so that

$$||\mathrm{id} - \Psi^{-1}\cdot\Psi'|| = ||\Psi - \Psi'|| < 2.$$

Thus $\Psi^{-1}\cdot\Psi'$ extends to a *-automorphism Ψ_0 of $\mathcal{B}(\mathcal{A},G)$; and $||\mathrm{id} - \Psi_0|| < 2$. If F is a non zero projection in $\mathcal{A}_1$ then $\Psi_0(F)$ is another non zero projection in $\mathcal{A}_1$ and $||F - \Psi_0(F)|| < 2$, hence $\Psi_0(F) = F$. Thus $\Psi_0(A) = A$ for each A in $\mathcal{A}_1$ and, by Lemma 4.16, Ψ_0 is in $\mathcal{E}(D(\mathcal{B}_1,\mathcal{A}_1))$; and, from Lemma 4.15, Ψ_0 is implemented by a unitary operator V in $\mathcal{A}_1$. Since Ψ is implemented by W; we have,

$$\Psi'(T) = \Psi(\Psi_0(T)) = W^*V^*TVW,$$

for each T in $\mathcal{G}_1$. Thus Ψ' is implemented by VW. Note that if Ψ is in $\mathcal{E}(D(\mathcal{B},\mathcal{A}))$ then, by Lemma 4.15, it is implemented by a unitary operator W in $\mathcal{A}$ hence, by what we have proved to this point, each *-automorphism Ψ' satisfying $||\Psi - \Psi'|| < 2$ is also implemented by some unitary operator in $\mathcal{A}$ and thus, by Lemma 4.15, is in $\mathcal{E}(D(\mathcal{B},\mathcal{A}))$.
This proves the last assertion of the corollary, ###

Let $\mathrm{Aut}_0(\mathcal{B},\mathcal{A})$ denote the connected component of the identity in $\mathrm{Aut}(\mathcal{B},\mathcal{A})$ (in the norm topology).

Proposition 4.18.: $\mathrm{Aut}_0(\mathcal{B},\mathcal{A}) = \mathcal{E}(D(\mathcal{B},\mathcal{A}))$.

Proof: Each Ψ in $\mathcal{E}(D(\mathcal{B},\mathcal{A}))$ is $\exp(i\delta)$ for some δ in $D(\mathcal{B},\mathcal{A})$. For every t in $\mathbb{R}$, $t\delta \in D(\mathcal{B},\mathcal{A})$ hence, by Lemma 4.14, $\exp(it\delta)$ $(=\beta(t))$ is in $\mathrm{Aut}(\mathcal{B},\mathcal{A})$. Since δ is bounded, the map $t \longrightarrow \beta(t)$ is norm continuous and $\beta(0) = \mathrm{id}$, $\beta(1) = \Psi$. Therefore Ψ lies in the connected component of the identity in $\mathrm{Aut}(\mathcal{B},\mathcal{A})$.

Conversely, by Lemma 4.17, the set $\mathcal{E}(D(\mathcal{B},\mathcal{A}))$ is open. This set, by Lemma 4.15, is the set of all the *-automorphisms in $\mathrm{Aut}(\mathcal{B},\mathcal{A})$ that are implemented by a unitary operator in $\mathcal{A}$; hence $\mathcal{E}(D(\mathcal{B},\mathcal{A}))$ is a subgroup of $\mathrm{Aut}(\mathcal{B},\mathcal{A})$. Since it is open, it is also closed (in the norm topology).
Since $\mathcal{E}(D(\mathcal{B},\mathcal{A})) \subseteq \mathrm{Aut}_0(\mathcal{B},\mathcal{A})$ and $\mathrm{Aut}_0(\mathcal{B},\mathcal{A})$ is connected,
$\mathcal{E}(D(\mathcal{B},\mathcal{A})) = \mathrm{Aut}_0(\mathcal{B},\mathcal{A})$. ###

Lemma 4.19.: Let δ, in $D(\mathcal{G}+\mathcal{G}^*,\mathcal{a})$, be implemented by a map C from $\bar{G}$ to $\mathcal{a}$. Let Ψ_t be $E(t\delta)$. Then Ψ_t is implemented by (I, φ_t) where $\varphi_t(U) = \exp(itC(U))$ for each t in $\mathbb{R}$; and the map $t \longrightarrow \Psi_t(T)$ is continuous for each T in $B(\mathcal{a},G)$.

Proof: By the definition of $E(t\delta)$ (see Lemma 4.14) Ψ_t is implemented by (I,φ_t).

For the continuity, let T be AU with A in $\mathcal{a}$ and U in $\bar{G}$, then $||\Psi_t(AU)-\Psi_s(AU)|| = ||A(\exp(itC(U)) - \exp(isC(U)))U|| \leq ||A||\ ||\exp(itC(U)) -\exp(isC(U))|| \leq ||A||\ |t-s|\ ||C(U)|| \longrightarrow 0$ (as $t \longrightarrow s$). This proves the continuity when T is in $\mathcal{G}+\mathcal{G}^*$. If T is in $B(\mathcal{a}, G)$, there is a sequence $\{S_n\}$ in $\mathcal{G}+\mathcal{G}^*$ such that $||S_n-T|| \longrightarrow 0$ as $n \to \infty$. Since, for all t in $\mathbb{R}$,

$$||\Psi_t(T) - \Psi_t(S_n)|| = ||T - S_n||,$$

the function $t \longrightarrow \Psi_t(T)$ is a uniform limit of the continuous functions $t \longrightarrow \Psi_t(S_n)$ on $\mathbb{R}$. Hence $t \longrightarrow \Psi_t(T)$ is continuous for each T in $B(\mathcal{a},G)$. ###

Theorem 4.20.: Let δ, in $D(\mathcal{G}+\mathcal{G}^*,\mathcal{a})$, be implemented by the map $U \longrightarrow C(U)$ with $\sup_{U \in \bar{G}}||C(U)|| < \infty$, then δ is in $D(B,\mathcal{a})$.

Proof: Let Ψ_t be $\exp(it\delta)$, then by the remark following Corollary 4.10, there is a bounded operator η on $B(\mathcal{a},G)$ such that $\exp(it\eta) = \Psi_t$ for t in $\mathbb{R}$. Since $\eta = \lim_{t\to 0} \frac{1}{t}(\Psi_t - id)$ we have, for A in $\mathcal{a}$ and U in $\bar{G}$:

$$\eta(AU) = \lim_{t\to 0} \frac{1}{t}A(\exp(itC(U))U-U) = A(\lim_{t\to 0} \frac{1}{t}(\exp(itC(U))-I))U = AC(U)U = \delta(AU)$$

where the limits are in the norm topology. Hence $\delta = \eta$ on $\mathcal{G}+\mathcal{G}^*$ and so δ is bounded on $\mathcal{G}+\mathcal{G}^*$, thus is in $D(B,\mathcal{a})$. ###

For a C*-algebra C, acting on a Hilbert space H, let $(C_+)^m$ denote the set of all oprators in $B(H)$ that are strong limits of monotone increasing nets of positive operators from C. Let $((C_+)^m)^-$ denotes its norm closure.

The next two results are Proposition 8.6.4 and Theorem 8.6.5 of [47

Proposition 4.21.: If δ is a *-derivation of a C*-algebra C, define Ψ_t to be $\exp(t\delta)$ for each t in $\mathbb{R}$. Then $\Psi: t \longrightarrow \Psi_t$ is a uniformly continuous one parameter group of automorphisms of $\mathcal{C}$ and $\sigma(\delta) = i\ sp(\Psi)$.

Theorem 4.22.: Let δ be a $*$-derivation of a C*-algebra $\mathcal{C}$. Then the spectral radius of δ equals $||\delta||$ and there is an element h in $((\mathcal{C}_+)^m)^-$ such that $\delta = ad(ih)$ and $||\delta|| = ||h||$.

Applying these results we get:

Corollary 4.23.: Let δ, in $D(\mathcal{G}+\mathcal{G}^*,\mathcal{A})$, be implemented by the map $U \to C(U)$ from $\bar{G}$ to $\mathcal{A}$, such that $\mathrm{Sup}_{U \in \bar{G}}||C(U)|| < \infty$. Then there is a self adjoint operator D in $\mathcal{A}$, such that $\delta = ad(D)$ and:

(1) $\sigma(\delta) = \overline{\cup_{U \in \bar{G}}\sigma(C(U))}$.

(2) $||D|| = ||\delta|| = \mathrm{Sup}_{U \in \bar{G}}||C(U)||$.

Proof: By Theorem 4.20, δ is in $D(\mathcal{B},\mathcal{A})$, hence, by Lemma 4.12, there is a self adjoint operator D in $\mathcal{A}$ such that $\delta = ad(D)$. Let Ψ be the map $t \longrightarrow \exp(it\delta)$. Since δ is skew adjoint, the derivation $i\delta$ is a $*$-derivation (i.e. a self adjoint derivation) hence, applying Proposition 4.21 we get $\sigma(i\delta) = i\ sp(\Psi)$; so that $\sigma(\delta) = sp(\Psi)$. Since δ is implemented by the map $U \longrightarrow C(U)$; by Lemma 4.19, $\exp(it\delta)$ is implemented by the map $U \longrightarrow \exp(itC(U))$.
Hence we can apply Theorem 4.6 to get

$$\sigma(\delta) = sp(\Psi) = \overline{\cup_{U \in \bar{G}}\sigma(C(U))}.$$

For the second part, note that $||C(U)|| = \mathrm{Sup}\{|t| : t \in \sigma(C(U))\}$ hence $\mathrm{Sup}\ \{|t|: t \in \sigma(\delta)\} = \mathrm{Sup}\{|t|: t \in \sigma(CU)),\ U \in \bar{G}\} = \mathrm{Sup}\{||C(U)||: U \in \bar{G}\}$.
By Theorem 4.22, the spectral radius of δ equals $||\delta||$. Hence

$$||\delta|| = \mathrm{Sup}_{U \in \bar{G}}||C(U))||.$$

By Theorem 4.22, there is a self adjoint operator D such that $\delta = ad(D)$ and $||\delta|| = ||D||$: by Lemma 4.12, D is in $\mathcal{A}$. ###

Thus far, in this chapter, we have dealt only with $*$-automorphisms. The following theorem discusses an automorphism that is not necessarily a $*$-automorphism.

Theorem 4.24.: Let Ψ be an automorphism (not necessarily a $*$-automorphism) of $\mathcal{G}$ leaving each A in $\mathcal{A}$ fixed. Assume also that Ψ is implemented by (I,φ) and that there are positive numbers N,M such that for each U in G, $NI \leq |\varphi(U)| \leq MI$. Then Ψ can be extended to a bounded automorphism Ψ' on $\mathcal{B}(\mathcal{A},G)$ and $\Psi' = \Psi_1' \cdot \Psi_2'$ where:

(1) Ψ_2' is in $\mathrm{Aut}(\mathcal{B},\mathcal{A})$.

(2) $\Psi_1'(T) = RTR^{-1}$ for each T in $\mathcal{B}(\mathcal{A},G)$, where R is some invertible operator in $\mathcal{A}$.

Proof: Using the polar decomopsition, we can define two maps, φ_1 and φ_2, from G into $\mathcal{A}$ such that $\varphi_1(U) = |\varphi(U)|$, $\varphi(U) = \varphi_1(U)\,\varphi_2(U)$, and $\varphi_2(U)$ is a partial isometry for each U in G. Since $\varphi(U)$ is invertible, $\varphi_2(U)$ is, in fact, a unitary operator. For each U,V in G we have:

$$\varphi(UV) = \varphi(U)U\,\varphi(V)U^* = \varphi_1(U)U\,\varphi_1(V)U^*\,\varphi_2(U)U\,\varphi_2(V)U^*.$$

Hence, by the uniqueness of the polar decomposition, we get:

$$\varphi_i(UV) = \varphi_i(U)U\,\varphi_i(V)U^* \qquad i = 1,2 \qquad \text{for } U,V \text{ in } G.$$

Therefore, by the discussion preceding Lemma 3.4, (I,φ_1) and (I,φ_2) implement two homomorphisms, Ψ_1 and Ψ_2, on $\mathcal{G}$, and $\Psi = \Psi_1 \cdot \Psi_2$. Since $\varphi_2(U)$ is a unitary operator for each U in G, the homomorphism implemented by (I, φ_2^*), where $\varphi_2^*(U) = \varphi_2(U)^*$, is the inverse homomorphism of Ψ_2. Hence Ψ_2 is an automorphism and so is $\Psi_1 (= \Psi \cdot \Psi_2^{-1})$. Since $\varphi_2(U)$ is a unitary operator for each U in G, Ψ_2 can be extended, by Corollary 3.14, to a *-automorphism Ψ_2' in $\mathrm{Aut}(\mathcal{B},\mathcal{A})$.

Each operator $|\varphi(U)|$ (in $\mathcal{A}$) has its spectrum contained in the interval $[N,M]$, $N > 0$. Thus, using Lemma 1 of [22], we can define the operator $\log|\varphi(U)|$ in $\mathcal{A}$, and we have:

$$\log|\varphi(UV)| = \log|\varphi(U)| + \log U|\varphi(V)|U^* =$$
$$\log|\varphi(U)| + U(\log|\varphi(V)|)U^*.$$

Let C(U) be $\log|\varphi(U)|$, then:

$$C(UV) = C(U) + UC(V)U^* \qquad (*)$$

for U and V in G.

The spectrum of C(U) lies in the interval $[\log(N), \log(M)]$, hence C(U) is self adjoint (it lies in $\mathcal{a}$ hence it is normal) and

$$\mathrm{Sup}_{U \in \bar{G}} ||C(U)|| < \infty.$$

For U in G, define $C(U^*) = -U^*C(U)U$, then for each U in $\bar{G}$, C(U) is self adjoint and

$$\mathrm{Sup}_{U \in \bar{G}} ||C(U)|| < \infty \qquad (**).$$

Note also that (*) holds for U,V in $\bar{G}$. We prove this for the case where $U \in G$, $V \in G^*$ and $UV \in G$. The other possible cases are handled similarly. Under these assumptions, it follows from (*) that

$$C(U) = C(UV) + UVC(V^*)V^*U^*.$$

Since $C(V) = -VC(V^*)V^*$, $C(U) = C(UV) - UC(V)U^*$.

Hence $C(UV) = C(U) + UC(V)U^*$.

Define a map $\delta\colon g+g^* \longrightarrow g+g^*$ by $\delta(\sum A_U U) = \sum C(U)A_U U$.

To see that δ is a derivation, note that, using (*), we have

$\delta(AUBV) = AUBU^*C(UV)UV = AUBU^*C(U)UV +$

$\delta(AUBU^*UC(V)U^*UV = AC(U)UBV + AUBC(V)V = \delta(AU)BV + AU\,\delta(BV)$ for A,B in $\mathcal{a}$ and U,V in $\bar{G}$. Since δ is linear, this implies that δ is a derivation on $g+g^*$. Since $C(I) = \log|\varphi(I)| = \log(I) = 0$, $\delta(A) = 0$ for each A in $\mathcal{a}$.

Also $\delta((AU)^*) = \delta(U^*A^*) = U^*A^*UC(U^*)U^* = - U^*A^*UU^*C(U)UU^*$

$$= -U^*A^*C(U) = -\delta(AU)^* ;$$ so that δ is in $D(g+g^*,\mathcal{a})$.

Moreover, by (**), the hypothesis of Corollary 4.23 is satisfied hence there is a self adjoint operator D in $\mathcal{a}$ such that $\delta = \mathrm{ad}(D)$; so that $C(U)U = DU - UD$ and $C(U) = D-UDU^*$.

Let the operator R, in $\mathcal{a}$, be exp(D) then $R^{-1} = \exp(-D)$ and

$|\varphi(U)| = \exp(C(U)) = \exp(D-UDU^*) = (\exp(D))U(\exp(-D))U^* = RUR^{-1}U^*$ for each U in $\bar{G}$.

Define a map τ on g by $\tau(T) = RTR^{-1}$ then, for A in $\mathcal{a}$, U in $\bar{G}$, we have:

$$\tau(AU) = RAUR^{-1} = ARUR^{-1} = A|\varphi(U)|U = \Psi_1(AU) \quad ;$$

so that, by linearity, $\tau = \Psi_1$ on g. Since τ can be extended to an automorphism Ψ_1' on $\mathcal{B}(\mathcal{a},G)$ so can Ψ_1. ###

Example 4.25. : Let $\mathcal{A}$ be the multiplication algebra of $L^2([-\Pi,\Pi])$ (i.e. $\mathcal{A} \cong L^\infty([-\Pi,\Pi])$). Let G be the semigroup generated by a single unitary operator U acting ergodically on $\mathcal{A}$. By Lemma 1.7, the algebra $\mathcal{G}$ generated by $\mathcal{A}$ and G is an irreducible triangular algebra.

Fix t in $[-\Pi,\Pi]$ and, for each integer k, let $\varphi_t(U^k)$ be $e^{itk}I$. Define a linear map α_t on $\mathcal{G}$ by: $\alpha_t(A_0+A_1U+\ldots+A_nU^n) = A_0 + e^{it}A_1U+\ldots+ e^{itn}A_nU^n$ where A_i is in $\mathcal{A}$.

For A,B in $\mathcal{A}$, we have

$$\alpha_t(AU^kBU^m) = e^{it(k+m)}AU^kBU^m = \alpha_t(AU^k)\ \alpha_t(BU^m) ;$$

so that, by linearity, α_t is a homomorphism on $\mathcal{G}$. Note that Λ is $\mathbb{T}$, in the present case.

We assume now that U arises from a measure-preserving transformation on $[-\Pi,\Pi]$ (with the Lebesgue measure dt). Let g be a state on $\mathcal{A}$ defined by $g(f) = \frac{1}{2\Pi}\int_{-\Pi}^{\Pi} f(t)dt$; then g is a faithful G-invariant state on $\mathcal{A}$. Since $\bar{G}$ is amenable (hence Φ is faithful), the remark preceding Corollary 3.14 implies that the conditions of that Corollary are satisfied.

Since α_t is implemented by φ_t, and $\varphi_t(U^k)$ is a unitary operator for each positive integer k, we can apply Corollary 3.14 and extend α_t to a *-automorphism on the C*-algebra $\mathcal{B}(\mathcal{A},G)$. Denote the extension, again, by α_t.

The map $t \longrightarrow \alpha_t(T)$ is continuous if T is of the form AU^k ($A \in \mathcal{A}$, $k \in \mathbb{Z}$) because $\alpha_t(AU^k) = e^{itk}AU^k$. Hence the map is continuous for each T in $\mathcal{G}+\mathcal{G}^*$. As in the proof of Lemma 4.19, the map $t \longrightarrow \alpha_t(T)$ is continuous for each T in $\mathcal{B}(\mathcal{A},G)$..

Thus, to each μ in $M([-\Pi,\Pi])$, we can associate an operator $\alpha_\mu(T)$ in $\mathcal{B}(\mathcal{A},G)$, (See Corollary 4.2 (1).) For every functional g in the dual of $\mathcal{B}(\mathcal{A},G)$, we have: $g(\alpha_\mu(T)) = \int_{-\Pi}^{\Pi} g(\alpha_t(T))d\mu(t)$.

Hence $|g(\alpha_\mu(T))| \leq ||g||\ ||T||\ ||\mu||$; so that

$$||\alpha_\mu(T)|| \leq ||T|| .$$

A sequence $\{K_n\}$ of functions in $L^1([-\Pi,\Pi])$ is called an <u>approximate</u>

identity if they satisfy:

(1) $K_n \geq 0$.

(2) $\frac{1}{2\Pi}\int_{-\Pi}^{\Pi} K_n(t)dt = 1$.

(3) If J is an open interval about $t = 0$ then

$$\lim_{n\to\infty} \operatorname{Sup}_{t\notin J} K_n(t) = 0.$$

Such a sequence is called an approximate identity since for every function f in $L^1([-\Pi,\Pi])$,

$$||K_n * f - f||_1 \underset{n}{\to} 0 .$$

We will now prove that $\alpha_{K_n}(T) \underset{n}{\longrightarrow} T$ in norm where K_n is an approximate identity. For This, let $\delta > 0$ and write, for each bounded linear functional g on $\mathcal{B}(\mathcal{a},G)$:

$$\begin{aligned} g(\alpha_{K_n}(T) - T) &= \frac{1}{2\Pi}\int_{-\Pi}^{\Pi} g(\alpha_t(T))K_n(t)dt - g(T) \\ &= \frac{1}{2\Pi}\int_{-\Pi}^{\Pi}(g(\alpha_t(T)) - g(T))K_n(t)dt \\ &= \frac{1}{2\Pi}\int_{-\delta}^{\delta}(g(\alpha_t(T)) - g(T))K_n(t)dt \\ &\quad + \frac{1}{2\Pi}\int_{|t|\geq\delta}(g(\alpha_t(T)) - g(T))K_n(t)dt. \end{aligned}$$

Therefore

$$|g(\alpha_{K_n}(T) - T| \leq \operatorname{Sup}_{-\delta\leq t\leq\delta}|g(\alpha_t(T)) - g(T)|$$
$$+ 2||g||\ ||T||\operatorname{Sup}_{|t|\geq\delta}K_n(t) \leq ||g||(\operatorname{Sup}_{-\delta\leq t\leq\delta}||\alpha_t(T) - T||$$
$$+ 2||T||\operatorname{Sup}_{|t|\geq\delta}K_n(t)).$$

Fix $\varepsilon > 0$. Since $t \longrightarrow \alpha_t(T)$ is continuous at $t = 0$ and $\alpha_0(T) = T$, we can choose $\delta(=\delta(\varepsilon))$ such that $\operatorname{Sup}_{-\delta\leq t\leq\delta}||\alpha_t(T) - T|| \leq \frac{1}{2}\varepsilon$.

Since $\lim_{n\to\infty} \operatorname{Sup}_{|t|\geq\delta}K_n(t) = 0$, there is an integer N such that for each $n \geq N$

$$\operatorname{Sup}_{|t|\geq\delta}K_n(t) \leq \frac{1}{4}\varepsilon||T|| \qquad \text{and thus}$$

$$|g(\alpha_{K_n}(T) - T)| \leq \varepsilon\ ||g|| .$$

Hence $\quad ||\alpha_{K_n}(T) - T|| \underset{n}{\longrightarrow} 0$.

We can choose K_n to be the trigonometric polynomial (the classical

Fejer's Kernel) $\sum_{k=-n}^{n} a_n(k)e^{ikt}$, where $a_n(k) = 1-\frac{k}{n}$.

Then K_n is an approximate identity and $K_n(t) = \frac{1}{n}(\frac{\mathrm{Sin}\ 1/2nt}{\mathrm{Sin}\ 1/2t})^2$ (see [28, pp. 16-17]).

With this choice of K_n we get:

$$\alpha_{K_n}(T) = \sum_{k=-n}^{n} a_n(-k)\ \Phi(TU^{-k})U^k \qquad (*).$$

To prove this, let us, first, define a linear bounded map from $\mathcal{B}(\mathcal{a},G)$ onto by $\Phi_k(T) = \Phi(TU^{-k})$ $k \in \mathbb{Z}$ and observe that $\Phi_k \cdot \alpha_t = e^{itk}\ \Phi_k$ for each k in $\mathbb{Z}$ and t in $[-\Pi,\Pi]$. (This last equality is clear on $g+g^*$ and extends to $\mathcal{B}(\mathcal{a},G)$ by continuity of each side).

Let g be any bounded linear functional on $\mathcal{B}(\mathcal{a},G)$, we have:

$$g(\Phi_k(\alpha_{K_n}(T))) = \frac{1}{2\Pi}\int_{-\Pi}^{\Pi} g(\Phi_k(\alpha_t(T)))K_n(t)dt = \frac{1}{2\Pi}\int_{-\Pi}^{\Pi} e^{itk} g(\Phi_k(T))K_n(t)dt$$
$$= g\ (\Phi_k(T))a_n(-k),$$

where we let $a_n(k)$ be 0 if $|k| \geq n$.

Therefore, for every k, $\Phi_k(\alpha_{K_n}(T)) = a_n(-k)\ \Phi_k(T)$.

Since $\Phi_k(\sum_{j=-n}^{n} a_n(-j)\ \Phi(TU^{-j})U^j) = a_n(-k)\ \Phi_k(T)$ we conclude that:

$$\Phi_k(\alpha_{K_n}(T)) = \Phi_k(\sum_{j=-n}^{n} a_n(-j)\ \Phi(TU^{-j})U^j)$$

for each k in $\mathbb{Z}$.

Using Lemma 2.10 this completes the proof of (*).

In fact, the above argument shows that for every function f in $L^1([-\Pi,\Pi])$

$$\Phi(\alpha_f(T)U^{-k}) = \mathbf{f}(k)\ \Phi(TU^{-k}).$$

With the exception of the discussion related to K_n, the representation $t \longrightarrow \alpha_t$ applies to the case where $\Lambda = \mathbb{R}$. In this case $C(U^k) = kI$, and, applying Theorem 4.6 and Corollary 4.10, we have:

(1) $sp(\alpha) = \mathbb{Z}$.

(2) For every t in $\mathbb{R}$, the spectrum of α_t as an operator on $\mathcal{B}(\mathcal{a},G)$ is the closure of the set $\{e^{ikt} : k \in \mathbb{Z}\}$.

Thus if e^{it} is not a root of 1, the spectrum is the whole circle group.

BIBLIOGRAPHY

1. W.B. Arveson, A density theorem for operator algebras. Duke Math J. 23 (1967), pp. 635-648.

2. W.B. Arveson, Analyticity in operator algebras. Amer. J. Math. 89 (1967), pp. 578-642.

3. W.B. Arveson, Operator algebras and measure preserving automorphisms. Acta Math. 118 (1967), pp. 95-109.

4. W.B. Arveson, Operator algebras and invariant subspaces. Ann. of Math. 100 (1974), pp. 433-532.

5. W.B. Arveson, On groups of automorphisms of operator algebras. J. Functional Anal. 15 (1974)

6. W.B. Arveson, Interpolation problems in nest algebras. J. Functional anal. 20 (1975), pp. 208-233.

7. W.B. Arveson and K.B. Josephson, Operator algebras and measure preserving automorphisms II. J. Functional Anal. 4 (1969), pp. 100-134.

8. G. Birkhoff, Lattice Theory. Amer. Math. Soc. Coll. Publ. v.5, third edition (1967).

9. E. Christensen, Derivations of nest algebras. Math. Ann. 229 (1977), pp. 155-161.

10. J.A. Deidens, Another description of nest algebras. Lecture Notes in Mathematics No. 693. Springer-Verlag, New York 1978, pp.77-86.

11. N. Dunford and J.T. Schwartz, Linear operators, Part 1: General theory. New York, N.Y., Interscience Publishers, Inc. 1958.

12. H.A. Dye, On groups of measure preserving transformations I. Amer. J. of Math. 81 (1959), pp. 119-159.

13. H.A. Dye, On groups of measure preserving transformations II. Amer. J. of Math. 85 (1963), pp. 551-576.

14. J.A. Erdos, Some results on triangular operator algebras, Amer. J. Math. 89 (1967), pp. 85-93.

15. J.A. Erdos, Unitary invariants for nests. Pacific J. Math. 23 (1967), pp. 229-256.

16. J.A. Erdos, Operators of finite rank in nest algebras. J. London Math. Soc. 43 (1968), pp. 391-397.

17. J.A. Erdos, An abstract characterization of next algebras. Quart. J. Math. Oxford 22 (1971), pp. 47-63.

18. J.A. Erdos, Some questions concerning triangular operator algebras. Proc. R. In. Acad. 74A (1974), pp. 223-232.

19. J.A. Erdos, On some ideals of nest algebras. Proc. London Math. Soc.

20. T. Fall, W.B. Arveson and P.S. Muhly, Perturbations of nest algebras. J. Operator Theory 1 (1979), pp. 137-150.

21. E. Følner, On groups with full Banach mean value. Math. Scand. 3 (1955), pp. 243-254.

22. T. Gardner, An invariance theorem for representations of Banach algebras. Proc. Amer. Math. Soc. 16 (1965), pp. 383.

23. F. Gilfeather and D.R. Larson, Nest subalgebras of von Neumann algebras. Advances in Math.

24. F. Gilfeather and D.R. Larson, Nest subalgebras of von Neumann algebras: commutants modulo compacts and distance estimates.

25. F. Gilfeather and D.R. Larson, Nest subalgebras of von Neumann algebras: commutants modulo the radical.

26. P.R. Halmos, Reflexive lattices of subspaces. J. London Math. Soc. (2) 4(1971), pp. 257-263.

27. P.R. Halmos, Measure theory. Springer-Verlag New York 1974.

28. K. Hoffman, Banach spaces of analytic functions, Prentice-Hall, Englewook Cliffs, N.J. 1962.

29. A. Hopenwasser, Isometries on irreducible triangular operator algebras. Math. Scand. 30 (1972), pp. 136-140.

30. A. Hopenwasser, The radical of a reflexive operator algebra. Pacific J. Math. 65 (1976), pp. 375-392.

31. A. Hopenwasser, The Cartan criterion fails for triangular subalgebras of a factor. Rocky Mountain J. Math. 9 (1979), pp. 441-445.

32. A. Hopenwasser, The equation Tx=y in a reflexive operator algebra. Indiana Univ. Math. J. 29 (1980), pp. 121-126.

33. R.V. Kadison and I.M. Singer, Triangular operator algebras. Amer. J. Math. 82 (1960), pp. 227-259.

34. E.C. Lance, Some properties of nest algebras. Proc. London Math. Soc. (3) 19 (1968), pp. 45-68.

35. E.C. Lance, Cohomology and perturbations of nest algebras.

36. D.R. Larson, On the structure of certain reflexive operator algebras. J. Functional Anal. 31 (1979), pp. 275-292.

37. W.E. Longstaff, Generators of nest algebras. Canadian J. Math.26 (1974), pp. 565-575.

38. W.E. Longstaff, Strongly reflexive lattices. J. London Math. Soc. (2) 11 (1975), pp. 491-498.

39. W.E. Longstaff, Generators of reflexive algebras. J. Australian Math. Soc. 20 (1975), pp. 159-164.

40. W.E. Longstaff, Operators of rank one in reflexive algebras. Canadian J. Math. 28 (1976), pp. 19-23.

41. F.J. Murray and J. von Neumann, On rings of operators. Ann. of Math. 37 (1936), pp. 116-229.

42. G.K. Pedersen, C*-algebras and their automorphism groups. Academic Press Inc. (London) 1979.

43. J.R. Ringrose, Algebraic isomorphisms between ordered bases. Amer. J. Math. 83 (1961), pp. 463-478.

44. R.J. Ringrose, On some algebras of operators. Proc. London Math. Soc. (3) 15 (1965), pp. 61-83.

45. J.R. Ringrose, On some algebras of operators II. Proc. London Math. Soc. (3) 16 (1966), pp. 385-402.

46. P. Rosental, Weakly closed maximal triangular algebras are hyperreducible. Proc. Amer. Math. Soc. 24 (1970), p.220.

47. S. Sakai, C*-algebras and W*-algebras. 'Ergebnisse der Mathematic' 60, Springer-Verlag, Berlin, Heidelberg, New York, 1971.

48. J.R. Schue, The structure of hyperreducible triangular algebras. Proc. Amer. Math. Soc. 15 (1964), pp. 766-772.

49. E. Størmer, Positive linear maps of operator algebras. Acta Math. 110 (1963), pp. 233-278.

School of Mathematical Sciences, Tel-Aviv University, Tel-Aviv, Israel

General instructions to authors for
PREPARING REPRODUCTION COPY FOR MEMOIRS

For more detailed instructions send for AMS booklet, "A Guide for Authors of Memoirs." Write to Editorial Offices, American Mathematical Society, P. O. Box 6248, Providence, R. I. 02940.

MEMOIRS are printed by photo-offset from camera copy fully prepared by the author. This means that, except for a reduction in size of 20 to 30%, the finished book will look exactly like the copy submitted. Thus the author will want to use a good quality typewriter with a new, medium-inked black ribbon, and submit clean copy on the appropriate model paper.

Model Paper, provided at no cost by the AMS, is paper marked with blue lines that confine the copy to the appropriate size. Author should specify, when ordering, whether typewriter to be used has PICA-size (10 characters to the inch) or ELITE-size type (12 characters to the inch).

Line Spacing – For best appearance, and economy, a typewriter equipped with a half-space ratchet – 12 notches to the inch – should be used. (This may be purchased and attached at small cost.) Three notches make the desired spacing, which is equivalent to 1-1/2 ordinary single spaces. Where copy has a great many subscripts and superscripts, however, double spacing should be used.

Special Characters may be filled in carefully freehand, using dense black ink, or INSTANT ("rub-on") LETTERING may be used. AMS has a sheet of several hundred most-used symbols and letters which may be purchased for $5.

Diagrams may be drawn in black ink either directly on the model sheet, or on a separate sheet and pasted with rubber cement into spaces left for them in the text. Ballpoint pen is *not* acceptable.

Page Headings (Running Heads) should be centered, in CAPITAL LETTERS (preferably), at the top of the page – just above the blue line and touching it.

LEFT-hand, EVEN-numbered pages should be headed with the AUTHOR'S NAME;

RIGHT-hand, ODD-numbered pages should be headed with the TITLE of the paper (in shortened form if necessary).

Exceptions: PAGE 1 and any other page that carries a display title require NO RUNNING HEADS.

Page Numbers should be at the top of the page, on the same line with the running heads.

LEFT-hand, EVEN numbers – flush with left margin;

RIGHT-hand, ODD numbers – flush with right margin.

Exceptions: PAGE 1 and any other page that carries a display title should have page number, centered below the text, on blue line provided.

FRONT MATTER PAGES should be numbered with Roman numerals (lower case), positioned below text in same manner as described above.

MEMOIRS FORMAT

It is suggested that the material be arranged in pages as indicated below.
Note: <u>Starred items</u> (*) <u>are requirements of publication.</u>

Front Matter (first pages in book, preceding main body of text).

Page i – *Title, *Author's name.

Page iii – Table of contents.

Page iv – *Abstract (at least 1 sentence and at most 300 words).

*1980 Mathematics Subject Classifications represent the primary and secondary subjects of the paper. For the classification scheme, see Annual Subject Indexes of MATHEMATICAL REVIEWS beginning in December 1978.

Key words and phrases, if desired. (A list which covers the content of the paper adequately enough to be useful for an information retrieval system.)

Page v, etc. – Preface, introduction, or any other matter not belonging in body of text.

Page 1 – Chapter Title (dropped 1 inch from top line, and centered).

Beginning of Text.

Footnotes: *Received by the editor date.

Support information – grants, credits, etc.

Last Page (at bottom) – Author's affiliation.

ABCDEFGHIJ–AMS–8987654

Number 291

Richard M. Hain

Iterated integrals and homotopy periods

Memoirs
of the American Mathematical Society

Providence · Rhode Island · USA

January 1984 · Volume 47 · Number 291 (third of six numbers) · ISSN 0065-9266

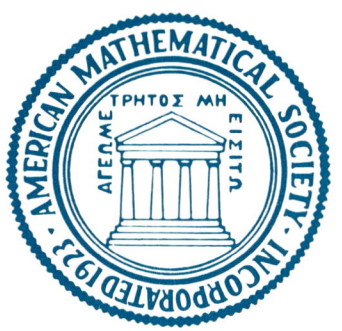

Memoirs of the American Mathematical Society

Number 291

Richard M. Hain

Iterated integrals and homotopy periods

Published by the

AMERICAN MATHEMATICAL SOCIETY

Providence, Rhode Island, USA

January 1984 · Volume 47 · Number 291 (third of six numbers)

MEMOIRS of the American Mathematical Society

This journal is designed particularly for long research papers (and groups of cognate papers) in pure and applied mathematics. It includes, in general, longer papers than those in the TRANSACTIONS.

Mathematical papers intended for publication in the Memoirs should be addressed to one of the editors. Subjects, and the editors associated with them, follow:

MEMOIRS are printed by photo-offset from camera-ready copy fully prepared by the authors. Prospective authors are encouraged to request booklet giving detailed instructions regarding reproduction copy. Write to Editorial Office, American Mathematical Society, P. O. Box 6248, Providence, Rhode Island 02940. For general instructions, see last page of Memoir.

SUBSCRIPTION INFORMATION. The 1984 subscription begins with Number 289 and consists of six mailings, each containing one or more numbers. Subscription prices for 1984 are $148 list; $74 member. A late charge of 10% of the subscription price will be imposed upon orders received from nonmembers after January 1 of the subscription year. Subscribers outside the United States and India must pay a postage surcharge of $10; subscribers in India must pay a postage surcharge of $15. Each number may be ordered separately; *please specify number* when ordering an individual number. For prices and titles of recently released numbers, refer to the New Publications sections of the NOTICES of the American Mathematical Society.

BACK NUMBER INFORMATION. For back issues see the AMS Catalogue of Publications.

TRANSACTIONS of the American Mathematical Society

This journal consists of shorter tracts which are of the same general character as the papers published in the MEMOIRS. The editorial committee is identical with that for the MEMOIRS so that papers intended for publication in this series should be addressed to one of the editors listed above.

Subscriptions and orders for publications of the American Mathematical Society should be addressed to American Mathematical Society, P. O. Box 1571, Annex Station, Providence, R. I. 02901. *All orders must be accompanied by payment.* Other correspondence should be addressed to P. O. Box 6248, Providence, R. I. 02940.

MEMOIRS of the American Mathematical Society (ISSN 0065-9266) is published bimonthly (each volume consisting usually of more than one number) by the American Mathematical Society at 201 Charles Street, Providence, Rhode Island 02904. Second Class postage paid at Providence, Rhode Island 02940. Postmaster: Send address changes to Memoirs of the American Mathematical Society, American Mathematical Society, P. O. Box 6248, Providence, RI 02940.

CONTENTS

ABSTRACT

Let M be a simply connected smooth manifold with finite Betti numbers and let p be a positive integer. A method of finding a finite list of iterated integrals that form a basis of $\mathrm{Hom}(\pi_p(M), \mathbb{R})$ is described.

A rational version of Chen's loop space de Rham theorem is proved and Cuadrado's rational version of Chen's method of power series connections is strengthened. We show that the set of primitive elements of Chen's model of a space has homology isomorphic to the rational homotopy groups of the space. We establish the naturality of the construction of this Lie algebra model. Minimal cofibrations of a rational space are shown to correspond to elementary extensions of Chen's Lie algebra model of the space.

A relationship between Sullivan's minimal models and Chen's iterated integrals and power series connections is described. We give a concise exposition of the construction and basic properties of Chen's iterated integrals.

AMS (MOS) Subject classification (1980). Primary 55P62; Secondary 57T30.

Library of Congress Cataloging in Publication Data

Hain, Richard M. (Richard Martin), 1953-
Iterated integrals and homotopy periods.

(Memoirs of the American Mathematical Society, ISSN 0065-9266 ; no. 291)
"January 1984, volume 47, number 291."
Bibliography: p.
1. Homotopy theory. 2. Integrals, Multiple.
I. Title. II. Series.
QA3.A57 no. 291 [QA612.7] 510s [514'.24] 83-22416
ISBN 0-8218-2291-8

1. INTRODUCTION

Of the various minimal algebraic models of a simply connected space that have been constructed in the last decade ([37], [10], [2], [3], [33]), possibly the least understood and the one most suitable for applications in geometry is K.-T. Chen's non-commutative algebra model. In this paper we give a complete exposition of Chen's methods and extend these in two directions: We establish a rational version of Chen's theory for simply connected semi-simplicial complexes, and we show that the set of primitive elements of Chen's model is a Lie algebra model of the space whose generators correspond to cells in the space that represent non trivial rational homology classes.

Differential forms and the aspects unique to Chen's approach are emphasized. This paper is written for the non specialist in the hope of making Chen's ideas more accessible. Those homotopy theorists wanting to understand Chen's theory and its relationship to the other models from a more algebraic point of view should consult Tanré's papers [42], [43] or the author's paper [25].

As a central theme in this paper we adopt the "homotopy period problem": For a simply connected manifold M with finite Betti numbers, give a method for writing down a finite list of integrals of differential forms on M that will detect all non-zero elements of $\pi_p(M) \otimes \mathbb{R}$.

The first obstacle to solving the homotopy period problem is that a manifold M does not support any p-forms when p exceeds the dimension of M, so that it is not at all clear how to detect non-trivial elements of $\pi_p(M) \otimes \mathbb{R}$ when $p > \dim M$. The first example of detecting non-trivial elements of $\pi_p(M) \otimes \mathbb{R}$ when $p > \dim M$ was given by J.H.C. Whitehead in

Received by the editors July 21, 1981 and in revised form September 17, 1981 and February 1, 1983.

1947 [41]: Suppose that $f\colon S^{2n-1} \to S^n$ is a smooth map where $n > 1$. Let w be a volume form on S^n. Since $n > 1$, there is an $n-1$ form ξ on S^{2n-1} such that $d\xi = f^*w$. Observe that $\xi\wedge f^*w$ is a top dimensional form on S^{2n-1}. Whitehead's result asserts that

$$\int_{S^{2n-1}} \xi\wedge f^*w = 0$$

if and only if the homotopy class of f is zero in $\pi_{2n-1}(S^n) \otimes \mathbb{R}$.

For the time being, let's drop the assumption that M is simply connected. Choose a base-point $*$ of M. Another obstacle to solving the homotopy period problem for M is that the homology class of smooth map $f\colon (S^1, 1) \to (M,*)$ may be trivial while the homotopy class $\{f\}$ of f in $\pi = \pi_1(M,*)$ may be non-trivial. For example, let $M = \mathbb{C} - \{-1,1\}$ and let $* = 0$. Suppose that $f\colon (S^1, 1) \to (M, 0)$ is a smooth map. If

$$\int_f \frac{dz}{z+1} = \int_f \frac{dz}{z-1} = 0,$$

then the homology class of f is trivial in $H_1(M,\mathbb{Z})$ so that $\{f\} \in [\pi,\pi]$. How can we determine whether $\{f\}$ is non-zero in $\pi/[[\pi,\pi]\pi]$? Since $\int_f (z+1)^{-1}dz = 0$, there is a smooth function $g\colon S^1 \to \mathbb{C}$ such that $dg = f^*(z+1)^{-1}dz$. One can show, without too much difficulty, that the image of $\{f\}$ in $\pi/[[\pi,\pi]\pi]$ is zero if and only if

$$\int_{S^1} g \wedge f^* \frac{dz}{z-1} = 0.$$

In fact, this procedure can be extended to detect all non-trivial elements of π (see [14]).

The above examples illustrate ad hoc approaches to the homotopy period problem. Our aim in this paper is to give a systematic procedure for solving the homotopy period problem when M is simply connected. Sullivan [38] has previously given a solution of the homotopy period problem that uses his minimal models. However, the author believes that his method is more explicit than Sullivan's.

In the case when M is not simply connected, both Sullivan [38] and Chen [11], [14] have given a solution to the homotopy period problem. In this case, all elements of $\pi_1(M)/\kappa$ can be detected by integrals of differential forms on M, where κ denotes the torsion free nilpotent residue of $\pi_1(M)$. (The torsion free nilpotent residue κ of a group π is the intersection of the kernels of all group homomorphisms of π into torsion free nilpotent groups.) A result of Baumslag (Trans. Amer. Math. Soc. 106, (1963)) implies that if π is free or the fundamental group of a Riemann surface, then κ is trivial.

Our approach to the homotopy period problem is to view a smooth map $f\colon\ S^p \to M$ as a smooth map $\hat{f}\colon\ [0,1] \times S^{p-1} \to M$ by composing f with a smooth map

$$([0,1] \times S^{p-1},\ \{0,1\} \times S^{p-1}) \to (S^p,*)$$

of degree 1. Chen's iterated integrals are differential forms that can be evaluated on smooth maps $[0,1] \times N \to M$, where N denotes a compact oriented manifold. They can naturally be viewed as differential forms on the space of piecewise smooth loops ΩM of M and are a natural generalization of line integrals, which can be thought of as smooth functions on ΩM. Their value on a smooth map $[0,1] \times N \to M$ is readily calculable by a multiple integral. For example, iterated integrals can be used to detect non-trivial elements of $\pi_{2n-1}(S^n) \otimes \mathbb{R}$ $(n > 1)$ as follows: Choose a volume form w on S^n. Given a smooth map

$$f\colon\ [0,1] \times S^{2n-2} \to S^n$$

that represents an element of $\pi_{2n-1}(S^n)$, write the pullback f^*w of w in the form

$$f^*w = dt \wedge w'(t,\xi) + w''(t,\xi),$$

where t denotes the coordinate in $[0,1]$, ξ the coordinates in S^{2n-2} and where, for each t, $w'(t,\xi)$ and $w''(t,\xi)$ are forms on S^{2n-2}. The homotopy class of f in $\pi_{2n-1}(S^n) \otimes \mathbb{R}$ is trivial if and only if the iterated integral

$$\int_{\xi \in S^{2n-2}} \left(\int_0^1 \int_0^t w'(s,\xi) \wedge w'(t,\xi)\, ds\, dt \right)$$

is zero.

Chen's loop space de Rham theorem (theorem (6.5)) asserts that (when M is simply connected) the cohomology of the complex of iterated integrals (a d.g. sub algebra of the de Rham complex of ΩM) is naturally isomorphic to the real singular cohomology of ΩM. A well known result of Cartan and Serre implies that each homotopy functional $\pi_p(\Omega M) \to \mathbb{R}$ can be represented by an iterated integral.

The problem is to give an efficient procedure for writing down closed iterated integrals whose cohomology classes form a basis of

$$\mathrm{Hom}\,(\pi_{p-1}(\Omega M),\ \mathbb{R}) \approx \mathrm{Hom}\,(\pi_p(M),\ \mathbb{R}).$$

This is achieved by using a strengthened version of Chen's method of power series connections. Roughly speaking, a power series connection on M defines a differential ∂ of degree -1 on the free graded Lie algebra $L = \mathbb{L}\,(\tilde{H}_{*-1}(M;\ \mathbb{R}))$ generated by the reduced real homology $\tilde{H}_*(M;\ \mathbb{R})$ of M (where the degree of each homology class has been reduced by one) and an L-valued iterated integral T_L on M, which defines a graded Lie algebra isomorphism

$$\pi_*(M) \otimes \mathbb{R} \to H_*(L)$$

via integration. By examining the coefficients of T_L carefully, a list of iterated integrals dual to $\pi_*(M) \otimes \mathbb{R}$ can be read off from T_L.

The author has attempted to make the basics of Chen's method of power series connections and iterated integrals as accessible as possible. As a result, the contents of several of the early chapters overlap. Provisional statements of several of the main results are given in these chapters to avoid lengthy technical digressions.

Chapter 2 is introductory. It contains an exposition of the method of power series connections. To avoid unnecessary technicalities, we restrict our attention to power series connections on smooth manifolds. A provisional version of Chen's loop space homology theorem is stated and several elementary and hopefully illuminating examples are worked.

Chapter 3 is a dictionary of notation and conventions used in this paper.

In chapter 4, power series connections are defined in a more general setting than in chapter 2. Provisional versions of the main results in the paper are stated and several applications are given: the rational homotopy groups of the wedge $M_1 \vee M_2$ and the connected sum $M_1 \# M_2$ of two simply connected closed manifolds, M_1 and M_2, are compared and a divided power property of the generator of $\pi_2(\mathbb{C}P^n)$ is obtained.

Chapter 5 contains a concise exposition of the construction and basic properties of iterated integrals. A reader only interested in the construction and properties of iterated integrals could read chapter 5 after reading the first section of chapter 4.

The main results of the paper are stated in full detail in chapter 6 and proved in chapters 6, 8 and 9. The main results comprise a strengthening of Chen's method of power series connections. We prove that the Lie elements of the d.g. algebra model associated to a space by Chen [15] has homology isomorphic to the rational homotopy Lie algebra of the space and that the association of this Lie algebra of the space, when suitably interpreted, is natural. We also prove that minimal cofibrations of a simply connected rational space correspond to elementary extensions of its Lie algebra model. The proofs of the parts of the main theorems not relevant to our discussion of homotopy periods in chapter 7 have been deferred to chapters 8 and 9.

In chapter 7 we outline our solution of the homotopy period problem and describe the relationship between Chen's iterated integrals and power series connections and Sullivan's minimal models.

This paper is a modified version of part of the author's doctoral dissertation written at the University of Illinois. The author would like to take this opportunity to express his sincere gratitude to his advisor, Professor Kou-Tsai Chen, for introducing him to iterated integrals and de Rham homotopy theory, and for guidance and encouragement given during the author's graduate studies.

The author would also like to thank Tom Duchamp for critically reading chapter 2, and the referee for helpful suggestions which led to improvements in the exposition, especially in chapter 6.

2. HOW TO COMPUTE $\pi_*(M) \otimes \mathbb{R}$ USING DIFFERENTIAL FORMS

Let M be a simply connected manifold with finite Betti numbers. In this chapter we describe a procedure for computing the real homotopy groups $\pi_*(M) \otimes \mathbb{R}$ of M and the Whitehead product

$$\pi_p(M) \otimes \mathbb{R} \times \pi_q(M) \otimes \mathbb{R} \to \pi_{p+q-1}(M) \otimes \mathbb{R},$$

from the complex of smooth forms on M. The method is a refinement of Kuo-Tsai Chen's method of power series connections [15].

The dual $\mathrm{Hom}(\pi^*(M), \mathbb{R})$ of the real homotopy groups of M and the dual of the Whitehead product can also be computed directly from the de Rham complex of M using Sullivan's minimal models [37], [19]. There is a direct and explicit relationship between our approach and Sullivan's [24], [25] which is described in chapter 7. This relationship allows one to pass back and forth between the two methods during computations, thereby sharpening the computational power of the methods of de Rham homotopy theory.

The Whitehead Product

Recall that for a topological space X and positive integers p and q, there is a $\mathbb{Z}$-bilinear pairing $[\ ,\ ]: \pi_p(X) \otimes \pi_q(X) \to \pi_{p+q-1}(X)$. The "bracket" $[\alpha,\beta]$ of the homotopy classes α in $\pi_p(X)$ and β in $\pi_q(X)$ is called the Whitehead product of α and β. Up to a sign, $[\alpha,\beta]$ is the obstruction to extending the map $f \vee g: S^p \vee S^q \to X$ to a map $S^p \times S^q \to X$ where $f: S^p \to X$ and $g: S^q \to X$ are representatives of α and β, respectively. The Whitehead product has several nice properties which are summarized in the following proposition, a proof of which can be found in [40].

(2.1) Proposition. Let X be a topological space and p, q, r be positive integers. If $\alpha \in \pi_{p+1}(X)$, $\beta \in \pi_{q+1}(X)$, $\gamma \in \pi_{r+1}(X)$, then

(a) $[\alpha,\beta] = -(-1)^{pq}[\beta,\alpha]$,

(b) $(-1)^{pr}[[\alpha,\beta],\gamma] + (-1)^{qp}[[\beta,\gamma],\alpha]$
$+ (-1)^{rq}[[\gamma,\alpha],\beta] = 0$.

If $\underline{k}$ is a field and if X is simply connected, then the desuspension $s^{-1}\pi_*(X) \otimes \underline{k}$ of the homotopy groups of X tensored with $\underline{k}$ is a graded Lie algebra over $\underline{k}$. (The desuspension of a graded vector space V is the graded vector space $s^{-1}V$ obtained by lowering the degree of each element of V by 1.)

We will compute the graded Lie algebra $s^{-1}\pi_*(M) \otimes \mathbb{R}$ as the homotopy of the free Lie algebra generated by the desuspension $s^{-1}\tilde{H}_*(M; \mathbb{R})$ of the reduced real homology of M endowed with suitable differential ∂ of degree -1.

<u>The de Rham Theorem</u>

Let M be a smooth manifold. Denote the chain complex generated by the smooth singular simplices $\sigma\colon \Delta^p \to M$ by $S^*(M)$ and the chain complex generated by the continuous singular simplices $\sigma\colon \Delta^p \to M$ by $S_*(|M|)$. The inclusion $S_*(M) \to S_*(|M|)$ induces an isomorphism

$$H_*(S_*(M)) \approx H_*(M; \mathbb{Z}).$$

(See [20] for example.)

Denote the de Rham complex of M by $E_{\mathbb{R}}(M)$. For a smooth map $\sigma\colon \Delta^p \to M$ and a q-form w on M, define

$$< w,\sigma > = \begin{cases} \int_\sigma w & \text{if } p = q \\ 0 & \text{if } p \neq q \end{cases}$$

(2.2) <u>The classical de Rham theorem</u>. Let M be a smooth manifold. The integration map

$$\int : \mathcal{E}_{\mathbb{R}}(M) \to \mathrm{Hom}\,(S_*(M),\ \mathbb{R})$$

defined by $w \to \{\sigma \to \langle w,\sigma\rangle\}$ induces a natural algebra isomorphism

$$\int^* : H^*(\mathcal{E}_{\mathbb{R}}(M)) \to H^*(M;\mathbb{R}). \qquad \square$$

Power Series Connections

The method of power series connections was introduced by Chen in [10] to study the real homology of the loop space of a simply connected smooth manifold. It is, in some sense, a generalization of the notion of a linear connection on a vector bundle. (For details, see Chen [12] and Lehmann [28].)

The method of power series connections defines a differential ∂ of degree -1 on the free graded Lie algebra L generated by $s^{-1} H_*(M;\mathbb{R})$. The quadratic terms of ∂ are given by the cup products in $H^*(M;\mathbb{R})$, the cubic terms by the Massey triple products in $H^*(M;\mathbb{R})$, and so on. The main theorem of this section asserts that there is a natural Lie algebra isomorphism

$$\tau:\ s^{-1}\pi_*(M) \otimes \mathbb{R} \to H_*(L,\partial),$$

called the holonomy map of the connection and that this isomorphism is defined by integrating an L-valued iterated integral T_L over each homotopy class in $\pi_*(M) \otimes \mathbb{R}$. In other words, $\tau(\alpha)$ equals the homology class of the closed element $\langle T_L, f\rangle$ of L, where $f\colon S^p \to M$ is a representative of α. A precise definition of T_L is given in (6.19).

We need some notation. Let L be a graded Lie algebra over $\mathbb{R}$ with a differential ∂ of degree -1. Denote by $\mathcal{E}_{\mathbb{R}}(M) \hat{\otimes} L$ the set of all formal sums $\Sigma w_i U_i$, where $w_i \in \mathcal{E}_{\mathbb{R}}(M)$ and $U_i \in L$ and, for each integer n, there is only a finite number of terms $w_i U_i$ such that $\deg w_i + \deg U_i = n$. One can think of $\mathcal{E}_{\mathbb{R}} \hat{\otimes} L$ as the set of L-valued forms on M. Extend the actions of the exterior derivative d in $E_{\mathbb{R}}(M)$ and the differential ∂ of L to $E_{\mathbb{R}}(M) \hat{\otimes} L$ by $d(\Sigma w_i U_i) = \Sigma(dw_i)U_i$ and $\partial(\Sigma w_i U_i) = \Sigma w_i(\partial U_i)$.

Define a linear automorphism J of $E_{\mathbb{R}}(M)$ by $Jw = (-1)^{\deg w} w$ and extend it to $E_{\mathbb{R}}(M) \hat{\otimes} L$ by defining $J(\Sigma w_i U_i) = \Sigma(Jw_i)U_i$. Finally, define a bracket in $E_{\mathbb{R}}(M) \hat{\otimes} L$ by

$$[\Sigma a_i A_i, \Sigma b_j B_j] = \Sigma a_i \wedge b_j [A_i, B_j].$$

Let M be a simply connected manifold with finite Betti numbers. Choose a graded basis (X_i) of the desuspension $s^{-1} \tilde{H}_*(M,\mathbb{R})$ of the reduced real homology of M. Observe that the free graded Lie algebra $\mathbb{L}(X_1, X_2, X_3, \ldots)$ generated by the X_i is isomorphic to $\mathbb{L}(s^{-1} \tilde{H}_*(M; \mathbb{R}))$. Below is a provisional definition of a power series connection. It will be generalized slightly in chapter 4.

(2.3) Definition. A power series connection on M is a differential ∂ of degree -1 on $L = \mathbb{L}(X_1, X_2, \ldots)$ such that

$$\partial[U, V] = [\partial U, V] + (-1)^{\deg U}[U, \partial V]$$

for all $U,V \in L$, and an element $\omega = \Sigma u_i U_i$ of $E_{\mathbb{R}}(M) \hat{\otimes} L$ such that

(a) $\deg u_i = 1 + \deg U_i$,

(b) if $\omega \equiv \Sigma w_i X_i \mod E_{\mathbb{R}}(M) \otimes [L, L]$, then each w_i is closed and their cohomology classes $(\{w_i\})$ form a basis of $\tilde{H}^*(M; \mathbb{R})$ dual to the basis (X_i) of $\tilde{H}_*(M; \mathbb{R})$,

(c) $\partial\omega + d\omega - \frac{1}{2}[J\omega, \omega] = 0$.

We shall denote a power series connection on M by (ω, L, ∂).

The definition of power series connections is not easy to digest and is best understood by referring to the following examples and the remarks that follow them.

(2.4) Examples. (a) Let X represent the fundamental homology class of the sphere S^n. Choose a volume form w on S^n such that $\langle w, X \rangle = 1$. A connection on S^n is given by setting $L = (\mathbb{L}(X), \partial)$ where $\deg X = n - 1$ and $\partial X = 0$. The connection form is $\omega = wX$.

(b) Choose a 2-form w on $\mathbb{C}P^n$ representing a generator of the integral cohomology group $H^2(\mathbb{C}P^n; \mathbb{Z})$ of $\mathbb{C}P^n$. Let $X_1, X_2, \ldots, X_n$ be the basis of $\tilde{H}_*(\mathbb{C}P^n; \mathbb{Q})$ dual to the basis of $H_*(\mathbb{C}P^n; \mathbb{Q})$ given by the cohomology classes of $w, w^2, \ldots, w^n$, respectively. Set $\deg X_k = 2k - 1$ and define $\partial X_1 = 0$ and $\partial X_k = \frac{1}{2} \sum_{i+j=k} [X_i, X_j]$. A connection on $\mathbb{C}P^n$ is given by setting $L = (\mathbb{L}(X_1, X_2, \ldots, X_n), \partial)$ and $\omega = wX_1 + w^2 X_2 + \ldots w^n X_n$.

(c) Let M be a compact simply connected Riemannian symmetric space. Choose a basis (X_i) of $s^{-1}\tilde{H}_*(M; \mathbb{R})$ and choose harmonic forms (w_i) on M such that $\langle w_i, X_j \rangle = \delta_{ij}$. Since, on a symmetric space, the product of harmonic forms is harmonic, there are real numbers c_{ij}^k such that

$$Jw_i \wedge w_j = \sum c_{ij}^k w_k .$$

A connection on M is given by setting $\partial X_k = \frac{1}{2} \sum c_{ij}^k [X_i, X_j]$ and $\omega = \sum w_i X_i$.

(d) Let $M = S^{p_1} \times S^{p_2} - \{\text{point}\}$ where $p_1, p_2 > 1$. Let X_1 be the generator of $H_{p_1}(M; \mathbb{R})$ that corresponds to S^{p_1} and let X_2 be the generator of $H_{p_2}(M; \mathbb{R})$ that corresponds to S^{p_2}. Choose closed forms w_1, w_2 on M such that $\langle w_i, X_j \rangle = \delta_{ij}$. Since $\{w_1\} \wedge \{w_2\} = 0$ in $H^*(M; \mathbb{R})$, there is a $p_1 + p_2 - 1$ form ξ such that $d\xi = Jw_1 \wedge w_2$. A connection (ω, ∂) on M is given by $\partial X_1 = \partial X_2 = 0$ and

$$\omega = w_1 X_1 + w_2 X_2 + \xi [X_1, X_2].$$

(2.5) Remarks. Let (ω, L) be a power series connection on a simply connected manifold M with finite Betti numbers. Suppose that $\omega \equiv \sum w_i X_i$

mod $E_{\mathbb{R}}(M) \hat{\otimes} [L,L]$.

(a) If we reduce the equation

$$\partial\omega + d\omega - \frac{1}{2}[J\omega, \omega] = 0$$

modulo $E_{\mathbb{R}}(M) \otimes [L,L]$, then we get

$$\Sigma w_i \partial X_i \equiv 0 \quad \text{mod} \quad E_{\mathbb{R}}(M) \hat{\otimes} [L,L].$$

Since (w_i) is a linearly independent set in $E_{\mathbb{R}}(M)$, it follows that $\partial X_i \in [L,L]$. That is, $\partial L \subseteq [L,L]$ so that L is a minimal chain Lie algebra. In fact, L is the real form of the minimal Lie algebra models of M defined by Allday [2], Baues-Lemaire [3] and Neisendorfer [33].

(b) Since the cohomology classes $(\{w_i\})$ of the (w_i) form a basis of $\tilde{H}^*(M;\mathbb{R})$, there are real numbers c_{ij}^k such that

$$\{Jw_i\} \wedge \{w_j\} = \Sigma\, c_{ij}^k \{w_k\}.$$

Reducing the equation

$$\partial\omega + d\omega - \frac{1}{2} [J\omega , \omega] = 0$$

modulo $E_{\mathbb{R}}(M) \hat{\otimes} [L,[L,L]]$, we see that

$$\Sigma w_k\, \partial X_k + d\omega \equiv \frac{1}{2} \Sigma J w_i \wedge w_j [X_i, X_j] \quad \text{mod} \quad E_{\mathbb{R}}(M) \hat{\otimes} [L,[L,L]] .$$

It follows that

$$\partial X_k \equiv \frac{1}{2} \Sigma\, c_{ij}^k [X_i, X_j] \text{ mod } [L,[L,L]].$$

(c) In chapter 6 we will prove that (L,∂) is unique up to isomorphism and that a smooth map $f: M \to N$ induces a d.g. Lie algebra map on the corresponding Lie algebras.

(2.6) <u>Theorem</u> (Chen [14]). Every simply connected manifold with finite

Betti numbers has a power series connection. □

In the appendix to this chapter a procedure for computing the differential ∂ and the connection form ω is given.

The Main Theorem

Here we state a provisional version of the principal result of this paper (theorem 6.23)). It is really a strengthened version of Chen's theorem on the real homology of the loop space of a simply connected manifold with finite Betti numbers (theorem 3.4.1, [15]).

(2.7) Theorem. Let M be a simply connected manifold with finite Betti numbers. If (ω, L, ∂) is a power series connection on M, then there is a natural Lie algebra isomorphism

$$\tau: s^{-1}\pi_*(M) \otimes \mathbb{R} \to H_*(L).$$

Moreover, (L,∂) is unique up to an isomorphism that respects τ. □

(2.8) Examples. From examples (2.4) and theorem (2.7), it follows that

(a) $s^{-1}\pi_*(S^n) \otimes \mathbb{R} \approx \mathbb{L}(X)$, where X is of degree $n - 1$. When n is even, $\mathbb{L}(X)$ is spanned by X, $[X,X]$ and when n is odd, $\mathbb{L}(X)$ is spanned by X. This gives the well known result

$$\pi_{2n-1}(S^n) \otimes \mathbb{R} \approx \begin{cases} 0 & n \text{ odd} \\ \mathbb{R} & n \text{ even.} \end{cases}$$

(b) $s^{-1}\pi_*(\mathbb{C}P^n) \otimes \mathbb{R} \approx H_*(\mathbb{L}(X_1, X_2, \ldots, X_n), \partial)$ where $\deg X_k = 2k-1$ and $\partial X_k = \frac{1}{2}\sum_{i+j=k} [X_i, X_j]$. In [25] (see also chapter 7), a procedure is given for computing the homology of a minimal chain Lie algebra. In this case, $H_*(\mathbb{L}(X_1,\ldots,X_n))$ is spanned by the homology classes of X_1 and $\sum_{i+j=n+1} [X_i, X_j]$.

(c) The real homotopy Lie algebra of a compact, simply connected Riemannian symmetric space is isomorphic to

$$H_*(\mathbb{L}(X_1, X_2, \ldots, X_n))$$

where $\partial X_k = \frac{1}{2} \Sigma c_{ij}^k [X_i, X_j]$ and where the c_{ij}^k are the structure constants of $\tilde{H}^*(M; \mathbb{R})$ as in (2.4) (c).

(d) $$s^{-1}\pi_*(S^2 \times S^2 - \{\text{point}\}) \otimes \mathbb{R} \approx \mathbb{L}(X_1, X_2)$$

where $\deg X_1 = \deg X_2 = 1$. Thus $\pi_p(S^2 \times S^2 - \{\text{point}\}) \otimes \mathbb{R}$ is non trivial for every $p > 1$. □

The real Hurewicz homomorphism

$$h: \pi_*(M) \otimes \mathbb{R} \to H_*(M; \mathbb{R})$$

can conveniently be described in terms of the Lie algebra model L of M.

Let M be a simply connected manifold with finite Betti numbers and let (ω, L, ∂) be a power series connection on M. There is a natural isomorphism

$$\sigma: s^{-1}\tilde{H}_*(M; \mathbb{R}) \to L/[L,L]$$

defined by taking each X_i in $s^{-1}\tilde{H}_*(M; \mathbb{R})$ to its image in $L/[L,L]$. Since $\partial L \subseteq [L,L]$, there is a natural map

$$H_*(L) \to L/[L,L]$$

(2.9) <u>Theorem</u>. If M is a simply connected manifold with finite Betti numbers and if (ω, L, ∂) is a power series connection on M, then the diagram

$$\begin{array}{ccc} s^{-1}\pi_*(M) \otimes \mathbb{R} & \xrightarrow{\tau} & H_*(L) \\ {\scriptstyle s^{-1}h}\downarrow & & \downarrow \\ s^{-1}\tilde{H}_*(M; \mathbb{R}) & \xrightarrow{\sigma} & L/[L,L] \end{array}$$

commutes.

Appendix

Here we give a recipe for computing power series connections. Let M be a simply connected manifold with finite Betti numbers. Choose a graded basis (X_i) of the desuspension $s^{-1}\tilde{H}_*(M;\mathbb{R})$ of the reduced real homology of M.

Let

$$L = \mathbb{L}(X_1, X_2, \ldots).$$

Set $I^2L = [L,L]$ and, for $r > 2$, set $I^rL = [L, I^{r-1}L]$. Next choose a basis

$$\bigcup_{n=1}^{\infty} \{U_\alpha : \alpha \in J(n)\}$$

of L such that $\bigcup_{n=r}^{\infty} \{U_\alpha : \alpha \in J(n)\}$ is a basis of I^rL and $\{U_\alpha : \alpha \in J(1)\} = \{X_i\}$. (In practice, it is unnecessary to find such a basis; we only need it to describe the procedure.)

Choose closed forms (w_i) in $E_{\mathbb{R}}(M)$ whose cohomology classes $(\{w_i\})$ form a basis of $\tilde{H}^*(M;\mathbb{R})$ dual to the basis (X_i) of $\tilde{H}_*(M;\mathbb{R})$. We will compute the connection form ω and the differential ∂ by finding a sequence of "successive approximations" (ω_s) of ω and (∂_s) of ∂. In fact, it will turn out that

$$\partial_s X_i \equiv \partial X_i \mod I^{s+1}L$$

and

$$\omega_s \equiv \omega \qquad \mod E_{\mathbb{R}}(M) \hat{\otimes} I^{s+1}L.$$

Set $\omega_1 = \Sigma\, w_i X_i$ and $\partial_1 X_i = 0$. Observe that

$$\partial_1\omega_1 + d\,\omega_1 - \frac{1}{2}[J\omega_1, \omega_1] \equiv 0 \mod E_{\mathbb{R}}(M) \hat{\otimes} I^2L.$$

Next, suppose that we have found ω_r and ∂_r for $1 \le r < s$ such that

(a) $\partial_r X_i \equiv \partial_{s-1} X_i \quad \bmod I^{r+1}L,$

(b) ∂_r is a derivation of L of degree -1,

(c) $\omega_r \equiv \omega_{s-1} \quad \bmod \mathcal{E}_{\mathbb{R}}(M) \hat{\otimes} I^{r+1}L,$

(d) $\partial_{s-1}\omega_{s-1} + d\omega_{s-1} - \frac{1}{2}[J\omega_{s-1},\omega_{s-1}] \equiv 0 \quad \bmod \mathcal{E}_{\mathbb{R}}(M) \hat{\otimes} I^{s}L.$

To find ω_s, set

$$\omega_s = \omega_{s-1} + \sum_{\alpha \in \mathcal{J}(s)} w_\alpha U_\alpha$$

and

$$\partial_s X_i = \partial_{s-1} X_i + \sum_{\alpha \in \mathcal{J}(s)} a_i^\alpha U_\alpha$$

where the w_α are forms on M and the a_i^α are real numbers yet to be determined. In order that

$$\partial_s \omega_s + d\omega_s - \frac{1}{2}[J\omega_s,\omega_s] \equiv 0 \quad \bmod \mathcal{E}_{\mathbb{R}}(M) \hat{\otimes} I^{s+1}L$$

it is necessary and sufficient that the w_α and the a_i^α satisfy the equation

$$(*) \quad \sum_{\alpha \in \mathcal{J}(s)} (\sum_i a_i^\alpha w_i + dw_\alpha)\, U_\alpha \equiv \partial_{s-1}\omega_{s-1} + d\omega_{s-1} - \frac{1}{2}[J\omega_{s-1},\omega_{s-1}]) \quad \bmod \mathcal{E}_{\mathbb{R}}(M) \hat{\otimes} I^{s+1}L.$$

It turns out that always

$$d(\partial_{s-1}\omega_{s-1} + d\omega_{s-1} - \frac{1}{2}[J\omega_{s-1},\omega_{s-1}] \equiv 0 \quad \bmod \mathcal{E}_{\mathbb{R}}(L) \hat{\otimes} I^{s+1}L.$$

(See Chen [14] for an analytic proof and Hain [25] for an algebraic proof.) Because the cohomology classes $(\{w_i\})$ of the (w_i) span $\tilde{H}^*(M;\mathbb{R})$ and because

$$\partial_{s-1}\omega_{s-1} + d\omega_{s-1} - \frac{1}{2}[J\omega_{s-1},\omega_{s-1}] \equiv 0 \quad \text{mod } \mathcal{E}_{\mathbb{R}}(M) \hat{\otimes} I^s L,$$

there exists a solution (a_i^α) and (w_α) of (*). Thus ω_s can be constructed.

Define ω and α by insisting that

$$\omega \equiv \omega_s \quad \text{mod } \mathcal{E}_{\mathbb{R}}(M) \hat{\otimes} I^{s+1}L,$$

$$\partial X_i \equiv \partial_s X_i \quad \text{mod } I^{s+1}L.$$

The equation $\partial\omega + d\omega - \frac{1}{2}[J\omega, \omega] = 0$ is automatically satisfied. This implies that $\partial^2 = 0$.

A good exercise is to compute a connection for M a tubular neighborhood of $S^2 \times S^2 \vee S^2$ in $S^2 \times S^2 \times S^2$.

3. NOTATION AND CONVENTIONS

We assume the reader is familiar with the definitions of and basic properties of graded algebras, graded Lie algebras, graded coalgebras and graded Hopf algebras. Our basic reference for this material is Milnor-Moore [30]. Another useful reference is Appendix B of Quillen's paper [34].

Let k denote either the field of rational numbers, $\mathbb{Q}$, or the field of real numbers, $\mathbb{R}$. A graded k-vector space V is a family of k-vector spaces $\{V_n\}$ where n runs through the non-negative integers. The degree of an element v of V will be denoted by $\deg v$. A graded vector space V is said to be of finite type if for each n, V_n has finite dimension.

When V is a differential graded vector space (hereafter written d.g. vector space), we shall use the prefix chain (resp. cochain) to indicate that the differential of V has degree -1 (resp. +1). If v is a closed element of V, we shall denote by $\{v\}$ its homology class in $H_*(V)$.

The r-fold suspension $(r \in \mathbb{Z})$ of a graded vector space V is the graded vector space s^rV defined by

$$(s^rV)_p = V_{p-r} .$$

We shall usually denote by s^rv the element of s^rV corresponding to the element v of V.

A graded vector space V is said to be n-connected if $V_p = 0$ whenever $p \le n$.

If V and W are d.g. vector spaces, then their tensor product $V \otimes W$ (over k) is a d.g. vector space with differential d defined by

$$d(v \otimes w) = (d_1v) \otimes w + (-1)^{\deg v}\, v \otimes (d_2w)$$

where d_1 denotes the differential in V and d_2 denotes the differential in W.

All algebras are graded and have a unit, augmentation and an associative multiplication. The augmentation ideal of an algebra A is the kernel of the augmentation $A \to k$ and will be denoted by IA. We say that the d.g. algebra A is r-connected if IA is r-connected as a d.g. vector space. If A is connected, then $IA = \bigoplus_{p>0} A_p$. We denote the rth power of the augmentation ideal by $I^r A$. The space of indecomposables of A is the graded vector space IA/I^2A and will be denoted by QA. An algebra A is said to be commutative if

$$xy = (-1)^{\deg x \deg y} yx$$

for all x,y in A.

A derivation of degree r of an algebra A is a linear map $\delta : A \to A$ such that

$$\delta(xy) = (\delta x)y + (-1)^{r \deg x} x(\delta y)$$

for all x,y in A.

A chain algebra (resp. cochain algebra) A is a graded algebra with a differential of degree -1 (resp. +1) which is also a derivation of A of degree -1 (resp. +1). In this paper all cochain algebras are assumed to be commutative! Cochain algebras will be denoted by capital script letters such as $\mathcal{A}$, $\mathcal{B}$, $\mathcal{M}$.

Define an automorphism $J\colon \mathcal{A} \to \mathcal{A}$ of each cochain algebra $\mathcal{A}$ by $Ja = (-1)^{\deg a} a$ for each a in $\mathcal{A}$.

The free graded commutative algebra on the graded vector space V (resp. the graded set $\{x_1, x_2, \ldots\}$) will be denoted by $\Lambda(V)$ (resp. $\Lambda(x_1, x_2, \ldots)$). That is, $\Lambda(V)$ is the tensor product of the polynomial algebra on the elements of V of even degree with the exterior algebra on the elements of V of odd degree. If W is a graded vector space with basis $\{x_1, x_2, \ldots\}$, then $\Lambda(x_1, x_2, \ldots) = \Lambda(W)$.

A chain Lie algebra L is a graded Lie algebra with a differential of degree -1 such that the bracket

$$[,]: \ L \otimes L \to L$$

is a chain map. We say that L is r-connected if it is r-connected as a d.g. vector space. Denote by I^2L the subspace $[L,L]$ of L and by I^rL $(r \geq 3)$ the subspace $[L,I^{r-1}L]$ of L. The space of indecomposables of L is the graded vector space L/I^2L and will be denoted by QL. The universal enveloping algebra of L will be denoted by UL.

The free Lie algebra on the graded vector space V (resp. the graded set $\{X_1,X_2,\ldots\}$) will be denoted by $L(V)$ (resp. $L(X_1,X_2,\ldots)$). The free product of the chain Lie algebras L_1 and L_2 will be denoted by $L_1 * L_2$. In the case when $L_1 = L(V_1)$ and $L_2 = L(V_2)$, then $L_1 * L_2 = L(V_1 \oplus V_2)$ endowed with the unique differential such that the canonical maps $L(V_1) \to L(V_1 \oplus V_2)$ and $L(V_2) \to L(V_1 \oplus V_2)$ are chain maps.

A chain coalgebra C is a graded coalgebra with a differential of degree -1 such that the comultiplication $\Delta: C \to C \otimes C$, the coaugmentation $k \to C$ and the counit $C \to k$ are all chain maps. The cokernel of the coaugmentation $k \to C$ will be denoted by $\overline{C}$. The comultiplication induces a linear map $\overline{\Delta}: \overline{C} \to \overline{C} \otimes \overline{C}$.

A coalgebra C is said to be cocommutative if the diagram

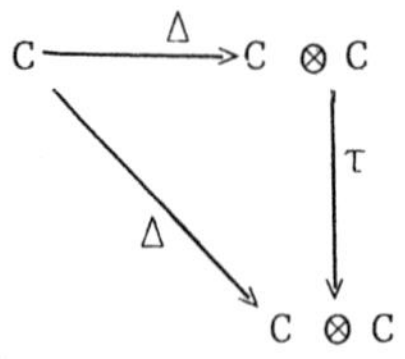

commutes where τ denotes the interchange map

$$\tau: c \otimes d \to (-1)^{\deg c \deg d} d \otimes c.$$

A chain Hopf algebra is a Hopf algebra A with a differential of degree -1 such that the underlying algebra is a chain algebra and the underlying coalgebra is a chain coalgebra. The set of primitive elements of a chain Hopf algebra A will be denoted by PA. That is,

$$PA = \{X \in A: \ \Delta X = X \otimes 1 + 1 \otimes X\} .$$

Note that PA has the structure of a chain Lie algebra with the bracket given by the commutator in A.

A Hopf algebra is said to be cocommutative if the uderlying coalgebra is cocommutative.

For a topological space X and a ring R we denote by $H_*(X; R)$ the singular homology groups of X with coefficients in R and by $\tilde{H}_*(X;R)$ the reduced singular homology groups of X with coefficients in R. We define the ith Betti number of X to be the dimension of the vector space $H_i(X;\mathbb{Q})$.

We denote the simplicial chain complex of a semisimplicial complex K by ΔK and denote by $H_*(K;R)$ the simplicial homology groups of K with coefficients in R.

Throughout this paper we will use the following convention: if A and B are vector spaces, algebras, coalgebras, etc., then $A \otimes B$ will denote their tensor product as $\mathbb{Z}$-modules. If A and B happen to be vector spaces over $\mathbb{Q}$, then

$$A \otimes B = A \otimes_{\mathbb{Q}} B$$

so that, in this case, $A \otimes B$ is unambiguous.

4. POWER SERIES CONNECTIONS ON SEMI SIMPLICIAL COMPLEXES

It is desirable to extend the results stated in chapter 2 so that they apply to singular manifolds, algebraic varieties, simplicial complexes and other naturally occurring spaces on which differential forms can be defined. In this chapter we state provisional versions of the principal results of this paper. These are rational versions of theorems (2.7) and (2.9) for simply connected semi-simplicial complexes with finite Betti numbers. Detailed proofs of these results appear in chapters 6 and 9.

Several applications of these theorems are given: a power series connection on the connected sum $M_1 \# M_2$ of two simply connected, closed manifolds, M_1 and M_2, is computed in terms of power series connections on M_1 and M_2. This is used to compare the rational homotopy groups of $M_1 \# M_2$ to the rational homotopy groups of the one point union $M_1 \vee M_2$ of M_1 and M_2. We also show that if ζ is a generator of $\pi_2(\mathbb{C}P^n)$, then the $(n + 1)$ st higher order Whitehead product $[\zeta, \zeta, \ldots, \zeta]$ is $(n + 1)!$ times a generator of $\pi_{2n+1}(\mathbb{C}P^n)$.

From this point on, all vector spaces, algebras etc. are over $\mathbb{Q}$ unless otherwise stated. All our results that are stated for semi-simplicial complexes are true for smooth manifolds provided that $\mathbb{Q}$ is replaced by $\mathbb{R}$. The proofs of these results for manifolds are similar to the proofs given for semi-simplicial complexes, but are often simpler.

Differentiable Spaces

Let n be a non-negative integer. By an n-dimensional convex set we shall mean a convex subset of $\mathbb{R}^n$ with non-empty interior. A convex set is simply an n-dimensional convex set for some non-negative integer n.

(4.1) Definition. A differentiable space is a set M and a family of maps $\{\alpha: M \to M\}$, called plots on M, each of whose domain is a convex set, which satisfy the following conditions:

(a) if $\alpha: U \to M$ is a plot, V a convex set and $\theta: V \to U$ a smooth map, then $\alpha \circ \theta: V \to M$ is also a plot,

(b) every constant map from a convex set into M is a plot,

(c) if U is a convex set, $\{U_i\}$ a cover of U by convex sets, each open in U, and if $\alpha: U \to M$ is a map such that for each i, the restriction $\alpha|U_i$ of α to U_i is a plot, then α is also a plot.

If M is a set and $\mathcal{U}$ is a family of maps into M, each of whose domain is a convex set, then there is a unique smallest family $\mathcal{U}'$ of maps, each from a convex set into M, such that $(M,\mathcal{U}')$ is a differentiable space. We shall call $\mathcal{U}'$ the differentiable space structure on M generated by $\mathcal{U}$.

Each n-dimensional convex set has natural coordinates $\{\xi_1, \xi_2, \ldots, \xi_n\}$ which are the restriction of the canonical coordinates of $\mathbb{R}^n$. It thus makes sense to speak of differential forms defined on a convex set.

(4.2) Definition. A smooth p-form w on a differentiable space M is a family (w_α) of smooth p-forms indexed by the plots $\alpha: U \to M$. The p-form w_α associated to the plot $\alpha: U \to M$ is a smooth p-form on U. The family (w_α) is required to satisfy the following compatability condition: if $\alpha: U \to M$ is a plot and $\theta: V \to U$ is a smooth map from a convex set V into U, then $\theta^* w_\alpha = w_{\alpha \circ \theta}$.

One can think w as being intrinsically defined on M and w_α as being the pullback $\alpha^* w$ of w along α.

The sum $w_1 + w_2$ and exterior product $w_1 \wedge w_2$ of two smooth forms w_1 and w_2 on a differentiable space M, and the exterior derivative dw and scalar multiple λw $(\lambda \in \mathbb{R})$ of a smooth form w on M can all be defined plotwise as follows: $(w_1 + w_2) = w_{1\alpha} + w_{2\alpha}$, $(w_1 \wedge w_2) = w_{1\alpha} \wedge w_{2\alpha}$, $(dw)_\alpha = dw_\alpha$ and $(\lambda w)_\alpha + \lambda w_\alpha$. With these operations, the set of all smooth forms on M forms a commutative cochain algebra $E_{\mathbb{R}}(M)$ that we shall call the <u>de Rham complex</u> of M. Its cohomology will be called the de Rham cohomology of M.

(4.3) <u>Definition</u>. Let M and N be differentiable spaces. A map $f\colon M \to N$ is said to be smooth if, for each plot $\alpha\colon U \to M$, the map $f \circ \alpha\colon U \to N$ is a plot on N.

A smooth map $f\colon M \to N$ induces a d.g. algebra map $f^*\colon E_{\mathbb{R}}(N) \to E_{\mathbb{R}}(M)$ defined as follows: let $\alpha\colon U \to M$ be a plot and w a smooth form on N. We define f^*w to be the form on M given by $(f^*w)_\alpha = w_{f \circ \alpha}$. The map $f^*\colon E_{\mathbb{R}}(N) \to E_{\mathbb{R}}(M)$ is then defined by $w \to f^*w$.

(4.4) <u>Examples</u>.

(a) Each differentiable manifold M has a natural differentiable space structure. Let U be a convex set. A map $\alpha\colon U \to M$ is a plot if and only if it is smooth. The usual de Rham complex of the manifold is isomorphic to the differentiable space de Rham complex of M. The smooth form w on the manifold M corresponds to the smooth form (w_α) on the differentiable space associated to M defined by $w_\alpha = \alpha^* w$ for each plot $\alpha\colon U \to M$.

(b) Each semisimplicial complex (s.s.c.) K gives rise to a natural differentiable space structure on $|K|$, Milnor's geometric realization of K. For each n-simplex σ of K, there is a canonical map $|\sigma|\colon \Delta^n \to |K|$ that maps the standard n-simplex Δ^n onto the cell in $|K|$ corresponding to σ. We shall call such maps <u>face maps</u>. The differentiable space structure on $|K|$ is the differentiable space structure generated by the face maps. We will abuse notation and denote this differentiable space by K. There is a natural bijection between the smooth forms on the differentiable space K and the smooth forms on K defined by Thom. (See [39] for Thom's definition of smooth forms on s.s.c.)

(c) The product of two differentiable spaces M, N has a natural differentiable space structure. Denote by p: $M \times N \to M$ and q: $M \times N \to N$ the canonical projections. Let U be a convex set. A map α: $U \times M \to N$ is a plot on $M \to N$ if and only if $p \circ \alpha$: $U \to M$ and $q \circ \alpha$: $U \to N$ are plots on M and N, respectively. We shall call this the *product differentiable structure* on $M \times N$. It is easy to verify that $M \times N$, with the product differentiable structure, is a product in the category of differentiable spaces.

(d) Each subset of a differentiable space has a natural differentiable space structure. Let N be a subset of a differentiable space M. A map α: $U \to N$ is a plot on N if and only if the composition $i \circ \alpha$: $U \to M$ of a with the inclusion i: $N \to M$ is a plot on M. With this differentiable structure, N has the following property: if Z is a differentiable space and f: $Z \to N$ is a map, then f is smooth if and only if $i \circ f$: $Z \to M$ is smooth. In particular, the inclusion i: $N \to M$ is smooth. We shall call this the *subspace differentiable structure* on N.

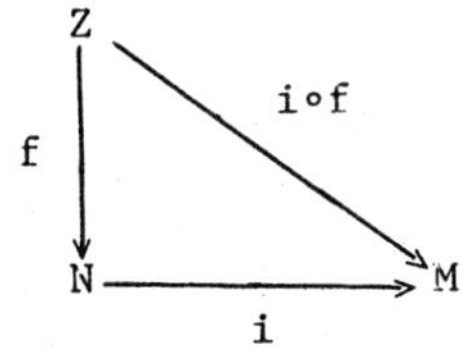

(e) If M is a differentiable space, N a set and if p: $M \to N$ is onto, then N inherits a natural differentiable space structure from M that we shall call the *quotient differentiable structure* on N. It is generated by the maps $p \circ \alpha$: $U \to N$, where α: $U \to M$ is a plot on M. With this differentiable structure N has the following property: if Z is a differentiable space and if f: $N \to Z$ is a map, then f is smooth if and only if $f \circ p$: $M \to Z$ is smooth.

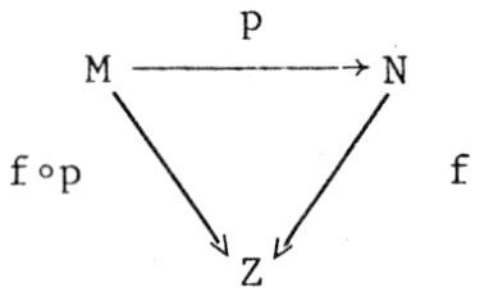

(f) Every topological space admits a differentiable space structure. Let χ be a topological space. A map $\alpha: U \to \chi$ from a convex set into χ is a plot if and only if it is continuous.

Let M be a differentiable space which is also a topological space. Denote the underlying topological space by $|M|$. Note that if every plot on M is continuous, then the natural map $M \to |M|$ is smooth.

Polynomial Forms on an s.s.c.

The piecewise linear structure of an s.s.c. K enables us to speak of the differential forms on K whose restriction to each face of K is a polynomial, with rational coefficients, in the barycentric coordinates of the face and their exterior derivatives. Sullivan introduced them in [37], showed that their homology is isomorphic to $H^*(K; \mathbb{Q})$ and, amazingly, that when K is simply connected they determine the rational homotopy type of K.

Denote the standard n-simplex by Δ^n and its barycentric coordinates by $(\xi_0,\ldots,\xi_n)$. Denote by $E(\Delta^n)$ the free graded commutative algebra over $\mathbb{Q}$ generated by the set $\{\xi_0,\ldots,\xi_n, d\xi,\ldots,d\xi_n\}$ with relations $\xi_0 + \xi_1 + \ldots + \xi_n = 1$, $d\xi_0 + d\xi_1 + \ldots + d\xi_n = 0$ where each ξ_j has degree 0 and each $d\xi_j$ has degree 1. Define a differential d on $E(\Delta^n)$ by $d: \xi_j \to d\xi_j$ and $d: d\xi_j \to 0$; extend d to all of $E(\Delta^n)$ by insisting that d be a derivation of $E(\Delta^n)$ of degree 1. We call the cochain algebra $E(\Delta^n)$ the <u>rational polynomial</u> (or rational) <u>de Rham complex of</u> Δ^n. Note that there is a natural injection of $E(\Delta^n)$ into the de Rham complex $E_{\mathbb{R}}(\Delta^n)$

of Δ^n: consider Δ^n as a subset of $\mathbb{R}^{n+1}$ so that the barycentric coordinates $(\xi_0,\ldots,\xi_n)$ of Δ^n are the restriction of the canonical coordinates on $\mathbb{R}^{n+1}$. The injection takes ξ_j to the corresponding coordinate function on Δ^n. We will identify $E(\Delta^n)$ with its image in $E_{\mathbb{R}}(\Delta^n)$ under this injection. Elements of $E(\Delta^n)$ will be called rational polynomial (or rational) forms on Δ^n.

Recall from (4.4) that each s.s.c. K induces a differentiable space structure on its geometric realization $|K|$. This differentiable structure is generated by the canonical face maps $|\sigma|: \Delta^n \to |K|$ corresponding to each simplex σ of K. For each p-form w on K, denote the form on Δ^n corresponding to the face map $|\sigma|: \Delta^n \to |K|$ by w_σ. This is a convenient abuse of notation.

(4.5) Definition. A rational polynomial (or rational) p-form w on an s.s.c. K is a smooth p-form w on K such that for each n and each n-simplex σ of K, w_σ is a rational polynomial p-form on Δ^n.

Denote the set of rational polynomial forms on the s.s.c. K by $E(K)$. Since, for each n, $E(\Delta^n)$ is a cochain algebra over $\mathbb{Q}$, $E(K)$ is a cochain algebra over $\mathbb{Q}$. The canonical inclusion $E(K) \to E_{\mathbb{R}}(K)$ is a d.g. algebra map. We call $E(K)$ the rational de Rham complex of K.

Observe that if w is a rational p-form on K and if σ is a p-simplex of K, then $\int_\sigma w$ is a rational number.

Let M be a differentiable space and U a compact oriented n-manifold or a compact convex set of dimension n. If $\alpha: U \to M$ is a smooth map and w is an n-form on M, then the pullback $\alpha^* w$ of w along α can be integrated over U. It is convenient to introduce the following notation: Let α: $U \to M$ be as above where the dimension of U is n. Let w be a smooth p-form on M. Define

$$< w,\alpha > = \begin{cases} \int_U \alpha^* w & \text{if } n = p \\ 0 & \text{if } n \neq p . \end{cases}$$

(4.6) Theorem (Sullivan). Let K be an s.s.c., $E(K)$ its rational de Rham complex and K its simplicial chain complex. The integration map

$$\int : E(K) \to \mathrm{Hom}_{\mathbb{Z}}(\Delta K, \mathbb{Q})$$

defined by $w \to \{\sigma \to < w,\sigma >\}$ induces a natural algebra isomorphism

$$\int^* : H^*(E(K)) \to H^*(K;\mathbb{Q}). \quad \square$$

Proofs of this theorem may be found in [4], [6], [26] and [38].

Connections on Cochain Algebras

In this section we generalize Chen's notion of power series connections to connections on cochain algebras. This generalization is necessary when studying the relationship between power series connections and Sullivan's minimal models (see Chapter 7).

Let V, W be graded vector spaces. Denote by $V \hat{\otimes} W$ the graded vector space $\prod_{n=0}^{\infty} \bigoplus_{p+q=n} V_p \oplus W_q$. A typical element of $V \hat{\otimes} W$ being the infinite sum $\sum_{j=1}^{\infty} v_j \otimes w_j$ where, for each n, there is only a finite number of terms $v_j \otimes w_j$ of degree n.

Let A be a cochain algebra with differential d and let L be a chain Lie algebra with differential ∂. We can extend the actions of d, ∂ and J to $A \hat{\otimes} L$ by setting $d(\Sigma a_i \otimes A_i) = \Sigma(da_i) \otimes A_i$, $\partial(\Sigma a_i \otimes A_i) = \Sigma a_i \otimes (\partial A_i)$ and $J(\Sigma a_i \otimes A_i) = \Sigma(Ja_i) \otimes A_i$, where $a_i \in A$ and $A_i \in L$. Define a bracket in $A \hat{\otimes} L$ by $[\Sigma a_i \otimes A_i, \Sigma b_j \otimes B_j] = \Sigma(a_i \wedge b_j) \otimes [A_i, B_j]$ where $a_i, b_j \in A$ and $A_i, B_j \in L$.

Usually we will omit the tensor sign and write the element $\Sigma a_i \otimes A_i$ of $A \hat{\otimes} L$ as $\Sigma a_i A_i$.

(4.7) Definition. Let A be a cochain algebra with differential d, and L a chain Lie algebra with differential ∂. A twisting cochain in $A \hat{\otimes} L$ is an element ω of $\prod_{p=0}^{\infty} A^{p+1} \otimes L_p$ $(\subseteq A \hat{\otimes} L)$ satisfying the "twisting cochain condition" $\partial\omega + d\omega - \frac{1}{2}[J\omega, \omega] = 0$.

If A is of finite type, then the dual $\mathrm{Hom}(A, \mathbb{Q})$ of A is a d.g. coalgebra. The map τ_ω: $\mathrm{Hom}(A, \mathbb{Q}) \to L$ defined by $\tau_\omega(\phi) = \Sigma\phi(a_i)A_i$, where $\omega = \Sigma a_i \otimes A_i$ and $\phi \in \mathrm{Hom}(A, \mathbb{Q})$ is a twisting cochain in the sense of Brown [5]. For our purposes there are two advantages in representing twisting cochains as elements of $A \hat{\otimes} L$ rather than as functions. The first is that, in our context, it is more natural to deal with A (usually a deRham complex) than its dual. Second, our twisting cochains take on a very explicit form when written as a elements of $A \hat{\otimes} L$. This is an advantage in computations.

(4.8) Definition. (a) Let A be a cochain algebra with 1-connected homology and finite Betti numbers. A connection on A is a free chain Lie algebra L and a twisting cochain ω in $A \hat{\otimes} L$ such that if (X_i) is a set that freely generates L and if $\omega \equiv \Sigma w_i X_i \bmod A \hat{\otimes} [L, L]$, then each w_i is closed in A and their homology classes $(\{w_i\})$ form a basis of $IH^*(A)$. We shall denote a connection on A by (ω, L) and shall call ω the connection form of the connection (ω, L).

(b) Let K be a 1-connected s.s.c. with finite Betti numbers. A power series connection on K is a connection on the rational de Rham complex $E(K)$ of K.

(4.9) Examples. In addition to the examples (2.8) we have:

(a) Let $p_1, p_2, \ldots, p_r$ be positive integers, and let $X_1, X_2, \ldots, X_r$ be indeterminates of degrees $p_1-1, p_2-1, \ldots, p_r-1$ respectively. Let $w_1, w_2,$

..., w_r be forms on the wedge W of the spheres $S^{p_1}, S^{p_2}, \ldots, S^{p_r}$ such that w_j restricted to S^{p_j} is a volume form on S^{p_j} and zero on the complement of S^{p_j} in W. If each $p_j \geq 2$, then W is 1-connected. A connection (ω, L) on W is defined by $L = \mathbb{L}(X_1, X_2, \ldots, X_r)$ with $\partial X_j = 0$ and $\omega = w_1 X_1 + w_2 X_2 + \ldots + w_r X_r$.

(b) Let K_1 and K_2 be two 1-connected s.s.c.'s, each with finite Betti numbers. Let (w_j, L_j) be a connection on K_j $(j = 1, 2)$. Observe that if $p \geq 1$, then each p-form w on K_j $(j = 1, 2)$ can be extended to a p-form $\tilde{w}$ on $K_1 \vee K_2$ by setting $\tilde{w} = 0$ on the complement of K_j in $K_1 \vee K_2$ and $\tilde{w} = w$ on K_j. This process defines inclusions

$$i_j: \bigoplus_{p \geq 1} E^p(K_j) \to E(K_1 \vee K_2)$$

$(j = 1, 2)$ such that the images of i_1 and i_2 in $E(K_1 \vee K_2)$ annihilate each other.

Set $L = L_1 * L_2$. (That is, L is the free product of L_1 and L_2 in the category of d.g. Lie algebras.) A twisting cochain ω in $\bigoplus_{p \geq 1} E^p(K_j) \hat{\otimes} L_j$ gives rise to twisting cochain $\tilde{\omega}$ in $E(K_1 \vee K_2) \hat{\otimes} (L_1 * L_2)$: if $\omega = \Sigma u_k U_k$, then $\tilde{\omega} = \Sigma \tilde{u}_k U_k$. Define a connection (ω, L) on $K_1 \vee K_2$ by setting $\omega = \tilde{\omega}_1 + \tilde{\omega}_2$. It is not hard to check that this does define a connection on $K_1 \vee K_2$.

The following theorem is an algebraic analogue of (2.6). A similar algebraic result has been proved by Gugenheim in [23], and a proof of a dual assertion can be found in [25]. The procedure given for computing a power series connection on a manifold, given in the appendix to Chapter 2, works equally well for computing connections on cochain algebras.

(4.10) Theorem. Every cochain algebra with 1-connected homology and finite Betti numbers has a connection. The chain Lie algebra associated to a cochain algebra by a connection is a connected minimal Lie algebra. □

The Main Theorem

The following theorem is a strengthened version of Chen's loop space homology theorem (Theorem 3.4.1 in [15]). It is proved in chapters 6 and 9.

(4.11) Theorem. Let K be a simply connected s.s.c. with finite Betti numbers. If (ω, L) is a power series connection on K, then there is a natural Lie algebra isomorphism τ: $s^{-1}\pi_*(|K|) \otimes \mathbb{Q} \to H_*(L)$. Moreover, τ is defined by integrating an L-valued iterated integral T_L over each element of $\pi_*(|K|) \otimes \mathbb{Q}$. □

A formula for T_L is given in (6.19). By carefully examining the coefficients of T_L, we will obtain a finite list of iterated integrals that comprise a basis of $\mathrm{Hom}(\pi_p(|K|),\mathbb{Q})$.

(4.12) Examples. From (4.9) it follows that:

(a) $s^{-1}\pi_*(S^{p_1} \vee S^{p_2} \vee \ldots \vee S^{p_r}) \otimes \mathbb{Q} \approx \mathbb{L}(X_1, X_2, \ldots, X_r)$, where $\deg X_j = p_j - 1$.

(b) $s^{-1}\pi_*(|K|) \vee |K|) \otimes \mathbb{Q} \approx s^{-1}\pi_*(|K_1|) \otimes \mathbb{Q} * s^{-1}\pi_*(|K_2|) \otimes \mathbb{Q}$, where $*$ denotes free product of Lie algebras. Here we used the fact (cf. [27]) that, if L_1 and L_2 are chain Lie algebras, then $H_*(L_1 * L_2) \approx H_*(L_1) * H_*(L_2)$.

Throughout the rest of this section, K will denote a fixed simply connected s.s.c. with finite Betti numbers. Choose a connection (ω, L) on K. Suppose that $\omega \equiv \Sigma w_i X_i \mod E(K) \hat{\otimes} I^2L$, where (X_i) is a set that freely generates L.

The connection form ω defines an isomorphism

$$\sigma\colon\ s^{-1} H^*(K; \mathbb{Q}) \to QL$$

as follows:

$$\sigma(s^{-1}z) = \sum_i \int_z w_i X_i \quad \text{for all} \quad z \in \tilde{H}_*(K; \mathbb{Q}).$$

That σ is an isomorphism follows from the definition (4.8) of a power series connection. Since $\partial L \subseteq [L, L]$, there is a natural map $H_*(L) \to QL$.

(4.13) Theorem. If (ω, L) is a power series connection on K as above, then the diagram

$$\begin{array}{ccc} s^{-1}\pi_*(|K|) \otimes \mathbb{Q} & \xrightarrow{\tau} & H_*(L) \\ {\scriptstyle s^{-1}h}\downarrow & & \downarrow \\ s^{-1}\tilde{H}_*(K; \mathbb{Q}) & \xrightarrow{\sigma} & QL \end{array}$$

commutes, where $h\colon \pi_*(|K|) \otimes \mathbb{Q} \to \tilde{H}_*(K; \mathbb{Q})$ denotes the rational Hurewicz homomorphism. Moreover, if (ω', L') is a power series connection on K', a simply connected s.s.c. with finite Betti numbers, and if $f\colon K \to K'$ is a simplicial map, then there is a d.g. Lie algebra map $\hat{f}\colon L \to L'$ such that the diagram

$$\begin{array}{ccccccc} s^{-1}\pi_*(|K|) \otimes \mathbb{Q} & & \xrightarrow{\quad\tau\quad} & & H_*(L) & & \\ & \searrow^{s^{-1}h} & & & \downarrow{\scriptstyle \hat{f}_*} & \searrow & \\ {\scriptstyle f_*}\downarrow & & s^{-1}\tilde{H}_*(K; \mathbb{Q}) & & \xrightarrow{\quad\sigma\quad} & & QL \\ & & \downarrow & & \downarrow & & \\ s^{-1}\pi_*(|K'|) \otimes \mathbb{Q} & & \xrightarrow{\quad\tau'\quad} & & H_*(L') & & \downarrow{\scriptstyle Q\hat{f}} \\ & \searrow^{s^{-1}h} & \downarrow{\scriptstyle f_*} & & & \searrow & \\ & & s^{-1}\tilde{H}_*(K'; \mathbb{Q}) & & \xrightarrow{\quad\sigma'\quad} & & QL' \end{array}$$

commutes. In particular, the Lie algebra associated to K by a connection is unique up to isomorphism. □

The Lie algebra L associated to K via a connection reflects the combinatorial structure of K as the following theorem shows. It is proved in chapter 6.

(4.14) Theorem. Let $n \geq 1$. If $f\colon S^n \to K$ is simplicial map (with respect to a suitable subdivision of S^n) such that $f_*\colon H_n(S^n; \mathbb{Q}) \to H_n(K; \mathbb{Q})$ is trivial, then there is a power series connection (ω', L') on the adjunction space $K \cup_f e^{n+1}$, where

$$L' = L * \mathbb{L}(Z) = \mathbb{L}(X_1, X_2, \ldots, Z)$$

and where $\deg Z = n$, the image of $s^{-1}\{f\}$ in $H_*(L)$ under the isomorphism

$$\tau\colon s^{-1}\pi_*(|K|) \otimes \mathbb{Q} \to H_*(L)$$

is $\{\partial Z\}$, and such that if z is a homology class in $H_{n+1}(K \cup_f e^{n+1})$ whose image in $H_{n+1}(K \cup_f e^{n+1}, K)$ is $\{e^{n+1}\}$, then $\sigma(s^{-1}z) \equiv Z \bmod QL$ under the isomorphism

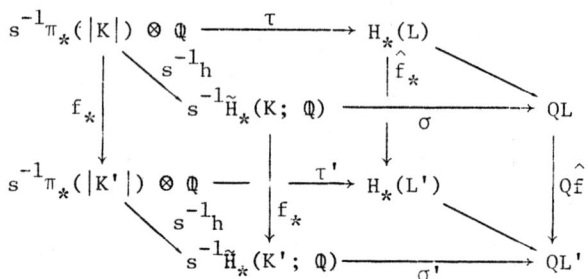

$$\sigma\colon\ s^{-1}\tilde{H}_*(K \cup_f e^{n+1}; \mathbb{Q}) \to QL'. \quad \square$$

(4.15) Remark. Allday [2], Baues-Lemaire [3], and Neisendorfer [33] each have a construction of a minimal chain Lie algebra model of a simply connected s.s.c. K with finite Betti numbers. Each has analogues of (4.11), (4.13), and (4.14) for his model. Each of these Lie algebra models is isomorphic to the Lie algebra model of K given by a power series connection (see Andrews-Arkowitz, *Notices A.M.S.*, 25 (1978), p. A142, and Hain [24]). The advantage of our construction of the Lie algebra model L of K is that it is constructed directly from the de Rham complex of K, whereas the other constructions of L are algebraic and require knowing either Sullivan's minimal model of K or Quillen's Lie algebra model (see [34]) of K.

(4.16) The Connected Sum of Closed Manifolds. In this example we compute a power series connection on the connected sum $M_1 \# M_2$ of two 1-connected closed manifolds M_1 and M_2 in terms of power series connections on M_1 and M_2. As an application, we prove the following theorem.

Theorem. If M_1 and M_2 are k-connected, n-dimensional closed manifolds with $k \geq 1$, and if neither M_1 nor M_2 is a rational homology sphere, then the map $f_*\colon \pi_p(M_1 \# M_2) \otimes \mathbb{Q} \to \pi_p(M_1 \vee M_2) \otimes \mathbb{Q}$ induced by the "pinch map" $f\colon M_1 \# M_2 \to M_1 \vee M_2$ is an isomorphism when $0 \leq p < n-1$ and $n \leq p < n+k-1$, and an epimorphism of nullity one when $p = n-1$.

Throughout this example M_1 and M_2 will denote fixed 1-connected closed manifolds of dimension n. Fix a coordinate neighborhood U_j in M_j and a diffeomorphism $\phi_j\colon U_j \to \mathbb{R}^n$ $(j = 1, 2)$. Denote by B_j the image of the unit ball of $\mathbb{R}^n$ in U_j under ϕ_j^{-1} $(j = 1, 2)$. Construct $M_1 \# M_2$ by cutting B_j from M_j $(j = 1, 2)$ and by smoothly gluing $S^{n-1} \times [0, 1]$ to $M_1 - B_1$ and $M_2 - B_2$, where $S^{n-1} \times \{0\}$ is identified with $\partial(M_1 - B_1)$ and $S^{n-1} \times \{1\}$ is identified with $\partial(M_2 - B_2)$.

Let $M_j' = M_j/B_j$ and denote by x_j the image of B_j in M_j' $(j = 1, 2)$. Denote by $\pi_j\colon M_j \to M_j'$ the canonical projection. Give M_j' the quotient differentiable space structure. The projection $\pi_j\colon M_j \to M_j'$ is smooth. Observe that M_j and M_j' are homeomorphic.

Define the pinch map $f\colon M_1 \# M_2 \to M_1' \vee M_2'$ by insisting that f takes $S^{n-1} \times [0, 1]$ into the base point of $M' \vee M'$ and that $f|(M_j - B_j) = \pi_j|(M_j - B_j)$ for $j = 1, 2$. It is not hard to check that f is a smooth map.

An elementary argument, using Mayer-Vietoris sequences, shows that whenever $0 \le p < n$, the map $f_*\colon H_p(M_1 \# M_2) \to H_p(M_1' \vee M_2')$ is an isomorphism. Recall that there is a natural isomorphism $\tilde{H}_*(M_1' \vee M_2') \approx \tilde{H}_*(M_1') \oplus \tilde{H}_*(M_2')$.

The key step in being able to write down a connection on $E(M_1 \# M_2)$ in terms of connections on $E(M_1)$ and $E(M_2)$ is to find nice subalgebras of $E(M_1)$ and $E(M_2)$. For $j = 1, 2$, define a d.g. subalgebra A_j of $E(M_j)$ by

$$A_j = \{w \in E(M_j)\colon w|B_j = 0\} \oplus \{g\colon M_j \to \mathbb{Q}\colon dg = 0\}.$$

It is not hard to show that integration induces an isomorphism

$$H^*(A_j) \approx H^*(M_j, B_j; \mathbb{Q}) \oplus \mathbb{Q},$$

and it follows immediately that the inclusion of A_j into $E(M_j)$ induces an isomorphism on homology.

Define inclusions $i_j\colon A_j \to E(M_1 \# M_2)$ $(j = 1, 2)$ by defining

$$i_j(w) = \begin{cases} w & \text{on } M_j - B_j \\ 0 & \text{on } (M_1 \# M_2) - (M_j - B_j) \end{cases}$$

if $w \in \{w \in E(M_j)\colon w|B_j = 0\}$, and by defining i_j of a constant function g on M_j to be the constant function on $M_1 \# M_2$ that extends $g|(M_j - B_j)$.

Let (ω_j, L_j) be a connection on A_j $(j = 1, 2)$. Suppose that

$$L_1 = (\mathbb{L}(X_1, X_2, \ldots, X_s, X), \partial_1)$$

and

$$L_2 = (\mathbb{L}(Y_1, Y_2, \ldots, Y_t, Y), \partial_2)$$

where X is the generator of L_1 that corresponds to the fundamental homology class of M_1 and where Y is the generator of L_2 that corresponds to the fundamental homology class of M_2. Set

$$L = (\mathbb{L}(X_1, \ldots, X_s, Y_1, \ldots, Y_t, Z), \partial)$$

where $\partial X_\ell = \partial_1 X_\ell$, $\partial Y_m = \partial_2 Y_m$ and $\partial Z = \partial_1 X + \partial_2 Y$. We will show that L is the Lie algebra model of $M_1 \# M_2$.

Let w_1 be the coefficient of X in ω_1 and w_2 be the coefficient of Y in ω_2. Since X and Y correspond to the fundamental classes of M_1 and M_2 respectively, it follows that $\langle w_1, M_1\rangle = \langle w_2, M_2\rangle = 1$. Consequently $\langle i_1 w_1 - i_2 w_2, M_1 \# M_2\rangle = 0$, and it follows from the de Rham theorem that there is an (n-1)-form ξ on $M_1 \# M_2$ such that $d\xi = i_1 w_1 - i_2 w_2$. Set

$$\omega = (i_1 \hat{\otimes} \mathrm{id})\omega_1 + (i_2 \hat{\otimes} \mathrm{id})\omega_2 - (i_1 w_1)X - (i_2 w_2)Y + \tfrac{1}{2}(i_1 w_1 + i_2 w_2)Z + \tfrac{1}{2}\xi(\partial_1 X - \partial_2 Y).$$

It is not hard to check that $\omega \in E(M_1 \# M_2) \hat{\otimes} L$, that $\partial\omega + d\omega - \frac{1}{2}[J\omega, \omega] = 0$ and that (ω, L) is a connection on $E(M_1 \# M_2)$.

From (4.9(b)) we know that the Lie algebra model of $M_1' \vee M_2'$ is $L_1 * L_2$. Let $\hat{f}: L \to L_1 * L_2$ be a map on the Lie algebra models induced by the pinch map $f: M_1 \# M_2 \to M_1' \vee M_2'$. The theorem stated at the beginning of this example will follow from the following lemma.

<u>Lemma</u>. Let M_1, M_2, L_1, L_2, L and $\hat{f}: L \to L_1 * L_2$ be as above. If neither M_1 nor M_2 is a rational homology sphere, then $\hat{f}_*: H_p(L) \to H_p(L_1 * L_2)$ is an isomorphism when $0 \le p < n-2$ and $n-1 \le p < n+k-2$, and an epimorphism of nullity one when $p = n-2$.

<u>Proof</u>. First note that $Q\hat{f}$ takes X_i to X_i $(i = 1, 2, \ldots, s)$, Y_i to Y_i $(i = 1, 2, \ldots, t)$, and Z to X + Y.

That $\hat{f}_*: H_p(L) \to H_p(L_1 * L_2)$ is an isomorphism whenever $0 \le p < n-2$ is a consequence of the fact that $\hat{f}_p: L_p \to (L_1 * L_2)_p$ is an isomorphism whenever $0 \le p < n-2$.

Denote by N the sub-Lie algebra of L generated by $X_1, X_2, \ldots, X_s, Y_1, Y_2, \ldots, Y_t$. Observe that the composite $N \to L \xrightarrow{\hat{f}} L_1 * L_2$ is injective.

To prove that $\hat{f}_*: H_{n-2}(L) \to H_{n-2}(L_1 * L_2)$ is an epimorphism of nullity one, first note that $H_{n-1}(L, N)$ is 1-dimensional and generated by the homology class of Z, and that $H_{n-1}(L_1 * L_2, N)$ is two-dimensional and spanned by the homology classes of X and Y. Since neither M_1 nor M_2 is a rational homology sphere, it follows that $\partial_1 X$, $\partial_2 Y$, and ∂Z are each nonzero. Consequently, the natural maps $H_{n-1}(L) \to H_{n-1}(L, N)$ and $H_{n-1}(L_1 * L_2) \to H_{n-1}(L_1 * L_2, N)$ are trivial. Since $H_{n-2}(L, N) = 0$ and $H_{n-2}(L_1 * L_2, N) = 0$, it follows that the following commutative diagram has exact rows.

$$\begin{array}{ccccccccc} 0 \to & H_{n-1}(L, N) & \longrightarrow & H_{n-2}(N) & \to & H_{n-2}(L) & \longrightarrow & 0 \\ & \downarrow \tilde{f}_* & & \downarrow \mathrm{id} & & \downarrow \hat{f}_* & & \\ 0 \to & H_{n-1}(L_1 * L_2, N) & \to & H_{n-2}(N) & \to & H_{n-2}(L_1 * L_2) & \to & 0 \end{array}$$

Since $\tilde{f}_*: H_{n-1}(L, N) \to H_{n-1}(L_1 * L_2, N)$ takes $\{Z\}$ to $\{X\} + \{Y\}$ and since $H_{n-1}(L_1 * L_2, N)$ is 2-dimensional, it follows that $\hat{f}_*: H_{n-2}(L) \to H_{n-2}(L_1 * L_2)$ is a surjection of nullity one.

To prove that $\hat{f}_*: H_p(L) \to H_p(L_1 * L_2)$ is an isomorphism when $n-1 \le p < n+k-2$, note that $H_p(L, N) = 0$ and $H_p(L_1 * L_2, N) = 0$ whenever $n-1 < p < n+k-2$. It follows that the diagram

$$\begin{array}{ccccccc} 0 \to & H_p(N) & \to & H_p(L) & \longrightarrow & 0 \\ & \downarrow \mathrm{id} & & \downarrow \hat{f}_* & & \\ 0 \to & H_p(N) & \to & H_p(L_1 * L_2) & \to & 0 \end{array}$$

commutes and has exact rows when $n-1 \le p < n+k-2$. □

(4.17) Fat Wedge of Spheres. In this example we discuss higher order Whitehead products. We calculate the Lie Algebra model of a fat wedge of spheres and identify the homology class of the model that corresponds to the universal rth order Whitehead product.

Allday [2] has previously computed the Lie algebra model of a fat wedge of spheres and used it to identify the higher order Whitehead products in the homotopy Lie algebra of a 1-connected rational space as the "Massey products" in the homology of the Lie algebra model of the space.

Let $S_1, S_2, \ldots, S_r$ be 1-connected oriented spheres of dimension $p_1, p_2, \ldots, p_r$ respectively. Denote their product $S_1 \times S_2 \times \ldots \times S_r$ by P. Choose a base point x_j of S_j ($j = 1, 2, \ldots, r$). The <u>fat wedge</u> $T(S_1, S_2, \ldots, S_r)$ of $S_1, S_2, \ldots, S_r$ is the subset

$$\{(\xi_1, \xi_2, \ldots, \xi_r) \in P\colon \text{for at least one } j,\ \xi_j = x_j\}$$

of P. We shall denote the fat wedge of $S_1, S_2, \ldots, S_r$ by T, and the inclusion of T into P by $i\colon T \to P$. Give T the subspace differentiable structure.

Choose a smooth map

$$\nu_j\colon ([0, 1]^{p_j}, \partial[0, 1]^{p_j}) \to (S_j, x_j)$$

of degree 1. Set $N = p_1 + p_2 + \ldots + p_r$ and write $[0, 1]^N = \prod_{j=1}^{r} [0, 1]^{p_j}$. A typical element of $[0, 1]^N$ is written $(\xi_1, \xi_2, \ldots, \xi_r)$, where $\xi_j \in [0, 1]^{p_j}$. Define a smooth map

$$\nu\colon ([0, 1]^N, \partial[0, 1]^N) \to (P, T)$$

by $\nu(\xi_1, \xi_2, \ldots, \xi_r) = (\nu_1(\xi_1), \nu_2(\xi_2), \ldots, \nu_r(\xi_r))$. Set $h = \nu|\partial[0, 1]^N$ and observe that ν induces a homeomorphism $T \cup_h [0, 1]^N \to P$.

Let ξ_j be the element of $\pi_{p_j}(T)$ which is the homotopy class of $S_j \to T$. The rth <u>order universal Whitehead product</u> $[\xi_1, \xi_2, \ldots, \xi_r]$ of $\xi_1, \xi_2, \ldots, \xi_r$ is the homotopy class of $h\colon \partial[0, 1]^N \to T$ in $\pi_{N-1}(T)$.

Suppose that χ is a topological space and that $\alpha_j \in \pi_{p_j}(\chi)$ ($j = 1, 2, \ldots, r$). For each j in $\{1, 2, \ldots, r\}$ choose a continuous map $f_j\colon S_j \to \chi$ such that $f_{j*}(S_j) = \alpha_j$. The (possibly empty) rth <u>order Whitehead product set</u> $[\alpha_1, \alpha_2, \ldots, \alpha_r]$ is the subset

$$\{f_*([\xi_1, \xi_2, \ldots, \xi_r]);\ f\colon T \to \chi \text{ extends } \vee f_j\colon \bigvee_{j=1}^{r} S_j \to \chi\}$$

of $\pi_{N-1}(\chi)$.

Observe that the set $[\alpha_1, \alpha_2, \ldots, \alpha_r]$ contains zero if and only if the map $\vee f_j\colon \vee S_j \to \chi$ extends to a continuous map $\tilde{f}\colon P \to \chi$.

Choose a volume form u_j on S_j such that $\langle u_j, S_j \rangle = 1$. Denote by $\pi_j \colon P \to S_j$ the canonical projection. For each j set $w_j = \pi_j^* u_j$. For each subset I of {1, 2, ..., r} set

$$w_I = w_{i_1} \wedge w_{i_2} \wedge \dots \wedge w_{i_s}$$

where $I = \{i_1, i_2, \dots, i_s\}$ and $i_1 < i_2 < \dots < i_s$.

Before writing down the Lie algebra models of P and T we need to define a permutation symbol. For subsets I, J, K of {1, 2, ..., r} let $\varepsilon(I, J; K)$ be the unique element of {-1, 0, 1} such that $(Jw_I) \wedge w_J = \varepsilon(I, J; K) w_K$. Set $\underset{\sim}{r} = \{1, 2, \dots, r\}$. The Lie algebra model L_P of P is given by

$$L_P = \mathbb{L}(X_I;\ I \subseteq \underset{\sim}{r})$$

where $\deg X_I = -1 + \sum_{i \in I} p_i$ and where $\partial X_K = \frac{1}{2} \sum_{I,J} \varepsilon(I, J; K)[X_I, X_J]$.

The Lie algebra model L_T of T is the sub-Lie algebra of L_P generated by $\{X_I;\ I \neq \underset{\sim}{r}\}$. A connection on $\mathcal{E}(P)$ is given by the connection form

$$\omega_P = \sum_I w_I X_I$$

and a connection on $\mathcal{E}(T)$ is given by the connection form

$$\omega_T = \sum_{I \neq \underset{\sim}{r}} w_I X_I .$$

It follows easily from definition (6.29) that the Lie algebra map $\hat{i} \colon L_T \to L_P$ induced by the inclusion $i \colon T \to P$ is just the natural inclusion $L_T \to L_P$. Consequently, the diagram

$$\begin{array}{ccc}
s^{-1}\pi_*(T) \otimes \mathbb{Q} & \xrightarrow{\tau_T} & H_*(L_T) \\
{\scriptstyle s^{-1} i_*}\downarrow & & \downarrow{\scriptstyle \hat{i}_*} \\
s^{-1}\pi_*(P) \otimes \mathbb{Q} & \xrightarrow[\tau_P]{} & H_*(L_P)
\end{array}$$

commutes.

Since $\partial X_{\underset{\sim}{r}} = \frac{1}{2} \sum_{I,J} \varepsilon(I, J\colon \underset{\sim}{r})[X_I, X_J]$, and since $P = T \cup_h [0, 1]^N$, it follows from (4.14) that $\tau_T(s^{-1}[\xi_1, \xi_2, \dots, \xi_r]) = \{\frac{1}{2} \sum_{I,J} \varepsilon(I, J\colon \underset{\sim}{r})[X_I, X_J]\}$. Thus we have identified the universal rth order Whitehead product in $H_*(L_T)$.

(4.18) Complex Projective Space. In this example we illustrate techniques which give information about the position of the integral homotopy lattice inside $\pi_*(M) \otimes \mathbb{Q}$. (The integral homotopy lattice is the image of the canonical map $\pi_*(M) \to \pi_*(M) \otimes \mathbb{Q}$.)

From example (2.4)(b) we know that $\mathbb{C}P^n$ has Lie algebra model

$$L = \mathbb{L}(X_1, X_2, \dots, X_n: \deg X_k = 2k - 1, \partial X_k = \frac{1}{2} \sum_{i+j=k} [X_i, X_j]).$$

Since the integral homotopy group $\pi_{2n+1}(\mathbb{C}P^{n+1})$ is trivial, it follows that the homotopy class of the Hopf map $h: S^{2n+1} \to \mathbb{C}P^n$ generates $\pi_{2n+1}(\mathbb{C}P^n)$. Since $\mathbb{C}P^{n+1} = \mathbb{C}P^n \cup_h e^{2n+2}$, it follows from (4.14) that the image of $\{h\}$ in $H_*(L)$ is $\frac{1}{2}\{\sum_{i+j=n+1} [X_i, X_j]\}$.

Let T be a fat wedge of n + 1 copies of S^2. Let $\zeta_1, \zeta_2, \dots, \zeta_{n+1}$ be the n + 1 generators of $\pi_2(T)$, one corresponding to each copy of S^2. Let ζ be a generator of $\pi_2(\mathbb{C}P^n)$ such that $\langle w, \zeta\rangle = 1$. An elementary obstruction theory argument shows that there is a smooth map $f: T \to \mathbb{C}P^n$ such that $f_*(\zeta_j) = \zeta$ for each $j \in \{1, 2, \dots, n+1\}$. The Lie algebra model of T is

$$L_T = \mathbb{L}(Z_I: I \subsetneq \{1, 2, \dots, n+1\}, \partial Z_K = \frac{1}{2} \sum_{I \dot\cup J=K} [Z_I, Z_J]),$$

where $\dot\cup$ denotes disjoint union. The map $f: T \to \mathbb{C}P^n$ induces the map $\hat{f}: L_T \to L$ defined by

$$\hat{f}(Z_I) = |I|!X_{|I|} \qquad I \subsetneq \underset{\sim}{n+1} .$$

A short calculation shows that

$$\hat{f}(\frac{1}{2} \sum_{I \dot\cup J=\underset{\sim}{n+1}} [Z_I, Z_J]) = \frac{(n+1)!}{2} \sum_{i+j=n+1} [X_i, X_j] .$$

It follows that in $\pi_{2n+1}(\mathbb{C}P^n)$

$$\{h\} = \frac{1}{(n+1)!} f_*([\zeta_1, \zeta_2, \dots, \zeta_{n+1}]) = \frac{1}{(n+1)!} [\zeta, \zeta, \dots, \zeta] .$$

That is, the (n+1)st order Whitehead product of a generator of $\pi_2(\mathbb{C}P^n)$ with itself divided by (n+1)! is a generator of $\pi_{2n+1}(\mathbb{C}P^n)$.

5. ITERATED INTEGRALS

Kuo-Tsai Chen's iterated integrals play a central role in our approach to de Rham homotopy theory. Let M be a simply connected smooth manifold with finite Betti numbers. In order to give a procedure for detecting a smooth map $f: S^p \to M$ using differential forms on M, we lift f to a smooth map $f': S^{p-1} \to \Omega M$, where ΩM denotes the space of piecewise smooth loops on M.

In this chapter we construct certain differential forms on ΩM from the smooth forms on M, namely Chen's iterated integrals. In Chapter 6 we show that there are enough iterated integrals on ΩM to detect all the nontrivial elements of $\pi_*(M) \otimes \mathbb{Q}$, and in Chapter 7 we will describe a procedure for finding a finite set of iterated integrals of forms on M that will detect each nontrivial element of $\pi_p(M) \otimes \mathbb{Q}$.

Iterated integrals enjoy many nice properties. In this chapter we define them and state their most useful properties.

Loop Spaces

The space of piecewise smooth paths on a differentiable space M has a natural differentiable space structure:

A path $\gamma: [0, 1] \to M$ is said to be piecewise smooth if there is a partition $0 = t_0 < t_1 < \ldots < t_m = 1$ of $[0, 1]$ such that the restriction of γ to each subinterval $[t_{j-1}, t_j]$ of $[0, 1]$ is a plot on M. Denote by PM the set of all piecewise smooth paths on M. For a set X and a map $\alpha: X \to PM$, define the <u>suspension</u> of α to be the map $\phi_\alpha: [0, 1] \times X \to M$ that takes (t, ξ) to $\alpha(\xi)(t)$. The differentiable space structure on M is generated by the maps $\alpha: U \to PM$ where U is a convex set and such that there is a partition $0 = t_0 < t_1 < \ldots < t_m = 1$ of $[0, 1]$ such that the restriction of the suspension ϕ_α: $[0, 1] \times U \to M$ of α to each $[t_{j-1}, t_j] \times U$ is a plot on M. We shall call such plots basic plots on PM.

Observe that if U is a compact convex set, and if α: $U \to PM$ is a plot on PM, then α is a basic plot.

For a point x in M, denote by P_xM the subset of PM consisting of those paths γ: $[0, 1] \to M$ such that $\gamma(0) = x$. Denote by Ω_xM the subset of P_xM consisting of those paths γ: $[0, 1] \to M$ such that $\gamma(0) = \gamma(1) = x$. According to (4.4)(d), both P_xM and Ω_xM inherit differentiable space structures from PM. Often we will suppress the base-point x and write ΩM. The space Ω_xM is called the loop space of M.

Iterated Integrals

Throughout this section M will denote a fixed differentiable space. Let $w_1, w_2, \ldots, w_r$ be smooth forms on M. The iterated integral $\int w_1w_2\ldots w_r$ is a smooth form on ΩM of degree $-r + \sum_{j=1}^{r} \deg w_j$.

When each w_j is a 1-form on M, $\int w_1w_2\ldots w_r$ is a smooth real-valued function on ΩM. Its value on the loop γ: $[0, 1] \to M$ is given as follows: if $\gamma^*w_j = f_j(t)dt$, then

$$<\int w_1w_2\ldots w_r, \gamma> = \int_0^1 \int_0^{t_n} \cdots \int_0^{t_2} f_1(t_1)f_2(t_2)\ldots f_r(t_r)dt_1dt_2\ldots dt_r \ .$$

In particular, when $r = 0$, $<\int w, \gamma> = \int_\gamma w$, the usual line integral.

We now define iterated integrals of forms of arbitrary degree. Let U be an n-dimensional convex set with coordinates $(\xi_1, \xi_2, \ldots, \xi_n)$ and $[b, c]$ a subinterval of the real line with coordinate t. An $\mathcal{E}_{\mathbb{R}}(U)$-valued function of t is a smooth form on $[b, c] \times U$ which can be written in the form

$$\Sigma a_{i_1\ldots i_p}(t, \xi)d\xi_{i_1} \wedge d\xi_{i_2} \wedge \ldots \wedge d\xi_{i_p} .$$

For each smooth form w on $[b, c] \times U$ there are unique $\mathcal{E}_{\mathbb{R}}(U)$-valued forms w' and w'' such that $w = dt \wedge w' + w''$. In fact, if $\frac{\partial}{\partial t}$ denotes the vector field on $[b, c] \times U$ with integral curves $t \to (t, \xi)$, then $w'(t, \xi) = \frac{\partial}{\partial t} \lrcorner\, w(t, \xi)$.

Let $\alpha: U \to PM$ be a basic plot. That is, there is a partition $0 = t_0 < t_1 < \dots < t_m = 1$ of $[0, 1]$ such that the restriction of the suspension ϕ_α of α to each $[t_{j-1}, t_j] \times U$ is smooth. Let $w_1, w_2, \dots, w_r$ be smooth forms on M. For each k in $\{1, \dots, r\}$ set $w_k'(t, \xi) = \frac{\partial}{\partial t} \lrcorner\, \phi_\alpha^* w_k$. Observe that for each k, the form w_k' is a piecewise smooth $E_{\mathbb{R}}(U)$-valued function of t. For each t in [0, 1] we inductively define forms $\int_0^t w_1, \int_0^t w_1 w_2, \dots, \int_0^t w_1 w_2 \dots w_r$ on ΩM as follows: set

$$\left(\int_0^t w_1\right)_\alpha (\xi) = \int_0^t w_1'(s, \xi) ds ,$$

$$\left(\int_0^t w_1 w_2\right)_\alpha (\xi) = \int_0^t \left(\int_0^s w_1\right)_\alpha (\xi) \wedge w_2'(s, \xi) ds ,$$

and

$$\left(\int_0^t w_1 w_2 \dots w_r\right)_\alpha (\xi) = \int_0^t \left(\int_0^s w_1 \dots w_{r-1}\right)_\alpha (\xi) \wedge w_r'(s, \xi) ds .$$

It is a straightforward exercise to check that this procedure does in fact define smooth forms on ΩM. One must check the compatibility condition of (4.2).

We now define the r-times iterated integral $\int w_1 w_2 \dots w_r$ to be $\int_0^1 w_1 w_2 \dots w_r$. It follows that $\int w_1 w_2 \dots w_r$ is a smooth form on ΩM of degree $-r + \sum_{j=1}^{r} \deg w_j$. It is convenient to define the zero-times interated integral, denoted 1, to be the smooth functional which takes the constant value 1 on ΩM.

Iterated integrals were first defined by Chen for 1-forms in [7] and for arbitrary forms in [8]. The definition given above defines a form on PM. However, to simplify our exposition, we only consider their restrictions to ΩM. For an account of iterated integrals on PM, see Chen [15].

Properties of Iterated Integrals

The remainder of this chapter is devoted to some basic and useful properties of iterated integrals. To demonstrate their use, a formula for the Hopf invariant of a smooth map $f: S^{2n-1} \to S^n$ is given in terms of iterated integrals.

Recall that for a graded commutative algebra A, the linear automorphism $J: A \to A$ of A is defined by $Ja = (-1)^{\deg a} a$ for each $a \in A$. Throughout this section, M will denote a fixed differentiable space.

(5.1) Proposition (Chen [10]). If $w_1, w_2, \ldots, w_r$ are smooth forms on M, then

$$d\int w_1 w_2 \ldots w_r = \sum_{i=1}^{r} (-1)^i \int Jw_1 \ldots Jw_{i-1} dw_i w_{i+1} \ldots w_r$$

$$- \sum_{i=1}^{r-1} (-1)^i \int Jw_1 \ldots Jw_{i-1} (Jw_i \wedge w_{i+1}) w_{i+2} \ldots w_r \ . \quad \square$$

In order to state the next proposition we need to introduce a weighted permutation symbol.

(5.2) For each permutation σ of $\{1, \ldots, r\}$ and for each family $(q_1, q_2, \ldots, q_r)$ of nonnegative integers, define the permutation symbol $\varepsilon(\sigma; q_1 \ldots, q_r)$ to be the element of $\{-1, 1\}$ defined by

$$\alpha_1 \wedge \alpha_2 \wedge \ldots \wedge \alpha_r = \varepsilon(\sigma; q_1, \ldots, q_r) \alpha_{\sigma(1)} \wedge \alpha_{\sigma(2)} \wedge \ldots \wedge \alpha_{\sigma(r)}$$

where $\alpha_1, \alpha_2, \ldots, \alpha_r$ are generators of the free graded commutative algebra $\Lambda(\alpha_1, \alpha_2, \ldots, \alpha_r)$ of degrees $q_1, q_2, \ldots, q_r$ respectively.

Let r and s be nonnegative integers. Recall that a permutation σ of the set $\{1, 2, \ldots, r+s\}$ of integers is a shuffle of type (r, s) if $\sigma^{-1}(1) < \sigma^{-1}(2) < \ldots < \sigma^{-1}(r)$ and $\sigma^{-1}(r+1) < \sigma^{-1}(r+2) < \ldots < \sigma^{-1}(r+s)$.

(5.3) Proposition (Ree [35], Chen [10]). If $w_1, w_2, \ldots, w_{r+s}$ are smooth forms on M of degrees $p_1, p_2, \ldots, p_{r+s}$ respectively, then

$$\int w_1 \ldots w_r \wedge \int w_{r+1} \ldots w_{r+s} = \sum_{\sigma} \varepsilon(\sigma; p_1 - 1, \ldots, p_{r+s} - 1) \int w_{\sigma(1)} w_{\sigma(2)} \ldots w_{\sigma(r+s)}$$

where σ ranges over the shuffles of type (r, s) of $\{1, 2, \ldots, r+s\}$. □

(5.4) Definition. The Pontrjagin product of the smooth maps $\alpha: U \to \Omega M$ and $\beta: V \to \Omega M$ is the smooth map $\alpha \times \beta: U \times V \to \Omega M$ that takes the point (ξ, η) in $U \times V$ to the product $\alpha(\xi) \cdot \beta(\eta)$ of the loops $\alpha(\xi)$ and $\beta(\eta)$.

(5.5) Proposition (Chen [10]). If U and V are each either a compact oriented manifold or a compact convex set, if $\alpha: U \to \Omega M$ and $\beta: V \to \Omega M$ are smooth maps, and if $w_1, w_2, \ldots, w_r$ are smooth forms on M, then

$$<\int w_1 w_2 \ldots w_r, \alpha \times \beta> = \sum_{i=0}^{r} <\int w_1 \ldots w_i, \alpha><\int w_{i+1} \ldots w_r, \beta> .$$

When $i = 0$ we interpret $\int w_1 \ldots w_i$ as 1, the 0-times iterated integral, and when $i = r$ we interpret $\int w_{i+1} \ldots w_r$ as 1, the 0-times iterated integral. □

(5.6) Corollary (Chen [10]). Let r and s be positive integers with $r < s$. Let each of $U_1, \ldots, U_s$ be either a compact convex set or a compact oriented manifold. Let $\alpha_j: U_j \to \Omega M$ be smooth maps $(j = 1, \ldots, s)$ and $w_1, w_2, \ldots, w_r$ smooth forms on M. If each U_j has positive dimension, then

$$<\int w_1 w_2 \ldots w_r, \alpha_1 \times \alpha_2 \times \ldots \times \alpha_s> = 0 . \quad \square$$

Let M and N be differentiable spaces, x a point in M, and y a point in N. Each smooth map $f: M \to N$ for which $f(x) = y$ induces a smooth map $\Omega f: \Omega_x M \to \Omega_y N$ defined by $\Omega f: \gamma \to f \circ \gamma$ for each $\gamma \in \Omega_x M$. Further, f induces a d.g. algebra map

$$(\Omega f)^*: E_{\mathbb{R}}(\Omega_y N) \to E_{\mathbb{R}}(\Omega_x M)$$

defined as in (4.3).

(5.7) Proposition. Let M and N be differentiable spaces with base points x and y respectively. If $f: M \to N$ is a smooth map taking x to y, and if $w_1, w_2, \ldots, w_r$ are smooth forms on N, then

$$(\Omega f)^* \int w_1 w_2 \ldots w_r = \int f^* w_1 f^* w_2 \ldots f^* w_r . \quad \square$$

Once-iterated integrals have a useful evaluation property.

(5.8) Proposition (Chen [15]). Let U be a compact convex set or a compact oriented manifold. If $\alpha\colon U \to \Omega M$ is a smooth map with suspension $\phi_\alpha\colon I \times U \to M$, and if w is a smooth form on M, then

$$\left\langle \int w, \alpha \right\rangle = \langle w, \phi_\alpha \rangle \quad . \quad \square$$

To illustrate the use of the above properties we present a familiar example, calculating the Hopf invariant, using iterated integrals.

(5.9) Example (Hopf invariant). Let $n \geq 2$ and $f\colon S^{2n-1} \to S^n$ be a smooth map. Define a smooth map $\alpha\colon S^{n-1} \to \Omega S^n$ as follows: Consider S^n as the subset $\{(t, \xi)\colon t^2 + \|\xi\|^2 = 1\}$ of $\mathbb{R} \times \mathbb{R}^n$. Fix a point ξ_0 in $\mathbb{R}^n$ such that $\|\xi_0\| = 1$. Define smooth maps $\alpha'_n, \alpha''_n\colon S^{n-1} \to PS^n$ by

$$\phi_{\alpha'}(t, \xi) = (\sin\{(2t - 1)\pi/2\}, \cos\{(2t - 1)\pi/2\}\xi)$$

and

$$\phi_{\alpha''}(t, \xi) = (\sin\{(1 - 2t)\pi/2\}, \cos\{(1 - 2t)\pi/2\}\xi_0) \ .$$

Define α by $\alpha(\xi) = \alpha'(\xi) \cdot \alpha''(\xi)$. Note that the map

$$\phi_\alpha\colon ([0, 1] \times S^{n-1}, \{0, 1\} \times S^{n-1}) \to (S^n, *)$$

of pairs has degree 1.

Choose a volume form w on S^n such that $\langle w, S^n \rangle = 1$. Since $n \geq 2$, f^*w is exact, and there is an (n-1)-form ξ on S^{2n-1} such that $d\xi = f^*w$. Now

$$\begin{aligned} d\int \xi f^*w &= -\int d\xi f^*w + \int J\xi \wedge f^*w \\ &= -\int f^*w f^*w + \int J\xi \wedge f^*w \\ &= -(\Omega f)^* \int ww + \int J\xi \wedge f^*w \ . \end{aligned}$$

Using this, Stokes' theorem, and (5.8), we have

$$\begin{aligned} \left\langle \int ww, (\Omega f) \circ \alpha \right\rangle &= \left\langle (\Omega f)^* \int ww, \alpha \right\rangle \\ &= \left\langle \int J\xi \wedge f^*w, \alpha \right\rangle - \left\langle d\int \xi f^*w, \alpha \right\rangle \\ &= \left\langle \int J\xi \wedge f^*w, \alpha \right\rangle \\ &= \langle J\xi \wedge f^*w, \phi_\alpha \rangle \\ &= \int_{S^{2n-1}} J\xi \wedge f^*w \quad . \end{aligned}$$

According to Whitehead's formula for the Hopf invariant γ_f of f (see [41]), we have

$$\gamma_f = \left\langle \int ww, (\Omega f) \circ \alpha \right\rangle . \quad \square$$

The inverse of the path $\gamma: [0, 1] \to M$ is the path $\gamma^{-1}: [0, 1] \to M$ defined by $\gamma^{-1}(t) = \gamma(1 - t)$. The map $i: \Omega M \to \Omega M$ defined by $\gamma \mapsto \gamma^{-1}$ is smooth.

(5.10) Proposition (Chen [9]). Let $w_1, w_2, \ldots, w_r$ be smooth forms on M. If q is the number of w_j of even degree, then

$$i^* \int w_1 w_2 \ldots w_r = (-1)^{r+\binom{q}{2}} \int w_r w_{r-1} \ldots w_1 \ . \quad \square$$

A reparametrization of a piecewise smooth path $\gamma: [0, 1] \to M$ is a piecewise smooth function $\tau: [0, 1] \to [0, 1]$ such that $\tau(0) = 0$, $\tau(1) = 1$. The corresponding reparametrization of γ is the piecewise smooth path $\gamma \circ \tau$. Recall from advanced calculus that if w is a smooth 1-form on M, then

$$\int_\gamma w = \int_{\gamma \circ \tau} w \ .$$

Let $\alpha: U \to \Omega M$ be a plot. A reparametrization of γ is a function $\tau: [0, 1] \times U \to [0, 1]$ such that

(a) for each $\xi \in U$, $\tau(0, \xi) = 0$ and $\tau(1, \xi) = 1$, and

(b) the map $\hat{\tau}: U \to P([0, 1])$, defined by $\hat{\tau}(\xi)(t) = \tau(t, \xi)$, is smooth.

The reparametrization of α via τ is the map $\alpha': U \to \Omega M$ whose suspension is $(t, \xi) \mapsto \alpha(\tau(t, \xi), \xi)$. Note that α' is not necessarily a smooth map $U \to \Omega M$ although, for each smooth form w on ΩM, we can evaluate $\langle w, \alpha' \rangle$.

(5.11) Proposition (Chen [16]). Let $w_1, w_2, \ldots, w_r$ be smooth forms on M. If $\alpha: U \to \Omega M$ is a plot, and if $\alpha': U \to \Omega M$ is a map obtained from α by a reparametrization, then

$$\langle \int w_1 w_2 \ldots w_r, \alpha \rangle = \langle \int w_1 w_2 \ldots w_r, \alpha' \rangle \ . \quad \square$$

(5.12) Proposition (Chen [10]). If $w_1, w_2, \ldots, w_r$ are smooth forms on M, and if $f: M \to \mathbb{R}$ is a smooth function, then

(a) $$\int df w_1 \ldots w_r = \int (f w_1) w_2 \ldots w_r - f(x) \int w_1 w_2 \ldots w_r \ ,$$

(b) $$\int w_1 \ldots w_i \, df w_{i+1} \ldots w_r = \int w_1 \ldots w_i (f w_{i+1}) w_{i+2} \ldots w_r - \int w_1 \ldots w_{i-1} (f w_i) w_{i+1} \ldots w_r \ ,$$

for $1 \le i < r$,

(c) $\int w_1 \ldots w_r df = f(x) \int w_1 w_2 \ldots w_r - \int w_1 \ldots w_{r-1}(fw_r)$,

where x denotes the base-point of M. □

For a d.g. subalgebra A of $E_{\mathbb{R}}(M)$, denote by $\int A$ the linear subspace of $E_{\mathbb{R}}(M)$ that is spanned by the iterated integrals $\int w_1 w_2 \ldots w_r$ where each $w_j \in A$. According to (5.1) and (5.3), $\int A$ is a cochain algebra. In fact, $\int A$ is a d.g. Hopf algebra and, as a d.g. Hopf algebra, $\int E_{\mathbb{R}}(M)$ has no other relations than (5.1), (5.3), and (5.12). These facts are most conveniently expressed in terms of the bar construction on $E_{\mathbb{R}}(M)$.

(5.13) <u>Definition</u>. Let A be a connected cochain algebra over a field k. The <u>bar construction</u> $B(A)$ on A is a d.g. Hopf algebra defined as follows: as a vector space, $B(A)$ is the tensor algebra $T(IA)$ on the augmentation ideal IA of A. Let $a_1, a_2, \ldots$ be elements of IA of degrees $p_1, p_2, \ldots$ respectively. We shall denote the element of $B(A)$ corresponding to $a_1 \otimes \ldots \otimes a_r$ by $[a_1|a_2|\ldots|a_r]$. The unit element 1 will sometimes be denoted by [ ]. The degree of $[a_1|a_2|\ldots|a_r]$ is defined to be $-r + p_1 + p_2 + \ldots + p_r$. Define the coproduct Δ, product $\wedge$, and differential d in $B(A)$ by:

(a) $\Delta[a_1|a_2|\ldots|a_r] = \sum_{i=0}^{r} [a_1|\ldots|a_i] \otimes [a_{i+1}|\ldots|a_r]$,

(b) $[a_1|\ldots|a_r] \wedge [a_{r+1}|\ldots|a_{r+s}] =$

$$\sum_\sigma \varepsilon(\sigma;\, p_1-1, \ldots, p_{r+s}-1)[a_{\sigma(1)}|a_{\sigma(2)}|\ldots|a_{\sigma(r+s)}]$$

where σ ranges over the shuffles of type (r, s) of $\{1, 2, \ldots, r+s\}$ and where $\varepsilon(\sigma)$ is the permutation symbol defined in (5.2), and

(c) $$d[a_1|a_2|\ldots|a_r] = \sum_{i=1}^{r} (-1)^i [Ja_1|\ldots|Ja_{i-1}|da_i|a_{i+1}|\ldots|a_r]$$
$$- \sum_{i=1}^{r-1} (-1)^i [Ja_1|\ldots|Ja_{i-1}|Ja_i \wedge a_{i+1}|a_{i+2}|\ldots|a_r] .$$

It follows from (5.1) and (5.3) that, if A is a d.g. subalgebra of $E_{\mathbb{R}}(M)$, then the linear map $\rho\colon B(A) \to \int A$ that takes $[w_1|w_2|\ldots|w_r]$ to $\int w_1 w_2 \ldots w_r$ is a d.g. algebra map.

(5.14) Proposition (Chen [13], [15]). The kernel of the natural map

$$\rho: B(E_{\mathbb{R}}(M)) \to \int E_{\mathbb{R}}(M)$$

is spanned by elements of $B(E_{\mathbb{R}}(M))$ of one of the following forms:

(a) $[df|w_1|\ldots|w_r] - [fw_1|w_2|\ldots|w_r] + f(x)[w_1|\ldots|w_r]$,

(b) $[w_1|\ldots|w_i|df|w_{i+1}|\ldots|w_r] - [w_1|\ldots|w_i|fw_{i+1}|\ldots|w_r]$
$+ [w_1|\ldots|fw_i|w_{i+1}|\ldots|w_r]$,

(c) $[w_1|\ldots|w_r|df] - f(x)[w_1|\ldots|w_r] + [w_1|\ldots|w_{r-1}|fw_r]$,

where $w_i \in E_{\mathbb{R}}(M)$, $f: M \to \mathbb{R}$ is a smooth map, and x is the base-point of M. Moreover, the kernel of ρ is a Hopf ideal in $B(E_{\mathbb{R}}(M))$. □

(5.15) Corollary. Let A be a d.g. subalgebra of $E_{\mathbb{R}}(M)$. The linear map

$$\Delta: \int A \to \int A \otimes \int A$$

defined by

$$\Delta \int w_1 \ldots w_r = \sum_{i=0}^{r} \int w_1 \ldots w_i \otimes \int w_{i+1} \ldots w_r$$

is well defined. With this coproduct, $\int A$ has the structure of a commutative d.g. Hopf algebra. □

According to (5.5), the coproduct Δ is dual to the Pontrjagin product of smooth oriented chains on ΩM.

Let A be a d.g. subalgebra of $E_{\mathbb{R}}(M)$. Define a descending filtration $\{F_s\}$ on $\int A$ by defining F_s to be the linear span of iterated integrals of the form $\int w_1 w_2 \ldots w_r$, where $r \le -s$ and each $w_j \in A$.

(5.16) Proposition (Chen [10]). If A is a d.g. subalgebra of $E_{\mathbb{R}}(M)$ such that the induced map $H^1(A) \to H^1(E_{\mathbb{R}}(M))$ is injective, then

$$\mathrm{Gr}\, F_* \approx T(s^{-1}\overline{A}) ,$$

where $\overline{A}$ is the graded vector space defined by:

$$\overline{A}^p = \begin{cases} 0 & p = 0 \\ A^1/dA^0 & p = 1 \\ A^p & p > 1 . \end{cases}$$ □

6. POWER SERIES CONNECTIONS REVISITED

In this chapter we state and prove final versions of theorems stated provisionally in chapter 4. These results give a refinement and strengthening of Chen's method of power series connections. In particular, we show that the Lie algebra model associated to a 1-connected s.s.c. by a power series connection is unique up to isomorphism and that this association is natural in some sense.

Central to this chapter is the study of the Lie transport associated to a power series connection (ω, L) on a 1-connected s.s.c. K, which is an L-valued iterated integral on K constructed from ω. It is used to define the Lie algebra isomorphism

$$\tau\colon s^{-1}\pi_*(|K|) \otimes \mathbb{Q} \to H_*(L)$$

of (4.11).

We show that minimal cofibrations of a 1-connected rational space correspond to elementary extensions of its Lie algebra model. We also state a rational version of Chen's loop space de Rham theorem [15] for s.s.c.'s (that we will prove in chapter 9). Roughly speaking, it asserts that if K is a simply connected s.s.c., then integration induces an isomorphism

$$H^*(\int E(K)) \approx H^*(\Omega|K|; \mathbb{Q}) .$$

A well-known theorem of Cartan and Serre (see [30]) implies that

$$QH^*(\Omega|K|; \mathbb{Q}) \approx s^{-1}\mathrm{Hom}(\pi_*(|K|), \mathbb{Q}) .$$

Consequently, all of the nontrivial rational homotopy of K can be detected by iterated integrals.

The Smoothing Lemma

In order to define a pairing between the iterated integrals on ΩK and the singular homology of $\Omega|K|$, we need to prove that the homology of the complex of smooth singular chains $\sigma: \Delta^p \to \Omega K$ is isomorphic to the singular homology $H_*(\Omega|K|)$ of $\Omega|K|$. This is achieved by means of the following technical smoothing lemma.

Let K be an s.s.c. Give $\Omega|K|$ (the space of continuous loops on $|K|$) the compact open topology. View ΩK (the space of piecewise smooth loops on K) as a subspace of $\Omega|K|$.

(6.1) Smoothing lemma. Let K be an s.s.c. If $\sigma: \Delta^p \to \Omega|K|$ is a continuous map such that $\sigma|\partial\Delta^p$ lands in ΩK and $\sigma|\partial\Delta^p: \partial\Delta^p \to \Omega K$ is smooth, then there is a smooth map $\sigma': \Delta^p \to \Omega K$ such that $\sigma'|\partial\Delta^p = \sigma|\partial\Delta^p$, and a homotopy

$$h: [0, 1] \times \Delta^p \to \Omega|K|$$

from σ to σ' rel $\partial\Delta^p$. □

The proof of (6.1) is the content of chapter 8. The following corollary is an immediate consequence of (6.1).

(6.2) Corollary. Let (L, L') be a pair of finite simplicial complexes. If $\phi: L \to \Omega|K|$ is a continuous map such that $\phi|L'$ lands in ΩK and $\phi|L'$ is smooth, then there is a smooth map $\hat{\phi}: L \to \Omega K$ such that $\hat{\phi}|L' = \phi|L$, and a homotopy

$$h: [0, 1] \times L \to \Omega|K|$$

from σ to σ' rel L'. □

The proof of the following corollary of (6.2) uses techniques from the proof of (8.3).

(6.3) Corollary. Let M be a smooth compact manifold, and let N be an imbedded submanifold. If $\phi: M \to \Omega|K|$ is a continuous map such that $\phi|N$ lands in ΩK and $\phi|N: N \to \Omega K$ is smooth, then there is a smooth map $\hat{\phi}: M \to \Omega K$ such that $\hat{\phi}|N = \phi|N$, and a homotopy

$$h: [0, 1] \times M \to \Omega|K|$$

from ϕ to $\hat{\phi}$ rel N. □

For an s.s.c. K (with base-point x), denote by $\pi_p(\Omega K)$ the set of smooth maps $(S^p, *) \to (\Omega K, \eta_x)$ modulo smooth homotopy, where η_x denotes the constant loop at x. Corollary (6.3) implies that the natural map $\pi_*(\Omega K) \to \pi_*(\Omega|K|)$ is an isomorphism.

For a differentiable space M denote by $C_*(M)$ the chain complex generated by the smooth singular cubes $[0, 1]^n \to M$ modulo the degenerate cubes. (A singular n-cube σ: $[0, 1] \to M$ is degenerate if there is a singular (n-1)-cube σ': $[0, 1]^{n-1} \to M$ such that $\sigma(\xi_1, \xi_2, \ldots, \xi_n) = \sigma'(\xi_2, \xi_3, \ldots, \xi_n)$ for all $(\xi_1, \xi_2, \ldots, \xi_n)$ in $[0, 1]^n$.) If X is a topological space, considered as a differentiable space as in (4.4), then a standard argument using acyclic models shows that the homology of $C_*(X)$ is naturally isomorphic to the singular homology of $H_*(X)$ of X.

Let K be an s.s.c. The natural inclusion $\Omega K \to \Omega|K|$ induces a natural chain map $C_*(\Omega K) \to C_*(\Omega|K|)$. Note that the homology of $C_*(\Omega|K|)$ is naturally isomorphic to $H_*(\Omega|K|)$. Denote the homology of $C_*(\Omega K)$ by $H_*(\Omega K)$.

(6.4) Lemma. If K is a connected s.s.c., then the chain map $C_*(\Omega K) \to C_*(\Omega|K|)$ induces a Hopf algebra isomorphism

$$H_*(\Omega K) \approx H_*(\Omega|K|) \ . \ \square$$

This lemma is proved by first showing that the smooth singular homology of ΩM is isomorphic to the smooth cubical homology $H_*(\Omega M)$ of ΩM. This is done using acyclic models. One can then use the smoothing lemma (6.1) to show that the smooth singular homology of ΩM is isomorphic to the singular homology of $\Omega|K|$.

Loop Space Cohomology

The following rational version of Chen's loop space de Rham theorem [15] is proved in chapter 9.

(6.5) Theorem. If K is a simply connected s.s.c. with finite Betti numbers, then there is a natural Hopf algebra isomorphism

$$\nu\colon H^*\left(\int E(K)\right) \to H^*(\Omega K; \mathbb{Q}) \ .$$

Furthermore, if

$$\int : \int E(K) \to \mathrm{Hom}\,(C_*(\Omega K),\ \mathbb{R})$$

denotes the integration map $w \mapsto \{\sigma \mapsto \langle w, \sigma\rangle\}$, then the diagram

$$\begin{array}{ccc} & & H^*(\Omega K;\ \mathbb{Q}) \\ & \overset{\nu}{\nearrow} & \downarrow \\ H^*(\int E(K)) & \xrightarrow[\int^*]{} & H^*(\Omega K;\ \mathbb{R}) \end{array}$$

commutes, where the vertical map is induced by the inclusion $\mathbb{Q} \to \mathbb{R}$. □

From our point of view, the most important consequence of (6.5) is that integration defines a natural, nonsingular pairing

$$QH^*(\int E(K)) \otimes (\pi_*(\Omega K) \otimes \mathbb{Q}) \to \mathbb{Q}\ .$$

Note that it is not clear *a priori* that this pairing lands in $\mathbb{Q}$.

The Transport of a Connection

A power series connection (ω, L) on an s.s.c. K determines a UL-valued iterated integral, called the transport of the connection. This form defines a natural Hopf algebra isomorphism

$$H_*(\Omega K;\ \mathbb{Q}) \approx H_*(UL)\ .$$

In this section we define the transport and use it to define the above isomorphism.

Throughout this section, K will denote a fixed simply connected s.s.c. with finite Betti numbers. Choose a basis (X_i) of $s^{-1}\tilde{H}_*(K;\ \mathbb{Q})$. Recall that we denote the universal enveloping algebra of a Lie algebra L by UL.

(6.6) Definition. Let (ω, L) be a power series connection on K. The transport of the connection is the element T of $\int E(K) \hat{\otimes} UL$ defined as follows: if

$$\omega = \sum w_i X_i + \sum w_{ij} X_i X_j + \ldots\ , \text{ then}$$

$$T = 1 + \sum \int w_i X_i + \sum \int (w_i w_j + w_{ij}) X_i X_j$$
$$+ \sum \int (w_i w_j w_k + w_{ij} w_k + w_i w_{jk} + w_{ijk}) X_i X_j X_k + \ldots\ .$$

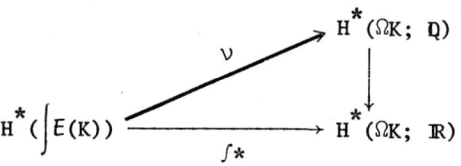

An alternative and convenient way of writing T is to view ω as an L-valued form on K and define T to be the UL-valued iterated integral

$$T = 1 + \int\omega + \int\omega\omega + \int\omega\omega\omega + \ldots = \sum_{r\geq 0}\int\omega^r .$$

Extend the action of the differential d of $\int E(K)$ and the differential ∂ of UL to $\int E(K) \hat{\otimes} UL$ as in the discussion preceding (4.7).

(6.7) Proposition (Chen [15]). If T is the transport of a power series connection on K, then $dT = \partial T$.

Proof. Write $T = \sum_{r\geq 0}\int\omega^r$. Now, using (5.1) and the fact that ω satisfies the twisting cochain condition,

$$\begin{aligned} dT &= \sum_{r\geq 0} d\int\omega^r \\ &= \sum_{r\geq 0}\sum_{i+j=r}(-1)^i\int(J\omega)^{i-1}d\omega\ \omega^j \\ &\quad - \sum_{r\geq 0}\sum_{i+j=r}(-1)^i\int(J\omega)^{i-1}(J\omega\wedge\omega)\omega^{j-1} \\ &= -\sum_{r\geq 0}\sum_{i+j=r}(-1)^{i-1}\int(J\omega)^{i-1}(d\omega - J\omega\wedge\omega)\omega^j \\ &= \sum_{r\geq 0}\sum_{i+j=r}(-1)^{i-1}\int(J\omega)^{i-1}\partial\omega\ \omega^j \\ &= \sum_{r\geq 0}\partial\int\omega^r \\ &= \partial T . \quad \square \end{aligned}$$

Because $dT = \partial T$, the transport defines a chain map, called the holonomy map, from the smooth chains on ΩM into $\mathbb{R} \otimes UL$.

(6.8) Definition. Let (ω, L) be a power series connection on K and let T be the associated transport. The holonomy map associated to ω is the chain map

$$\Theta: C_*(\Omega K) \to \mathbb{R} \otimes UL$$

defined by $c \to \langle T, c\rangle$, where

$$\langle T, c\rangle = \langle 1, c\rangle + \sum\langle\int w_i, c\rangle X_i + \sum\langle\int(w_iw_j + w_{ij}), c\rangle X_iX_j + \ldots .$$

That Θ is a chain map follows from Stokes' theorem and (6.7).

If $\alpha\colon [0, 1]^p \to \Omega K$ and $\beta\colon [0, 1]^q \to \Omega K$ are smooth cubes, then it is not hard to show, using (5.5), that $\Theta(\alpha \times \beta) = \Theta(\alpha)\Theta(\beta)$.

The holonomy map gives an explicit isomorphism between $H_*(\Omega K; \mathbb{Q})$ and $H_*(UL)$.

(6.9) <u>Theorem</u>. Let K be a 1-connected s.s.c. with finite Betti numbers. If (ω, UL) is a power series connection on K, then there is a natural Hopf algebra isomorphism $\Psi\colon H_*(\Omega K; \mathbb{Q}) \to H_*(UL)$ such that the diagram

$$\begin{array}{ccc} & & H_*(UL) \\ & \overset{\Psi}{\nearrow} & \downarrow \\ H_*(\Omega K; \mathbb{Q}) & \xrightarrow[\Theta_*]{} & H_*(\mathbb{R} \otimes UL) \end{array}$$

commutes, where the vertical map is induced by the canonical inclusion $UL \to \mathbb{R} \otimes UL$ and where $\Theta\colon C_*(\Omega K) \otimes \mathbb{Q} \to \mathbb{R} \otimes UL$ is the holonomy map associated to ω. □

The proof that Θ_* is a Hopf algebra map and the proof of the naturality of Θ_* occupy the rest of this chapter. That the lifting Ψ of Θ_* exists and that Ψ is an isomorphism are proved in Chapter 9.

(6.10) <u>Remarks</u>. Chen [12] first proved that, for a class of differentiabl spaces (that included manifolds and loop spaces of manifolds), the holonomy map associated to a connection (ω, L) on such a space M induces an algebra isomorphism $H_*(\Omega M; \mathbb{R}) \approx \mathbb{R} \otimes H_*(UL)$. Cuadrado [18] then extended this to the rational case by proving that, if (ω, L) is a connection on a simply connected simplicial complex K, then there is an algebra isomorphism $H_*(\Omega K; \mathbb{Q}) \approx H_*(UL)$. That Θ_* is a Hopf algebra isomorphism and the uniqueness and naturality of power series connections were established by the author in [24].

The Lie Transport

To prove that the holonomy map associated to a connection on a simply connected s.s.c. is a Hopf algebra map, it is necessary to study the transport of the connection in greater detail. Just as the transport of a connection on K is a UL-valued iterated integral and defines a map $H_*(\Omega K) \to \mathbb{R} \otimes H_*(UL)$, the Lie transport of the connection is an L-valued iterated integral and defines a Lie algebra map $\pi_*(\Omega K) \to \mathbb{R} \otimes H_*(L)$.

Central to this discussion are the Poincaré-Birchoff-Witt theorem (hereinafter called the PBW theorem) and the Milnor-Moore theorem. These are stated below for the convenience of the reader.

Let V be a graded vector space. The free graded commutative algebra $\Lambda(V)$ on V admits a Hopf algebra structure: the comultiplication $\Delta: \Lambda(V) \to \Lambda(V) \otimes \Lambda(V)$ is defined by $\Delta X = X \otimes 1 + 1 \otimes X$ for all $X \in V$. We denote by S(V) the underlying coalgebra. We call S(V) the symmetric coalgebra on V. If V is a chain vector space, then $\Lambda(V)$ is a chain algebra, and the differential induced on S(V) gives S(V) the structure of a cocommutative chain coalgebra.

The following version of the PBW theorem is proved in appendix B of [34].

(6.11) Theorem (PBW theorem). Let L be a chain Lie algebra and $i: L \to UL$ the canonical map. Let $X_1, X_2, \ldots, X_n$ be elements of L of degrees $p_1, p_2, \ldots, p_n$ respectively. The linear map

$$S(L) \to UL$$

defined by

$$X_1 \wedge X_2 \wedge \ldots \wedge X_n \mapsto \frac{1}{n!}\sum_{\sigma}\varepsilon(\sigma; p_1, \ldots, p_n) i(X_1) i(X_2) \ldots i(X_n),$$

where σ ranges over all permutations of $\{1, 2, \ldots, n\}$ and where ε is the permutation symbol defined in (5.2), is an isomorphism of chain coalgebras. □

Recall that the set of primitive elements PA of a Hopf algebra A with comultiplication Δ is the subspace $\{X: \Delta X = X \otimes 1 + 1 \otimes X\}$ of A. Recall also that the commutator $[U, V] = UV - (-1)^{\deg U \deg V} VU$ in A induces a Lie algebra structure on PA.

(6.12) Theorem (Milnor-Moore [30]). (a) If L is a chain Lie algebra, then the natural map $L \to PUL$ is a chain Lie algebra isomorphism.

(b) If A is a cocommutative chain Hopf algebra, then the natural map $UPA \to A$ induced by the inclusion $PA \to A$ is a chain Hopf algebra isomorphism. □

Together, the PBW theorem and the Milnor-Moore theorem yield the following corollaries.

(6.13) Corollary. Each cocommutative chain Hopf algebra A possesses a unique idempotent endomorphism $\eta: A \to A$ with the properties:

(a) the image of η is PA;

(b) $IA \cap \ker \eta$ is spanned by the symmetric polynomials on L of degree ≥ 2;

(c) η commutes with the differential of A.

Moreover, if A and B are chain Hopf algebras, with idempotents η_A and η_B respectively, and if $\Phi: A \to B$ is a d.g. Hopf algebra map, then $\Phi \circ \eta_A = \eta_B \circ \Phi$. □

(6.14) Corollary. The bar construction $B(A)$, on a 1-connected cochain algebra A, possesses an idempotent endomorphism $\gamma: B(A) \to B(A)$ with the properties:

(a) $\ker \gamma = \mathbb{Q} \oplus I^2 B(A)$;

(b) $\operatorname{im} \gamma \subseteq IB(A)$;

(c) γ commutes with the differential of $B(A)$.

Moreover, if A_1 and A_2 are 1-connected cochain algebras, and if $\phi: A_1 \to A_2$ is a d.g. algebra map, then $B(\phi) \circ \gamma_1 = \gamma_2 \circ B(\phi)$, where γ_1 and γ_2 are the idempotents associated to $B(A_1)$ and $B(A_2)$ respectively. □

The idempotent η of (6.13) is easily understood from the following examples. The idempotent of (6.14) is obtained by dualizing the idempotent $\eta: \operatorname{Hom}(B(A), \mathbb{Q}) \to \operatorname{Hom}(B(A), \mathbb{Q})$ when A is of finite type and using naturality when A is not.

(6.15) Examples. (a) Let $L = \mathbf{L}(X_1, X_2, X_3, X_4)$ where $\deg X_i = p_i$. Observe that in UL

$$X_1X_2 = \frac{1}{2}(X_1X_2 - (-1)^{p_1p_2}X_2X_1) + \frac{1}{2}(X_1X_2 + (-1)^{p_1p_2}X_2X_1)$$
$$= \frac{1}{2}[X_1, X_2] + \frac{1}{2}S(X_1, X_2)$$

where $S(X_1, X_2)$ denotes the symmetric polynomial $X_1X_2 + (-1)^{p_1p_2}X_2X_1$ in X_1 and X_2. It follows that

$$\eta(X_1X_2) = \frac{1}{2}[X_1, X_2] .$$

Next,

$$X_1X_2X_3 = \frac{1}{3!}([X_1[X_2, X_3]] + [[X_1, X_2]X_3])$$
$$+ \frac{3}{2} S(X_1, [X_2, X_3]) + \varepsilon\frac{3}{2}S(X_2, [X_1, X_3])$$
$$+ \varepsilon\frac{3}{2}S(X_3, [X_1, X_2]) + \frac{1}{3!}S(X_1, X_2, X_3)$$

where $S(X_1, X_2, X_3)$ denotes the symmetric polynomial

$$\sum_{\sigma}\varepsilon(\sigma; p_1, p_2, p_3)X_{\sigma(1)}X_{\sigma(2)}X_{\sigma(3)}$$

and where ε denotes the permutation symbol defined in (5.2). It follows that

$$\eta(X_1X_2X_3) = \frac{1}{3!}([X_1[X_2, X_3]] + [[X_1, X_2]X_3]) .$$

Similarly, one can show that

$$\eta(X_1X_2X_3X_4) = \frac{1}{12}([X_1[X_2[X_3, X_4]]] + \varepsilon[X_3[[X_1, X_4]X_2]]$$
$$+ [[X_1[X_2, X_3]]X_4] + [[[X_1, X_2]X_3]X_4]) .$$

(b) Let $\mathcal{B} = B(A)$, where $B(A)$ denotes the bar construction on a 1-connected cochain algebra A of finite type. Let $a_1, a_2, a_3 \in A$ where $\deg a_i = 1 + p_i$. By dualizing the formulas in (a) above, one can show that

$$\gamma[a_1] = [a_1]$$

$$\gamma[a_1|a_2] = \frac{1}{2}([a_1|a_2] - (-1)^{p_1p_2}[a_2|a_1])$$

$$\gamma[a_1|a_2|a_3] = \frac{1}{2}([a_1|a_2|a_3] + \varepsilon[a_3|a_2|a_1])$$
$$- \frac{1}{3!}\sum_{\sigma}\varepsilon(\sigma; p_1, p_2, p_3)[a_{\sigma(1)}|a_{\sigma(2)}|a_{\sigma(3)}].$$

Throughout the rest of this section K denotes a fixed simply connected s.s.c. with finite Betti numbers. It is convenient to introduce the formal transport of a connection on K.

(6.16) Definition. The formal transport F of a connection (ω, L) on K is the element

$$1 + [\omega] + [\omega|\omega] + [\omega|\omega|\omega] + \dots$$

of $B(E(K)) \hat{\otimes} UL$.

(6.17) Lemma. If F is the formal transport of a connection (ω, L) on K, then the map

$$\Phi\colon \mathrm{Hom}(UL, \mathbb{Q}) \to B(E(K))$$

defined by $\Phi(\varphi) = \langle F, \varphi\rangle$ is a d.g. Hopf algebra map that induces an isomorphism on homology.

Proof. As in (6.7), one can show that $\partial F = dF$. It follows immediately that Φ is a chain map. To prove that Φ is a Hopf algebra map, we have to show that

(a) $$(\Delta \hat{\otimes} 1)F = (1 \otimes \mu)F \otimes F$$

(b) $$(1 \hat{\otimes} \Delta)F = (\wedge \otimes 1)F \otimes F ,$$

where $\mu\colon UL \otimes UL \to UL$ and $\wedge\colon B(E(K)) \otimes B(E(K)) \to B(E(K))$ denote the multiplications in UL and B(E(K)) respectively.

To establish these identities, write ω in the form $\omega = \sum_{i\in S} a_iA_i$, where $a_i \in E(K)$ and $A_i \in L$. Observe that

$$F = 1 + \sum[a_i]A_i + \sum[a_i|a_j]A_iA_j + \sum[a_i|a_j|a_k]A_iA_jA_k + \dots$$

$$= \sum[a_I]A_I$$

where for each finite sequence $I = (i_1, i_2, \dots, i_p)$ of elements of S,

$$[a_I] = [a_{i_1}|a_{i_2}|\dots|a_{i_p}]$$

and

$$A_I = A_{i_1}A_{i_2}\dots A_{i_p} .$$

For finite sequences $I = (i_1, i_2, \ldots, i_p)$ and $J = (j_i, j_2, \ldots, j_q)$ in S, denote by $I * J$ their juxtaposition $(i_1, i_2, \ldots, i_p, j_1, j_2, \ldots, j_q)$. We now have

$$(1 \otimes \mu)F \otimes F = \sum_{I,J} [a_I] \otimes [a_J]A_{I*J}$$

$$= \sum_K \sum_{I*J=K} [a_I] \otimes [a_J]A_K$$

$$= \sum_K (\Delta[a_K])A_K$$

$$= (\Delta \hat{\otimes} 1)F .$$

To prove the second identity (b), we need some additional notation. If I, J, and K are finite sequences of elements of S, and if there are order-preserving inclusions $I \to K$ and $J \to K$ such that $I \cup J = K$ and $I \cap J = \phi$, we write $K = I \cdot J$. Recall the definition of the permutation symbol $\varepsilon(I, J; K)$ from (4.17). Identity (b) now follows directly from the formulas

$$\Delta A_K = \sum_{I \cdot J=K} \varepsilon(I, J; K) A_I \otimes A_J$$

and

$$[a_I] \wedge [a_J] = \sum_{I \cdot J=K} \varepsilon(I, J; K)[a_K] .$$

Finally, to show that Φ induces an isomorphism on homology, define filtrations F_s and G_s on $\mathrm{Hom}(UL, \mathbb{Q})$ and $B(E(K))$ as follows:

$$F_{-s} = \{\varphi \in \mathrm{Hom}(UL, \mathbb{Q}) : \varphi | I^{s+1}UL = 0\}$$

$$G_{-s} = \mathrm{span}\{[w_1|\ldots|w_r] : r \le s\} .$$

It is easy to check that Φ is filtration preserving and that the E^1 terms of the corresponding spectral sequences are

$$T(\mathrm{Hom}(QL, \mathbb{Q}))$$

and

$$T(s^{-1}\tilde{H}^*(K, \mathbb{Q})) .$$

Further, Φ induces the map

$$T(\mathrm{Hom}(QL, \mathbb{Q})) \to T(s^{-1}\tilde{H}^*(K, \mathbb{Q}))$$

induced by the isomorphism

$$\sigma^*: \mathrm{Hom}(QL, \mathbb{Q}) \to s^{-1}\tilde{H}^*(K; \mathbb{Q})$$

dual to the isomorphism σ defined in the discussion preceding (4.13). It follows that Φ induces an isomorphism on homology. □

(6.18) Remark. Let (ω, L) be a connection on K. If $\omega = \Sigma a_i A_i$, where $a_i \in E(K)$ and $A_i \in L$, then the subalgebra A of $E(K)$ generated by the coefficients a_i of ω is 1-connected and of finite type. Consequently, $B(A)$ is connected and of finite type and the map $\Phi: \mathrm{Hom}(UL, \mathbb{Q}) \to B(E(K))$ lands in $B(A)$. We can dualize to get a d.g. Hopf algebra map

$$\Phi^*: \mathrm{Hom}(B(A), \mathbb{Q}) \to UL$$
$$\varphi \to \langle T, \varphi\rangle .$$

Denote by

$$I: C_*(\Omega K) \to \mathrm{Hom}(B(A), \mathbb{Q})$$

the integration map $c \mapsto \{[a_1 \ldots a_r] \mapsto \langle \int w_1 \ldots w_r, c\rangle\}$. It follows from Stokes' theorem that I is a chain map and from (5.5) that I is multiplicative. The holonomy map Θ associated to the connection (ω, L) on K then factors as $\Theta = (\mathbb{R} \otimes \Phi^*) \circ I$.

$$\begin{array}{ccc} C_*(\Omega K) \otimes \mathbb{R} & \xrightarrow{\ I\ } & \mathrm{Hom}(B(A), \mathbb{R}) \\ & \searrow^{\Theta} & \downarrow{\scriptstyle \mathbb{R}\otimes\Phi^*} \\ & & \mathbb{R} \otimes UL \end{array}$$

One can show that the inclusion $A \to E(K)$ induces on isomorphism on homology. Consequently $B(A) \to B(E(K))$ also induces an isomorphism on homology. So theorem (6.9) essentially says that the integration map induces a Hopf algebra isomorphism on homology. The proof that I induces an isomorphism on homology depends heavily on Adam's fundamental result [1] as well as the evaluation properties (5.6) and (5.8) of iterated integrals. The proof that I induces a Hopf algebra map on homology uses the Lie transport which we are about to define.

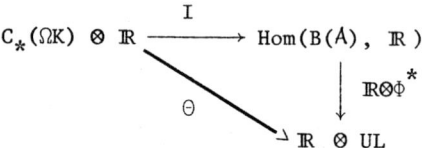

Choose a map $\mu\colon \mathcal{F}(\Delta K) \to C_*(\Omega K) \otimes \mathbb{R}$ that induces an isomorphism on homology, where $\mathcal{F}(\Delta K)$ denotes the cobar construction on ΔK (see, for example, chapter 9). One can identify $\mathrm{Hom}(B(\mathcal{A}), \mathbb{R})$ with the cobar construction $\mathcal{F}(\mathcal{A}^*)$ on the dual $\mathcal{A}^*$ of $\mathcal{A}$. Iterated integrals thus provide, via integration, a d.g. algebra map

$$I \circ \mu\colon \mathcal{F}(\Delta K) \to \mathcal{F}(\mathcal{A}^*)$$

that induces a Hopf algebra isomorphism on homology. (All the above can be done over $\mathbb{Q}$ using the techniques in chapter 9.)

Let $\eta\colon UL \to L$ and $\gamma\colon B(\mathcal{E}(K)) \to B(\mathcal{E}(K))$ be the idempotents given by (6.13) and (6.14). Let (ω, L) be a connection on K with transport T and formal transport F. Since Φ is a d.g. Hopt algebra map, it follows that $(1 \hat{\otimes} \eta)F = (\gamma \hat{\otimes} 1)F$. Recall that $\rho\colon B(\mathcal{E}(K)) \to \int \mathcal{E}(K)$ denotes the natural map $[w_1|\ldots|w_r] \mapsto \int w_1 \ldots w_r$. Since γ commutes with ρ, it follows that $(1 \hat{\otimes} \eta)T = (\gamma \hat{\otimes} 1)T$.

(6.19) Definition. The Lie transport of a power series connection (ω, L) on K is the element T_L of $\int \mathcal{E}(K) \hat{\otimes} L$ defined by

$$T_L = (1 \hat{\otimes} \eta)T .$$

The element $F_L = (1 \hat{\otimes} \eta)F$ of $B(\mathcal{E}(K)) \hat{\otimes} L$ will be called the formal Lie transport of (ω, L).

(6.20) Example. Let $M = S^3 \times S^3 - \{\text{point}\}$. As in (2.4), a connection (ω, L) on M is given by

$$L = \mathbb{L}(X_1, X_2\colon \deg X_1 = \deg X_2 = 2,\ \partial X_1 = \partial X_2 = 0)$$

$$\omega = w_1 X_1 + w_2 X_2 + w_{12}[X_1, X_2]$$

where $dw_{12} = Jw_1 \wedge w_2 = -w_1 \wedge w_2$. The transport T of the connection satisfies

$$T \equiv 1 + \int w_1X_1 + \int w_2X_2 + \int w_{12}[X_1X_2] + \int w_1w_1X_1^2 + \int w_2w_2X_2^2 + \int w_1w_2X_1X_2 +$$

$$\int w_2w_1X_2X_1 + \int w_1w_{12}X_1[X_1, X_2] + \int w_{12}w_1[X_1, X_2]X_1 + \int w_2w_{12}X_2[X_1, X_2] +$$

$$\int w_{12}w_2[X_1, X_2]X_2 + \int w_1w_1w_1X_1^3 + \int w_1w_1w_2X_1^2X_2 + \int w_1w_2w_1X_1X_2X_1 +$$

$$\int w_2w_1w_1X_2X_1^2 + \int w_1w_2w_2X_1X_2^2 + \int w_2w_1w_2X_2X_1X_2 + \int w_2w_2w_1X_2^2X_1 + \int w_2w_2w_2X_2^3$$

$$\operatorname{mod} \int E(M) \hat{\otimes} I^4(UL) .$$

Using the formulas in (6.15) we have

$$T_L \equiv \int w_1X_1 + \int w_2X_2 + \int (w_{12} + \tfrac{1}{2}(w_1w_2 - w_2w_1))[X_1, X_2] +$$

$$\frac{1}{6}\int (w_1w_1w_2 - 2w_1w_2w_1 + w_2w_1w_1 + 3w_1w_{12} - 3w_{12}w_1)[X_1[X_1, X_2]] +$$

$$\frac{1}{6}\int (w_2w_2w_1 - 2w_2w_1w_2 + w_1w_2w_2 - 3w_2w_{12} + 3w_{12}w_2)[X_2[X_1, X_2]]$$

$$\operatorname{mod} \int E(M) \hat{\otimes} I^4L .$$

(6.21) Proposition. The Lie transports T_L and F_L of a connection on K satisfy $\partial T_L = dT_L$ and $\partial F_L = dF_L$.

Proof. These follow immediately from (6.7), (6.13) and (6.17). □

(6.22) Proof of theorem (6.9). Let (ω, L) be a connection on K with associated holonomy map

$$\Theta\colon C_*(\Omega K) \to \mathbb{R} \otimes UL .$$

That $\Theta_*\colon H_*(\Omega K; \mathbb{Q}) \to H_*(UL)$ is an algebra isomorphism is Cuadrado's [18] rational version of Chen's [15] loop space homology theorem. We give a proof of it in chapter 9. We need only show that Θ_* is a coalgebra map. To do this, it suffices to show that the image of $PH_*(\Omega K; \mathbb{Q})$ under Θ_* is contained in $H_*(\mathbb{R} \otimes L)$.

Let c be a cycle in $C_*(\Omega K) \otimes \mathbb{R}$ such that $\{c\} \in PH_*(\Omega K; \mathbb{Q})$. To prove that the homology class of $\Theta(c)$ in $H_*(\mathbb{R} \otimes UL)$ is primitive, we have to show that

$$\Theta(c) \equiv \langle T_L, c\rangle \mod \partial(\mathbb{R} \otimes UL) .$$

Set $S = \ker \eta \cap IUL$, where $\eta: UL \to UL$ denotes the idempotent of (6.13). Since η commutes with ∂, it follows that $\partial S \subseteq S$. Since η is an idempotent, it follows that $IUL = L \oplus S$. Thus we can decompose T as

$$T = 1 + T_L + T_S ,$$

where $T_S \in \int E(K) \hat{\otimes} S$. Since $\partial S \subseteq S$, and since $dT = \partial T$, it follows that $\partial T_S = dT_S$. To prove that

$$\Theta(c) \equiv \langle T_L, c\rangle \mod \partial(\mathbb{R} \otimes UL)$$

it suffices to show that

$$\langle T_S, c\rangle \in \partial(\mathbb{R} \otimes UL) .$$

Choose a subspace H of S that consists of closed elements and such that the inclusion of H into S induces an isomorphism on homology. There is a subspace M of S such that

$$S = H \oplus M \oplus \partial M .$$

We can now decompose T_S as follows:

$$T_S = T_H + T_M + T_{\partial M} ,$$

where $T_H \in \int E(K) \hat{\otimes} H$, $T_M \in \int E(K) \hat{\otimes} M$, and $T_{\partial M} \in \int E(K) \hat{\otimes} (\partial M)$.

Since $\partial T_S = dT_S$, it follows that $dT_H = 0$, $\partial T_M = dT_{\partial M}$, and $dT_M = 0$. It is easy to check that $\partial|M: M \to \partial M$ is a linear isomorphism. Consequently,

$$T_M \in (d\int E(K)) \hat{\otimes} M .$$

It follows from the fact that $(\gamma \hat{\otimes} 1)T = (1 \hat{\otimes} \eta)T = T_L$ that

$$1 + T_S = ((1 - \gamma) \hat{\otimes} 1)T ,$$

and, since the image of $1 - \gamma$ is $I^2\int E(K) \oplus \mathbb{Q}$, it follows that the coefficients of T_H represent decomposable cohomology classes of ΩK. This, combined with the fact that c is a primitive homology class, implies that

$$\langle T_S, c\rangle = \langle T_{\partial M}, c\rangle$$

which lies in $\partial(\mathbb{R} \otimes UL)$. □

Denote by

$$\mathcal{H}: \pi_*(\Omega K) \to H_*(\Omega K)$$

the Hurewicz homomorphism. There is a $\mathbb{Z}$-bilinear pairing (the Samelson product)

$$[\ ,\ ]: \pi_p(\Omega K) \otimes \pi_q(\Omega K) \to \pi_{p+q}(\Omega K)$$

such that

(a) $\pi_*(\Omega K)$ is a graded Lie algebra over $\mathbb{Z}$ with bracket $[\ ,\ ]$;

(b) if $a \in \pi_p(\Omega M)$ and $b \in \pi_q(\Omega M)$, then

$$H([a, b]) = H(a)H(b) - (-1)^{pq}H(b)H(a);$$

(c) the natural isomorphism

$$\Sigma: s^{-1}\pi_*(K) \to \pi_*(\Omega K)$$

is a Lie algebra isomorphism. Detailed proofs of these assertions can be found in [36] and [40].

Define a Lie algebra map

$$\tau: s^{-1}\pi_*(K) \otimes \mathbb{Q} \to H_*(L)$$

by $\tau = P\Psi \circ H \circ \Sigma$, where Ψ is the isomorphism defined in (6.9). Since the image of H lies in $PH_*(\Omega K; \mathbb{Q})$, τ is well defined.

Let T_L be the Lie transport of the power series connection on K. Let $g: S^q \to \Omega K$ be a smooth map. Since $dT_L = \partial T_L$, it follows from Stokes' theorem that $\langle T_L, g\rangle$ is a cycle in $\mathbb{R} \otimes L$ and that the homology class of $\langle T_L, g\rangle$ depends only on the homotopy class of g in $\pi_*(\Omega K)$. Consequently T_L determines a linear map

$$\hat{\tau}: s^{-1}\pi_*(K) \otimes \mathbb{Q} \to H_*(\mathbb{R} \otimes L)$$

as follows: for each a in $s^{-1}\pi_*(K)$, choose a smooth map $f: S^p \to \Omega K$ that is a representative of the element $\Sigma(a)$ of $\pi_*(\Omega M)$. Define $\hat{\tau}(a)$ to be the homology class of $\langle T_L, f\rangle$ in $H_*(\mathbb{R} \otimes L)$.

(6.23) Theorem. Let K be a simply connected s.s.c. with finite Betti numbers. If (ω, L) is a power series connection on L, then

$$\hat{\tau}: s^{-1}\pi_*(K) \otimes \mathbb{Q} \to H_*(\mathbb{R} \otimes L)$$

is a Lie algebra map,

$$\tau: s^{-1}\pi_*(K) \otimes \mathbb{Q} \to H_*(L)$$

is a Lie algebra isomorphism, and the diagram

$$\begin{array}{ccc} & \overset{\tau}{\nearrow} & H_*(L) \\ & & \downarrow \\ s^{-1}\pi_*(K) \otimes \mathbb{Q} & \xrightarrow[\hat{\tau}]{} & H_*(\mathbb{R} \otimes L) \end{array}$$

commutes, where the vertical map is induced by the natural inclusion $\mathbb{Q} \to \mathbb{R}$.

<u>Proof</u>. This theorem follows immediately from (6.22) and the fact that the Hurewicz homomorphism induces a natural Lie algebra isomorphism

$$H\colon \pi_*(\Omega K) \otimes \mathbb{Q} \to PH_*(\Omega K, \mathbb{Q}) \ .$$

(For a proof of this last fact, see [30].) □

<u>Uniqueness and Naturality of Power Series Connections</u>

Let A be a commutative graded Hopf algebra with coproduct $\Delta\colon A \to A \otimes A$. Define a new coproduct $\Delta'\colon A \to A \otimes A$ by

$$\Delta' = \Delta - \tau \circ \Delta \ ,$$

where $\tau\colon A \otimes A \to A \otimes A$ denotes the interchange map $v \otimes w \mapsto (-1)^{\deg v \deg w} w \otimes v$. The cobracket Δ' induces a map

$$\overline{\Delta'}\colon IA \to IA \otimes IA$$

which, in turn, induces a cobracket

$$\Delta''\colon QA \to QA \otimes QA \ .$$

(6.24) <u>Definition</u>. A <u>Lie coalgebra</u> is a graded vector space Q together with a coproduct $\Delta\colon Q \to Q \otimes Q$ such that the diagrams

$$\begin{array}{ccc} & \overset{\Delta}{\nearrow} & Q \otimes Q \\ Q & & \downarrow -\tau \\ & \underset{\Delta}{\searrow} & Q \otimes Q \end{array}$$

and

$$\begin{array}{ccccc} & \overset{\Delta}{\nearrow} & Q \otimes Q & \xrightarrow{1 \otimes \Delta} & Q \otimes Q \otimes Q \\ Q & & & & \downarrow \tau \otimes 1 \\ & \underset{\Delta}{\searrow} & Q \otimes Q & \xrightarrow[1 \otimes \Delta - \Delta \otimes 1]{} & Q \otimes Q \otimes Q \end{array}$$

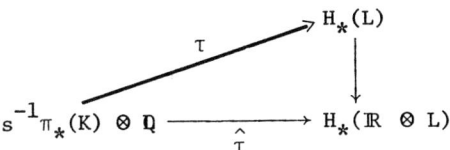

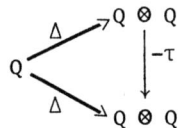

commute, where $\tau: Q \otimes Q \to Q \otimes Q$ denotes the interchange map.

It is easy to check that the dual $Q^* = \mathrm{Hom}(Q, \mathbb{Q})$ of a Lie coalgebra Q is a Lie algebra whose bracket is the composite

$$Q^* \otimes Q^* \to (Q \otimes Q)^* \xrightarrow{\Delta^*} Q^* .$$

Straightforward but tedious calculations show that (QA, Δ'') is a Lie coalgebra. In particular, if K is a simply connected s.s.c. with finite Betti numbers, then $QB(\mathcal{E}(K))$ is a Lie coalgebra. Denote its dual Lie algebra by $QB(\mathcal{E}(K))^*$. The canonical inclusion $i: s^{-1}\mathcal{E}(K) \to IB(\mathcal{E}(K))$, which takes $s^{-1}w$ to $[w]$, induces a map

$$s^{-1}\tilde{H}^*(K; \mathbb{Q}) \to H^*(IB(\mathcal{E}(K))) \to H^*(QB(\mathcal{E}(K)))$$

(6.25) Proposition. If (ω, L) is a connection on K, then the map

$$\nabla: QB(\mathcal{E}(K))^* \to L$$

$$\varphi \mapsto \langle F_L, \varphi\rangle ,$$

given by the formal Lie transport of ω, induces a Lie algebra isomorphism on homology. Moreover the diagram

$$\begin{array}{ccc} H_*(QB(\mathcal{E}(K))^*) & \xrightarrow{\nabla_*} & H_*(L) \\ \downarrow & & \downarrow \\ s^{-1}\tilde{H}_*(K; \mathbb{Q}) & \xrightarrow{\sigma} & QL \end{array}$$

commutes, where σ is the map defined by the connection form (see (4.13)).

Proof. According to (6.17), the map

$$\Phi: \mathrm{Hom}(UL, \mathbb{Q}) \to B(\mathcal{E}(K))$$

is a d.g. Hopf algebra map that induces an isomorphism on homology. Since $Q\,\mathrm{Hom}(UL, \mathbb{Q}) = L^*$, it follows from (6.11) and the naturality of the construction of a Lie coalgebra structure on QA that

$$Q\Phi: L^* \to QB(\mathcal{E}(K))$$

is a Lie coalgebra map that induces an isomorphism on homology. This implies that

$$\nabla: QB(\mathcal{E}(K))^* \to L$$

is a Lie algebra map that induces an isomorphism on homology.

Choose a set (X_i) that freely generates L. If $\omega \equiv \Sigma w_i X_i \mod \mathcal{E}(K) \hat{\otimes} I^2 L$, then

$$F_L \equiv \sum [w_i] X_i \mod B(\mathcal{E}(K)) \hat{\otimes} I^2 L .$$

It follows that the diagram

$$\begin{array}{ccc} H_*(QB(\mathcal{E}(K))^*) & \xrightarrow{\nabla_*} & H_*(L) \\ {\scriptstyle i^*}\downarrow & & \downarrow \\ s^{-1}\tilde{H}_*(K; \mathbb{Q}) & \xrightarrow[\sigma]{} & QL \end{array}$$

commutes. □

(6.26) Remark. It follows from (5.8) and the discussion in (6.18) that the map $\tau: s^{-1}\pi_*(K) \otimes \mathbb{Q} \to H_*(L)$ factors as $\tau = \nabla_* \circ I_* \circ \Sigma$,

$$\begin{array}{ccccc} s^{-1}\pi_*(K) \otimes \mathbb{Q} & \xrightarrow{\Sigma} & \pi_*(\Omega K) \otimes \mathbb{Q} & \xrightarrow{I_*} & H_*(QB(\mathcal{E}(K))^*) \\ & {\scriptstyle \tau}\searrow & & \swarrow{\scriptstyle \nabla_*} & \\ & & H_*(L) & & \end{array}$$

where Σ denotes the natural isomorphism and I_* denotes the map induced by the integration map

$$I: C_*(\Omega K) \otimes \mathbb{Q} \to \mathrm{Hom}(B(\mathcal{E}(K)), \mathbb{Q}) .$$

(6.27) Proposition. With the notation of (6.25), the map

$$\nabla: QB(\mathcal{E}(K))^* \to L$$

splits.

Proof. Let $\rho: L' \to QB(\mathcal{E}(K))^*$ be a minimal model of $QB(\mathcal{E}(K))^*$ (see [3] or [33]). Since the map $\nabla \circ \rho: L' \to L$ induces an isomorphism on homology, and since both L and L' are connected and minimal, $\nabla \circ \rho: L' \to L$ is a d.g. Lie algebra isomorphism. The d.g. Lie algebra map

$$\rho \circ (\nabla \circ \rho)^{-1}: L \to QB(\mathcal{E}(K))^*$$

is a splitting of ∇. □

We can now establish the uniqueness of power series connections.

(6.28) Theorem. Let K be a simply connected s.s.c. with finite Betti numbers. If (ω_1, L_1) and (ω_2, L_2) are power series connections on K, then there is a d.g. Lie algebra isomorphism $f\colon L_1 \to L_2$ such that the diagram

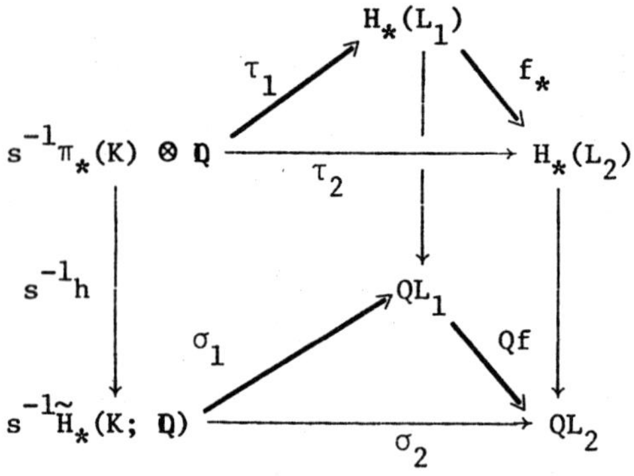

commutes, where h denotes the Hurewicz homomorphism.

Proof. Denote by $\nabla_j\colon QB(E(K))^* \to L_j$ the d.g. Lie algebra map associated to ω_j $(j = 1, 2)$ that is defined in (6.25). Choose a splitting $\rho\colon L_1 \to QB(E(K))^*$ of ∇_1. Define $f\colon L_1 \to L_2$ by $f = \nabla_2 \circ \rho$. Since $(\nabla_1)_*$ is an isomorphism, it follows that

$$(\rho \circ \nabla_1)_*\colon H_*(QB(E(K))^*) \to H_*(QB(EK))^*)$$

is the identity. Consequently, the diagram

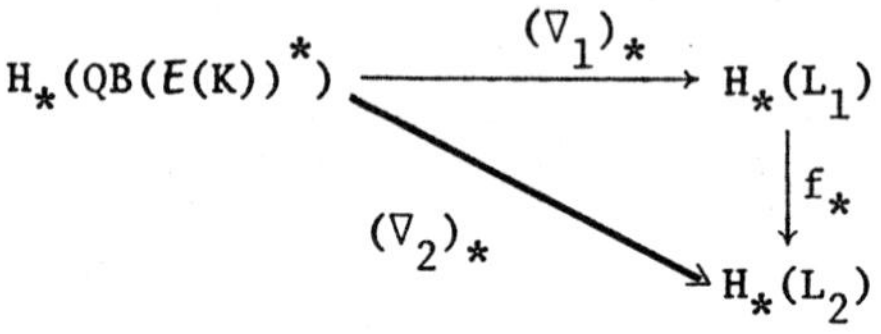

commutes.

We know from (6.26) that the diagram

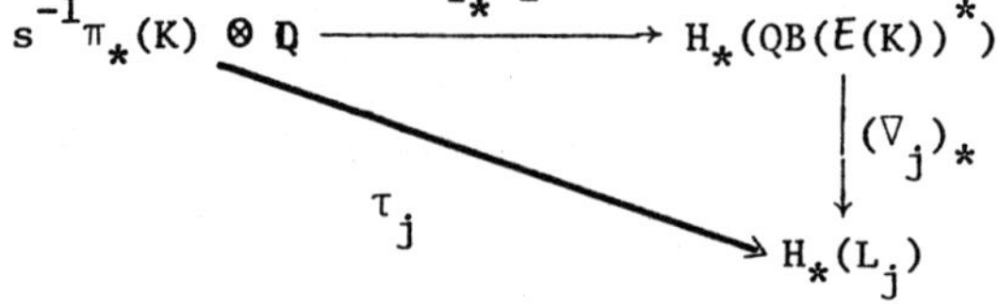

commutes, where $j = 1, 2$.

Denote by

$$\Sigma'\colon H_*(\Omega K;\mathbb{Q}) \to s^{-1}H_*(K;\mathbb{Q})$$

the homology suspension associated to the fibration

$$\begin{array}{ccc} K & \longrightarrow & P_xK \\ & & \downarrow \\ & & K \end{array}$$

where x denotes the base-point of K, P_xK is the space of paths originating at x, and the projection $P_xK \to K$ takes a path γ to its end point $\gamma(1)$. The diagram

$$\begin{array}{ccc} & & H_*(\Omega K;\, \mathbb{Q}) \\ & \overset{H\circ\Sigma}{\nearrow} & \downarrow{\scriptstyle \Sigma'} \\ s^{-1}\pi_*(K)\otimes\mathbb{Q} & \xrightarrow[s^{-1}h]{} & s^{-1}H_*(K;\, \mathbb{Q}) \end{array}$$

commutes, where H denotes the Hurewicz homomorphism $\pi_*(\Omega K) \to H_*(\Omega K)$. (For a proof of this, see Moore [31].) It follows from (5.8) that the inclusion $i\colon s^{-1}E(K) \to \int E(K)$ defined by $w \mapsto \int w$ is dual to the homology suspension Σ'. Thus, for j = 1, 2, the diagram

$$\begin{array}{ccc} s^{-1}\pi_*(K)\otimes\mathbb{Q} & \overset{h}{\searrow} & \\ \downarrow{\scriptstyle I_*\circ\Sigma} & & s^{-1}\tilde{H}_*(K;\, \mathbb{Q}) \\ H_*(QB(E(K))^*) & \underset{i^*}{\nearrow} & \end{array}$$

commutes. That the diagram

$$\begin{array}{ccc} s^{-1}\pi_*(K)\otimes\mathbb{Q} & \xrightarrow{\tau_j} & H_*(L_j) \\ \downarrow{\scriptstyle s^{-1}h} & & \downarrow \\ s^{-1}\tilde{H}_*(K;\, \mathbb{Q}) & \xrightarrow[\sigma_j]{} & QL_j \end{array}$$

commutes now follows directly from (6.25) and (6.26).

Next, we prove that the diagram

$$\begin{array}{ccc} & \overset{\sigma_1}{\nearrow} & QL_1 \\ s^{-1}\tilde{H}_*(K;\, \mathbb{Q}) & & \downarrow{\scriptstyle Qf} \\ & \underset{\sigma_2}{\searrow} & QL_2 \end{array}$$

commutes. The dual i^* of the canonical injection $i\colon s^{-1}E \to QB(E(K))$ is surjective so that, for each cycle ϕ in $s^{-1}\mathrm{Hom}(E(K),\, \mathbb{Q})$, there is an element $\tilde{\phi}$ of

$(QB(E(K))^*$ such that $\delta\tilde{\phi}$ vanishes on $i(s^{-1}E(K))$. That is, $\tilde{\phi}$ vanishes on the image of $s^{-1}dE(K)$ in $QB(E(K))$.

Given $X \in s^{-1}\tilde{H}_*(K; \mathbb{Q})$, choose a cycle ϕ in $s^{-1}\mathrm{Hom}(E(K), \mathbb{Q})$ such that $\{\phi\} = X$. Let $\tilde{\phi}$ be as above. It follows from the definition of ∇_j that

$$\nabla_j(\tilde{\phi}) \equiv \sigma_j X \quad \mathrm{mod}\ I^2L_j \qquad j = 1, 2 .$$

That is, $Qf \circ \sigma_1(X) = \sigma_2(X)$.

Finally, since L_1 and L_2 are minimal Lie algebras and since Qf is an isomorphism, it follows that f is an isomorphism. □

Let K_1 and K_2 be simply connected s.s.c.'s with finite Betti numbers. Choose a power series connection (ω_1, L_1) on K_1 and (ω_2, L_2) on K_2.

(6.29) Theorem. If $f\colon K_1 \to K_2$ is a simplicial map, then there is a d.g. Lie algebra map $\hat{f}\colon L_1 \to L_2$ such that the diagram

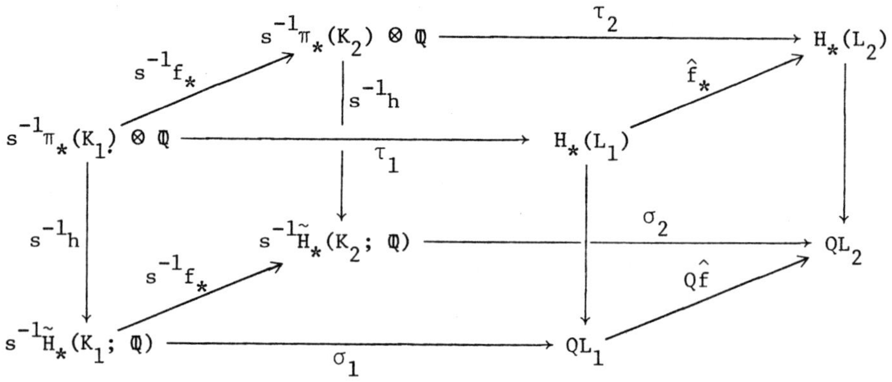

commutes.

Proof. Choose a splitting $\rho\colon L_1 \to (QE(K_1))^*$ of $\nabla_1\colon (QE(K_1))^* \to L_1$. Define $\hat{f}\colon L_1 \to L_2$ by $\hat{f} = \nabla_2 \circ QB(f^*) \circ \rho$, where

$$QB(f^*)\colon QB(E(K_2)) \to QB(E(K_1))$$

is the natural coalgebra map induced by $f\colon K_1 \to K_2$. The proof proceeds by an argument very similar to the proof of (6.28). □

(6.30) Remark. Baues and Lemaire [3] have defined a notion of homotopy between d.g. Lie algebra maps from a free chain Lie algebra into a chain Lie algebra. The map $\hat{f}\colon L_1 \to L_2$ defined in the proof of (6.29) is unique up to homotopy. This follows from the fact that the splitting ρ is unique up to homotopy.

Topological Interpretation of the Lie Algebra Model

In this section we prove that elementary extensions of the Lie algebra model of a space K correspond to attaching a cell to K which does not kill any rational homology of K. Similar assertions have been proved by Neisendorfer [33].

(6.31) Definition. We say that the chain Lie algebra L' is an *elementary extension* of a d.g. subalgebra L if there is an element Z of L' such that $\partial Z \in L$ and $L' = L * \mathbb{L}(Z)$.

We shall usually denote L' by $L *_\partial \mathbb{L}(Z)$. Observe that each minimal chain Lie algebra can be built up from the trivial Lie algebra by a sequence of elementary extensions.

(6.32) Theorem. Let K be a 1-connected space with Lie algebra model L. If $n \geq 1$ and if $f: S^n \to K$ is a simplicial map (with respect to a suitable subdivision of S^n) such that $f_*: H_n(S^n; \mathbb{Q}) \to H_n(K; \mathbb{Q})$ is trivial, then the adjunction space $K \cup_f e^{n+1}$ has Lie algebra model $L *_\partial \mathbb{L}(Z)$, where deg Z = n, the image of $s^{-1}\{f\}$ in $H_*(L)$ under the isomorphism

$$\tau: s^{-1}\pi_*(|K|) \otimes Q \to H_*(L)$$

is $\{\partial Z\}$, and such that if z is a homology class in $H_{n+1}(K \cup_f e^{n+1})$ whose image in $H_{n+1}(K \cup_f e^{n+1}, K)$ is $\{e^{n+1}\}$, then $\sigma(s^{-1}z) \equiv Z \bmod QL$ under the isomorphism

$$\sigma: s^{-1}\tilde{H}_*(K \cup_f e^{n+1}; \mathbb{Q}) \to Q(L *_\partial \mathbb{L}(\mathbb{Z})) .$$

Proof. Set $K' = K \cup_f e^{n+1}$ and denote the canonical inclusion of K into K' by $i: K \to K'$. Since $f_*: H_n(S^n; \mathbb{Q}) \to H_n(K; \mathbb{Q})$ is trivial, we can choose a basis $(X_1, X_2, \ldots)$ of $s^{-1}\tilde{H}_*(K; \mathbb{Q})$ and a basis $(Z, Y_1, Y_2, \ldots)$ of $s^{-1}\tilde{H}_*(K'; \mathbb{Q})$ such that $(s^{-1}i_*)X_j = Y_j$ for each j and such that the image of sZ in $H_{n+1}(K', K, \mathbb{Q})$ is the homology class $\{e^{n+1}\}$ of e^{n+1}.

Choose an (n+1)-form w on K' such that $i^*w = 0$ and $\langle w, e^{n+1}\rangle = 1$. There is a connection (ω', L') on $E(K')$ and a connection (ω, L) on $E(K)$ such that

$$\omega' \equiv wZ + \sum w_j Y_j \mod E(K') \hat{\otimes} I^2 L'$$

and

$$\omega \equiv \omega' - wZ \mod \bigoplus_{p \geq n+1} (E^{p+1}(K) \otimes L'_p) ,$$

where L is considered as a sub-Lie algebra of L' by identifying X_j with Y_j.

Let T and T' be the respective transports of ω and ω'. Let T_L and T_L' be the corresponding Lie transports. Note that

$$T_L \equiv T'_L \mod \bigoplus_{p \geq n+1} (E^p(\Omega K) \otimes L'_p) .$$

Choose a smooth map

$$h: e^n \to \Omega K'$$

such that the suspension ϕ_h of h takes $\partial([0,1] \times e^n)$ into K and such that the homology class of

$$\phi_h: ([0,1] \times e^n, \partial([0,1] \times e^n)) \to (K',K)$$

in $H_{n+1}(K',K)$ equals the homology class of e^{n+1}. Denote the restriction of h to ∂e^{n+1} by $\partial h: S^{n-1} \to \Omega K$.

The element $\langle T_L, \partial h\rangle$ of L is closed and a representative of $\tau(s^{-1}\{f\})$ in $H_*(L)$. Observe that in L'

$$\langle T'_L, h\rangle \equiv \langle \int w, h\rangle Z \mod L$$

$$\equiv \langle w, \phi_h\rangle Z \mod L$$

$$\equiv Z \mod L .$$

That is, there is an element U of L such that

$$\langle T'_L, h\rangle = Z + U .$$

Now, using Stokes' theorem and (6.7), we have

$$\begin{aligned} \langle T_L, \partial h\rangle &= \langle T'_L, \partial h\rangle \\ &= \langle dT'_L, h\rangle \\ &= \langle \partial T'_L, h\rangle \\ &= \partial(Z + U) \\ &\equiv \partial Z \mod \partial L . \end{aligned}$$

That is, $\tau(s^{-1}\{f\}) = \{\partial Z\}$ in $H_*(L)$. □

The following theorem is a converse of (6.32).

(6.33) <u>Theorem</u>. Let K be a 1-connected space with Lie algebra model L. If $L *_\partial \mathbb{L}(Z)$ is an elementary extension of L such that $\partial Z \in I^2L$, then there is a simplicial map $f: S^n \to K$ (with respect to a suitable subdivision of S^n) and a non-zero rational number λ such that $K \cup_f e^{n+1}$ has Lie algebra model $L *_\partial \mathbb{L}(Z)$, such that the image of $s^{-1}\{f\}$ under the isomorphism $\tau: s^{-1}\pi_*(|K|) \otimes \mathbb{Q} \to H_*(L)$ is $\lambda\{\partial Z\}$ and such that if z is an element of $H_{n+1}(K \cup_f e^{n+1})$ whose image in $H_{n+1}(K \cup_f e^{n+1}, K)$ is $\{e^{n+1}\}$, then $\sigma(s^{-1}z) \equiv \lambda Z \mod QL$ in $Q(L *_\partial \mathbb{L}(Z))$.

<u>Proof</u>. If the homology class $\{\partial Z\}$ is trivial in $H_*(L)$, we may take $\lambda = 1$ and f to be a constant map. In this case $K \cup_f e^{n+1} = K \vee S^{n+1}$ which has Lie algebra model $L *_\partial \mathbb{L}(Z)$ by (4.9).

Suppose that $\{\partial Z\}$ is non-zero in $H_*(L)$. Let $j: \pi_*(|K|) \to \pi_*(|K|) \otimes_Z \mathbb{Q}$ denote the canonical inclusion. Since τ is an isomorphism and since $\{\partial Z\}$ is non-zero in $H_*(L)$, there is a non-zero rational number λ such that $\lambda\{\partial Z\}$ lies in the image of $\tau \circ j$. That is, there is a simplicial map $f: S^n \to K$ (with respect to a suitable subdivision of S^n) such that $\tau(s^{-1}\{f\}) = \lambda\{\partial Z\}$. It now follows from (6.32) that $K \cup_f e^{n+1}$ has Lie algebra model $L *_\partial \mathbb{L}(Z)$. □

7. ITERATED INTEGRALS AND HOMOTOPY PERIODS

In this chapter we demonstrate, by examples, how to write down a finite list of iterated integrals dual to $\pi_p(K) \otimes \mathbb{Q}$, where K is a simply connected s.s.c. with finite Betti numbers. We also describe a relationship between Sullivan's minimal models and Chen's power series connections. In particular, a method is given for representing the homotopy functional

$$x: \pi_p(K) \to \mathbb{Q} ,$$

associated to an indecomposable of the minimal model of K, by an iterated integral.

Throughout this chapter we will use the following notation. If $f: S^p \to K$ is a smooth map, then denote by $f': S^{p-1} \to \Omega K$ the smooth map whose suspension is the map

$$[0, 1] \times S^{p-1} \to S^p \xrightarrow{f} K$$

(cf. example (5.9)).

Let (ω, L) be a power series connection on K, a simply connected s.s.c. with finite Betti numbers. Let H be a subset of the cycles of L for which the inclusion $H \to L$ induces an isomorphism $H \to H_*(L)$ on homology. For each such H, there is a subspace M of L such that

$$L = H \oplus M \oplus \partial M .$$

One can think of this as "Hodge decomposition" of L.

The Lie transport T_L of ω can be decomposed as follows:

$$T_L = T_H + T_M + T_{\partial M}$$

where $T_H \in \int E(K) \hat{\otimes} H$, $T_M = \int E(K) \hat{\otimes} M$, and $T_{\partial M} \in \int E(K) \hat{\otimes} \partial M$. Choose a basis (W_i) of H. The following lemma is the key to writing down a list of closed iterated integrals dual to $s^{-1}\pi_*(K) \otimes \mathbb{Q}$.

(7.1) <u>Lemma</u>. If

$$T_H = \Sigma \zeta_i W_i ,$$

where $\zeta_i \in \int E(K)$, then each ζ_i is closed, and the images of their cohomology classes $(\{\zeta_i\})$ in $QH^*(\int E(K))$ form a basis of $QH^*(\int E(K))$ dual to the basis $(\{W_i\})$ of $H_*(L)$. □

<u>Proof</u>. Since $\partial T_L = dT_L$ and since $\partial | M\colon\ M \to \partial M$ is a linear isomorphism, it follows that $dT_H = 0$, $dT_{\partial M} = \partial T_M$ and

$$T_M \in d(\int E(K)) \mathbin{\hat{\otimes}} L .$$

Because $dT_H = 0$, each ζ_i is closed.

Observe that the isomorphism

$$P\Theta_*\colon\ PH_*(\Omega K; \mathbb{Q}) \to H_*(L)$$

is defined by $\{c\} \mapsto \langle T_L, c\rangle$, where $c \in C_*(\Omega K) \otimes \mathbb{Q}$ and $\partial c = 0$. Since $T_M \in d(\int E(K)) \mathbin{\hat{\otimes}} L$, $\langle T_M, c\rangle = 0$ and

$$\begin{aligned} P\Theta(c) &= \langle T_L, c\rangle \\ &= \langle T_H, c\rangle + \langle T_M, c\rangle + \langle T_{\ M}, c\rangle \\ &\equiv \langle T_H, c\rangle \bmod \partial(\mathbb{R}\ \ L) . \end{aligned}$$

Since $QH^*(\int E(K)) \approx \mathrm{Hom}(PH_*(\Omega K; \mathbb{Q}), \mathbb{Q})$ and since $P\Theta_*$ is an isomorphism, it follows that $(\{\zeta_i\})$ is a basis of $QH^*(\int E(K))$ dual to the basis $(\{W_i\})$ of $H_*(L)$. □

(7.2) <u>Example</u>. Let S^n be a simply connected sphere. A connection (ω, L) on S^n is given by $\omega = wX$ and $L = \mathbb{L}(X)$, where w is a volume form on S^n, $\deg X = n - 1$, and $\partial X = 0$. The transport of ω is

$$T = 1 + \int wX + \int wwX^2 + \int wwwX^3 + \ldots$$

and the Lie transport of ω is given by

$$T_L = \begin{cases} \int wX & n \text{ odd} \\ \int wX + \frac{1}{2}\int ww[X, X] & n \text{ even} . \end{cases}$$

Since the map

$$\tau: s^{-1}\pi_*(S^n) \otimes \mathbb{Q} \to H_*(L)$$

is given by $s^{-1}\{f\} \to \{\langle T_L, f'\rangle\}$, it follows that $\int w$ detects the generator ζ of $\pi_n(S^n)$ and, when n is even, $\int ww$ detects $[\zeta, \zeta]$.

(7.3) <u>Example</u>. Let $M = S^3 \times S^3 - \{\text{point}\}$. As in examples (2.4) and (6.18), a connection on M is given by

$$L = \mathbb{L}(X_1, X_2)$$

where $\deg X_1 = \deg X_2 = 2$ and $\partial X_1 = \partial X_2 = 0$, and

$$\omega = w_1X_1 + w_2X_2 + w_{12}[X_1, X_2]$$

where $dw_{12} = - w_1 \wedge w_2$. The Lie transport T_L of ω satisfies

$$\begin{aligned} T_L \equiv & \int w_1X_1 + w_2X_2 + (w_{12} + \tfrac{1}{2}(w_1w_2 - w_2w_1))[X_1, X_2] \\ & + \frac{1}{6}\int (w_1w_1w_2 - 2w_1w_2w_1 + w_2w_1w_1 + 3w_1w_{12} - 3w_{12}w_1)[X_1[X_1, X_2]] \\ & + \frac{1}{6}\int (w_2w_2w_1 - 2w_2w_1w_2 + w_1w_2w_2 - 3w_2w_{12} + 3w_{12}w_2)[X_2[X_1, X_2]] \\ & \mod \int E(M) \hat{\otimes} I^4L . \end{aligned}$$

It follows, for example, that $[X_1, X_2]$ is detected by $\int w_{12} + \frac{1}{2}(w_1w_2 - w_2w_1)$ and that $[X_1[X_1, X_2]]$ is detected by

$$\frac{1}{6}\int (w_1w_1w_2 - 2w_1w_2w_1 + w_2w_1w_1 + 3w_1w_{12} - 3w_{12}w_1) .$$

Since decomposable cohomology classes vanish on spherical cycles, the above formulas can be simplified as follows:

Since $\int w_1$ and $\int w_2$ are closed in $\int E(M)$, and since

$$\int (w_{12} + \tfrac{1}{2}(w_1w_2 - w_2w_1) + \tfrac{1}{2}\int w_1 \wedge \int w_2 = \int (w_{12} + w_1w_2) ,$$

it follows that, for all smooth maps $f\colon S^4 \to \Omega M$,

$$<\int w_{12} + w_1w_2,\ f> \;=\; <\int w_{12} + \frac{1}{2}(w_1w_2 - w_2w_1),\ f> .$$

In the second case,

$$\frac{1}{6}\int (w_1w_1w_2 - 2w_1w_2w_1 + w_2w_1w_1 + 3w_1w_{12} - 3w_{12}w_1)$$
$$+ \frac{1}{2}\int (w_{12} + \frac{1}{2}(w_1w_2 - w_2w_1)) \wedge \int w_1 + \frac{1}{3}\int w_1w_1 \wedge \int w_2$$
$$= \int (w_1w_1w_2 + w_1w_{12}) .$$

Since we have altered the integral only by products of closed forms in $\int E(M)$, for all smooth maps $f\colon S^6 \to \Omega M$,

$$<\int (w_1w_1w_2 + w_1w_{12}),\ f> =$$
$$<\frac{1}{6}\int (w_1w_1w_2 - 2w_1w_2w_1 + w_2w_1w_1 + 3w_1w_{12} - 3w_{12}w_1),\ f> .$$

(7.4) <u>Example</u>. In this example, we compute an iterated integral that will detect a specific nontrivial element of $\pi_4(\mathbb{C}P^2 \# \mathbb{C}P^2 \# \mathbb{C}P^2) \otimes \mathbb{Q}$.

Choose closed 2-forms w_1, w_2, w_3 on $M = \mathbb{C}P^2 \# \mathbb{C}P^2 \# \mathbb{C}P^2$ whose cohomology classes form a basis of $H^2(M; \mathbb{Q})$, and where w_1 is supported in the first copy of $\mathbb{C}P^2$, w_2 in the second, and w_3 in the third (cf. example (4.16)). Since the supports of the w_j are mutually disjoint, $w_i \wedge w_j = 0$ when $i \neq j$. Normalize w_1, w_2, w_3 so that

$$\int_M w_i^2 = 1 \qquad\qquad i = 1, 2, 3 .$$

Consequently,

$$\int_M (2w_1^2 - w_2^2 - w_3^2) = 0 .$$

By the de Rham theorem, there is a 3-form ξ_1 on M such that

$$d\xi_1 = \frac{1}{3}(2w_1^2 - w_2^2 - w_3^2) .$$

Similarly, there are 3-forms ξ_2, ξ_3 on M such that

$$d\xi_2 = \frac{1}{3}(2w_2^2 - w_1^2 - w_3^2)$$

$$d\xi_3 = \frac{1}{3}(2w_3^2 - w_1^2 - w_2^2) \ .$$

Set $w = \frac{1}{3}(w_1^2 + w_2^2 + w_3^2)$. A connection (ω, L) on M is given by

$$\omega = w_1X_1 + w_2X_2 + w_3X_3 + wZ + \frac{1}{2}\xi_1[X_1, X_1] + \frac{1}{2}\xi_2[X_2, X_2] + \frac{1}{2}\xi_3[X_3, X_3] \ ,$$

$$L = \mathbf{L}(X_1, X_2, X_3) \ ,$$

where $\deg X_i = 1$ $(i = 1, 2, 3)$, $\deg Z = 3$, $\partial X_i = 0$, and $\partial Z = \frac{1}{2}([X_1, X_1] + [X_2, X_2] + [X_3, X_3])$.

We will write down an iterated integral that will detect $[X_1[X_2, X_2]]$ in $\pi_4(M)$.

There is a Hodge decomposition

$$L = H \oplus M \oplus \partial M$$

of L such that $L_3 \cap M$ is spanned by Z, $L_3 \cap \partial M$ is spanned by $\partial[X_1, Z]$, $\partial[X_2, Z]$, and $\partial[X_3, Z]$, and $L_3 \cap H$ is spanned by $[X_1[X_2, X_2]]$, $[X_2[X_3, X_3]]$, $[X_3[X_1, X_1]]$, $[X_1[X_2, X_3]]$, $[X_2[X_3, X_3]]$, $\dots$.

The relevant part of the transport of ω is

$$\begin{aligned} T = 1 &+ \Sigma\int w_iX_i + \int wZ + \frac{1}{2}\Sigma\xi_i[X_i, X_i] + \Sigma\int w_iw_jX_iX_j \\ &+ \frac{1}{2}\Sigma\int w_i\xi_jX_i[X_j, X_j] + \frac{1}{2}\Sigma\int \xi_iw_j[X_i, X_i]X_j \\ &+ \int w_1w_2w_2X_1X_2X_2 + \int w_2w_1w_2X_2X_1X_2 + \int w_2w_2w_1X_2X_2X_1 + \dots \ . \end{aligned}$$

Using the formulas in (6.15), we obtain

$$\begin{aligned} T_L = \Sigma\int w_iX_i &+ \int wZ + \frac{1}{2}\Sigma\int(w_iw_i + \xi_i)[X_i, X_i] \\ &+ \frac{1}{2}\sum_{i<j}\int(w_iw_j + w_jw_i)[X_i, X_j] \\ &+ \frac{1}{4}\int(w_1w_2w_2 - w_2w_2w_1 + w_1\xi_2 - \xi_2w_1 - w_1w_3w_3 \\ &\qquad + w_3w_3w_1 - w_1\xi_3 + \xi_3w_1)[X_1[X_2, X_2]] \\ &+ \frac{1}{4}\int(w_1w_3w_3 - w_3w_3w_1 + w_1\xi_3 - \xi_3w_1)\partial[X_1, Z] + \dots \ . \end{aligned}$$

It follows from (7.1) that

$$I = \frac{1}{4}\int(w_1w_2w_2 - w_2w_2w_1 + w_1\xi_2 - \xi_2w_1 - w_1w_3w_3 + w_3w_3w_1 - w_1\xi_3 + \xi_3w_1)$$

is closed and that it detects $[X_1[X_2, X_2]]$.

This formula can be simplified, as in (7.3), by adding

$$\frac{1}{4}\int w_1 \wedge \int(w_2w_2 + \xi_2) + \frac{1}{8}\int w_2 \wedge \int(w_1w_2 + w_2w_1)$$
$$- \frac{1}{4}\int w_1 \wedge \int(w_3w_3 + \xi_3) - \frac{1}{8}\int w_3 \wedge \int(w_1w_3 + w_3w_1)$$

to I. After simplification, we see that the iterated integral

$$I' = \frac{1}{2}\int(w_1w_2w_2 - w_1w_3w_3 + w_1\xi_2 - w_1\xi_3)$$

differs from I by a representative of a decomposable cohomology class of ΩM, so that I' also detects $[X_1[X_2, X_2]]$.

Iterated Integrals and Minimal Models

In this section we assume that the reader is familiar with the basic results of Sullivan's theory of minimal models. Good references include [19], [21], [37], and [38].

A direct and explicit relationship between the minimal model $\mathcal{M}$ of a space K and the complex of iterated integrals on K is given by taking a connection on $\mathcal{M}$. Specifically, let K be a simply connected s.s.c. with finite numbers. According to (4.10), there is a connection (ω, L) on $\mathcal{M}$. Choose a set (x_i) that freely generates $\mathcal{M}$.

(7.5) Theorem (Hain [25]). If

$$\omega \equiv \Sigma x_i W_i \qquad \text{mod } I^2\mathcal{M} \hat{\otimes} L ,$$

then each W_i is closed in L, and their homology classes form a basis of $H_*(L)$. □

(7.6) Example. Let $K = \mathbb{C}P^n$. The minimal model of $\mathbb{C}P^n$ is

$$\mathcal{M} = \Lambda(a, b\colon \deg a = 2, \deg b = 2n + 1, da = 0, db = a^{n+1}) .$$

A connection (ω, L) on $\mathcal{M}$ is given by

$$L = \mathbb{L}(X_1, X_2, \ldots, X_n)$$

where $\deg X_k = 2k-1$ and $\partial X_k = \frac{1}{2}\sum_{i+j=k}[X_i, X_j]$, and

$$\omega = \sum_{k=1}^{n} a^k X_k + \frac{1}{2}\sum_{r=1}^{n} a^{r-1} b \sum_{i+j=n+r}[X_i, X_j] .$$

Observe that

$$\omega \equiv aX_1 + \frac{1}{2} b \sum_{i+j=n+1}[X_i, X_j] \qquad \mathrm{mod}\ I^2 M \hat{\otimes} L .$$

According to (7.5), $\{X_1\}$ and $\{\sum_{i+j=n+1}[X_i, X_j]\}$ span $H_*(L)$.

Observe that, if $\rho: M \to E(K)$ is a minimal model of K, and if (ω, L) is a connection on M, then $((\rho \hat{\otimes} 1)\omega, L)$ is a power series connection on K. Theorem (7.5) thus provides a link between Sullivan's minimal model of K and the Lie algebra associated to K via a connection. The following lemma, due to Chen, relates M to the complex of iterated integrals on K.

First we introduce some notation. Let M be a 1-connected minimal algebra. Define a minimal algebra ΩM by $\Omega M = \Lambda(s^{-1}(QM))$ endowed with the trivial differential. Denote the element of $s^{-1}QM$ corresponding to the element x of QM by $\overline{x}$.

Recall from (5.13) that the bar construction $B(M)$ on M is spanned by elements of the form $[a_1|a_2|\dots|a_r]$ where each $a_j \in IM$. Let U be the subspace of $B(M)$ spanned by the elements of the form $[a_1|a_2|\dots|a_r]$ where $r \geq 2$, and by elements of the form $[a]$ where $a \in I^2M$.

(7.7) Lemma (Chen [17]). If M is a 1-connected minimal algebra, then there is a d.g. algebra map $\phi: \Omega M \to B(M)$ that induces an isomorphism on homology and such that $\phi(\overline{x}) \equiv [x]$ mod U for all $x \in QM$. □

(7.8) Corollary. If $\rho: M \to E(K)$ is a minimal model of K, then the composite

$$\Omega\rho: \Omega M \to \int E(K)$$

of $\phi: \Omega M \to B(M)$ with the natural map $B(M) \to B(E(K)) \to \int E(K)$ is a minimal model of $\int E(K)$. □

Fix a minimal model $\rho: M \to E(K)$ of K and a connection (ω, L) on M.

Define a linear map

$$\psi\colon QM \to \mathrm{Hom}_{\mathbb{Z}}(s^{-1}\pi_*(K), \mathbb{Q})$$

by $\psi(x)(\alpha) = \langle \Omega\rho(\bar{x}), f \rangle$ for each $x \in QM$ and $\alpha \in s^{-1}\pi_*(K)$, where $f\colon S^n \to \Omega K$ is a smooth map whose homology class is $\Sigma(\alpha)$.

Choose a set (x_i) that freely generates M and suppose that $\omega \equiv \Sigma x_i W_i$ mod $I^2 M \hat{\otimes} L$. Recall that each W_i is closed in L and that their homology classes $(\{W_i\})$ form a basis of $H_*(L)$. Define a linear map

$$\psi'\colon QM \to \mathrm{Hom}(H_*(L), \mathbb{Q})$$

by $\psi'(x_i)(\{W_j\}) = \delta_{ij}$. The definition of ψ' is independent of the choice of basis of QM.

The following theorem provides a means of finding an iterated integral to represent a map

$$x\colon \pi_*(K) \to \mathbb{Q}$$

where $x \in QM$. The proof is an algebraic analogue of (6.22) and the proof of (6.23) and uses (7.5) and (7.7). A detailed proof of it can be found in [24].

(7.9) Theorem. Let K be a 1-connected space with minimal model M and Lie algebra model L. With notation as in the preceding discussion, the diagram

$$\begin{array}{ccc} & & \mathrm{Hom}_{\mathbb{Z}}(s^{-1}\pi_*(K), \mathbb{Q}) \\ & \overset{\psi}{\nearrow} & \big\uparrow \tau^* \\ QM & & \\ & \underset{\psi'}{\searrow} & \\ & & \mathrm{Hom}(H_*(L), \mathbb{Q}) \end{array}$$

commutes, and ψ and ψ' are isomorphisms.

(7.10) Examples. (a) Let n be an even integer. The minimal model of S^n is

$$M = \Lambda(a, b\colon \deg a = n,\ \deg b = 2n - 1,\ da = 0,\ db = a^2)$$

and $\rho\colon M \to E(S^n)$ is defined by $\rho(a) = w$ and $\rho(b) = 0$. A connection (ω, L) on M is given by

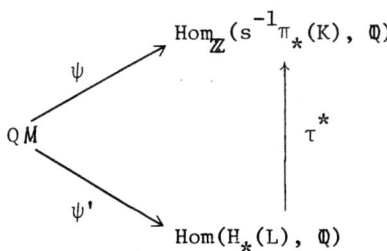

$$L = \mathbf{L}(X;\ \deg X = n-1,\ \partial X = 0)$$
$$\omega = aX + \frac{1}{2}b[X, X] \quad .$$

To find integrals that represent a and b as functionals on $\pi_*(S^n) \otimes \mathbb{Q}$, first complete the elements [a] and [b] of $B(M)$ to cocycles by adding elements of U (see (7.7)). In this case $d[a] = 0$ and $d([b] + [a|a]) = 0$. The image of [a] in $\int E(S^n)$ is $\int w$. Thus, if $f\colon S^n \to S^n$ is a smooth map, then

$$\langle\psi(a),\ \{f\}\rangle = \langle\int w,\ f'\rangle = \langle w,\ f\rangle \quad .$$

The image of $[b] + [a|a]$ in $\int E(S^n)$ is $\int ww$. Let $f\colon S^{2n-1} \to S^n$ be a smooth map. It follows from (7.9) that

$$\langle\psi(b),\ \{f\}\rangle = \langle\int ww,\ f'\rangle \quad .$$

(b) Let A be the truncated polynomial algebra

$$\Lambda(c_1, c_2\colon \deg c_1 = 2,\ \deg c_2 = 4)/J$$

where J is the ideal of $\Lambda(c_1, c_2)$ generated by c_1^3, $c_1 \wedge c_2$, and c_2^2.

There is an inclusion of A into the de Rham complex of the 4-skeleton $BU^{(4)}$ of BU that induces an isomorphism on cohomology. It is not hard to check that the subalgebra of the minimal model M of $BU^{(4)}$ generated by the elements of M of degree ≤ 8 is

$$M' = \Lambda(x_1, x_2, u_{1,11}, u_{1,2}, u_{12,11}, u_{12,2})$$

where $\deg x_1 = 2$, $\deg x_2 = 4$, $\deg u_{1,11} = \deg u_{1,2} = 5$, $\deg u_{2,2} = 7$, $\deg u_{12,11} = \deg u_{12,2} = 8$, and where $dx_1 = dx_2 = 0$, $du_{1,11} = x_1^3$, $du_{1,2} = x_1 \wedge x_2$, $du_{2,2} = x_2^2$, $du_{12,11} = x_1^2 \wedge u_{1,2} - x_2 \wedge u_{1,11}$, $du_{12,2} = u_{1,2} \wedge x_2 - x_1 \wedge u_{2,2}$. Define a d.g. algebra map $\rho\colon M' \to A$ by $\rho'(x_1) = c_1$, $\rho'(x_2) = c_2$, and $\rho'(u_{I,J}) = 0$ for all I, J.

In [25] it is shown that there is a connection (ω, L) on M such that

$$L = \mathbf{L}(X_1, X_{11}, X_2;\ \deg X_1 = 1,\ \deg X_{11} = \deg X_2 = 3,$$
$$\partial X_1 = \partial X_2 = 0,\ \partial X_{11} = \frac{1}{2}[X_1, X_1]) \ ,$$

and

$$\omega \equiv x_1X_1 + x_2X_2 + \tfrac{1}{2}u_{2,2}[X_2, X_2] + u_{1,11}[X_1, X_{11}] + u_{1,2}[X_1, X_2] + u_{12,2}[[X_1, X_2]X_2] + u_{12,11}[X_2[X_1, X_{11}]] \mod (I^2M \hat{\otimes} L + \bigoplus_{p\geq 9} M^p \otimes L_{p-1}) .$$

The following table gives the generators of M of degree ≤ 8, the corresponding iterated integrals, and a basis of $s^{-1}\pi_*(BU^{(4)}) \otimes \mathbb{Q}$ in low dimensions, dual to the basis given for QM.

Basis of $\bigoplus_{p\leq 8} (QM)^p$	Corresponding iterated integrals	Dual basis of $\bigoplus_{p\leq 7} H_p(L)$
x_1	$\int c_1$	$\{X_1\}$
x_2	$\int c_2$	$\{X_2\}$
$u_{1,11}$	$\int c_1^2 c_1$	$\{[X_1, X_{11}]\}$
$u_{1,2}$	$\int c_1 c_2$	$\{[X_1, X_2]\}$
$u_{2,2}$	$\int c_2 c_2$	$\frac{1}{2}\{[X_2, X_2]\}$
$u_{12,11}$	$\int c_1^2 c_1 c_2$	$\{[X_2[X_1, X_{11}]]\}$
$u_{12,2}$	$-\int c_1 c_2 c_2$	$\{[[X_1, X_2]X_2]\}$

8. A PROOF OF THE SMOOTHING LEMMA

In this chapter we prove the smoothing lemma (6.1) that we state below. Throughout this chapter, K will denote a fixed s.s.c. Recall from the discussion preceding (6.1) that we view ΩK as a subspace of $\Omega|K|$.

<u>Lemma</u>. If $\sigma: \Delta^p \to \Omega|K|$ is a continuous map such that $\sigma|\partial\Delta^p$ lands in ΩK, and if $\sigma|\partial\Delta^p: \partial\Delta^p \to \Omega K$ is smooth, then there is a smooth map $\sigma': \Delta^p \to \Omega K$ such that $\sigma'|\partial\Delta^p = \sigma|\partial\Delta^p$, and a homotopy $h: [0, 1] \times \Delta^p \to \Omega|K|$ from σ to σ' rel $\partial\Delta^p$.

The proof of the smoothing lemma is broken down into several propositions. We assume that the reader is familiar with triangulating s.s.c.'s. A good reference is [29].

The next proposition is an easy consequence of the definitions of subdivision and smoothness and will not be proved.

(8.1) <u>Proposition</u>. If K' is a subdivision of K, then the natural map $K' \to K$ is smooth. □

Let X be an s.s.c. Denote by $[0, 1] \times X$ the differentiable space whose plots are generated by the maps $id \times |\sigma|: [0, 1] \times \Delta^p \to |K|$ for each p-simplex σ of K.

Let X be an s.s.c., and A a subcomplex of X. A subdivision of X rel A is a subdivision of X such that the simplices of A are not subdivided.

The next proposition is an analogue of the simplicial approximation theorem.

(8.2) <u>Proposition</u>. Let X be a finite simplicial complex, and let A, B be subcomplexes of X with $B \subseteq A$. Let L be an s.s.c. such that $|L|$ is a finite CW-complex. If $\phi: |X| \to |L|$ is a continuous map, such that the restriction of ϕ to A is smooth, and such that the restriction of ϕ to B is simplicial, then there are subdivisions X' of X rel B and L' of L, and there is a simplicial map $\psi: X' \to L'$ and a homotopy $h: [0, 1] \times |X| \to |L|$ from ϕ to ψ such that

(a) $h(s, b) = \phi(b) = \psi(b)$ for all $b \in |B|$ and $s \in [0, 1]$, and

(b) $h[0, 1] \times A'$: $[0, 1] \times A' \to L$ is smooth, where A' is the subdivision of A induced by X'.

Proof. According to Theorem (6.1) in [29], there is a subdivision L' of L such that L' is a simplicial complex. By the simplicial approximation theorem, there is a subdivision X' of X rel B and a simplicial map ψ: $X' \to L'$ which is a simplicial approximation to ϕ and such that $\psi(x) = \phi(x)$ whenever $x \in |B|$.

By (8.1), the composite $X' \xrightarrow{\psi} L' \to L$ is smooth. Since ψ is a simplicial approximation to ϕ, it follows that $\psi(x)$ and $\phi(x)$ lie in the same simplex of L' for all $x \in |X|$. We can define a homotopy h: $[0, 1] \times |X| \to |L|$ from ϕ to ψ by

$$h(s, x) = (1 - s)\phi(x) + s\psi(x) .$$

Since the restriction of ϕ to A' is smooth, it follows that the restriction of h to $[0, 1] \times A'$ is smooth. □

Proposition (8.1) asserts that, if K is an s.s.c. and K' a subdivision of K, then the natural map $K' \to K$ is smooth. In general, the natural map $K \to K'$ is not smooth. The next proposition shows how to smooth $K \to K'$ when K is a simplicial complex.

(8.3) Proposition. Let L be a simplicial complex. If L' is a subdivision of L, then there is a smooth map ϕ: $L' \to L'$ such that ϕ is smoothly homotopic to id: $L' \to L'$ and such that the composition $L \to L' \xrightarrow{\phi} L'$ of the natural map $L \to L'$ with ϕ is smooth.

Proof. We begin by constructing a sequence $(\phi_n: \Delta^n \to \Delta^n)_{n\geq 0}$ of smooth maps with the following properties:

(a) if d: $\Delta^{n-1} \to \Delta^n$ is a face map of Δ^n, then $\phi_n \circ d(\Delta^{n-1}) \subseteq d(\Delta^{n-1})$ and $\phi_n \circ d = \phi_{n-1}$;

(b) each ϕ_n is smoothly homotopic to id: $\Delta^n \to \Delta^n$;

(c) if σ is a simplex of Δ^n, then $\phi_n^{-1}(\sigma)$ is a closed neighborhood of σ in Δ^n.

We construct the sequence (ϕ_n) inductively. First, choose a smooth function $\mu: [0, 1] \to [0, 1]$ such that $\mu(t) = 0$ when t is in some neighborhood of 0 and $\mu(t) = 1$ when t is in some neighborhood of 1.

When $n = 0$, take ϕ_0 to be the unique map $\Delta^0 \to \Delta^0$. Suppose that $n \geq 1$ and that $\phi_0, \phi_1, \ldots, \phi_{n-1}$ have been defined and satisfy the conditions (a), (b), and (c) above. Let b be the barycenter of Δ^n. For each $\xi \in \Delta^n \backslash \{b\}$, let $\pi(\xi)$ be the radical projection of ξ onto $\partial\Delta^n$.

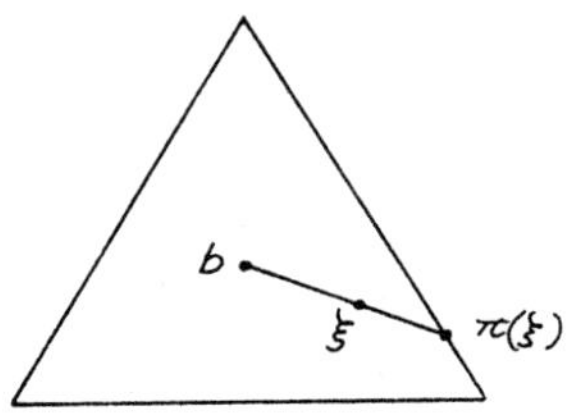

For each ξ in $\Delta^n\backslash\{b\}$, there is a unique number t in [0, 1] such that $\xi = tb + (1 - t)\pi(\xi)$. Using (a), define $\phi_n|\partial\Delta^n: \partial\Delta^n \to \partial\Delta^n$. Observe that $\partial\phi_n \circ \pi: \Delta^n\backslash\{b\} \to \partial\Delta^n$ is a smooth map. Now define $\phi_n: \Delta^n \to \Delta^n$ by $\phi_n(b) = b$, and for $\xi \in \Delta^n\backslash\{b\}$

$$\phi_n(\xi) = \mu(t)b + (1 - \mu(t))\phi_n \circ \pi(\xi)$$

where $\xi = tb + (1 - t)\pi(\xi)$. It is not hard to check that ϕ_n is smooth at b, that condition (c) is satisfied, and that ϕ_n is smoothly homotopic to id: $\Delta^n \to \Delta^n$.

Now define $\phi: L' \to L'$ by defining the restriction of ϕ to each p-simplex to be ϕ_p. It is not hard to check, using condition (c) above, together with (4.1(c)), that the composite $L \to L' \xrightarrow{\phi} L'$ is smooth. A smooth homotopy from ϕ to id: $L' \to L'$ can be defined "simplex-wise." □

We can now prove the smoothing lemma. Let $\sigma: \Delta^p \to \Omega|K|$ be a continuous map such that $\sigma|\partial\Delta^p$ lands in ΩK and $\sigma|\partial\Delta^p: \partial\Delta^p \to \Omega K$ is smooth. That is, there is a partition $0 = t_0 < t_1 < \dots < t_m = 1$ of $[0, 1]$ such that the restriction of the suspension ϕ_σ of σ to each $[t_{j-1}, t_j] \times \partial\Delta^p$ is smooth. Let v_0 be the distinguished vertex of K. Observe that ϕ_σ takes $\{0, 1\} \times \Delta^p$ into $\{v_0\}$. Triangulate $[0, 1] \times \Delta^p$ so that each $[t_{j-1}, t_j] \times \partial\Delta^p$ is a subcomplex of $[0, 1] \times \Delta^p$. (This is possible: see [32].) Denote the resulting simplicial complex by X. Set

$$A = [0, 1] \times \partial\Delta^p \cup \{0, 1\} \times \Delta^p ,$$

$$B = \{0, 1\} \times \Delta^p ,$$

$$X_j = [t_{j-1}, t_j] \times \Delta^p , \text{ and}$$

$$A_j = [t_{j-1}, t_j] \times \partial\Delta^p .$$

Since $|X|$ is compact, there is a subcomplex $\overline{K}$ of K such that $|\overline{K}|$ is a finite CW-complex and the image of ϕ_σ lies in $|\overline{K}|$. Without loss of generality, we assume that $|K|$ is a finite CW-complex.

By (8.2), there are subdivisions X' of X (rel B) and K' of K, a simplicial map $\psi\colon X' \to K'$, and a homotopy $h\colon [0, 1] \times |X'| \to |K|$ from ϕ_σ to ψ such that $h([0, 1] \times |B|) \subseteq \{v_0\}$, and such that the restriction of h to each $[0, 1] \times A'_j$ is smooth.

Denote the barycentric coordinates of Δ^p by $(\xi_0, \xi_1, \dots, \xi_p)$. Set

$$D = \{(\xi_0, \xi_1, \dots, \xi_p)\colon \xi_j \ge \frac{1}{2(p+1)} \text{ for all } j\}$$

$$E_i = \{(\xi_0, \xi_1, \dots, \xi_p)\colon \xi_i \le \frac{1}{2(p+1)} \text{ and } \xi_j \ge \xi_i \text{ for } j = 0, 1, \dots, p\} .$$

Observe that

$$\Delta^p = (\bigcup_{i=1}^{p} E_i) \cup D ,$$

that D is a copy of Δ^p, and that each E_i is homeomorphic to $[0, 1] \times \Delta^{p-1}$ via an affine map.

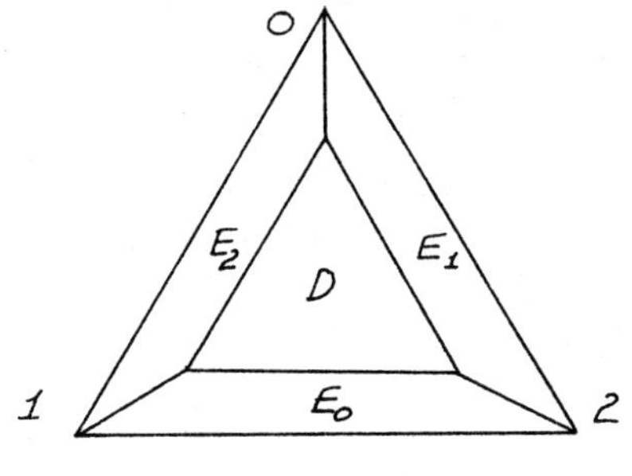

Define a homeomorphism ρ from Δ^p onto the subspace $[0, 1] \times \partial\Delta^p \cup \{1\} \times \Delta^p$ of $[0, 1] \times \Delta^p$ by insisting that the restriction of ρ to each E_i and D be an affine map, and by insisting that ρ take E_i onto the product of $[0, 1]$ with the ith face of Δ^p, and that ρ take D onto $\{1\} \times \Delta^p$.

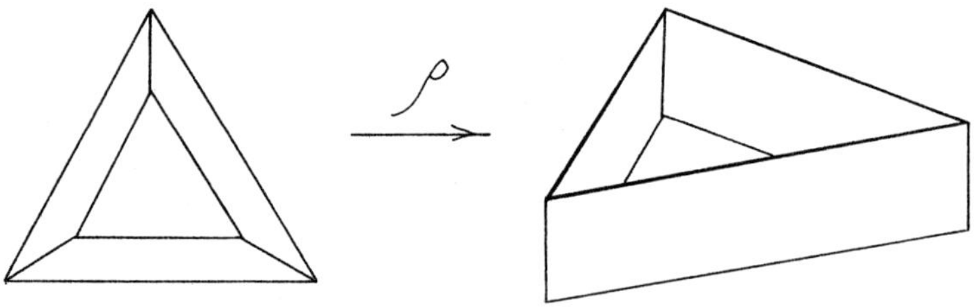

Let J be the subspace $\{1\} \times X' \cup [0, 1] \times A'$ of $[0, 1] \times X'$ endowed with the subspace differentiable structure. Set $J_j = \{1\} \times X'_j \cup [0, 1] \times A'_j$ endowed with the subspace differentiable structure.

Define a map $\gamma\colon J \to K$ by $\gamma(s, \xi) = h(s, \xi)$ whenever $\xi \in |A'|$ and $\gamma(1, \xi) = \psi(\xi)$ for all $\xi \in |X'|$. Since the restriction of h to each $[0, 1] \times A'_j$ is smooth, and since $h(1, \xi) = \psi(\xi)$ for all $\xi \in |X'|$, it follows that γ is well defined and that the restriction of γ to each J_j is smooth.

The map $\mathrm{id} \times \rho\colon [0, 1] \times \Delta^p \to J$ is a homeomorphism. However, the composite $\gamma \circ (\mathrm{id} \times \rho)\colon [0, 1] \times \Delta^p \to K$ is not necessarily the suspension of a smooth map $\Delta^p \to \Omega K$, but it can be smoothed. We will define a smooth map $J\theta\colon J \to J$ such that the composite $\gamma \circ J\theta \circ (\mathrm{id} \times \rho)\colon [0, 1] \times \Delta^p \to K$ is the suspension of a smooth map $\Delta^p \to \Omega K$.

Let $\theta\colon X' \to X'$ be a smoothing map as given by the proof of (8.3). Let $\mu\colon [0, 1] \to [0, 1]$ be a smooth function such that $\mu(s) = 0$ when s is in some small neighborhood of 0 and $\mu(s) = 1$ when s is in some small neighborhood of 1. Define $J\theta\colon J \to J$ by

$$J\theta(s, \xi) = (\mu(s), s\theta(\xi) + (1 - s)\xi) .$$

Since $\theta(\xi)$ and ξ lie in the same simplex of X', it follows that $J\theta$ is well defined. It is not hard to check that $J\theta$ is smooth and that the restriction of

$$\gamma \circ J\theta \circ (\mathrm{id} \times \rho): [0, 1] \times \Delta^p \to K$$

to each $[t_{j-1}, t_j] \times \Delta^p$ is smooth. Define a smooth map $\sigma': \Delta^p \to \Omega K$ by $\phi_{\sigma'} = \gamma \circ J\theta \circ (\mathrm{id} \times \rho)$. It is not hard to check that $\partial\sigma' = \partial\sigma: \partial\Delta^p \to \Omega K$. It is an exercise to construct a homotopy from σ to σ' relative to $\partial\Delta^p$. □

9. PROOFS OF THE RATIONAL LOOP SPACE HOMOLOGY AND COHOMOLOGY THEOREMS

In this chapter we prove the rational versions (6.5) and (6.9) of Chen's loop space homology and cohomology theorems. Another proof of Chen's loop space cohomology theorem has been given by Gugenheim in [22].

(9.1) <u>Theorem</u>. Let K be a simply connected s.s.c. with finite Betti numbers. If (ω, L) is a power series connection on K, then there is a Hopf algebra isomorphism

$$\Psi\colon H_*(\Omega K;\, \mathbb{Q}) \to H_*(UL)$$

such that the diagram

$$\begin{array}{ccc} & & H_*(UL) \\ & \overset{\Psi}{\nearrow} & \downarrow \\ H_*(\Omega K;\, \mathbb{Q}) & \xrightarrow[\theta_*]{} & H_*(\mathbb{R} \otimes UL) \end{array}$$

commutes, where the vertical map is induced by the canonical inclusion $UL \to \mathbb{R} \otimes UL$ and where $\theta\colon C_*(\Omega K) \otimes \mathbb{Q} \to \mathbb{R} \otimes UL$ is the holonomy map associated to ω.

(9.2) <u>Theorem</u>. If K is a simply connected s.s.c. with finite Betti numbers, then there is a Hopf algebra isomorphism

$$\nu\colon H^*\left(\int E(K)\right) \to H^*(\Omega K;\, \mathbb{Q}) .$$

Furthermore, if

$$\int : \int E(K) \to \mathrm{Hom}(C_*(\Omega K),\, \mathbb{R})$$

denotes the integration map $w \mapsto \{\sigma \mapsto \langle w, \sigma\rangle\}$, then the diagram

$$\begin{array}{ccc} & & H^*(\Omega K;\, \mathbb{Q}) \\ & \overset{\nu}{\nearrow} & \downarrow \\ H^*\left(\int E(K)\right) & \xrightarrow[\int^*]{} & H^*(\Omega K;\, \mathbb{R}) \end{array}$$

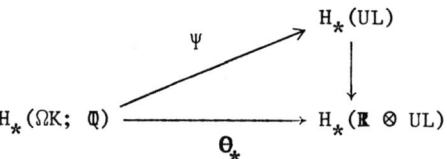

commutes, where the vertical map is induced by the inclusion $\mathbb{Q} \to \mathbb{R}$.

Recall the definition of Adam's cobar construction.

(9.3) Definition. Let C be a connected chain coalgebra with coaugmentation η: $\mathbb{Q} \to C$ and differential δ. The cobar construction on C is the chain algebra $\mathcal{F}(C)$ defined as follows:

Let $\overline{C}$ = coker η and observe that the comultiplication Δ: $C \to C \otimes C$ induces a map $\overline{\Delta}$: $\overline{C} \to \overline{C} \otimes \overline{C}$. As a graded algebra, $\mathcal{F}(C)$ is the tensor algebra $T(s^{-1}\overline{C})$ on the desuspension $s^{-1}\overline{C}$ of $\overline{C}$. We follow convention and write the element $s^{-1}c_1 \otimes s^{-1}c_2 \otimes \dots \otimes s^{-1}c_r$ of $\mathcal{F}(C)$ as $[c_1|c_2|\dots|c_r]$. Let $c \in \overline{C}$ and suppose that $\overline{\Delta}c = \Sigma a_i \otimes b_i$. Define the differential $\partial[c]$ of $[c]$ by

$$\partial[c] = -[\delta c] + \Sigma(-1)^{\deg a_i}[a_i|b_i] .$$

Extend ∂ to all of $\mathcal{F}(C)$ by insisting that ∂ be a derivation of degree -1 of $\mathcal{F}(C)$. It is not hard to check that $\partial^2 = 0$.

The simplicial chain complex ΔK of an s.s.c. K has the structure of a coalgebra. Define a coproduct Δ by

$$\Delta\sigma = \sum_{i+j=n} {}_{(i)}\sigma \otimes \sigma_{(j)}$$

where ${}_{(i)}\sigma$ denotes the front ith face and $\sigma_{(j)}$ the rear jth face of the n-simplex σ.

We first prove (9.1) and (9.2) in the case when K has only one 0-simplex. Let K be a simply connected s.s.c. with finite Betti numbers and only one 0-simplex, v.

Let $v_0, v_1, \dots, v_n$ be the vertices of the standard n-simplex Δ^n. For each n, define a smooth map

$$\theta_n: [0, 1]^{n-1} \to P(\Delta^n; v_0, v_n)$$

exactly as in [10, pp. 239-240]. This map has the following properties: if $(\xi_1, \dots, \xi_{n-1})$ are the canonical coordinates of $[0, 1]^{n-1}$ and $(\eta_0, \dots, \eta_n)$ are the barycentric coordinates of Δ^n, and if

$$\phi_{\theta_n}(t, \xi) = (\eta_0(t, \xi), \dots, \eta_n(t, \xi)) ,$$

then each $\eta_j(t, \xi)$ is a polynomial in the variables $(t, \xi_1, \ldots, \xi_{n-1})$ with rational coefficients. Secondly, $\phi_{\theta_n}(\partial[0, 1]^n) \subseteq \partial\Delta^n$ and the induced map of pairs

$$\phi_{\theta_n} : ([0, 1]^n, \partial[0, 1]^n) \to (\Delta^n, \partial\Delta^n)$$

is of degree 1.

Now define, for each n-simplex σ of K, a smooth map

$$\hat{\sigma}: [0, 1]^{n-1} \to \Omega K$$

by $\hat{\sigma} = P(|\sigma|) \circ \theta_n$, where $P(|\sigma|)$ is the map $P(\Delta^n; v_0, v_n) \to P(K; v, v)$ induced by the face map $|\sigma|: \Delta^n \to |K|$. Now define a chain map

$$\mu: F(\Delta K) \to C_*(\Omega K) \otimes \mathbb{Q}$$

exactly as in [15, pp. 872-873]. In fact, if σ is a p-simplex of K with $p \geq 1$, then

$$\mu([\sigma]) = \begin{cases} \hat{\sigma} & \text{if } p \geq 2 \\ \hat{\sigma} - \eta_v & \text{if } p = 1 , \end{cases}$$

where η_v denotes the constant loop at v. Further, $\mu([\sigma_1|\ldots|\sigma_r])$ and $\mu([\sigma_1]) \times \ldots \times \mu([\sigma_r])$ differ only by a piecewise linear reparameterization.

It follows from a theorem of Adams [1] (see also [15, p. 873]) and the smoothing lemma that μ induces an algebra isomorphism

$$\mu_*: H_*(F(\Delta K)) \to H_*(\Omega K; \mathbb{Q}) .$$

Since, for each p-simplex σ of K, the suspension $\phi_{\hat{\sigma}}: [0, 1]^p \to K$ of $\hat{\sigma}$ is given by rational polynomials, and since, for simplices $\sigma_1, \sigma_2, \ldots, \sigma_r$ of K, $\mu([\sigma_1|\ldots|\sigma_r])$ and $\mu([\sigma_1]) \times \ldots \times \mu([\sigma_r])$ differ only by a piecewise linear reparameterization, it follows from (5.11) that, if $w_1, w_2, \ldots, w_s \in E(K)$ and $a \in F(\Delta K)$, then

$$<\int w_1 w_2 \ldots w_s, \mu(a)> \in \mathbb{Q} .$$

Since $\phi_{\theta_n} : ([0, 1]^n, \partial[0, 1]^n) \to (\Delta^n, \partial\Delta^n)$ has degree 1, it follows from (5.8) that, if w is a p-form on K and $p \geq 2$, and if σ is a simplex of K, then

$$<\int w,\ \mu([\sigma])> \ = \ <w,\ \sigma> \quad .$$

Let $(\omega,\ L)$ be a power series connection on K. Let $\Theta\colon C_*(\Omega K) \otimes \mathbb{Q} \to \mathbb{R} \otimes UL$ be the associated holonomy map. Since Θ is multiplicative and since $\omega \in E(K) \hat{\otimes} UL$, it follows that $\Theta \circ \mu$ lands in UL and yields a d.g. algebra map

$$\Theta \circ \mu\colon F(\Delta K) \to UL \quad .$$

Choose a set (X_i) that freely generates L. If $\omega \equiv \Sigma w_i X_i \mod E(K) \hat{\otimes} I^2 UL$, then for each simplex σ of K

$$Q(\Theta \circ \mu)([\sigma]) = \Sigma <w_i,\ \sigma> X_i \quad .$$

Since each w_i is closed in $E(K)$, and since their homology classes form a basis of $\tilde{H}^*(K;\ \mathbb{Q})$ dual to the basis (sX_i) of $\tilde{H}_*(K;\ \mathbb{Q})$, it follows that $Q(\Theta \circ \mu)$ induces an isomorphism on homology. From (1.5) in [3] it follows that $\Theta \circ \mu$ induces an isomorphism

$$(\Theta \circ \mu)_*\colon H_*(F(\Delta K)) \to H_*(UL) \quad .$$

Define $\Psi\colon H_*(\Omega K;\ \mathbb{Q}) \to H_*(UL)$ by $\Psi = (\Theta \circ \mu)_* \circ (\mu_*)^{-1}$. The diagram

$$\begin{array}{ccc} H_*(F(\Delta K)) & \xrightarrow{(\Theta \circ \mu)_*} & H_*(UL) \\ \mu_* \downarrow & \overset{\Psi}{\nearrow} & \downarrow \\ H_*(\Omega K;\ \mathbb{Q}) & \xrightarrow[\Theta_*]{} & H_*(\mathbb{R} \otimes UL) \end{array}$$

commutes. That Ψ is a Hopf algebra map follows from (6.22). This proves (9.1) in the case when K has only one 0-simplex.

Using an argument identical to that in [15, pp. 850-851], one can show that the map

$$\lambda\colon \int E(K) \to \mathrm{Hom}\ (F(\Delta K),\ \mathbb{Q}) \ ,$$

defined by $w \mapsto \{a \mapsto <w,\ \mu(a)>\}$, for $w \in E(K)$ and $a \in F(\Delta K)$, induces an isomorphism on homology. Define

$$\nu\colon H^*(\int E(K)) \to H^*(\Omega K;\ \mathbb{Q})$$

by $\nu = (\mu^*)^{-1} \circ \lambda^*$. That is, the diagram

$$\begin{array}{ccc}
H^*(\int \mathcal{E}(K)) & \xrightarrow{\quad\lambda^*\quad} & H^*(\mathrm{Hom}\,(\mathcal{F}(\Delta K),\ \mathbb{Q})) \\
{\scriptstyle \int^*}\big\downarrow & \searrow^{\nu} & \big\uparrow{\scriptstyle \mu^*} \\
H^*(\Omega K;\ \mathbb{R}) & \longleftarrow & H^*(\Omega K;\ \mathbb{Q})
\end{array}$$

commutes. That ν is a Hopf algebra map follows from (5.5). This proves (9.2) in the case when K has only one 0-simplex.

Now suppose that K is a simply connected s.s.c. with finite Betti numbers. Choose a maximal tree Γ in K. The quotient s.s.c. K/Γ has only one 0-simplex. The canonical projection $\pi\colon K \to K/\Gamma$ is a simplicial map, and hence smooth. The induced map

$$\pi^*\colon \mathcal{E}(K/\Gamma) \to \mathcal{E}(K)$$

induces an isomorphism on homology. Observe that if $p \geq 2$ and w is a p-form on K, then the restriction of w to Γ is zero. Consequently, $\pi^*\colon \mathcal{E}^p(K/\Gamma) \to \mathcal{E}^p(K)$ is an isomorphism whenever $p \geq 2$.

Let (ω, L) be a power series connection on K. Since $\omega \in (\bigoplus_{p\geq 2} \mathcal{E}^p(K))\ \hat{\otimes}\ L$, and since π induces an isomorphism on homology, it follows that $(\tilde{\omega}, L)$ is a power series connection on K/Γ, where $\tilde{\omega} = ((\pi^*)^{-1}\ \hat{\otimes}\ \mathrm{id})\omega$. Denote the holonomy maps associated to ω, $\tilde{\omega}$ respectively by Θ, $\tilde{\Theta}$ respectively. The diagram

$$\begin{array}{ccc}
C_*(\Omega K) \otimes \mathbb{Q} & \xrightarrow{\quad\Theta\quad} & \mathbb{R} \otimes UL \\
{\scriptstyle (\Omega\pi)_*}\big\downarrow & & \big\downarrow{\scriptstyle \mathrm{id}} \\
C_*(\Omega(K/\Gamma)) \otimes \mathbb{Q} & \xrightarrow[\quad\tilde{\Theta}\quad]{} & \mathbb{R} \otimes UL
\end{array}$$

commutes. By the first part of the proof, there is a Hopf algebra isomorphism

$$\Psi'\colon H_*(\Omega(K/\Gamma);\ \mathbb{Q}) \to H_*(UL)$$

such that the diagram

$$\begin{array}{ccc}
H_*(\Omega K;\ \mathbb{Q}) & \xrightarrow{\quad\Theta_*\quad} & H_*(\mathbb{R} \otimes UL) \\
{\scriptstyle (\Omega\pi)_*}\big\downarrow & & \big\uparrow \\
H_*(\Omega(K/\Gamma);\ \mathbb{Q}) & \xrightarrow[\quad\Psi'\quad]{} & H_*(UL)
\end{array}$$

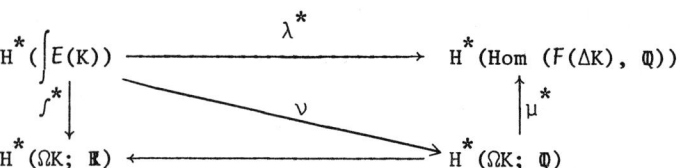

commutes, where the right-hand vertical map is induced by the inclusion $A \to \mathbb{R} \otimes UL$. Define an algebra isomorphism

$$\Psi\colon H_*(\Omega K;\ \mathbb{Q}) \to H_*(UL)$$

by $\Psi = \Psi' \circ (\Omega\pi)_*$. This completes the proof of (9.1).

The first step toward proving (9.2) is to show that the induced map

$$(\textstyle\int \pi)^*\colon\ \int E(K/\Gamma) \to \int E(K)$$

induces an isomorphism on homology. This follows from a straightforward spectral sequence argument combined with (5.16).

By the first part of the proof, there is a Hopf algebra isomorphism

$$\nu'\colon H^*(\textstyle\int E(K/\Gamma)) \to H^*(\Omega(K/\Gamma);\ \mathbb{Q})$$

such that the diagram

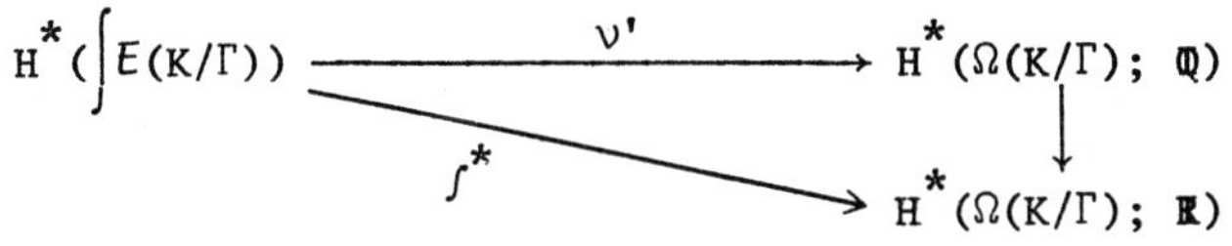

commutes. The following diagram commutes:

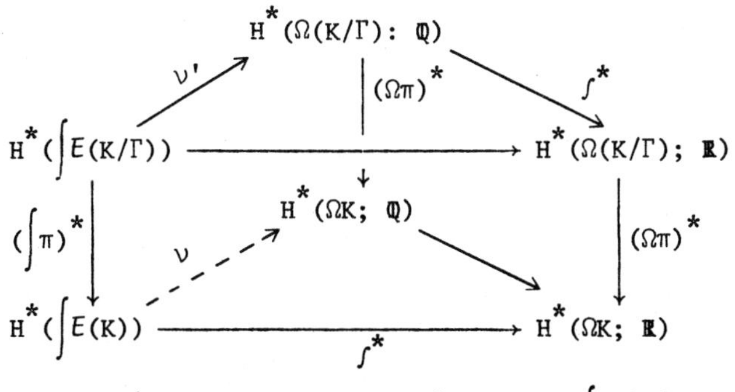

Define $\nu\colon H^*(\int E(K)) \to H^*(\Omega K;\ \mathbb{Q})$ by $\nu = (\Omega\pi)^* \circ \nu' \circ (\int \pi)^{*-1}$. This completes the proof of (9.2). □

REFERENCES

[1] J.F. Adams, On the cobar construction, *Colloque de topologie algébraique (Louvain, 1956)*, George Thone, Liège, Masson, Paris, 1957, 81-87.

[2] C. Allday, Rational Whitehead products and a spectral sequence of Quillen, II, *Houston J. Math.* 3 (1977), 301-308.

[3] H.J. Baues & J.M. Lemaire, Minimal models in homotopy theory, *Math. Ann.* 225 (1977), 219-242.

[4] A.K. Bousfield & V.K.A.M. Gugenheim, On PL de Rham theory and rational homotopy type, *Mem. Amer. Math. Soc.* 179 (1976).

[5] E.H. Brown, Jr., Twisted tensor products, I, *Ann. of Math.* (2) 69 (1959), 223-246.

[6] H. Cartan, Théories cohomologiques, *Invent. Math.* 35 (1976), 261-271.

[7] K.-T. Chen, Integration of paths, geometric invariants and a generalized Baker-Hausdorff formula, *Ann. of Math.* (2) 65 (1957), 163-178.

[8] K.-T. Chen, Differential forms and homotopy groups, *J. Differential Geometry* 6 (1971), 231-246.

[9] K.-T. Chen, Algebras of iterated path integrals and fundamental groups, *Trans. Amer. Math. Soc.* 156 (1971), 359-379.

[10] K.-T. Chen, Iterated integrals of differential forms and loop space homology, *Ann. of Math.* (2) 97 (1973), 217-246.

[11] K.-T. Chen, Iterated integrals, fundamental groups and covering spaces, *Trans. Amer. Math. Soc.* 206 (1975), 83-98.

[12] K.-T. Chen, Connections, holonomy and path space homology, *Differential Geometry*, Proc. Sympos. Pure Math., vol. 27, part 1, Amer. Math. Soc., Providence, R.I., 1975, 39-52.

[13] K.-T. Chen, Reduced bar constructions on de Rham complexes, *Algebra, Topology and Category Theory, A Collection of Papers in Honor of Samuel Eilenberg*, Academic Press, New York, 1976, 19-32.

[14] K.-T. Chen, Extension of C^∞ function algebra by integrals and Malcev completion of π_1, *Advances in Math.* 23 (1977), 181-210.

[15] K.-T. Chen, Iterated path integrals, *Bull. Amer. Math. Soc.* 83 (1977), 831-879.

[16] K.-T. Chen, Path space differential forms and transports of connections, *Bull. Inst. Acad. Sinica* 6 (1978), 457-477.

[17] K.-T. Chen, Circular bar construction, *J. Algebra* 57 (1979), 466-483.

[18] J.L. Cuadrado, *Rational iterated integrals and formal power series connections*, thesis, University of Illinois, 1977.

[19] P. Deligne, P. Griffiths, J. Morgan & D. Sullivan, Real homotopy theory of Kähler manifolds, *Invent. Math.* 29 (1975), 245-274.

[20] S. Eilenberg, Singular homology in differentiable manifolds, *Ann. of Math.* (2) 48 (1947), 670-681.

[21] E. Friedlander, P. Griffiths & J. Morgan, *Homotopy theory and differential forms*, Seminario di Geometria, mimeographed, Firenze, Italy, 1972.

[22] V.K.A.M. Gugenheim, On Chen's iterated integrals, *Ill. J. Math.* 21 (1977), 703-715.

[23] V.K.A.M. Gugenheim, On a perturbation theory for the homology of the loop space, preprint, 1979.

[24] R.M. Hain, *Iterated integrals, minimal models and rational homotopy theory*, thesis, University of Illinois, Champaign-Urbana, 1980.

[25] R.M. Hain, A duality theory between minimal algebras and minimal Lie algebras, to appear in *Trans. Amer. Math. Soc.*, 1983.

[26] S. Halperin, *Lectures on minimal models*, Publications internes de l'U.E.R. de Mathématiques, Université de Lille, 1977.

[27] T.W. Hungerford, The free product of algebras, *Ill. J. Math.* 12 (1968), 312-324.

[28] D. Lehmann, Théorie homotopique des formes differentielles, *Asterisque* 45, Soc. Math. de France, 1977.

[29] A. Lundell & S. Weingram, *The Topology of CW Complexes*, Van Nostrand Reinhold Co., New York, 1969.

[30] J. Milnor & J.C. Moore, On the structure of Hopf algebras, *Ann. of Math.* (2) 81 (1965), 211-264.

[31] J.C. Moore, The suspension, *Seminaire Cartan*, t. 12, exposé 6 (1959-60).

[32] J.R. Munkres, *Elementary Differential Topology*, rev. ed., Princeton University Press, Princeton, New Jersey, 1966.

[33] J. Neisendorfer, Lie algebras, coalgebras and rational homotopy theory for nilpotent spaces, *Pacific J. Math.* 74 (1978), 429-460.

[34] D. Quillen, Rational homotopy theory, *Ann. of Math.* (2) 90 (1969), 205-295.

[35] R. Ree, Lie elements and an algebra associated with shuffles, *Ann. of Math.* (2) 68 (1958), 210-220.

[36] H. Samelson, A connection between the Whitehead and Pontrjagin product, *Amer. J. Math.* 75 (1953), 744-752.

[37] D. Sullivan, Topology of manifolds and differential forms, *Proceedings of conference on manifolds*, Tokyo, 1973.

[38] D. Sullivan, Infinitesimal computations in topology, *Publications de IHES*, no. 47 (1977), 269-331.

[39] R.G. Swan, Thom's theory of differential forms on simplicial sets, *Topology* 14, 271-273.

[40] G. Whitehead, *Elements of Homotopy Theory*, Springer Verlag, Berlin, Heidelberg, New York, 1978.

[41] J.H.C. Whitehead, An expression of Hopf's invariant as an integral, *Proc. Nat. Acad. Sci. U.S.A.* 33 (1947), 117-123.

[42] D.Tanré, Modeles de Chen, Quillen, Sullivan. *Publ. U.E.R. Math. Pures Appl. IRMA* 2 (1980) No. 1, exp. 2, 87 pp.

[43] D. Tanré, Connexion homologique de Chen et modèle de Quillen. *C.R. Acad. Sci Paris Ser. A-B* 290 (1980), 1099-1102.

Department of Mathematics GN-50
University of Washington
Seattle, WA 98195
U.S.A.

General instructions to authors for

PREPARING REPRODUCTION COPY FOR MEMOIRS

For more detailed instructions send for AMS booklet, "A Guide for Authors of Memoirs." Write to Editorial Offices, American Mathematical Society, P. O. Box 6248, Providence, R. I. 02940.

MEMOIRS are printed by photo-offset from camera copy fully prepared by the author. This means that, except for a reduction in size of 20 to 30%, the finished book will look exactly like the copy submitted. Thus the author will want to use a good quality typewriter with a new, medium-inked black ribbon, and submit clean copy on the appropriate model paper.

Model Paper, provided at no cost by the AMS, is paper marked with blue lines that confine the copy to the appropriate size. Author should specify, when ordering, whether typewriter to be used has PICA-size (10 characters to the inch) or ELITE-size type (12 characters to the inch).

Line Spacing – For best appearance, and economy, a typewriter equipped with a half-space ratchet – 12 notches to the inch – should be used. (This may be purchased and attached at small cost.) Three notches make the desired spacing, which is equivalent to 1-1/2 ordinary single spaces. Where copy has a great many subscripts and superscripts, however, double spacing should be used.

Special Characters may be filled in carefully freehand, using dense black ink, or INSTANT ("rub-on") LETTERING may be used. AMS has a sheet of several hundred most-used symbols and letters which may be purchased for $5.

Diagrams may be drawn in black ink either directly on the model sheet, or on a separate sheet and pasted with rubber cement into spaces left for them in the text. Ballpoint pen is *not* acceptable.

Page Headings (Running Heads) should be centered, in CAPITAL LETTERS (preferably), at the top of the page – just above the blue line and touching it.

LEFT-hand, EVEN-numbered pages should be headed with the AUTHOR'S NAME;

RIGHT-hand, ODD-numbered pages should be headed with the TITLE of the paper (in shortened form if necessary).

Exceptions: PAGE 1 and any other page that carries a display title require NO RUNNING HEADS.

Page Numbers should be at the top of the page, on the same line with the running heads.

LEFT-hand, EVEN numbers – flush with left margin;

RIGHT-hand, ODD numbers – flush with right margin.

Exceptions: PAGE 1 and any other page that carries a display title should have page number, centered below the text, on blue line provided.

FRONT MATTER PAGES should be numbered with Roman numerals (lower case), positioned below text in same manner as described above.

MEMOIRS FORMAT

It is suggested that the material be arranged in pages as indicated below.
Note: Starred items (*) are requirements of publication.

Front Matter (first pages in book, preceding main body of text).

Page i – *Title, *Author's name.

Page iii – Table of contents.

Page iv – *Abstract (at least 1 sentence and at most 300 words).

*1980 Mathematics Subject Classifications represent the primary and secondary subjects of the paper. For the classification scheme, see Annual Subject Indexes of MATHEMATICAL REVIEWS beginning in December 1978.

Key words and phrases, if desired. (A list which covers the content of the paper adequately enough to be useful for an information retrieval system.)

Page v, etc. – Preface, introduction, or any other matter not belonging in body of text.

Page 1 – Chapter Title (dropped 1 inch from top line, and centered).

Beginning of Text.

Footnotes: *Received by the editor date.
Support information – grants, credits, etc.

Last Page (at bottom) – Author's affiliation.

ABCDEFGHIJ–AMS–8987654

Number 292

Henry Rose

Nonmodular lattice varieties

Memoirs
of the American Mathematical Society

Providence · Rhode Island · USA

January 1984 · Volume 47 · Number 292 (fourth of six numbers) · ISSN 0065-9266

Memoirs of the American Mathematical Society

Number 292

Henry Rose

Nonmodular lattice varieties

Published by the

AMERICAN MATHEMATICAL SOCIETY

Providence, Rhode Island, USA

January 1984 · Volume 47 · Number 292 (fourth of six numbers)

MEMOIRS of the American Mathematical Society

This journal is designed particularly for long research papers (and groups of cognate papers) in pure and applied mathematics. It includes, in general, longer papers than those in the TRANSACTIONS.

MEMOIRS are printed by photo-offset from camera-ready copy fully prepared by the authors. Prospective authors are encouraged to request booklet giving detailed instructions regarding reproduction copy. Write to Editorial Office, American Mathematical Society, P. O. Box 6248, Providence, Rhode Island 02940. For general instructions, see last page of Memoir.

SUBSCRIPTION INFORMATION. The 1984 subscription begins with Number 289 and consists of six mailings, each containing one or more numbers. Subscription prices for 1984 are $148 list; $74 member. A late charge of 10% of the subscription price will be imposed upon orders received from nonmembers after January 1 of the subscription year. Subscribers outside the United States and India must pay a postage surcharge of $10; subscribers in India must pay a postage surcharge of $15. Each number may be ordered separately; *please specify number* when ordering an individual number. For prices and titles of recently released numbers, refer to the New Publications sections of the NOTICES of the American Mathematical Society.

BACK NUMBER INFORMATION. For back issues see the AMS Catalogue of Publications.

TRANSACTIONS of the American Mathematical Society

This journal consists of shorter tracts which are of the same general character as the papers published in the MEMOIRS. The editorial committee is identical with that for the MEMOIRS so that papers intended for publication in this series should be addressed to one of the editors listed above.

Subscriptions and orders for publications of the American Mathematical Society should be addressed to American Mathematical Society, P. O. Box 1571, Annex Station, Providence, R. I. 02901. *All orders must be accompanied by payment.* Other correspondence should be addressed to P. O. Box 6248, Providence, R. I. 02940.

MEMOIRS of the American Mathematical Society (ISSN 0065-9266) is published bimonthly (each volume consisting usually of more than one number) by the American Mathematical Society at 201 Charles Street, Providence, Rhode Island 02904. Second Class postage paid at Providence, Rhode Island 02940. Postmaster: Send address changes to Memoirs of the American Mathematical Society, American Mathematical Society, P. O. Box 6248, Providence, RI 02940.

TABLE OF CONTENTS

ABSTRACT

It is shown that there are eight infinite sequences of join irreducible lattice varieties with the following property: each term of every sequence has the next term as its unique join irreducible cover. The description of these sequences is based on a detailed study of subdirectly irreducible lattices with the unique critical quotients.

1980 Mathematics subject classification. Primary and secondary: 03C05, 03G10, 06B20, 06B25, 08B15.

Key words and phrases. Bijective transposition, bounded homomorphism, critical quotient, isolated subset of a finite lattice, semidistributivity, splitting, weak projection.

Library of Congress Cataloging in Publication Data

Rose, Henry, 1941-
Nonmodular lattice varieties.

(Memoirs of the American Mathematical Society, ISSN 0065-9266 ; no. 292)
"January 1984, volume 47, number 292."
Bibliography: p.
1. Lattice theory. 2. Algebraic varieties.
I. Title. II. Series.
QA3.A57 no. 292 [QA171.5] 510s [511.3'3] 83-22449
ISBN 0-8218-2292-6

ACKNOWLEDGEMENT

This work is an extended version of author's dissertation which was written at Vanderbilt University under the supervision of Professor Bjarni Jónsson. To him I would like to express my deep gratitude. There is no doubt that without his valuable suggestions and incisive criticism this work would never have been completed.

Grants to the Topology Research Group from the University of Cape Town and the South African Council for Scientific and Industrial Research are acknowledged.

INTRODUCTION

The most part of this work is concerned with nonmodular lattice varieties whose members satisfy two semidistributive laws (see Definition 0.2.1(ii)).

The collection of these varieties forms an ideal in the lattice of all subvarieties. We show that there are eight infinite sequences of varieties in that ideal with the following property: each term of every sequence has the next term as its unique join irreducible cover.

Every variety of each sequence mentioned above is generated by a semi-distributive, nonmodular, subdirectly irreducible lattice which has a unique critical quotient. A detailed study of lattices with such properties can be found in Chapters 1 and 5 of this work.

The first section of Chapter 0 contains a list of known facts about the lattice of subvarieties Λ. The second section of Chapter 0 provides some information about free lattices and introduces such notions as bounded homomorphism, splitting, semidistributivity and critical quotient.

Chapter 1 is devoted to a detailed study of subdirectly irreducible lattices. The main results here are Theorem 1.2.7 and Corollaries 1.2.8 and 1.2.9. It is shown that if a subdirectly irreducible semidistributive lattice L does not have a sublattice isomorphic to L_{11} or L_{12} (see Figure 0.4) then L has a unique critical quotient c/a, and the principal filter generated by a and the principal ideal generated by c are distributive. Corollary 1.2.8 establishes a strong connection between pentagons of L and the critical quotient c/a.

The results of the third section of Chapter 1 are concerned with finite, subdirectly irreducible lattices. Most of the results here are technical. Lemma 1.4.3 is stated for lattices. However, it is valid for arbitrary algebras of a finitary type. Thus lemma tells us that every projective subdirectly irreducible member of a variety is embeddable in a generator of this variety.

It is known that the variety generated by the pentagon has precisely fifteen join irreducible covers (see Theorem 0.1.11), which are generated by finite subdirectly irreducible lattices $L_1, L_2, \ldots, L_{15}$ (see Figures 0.2, 0.3 and 0.4). The semidistributive laws fail in the first five of those, but hold in the remaining ten. As was mentioned before, we show that there are eight infinite sequences of join irredicible varieties $\{L_i^n\}^V$ $(i \in \{6,7,8,9,$

Received by the editors March 29, 1982.

10,13,14,15} and $n = 0,1,\ldots$) with $L_i^0 = L_i$ such that $\{L_i^{n+1}\}^v$ is the unique join irreducible cover of $\{L_i^n\}^v$ (see Chapters 2,3,4,5). On the other hand, for $i = 11$ and for $i = 12$, $\{L_i^n\}^v$ has at least two join irreducible covers; for $n \geq 1$ this is unknown (Problem 6.1.2).

Theorems 5.1.2 and 5.1.4 characterize subdirectly irreducible lattices obtained from finite distributive lattices by doubling some element which is neither the greatest nor the smallest element of the lattice.

Chapter 6 contains an overview of results obtained and a short list of open problems that are suggested by these results. It is shown there (see Theorem 6.2.10) that if a finite semidistributive lattice L has no sublattices isomorphic to L_{11} or L_{12}, then it is a bounded homomorphic image of a finitely generated free lattice. In addition if L satisfies the Whitman condition (see Definition 0.2.1 (i)) then L is a retract of a free lattice and, therefore, projective. Thus, any finite subdirectly irreducible semidistributive lattice which has no sublattices isomorphic to L_{11} or L_{12} is splitting.

The characterization of some conjugate varieties can be found in the last section of Chapter 6.

For standard concepts and facts from lattice theory and universal algebra we refer the reader to G. Grätzer [12] and [13], and to P. Crawley and R. P. Dilworth [2]. Note, however, that we use the plus, dot notation for the lattice operations rather than the symbols $\vee$ and $\wedge$ used there.

CHAPTER 0

PRELIMINARY RESULTS

0.1 The Lattice Λ. For a given set Σ of lattice identities we denote by Mod (Σ) the class of those lattices which satisfy every identity in Σ. If a class of V of lattices has the property that $V = \text{Mod}(\Sigma)$ for some set of identities Σ, we shall say that V is a variety.

When $\Sigma = \phi$, Mod (Σ) is the class (= variety) of all lattices and hence includes every other variety. On the other hand, if Σ consists of the single identity $x = y$, then Mod (Σ) is the class of all one-element lattices, which is included in every other variety. Further, if $\{\Sigma_i\}_{i \in I}$ is a family of sets of identities, then

$$\text{Mod}\,(\bigcup_{i \in I} \Sigma) = \bigcap_{i \in I} \text{Mod}\,(\Sigma_i),$$

and so the intersection of a family of varieties is again a variety. It follows that the varieties form a complete lattice, which we shall refer to as the lattice. Λ.

Theorem 0.1.1. (i) (B. H. Nueman [24]). The lattice Λ is isomorphic to the dual of the lattice of fully invariant congruences of the free lattice having $\aleph_0$ generators.

(ii) Λ is a dually algebraic lattice. The dually compact elements of Λ are exactly the finitely based lattice varieties.

Since lattices are congruence distributive algebras (see N. Funayama and T. Nakayama [10]), we have the following result concerning the lattice Λ.

Theorem 0.1.2. Λ is a distributive lattice.

Notation. For a given class K of lattices, we denote by

SK - the class of all sublattices of members of K.
HK - the class of all homomorphic images of members of K.
P_uK - the class of all ultraproducts of members of K.
P_sK - the class of all subdirect products of members of K.
K^v - the variety generated by K.

Using congruence distributivity, one can derive many very important results for the theory of lattice varieties. The following are due to B. Jónsson [15].

Theorem 0.1.3. Let K be a class of lattices. Then,

(i) Every subdirectly irreducible member of K^V belongs to HSP_uK.

(ii) $K^V = P_sHSP_uK$.

Theorem 0.1.4. Let K be a finite set of finite lattices. Then,

(i) Every subdirectly irreducible member of K^V belongs to HSK.

(ii) $K^V = P_sHSK$.

Corollary 0.1.5. Under the assumption of Theorem 0.1.4, K^V has, up to isomorphism, only a finite number of subdirectly irreducible members, and they are all finite. Furthermore, K^V has only a finite number of subvarieties.

Theorem 0.1.6. (i) Let A and B be finite, nonisomorphic, subdirectly irreducible lattices. If $|A| \leq |B|$ then there is an identity which holds in A but not in B.

(ii) Suppose V_1 is a lattice variety generated by its finite members, and V_2 is a subvariety of V_1. Then V_1 covers V_2 if and only if V_1 contains exactly one subdirectly irreducible lattice that is not in V_2.

Theorem 0.1.7. Given two lattice varieties V_1 and V_2, every subdirectly irreducible member of $V_1 + V_2$ belongs to either V_1 or V_2.

The next result can be found in R. McKenzie [23].

Theorem 0.1.8. (i) Every strictly join prime variety is generated by a finite subdirectly irreducible lattice.

(ii) If the variety V is generated by a finite subdirectly irreducible lattice, then V is a strictly join irreducible member of Λ.

(iii) If V is a strictly join irreducible variety, then it can be generated by a single finitely generated subdirectly irreducible lattice.

(iv) If the variety V is generated by a single subdirectly irreducible lattice, then it is join irreducible.

How large is the lattice Λ? The following theorem gives the answer to this question.

Theorem 0.1.9. (K. Baker [1], R. McKenzie [22] and R. Wille [27].) $|\Lambda| = 2^{\aleph_0}$.

We shall now turn our attention to the description of the structure of the lattice Λ.

Since any nontrivial lattice has $\mathfrak{2}$ as a sublattice, and since $\mathfrak{2}$ is the unique distributive, subdirectly irreducible lattice, we have that the variety of all distributive lattices D is the unique cover of the variety T of all trivial lattices. Thus, D is the unique atom of Λ, and since any nondistributive variety has a pentagon or a diamond as a member, $\mathcal{D}$ has only two covers in Λ.

Theorem 0.1.10. (G. Gratzer [11] and B. Jónsson [16]). The variety generated by a diamond - $\{M_3\}^V$ - has exactly two join irreducible covers, $\{M_4\}^V$ and $\{M_{3,3}\}^V$ (see Figure 0.1).

The varieties generated by a pentagon and by a diamond both have the same unique join reducible cover, namely $\{M_3,N_5\}^V$. In R. McKenzie [23], fifteen join irreducible covers of the variety generated by a pentagon were listed. The next theorem shows that McKenzie's list is complete.

Theorem 0.1.11. (B. Jónsson and I. Rival [20]). The variety generated by a pentagon - $\{N_5\}^V$ - has exactly fifteen join irreducible covers, $\{L_1\}^V$, ..., $\{L_{15}\}^V$ (see Figures 0.2, 0.3, 0.4).

0.2 Free Lattices, Bounded Homomorphisms, Semidistributivity, and the Concept of Splitting.

Definition 0.2.1. (i) We shall say that a lattice L satisfies the Whitman condition if for any a, b, c, d $\in$ L we have

$$ab \leq c + d \text{ if and only if } a \leq c + d \text{ or } b \leq c + d \tag{W}$$

or $ab \leq c$ or $ab \leq d$.

(ii) We shall say that a lattice L is semidistributive if for any u, a, b, c $\in$ L we have

$$u = a + b = a + c \text{ implies } u = a + bc; \tag{SD}$$

$$u = ab = ac \text{ implies } u = a(b + c). \tag{SD'}$$

A lattice variety V is said to be semidistributive if each of its members is a semidistributive lattice.

Theorem 0.2.2. (Ph. Whitman [26] and B. Jónsson [19]). Every free lattice satisfies the Whitman condition and is semidistributive.

Definition 0.2.3. (i) (R. McKenzie [23]). An ordered pair (V_1,V_2) of lattice varieties is said to be splitting if, for every variety V, either $V \subseteq V_1$ or $V_2 \subseteq V$, but not both.

(ii) (R. McKenzie [23]). A lattice epimorphism f: A $\to$ B is said to be bounded if $f^{-1}(b)$ is a closed interval for every b $\in$ B. That is, there are order monomorphisms α,β: B $\to$ A (where α is join preserving and β is meet preserving) such that for all b $\in$ B we have $f^{-1}(b) = \beta(b)/\alpha(b)$.

Remark 0.2.4. Let (V_1,V_2) be a splitting pair of varieties. It follows from the definition that V_2 is a strictly join prime variety, and therefore,

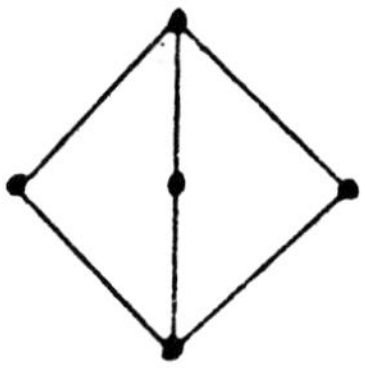

Diamond

M_3

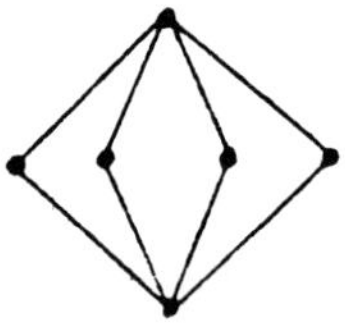

M_4

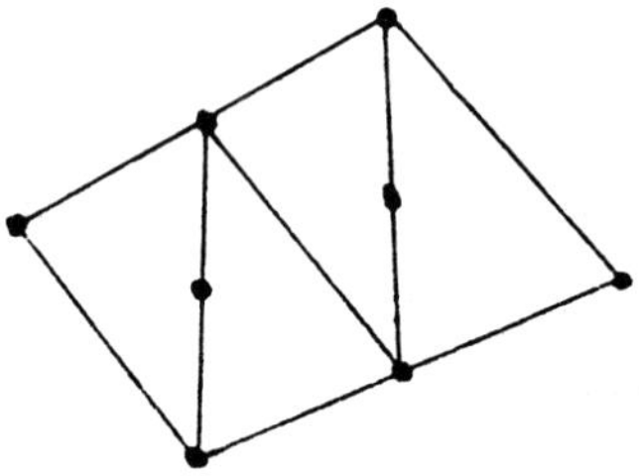

$M_{3,3}$

Figure 0.1

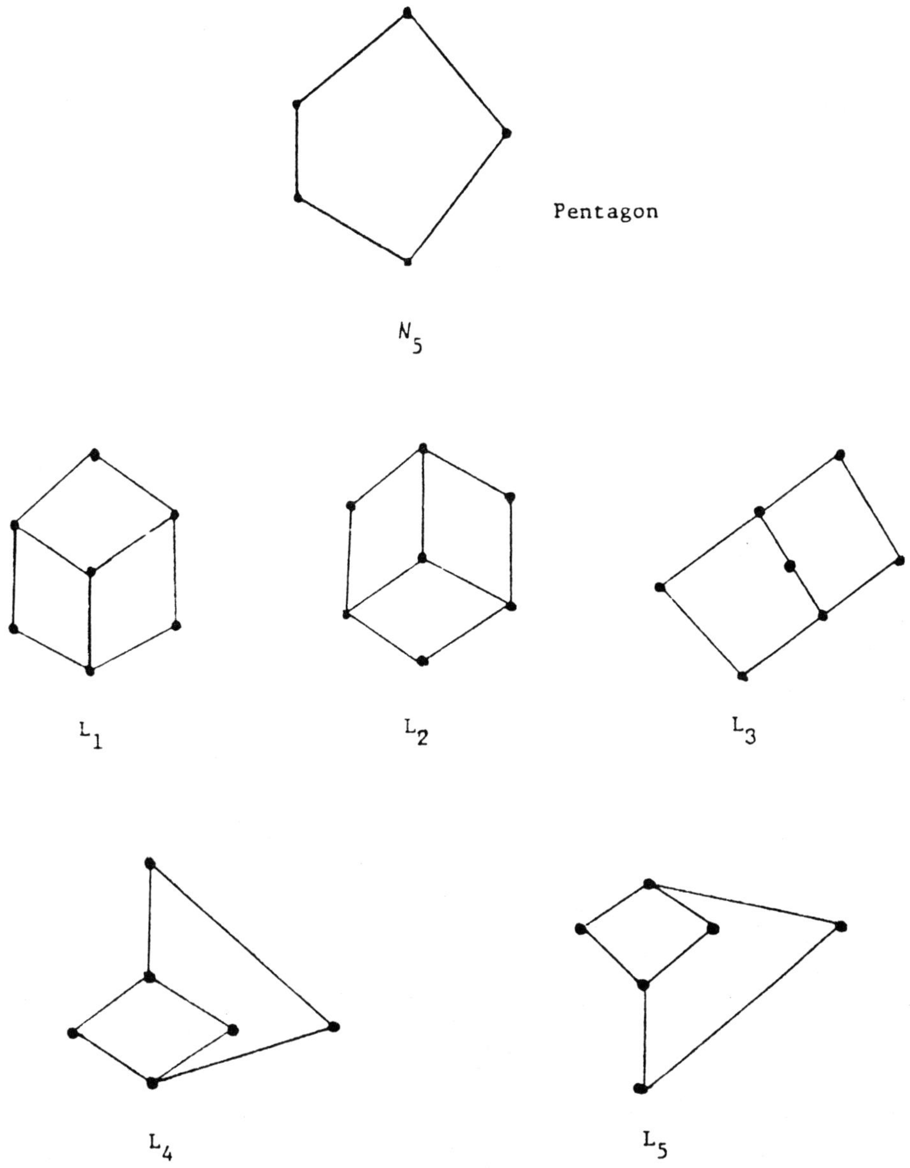

Figure 0.2

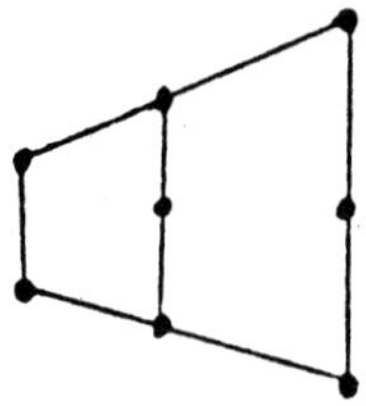

L_6

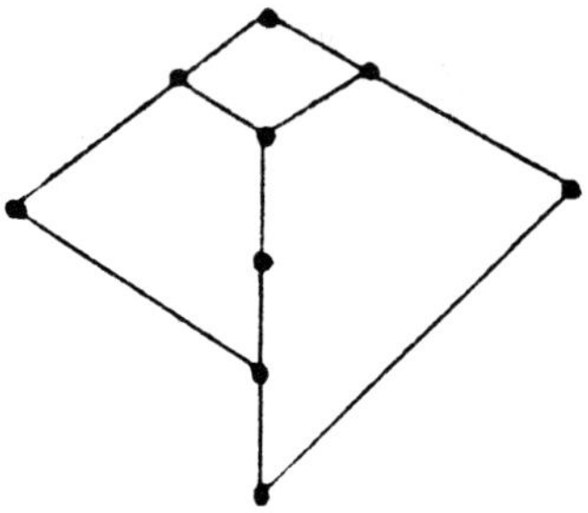

L_7

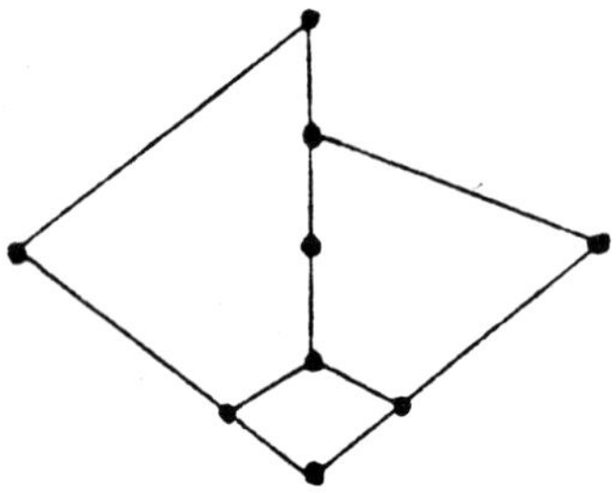

L_8

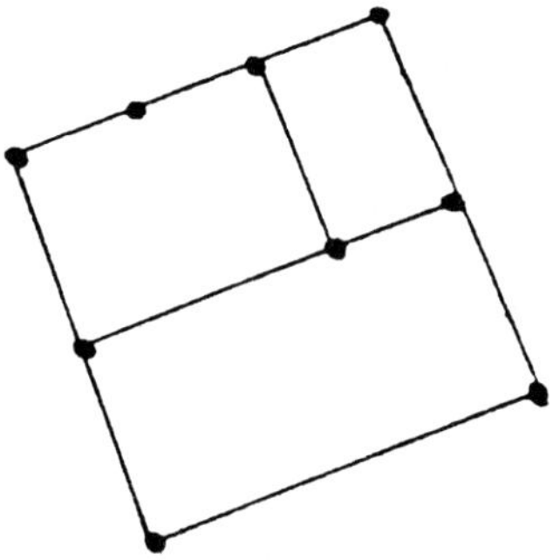

L_9

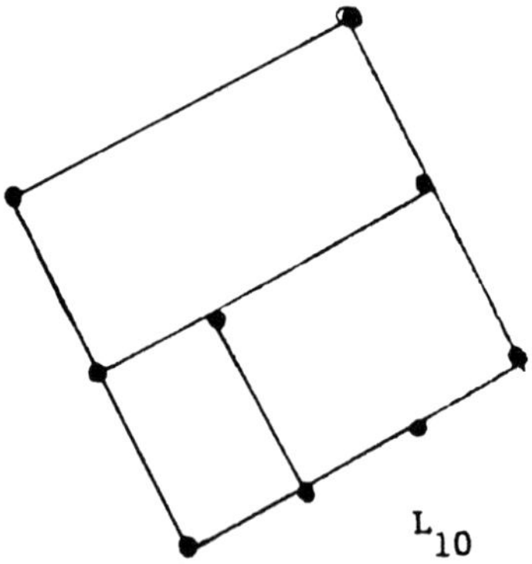

L_{10}

Figure 0.3

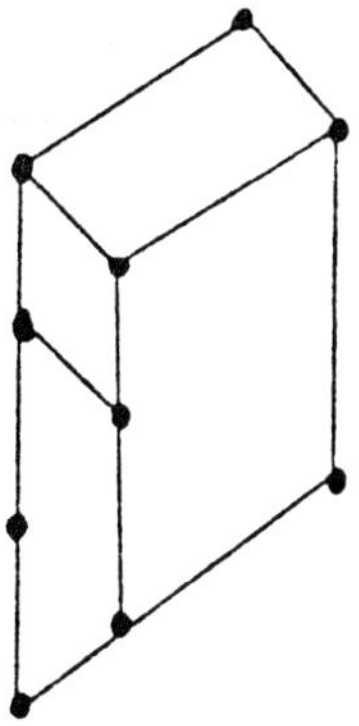

L_{11}

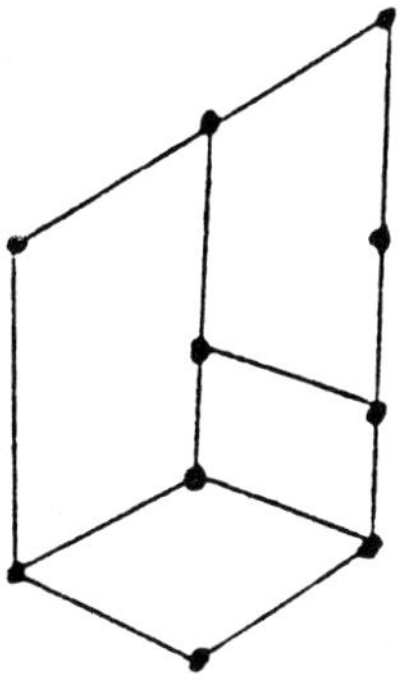

L_{12}

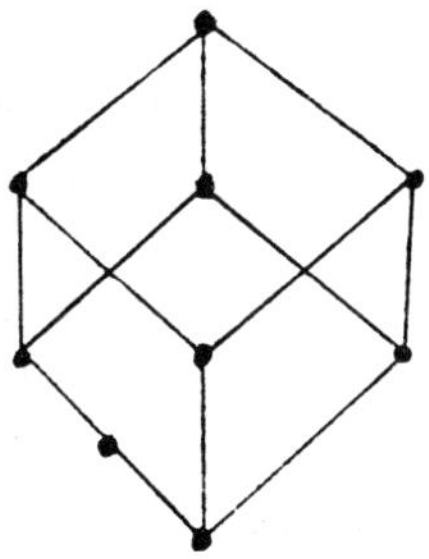

L_{15}

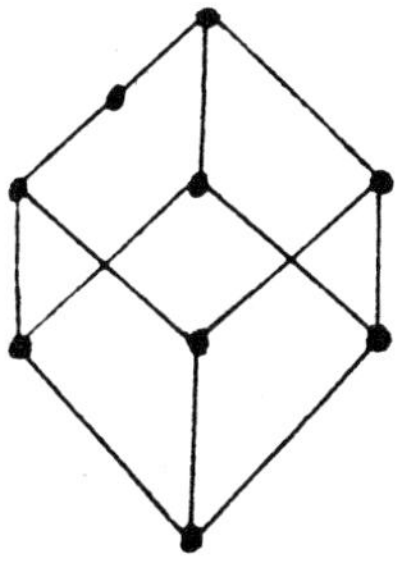

L_{14}

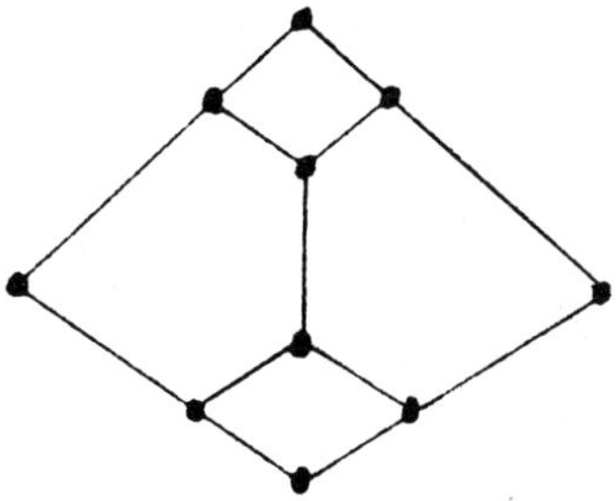

L_{16}

Figure 0.4

by Theorem 0.1.8 (i), is generated by a finite, subdirectly irreducible lattice. We shall refer to such a lattice as a splitting lattice, and the variety V_1 as a conjugate variety. It follows from Theorem 0.2.8 below that every conjugate variety is determined by a single identity. We refer to this identity as a conjugate identity.

Theorem 0.2.5. (R. McKenzie [23]). A finite subdirectly irreducible lattice is splitting if and only if it is a bounded homomorphic image of a finitely generated (especially free) lattice.

Corollary 0.2.6. (R. McKenzie [23]). (i) Bounded homomorphisms preserve semidistributivity, and hence every splitting lattice is semi-distributive.

(ii) Let $S \neq \underset{\sim}{2}$ be a splitting lattice. Then $\{S\}^V \supseteq \{N_5\}^V$, and hence S has a pentagon as a sublattice.

Definition 0.2.7. Let Con (a,c) be the smallest congruence relation which identifies a and c. We say that the quotient c/a of a subdirectly irreducible lattice L is critical if Con (a,c) is the unique atom of the congruence lattice of L.

Theorem 0.2.8. (R. McKenzie [23]). Let c/a be a prime critical quotient of a splitting lattice L. Suppose further that $F(n)$ is a finitely generated free lattice and $f: F(n) \to L$ is an epimorphism bounded below and above by $\alpha,\beta: L \to F(n)$, respectively. Then, for any variety V, we have that $V \models \alpha(c) \leq \beta(a)$ if and only if $L \notin V$.

The final theorem of this section gives a characterization of semidistributive varieties.

Theorem 0.2.9. (B. Jónsson and I. Rival [20]). For a given lattice variety V, the following statements are equivalent:

(i) V is semidistributive;

(ii) $M_3, L_1, \ldots, L_5 \notin V$ (see Figures 0.1, 0.2);

(iii) For $n = 0, 2, \ldots$ put $y_0 = y$, $z_0 = z$, $y_{n+1} = y + xz_n$ and $z_{n+1} = z + xy_n$. Then for some natural number m the identity $x(y + z) = xy_m$ and its dual hold in V.

CHAPTER 1

SEMIDISTRIBUTIVE SUBDIRECTLY IRREDUCIBLE LATTICES

1.1. Weak Projection.

Definition 1.1.1. (i) Given two quotients p/q and r/s in a lattice L, we say that p/q transposes weakly up onto r/s (in symbols $p/q \nearrow_w r/s$) if $q = ps$ and $r \geq p$ (see Figure 1.1.A). Dually, we say that p/q transposes weakly down onto r/s (in symbols $p/q \searrow_w r/s$) if $p = r + q$ and $q \geq s$ (see Figure 1.1.B). If both $p/q \nearrow_w r/s$ and $r/s \searrow_w p/q$, that is, if $q = ps$ and $r = p + s$, then we say that p/q transposes up onto r/s and that r/s transposes down onto p/q (in symbols $p/q \nearrow r/s$ or $r/s \searrow p/q$) (see Figure 1.1.C). We shall write $p/q \sim_w r/s$ $(p/q \sim r/s)$ if the quotient p/q transposes weakly (transposes) up or down onto the quotient r/s. We say that the quotient p/q projects weakly (projects) onto the quotient r/s in n steps, where n is a natural number, if there exists a sequence of quotients

$$p/q = x_0/y_0,\ x_1/y_1,\ldots,\ x_n/y_n = r/s$$

such that, for any $i \in \{0,1,\ldots,n-1\}$, $x_i/y_i \sim_w x_{i+1}/y_{i+1}$ $(x_i/y_i \sim x_{i+1}/y_{i+1})$.

(ii) We say that the quotient p/q transposes bijectively up onto r/s (in symbols $p/q \nearrow_\beta r/s$) if $p/q \nearrow r/s$ and, for $t \in p/q$ and $t' \in r/s$, we have $t = (t+s)p$ and $t' = t'p + s$. In that case the map $t \to t + s$ is an isomorphism from p/q to r/s. Dually we can define $p/q \searrow_\beta r/s$.

Our first lemma follows immediately from the definition of a weak projection.

Lemma 1.1.2. Let s, r, u and t be elements of a lattice L with $s < r \leq u < t$. Then neither of the quotients t/u or r/s projects weakly onto the other in two steps.

Proof. Trivial.

The next theorem shows how important the concept of a weak projection is.

Theorem 1.1.3. (R. P. Dilworth [6]). Given quotients r/s and p/q in the lattice L, Con (s,r) identifies p and q if and only if, for some chain $p = t_0 > t_1 > \ldots t_m = q$, the quotient t_i/t_{i+1} projects weakly onto r/s $(i \in \{0,1,\ldots,m-1\})$.

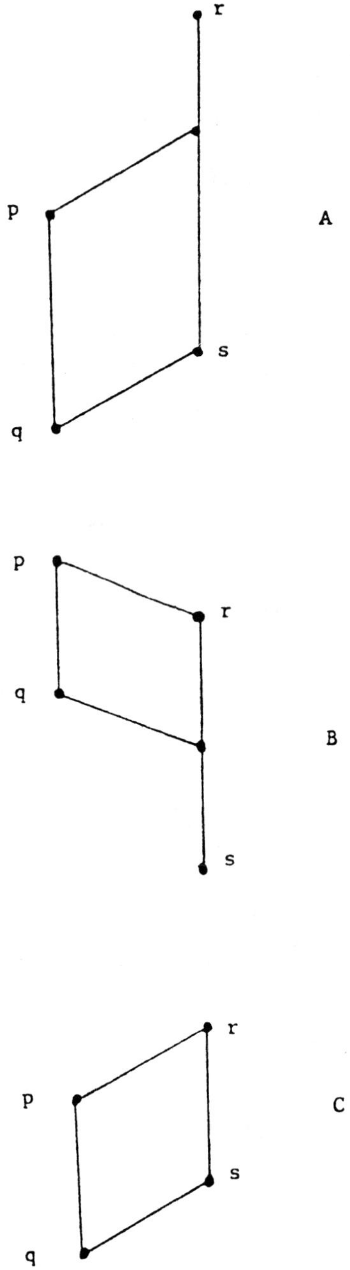

Figure 1.1

1.2 Semidistributive Subdirectly Irreducible Lattices with a Unique Critical Quotient. We write $N(c/a,b)$ to indicate that the elements a,b,c of a lattice L generate a pentagon (a five element nonmodular lattice (see Figure 1.2) with c/a as a critical quotient. (We shall refer to this quotient as an N-quotient.) Also, we use the expression $N(c/a,b)$ to denote the sublattice of L consisting of the five elements a,b,c, $a + b$ and bc.

If L and L' are lattices, we shall say that L excludes L' if L has no sublattice isomorphic to L'. (Otherwise we say that L includes L'.)

The following result is Lemma 2.2 in B. Jónsson and I. Rival [20].

Lemma 1.2.1. If, in a semidistributive lattice L, $x_0/y_0 \nearrow_w x_1/y_1 \searrow_w x_2/y_2$, then one of the following conditions holds:

(i) There exists a subquotient p/q of x_2/y_2 such that $x_0/y_0 \searrow u/v \nearrow p/q$ for some quotient u/v of L.

(ii) There exist $a,b,c \in L$ with $N(c/a,b)$ such that b/bc is a subquotient of x_2/y_2 (see Figure 1.3.A).

(iii) There exist $a,b,c \in L$ with $N(c/a,b)$ such that $(a + b)/b$ transposes down onto a subquotient of x_2/y_2 (see Figure 1.3.B).

In the proof of the next lemma we borrow ideas from the proof of Lemma 3.5 in B. Jónsson and I. Rival [20].

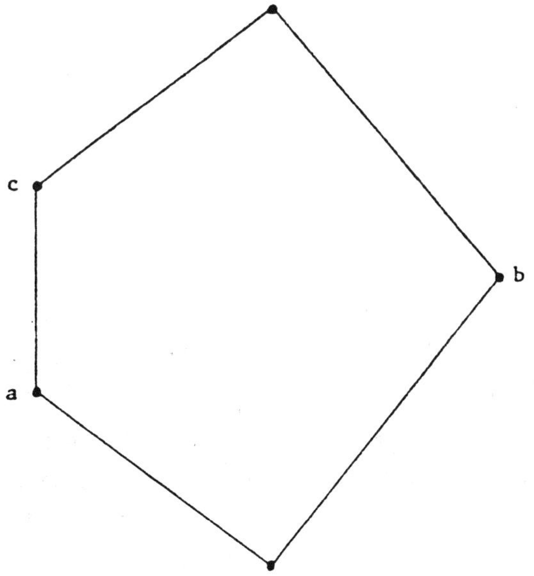

Figure 1.2

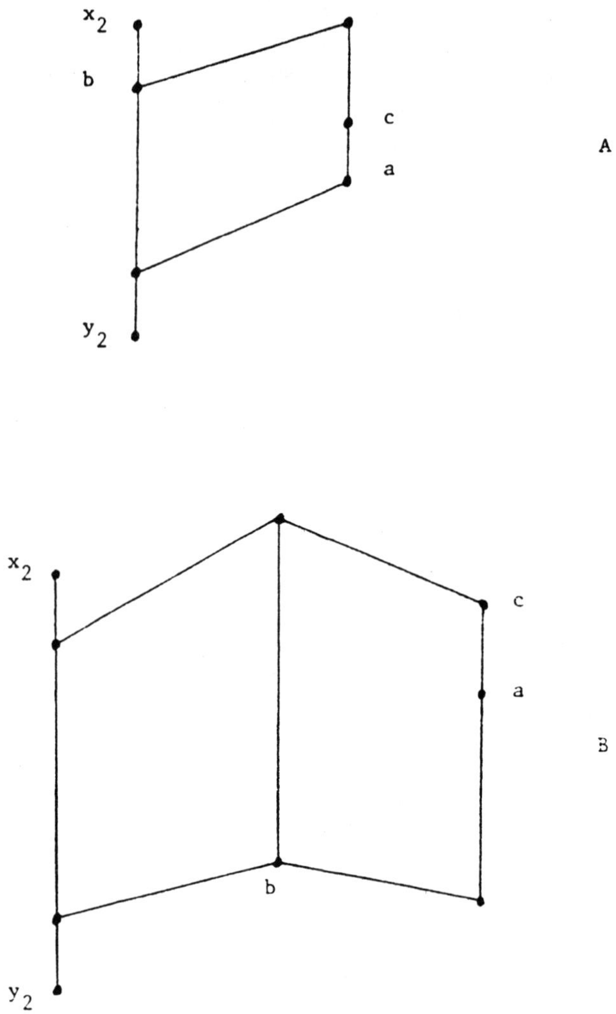

Figure 1.3

Lemma 1.2.2. Let x_0/x_0, x_1/y_1 and x_2/x_2 be quotients of a semidistributive lattice L such that $x_0/y_0 \nearrow_\beta x_1/y_1 \searrow_\beta x_2/y_2$. Then $x_0/y_0 \searrow x_0x_2/y_0y_2 \nearrow x_2/y_2$.

Proof. We have $x_1 = y_1 + x_0 = y_1 + x_2$, and hence by semidistributivity $x_1 = y_1 + x_0x_2$. Next, by the bijectivity of the transpositions, $y_0 + x_0x_2 = (y_0 + x_0x_2 + y_1)x_0 = x_1x_0 = x_0$, and similarly $y_2 + x_0x_2 = x_2$. Also, $y_0(x_0x_2) = x_0y_1x_2 = y_0y_2$ and $y_2(x_0x_2) = y_0y_2$.

Corollary 1.2.3. Suppose that for $n \geq 3$ we have a sequence $x_1/y_1 \sim_w x_2/y_2 \sim_w \cdots \sim_w x_n/y_n$ in a semidistributive lattice L. If $x_{n-2}/y_{n-2} \nearrow_\beta x_{n-1}/y_{n-1} \searrow_\beta x_n/y_n$, then x_0/y_0 can be projected weakly onto

x_n/y_n in $n - 1$ steps.

Proof. By the preceding lemma,

$$x_{n-2}/y_{n-2} \searrow x_{n-2}x_n/y_{n-2} \nearrow x_n/y_n,$$

and therefore

$$x_{n-3}/y_{n-3} \searrow_w x_{n-2}x_n/y_{n-2}y_n \nearrow x_n/y_n$$

(see Figure 1.4).

Lemma 3.1 in B. Jónsson and I. Rival [20] concerns a semidistributive lattice which excludes L_7, L_8 and L_{12}. By examining the proof we see that valuable information can be obtained by excluding some, but not all, of these lattices. The lemma below is a more detailed account of the results proved there.

Lemma 1.2.4. Let L be a semidistributive lattice generated by three elements, x, y and z, with $x \leq xy + z$ and $xz \leq y$. If L excludes L_{12}, then L is a homomorphic image of the lattice in Figure 1.5.A. If L also excludes L_7, respectively L_8, then L is a homomorphic image of the lattice in Figure 1.5.B, respectively in Figure 1.5.C. Finally, if L excludes L_{12}, L_7 and L_8, then L is a homomorphic image of the lattice in Figure 1.5.D.

Observe that under the hypothesis of Lemma 1.2.4 $N(x/xy,z)$ and $N((x + y)/y,z)$, unless the quotients are degenerate. This is the basis for the next result.

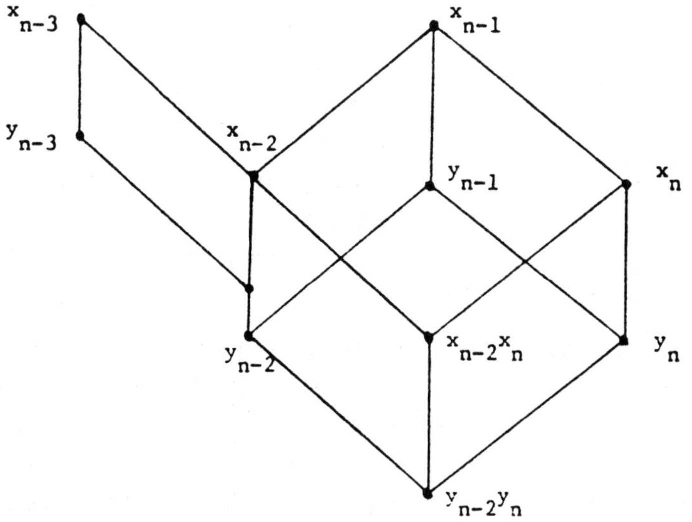

Figure 1.4

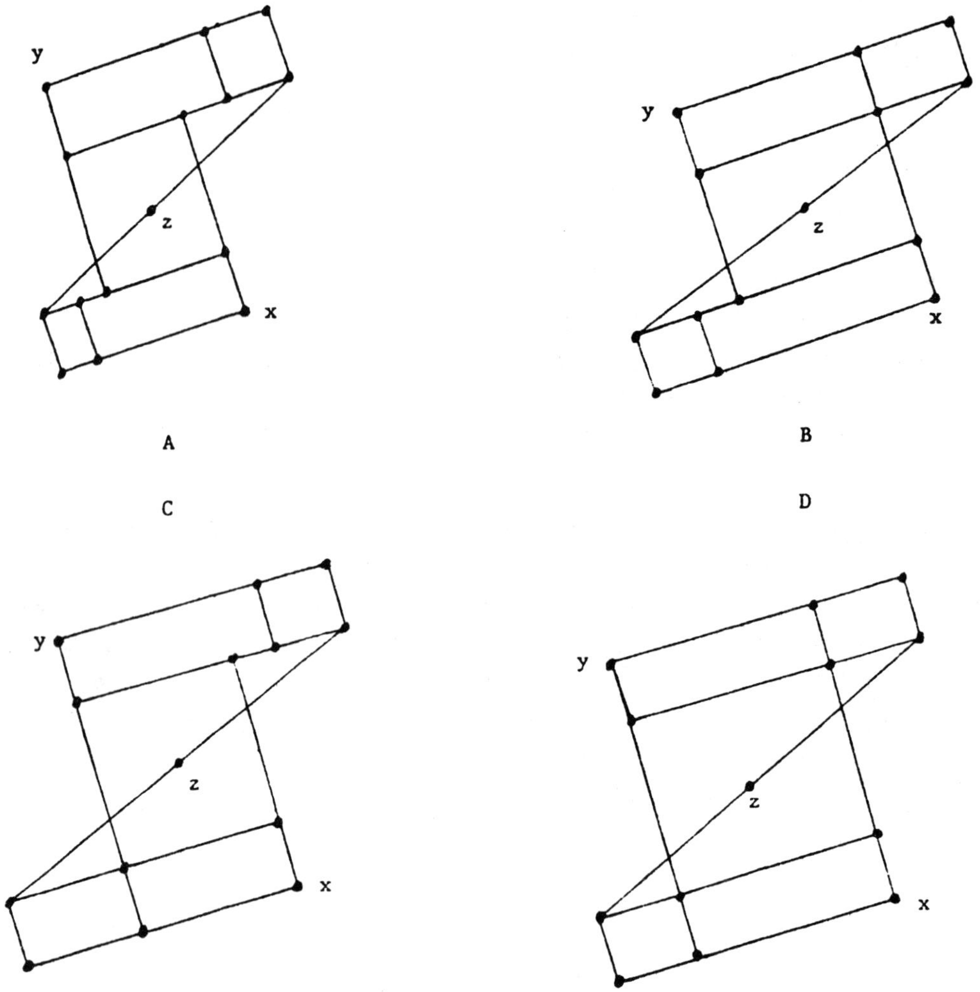

Figure 1.5

<u>Corollary 1.2.5</u>. Suppose L is a semidistributive lattice that excludes L_{11} and L_{12}. If a, b, c, a', c' $\in$ L, with N(c/a,b), and if c'/a' projects weakly onto c/a, then N(c'/a',b). Hence, if p/q is a quotient of L such that (q,p) $\in$ Con(a,c), then N(p/q,b).

<u>Proof</u>. It suffices to consider the case in which c'/a' is a transpose of a subinterval c"/a" of c/a, and since we then have N(c"/a",b), we may assume that c'/a' is a transpose of c/a. If c'/a' $\searrow$ c/a, then we apply the preceding lemma with x = c, y = a', and z = b, but if c'/a' $\nearrow$ c/a, then we apply the dual with x = a, y = c', and z = b. In either case we obtain N(c'/a',b). The last statement of the corollary follows immediately from Theorem 1.1.3.

Lemma 1.2.6. (Cf. B. Jónsson and I. Rival [20], Lemma 3.2) Let L be a semidistributive lattice which excludes L_{12}, and suppose that $a,b,c,a',c' \in L$ with $N(c/a,b)$ and $c/a \nearrow c'/a'$. Then

(i) $c/a \nearrow_\beta (a'b + c)/(a'b + c)a'$ or L includes L_{10} or L_8.

(ii) $c'/a' \searrow_\beta (c + (a + b)a')/(a + b)a'$ or L includes L_9 or L_7.

(iii) $(a'b + c)/(a'b + c)a' \nearrow_\beta (c + (a + b)a')/(a + b)a'$ or L includes L_6.

Theorem 1.2.7. Suppose L is a subdirectly irreducible semidistributive lattice that excludes L_{11} and L_{12}. Then L has a critical quotient c/a such that $\mathrm{Con}(a,c)$ identifies no two distinct elements of L except a and c. Hence c/a is a prime quotient, a is meet irreducible, and c is join irreducible, and therefore c/a is the only critical quotient of L.

Proof. Consider a critical quotient c/a of L, and suppose that for some nontrivial quotient p/q of L with $p/q \neq c/a$ we have $(q,p) \in \mathrm{Con}(a,c)$. By Theorem 1.1.3 there exists a subquotient p'/q' of p/q that projects weakly onto c/a in k steps. Since we may assume that $p'/q' \neq c/a$, we have that $k \geq 1$. Thus, there exists $u/v \neq c/a$ such that $u/v \sim_w c/a$. By duality suppose that $u/v \searrow_w c/a$. Put $a' = cv$. Since c/a' is also a critical quotient of L, we have that $(a'c) \in \mathrm{Con}(a',v)$. Thus, again by Theorem 1.1.3 there exists a chain $a' = e_0 < e_1 < \dots < e_m = c$ such that e_{j+1}/e_j projects weakly onto v/a' for $j \in \{0,1,\dots,m-1\}$. Put $e_1 = c'$. Then $a' = cv = c'v$. Consider a shortest sequence $c'a' = x_0/y_0 \sim_w \cdots \sim_w x_n/y_n = v/a'$. Clearly $n \geq 2$. Observe that if $n = 2$, then we cannot have $c'/a' \searrow_w x_1/y_1 \nearrow_w v/a'$ since that would imply $c' = a' + x_1 \leq v$, which contradicts $vc' = a'$.

First suppose that $x_{n-2}/y_{n-2} \nearrow_w x_{n-1}/y_{n-1} \searrow_w v/a'$. Then we can only apply parts (ii) or (iii) of Lemma 1.2.1. This is obvious if $n \geq 3$, and for $n = 2$ it follows from the observation made above. So by Lemma 1.2.1. (ii) and (iii), there exists $a'',b,c'', t \in L$ with $N(c''/a'',b)$ and $a' < t \leq v$ such that either $b/bc'' \subseteq v/a'$, or $(a'' + b)/b \searrow_w t/a'$. It follows from Corollary 1.2.5 that $N(c'/a',b)$. However, this is clearly impossible, since in both cases $b \geq a'$.

Now suppose that $x_{n-2}/y_{n-2} \searrow_w x_{n-1}/y_{n-1} \nearrow_w v/a'$. As we have already noted, this implies that $n \geq 3$, so we may only apply the dual parts of (ii) or (iii) of Lemma 1.2.1. That is, there exist $a'',b,c'',t \in L$ with $N(c''/a'',b)$ and $a' \leq t \leq v$ such that $(a'' + b)/b \subseteq v/a'$ or $b/bc'' \nearrow v/t$. Again by Corollary 1.2.5, $N(c'/a',b)$ so $(a'' + b)/b$ cannot be a subquotient of v/a', since this contradicts the noncomparibility of b and a'. Also, $b/bc'' \nearrow v/t$ implies $v \geq a' + b = c' + b \geq c'$, contradicting $a' = vc'$.

Thus, we have shown that $(p,q) \in \mathrm{Con}(a,c)$ implies $p/q = c/a$. This implies that $a \prec c$, since for $a < s < c$ we would otherwise have $(s,c) \in \mathrm{Con}(a,c)$. Finally, the assumption $a < s$ and $a = cs$ implies $c/a \nearrow (c+s)/s$ and so $(s,c+s) \in \mathrm{Con}(a,c)$, which again leads to a contradiction. The theorem is proven.

Corollary 1.2.8. Let L and c/a be as in Theorem 1.2.7. Then for $b \in L$ the following conditions are equivalent:

(i) $N(u/v,b)$ for some quotient u/v of L;

(ii) $N(c/a,b)$;

(iii) b is noncomparible with a and c.

Proof: (i) implies (ii) by Corollary 1.2.5, and clearly (ii) implies (iii). Finally, if (iii) holds, then it follows from Theorem 1.2.7 that the elements a, c, and b generate a pentagon.

Corollary 1.2.9. Let L and c/a be as in Theorem 1.2.7. Then the sublattices $[a)$ and $(c]$ of L are distributive.

Proof. Since L is a semidistributive lattice, the sublattices $[a)$ and $(c]$ exclude the diamond. Suppose that for some $u,v,b \in L$ we have $N(u/v,b)$, and that this pentagon is a sublattice of $[a)$ or $(c]$. Then $b \geq a$ or $b \leq c$. However, this leads to a contradiction, since by Corollary 1.2.8 we must have $N(c/a,b)$.

Lemma 1.2.10. Let L and c/a be as in Theorem 1.2.7, and suppose that u/v is a nontrivial quotient of $[c)$. Then there exist $b,v' \in L$ with $v \leq v' < u$ such that $N(c/a,b)$, $b \leq u$, $b \not\leq v'$, and $(v'+b)/v' \searrow_{\beta} (a+b)/(a+b)v'$.

Proof. Choose a shortest possible sequence

$$c/a = x_0/y_0 \sim_w x_1/y_1 \sim_w \cdots \sim_w x_n/y_n = u/v.$$

It follows from Lemma 1.1.2 that $n \geq 3$. Suppose that $x_{n-2}/y_{n-2} \nearrow_w x_{n-1}/y_{n-1} \searrow_w u/v$. Since n was chosen as small as possible, we can only apply parts (ii) or (iii) of Lemma 1.2.1. That is, there exist $a', b, c', u' \in L$ with $N(c'/a',b)$ and $v < u' \leq u$ such that $b/bc' \subseteq u/v$ or $(a'+b)/b \searrow_w u'/v$. It follows from Corollary 1.2.8 that $N(c/a,b)$, but this is clearly impossible, since in both cases $b \geq a$.

Thus we must have $x_{n-2}/y_{n-2} \searrow_w x_{n-1}/y_{n-1} \nearrow_w u/v$. By the dual of Lemma 1.2.1 (ii), (iii), there exist $a', b, c', v' \in L$ with $N(c'/a',b)$, and $v \leq v' < u$ such that either $(a'+b)b \subseteq u/v$ or $b/bc' \nearrow_w u/v'$. Again by Corollary 1.2.8, $N(c/a,b)$, so $(a'+b)/b$ cannot be a subquotient of u/v, since in that case $c \leq v \leq b$.

Now $a,b < u$ implies $a + b \leq u$, and $a < v'$ implies $v' + b = v' + (a + b)$. Since b and v' are noncomparable, the intervals $(v' + b)/b$ and $(a + b)/(a + b)v'$ are nontrivial, and we have $(a + b)/(a + b)v' \nearrow (v' + b)/v'$. The bijectivity of the transposition follows from the fact that the sublattice $[a)$ is distributive (see Corollary 1.2.9).

The last result of this section concerns a finitely generated subdirectly irreducible lattice L all of whose critical quotients are prime. In particular, L can be assumed to satisfy the conditions of Theorem 1.2.7.

Lemma 1.2.11. Let L be a finitely generated subdirectly irreducible lattice all of whose critical quotients are prime. If c/a is a critical quotient of L, and if $L/\mathrm{Con}(a,c)$ belongs to a variety generated by a finite lattice, then L is finite.

Proof. Since every critical quotient of L is prime, each congruence class of $\mathrm{Con}(a,c)$ has at most two elements. Thus the assumption that L is infinite implies that $L/\mathrm{Con}(a,c)$ is infinite as well. However, this leads to a contradiction, since the lattice $L/\mathrm{Con}(a,c)$ is finitely generated and belongs to the variety generated by a finite lattice, and therefore must be finite.

1.3 Finite, Semidistributive, Subdirectly Irreducible Lattices Which Exclude L_{11} and L_{12}. Let L be a finite, semidistributive, subdirectly irreducible lattice which excludes L_{11} and L_{12}. We denote by c/a the unique critical quotient of L. Recall that c/a is prime.

If X is a subset of L, we say that the element $s \in L$ is X-join isolated if $s = x + y$ and $x,y < s$ implies $x,y \in X$. Dually we can define X-meet isolated. The quotient u/v is said to be isolated if every element of u/v is u/v-doubly isolated.

For the rest of this section we suppose that c'/a' is an interval of L such that the following holds:

(i) $a' \leq a < c \leq c'$;

(ii) Any $s \in (c'/a' - \{a'\})$ is c'/a'-join isolated;

(iii) Any $s \in (c'/a' - \{c'\})$ is c'/a'-meet isolated.

Observe that if $b \notin c'/a'$ and b is noncomparable with some $s \in c'/a'$, then b is noncomparable with all the elements of c'/a'. Moreover, $a' + b = s + b = c' + b$ and $a'b = sb = c'b$, and hence $N(c'/a',b)$. Thus, for any $b \notin c'/a'$, the conditions $N(c'/a',b)$ and $N(c/a,b)$ are equivalent.

Lemma 1.3.1. Suppose that u/v is a prime quotient of L, with $c \leq v$. Then there exists $b \in L$ such that $N(c/a,b)$, $(a + b)/(a + b)v \nearrow u/v$ and $a + b \succ (a + b)v$. Hence, if $c' = v$, then $u = a' + b = a + b$ and $NN(c'/a',b)$.

Proof. Follows from Lemma 1.2.10.

Lemma 1.3.2. If L excludes L_7, then for any $b \in L$ the conditions

$$N(c'/a',b), \quad c' \prec a' + b, \text{ and } \quad a''b \prec b \prec a' + b$$

jointly imply that $a'b \prec a'$.

Proof. Suppose the contrary. Take $y \in L$ with $a'b < y \prec a'$. By the dual of Lemma 1.3.1 there exists $b_0 \in L$ with $N(c'/a',b_0)$ and $y = a'b_0$. Since for $y < s \leq b_0$, $N(c/a,s)$ (Corollary 1.2.8), we must have $N(c'/a',s)$. So we may assume that $y \prec b_0$. Now the interval $(a' + b_0)/b_0$ is prime, since for $b_0 < t < a' + b_0$ we would have $N(t/b_0,a)$, contrary to Corollary 1.2.8. Since y is noncomparable with $b, a' + b \succ b$ and $y < a' + b$, we have $y + b = a' + b$. Thus $N(a'/y,b)$. Since $a'/y \nearrow (a' + b_0)/b_0$, we have $N((a' + b_0)/b_0,b)$ (Corollary 1.2.5). Thus $a' + b_0 \not\geq a' + b$, which clearly implies that b_0 and $a' + b_0$ are noncomparable with $a' + b$. Since $a' + b \succ c, b \succ a'b$ and $b_0 \succ y$, we must have $(a' + b)(a' + b_0) = c'$, $(a' + b_0)b = a'b$ and $(a' + b)b_0 = y$. Thus the elements a', b and b_0 generate L_7 (see Figure 1.6). This contradiction completes the proof of the lemma.

Corollary 1.3.3. Given $c' \prec x \in L$, there exists $b \in L$ with $N(c'/a',b)$, $x = a' + b$, and $a'b \prec b \prec x$. If L excludes L_7, then any such element b also satisfies the condition $a'b \prec a'$.

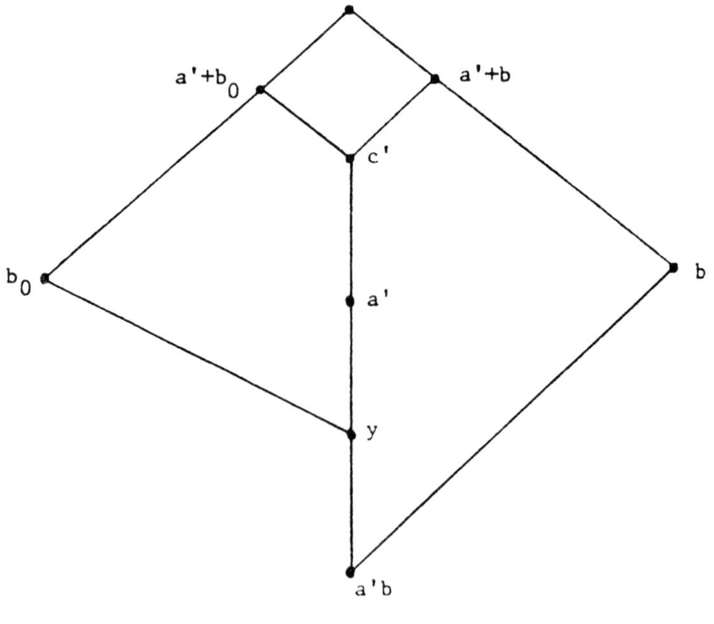

Figure 1.6

Proof. By Lemma 1.3.1 there exists $b \in L$ such that $N(c'/a',b)$ and $x = a' + b$. We may choose b so that $b \prec x$. Since for $a'b < s < b$ we would have $N(b/s,a')$ and $N(b/s,a)$, contrary to Corollary 1.2.8, b must cover $a'b$. If L excludes L_7, by Lemma 1.3.2 we must have $a'b \prec a'$.

Lemma 1.3.4. Suppose $N(u/v,z)$, $u/v \nsubseteq c'a'$ and $z \notin c'/a'$. Then there exists $y \in L$ with $N(c'/a',y)$ such that $N((a' + y)/a',z)$, $N(y/a'y,z)$ and $a' + y \succ c'$ or, dually, $N(c'/a'y,z)$, $N((a' + y)/y,z)$ and $a' \succ a'y$.

Proof. Consider a sequence

$$c/a = x_0/y_0 \sim_w x_1/y_1 \sim_w \cdots \sim_w x_n/y_n = u/v.$$

Since c/a is a subquotient of c'/a' and u/v is not, there is an index $i < n$ with $x_i/y_i \subseteq c'/a'$ and $x_{i+1}/y_{i+1} \nsubseteq c'/a'$. By duality, suppose that $x_i/y_i \nearrow_w x_{i+1}/y_{i+1}$. Since y_i is c'/a'-meet isolated, $y_{i+1} \in c'/a'$. Thus $x_{i+1} > c' \geq y_{i+1}$. Since x_{i+1}/y_{i+1} projects weakly onto u/v, by Corollary 1.2.5 $N(x_{i+1}/y_{i+1},z)$, and so $N(c'/a',z)$, since $z \notin c'/a'$. Take $x \in L$ with $c' \prec x \leq x_{i+1}$. We have $N(x/a',z)$. By Corollary 1.3.3 there exists y with $N(c'/a',y)$ and $x = a' + y$. Since $(a' + y)/a' = x/a' \searrow y/a'y$, again by Corollary 1.2.5 $N(y/a'y,z)$. The lemma is proven.

For the rest of this section we suppose that b is an element of L such that $N(c'/a',b)$ and the set $c'/a' \cup \{b, a' + b, a'b\}$ is an interval in L.

Lemma 1.3.5. Assume that for some $b_0 \in L$ we have $N(c'/a',b_0)$ and $a' + b = a' + b_0$, and the elements b and b_0 are noncomparable. Then the element b_0 can be chosen so that the set $\{a',c',b,b_0\}$ generates L_{14} (see Figure 1.7).

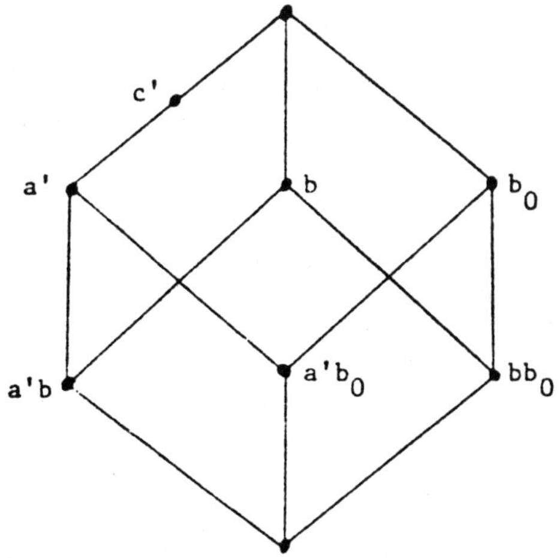

Figure 1.7

Proof. We may assume that $b_0 \prec a' + b_0$. Since for $a'b_0 < s < b_0$ we would have $N(b_0/s,a')$ and $N(b_0/s,a)$, contrary to Corollary 1.2.8 the interval $b_0/a'b_0$ must be prime. By semidistributivity,

$$a' + b = a' + b_0 = b + b_0 = a'b + a'b_0 + bb_0.$$

From this it follows that the elements $a'b = c'b$, $a'b_0 = c'b_0$ and bb_0 are noncomparable and, therefore,

$$a' = a'b + a'b_0,\ b = a'b + bb_0,\ b_0 = a'b_0 + bb_0.$$

This shows that a', b and b_0 generate an eight element Boolean algebra. Since $N(c'/a',b)$ and $N(c'/a',b_0)$, this completes the proof.

Corollary 1.3.6. If L excludes L_{14}, then for $x,y \in L$,

(i) $a' + b = a' + y > y$ implies $y \leq b$;

(ii) $a' + b = x + b > x$ implies $x \leq c'$.

Proof. (i) follows directly from Lemma 1.3.5, and (ii) reduces to (i) by observing that if $x \not\leq c'$, then $a' + x = a' + b$.

Lemma 1.3.7. If L excludes L_7, by L_{13} and L_{15}, then c' is meet irreducible.

Proof. Suppose c' is meet reducible. Then there exists an element x with $c' \prec x$ and $c' = x(a' + b)$. By Lemma 1.3.1, there exists $b_0 \in L$ with $N(c'/a',b_0)$ and $x = a' + b_0$. We may assume that $b_0 \prec x$.

The elements $a' + b$, $a' + b_0$ and $b + b_0$ generate a lattice K that is a homomorphic image of the lattice in Figure 1.8.A. If K is isomorphic to that lattice, then $bb_0 \leq a'$, since any $s \in (c'/a' - \{a'\})$ is c'/a'-join isolated and equality is excluded because a' is c'/a'-meet isolated. Thus, $K \cup \{a'\}$ is a sublattice of L isomorphic to L_{13}, contrary to our hypothesis. We infer that K is a proper homomorphic image of the lattice in Figure 1.8.A, and since $a' + b$, $a' + b_0$ and c' are distinct, this implies that $c' < b + b_0$.

We have $bb_0 \leq (a' + b)(a' + b_0) = c'$, and the inclusion must be strict because b and b_0 are not comparable with c'. The elements $a'b$ and $a'b_0$ must be comparable, for otherwise $a' + b = a'b_0 + b$ and $a' + b_0 = a'b + b_0$ and L includes L_{15} (see Figure 1.8.B). However, strict inclusions, $a'b < a'b_0$ and $a'b_0 < a'b$, are excluded because L_7 is not a sublattice of L, and an equality violates the semidistributivity of L, since $(b + b_0)c' = c' > c'b_0$. The lemma is proven.

Lemma 1.3.8. Suppose that L excludes L_{15}, and assume that for some $u,v,z \in L$ with $z \geq b$ we have $N(u/v,z)$. Then $u/v \subseteq c'/a'$.

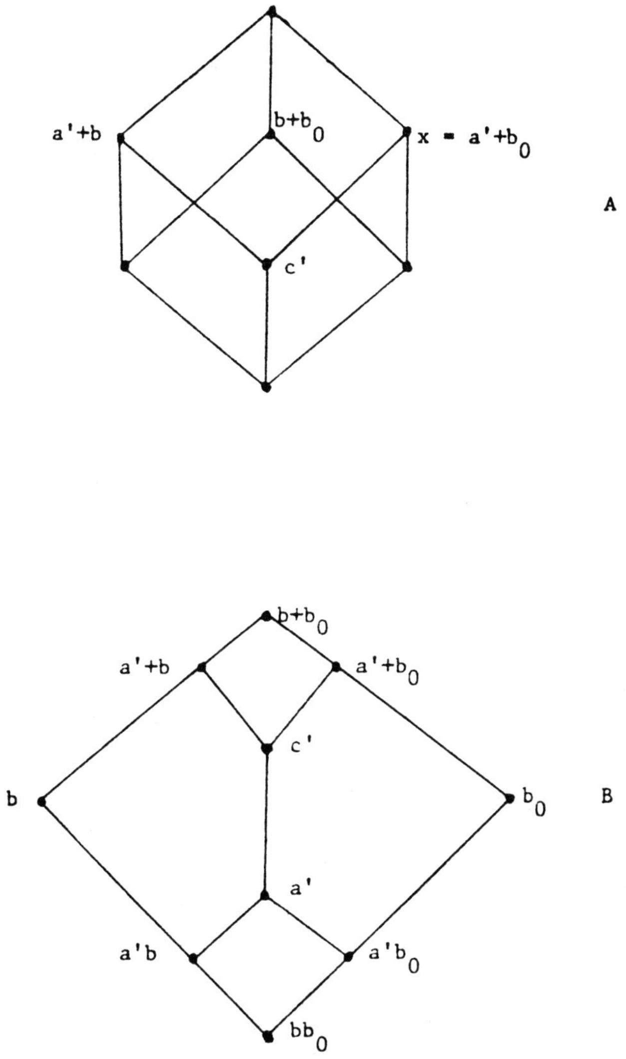

Figure 1.8

Proof. Suppose that $u/v \nleq c'/a'$. Since clearly $z \notin c'/a'$, by Lemma 1.3.4 there exists $b_0 \in L$ such that either

(1) $N((a' + b_0)/a', z)$, $N(b_0/a'b_0, z)$ and $c' \prec a' + b_0$; or

(2) $N(c'/a'b_0, z)$ $N((a' + b_0)/b_0, z)$ and $a'b_0 \prec a'$.

We are going to show that the elements a', c', b and b_0 generate L_{15}. Since we already know that $N(c'/a', b)$ and $N(c'/a', b_0)$, it suffices to check that

(3) $a'b + a'b_0 = a'$;
(4) $(a' + b)(a' + b_0) = c'$.

Regardless of whether it is (1) or (2) that is satisfied, the elements $a' + b_0$ and $a'b_0$ are noncomparable with z. Since $a'b \leq z$, this implies that $a'b_0 \not\leq a'b$. Strict inclusion, $a'b < a'b_0$, is also excluded because $a'b \prec a'$ and $a'b_0 < a'$. Thus $a'b$ and $a'b_0$ are noncomparable, and since $a'b \prec a'$, this implies that (3) holds. Next note that $a'z = a'b$, because $a'b \prec a'$ and $a'b \leq a'z < a'$. Thus $a'z = a'b > a'bb_0 = a'b_0z$, which shows that (2) fails, and (1) must therefore hold. In particular, $N((a' + b_0)/a'z)$, whence it follows that $a' + b_0 \not\geq b$, hence $c' \leq (a' + b)(a' + b_0) < a' + b$. Since $c' \prec a' + b$, this gives (4).

Lemma 1.3.9. Suppose that L excludes L_i for $i \in \{9,11,\ldots,15\}$. Then b is meet irreducible.

Proof. Let $z \succ b$ and $z \neq a' + b$, and consider a shortest sequence

$$c/a = x_0/y_0 \sim_w x_1/y_1 \sim_w \cdots \sim_w x_n/y_n = z/b. \tag{1}$$

Clearly $n \geq 2$. The case $n = 2$ is easily ruled out, for c/z is a subinterval of x_1/y_1 by Theorem 1.2.7, and x_{n-1}/y_{n-1} is a transpose of z/b since $b \prec z$. Thus $n \geq 3$.

Suppose $x_{n-2}/y_{n-2} \nearrow_w x_{n-1}/y_{n-1} \searrow z/b$. The quotient x_{n-1}/y_{n-1} is prime. Indeed, $y_{n-1} < t < x_{n-1}$ would imply $N(t/y_{n-1},z)$, contradicting Lemma 1.3.8. By a similar argument, x_{n-2}/y_{n-2} is prime. Thus $x_{n-2}/y_{n-2} \nearrow_\beta x_{n-1}/y_{n-1} \searrow_\beta z/b$, and by Corollary 1.2.3 the sequence (1) can be shortened, contrary to our choice of n. Thus, we must have $x_{n-2}/y_{n-2} \searrow_w x_{n-1}/y_{n-1} \nearrow z/b$. Observe that $x_{n-1} \notin c'/a'$, for otherwise $z = x_{n-1} + b = a' + b$.

The quotient x_{n-1}/y_{n-1} is prime, for $y_{n-1} < t < x_{n-1}$ would imply $N(x_{n-1}/t,b)$, contradicting Lemma 1.3.8. However, in this case the quotient x_{n-2}/y_{n-2} cannot be prime, because of the minimality of n. Hence for some $u,v \in L$ with $y_{n-2} \leq v < x_{n-2}$ we have $N(u/v,x_{n-1})$, since $x_{n-1} \succ y_{n-1}$. Thus by Corollary 1.2.8 $N(c/a,x_{n-1})$ and, since $x_{n-1} \notin c'/a'$, $N(c'/a',x_{n-1})$.

We claim that $a'x_{n-1} = bx_{n-1}$. Suppose the contrary. We have $bx_{n-1} = (a' + b)zx_{n-1} = (a' + b)x_{n-1} \geq a'x_{n-1}$. Hence, if bx_{n-1} and $a'x_{n-1}$ are not equal, then the last inequality must be strict. Also, since $y_{n-1} = ux_{n-1} = bx_{n-1} \neq a'x_{n-1}$, we have that $u/v \notin c'/a'$. By Lemma 1.3.4 there exists b_0 L with $N(c'/a',b_0)$ such that $N((a' + b_0)/a',x_{n-1})$ or $N(c'/a'b_0,x_{n-1})$.

First suppose that $N((a' + b_0)/a',x_{n-1})$. Then $a' + b_0$ is noncomparable with $a' + b$. Indeed, since $a' + b \succ c'$ we must otherwise have $a' + b_0 \geq a' + b$ and hence $N((a' + b)/a',x_{n-1})$. This would imply $a'x_{n-1} = (a' + b)x_{n-1} = (a' + b)zx_{n-1} = bx_{n-1}$, contrary to the assumption

$a'x_{n-1} \neq bx_{n-1}$. Thus $c' = (a' + b)(a' + b_0)$. Since L excludes L_{13} and L_{15}, it follows from theproof of Lemma 1.3.7 that the elements a', c', b and b_0 generate L_7. Hence $a'b_0 < a'b$ and $a' + b < b + b_0$. Now $N((a' + b_0)/a', x_{n-1})$ and $(a' + b_0)/a' \searrow b_0/a'b_0$ implies $N(b_0/a'b, x_{n-1})$ (Corollary 1.2.5). Thus $a'b_0 + x_{n-1} = b_0 + x_{n-1}$. This together with $a'b_0$, $x_{n-1} \leq z$ implies $b_0 \leq b_0 + x_{n-1} = a'b_0 + x_{n-1} \leq z$, and therefore $a' + b < b + b_0 < z$, a contradiction.

Now suppose that $N(c'/a'b_0, x_{n-1})$. Then $a'b_0$ is noncomparable with $a'b$. Indeed, since a' covers $a'b$ we would otherwise have $a'b_0 \leq a'b$ implying $a' \leq a' + x_{n-1} = a'b_0 + x_{n-1} \leq z$. Thus $a' = a'b + a'b_0$. Since L excludes L_{14} and L_{15}, it follows from the proof of the dual of Lemma 1.3.7 that the elements a', c', b and b_0 generate L_8 and therefore $c'/a'b_0 \nearrow (a + b_0)/b_0 \searrow b_0/bb_0$. Since $N(c'/a'b_0, x_{n-1})$ we have then $N(b/bb_0, x_{n-1})$ (Corollary 1.2.5). This together with $a'b \in b/bb_0$ and $x_{n-1} < z$ implies $bx_{n-1} = a'bx_{n-1} \leq a'x_{n-1} \leq (a' + b)x_{n-1} = bx_{n-1}$ contradicting the assumption $a'x_{n-1} \neq bx_{n-1}$.

Thus we have shown that $a'x_{n-1} = bx_{n-1}$. If $a'b = a'x_{n-1} = bx_{n-1}$, then it follows from the dual of Lemma 1.3.5 and L includes L_{13}. So suppose that $a'b \neq a'x_{n-1}$. Since $a'b = a'(a'b + x_{n-1})$, the elements b and $a'b + x_{n-1}$ must be comparable, for otherwise by the dual of Lemma 1.3.5 L would include L_{13}. Thus $a'b + x_{n-1} = z$, implying $N(b/a'b, x_{n-1})$. Since $b/a'b$ $(a' + b)/b$, by Corollary 1.2.5 $N((a' + b)/b, x_{n-1})$, whence $a'x_{n-1} = (a' + b)x_{n-1}$ and therefore the elements a', c', b and x_{n-1} generate L_9. The lemma is proven.

1.4 Projective, Subdirectly Irreducible Lattices.

Definition 1.4.1. Let V be a variety of lattices, and suppose that $P \in V$. We say that P is projective (in V) if for any $A, B \in V$ and any lattice homomorphisms $h: P \to A$ and $g: A \to B$ (g onto) there exists a lattice homomorphism $f: P \to A$ such that $h = fg$.

We state without proof the following well known result about projective lattices.

Lemma 1.4.2. For a variety V and a lattice $P \in V$, the following three conditions are equivalent:

(i) P is projective in V;

(ii) For any lattice $M \in V$ and any onto homomorphism $g: M \to P$, there exists an embedding $h: P \to M$ such that hg is the identity map on P;

(iii) P is a retract of a V-free lattice.

Our next result is valid for arbitrary algebras of finitary type.

Lemma 1.4.3. Let K be a class of lattices, and suppose that P is a projective, subdirectly irreducible member of K^V. Then P is isomorphic to a sublattice of some member of K.

Proof. Since $P \in K^V$, we have that for some index set $I, P \in HS\Pi(L_i)_{i \in I}$, where for any $i \in I$, $L_i \in K$. Thus, by Lemma 1.4.2 (ii), $P \in S\Pi(L_i)_{i \in I}$. We may, therefore, assume that P is a sublattice of $\Pi(L_i)_{i \in I}$.

Thus P is a subdirect product of the family $\pi_i(P)_{i \in I}$ of lattices, where $\pi_i: P \to L_i$ is a natural projection for any $i \in I$. But, since P is subdirectly irreducible, there exists $j \in I$ such that $\pi_j(P) \cong P$, and so $\pi_j: P \to L_j$ is an embedding.

Remark 1.4.4. Projective lattices were studied in R. Freese and J. B. Nation [9], B. Jónsson and J. B. Nation [18] and A. Kostinsky [21]. Since the variety of all lattices is generated by its finite members, it follows from Lemma 1.4.3 that every projective, subdirectly irreducible lattice is finite. On the other hand, since every finite projective lattice is a bounded homomorphic image of a free lattice, we have that every projective, subdirectly irreducible lattice is splitting. (One may infer from Lemma 1.4.3 that every projective subdirectly irreducible algebra of finitary type is splitting.)

The next result is also valid for arbitrary algebras of finitary type.

Corollary 1.4.5. Let P be a projective, subdirectly irredudible lattice, and suppose that p is its conjugate identity. Then the lattice L satisfies p if and only if L has no sublattice isomorphic to P.

Proof. Obviously, if $L \models p$, then L excludes P. Conversely, suppose L excludes P. Then by Lemma 1.4.3 $\{P\}^V \nsubseteq \{L\}^V$, and since P is a splitting lattice we have that $L \in Mod(p)$.

Example 1.4.6. It was shown in R. McKenzie [23] that the lattices L_i ($i \in \{7,\ldots,15\}$) and L_6^n (see Figures 0.2, 0.3. 2.1) are embeddable in free lattices. Hence all of them, as finite sublattices of a free lattice, are projective (see A. Kostinsky [21]).

CHAPTER 2

THE VARIETIES $\{L_6^n\}^V$

Definition 2.1. We say that the quotient c/a of a lattice L is an L_6^n-quotient if for some $b, b_0, \ldots, b_n \in L$ the set $\{a, c, b, b_0, \ldots, b_n\}$ generates a sublattice of L isomorphic to L_6^n, with c/a as a critical quotient (see Figure 2.1). In that case we shall write $L_6^n(c/a, b, b_0, \ldots, b_n)$.

Using Theorem 0.1.6 it is easy to check that for any $n = 0,1,\ldots,$ the variety $\{L_6^n\}^V$ has at least fifteen join redudible covers, $\{L_6^n, M_3\}^V$, $\{L_6^n, L_1\}^V, \ldots, \{L_6^n, L_5\}^V, \{L_6^n, L_7\}^V, \ldots, \{L_6^n, L_{15}\}^V$, and at least one join irreducible cover: the variety $\{L_6^{n+1}\}^V$. It turns out that for any natural number n, the above list of covers of $\{L_6^n\}^V$ is complete. This chapter is devoted to the proof of this result.

Theorem 2.2. For any natural number n, the variety $\{L_6^n\}^V$ has only one join irredicible cover, namely the variety $\{L_6^{n+1}\}^V$.

The theorem is a corollary of the following two propositions.

Proposition 2.3. Let L be a subdirectly irredicible lattice, and assume that the variety $\{L\}^V$ does not have the lattices M_3 and L_i $(i \in \{1, 2, \ldots, 5, 7, \ldots, 15\})$ as its members. Suppose further that k is a natural number such that c/a is an L_6^k-quotient of L, and L does not have any L_6^{k+1}-quotients. Then c/a is a critical quotient of L. Moreover, $L/\mathrm{Con}(a,c)$ does not have L_6^k-quotients.

Proposition 2.4. Let L be a finite subdirectly irredicible lattice with c/a as a critical quotient, and assume that the variety $\{L\}^V$ does not have the lattices M_3 and L_i $(i \in \{1, \ldots, 5, 7, \ldots, 15\})$ as its members. If c/a is an L_6^k-quotient and $L \neq L_6^k$, then c/a is an L_6^{k+1}-quotient.

Proof of Proposition 2.3. By Theorem 0.2.9 the variety $\{L\}^V$ is semidistributive, and by Theorem 1.2.7 L has a unique critical quotient, We denote it by x/y. Choose $b, b_0, \ldots, b_k \in L$ such that $L^k(c/a,b, b_0, \ldots, b_k)$. We are going to show that $x/y = c/a$.

Our first lemma is valid for arbitrary lattices.

Lemma 2.3.1. (i) Any nontrivial subquotient c'/a' is of c/a is an L_6^k-quotient.

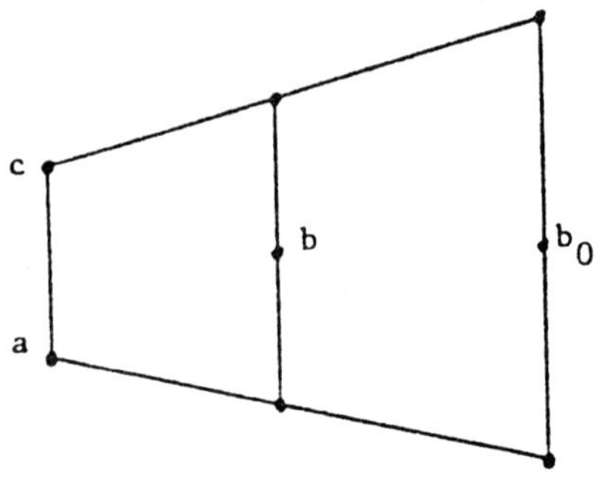

$L_6^0 = L_6$

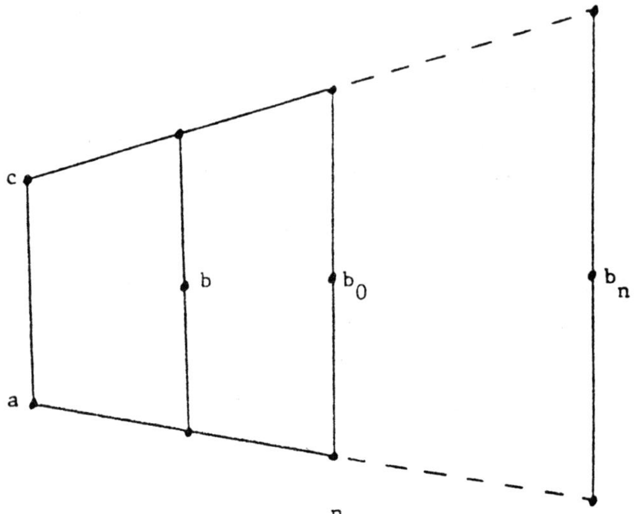

L_6^n

Figure 2.1

(ii) Suppose that for some a', c', z we have $N(c'/a', z)$ with $a \leq a'z < a' + z \leq c$. Then $L_6^{k+1}(c'/a', z, b, b_0, \ldots, b_k)$.

(iii) Suppose that for some $z \in L$ we have $N((a + b_i)/ab_i, z)$ $(i \in \{0, 1, \ldots, k\})$. Then $L_6^{i+1}(c/a, b, b_0, \ldots, b_i, z)$ and similarly, if $N((a + b)/ab, z)$, then $L_6^0(c/a, b, z)$.

Proof. Since the proofs of all three parts of the lemma are similar, we shall prove only part (ii). It is clear that for $s \in N(c'/a', z)$ and

$t \in \{b, b_0, \ldots, b_k\}$ we have $s + t = a + t$, since $a \leq s < a + t$. Dually, since $c \geq s > ct$, we must have $st = ct$ (see Figure 2.2).

Lemma 2.3.2. For any quotient u/v and p/q, if $u/v \nearrow p/q \searrow c/a$, then $u/v \searrow uc/va \nearrow c/a$, and all four transpotions are bijective.

Proof. By Lemma 1.2.4 the lattice generated by q, c, and b is a homomorphic image of the lattice in Figure 2.3.A. The pentagon $N(r/g, b)$ is contained in $(a + b)/ab$, whence it follows that $L_6^k(r/g, b, b_0, \ldots, b_k)$. From this we infer that r/g is distributive, for otherwise r/g would contain a pentagon $N(c'/a', b')$ (since $M_3 \notin \{L\}^V$), and we would have $L_6^{k+1}(c'/a', b', b, b_0, \ldots, b_k)$. In particular, therefore, the transposition $r/s \searrow f/g$ is bijective. By Lemma 1.2.6, the transpositions $p/q \searrow r/s$ and $f/g \searrow c/a$ are also bijective, and we consequently have $p/q \searrow_\beta c/a$.

Again by Lemma 1.2.4, the lattice generated by q, u and b is a homomorphic image of the lattice in Figure 2.3.B. Note that $ab \leq bq < b \leq a + b$, whence $N(b/bq, b_0)$. Since $(v + b)/g' \searrow b/bq$, it follows by still another application of Lemma 1.2.4 that the lattice generated by g', b and b_0 is a homomorphic image of the lattice in Figure 2.3.C, and by Lemma 1.2.6 the transposition $(v + b)/g' \searrow r''/s''$ is bijective. Letting $t = r'(b + b_0)$, we

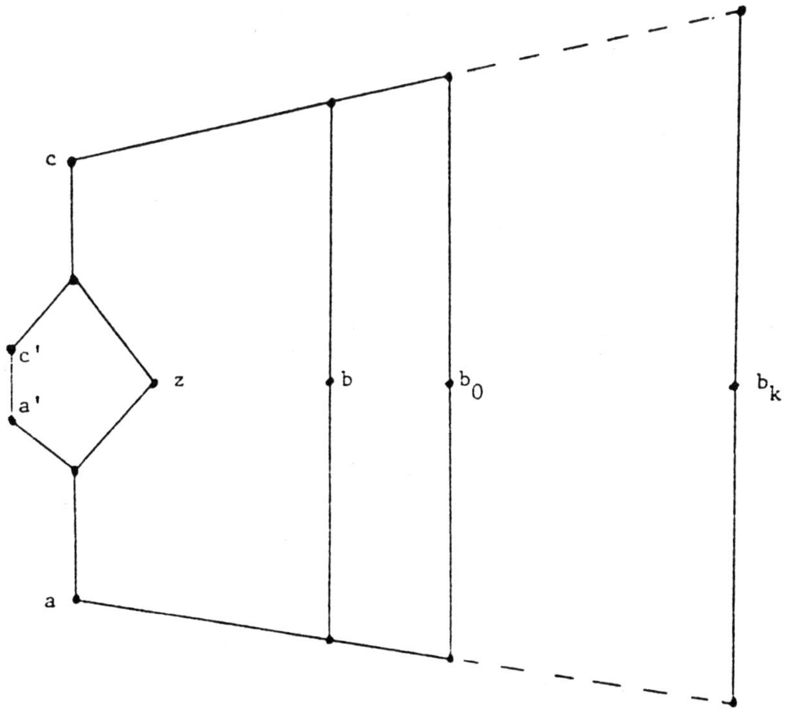

Figure 2.2

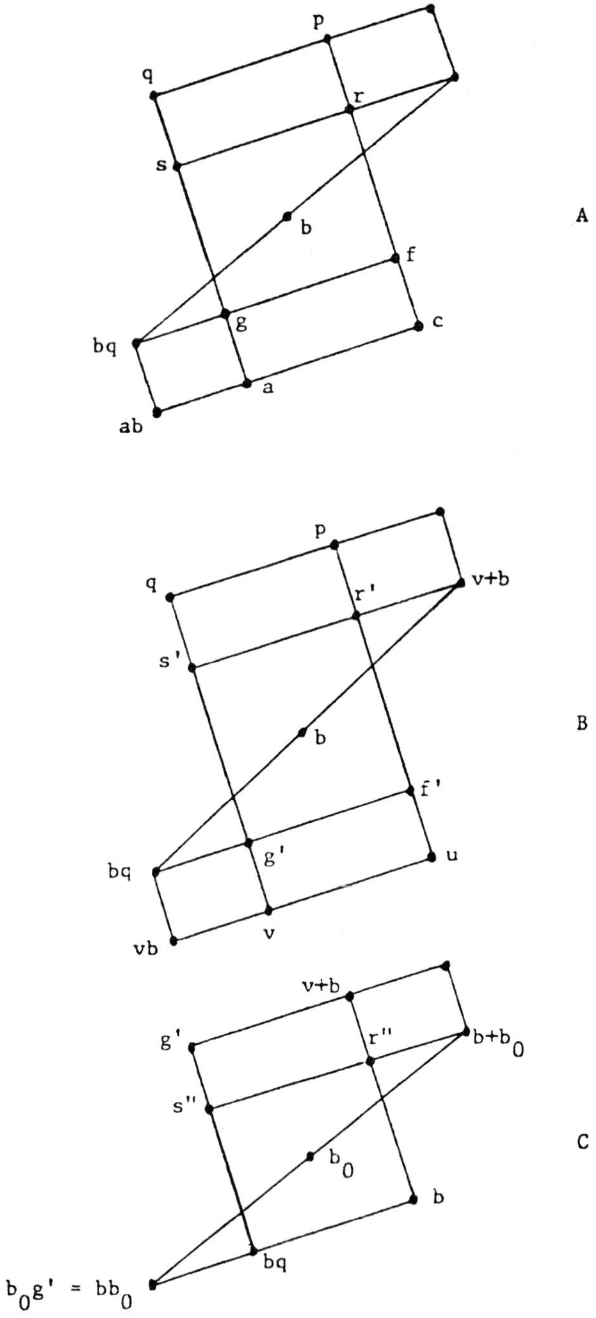
p
q
r
s
b
A
f
g
c
bq
a
ab
p
q
r'
v+b
s'
b
B
f'
g'
u
bq
v
vb
v+b
g'
r''
b+b0
s''
C
b0
b
bq
b0g' = bb0

Figure 2.3

have $N(t/s'', b)$ and therefore $L_6^k(t/s, b, b_0, \ldots, b_k)$. This implies that t/s'' is distributive, and hence so is r'/g', since the two quotients are isomorphic. The transposition $f'g' \nearrow r'/s'$ is therefore bijective, and by Lemma 1.2.6 so are the transpositions $u/v \nearrow f'/g'$ and $r'/s' \nearrow p/q$. Consequently, $u/v \nearrow_\beta p/q$.

Using Lemma 1.2.2, we conclude that $u/v \searrow uc/va \nearrow c/a$. By duality, these two transpositions must also be bijective.

Corollary 2.3.3. If u/v projects weakly onto a subquotient of c/a, then $u/v \searrow uc'/va' \nearrow c'/a'$ for some subquotient c'/a' of c/a.

Proof. Assume that $u/v = x_0/y_0 \sim_w x_1/y_1 \sim_w \cdots \sim_w x_n/y_n \subseteq c/a$. We use induction on n. The cases $n = 0,1$ being trivial, assume that $x_{n-2}/y_{n-2} \nearrow x'_{n-1}y'_{n-1} \subseteq x_{n-1}/y_{n-1} \searrow x_n/y_n$. By the preceding lemma, with c/a replaced by x_n/y_n, the latter transposition is bijective, and hence x'_{n-1}/y'_{n-1} transposes bijectively onto a subquotient x'_n/y'_n of x_n/y_n. By a second application of the same lemma, $x_{n-2}/y_{n-2} \searrow x_{n-2}x'_n/y_{n-2}y'_n \nearrow x'_n/y'_n$. For the case $n = 2$ this completes the proof, but for $n > 2$ it reduces the problem to the corresponding problem with n replaced by $n - 1$ (see Corollary 1.2.3).

Corollary 2.3.4. $x/y = c/a$.

Proof. By the preceding corollary x/y is projective to a subquotient c'/a' of c/a, and by Theorem 1.2.7 this implies that $x/y = c'/a'$, If $x < c$, then the hypothesis of the proposition is satisfied with a replaced by x, and we infer that x/y is a subinterval of c/x, a contradiction. Thus $x = c$ and similarly $y = a$. The corollary is proven.

We complete the proof of Proposition 2.3 by showing that $L/\mathrm{Con}\,(a,c)$ does not have L_6^k quotients. So, suppose that for some $u, v, d, d_0, \ldots, d_k \in L$ we have $L_6^k(u'/v', d', d'_0, \ldots, d'_k)$ in $L/\mathrm{Con}\,(a,c)$ (for $s \in L$, $s' = s/\mathrm{Con}\,(a,c)$). If $c = u$ in L, then $u = c > a > v$ and $L_6^k(u/v, d, d_0, \ldots, d_k)$, which would contradict the fact that c/a is the only L_6^k-quotient of L. Thus $c \neq u$ and, similarly, $a \neq u$ and $c, a \neq v$. If $a = d$, then we must have $N(u/v, a)$ in L, which contradicts Corollary 2.1.8. Thus, $a \neq d$ and, more generally, $c,a \notin \{d, d_0, \ldots, d_k\}$. Since $\mathrm{Con}\,(a,c)$ identifies only a and c, we infer that $L_6^k(u/v, d, d_0, \ldots, d_k)$ in L with $u/v \neq c/a$, a contradiction.

Proof of Proposition 2.4. Let c'/a' be an isolated quotient of L (see Chapter 1, Section 1.3) such that $c/a \subseteq c'/a'$.

Lemma 2.4.1. Suppose that for some $b \in L$ we have $N(c'/a', b)$ with $a'b \prec a'$, $c' \prec a' + b$ and $a'b \prec b \prec a' + b$. Then

(i) $(a' + b)/a'b = c'/a' \cup \{a'b, b, a' + b\}$;

(ii) $(a' + b)/a'b$ is an isolated quotient of L.

Proof. Assume that (i) fails. Then there exists $x \in L$ such that $x \in (a' + b)/a'b$ but $x \notin (c'/a' \cup \{a'b, b, a' + b\})$. Since $a'b < x < a' + b$, and since $a'b \prec b \prec a' + b$, it follows that b and x are noncomparable, and $bx = a'b$ and $b + x = a' + b$. Furthermore, x must be noncomparable with a' and c', whence $a' + x = a' + b$. However, this contradicts the semidistributivity of L, since $a' + b \neq a' = a' + bx$. Thus (i) holds.

To prove (ii) it suffices to show that

(1) a' is join irreducible;

(2) c' is meet irreducible'

(3) b is doubly irreducible;

(4) For every $x \in L$, $a' + b = x + b > x$ implies $x \in c'/a'$;

(5) For every $y \in L$, $a' + b = a' + y > y$ implies $y = b$;

(6) For every $x \in L$, $a'b = xb < x$ implies $x \in c'/a'$;

(7) For every $y \in L$, $a'b = ay < y$ implies $y = b$.

(1) and (2) follow from Lemma 1.3.7 and its dual. (3) follows from Lemma 1.3.9 and its dual. Suppose $a' + b = x + b > x$. Then $x \leq c'$ by Corollary 1.3.6. We cannot have $x < a'$, for clearly $x \nleq c'b = a'b$, and $a'b$ is the unique element covered by a'. Hence $x \in c'/a'$. Thus (4) holds. Suppose $a' + b = a' + y > y$. By Corollary 1.3.6 this implies that $y \leq b$, and using the join irreducibility of b we infer that $y = b$. Thus (5) holds. Finally, (6) and (7) are the duals of (4) and (5).

Let $b, b_o, \ldots, b_k \in L$ be such that $L_6^k(c/a, b, b_o, \ldots, b_k)$.

Lemma 2.4.2. The elements $b, b_o, \ldots, b_k \in L$ can be chosen to that the following holds:

(i) $(a + b)/ab = c/a \cup \{ab,b,a + b\}$;

$(a + b_o)/ab_o = (a + b)ab \cup \{ab_o,b_o,a + b_o\}$;

$(a + b_i)/ab_i = (a + b_{i-1})/ab_{i-1} \cup \{ab_i,b_i,a + b_i\}$

for $i \in \{1,2,\ldots,k\}$;

(ii) The quotients c/a, $(a + b)/ab$, $(a + b_o)/ab_o, \ldots, (a + b_k)/ab_k$ are isolated.

(iii) For $z \notin L_6^k(c/a, b, b_o, \ldots, b_k)$, if $N(c/a, z)$, then, $N((a + b_k)/ab_k, z)$ and hence $L_6^{k+1}(c/a, b, b_o, \ldots, b_k, z)$.

Proof. By Lemma 1.3.7 and its dual, the quotient c/a is isolated. Take $x \in L$ with $c \prec x \leq a + b$. Since L excludes L_7, by Corollary 1.3.3 and Lemma 2.4.1 there exists b' such that $N(c/a, b')$ and $a + b' = x$, and such that this sublattice is an interval in L. Since a is join irreducible, the elements ab' and ab must be comparable. From the fact that $a \succ a'b$ we infer that $ab' \geq ab$. Thus, $ab \leq ab' < b' < x \leq a + b$, whence it follows that $L_6^k(c/a, b', b_0, \ldots, b_k)$. So, we may assume that $b = b'$. By Lemma 2.4.1 $(a + b)/ab = c/a \cup \{ab, b, a + b\}$, and this quotient is isolated. By continuing in the same manner, we prove (i) and (ii).

To prove (iii) we only need to observe that for $z \notin L_6^k(c/a, b, b_0, \ldots, b_k)$ the conditions $N(c/a, z)$ and $N((a + b_k)/ab_k, z)$ are equivalent, and apply Lemma 2.3.1 (iii).

Lemma 2.4.3. There exists $z \in L$ such that $L_6^{k+1}(c/a, b, b_0, \ldots, b_k, z)$.

Proof. By Lemma 2.3.1 it is enough to show that for some $z \notin L_6^k(c/a, b, b_0, \ldots, b_k)$, $N(c/a, z)$. Since $L \neq L_6^k$, there exists $u \in L$ with $u \succ a + b_k$ or $u \prec ab_k$. The result now follows from Lemma 1.3.1 or its dual. Lemma 2.4.3 and Proposition 2.4 are proven.

Proof of Theorem 2.2. By way of contradiction, suppose that for some natural number n, the variety $\{L_6^n\}^V$ has a join irreducible cover $V \neq \{L_6^{n+1}\}^V$. Choose n as small as possible. Since V has a finite height in Λ, it is strictly join irreducible. It follows from Theorem 0.1.8 that $V = \{L\}^V$ for some finitely generated subdirectly irreducible lattice L. Since $L_6^n \in \{L\}^V$, and since L_6^n is a projective lattice (see Example 1.4.6), it follows from Lemma 1.4.3 that for some $a, c, b, b_0, \ldots, b_n \in L$ we have $L_6^n(c/a, b, b_0, \ldots, b_n)$. By Proposition 2.3, c/a is a critical quotient, and $L/\mathrm{Con}(a,c)$ does not have an L_6^n-quotient. Again, by the projectivity of L_6^n and Lemma 1.4.3, we have that L_6^n does not belong to the variety generated by $L/\mathrm{Con}(a,c)$. This, together with minimality of n, implies the following: $L/\mathrm{Con}(a,c)$ is in the variety generated by the pentagon if $n = 0$ and it is in the variety generated by L_6^{n-1} if $n \geq 1$. Thus L is a finite lattice (Lemma 1.2.11). However, since L_6^n is a sublattice of L, and since $L \neq L_6^n$, it follows from Proposition 2.4 that L includes L_6^{n+1}. This contradiction completes the proof.

CHAPTER 3

THE VARIETIES $\{L_7^n\}^v$ AND $\{L_8^n\}^v$

Since for any $n = 0, 1, \ldots,$ the lattices L_7^n and L_8^n are mutually dual, we shall consider only the lattices L_7^n and the varieties generated by them.

<u>Definition 3.1</u>. We say that the quotient c/a of a lattice L is an <u>L_7^n-quotient</u> if for some $b, b_0, \ldots, b_n \in L$ the set $\{a, c, b, b, \ldots, b_n\}$ generates a sublattice of L isomorphic to L_7^n with c/a as a critical quotient (see Figure 3.1). In that case we shall write $L_7^n(c/a, b, b_0, \ldots, b_n)$.

Using Theorem 0.1.6 it is easy to check that for any $n = 0, 1, \ldots,$ the variety $\{L_7^n\}^v$ has at least fifteen join reducible covers, $\{L_7^n, M_3\}^v$, $\{L_7^n, L_1\}^v, \ldots, \{L_7^n, L_6\}^v$, $\{L_7^n, L_8\}^v, \ldots, \{L_7^n, L_{15}\}^v$, and at least one join irreducible cover: the variety $\{L_7^{n+1}\}^v$. It turns out that for any natural number n, the above least of covers of $\{L_7^n\}^v$ is complete. This chapter is devoted to the proof of this result.

<u>Theorem 3.2</u>. For any natural number n, the variety $\{L_7^n\}^v$ ($\{L_8^n\}^v$) has only one join irreducible cover, namely the variety $\{L_7^{n+1}\}^v$ ($\{L_8^{n+1}\}^v$).

The theorem is a corollary of the following two propositions.

<u>Proposition 3.3</u>. Let L be a subdirectly irreducible lattice, and assume that the variety $\{L\}^v$ does not have the lattices M_3 and L_i $(i \in \{1, 2, \ldots, 6, 8, \ldots, 15\})$ as its members. Suppose further that k is a natural number such that c/a is an L_7^k-quotient of L, and L does not have any L_7^{k+1}-quotients. Then c/a is a critical quotient of L. Moreover, none of the proper epimorphic images of L have L_7^k-quotients.

<u>Proposition 3.4</u>. Let L be a finite subdirectly irreducible lattice with c/a as a critical quotient, and assume that the variety $\{L\}^v$ does not have the lattices M_3 and L_i $(i \in \{1, \ldots, 6, 8, \ldots, 15\})$ as its members. If c/a is an L_7^k-quotient and $L \neq L_7^k$, then c/a is an L_7^{k+1}-quotient.

<u>Proof of Proposition 3.3</u>. By Theorem 0.2.9 the variety $\{L\}^v$ is semi-distributive, and by Theorem 1.2.7 L has a unique critical quotient. We denote it by x/y. We are going to show that $x/y = c/a$.

Our first lemma is valid for arbitrary lattices.

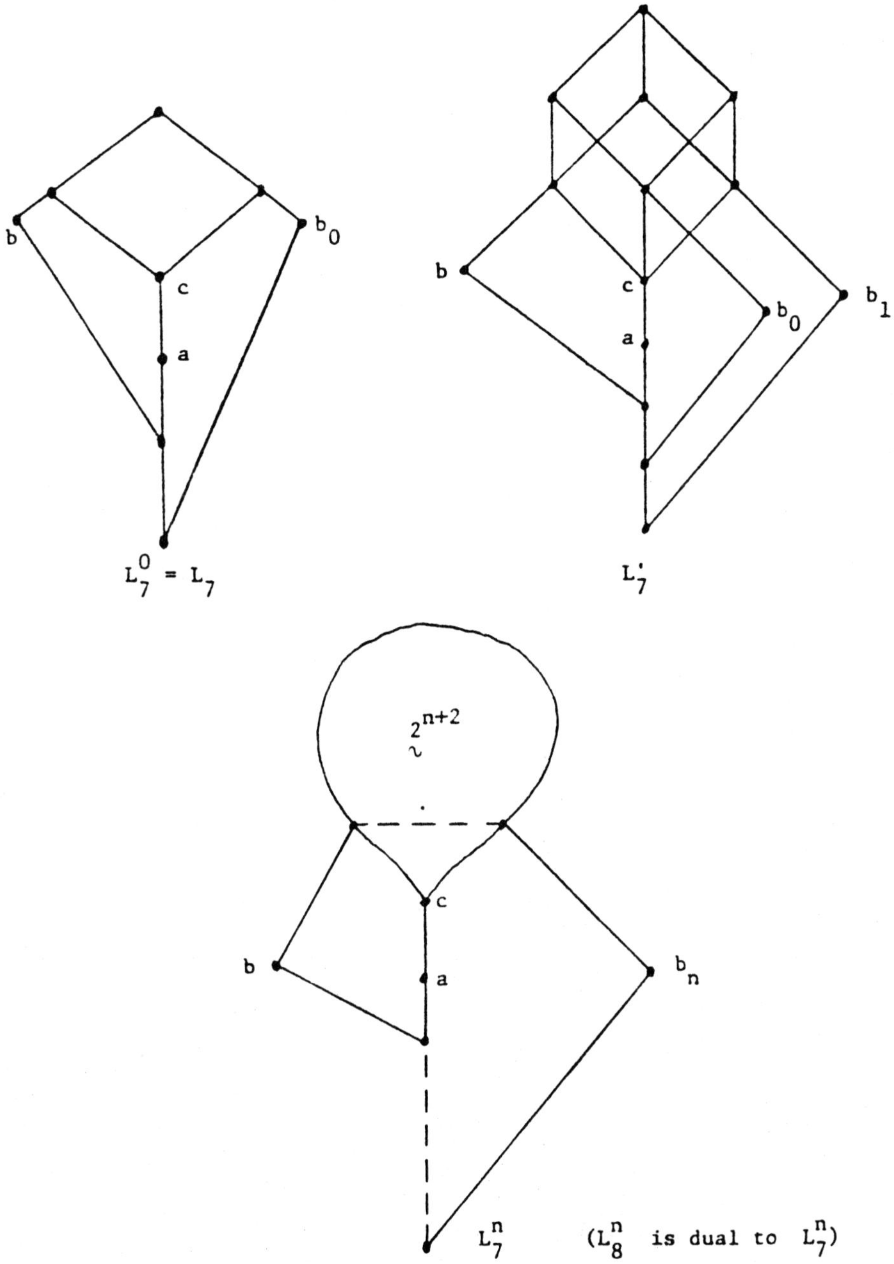

Figure 3.1

Lemma 3.3.1. For $a \leq a' < c$, the quotient c/a' is an L_7^k-quotient.

Proof. Trivial.

Lemma 3.3.2. Let $N(u/v, z)$ be a sublattice of L, and assume that u/v transposes down onto a quotient p/q. Then

(i) For any $t \in u/v$, $tp + v = t$. Hence, if v is comparable with x or y, then $u/v \searrow_\beta p/q$.

(ii) If for some $z_0 \in L$ we have $N(u/vz, z_0)$ (especially, if u/v is a subquotient of L_7-quotient), then $u/v \searrow_\beta p/q$.

Proof. (i) Since $L_i \notin \{L\}^V$ for $i \in \{6,8,9,10\}$, the equality $tp + v = t$ follows from Lemma 1.2.6. Suppose that v is comparable with x or y. To prove that $u/v \searrow_\beta p/q$ we just observe that the failure of the equality $(t' + v)p = t'$ for $t' \in p/q$ implies $N(t'/(t' + v)p, v)$. However, this leads to a contradiction since $N(x/y, v)$ (see Corollary 1.2.8). (ii) By virtue of the Lemma 1.2.6 it suffices to show that for $s \in p + (q+z)v/v(q+z)$ $(s + v)(q + z) = s$. This equality holds indeed, since its failure would oimply $L_6((s+v)(q+z)/s, v, z_0)$.

Lemma 3.3.3. Let $N(u/v, z)$ be a sublattice of L, and assume that $p/q \searrow r/s \nearrow u/v$. Then $p/q \nearrow (p+u)/(q+v) \searrow u/v$.

Proof. Since $s = rq = rv = r(q + v)$, but $s \neq r = r(p + u)$, the quotient $(p+u)/(q+v)$ must be nontrivial. Since $v = s + v = ru(q+v) + v$, it follows from the part (i) of the preceding lemma that $u(q + v) = v$. Similarly, $p(q + v) = q$. Finally, $u + (q + v) = u + r + (q + v) = u + q + r + v = u + p$, and similarly $p + (q + u) = p + u$.

Lemma 3.3.4. Let $L_7(u/v, z, z_0)$ be a sublattice of L, and assume that $x \in u/v$ or $y \in u/v$. Then $v \leq y < x = u$ and $L_7(x/y, z, z_0)$.

Proof. If x or y belongs to u/v, then since $N(x/y, z)$ and $N(x/y, z_0)$, we have $uz = yz < y < x < x + z = u + z$ and $uz_0 = yz_0 < y < x < x + z_0 = u + z_0$. Thus $u = (u + z)(u + z_0) \geq x$. Suppose that $u > x$, and consider a shortest possible sequence

$$x/y = x_0/y_0 \sim_w x_1/y_1 \sim_w \cdots \sim_w x_n/y_n = u/x. \tag{1}$$

As in the proof of Lemma 1.2.10, we have $n \geq 3$ and $x_{n-2}/y_{n-2} \searrow_w x_{n-1}/y_{n-1} \nearrow_w u/x$. Put $x'_{n-2} = x_{n-3} + y_{n-2}$

$$x'_{n-1} = x'_{n-2}x_{n-1}$$

$$y'_{n-1} = y_{n-2}x_{n-1}$$

$$u' = x'_{n-1} + x$$
$$x' = y_{n-1} + x$$

It follows from Lemma 3.3.2 that the intervals x'_{n-1}/y'_{n-1} and u'/x' are nontrivial and $x'_{n-2}/y_{n-2} \searrow x'_{n-1}/y'_{n-1} \nearrow u'/x'$. By the preceding lemma $x'_{n-3}/y_{n-3} \nearrow (x'_{n-3} + u')/(y_{n-3} + x') \searrow u'/x'$. This implies that the sequence (1) can be shortened which contradicts our choice of n. Thus $u = x$, and since y is the only dual cover of x, we have $v \leq y$. Thus, by Lemma 3.3.1 $L_7(x/y, z, z_0)$.

<u>Lemma 3.3.5</u>. Let $L_7(u/v, z, z_0)$ be a sublattice of L, and assume that x/y projects weakly onto a nontrivial subquotient p/q of u/v in three steps. Then $v \leq y < x = u$ and $L_7(x/y, z, z_0)$.

<u>Proof</u>. Suppose that for some quotients x_1/y_1 and x_2/y_2 of L we have $x/y \sim_w x_1/y_1 \sim_w x_2/y_2 \sim_w p/q$. Without loss of generality, we may assume that x_2/y_2 transposes onto p/q. We are going to show that $x \in u/v$. The result will then follow from the preceding lemma.

If $x/y \nearrow_w x_1/y_1 \searrow_w x_2/y_2 \nearrow p/q$, then since x/y is the only critical quotient of L we have $y_1 = y < x \leq x_1$. Letting $y'_2 = x_2 y$, $q' = y'_2 + q$ and applying both parts of Lemma 3.3.2 we get that $x'/y \searrow_\beta x_2/y'_2 \nearrow_\beta p/q'$. Again, using the fact that x/y is the only critical quotient of L we infer that $q' = y < x \leq p$. Thus $x \in u/v$.

Now suppose that $x/y \searrow_w x_1/y_1 \nearrow_w x_2/y_2 \searrow p/q$. Then $x_1 = x > y \geq y_1$. Put $x'_2 = x_1 + y_2$ and $p' = x'_2 p$. By Lemma 3.3.2 (i) $x'_2 = y_2 + p'$, and therefore $x/y_1 \nearrow x'_2/y_2 \searrow p'/q$. Since $x'_2 = y_2 + (x + q) = y_2 + (p' + y_1) = y_2 + (x + q)(p' + y_1)$, but $y_1 + q \leq y_2$, the interval $(x+q)(p'+y_1)/(y_1+q)$ must be nontrivial. Put $p'' = (x + q)(p' + y_1)p'$. Since $N(p'/q, z)$ and $(p'+y_1)/(y_1+q) \searrow p'/q$ by Corollary 1.2.5 $N((p'+y_1)/(y_1+q),z)$. By Lemma 3.3.2 (i) $(x + q)(p' + y_1) = (y_1 + q) + p''$ and therefore $(x+q)(p' + y_1)$ $(y_1+q) \searrow p''/q$. We have

$$(x + q)(p' + y_1) = x + q \tag{1}$$

or

$$(x + q)(p' + y_1) < x + q. \tag{2}$$

Suppose that (1) holds. Then the elements $xp'' + y_1$, $xp'' + q$ and $q + y_1$ generate a lattice K which is a homomorphic image of the lattice in Figure 3.2.A. We claim that $x = xp'' + y_1$. Suppose the contrary. Then K must be isomorphic to the lattice in Figure 3.2.A. Indeed since, $x + q >$ $y_1 + q$ we would have otherwise $xp'' + q = x + q$ or $xp'' + y_1 = x + q$, in either case implying $x = xp'' + y_1$. However, this leads to a contradiction since $K \cup \{x\}$ is isomorphic to L_{14}. Thus $x = xp'' + y_1$. This implies $x/y_1 \searrow_\beta xp''/y_1q \nearrow_\beta (xp'' + q)/q$ (Lemma 3.3.2 (i) and (ii)), and therefore $x \in u/v$.

Finally, suppose that (2) holds. We have $p'/q \nearrow x_2'/y_2 \searrow (x+q)/y_2(x+q)$ and therefore by Corollary 1.2.5 $N((x+q)/y_2(x+q),d)$ for $d \in \{z,z_o\}$. Thus by Lemma 1.2.4 the elements $x + q$, y_2 and d generate a sublattice of L which is a homomorphic image of the lattice in Figure 3.2.B. Put $r = y_2(x + q + d) + (x + q)(p' + y_1)$. Since $L_6, L_8, L_{10} \notin \{L\}^V$ we have $y_2(x+q+d) + (x+q)/y_2(x+q+d) \searrow_\beta (x+q)/y_2(x+q)$ (Lemma 1.2.6). This together with $(x + q)(p' + y_1) < x + q$ and $y_1 + q < (x + q)(p' + y_1) \leq r$ implies $r < r + x + q = r + x$. Since $(r+x)/r$ is a subquotient of L_7-quotient (see Figure 3.2.B), it follows from Lemma 3.3.2 (ii) that $x/rx \nearrow_\beta (r+x)/r$. Thus $x_2'(x + q + d) \geq x > r$, and by the preceding lemma $x = x_2'(x + q + d) \geq x+q \geq q$. To prove that $x \in u/v$ it suffices to show that $x \leq q + d$. Observe that if $x_2' = x$, then $x/y_2 \searrow_\beta p'/q$ (Lemma 3.3.2 (i)), and therefore $x = p'$. Suppose that $x_2' > x$. Then $N(x/y, y_2)$. If $x \not\leq q + d$, then since $N(x/y, d)$ the elements x and $q + d$ must be noncomparable. Thus $N(x/y,(q + d))$. However, this leads to a contradiction since the elements x, y_2 and $q + d$ generate L_{15} (see Figure 3.2.C). The lemma is proven.

<u>Lemma 3.3.6</u>. Suppose that $N(u/v, z)$ is a sublattice of L. Then x/y projects weakly onto a subquotient of u/v in three (or less) steps.

<u>Proof</u>. For $n \geq 4$, consider a shortest possible sequence

$$x/y = x_o/y_o \sim_w x_1/y_1 \sim_w \cdots \sim_w x_n/y_n = u/v. \tag{1}$$

It follows from the Corollary 1.2.5, that if p/q is a nontrivial subquotient of x_i/y_i $(i \leq n)$ then $N(p/q, z)$.

If $x/y \nearrow_w x_1/y_1 \searrow_w x_2/y_2 \nearrow_w x_3/y_3 \searrow_w x_4/y_4$, then $y_1 = y < x \leq x_1$ because x/y is the only critical quotient of L. By Lemma 3.3.2 (i) $x_1/y \searrow_\beta x_2/yx_2$, and therefore $y_2 \leq y < x \leq x_2$. It follows from another application of Lemma 3.3.2 (i) that $x + y_3 = (x + y_3)x_4 + y_3$. Thus $x/y_2 \nearrow (x+y_3)/y_3 \searrow_w (x+y_3)x_4/y_4$, and therefore the sequence (1) can be shortened by one step.

Now suppose that $x/y \searrow_w x_1/y_1 \nearrow_w x_2/y_2 \searrow_w x_3/y_3 \nearrow_w x_4/y_4$. Then $x_1 = x > y \geq y_1$. Put

$$x_2' = x + y_2$$
$$x_3' = x_2'x_3$$
$$y_3' = y_2x_3$$
$$x_4' = x_3' + y_4$$
$$y_4' = y_3' + y_4$$

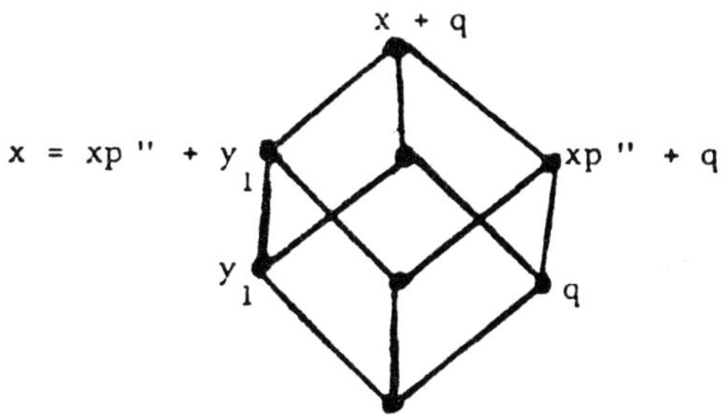

A

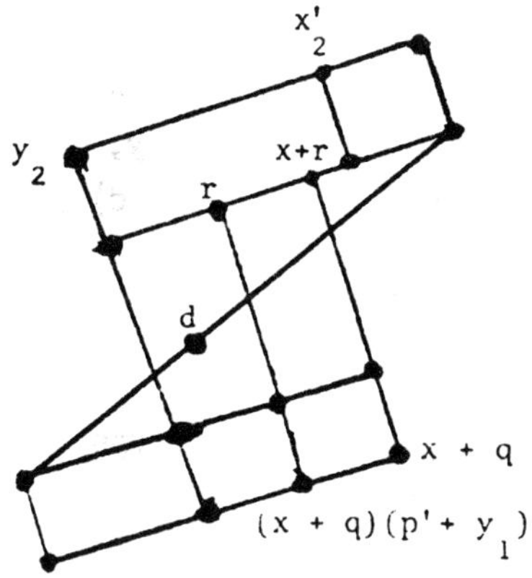

B

$r = y_2(x + q + d) + (x + q)(p' + y_1)$

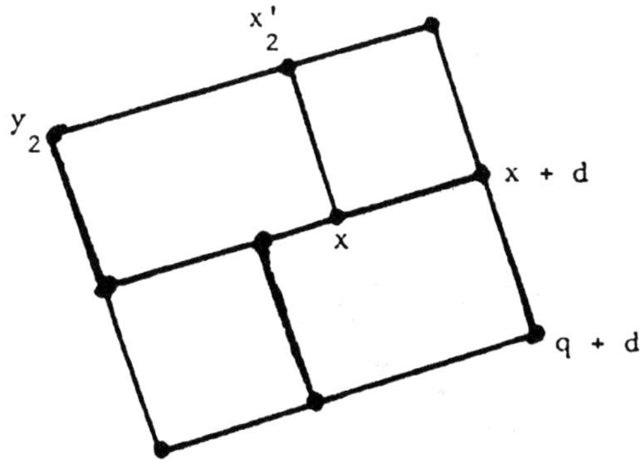

C

Figure 3.2

We have

$$x_4' = y_4' \tag{α}$$

or

$$x_4' > y_4' \tag{β}$$

Assume that (α) holds. By Lemma 1.2.4 the elements x_3', y_4 and z generate a lattice which is a homomorphic image of the lattice in Figure 3.3. Since $L_6, L_8, L_{10} \notin \{L\}^V$, it follows from Lemma 1.2.6 that $y_4(y_3+z) + x_3'/y_4(y_3+z) \searrow_\beta x_3'/y_3$. Letting $r = y_4(y_3 + z) + x_3'$ and $s = y_4(y_3 + z) + y_3'$ we have $x_2'/y_2 \searrow x_3'/y_3' \nearrow r/s$. It follows from the application of the Lemma 3.3.3 that $x/y_1 \nearrow (x+z)/(y_1+s) \searrow r/s$. Since r/s is a subquotient of L_7-quotient (see Figure 3.3) by the preceding lemma $s \leq y < x = x_3'(y_3 + z)$, and therefore x/y can be projected weakly onto x_4/y_4 in two steps.

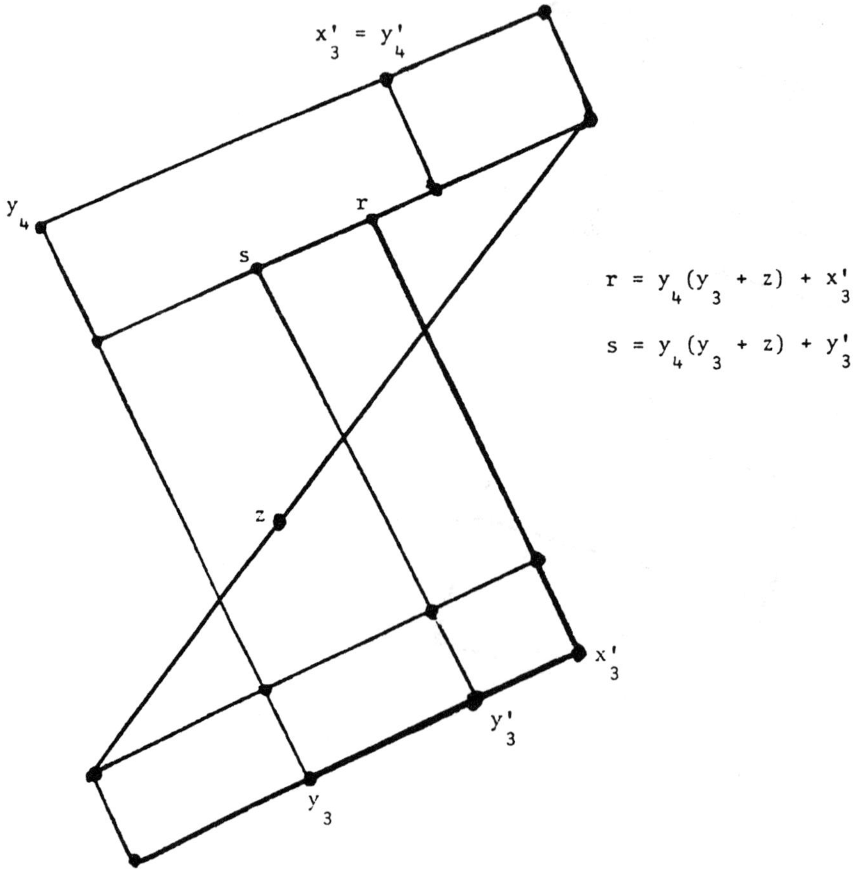

Figure 3.3

Now assume that (β) holds. If $y_3' = x_3y_4'$, then $x_2/y_2 \searrow x_3'/y_3' \nearrow x_4'/y_4'$. Again applying Lemma 3.3.3 we get that $x/y_1 \nearrow (x+x_4')/(y_1+y_4') \searrow x_4'/y_4'$, and therefore the sequence (1) can be shortened.

Finally, letting $f = x_3'y_4'$, we assume that $f > y_3'$. The case $x_2' = y_2 + f$ is similar to (α) since here we have $x/y' \nearrow x_2'/y_2' \searrow f/y_3'$ and f/y_3' is a lower transpose of a subquotient of $y_4'(y_3+z)/y_4(y_3+z) + y_3'$ which is an L_7-quotient. If $x_2' > y_2 + f$, then $f = x_3'(y_2 + f)$. Indeed, since $N(f/y_3',y_4)$ and $f/y_3' \nearrow (y_2+f)/y_2 \searrow x_3'(y_2+f)/y_3'$, by Corollary 1.2.5 $N(x_3'(y_2+f)/y_3', y_4)$, implying $y_4' = f + y_4 = x_3'(y_2 + f) + y_4 \geq x_3'(y_2 + f)$. Thus $f = x_3'y_4' \geq x_3'(y_2 + f) \geq f$. We have $x/x(y_2 + f) \nearrow x_2'/(y_2 + f) \searrow x_3'/f \nearrow x_4'/y_4'$, and again, by Lemma 3.3.3 $x/x(y_2 + f) \nearrow (x_2'+x_4')/(y_2 + f) + y_4' \searrow x_4'/y_4'$. The lemma is proven.

Corollary 3.3.7. (i) If u/v is an L_7-quotient of L, then $v \leq y < x = u$; (ii) $x/y = c/a$.

Proof. (i) Since u/v is an N-quotient, by the preceding lemma x/y projects weakly onto u/v in three steps. The result follows from Lemma 3.3.5. (ii) Since c/a is an L_7-quotient, by (i) $a \leq y < x = c$. Suppose that $y > a$. It follows from the other application of the preceding lemma and Lemma 3.3.5 that $x \leq y$, a contradiction.

We complete the proof of the Proposition 3.3 by showing that none of the proper epimorphic images of L have L_7^k-quotients. So, suppose that for some $u, v, d, d_0, \ldots, d_k \in L$ and $\Theta \in \mathrm{Con}(L)$ with $\mathrm{Con}(a,c) \subseteq \Theta$ we have $L_7^k(u'/v', d', d', \ldots, d_k')$ in L/Θ (for $s \in L$, $s' = s/\Theta$). Let A be a sublattice of L generated by the set $\{u, v, d, d, \ldots, d_k\}$. It follows from the Theorem 6.2.10 below that L_7^k is a splitting lattice, and therefore $L_7^k(u'/v', d', d_0', \ldots, d_k')$ is a boundedepimorphic image of A (see Theorem 0.2.5). Denote by $\bar{s}$ the largest element of $s' \in A/\Theta$. We shall show that $L_7^k(c/c\bar{v}, \bar{d}\ \bar{d}_0, \ldots, \bar{d}_k)$ in A. Let X be a sublattice of $L_7^k(u'/v', d', d', \ldots, d_k')$ isomorphic to L_7. Then $u' \in X$. Since L_7 is a projective lattice (see Example 1.4.6) X is embeddable in A. By the preceding corollary, the image of u' for this embedding is c. Since the map $s' \to \bar{s}$ is order preserving we have $c > c\bar{v} > c\bar{d} > c\bar{d}_0 > \ldots > c\bar{d}_k$. On the other hand, for $f', g' \in \{d', d_0', \ldots, d_k'\}$, if $u'f' > u'g'$, then $L_7(c/v_0,f,g)$ for some v_0, $f, g \in A$. This implies $c < (v_0 + f), (cf + g)$. Hence $c < (c\bar{v} + \bar{f})$, $(c\bar{f} + \bar{g})$, and therefore $L_7(c/c\bar{v},\bar{f},\bar{g})$. Since $[c)$ is a distributive sublattice of L (Corollary 1.2.9) the elements $c + \bar{d}, c + \bar{d}_0, \ldots, c + \bar{d}_k$ generate a Boolean algebra. Thus $L_7^k(c/c\bar{v}, \bar{d}, \bar{d}_0, \ldots, \bar{d}_k)$. However $c/c\bar{v} \neq c/a$ because $\mathrm{Con}(a,c) \subseteq \Theta$. This contradiction completes the proof.

Proof of Proposition 3.4.

Lemma 3.4.1. If $c \leq v < u$, then there is no $z \in L$ such that $N(u/v,z)$.

Proof. Suppose the contrary. Consider a shortest possible sequence

$$c/a = x_0/y_0 \sim_w x_1/y_0 \sim_w \cdots \sim_w x_n/y_n = u/v. \qquad (\alpha)$$

As in the proof of the Lemma 1.2.10 $n \geq 3$ and $x_{n-2}/y_{n-2} \searrow_w x_{n-1}/y_{n-1} \nearrow_w u/v$. We may assume that u covers v. Then $x_{n-1}/y_{n-1} \nearrow u/v$. Since $v \geq c$, it follows from the Corollary 1.2.8 that x_{n-1} covers y_{n-1}. Thus $x_{n-2}/y_{n-2} \searrow x_{n-1}/y_{n-1}$. Since $N(x_{n-2}/y_{n-2},z)$ (Corollary 1.2.5), it follows from the Lemma 3.3.2 (i) that the interval x_{n-2}/y_{n-2} is prime. Thus by the dual of Corollary 1.2.3 the sequence (α) can be shortened which contradicts our choice of n. The lemma is proven.

Let $b, b_0, \ldots, b_k \in L$ such that $L_7^k(c/a, b, b_0, \ldots, b_k)$. For the Lemmas 3.4.2 - 3.4.5 below, we suppose that there exists $e \in \{b, b_0, \ldots, b_k\}$ such that for any $d \in \{b, b_0, \ldots, e\}$

(1) $(a+d)/ad = c/a \cup \{a+d, d, ab, ab_0, \ldots, ad\}$;

(2) If $t \in a/ad$ then every cover of t in L belongs to either $c/ad - \{ad\}$ or $\{b, b_0, \ldots, d\}$;

(3) If $s \in ((a+d)/ad - \{ad\})$, then every dual cover of s in L belongs to $(a+d)/ad$.

Lemma 3.4.2. Suppose that $N(c/a, z)$ for $z \notin \{b, b_0, \ldots, e\}$. Then $L_7(c/a,e,z)$. Hence $L_7^{i+1}(c/a, b, b_0, \ldots, b_i,z)$ if $e = b_i$ $(i \leq k)$.

Proof. For $d \in \{b, b_0, \ldots, e\}$ we have $(a + d)z < ad$. To avoid L_6 the element $ad + z = c + z$ must be noncomparable with $a + d$. Thus $L_7(c/a,d,z)$. Since $[c)$ is a distributive sublattice of L (Corollary 1.2.9), the elements $a + b, a + b_0, \ldots, a + e, a + z$ generate a Boolean algebra, and therefore $L_7^{i+1}(c/a, b, b_0, \ldots, b_i,z)$.

Lemma 3.4.3. Suppose that $N(u/v,z)$ and $u/v \not\subseteq c/ad$ for $d \in \{b, b_0, \ldots, e\}$. Then there exists $x \in L$ such that $N(ae/x,z)$.

Proof. Consider a sequence

$$c/a = x_0/y_0 \sim_w x_1/y_1 \sim_w \cdots \sim_w x_n/y_n = u/v.$$

Since for $d \in \{b, b_0, \ldots, e\}$ $c/a \subseteq (a+d)/ad$ and $u/v \not\subseteq (a+d)/ad$ there is an index $i < n$ such that $x_{i+1}/y_{i+1} \not\subseteq (a+d)/ad$ and $x_i/y_i \subseteq (a+f)/af$ for some $f \in \{b, b_0, \ldots, e\}$. Because $N(x_{i+1}/y_{i+1},z)$ (Corollary 1.2.5) for $y_{i+1} \leq q < p \leq x_{i+1}$ we have $N(p/q,z)$. Suppose that $x \in x_{i+1}/y_{i+1}$ such that $x \notin (a+d)/ad$ for $d \in \{b, b_0, \ldots, e\}$. If for some $y \in x_i/y_i$, $y < x$, then using (1), (2) and (3) on page 42, one can easily show that there exists

$y' \in x_{i+1}/y_{i+1}$ with $c \le y' < x$, and therefore $N(x/y',z)$ contradicting Lemma 4.4.1. This implies that x_{i+1}/y_{i+1} is a lower weak transpose of x_i/y_i. Again by (1), (2) and (3) $y_i x_{i+1} \ge ae > x \ge y_{i+1}$, from which the desired result readily follows.

Lemma 3.4.4. Suppose that x is a dual cover of ae in L. Then there exists $z \in L$ such that the following holds:

(i) $L_7(c/a,e,z)$ and $L_7^{i+1}(c/a,b,b_0,\ldots,b_i,z)$ if $e = b_i$ $(i \le k)$;

(ii) $(a+z)/az = c/ae \cup \{z, a+z, az\}$;

(iii) c and z are the only dual covers of $a + z$;

(iv) ae and z are the only covers of az;

(v) ae is join irreducible;

(vi) z is doubly irreducible.

Proof. (i) By the dual of Lemma 1.3.1 there exists $z \in L$ such that $N(c/a,z)$ and $x = az$. Since clearly $z \notin \{b, b_0, \ldots, e\}$, (i) follows from Lemma 3.4.2.

(ii) We may assume that z covers x. Since for $z < f < a + z$ we would have $N(f/z,a)$ contrary to the Corollary 1.2.8, the interval $(a+z)/z$ must be prime. The interval $(a+z)/c$ also is prime because for $c < f < a + z$ would imply $N(f/c,z)$ contradicting Lemma 3.4.1. Since L excludes diamond we infer that (ii) holds.

(iii) If $z_0 \notin \{c,z\}$ is a dual cover of $a + z$, then $N(c/ae,z_0)$. As in the proof of Lemma 1.3.5 one can show that the elements c, ae, z and z_0 generate L_{14}.

(iv) is dual to (iii).

(v) Let $y \ne x$ be a dual cover of ae. By the dual of Lemma 1.3.1 there exists $z_0 \in L$ such that $y = az_0$ and $N(c/a,z_0)$. Hence $N(c/ae,z_0)$. As in the proof of the dual of Lemma 1.3.5 one can show that L includes at least one of the lattices L_8, L_{14} or L_{15}.

(vi) Suppose that $f \ne a + z$ is a cover of z and consider a shortest possible sequence

$$c/a = x_0/y_0 \sim_w x_1/y_1 \sim_w \cdots \sim_w x_n/y_n = f/z. \qquad (\alpha)$$

Since f and z are both noncomparable with a and c we have $n \ge 3$.

Suppose that $x_{n-2}/y_{n-2} \nearrow_w x_{n-1}/y_{n-1} \searrow f/z$. Since by (v) az is the only dual cover of ae, and $z \le f$, y_{n-1}, it follows from the preceding lemma that for $u,v,z \in L$, $N(u/v,z)$ and $z \in \{f, y_{n-1}\}$ implies $u/v \subseteq (a+d)/ad$ for some $d \in \{b, b_0, \ldots, e\}$. Thus, because none of the elements of $(a+d)/ad$ is comparable with z, the interval x_{n-1}/y_{n-1} must be prime. Whence $x_{n-2}/y_{n-2} \nearrow x_{n-1}/y_{n-1}$. If $u \in x_{n-2}/y_{n-2}$, then $uf = az \le z \le y_{n-1}$. However, this contradicts the semidistributivity since $x_{n-1} = y_{n-1} + u = y_{n-1} + f$ but $x_{n-1} \neq y_{n-1} = y_{n-1} + uf$. Thus $x_{n-2}/y_{n-2} \nearrow_\beta x_{n-1}/y_{n-1} \searrow_\beta f/z$. It follows from the Corollary 1.2.3 that the sequence (α) can be shortened contradicting our choice of n.

Now assume that $x_{n-2}/y_{n-2} \searrow_w x_{n-1}/y_{n-1} \nearrow f/z$. Since for $d \in \{b, b_o, \ldots, e\}$ none of the elements of $(a+d)/ad$ are comparable with f, it follows from (v), the preceding lemma and $f \geq az$ that the interval x_{n-1}/y_{n-1} is prime. Whence $x_{n-2}/y_{n-2} \searrow x_{n-1}/y_{n-1}$. Suppose that $g \in x_{n-2}/y_{n-2}$ where $g \in (a+d)/ad$ for some $d \in \{b, b_o, \ldots, e\}$. Then $y_{n-1} = gx_{n-1} \leq az$. Moreover, $y_{n-1} \neq az$. Indeed since ae is the only cover of az different from z the contrary assumption would imply $ae = x_{n-1} \leq f$. Thus $N(z/az, x_{n-1})$ implying $N((a+z)/c, x_{n-1})$ (Corollary 1.2.5). However this contradicts Lemma 3.4.1. Thus $g \notin (a+d)/ad$. If $x_{n-2} < g < x_{n-2}$, then $N(g/x_{n-2}, x_{n-1})$. By the preceding lemma $N(ae/az, x_{n-1})$ implying $f = x_{n-1} + az = x_{n-1} + ae \geq ae$ a contradiction. Thus $x_{n-2}/y_{n-2} \searrow_\beta x_{n-1}/y_{n-1} \nearrow_\beta f/z$. It follows from the dual of Corollary 1.2.3 that the sequence (α) can be shortened which contradicts our choice of n. Thus z is meet irreducible.

Finally, assume that $h \neq az$ is a dual cover of z, and consider a shortest possible sequence.

$$c/a = x_o/y_o \sim_w x_1/y_1 \sim_w \cdots \sim_w x_n/y_n = z/h.$$

As before $n \geq 3$. If $x_{n-1}/y_{n-1} \searrow z/h$, then since clearly $h \notin \{b, b_o, \ldots, e\}$ and because $a + z$ is the only cover of z, we have $N((a+z)/z, x_{n-1})$, and therefore $N(c/az, x_{n-1})$ (Corollary 1.2.5), implying that the elements a, c, z and y_{n-1} generate L_{10}.

Thus $x_{n-2}/y_{n-2} \searrow_w x_{n-1}/y_{n-1} \nearrow z/h$. As before, using the preceding lemma, semidistributivity and the dual of Corollary 1.2.3 one can easily show that this leads to contradiction. (We leave the details for the reader.) This completes the proof of (vi) and the proof of the lemma.

<u>Lemma 3.4.5</u>. Let $g = b_o$ if $e = b$ and $g = b_{i+1}$ if $e = b_i$ $(i < k)$. The g can be chosen so that (1), (2) and (3) holds (see pg. 42).

<u>Proof</u>. Apply the preceding lemma with $x \geq ag$, replace z by g and use Lemma 3.4.2 if $g \neq b_k$.

<u>Lemma 3.4.6</u>. The element b can be chosen so that (1), (2) and (3) holds.

<u>Proof</u>. Let $x \geq ab$ be a dual cover of a. By the dual of Lemma 1.3.1 there exists $b' \in L$ such that $N(c/a, b')$ and $x = ab'$. We may assume that b' covers x. To prove the lemma it suffices to show that:

(i) $N(c/a,b') = (a+b')/ab'$;

(ii) a is join irreducible;

(iii) c and b' are the only dual covers of $a + b'$, and a and b' are the only covers of ab';

(iv) b' is doubly irreducible;

(v) $L_7^k(c/a, b', b_0, \ldots, b_k)$.

To prove (i) first observe that $a + b'$ must cover b' since for $b' < f < a + b'$ we would otherwise have $N(b'/f,a)$ contradicting Corollary 1.2.8. Since L excludes L_8 by the dual of Corollary 1.3.3 the interval $(a+b')/c$ must be prime. Thus since the diamond is also excluded we infer that (i) holds.

(ii) follows from the dual of Lemma 1.3.7.

(iii) follows from the Corollary 1.3.6 and its dual.

(iv) follows from the Lemma 1.3.9 and its dual.

(v) Since $ab \leq ab' < a < c$ we have $N(c/ab',b_i)$ for $0 \leq i \leq k$. By Corollary 1.2.5 $N((a+b')/b',b_i)$. Thus $L_7(c/a,b',b_i)$, and therefore $L_7^k(c/a, b', b_0, \ldots, b_k)$. The lemma is proven.

We are now ready to complete the proof of Proposition 3.4. It follows from the preceding lemma and Lemma 3.4.5 that the elements $b, b_0, \ldots, b_k$ can be chosen so that (1), (2) and (3) holds for any $e \in \{b, b_0, \ldots, b_k\}$. To prove that c/a is an L_7^{k+1}-quotient, by Lemma 3.4.2 it suffices to show that for some $z \notin \{b, b_0, \ldots, b_k\}$ we have $N(c/a,z)$. Since $L \neq L_7^k$ there exists $u \in L$ such that $u \notin L_7^k(c/a, b, b_0, \ldots, b_k)$ and either u is a dual cover of ae or u covers some $v \in (b + b_0 + \ldots + b_k)/c$. The result follows from the Lemma 1.3.1 or its dual.

Proof of Theorem 3.2.* Let L and c/a be as in Proposition 3.3, and assume that L is finitely generated. For $0 \leq m < \omega$ we shall write $P_{(m)}$ if $L_7^m \in \{L\}^V$ implies that L includes L_7^m, and $T_{(m)}$ if $\{L_7^{m+1}\}^V$ is the only join irreducible cover of $\{L_7^m\}^V$. We claim that

$$\text{For } n \geq 1, \text{ if } P_{(m)} \text{ and } T_{(m)} \ (m < n), \text{ then } P_{(n)} \text{ and } T_{(n)}. \qquad (\alpha)$$

To prove (α) first suppose that $L_7^n \in \{L\}^V$ and L does not have L_7^n-quotients. Then $P_{(n-1)}$ together wity Proposition 3.3 imply that c/a is the only L_7^{n-1}-quotient of L. Let $\{A_i\}_{i\in I}$ be a collection of subdirectly irreducible epimorphic images of $L/\mathrm{Con}(a,c)$ such that $\{A_i\}_{i\in I}^V = \{L/\mathrm{Con}(a,c)\}^V$. Since for any $i \in I$, A_i is a proper epimorphic image of L, by Proposition 3.3 A_i does not have L_7^{n-1}-quotients. This together with

*Because L_7^n is not projective for $n > 0$, the proof of Theorem 3.2 differs from that of Theorem 2.2.

$P_{(m)}$ and $T_{(m)}$ $(m < n)$ implies that $A_i \in \{L_7^{n-1}\}^V$ for any $i \in I$. Thus $L/\mathrm{Con}\,(a,c) \in \{L_7^{n-1}\}^V$ and therefore by Lemma 1.2.11 L is a finite lattice. On the other hand, because $L_7^n \in \{L\}^V$ we have that $L \neq L_7^{n-1}$. However this contradicts Proposition 3.4. Thus $P_{(n)}$ holds.

Now suppose that the variety $\{L_7^n\}^V$ has a join irreducible cover $V \neq \{L_7^{n+1}\}^V$. Since V has a finite height in Λ, it is strictly join irreducible. It follows from Theorem 0.1.8 that $V = \{L\}^V$ for some finitely generated subdirectly irreducible lattice L. Since $P_{(n)}$ holds, L_7^n is a sublattice of L. By the Proposition 3.3 c/a is the only L_7^n-quotient of L and none of the proper homomorphic images of L have L_7^n-quotients. As before, one can show that this contradicts Proposition 3.4. Thus $T_{(n)}$ holds.

By virtue of (α) to complete the proof of the theorem it suffices to show that $P_{(0)}$ and $T_{(0)}$. Since L_7^0 is a projective lattice (see Example 1.4.6) $P_{(0)}$ follows from the Lemma 1.4.3, and the proof that $T_{(0)}$ holds is similar to the proof of Theorem 2.2 (see page 33).

CHAPTER 4

THE VARIETIES $\{L_9^n\}^V$ AND $\{L_{10}^n\}^V$

Since for any $n = 0,1, \ldots,$ the lattices L_9^n and L_{10}^n are mutually dual, we shall consider only the lattices L_9^n and the varieties generated by them.

Definition 4.1. We say that the quotient c/a of a lattice L is an L_9^n-quotient if for some $b, b_0, \ldots, b_n \in L$ the set $\{a,c,b,b_0, \ldots, b_n\}$ generates a sublattice of L isomorphic to L_9^n with c/a as a critical quotient (see Figure 4.1). In that case we shall write $L_9^n(c/a,b,b_0, \ldots, b_n)$.

Using Theorem 0.1.6 it is easy to check that for any $n = 0,1,\ldots$, the variety $\{L_9^n\}^V$ has at least fifteen join reducible covers, $\{L^n,M_3\}^V$, $\{L_9^n,L_1\}^V$, $\ldots$, $\{L_9^n,L_8\}^V$, $\{L_9^n,L_{10}\}^V$, $\ldots$, $\{L_9^n,L_{15}\}^V$, and at least one join irreducible cover: the variety $\{L_9^{n+1}\}^V$. It turns out that for any natural number n, the above list of covers of $\{L_9^n\}^V$ is complete. This chapter is devoted to the proof of this result.

Theorem 4.2. For any natural number n, the variety $\{L_9^n\}^V$ ($\{L_{10}^n\}^V$) has only one join irreducible cover, namely the variety $\{L_9^{n+1}\}^V$ ($\{L_{10}^n\}^V$).

The theorem is a corollary of the following two propositions.

Proposition 4.3. Let L be a subdirectly irreducible lattice and assume that the variety $\{L\}^V$ does not have the lattices M_3 and L_i ($i \in \{1,2, \ldots, 8,10, \ldots, 15\}$) as its members. Suppose further that k is a natural number such that c/a is an L_9^k-quotient of L and L does not have any L_9^{k+1}-quotients. The c/a is a critical quotient of L. Moreover, none of the proper epimorphic images of L have L_9^k-quotients.

Proposition 4.4. Let L be a finite subdirectly irreducible lattice with c/a as a critical quotient, and assume that the variety $\{L\}^V$ does not have the lattices M_3 and L_i ($i \in \{1,\ldots,8,10,\ldots,15\}$) as its members. If c/a is an L_9^k-quotient and $L \neq L_9^k$, then c/a is an L_9^{k+1}-quotient.

Proof of Proposition 4.3. By Theorem 0.2.9 the variety $\{L\}^V$ is semidistributive, and by Theorem 1.2.7 L has a unique critical quotient. We denote it by x/y. Choose $b, b_0, \ldots, b_k \in L$ such that $L_9^k(c/a,b,b_0,\ldots,b_k)$. We are going to show that $x/y = c/a$.

Our first lemma is valid for arbitrary lattices.

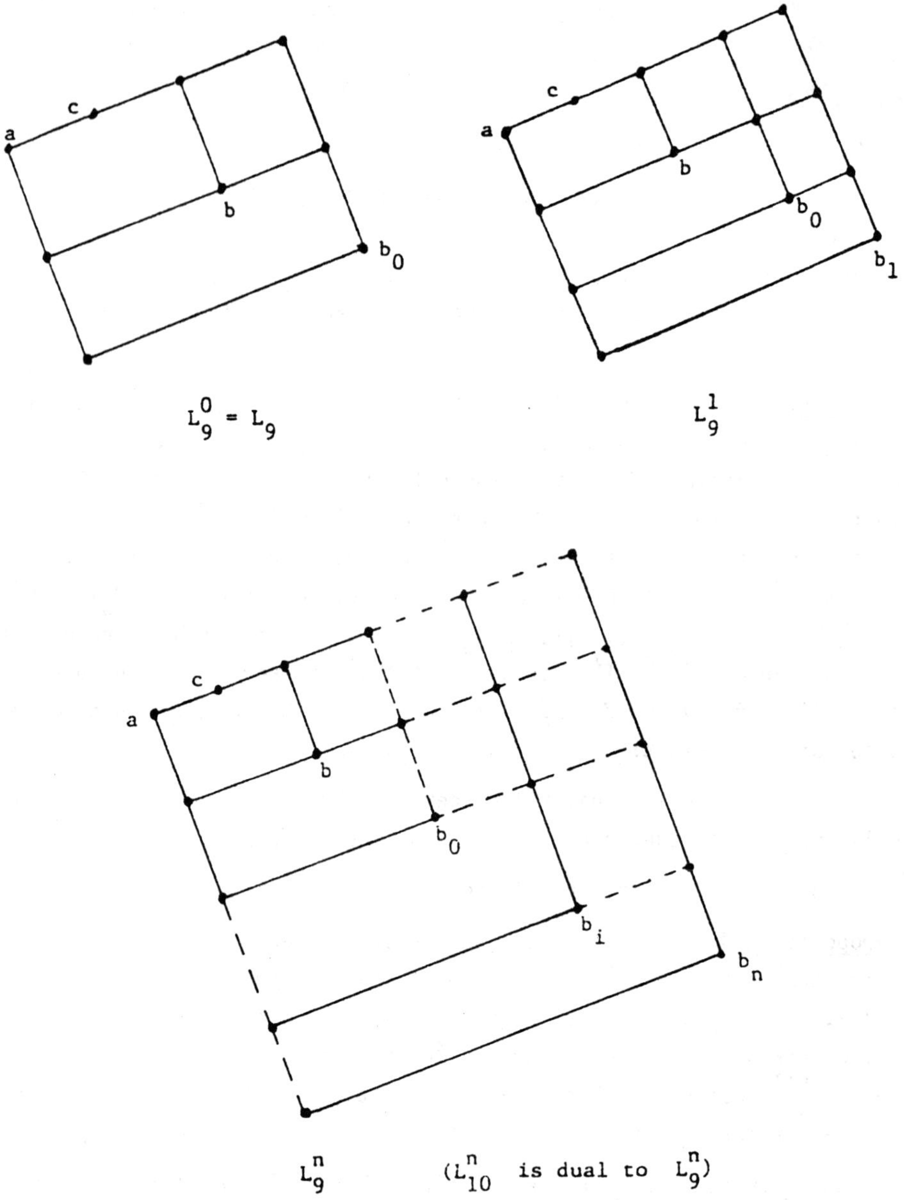

Figure 4.1

Lemma 4.3.1. Any nontrivial subquotient c'/a' of c/a is an L_9^k-quotient.

Proof. Trivial.

Lemma 4.3.2. Let $N(p/q,d)$ be a sublattice of L, and assume that p/q transposes down onto a quotient u/v. Then $p(v+d)/q(v+d) \searrow_\beta u/v$ and for $s \in u/v$, $s = (s + q)u$. Hence either $p/q \searrow_\beta u/v$ or there exists $t \in p/q$ such that $t > tu + q$.

Proof. It follows from Lemma 1.2.6 since $L_i \notin \{L\}^V$ for $i \in \{6,7,8,10\}$.

Lemma 4.3.3. Suppose that $N(p/q,d)$ and $N((q+d)/q,d_0)$ in L. If p/q transposes down onto a quotient u/v, then either this transposition is bijective, or else p/q has a subquotient which is an L_9^1-quotient.

Proof. Since $L_7, L_8 \notin \{L\}^V$, by the dual of Lemma 1.2.4 the elements q, u and d generate a lattice, which is a homomorphic image of a lattice in Figure 4.2.A. Suppose that transposition $p/q \searrow u/v$ is not bijective. Then, by the preceding lemma for some $t \in p/q$ we have $t > tu + q$.

Letting $s = tu + q$, we have $L_9(t/s,z,d)$. Put $f = p(v + d + d_0)$ and $z' = (q + d)(d + d_0)$. We are going to show that $L_9^1(t/s,f,z'd_0)$ (see Figure 4.2.F). We prove this by showing that the following holds:

(1) $q + d_0 > v + d + d_0 > d + d_0$;
(2) $v + d + d_0$ is noncomparable with $q + d$;
(3) $s(v + d + d_0) = t(v + d + d_0) < p(v + d + d_0) < (q + d)(v + d + d_0)$;
(4) $p(d + d_0) = q(d + d_0)$;
(5) For $m \in p/q$, $m(v + d + d_0) + (d + d_0) = v + d + d_0$;
(6) $p(d + d_0) < s(v + d + d_0)$;
(7) $(q + d)(v + d + d_0) = s(v + d + d_0) + (q + d)(d + d_0)$.

First observe that since $N((q+d)/q, d_0)$, $(q+d)/q \searrow d/q$ and $(q+d)/q \searrow (v + d)/r$ (see Figure 4.2.A), again by the dual of the Lemma 1.2.4 the lattice L has the sublattices which are the homomorphic images of the lattices in Figure 4.2.B and C. By the preceding lemma $z'/r' \searrow_\beta d/qd$ and $z''/r'' \searrow_\beta (v+d)/r$. Also for $t' \in d/qd$ and $t'' \in (v+d)/r$ we have $t' = (t' + q)d$ and $t'' = (t'' + q)(v + d)$.

To prove (1), assume that $d + d_0 = v + d + d_0$. Then $v + d \leq d + d_0$. Since $pd = qd$ and $z'/r' \searrow_\beta d/qd$, we have $q(d + d_0) = p(d + d_0)$ (see Figure 4.2.B). Thus $q(v + d) = q(d + d_0)(v + d) = p(d + d_0)(v + d) = p(v + d)$ which leads to a contradiction (see Figure 4.2.A). To show that $q + d_0 > v + d + d_0$, first observe that $N((q + d)/q,d_0)$ and $q \geq v$ jointly imply $q + d_0 = q + d + d_0 \geq v + d + d_0$. Suppose that $q + d + d_0 = v + d + d_0$. Since $(q+d)/q \searrow (v+d)/r$ (see Figure 4.2.A) again by the dual

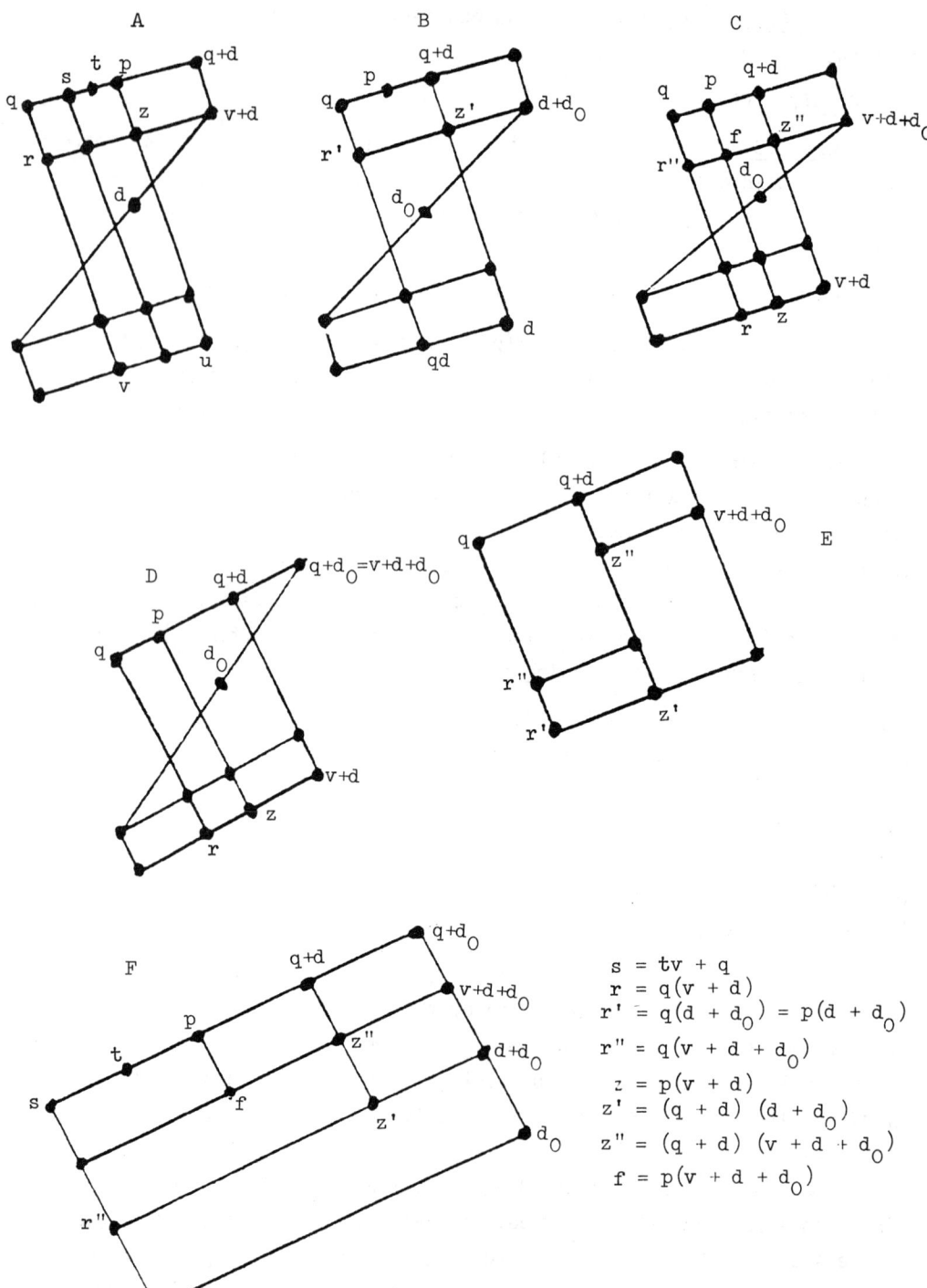

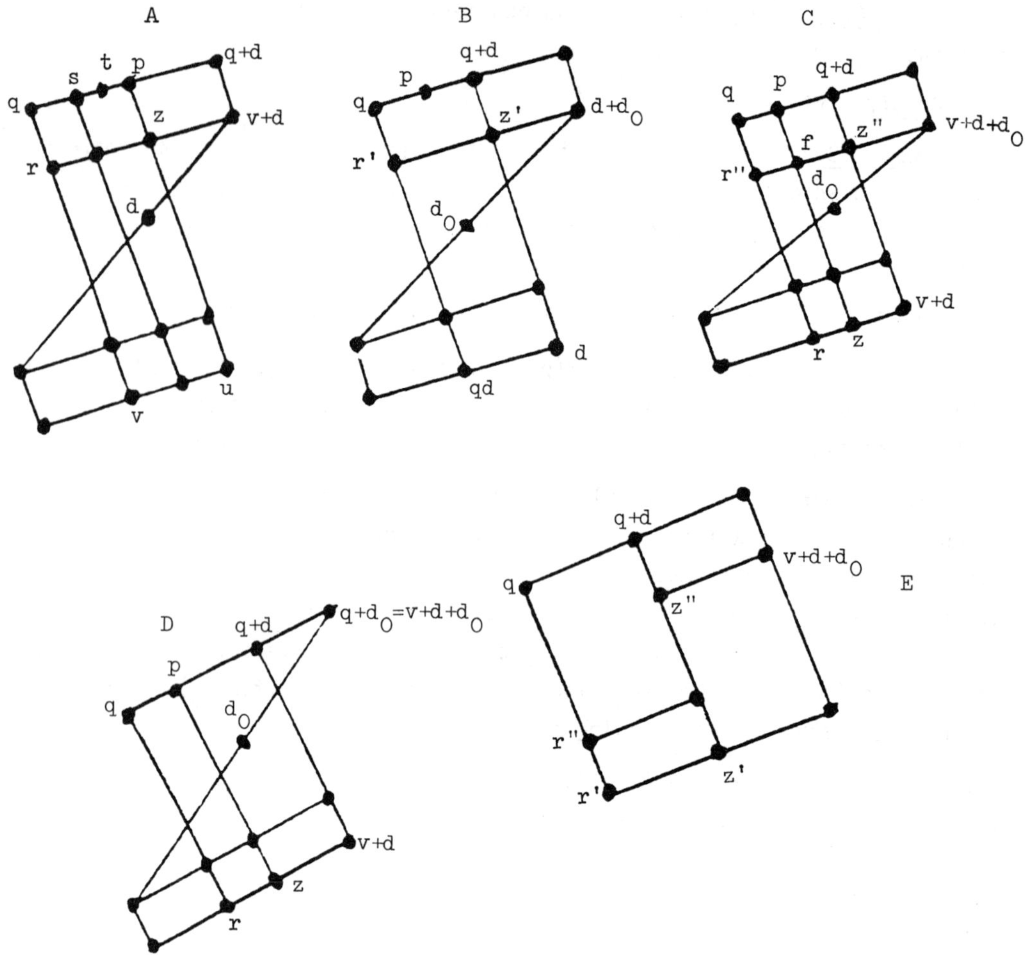

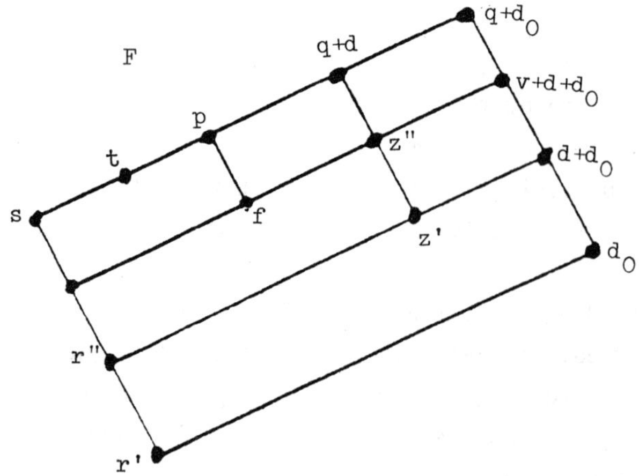

$$s = tv + q$$
$$r = q(v + d)$$
$$r' = q(d + d_0) = p(d + d_0)$$
$$r'' = q(v + d + d_0)$$
$$z = p(v + d)$$
$$z' = (q + d)\ (d + d_0)$$
$$z'' = (q + d)\ (v + d + d_0)$$
$$f = p(v + d + d_0)$$

Figure 4.2

of the Lemma 1.2.4, the elements q, $v + d$ and d_0 generate a lattice, which is a homomorphic image of the lattice in Figure 4.2.D. By the preceding lemma $(q+d)/q \searrow_\beta (v+d)/r$ implying $p/q \searrow_\beta z/r$ which contradicts our assumption. Thus (1) holds.

(2) holds since $v + d + d_0 \leq q + d$ implies $d_0 \leq q + d$ contradicting $N((q+d)/q, d_0)$ and $q + d < v + d + d_0$ implies $q + d_0 = q + d + d_0 \leq v + d + d_0$ contradicting (1).

(3) follows from $z''/r'' \searrow_\beta (v+d)/r$ and $q(v + d) \leq s(v + d) = t(v + d) < p(v + d)$ (see Figure 4.2.A and C).

(4) follows from $z'/r' \searrow_\beta d/qd$ and $qd = pd$ (see Figure 4.2.B).

(5) holds since for $m \in p/q$, $m > v$ and therefore $v + (d + d_0) \leq m(v + d + d_0) + (d + d_0) \leq v + d + d_0$.

To prove (6) observe that by (4) $p(d + d_0) = q(d + d_0) \leq q(v + d + d_0) \leq s(v + d + d_0)$. If $p(d + d_0) = q(v + d + d_0)$, then using (5) we get that $d + d_0 = p(d + d_0) + (d + d_0) = q(v + d + d_0) + (d + d_0) = v + d + d_0$ contradicting (1).

Finally, to avoid L_{15}, we must have $r'' + z' = z''$ (see Figure 4.2.E). Thus (7) holds. The lemma is proven.

<u>Corollary 4.3.4</u>. Suppose that for $p, q, d, d_0, \ldots, d_j \in L$ we have $N(p/q,d)$, $N((q+d)/q,d_0)$ and $N((q+d_i)/q,d_{i+1})$ for $j \geq 1$ and $0 \leq i < j$. If p/q transposes down onto a quotient u/v, then either this transposition is bijective, or else, p/q has a subquotient which is an L_9^{j+1}-quotient. Hence $j = k$ implies $p/q \searrow_\beta u/v$.

<u>Proof</u>. Since for $j = 0$ the corollary follows from the preceding lemma, we assume that $j \geq 1$. If the transposition $p/q \searrow u/v$ is not bijective, then for some $t \in p/q$, $t > tu + q$. Put $s = tu + q$, $g = p(v + d + d_0)$, $g_0 = (q + d)(d + d_i)$ and $g_{i+1} = (q + d_i)(d_i + d_j)$ for $0 \leq i < j$. To prove that $L_9^{j+1}(t/s,g,g_0,\ldots,g_j,d_j)$, it suffices to show that if $L_9^{i+1}(t/s,g,g_0,\ldots,g_i,d_j)$, then $L_9^{i+2}(t/s,g,g_0,\ldots,g_i,g_{i+1},d_j)$. We have $N((s+d_{j+1})/s, d_j)$. Also, for $e \in \{g,g_0,\ldots,g_i\}$, $N((s+e)/s,d_{i+1})$ and $t > s = td_{i+1} + s$. It follows from the preceding lemma that $L_9^1(t/s,e,g_{i+1},d_j)$, which implies the desired result.

<u>Lemma 4.3.5</u>. For any quotients u/v and p/q of L

(i) If $p/q \nearrow u/v \searrow c/a$, then these transpositions are bijective and $p/q \searrow pc/qa \nearrow c/a$.

(ii) If $p/q \searrow u/v \nearrow c/a$, then these transpositions are bijective and $p/q \nearrow (P+c)/(q+a) \searrow c/a$.

<u>Proof</u>. We show first that

(α) If $f/g \nearrow r/s$, and $N(f/g,b), N((g+b)/g,b_0)$ and $N((g+b_i)/g,b_{i+1})$ $(i < k)$, then $N(r/s,b)$, $N((s+b)/s,b_0)$ and $N((s+b_i)/s,b_{i+1})$.

By the Lemma 1.2.4 the elements s, f and b generate a lattice which is a homomorphic image of the lattice in Figure 4.3.A, and therefore $N(r/s,b)$. Since $(g+b)/s(g+b) \subseteq (g+b)/g$ and $N((g+b)/g,b_0)$ we have $N((g+b)/s(g+b),b_0)$. Also, $(g+b)/s(g+b) \nearrow (s+b)/s$ implies $N((s+b)/s,b_0)$, and similarly $N((s+b_i)/s,b_{i+1})$ for $i < k$.

(i) follows from (α), the preceding corollary and Lemma 1.2.2, since $N(c/a,b)$, $N((a+b)/a,b_0)$ and $N((a+b_i)/a,b_{i+1})$ for $i < k$.

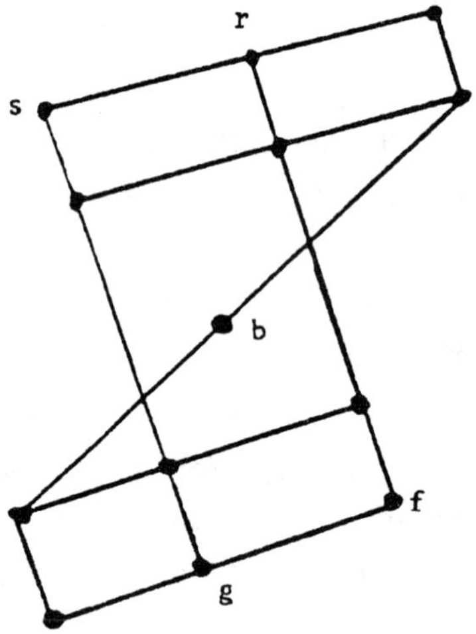

A

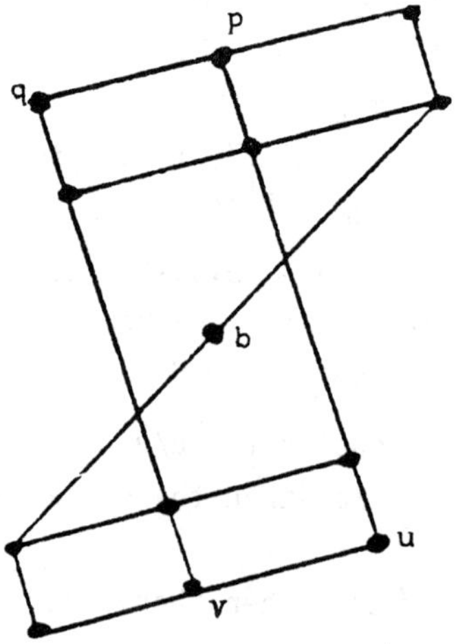

B

Figure 4.3

To prove (ii), first observe that since $v = uq = ua = u(q + a)$ but $u \leq p + c$ we have $p + c > q + a$. Also $p + c \geq (q + a) + c \geq (q + a) + u = (q + u) + (a + u) = p + c$, and therefore, $(p+c)/(q+a) \searrow c/c(q+a)$. Since $c/c(q+a)$ is an L_g^k-quotient (Lemma 4.3.1) it follows from (α) that $N((p+c)/(q+a),b)$ $N(((q+a)+b)/(q+a),b_0)$ and $N(((q+a)+b_i)/(q+a),b_{i+1})$ for $i < k$. On the other hand (again by Lemma 1.2.4) the elements q, u and b generate the lattice which is a homomorphic image of the lattice in Figure 4.3.B. Thus $N(p/q,b)$. Since $(v+b)/q(v+b) \searrow_\beta u/v$ (Lemma 4.3.2) and $v = u(q + a)$ we have $q(v + b) = (q + a)(v + b)$. Using $(q + a) + (v + b) = (q + a) + (u + b) = p + c + b$ we get that $((p+c)+b)/(q+a) \searrow (v+b)/q(v+b) \nearrow (q+b)/q$, and therefore, by Corollary 1.2.5 $N((q+b)/q,b_0)$. Similarly, $N((q+b_i)/q,b_{i+1})$ $(i < k)$. (ii) follows from the preceding corollary and the dual of Lemma 1.2.2. The lemma is proven.

Corollary 4.3.6. If u/v projects weakly onto a subquotient of c/a, then $u/v \searrow uc'/va' \nearrow c'/a'$ for some subquotient c'/a' of c/a.

Proof. It is similar to the proof of Corollary 2.3.3.

Corollary 4.3.7. $x/y = c/a$.

Proof. It is similar to the proof of Corollary 2.3.4.

We complete the proof of the Proposition 4.3 by showing that none of the proper epimorphic images of L have L_g^k-quotients. So, suppose that for some $u,v,d,d_0,\ldots,d_k \in L$ and $\Theta \in \mathrm{Con}(L)$ with $\mathrm{Con}(a,c) \subseteq \Theta$ we have $L_g^k(u'/v', d', d_0',\ldots, d_k')$ in L/Θ (for $s \in L$, $s' = s/\Theta$). Let A be a sublattice of L generated by the set $\{u,v,d,d_0,\ldots,d_k\}$. It follows from the Theorem 6.2.10 below that L_g^k is a splitting lattice, and therefore $L_g^k(u'/v', d', d_0',\ldots, d_k')$ is a bounded epimorphic image of A (see Theorem 0.2.5). Denote by $\overline{s}$ the largest element of $s' \in A/\Theta$. Let $f',g' \in \{d', d_0',\ldots, d_k'\}$ such that $(v + f)' < (v + g)'$. Since the map $s' \to \overline{s}$ preserves order and meets, we have

$$\overline{v + f} < \overline{v + g} \tag{1}$$

and

$$\overline{v}\,\overline{g} = (\overline{v + f})\overline{g} \geq (\overline{v + f})\overline{g} \geq \overline{v}\,\overline{g}. \tag{2}$$

Also, since $L_g(u'/v',f',g')$ is a projective lattice (see Example 1.4.6) for some u_0, v_0, f, $g \in A$ we have $L_g(u_0/v_0,f,g)$, and therefore $v_0 + f < v_0 + g$. This together with (1) implies $\overline{v} + \overline{f} < \overline{v} + \overline{g}$. Using (2) we get that $N((\overline{v}+\overline{f})/\overline{v},\overline{g})$. Thus $N((\overline{v}+\overline{d})/\overline{v},\overline{d}_0)$ and $N((\overline{v}+\overline{d}_i)/\overline{v},\overline{d}_{i+1})$ for $i < k$. Further, for $u_1 \in u'$ with $\overline{v} < u_1 < \overline{v} + \overline{d}$ we have $N(u_1/\overline{v},\overline{d})$. It follows from the proof of Corollary 4.3.4 that $u_1/\overline{v}$ is an L_g^k-quotient. However,

$u_1/v \neq c/a$ because $\mathrm{Con}(a,c) \subseteq \Theta$. This contradiction completes the proof.

Proof of Proposition 4.4.

Lemma 4.4.1. If $v < u \leq a$, then there is no $z \in L$ such that $N(u/v,z)$.

Proof. Consider a shortest possible sequence

$$(\alpha) \qquad c/a = x_0/y_0 \sim_w x_1/y_1 \sim_w \cdots \sim_w x_n/y_n = u/v.$$

As in the proof of dual of Lemma 1.2.10 one can show that $n \geq 3$ and $x_{n-2}/y_{n-2} \nearrow_w x_{n-1}/y_{n-1} \searrow_w u/v$. We may assume that u covers v. Then $x_{n-1}/y_{n-1} \searrow u/v$. Since $u \leq a$, it follows from the Corollary 1.2.8 that x_{n-1} covers y_{n-1}. Thus $x_{n-2}/y_{n-2} \nearrow x_{n-1}/y_{n-1}$. Since $N(x_{n-1}/y_{n-1},z)$ (Corollary 1.2.5), it follows from the Lemma 4.3.2 that the interval x_{n-2}/y_{n-2} is prime. Thus by Corollary 1.2.3 the sequence (α) can be shortened which contradicts our choice of n. The lemma is proven.

Let $b, b_0, \ldots, b_k \in L$ such that $L_9^k(c/a,b,b_0,\ldots,b_k)$. For the Lemmas 4.4.2 - 4.4.6 below, we suppose that there exists $e \in \{b,b_0,\ldots,b_k\}$ such that

(1) For $d \in \{b,b_0,\ldots,e\}$, $d = b$ implies $(a+d)/ad = N(c/a,d)$ and $d = b_i$ $(i \leq k)$ implies $(a+d)/ad = L_9^i(c/a,b,b_0,\ldots,b_i)$;
(2) If $t \in ((a+e)/ae - \{a+e, b+e,\ldots,e\})$ then every cover of t in L belongs to $(a+e)/ae$;
(3) If $s \in ((a+e)/ae - \{ae\})$, then every dual cover of s in L belongs to $(a+e)/ae$.

Lemma 4.4.2. Suppose that $N(c/a,z)$ for $z \notin (a+e)/ae$. Then $L_9(c/a,e,z)$. Hence $L_9^{i+1}(c/a,b,b_0,\ldots,b_i,z)$ if $e = b_i$ $(i \leq k)$.

Proof. Since ae is the only dual cover of e (see (3)) we have $az = ez < ae$. It follows from (2) that $ae + z > e$. To avoid L_6, for $e \leq q < p \leq a + e$ we must have $q + z < p + z$. Also if p covers q, then $q = p(q+z)$. Thus $L_9(c/a,e,z)$ and therefore $L_9^{i+1}(c/a,b,b_0,\ldots,b_i,z)$ if $d = b_i$ $(i \leq k)$.

Lemma 4.4.3. Suppose that $N(u/v,z)$ and $u/v \nsubseteq (a+d)/d$ for some $d \in \{b,b_0,\ldots,e\}$. Then there exist $x,y \in L$ with $a \leq y < a + d < x$, such that $N(x/y,z)$.

Proof. Consider a sequence $c/a = x_0/y_0 \sim_w \cdots \sim_w x_n/y_n = u/v$. Since c/a is a subquotient of $(a+d)/ad$ and u/v is not, there is an index $i < n$ with $x_i/y_i \subseteq (a+d)/ad$ and $x_{i+1}/y_{i+1} \nsubseteq (a+d)/ad$. Assume that $ax_i > ay_i$. Then $x_i/y_i \searrow ax_i/ay_i$ and therefore $N(ax_i/ay_i,z)$ (Corollary 1.2.5), contradicting the Lemma 4.4.1. Thus $ax_i = ay_i$, and therefore, for some $g \in \{b, b_0, \ldots, d\}$ we have $x_i \in (a+g)/g$ and $y_i \geq ax_i$.

Suppose that $x_i/y_i \searrow_w x_{i+1}/y_{i+1}$. It follows from (3) that $x_{i+1} \geq g$. Let $r \in x_{i+1}/y_{i+1}$ such that $r \notin (a+d)/ad$. Again, by (3) we have that $x_{i+1} \geq g > ad > r$. However this contradicts the Lemma 4.4.1, since $N(x_{i+1}/y_{i+1}, z)$ (Corollary 1.2.5) implies $N(ad/r, z)$.

Thus $x_i/y_i \nearrow_w x_{i+1}/y_{i+1}$. By (2) $y_{i+1} \leq a + y_i = a + y_{i+1}$. Let $p \in x_{i+1}/y_{i+1}$ such that $p \notin (a+d)/ad$. Then for some $t \in (a+d)/d$, $t < p$. Letting $y = a + y_{i+1}$ and $x = a + p$ we have $y < a + d < x$. Since $N(x_{i+1}/y_{i+1}, z)$, $p/py \subseteq x_{i+1}/y_{i+1}$ and $p/py \nearrow x/y$, by Corollary 1.2.5. The lemma is proven.

Lemma 4.4.4. Suppose that x covers $a + e$ in L. Then there exists $z \in L$ such that $z(a + e) < ae$ and $x/(a+e) \searrow_\beta z/z(a+e)$.

Proof. By Lemma 1.3.1 there exists $r \neq x$ such that $x/(a+e) \searrow r/r(a+e)$, and this transposition must be bijective since for $r(a + e) < f < r$ we would have $N(r/f, (a + e))$ contrary to the Corollary 1.2.8. If $r(a + e) \nleq ae$, then for some $d \in \{b, b_0, \ldots, e\}$, $e + d = r(a + e)$. Since by (3) e is join irreducible, the existence of $z \in L$ with $z(a + e) < ae$ and $x/(a+e) \searrow_\beta z/z(a+e)$ will follow from the following statement:

(α) For any $d \in \{b, b_0, \ldots, e\}$ if $p < x$ is a cover of $e + d$ and $p \neq a + e$, then there exists $q < p$ such that $x/(a+e) \searrow_\beta q/q(a+e)$.

To prove (α) consider a shortest possible sequence

$$\text{(i)} \qquad c/a = x_0/y_0 \sim_w \cdots \sim_w x_n/y_n = p/(e+d).$$

Since $e + d$ is noncomparable with a and c we have $n \geq 3$. Suppose that $x_{n-2}/y_{n-2} \nearrow_w x_{n-1}/y_{n-1} \searrow p/(e+d)$. Then the interval x_{n-1}/y_{n-1} must be prime. Indeed, for $y_{n-1} < f < x_{n-1}$ we would have $N(f/y_{n-1}, p)$. Since $p \geq d$; it follows from the preceding lemma that $ad < y_{n-1} < f < a + d$. This together with $a \leq e + d \leq y_{n-1}$ implies $ay_{n-1} < af$ and therefore $af/ay_{n-1} \nearrow f/y_{n-1}$. However this contradicts Lemma 4.4.1 since $N(af/ay_{n-1}, p)$ (Corollary 1.2.5). If x_{n-2} covers y_{n-2}, then by Corollary 1.2.3 the sequence (i) can be shortened by one step contradicting our choice of n. Thus for $y_{n-2} < f < x_{n-2}$ we have $N(x_{n-2}/f, y_{n-1})$. Since $d \leq y_{n-1}$, again by the preceding lemma $x_{n-2} < a + d$, and therefore $x_{n-2}p \leq (a + d)p = e + d \leq y_{n-1}$. However this contradicts semidistributivity since $x_{n-1} = y_{n-1} + x_{n-2} = y_{n-1} + p$ but $y_{n+1} + x_{n-1}p = y_{n-1}$. Thus $x_{n-1}/y_{n-1} \nearrow p/(e+d)$, and $x_{n-1} < p$ by the minimality of n. Put $q = x_{n-1}$. Since p covers $e + d$ we have $y_{n-1} = q(e + d) = qp(a + e) = q(a + e)$. Since x covers $a + e$, $x/(a+e) \searrow q/q(a+e)$, and this transposition must be bijective since for $q(a + e) < f < q$ we would have $N(q/f,(a+e))$ contradicting Corollary 1.2.8. The lemma is proven.

Lemma 4.4.5. Suppose that x covers $a + e$ in L. Then there exists $z \in L$ such that the following holds:

(i) $L(c/a,e,z)$ and $L_9^{i+1}(c/a,b,b_0,\ldots,b_i,z)$ if $e = b_i$ $(i \leq k)$;

(ii) $(a+z)/e = (a+e)/e \cup \{e + z,\ldots,b + z, a + z\}$;

(iii) $e + z$ covers z and if z_0 is a dual cover of $e + z$, then $z_0 \in \{e,z\}$;

(iv) ae and z cover ez and these elements are the only covers of ez;

(v) ae is join irreducible;

(vi) If $q \in (a+e)/e$ and p is a cover of q in L, then $p \not\leq a + e$ implies $e + z \leq p \leq a + z$;

(vii) If $p \in (a+z)/(e+z)$ and q is a dual cover of p in L, then $p \not\geq z$ implies $e \leq q \leq a + e$;

(viii) z is join irreducible.

Proof. (i) follows from the preceding lemma and Lemma 4.4.2.

To prove (ii) observe that for $p \in (a+z)/(e+z)$ the interval $p/p(a+e)$ must be prime since for $p(a + e) < f < p$ we would have $N(p/f,a)$ contrary to Corollary 1.2.8. By the similar argument if $p,q \in \{e + z,\ldots,b + z, a + z\}$ and p covers q in this chain then p covers q in L. Since L excludes diamond we infer that (ii) holds.

To prove (iii) first observe that we may assume that $e + z$ covers z. If $z_0 \notin \{e,z\}$ is a dual cover of $e + z$, then $N(e/ae,z_0)$. As in proof of Lemma 1.3.5 one can show that the elements e, ae, z and z_0 generate L_{14}.

To prove (iv) first observe that since $e + z$ covers z, it follows from Lemma 4.4.1 that ae covers ez. Since for $ez < f < z$ we would have $N(z/f,(ae))$ contrary to Corollary 1.2.8, z must cover ez. If $z_0 \notin \{ae,z\}$ is a cover of ez, then as in the proof of the dual of Lemma 1.3.5 one can show that the elements e, ae, z and z_0 generate L_{13}.

To prove (v), suppose that $y \neq az$ is a dual cover of ae. By the dual of Lemma 1.3.1 there exists $z_0 \in L$ such that $y = az_0$. We have $N(e/ae,z_0)$. As in the proof of the dual of Lemma 1.3.7 one can show that L includes at least one of the lattices L_8, L_{14} or L_{15}.

To prove (vi) suppose that $p \not\leq a + e$ covers $q \in (a+e)/e$ and $p \notin (a+z)/(e+z)$. If $a + p > a + z$, then $N((a+z)/(a+e),p)$. However, $(a+z)/(a+e) \searrow (q+z)/q$ implies $N((q+z)/q,p)$ (Corollary 1.2.5) contradicting $q < p$. Thus since $a + z$ covers $a + e$ the elements $a + p$ and $a + z$ must be noncomparable. We may assume that $a + p$ covers $a + e$. By the preceding lemma there exists $z_0 \in L$ such that $ae < (a + e)z_0$. It follows from (iv) that $(a + e)z_0 \neq ez$. Since ae covers az, it follows from (v) that $(a + e)z_0 < ez$ implying $N(ae/ez, z_0)$. However, this contradicts Lemma 4.4.1. Thus (vi) holds.

To prove (vii) suppose that $q \not\geq z$ is a dual cover of $p \in (a+z)/(e+z)$, and $e \not\leq q$. It follows from (iv), (v) and (vi) and $eq < ez$. Thus $N(ae/ez, q)$. However, this contradicts the Lemma 4.4.1.

To prove (viii) suppose that $f = ez$ is a dual cover of z, and consider a shortest possible sequence

$$(\alpha) \qquad c/a = x_0/y_0 \sim_w x_1/y_1 \sim_w \cdots \sim_w x_n/y_n = z/f.$$

Since f and z are both noncomparable with a and c we have $n \geq 3$.

Suppose that $x_{n-2}/y_{n-2} \nearrow_w x_{n-1}/y_{n-1} \searrow z/f$. Then the interval x_{n-1}/y_{n-1} is prime. Indeed for $y_{n-1} < g < x_{n-1}$ we would otherwise have $N(g/y_{n-1}, z)$. Since by (vi) $a + z$ is the only cover of $a + e$, it follows from Lemma 4.4.3 that $y_{n-1} \in (a+e)/ae$ implying $f = y_{n-1}z \geq ez$, a contradiction. Thus $x_{n-2}/y_{n-2} \nearrow x_{n-1}/y_{n-1}$. If x_{n-2} covers y_{n-2}, then by Corollary 1.2.3 the sequence (α) can be shortened which contradicts our choice of n. Thus for $y_{n-2} < g < x_{n-2}$ we have $N(x_{n-2}/g, y_{n-1})$. Suppose that $x_{n-2} \in (a+e)/ae$. Then $x_{n-1} = x_{n-2} + y_{n-1} = x_{n-2} + ae + f + y_{n-1}$, and therefore $x_{n-1} \geq e + z$ because $ae + f = e + z$. Since ez is the only dual cover of ae and $y_{n-1} \notin (a+e)/ae$ we have $y_{n-2} = x_{n-2}y_{n-1} \leq ez$, and therefore $y_{n-2} = x_{n-2}(y_{n-1}z)(ez) = y_{n-2}(y_{n-1}z)(ez) = y_{n-2}f(ez) < ez$. Hence, $N(ae/ez, y_{n-1})$ contradicting Lemma 4.4.1. Thus $x_{n-2} \notin (a+e)/ae$. Again, since $a + z$ is the only cover of $a + e$, it follows from Lemma 4.4.3 that $N(a+z)/(a+e), y_{n-1})$. The contradiction follows since $(a + z)y_{n-1} \geq f$ but $(a + e)y_{n-1} = aef < f$.

Finally, assume that $x_{n-2}/y_{n-2} \searrow_w x_{n-1}/y_{n-1} \nearrow z/f$. Since $z \geq f, x_{n-1}$ and again because $a + z$ is the only cover of $a + e$, it follows from Lemma 4.4.3 that if $N(u/v, r)$ for $r \in \{f, x_{n-1}\}$, then $u/v \subseteq (a+e)/ae$. Because none of the elements of $(a+e)/ae$ is comparable with z this implies that x_{n-1} covers y_{n-1}. Now if $y_{n-2} \in (a+e)/ae$, then $y_{n-2} + f = y_{n-2} + ez + f = y_{n-2} + z \geq z \geq x_{n-1}$. However, this contradicts semidistributivity since $y_{n-1} = x_{n-1}y_{n-2} = x_{n-1}f$, but $x_{n-1} = x_{n-1}(y_{n-2} + f)$. Thus $x_{n-2}/y_{n-2} \searrow_\beta x_{n-1}/y_{n-1} \nearrow_\beta z/f$. It follows from the dual of Corollary 1.2.3 that the sequence (α) cqn be shortened. This contradiction completes the proof.

<u>Lemma 4.4.6</u>. Let $g = b_0$ if $e = b$ and $g = b_{i+1}$ if $e = b_i$ $(i < k)$. Then g can be chosen so that (1), (2) and (3) holds (see page 54).

Proof. Apply the preceding lemma with $x \leq a + g$, replace z by g and use Lemma 4.4.2.

Lemma 4.4.7. The element b can be chosen so that (1), (2) and (3) holds.

Proof. Let $x \leq a + b$ be a cover of c. By Lemma 1.3.1 there exists $b' \in L$ such that $N(c/a,b')$ and $x = a + b'$. We may assume that x covers b'. To prove the lemma it suffices to show that:

(i) $N(c/a,b') = (a+b')/ab'$;

(ii) c is meet irreducible and a is join irreducible;

(iii) c and b' are the only dual covers of $a + b'$ and a and b' are the only covers of ab';

(iv) b' is join irreducible;

(v) $L_9^k(c/a,b',b ,\ldots, b_k)$.

To prove (i) first observe that b' must cover ab' since for $ab' < f < b'$ we otherwise have $N(b'/f,a)$ contradicting Corollary 1.2.8. Since L excludes L_7 the interval a/ab' must be prime (Corollary 1.3.3). Thus since the diamond is also excluded we infer that (i) holds.

(ii) follows from the Lemma 1.3.7 and its dual.

(iii) follows from the Corollary 1.3.6 and its dual.

(iv) follows from the dual of Lemma 1.3.9.

(v) follows from the Corollary 4.3.4 since $N(a + b')/a,b_i)$ for $i \in \{0,1,\ldots,k\}$. The lemma is proven.

We are now ready to complete the proof of Proposition 4.4. It follows from the preceding lemma and Lemma 4.4.6 that the elements $b, b_o ,\ldots, b_k$ can be chosen so that (1), (2) and (3) holds for any $e \in \{b,b_o ,\ldots, b_k\}$. To prove that c/a is an L_9^{k+1}-quotient, by Lemma 4.4.2 it suffices to show that for some $z \notin (a+b_k)/ab_k$ we have $N(c/a,z)$. Since $L \neq L_9^k$, there exists $u \in L$ such that u is a cover of $a + b_k$ or it is a dual cover of ab_k. The result follows from the Lemma 1.3.1 or its dual.

The proof of Theorem 4.2 is similar to the proof of Theorem 3.2 (see pages 45 and 46).

CHAPTER 5

SPLITTING LATTICES OBTAINED FROM FINITE DISTRIBUTIVE LATTICES

5.1. The Characterization Theorems. In [3] and [4], Alan Day introduced a construction that has proved to be extremely useful, the splitting of an interval in a lattice L. Here we need only the special case in which the interval consists of a single element d. In this case the new lattice is the set $L[d] = (L = \{d\}) \cup \{a,c\}$ with $a = (d,0)$ and $c = (d,1)$, and with the partial order defined as follows. Given x and y, $x \leq y$ if and only if one of the following conditions holds:

(i) $x,y \in L - \{d\}$ and $x \leq y$ in L;

(ii) $x \in \{a,c\}$, $y \in L - \{d\}$ and $d \leq y$;

(iii) $x \in L - \{d\}$, $y \in \{a,c\}$ and $x \leq d$;

(iv) $(x,y) = (a,a)$, (a,c), or (c,c).

It is easy to check that L[d] is indeed a lattice, and that there is epimorphism from L[d] to L. In this chapter we investigate the class *K* of subdirectly irreducible lattices that are obtained from finite distributive lattices by splitting an element. Observe that the pentagon is in *K*, and also the lattices L_{13}, L_{14} and L_{15}. By Alan Day [3], every lattice in *K* is splitting.

Lemma 5.1.1. Suppose L is a semidistributive lattice that excludes $L_6, L_7, \ldots, L_{12}$, and u/v is an N-quotient in L. Then:

(i) Every transposition $u'/v' \nearrow u/v$ or $u'/v' \searrow u/v$ is bijective;

(ii) Every quotient that is weakly projective to u/v is projective to a subquotient of u/v.

Proof. Follows from Lemmas 1.2.4 and 1.2.6.

The next two results are implicitly contained in B. Jónsson and I. Rival [20].

Theorem 5.1.2. Suppose L is a nondistributive, subdirectly irreducible, semidistributive lattice, and c/a is a critical quotient of L. Then the following conditions are equivalent:

(i) L excludes $L_6, L_7, \ldots, L_{12}$;

(ii) c/a is the only N-quotient of L;

(iii) Con(a,c) identifies no two distinct elements of L except a and c, and $L/\mathrm{Con}(a,c)$ is distributive;

(iv) $L \cong D[d]$ for some distributive lattice D and some $d \in D$.

Proof. Assume (i), and consider an N-quotient u/v in L. By Lemma 5.1.1 c/a is projective to a subquotient of u/v, and in view of Theorem 1.2.7 this implies that c/a is a subquotient of u/v. We must have $c = u$, for otherwise u/c would be an N-quotient, and c/a would be a subquotient of u/c. Similarly, $a = v$. Thus (ii) holds.

Assume (ii). Then L excludes L_{11} and L_{12}, whence it follows by Theorem 1.2.7 that $\mathrm{Con}(a,c)$ identifies no two distinct elements other than a and c. Furthermore, $L/\mathrm{Con}(a,c)$ must be distributive, for an N-quotient in $L/\mathrm{Con}(a,c)$ would be the image of an N-quotient in L. Thus (iii) holds.

Assume (iii). Let $D = L/\mathrm{Con}(a,c)$ and $d = \{a,c\}$. Define $a' = (d,0)$, $c' = (d,1)$, and $x' = x$ for $a,c \neq x \in L$ (where an element $x \neq a,c$ of L is identified with the member $\{x\}$ of D and of $D[d]$). The map $x \to x'$ is obviously a bijection from L to $D[d]$, and we claim that it is in fact an isomorphism. To prove this we must show that, for $x,y \in L$, the conditions $x < y$ and $x' < y'$ are equivalent. For $x,y \in L - \{a,c\}$ this is obvious, for $x < y$ then holds either in all three lattices L, D and $D[d]$ or in none. The case $x,y \in \{a,c\}$ is trivial, since $a < c$ and $a' < c'$. The remaining cases are taken care of by noting that, for $x \neq a,c$, the five conditions

$$x < c,\ x < a,\ x < d,\ x < a',\ x < c'$$

are equivalent, and also the conditions

$$x > c,\ x > a,\ x > d,\ x > a',\ x > c'.$$

Thus (iv) holds.

Assume (iv). The canonical homomorphism from $D[d]$ to D must collapse every N-quotient in $D[d]$, and this implies that $(d,1)/(d,0)$ is the only N-quotient. Inasmuch as each of the lattices $L_6, L_7, \ldots, L_{12}$ has at least two N-quotients, we conclude that (i) holds.

Corollary 5.1.3. If the lattice L in the preceding theorem is finitely generated, then $L \in K$.

Proof. Follows from the preceding theorem and Lemma 1.2.11.

Theorem 5.1.4. Suppose D is a finite distributive lattice and $0,1 \neq d \in D$. Then $D[d]$ is subdirectly irreducible if and only if all of the following conditions hold:

(i) every cover of d is join reducible;

(ii) every dual cover of d is meet reducible;

(iii) every prime quotient in D is projective to a prime quotient p/q with $p = d$ or $q = d$.

Proof. Suppose $L = D[d]$ is subdirectly irreducible. Let $a = (d,0)$ and $c = (d,1)$. If $x \in D$ covers d, then x covers c in L, whence by Lemma 1.3.1 there exists $b \in L$ with $N(c/a,b)$ and $x = a + b$. It follows that, in D, $x = d + b$ and $b < x$, so that x is join reducible. Dually, every element that is covered by d is meet reducible.

Consider a prime quotient $u/v \neq c/a$ in L, and pick a sequence $c/a \subseteq x_0/y_0 \sim_w x_1/y_1 \sim_w x_2/y_2 \sim_w \cdots \sim x_n/y_n = u/v$ with n as small as possible. For $i > 0$, x_i/y_i does not contain c/a as a subquotient, and is therefore isomorphic to its image x_i'/y_i' in D. Since x_n/y_n is prime, it follows that x_n'/y_n' is prime, hence so are x_i'/y_i' and x_i/y_i for $i > 0$. Consequently, $x_0'/y_0' \sim x_1'/y_1' \sim x_2'/y_2' \sim \cdots \sim x_n'/y_n'$. Therefore $y_0' \prec x_0'$, which shows that we cannot have both $y_0 < a$ and $c < x_0$. Thus (iii) holds with $p/q = x_0'/y_0'$.

Now suppose (i), (ii) and (iii) hold and consider a prime quotient $u/v \neq c/a$ of L. We begin by showing that u/v is projective to a prime quotient x/y with $x = a$ or $y = c$. Observe that $v \neq a$, because c is the only member of L that covers a. Similarly $u \neq c$. We also dismiss as trivial the cases in which $v = c$ or $u = a$.

Using (iii), we may assume by duality that u'/v' is projective to a prime quotient x'/d with $c \prec x$. Since D is distributive, this means that $u'/v' \nearrow (u' + x')/(v' + c') \searrow x'/c'$, i.e., $u' + c' = u' + x'$, $u'(v' + c') = v'$, $x' + c' = u' + x'$, $x'(v' + c') = c'$. Since $v' \neq d$ and $u' \nleq d$, we infer from the first three of these equations that $u + c = u + x$, $u(v + c) = v$ and $x + c = u + x$, and the fourth equation shows that $x(v + c)$ is either a or c. Inasmuch as $x > c > a$, we must in fact have $x(v + c) = c$. Thus $u/v \nearrow (u + x)/(v + c) \searrow x/c$.

By (i), there exists $b \in L$ with $b' < x'$ and $z' = c' + b'$, hence $x = c + b$. Hence $N(c/a, b)$, and since $\mathrm{Con}(v,u)$ identifies x and c, it also identifies c and a. L is, therefore, subdirectly irreducible, and the proof is completed.

5.2. The Varieties $\{L_{13}^n\}^V$ and $\{L_{14}^n\}^V$. Since for any $n = 0, 1, \ldots$ the lattices L_{13}^n and L_{14}^n are mutually dual, we shall consider only the lattices L_{13}^n and the varieties generated by them.

Definition 5.2.1. We say that the quotient c/a of a lattice L is an L_{13}^n-quotient if for some $b, b_0, \ldots, b_n \in L$ the set $\{a,c,b,b_0, \ldots, b_n\}$ generates a sublattice of L isomorphic to L_{13}^n, with c/a as a critical quotient (see Figure 5.1).

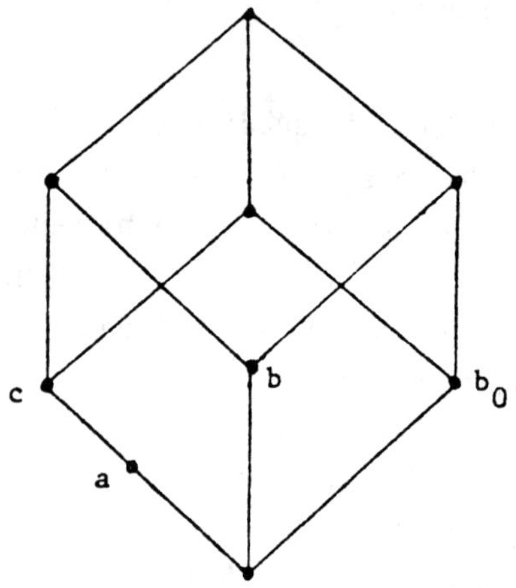

$L_{13} = L_{13}^0$

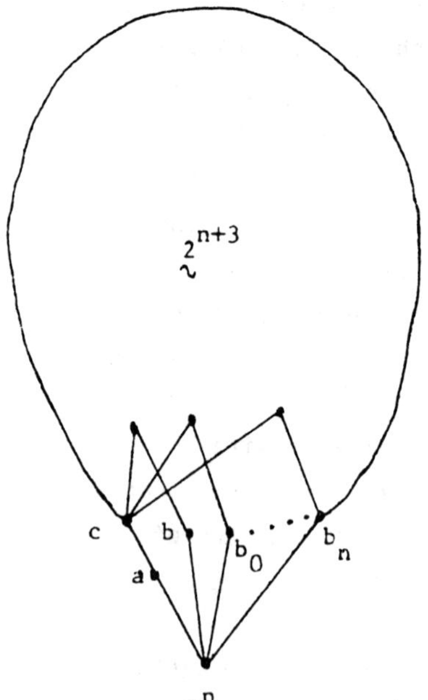

L_{13}^n

Figure 5.1

Using Theorem 0.1.6 it is easy to check that for any $n = 0,1,\ldots,$ the variety $\{L_{13}^n\}^V$ has at least fifteen join reducible covers $\{L_{13}^n, M_3\}^V$, $\{L_{13}^n, L_1\}^V, \ldots, \{L_{13}^n, L_{12}\}^V$, $\{L_{13}^n, L_{14}\}^V$, $\{L_{13}^n, L_{15}\}^V$, and at least one join irreducible: the variety $\{L_{13}^{n+1}\}^V$. It turns out that, for any natural number n, the above list of covers of $\{L_{13}^n\}^V$ is complete. In this section we shall prove this result.

<u>Theorem 5.2.2</u>. For any natural number n, the variety $\{L_{13}^n\}^V$ $(\{L_{14}^n\}^V)$ has only one join irreducible cover, namely the variety $\{L_{13}^{n+1}\}^V$ $(\{L_{14}^{n+1}\}^V)$.

The theorem is a corollary of the following proposition.

<u>Proposition 5.2.3</u>. Suppose L is a finite, subdirectly irreducible lattice such that $M_3 \notin \{L\}^V$ and $L_i \notin \{L\}^V$ for $i \neq 13$. If $L \neq \mathfrak{L}, N_5$, then $L \cong L_{13}^k$ for some k.

<u>Proof</u>. By Theorem 5.1.2 $L \cong D[d]$ for some finite distributive lattice D and some element $d \in D$. We need to show that D is a Boolean algebra and $0 \prec d$.

Assuming that d is not an atom, choose $x,y \in D$ with $x \prec y \prec d$. By Theorem 5.1.4 y/z is projective to an interval u/v with $u = d$ or $v = d$. Since D is distributive and $y < d$, the case $v = d$ is excluded, and hence y/z is projective to d/v. Again, by the distributivity of D, $y \neq v$ and hence $d = y + v$.

Again, by Theorem 5.1.4 y and v are meet reducible. Hence there exist $z,w \neq d$ that cover y and v, respectively. The lattice K generated by z, w and d is a homomorphic image of the lattice in Figure 5.2.A (the distributive lattice with generators z, w and d, and defining relation $d = dz + dw$). Since $y \prec z$ and $v \prec w$, K must in fact be either the lattice in Figure 5.2.B or C. Consequently, the sublattice $K[d]$ of $D[d]$ is either L_{14} or L_{15}, a contradiction. We conclude that $0 \prec d$.

Let s be the join of the atoms in D. To complete the proof it suffices to show that $s = 1$. Assuming that $s \neq 1$, choose an element t that covers s. Then t/s is projective to a quotient u/v with $u = d$ or $v = d$. Because of the distributivity of D, we have $u \nleq s$. This rules out the case $u = d$. Thus $d \prec u$ and u is join reducible. Hence $u = d + w$ for some $w < u$. Since D is distributive and $0 \prec d \prec u$, this implies that $0 \prec w \prec u$, hence $w \leq s$, and consequently $u \leq s$. This contradiction completes the proof.

<u>Proof of Theorem 5.2.2</u>. Let V be a join irreducible variety that covers $\{L_{13}^n\}^V$. Then there exists a finitely generated subdirectly irreducible lattice L such that $\{L\}^V = V$. By Corollary 5.1.3, L is finite. The theorem follows by Proposition 5.2.3.

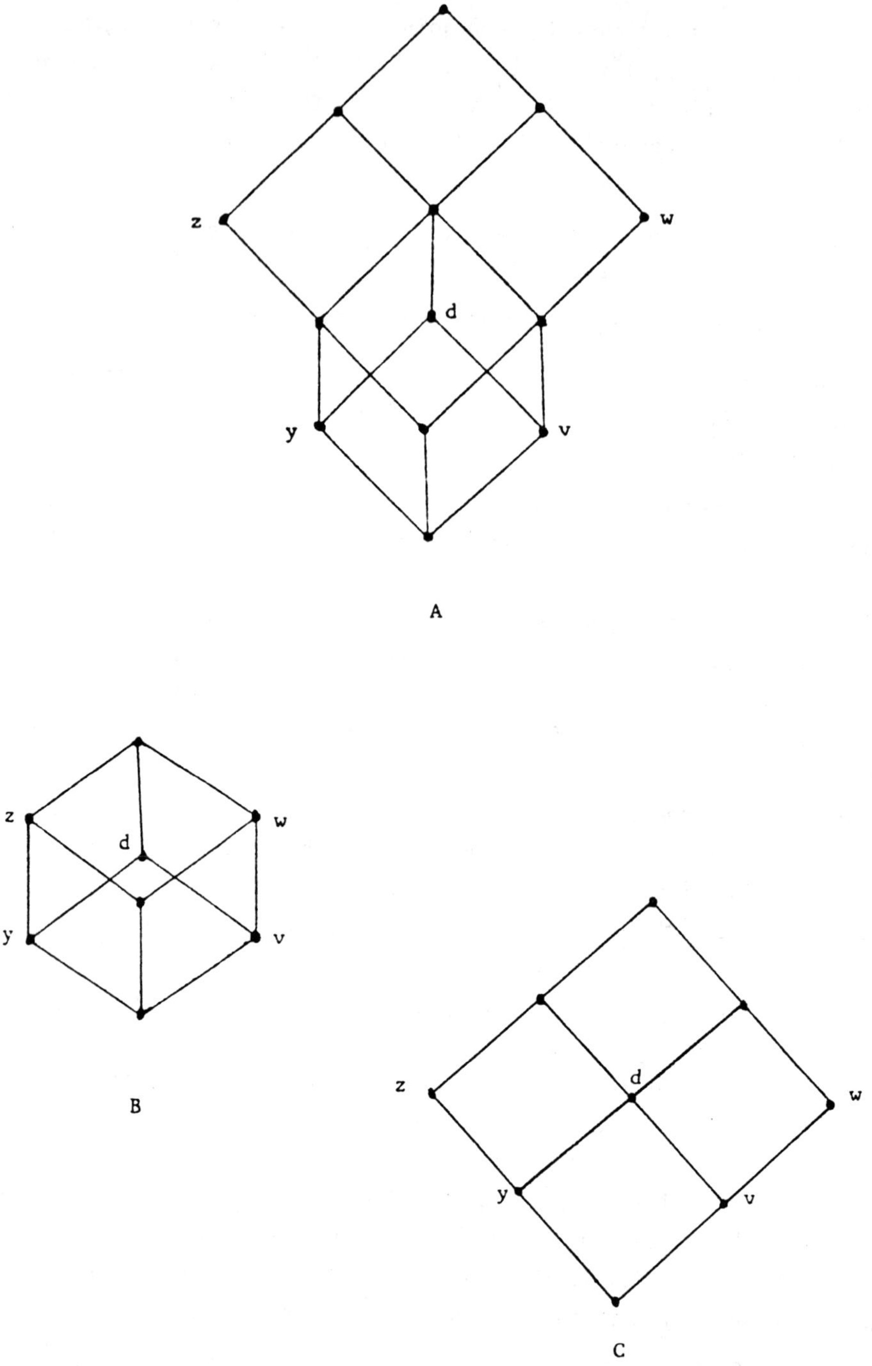

Figure 5.2

5.3. The Varieties $\{L_{15}^n\}^v$.

Definition 5.3.1. We say that the quotient c/a of the lattice L is an L_{15}^n-quotient if, for some $b, b_0, \ldots, b_n \in L$, the set $\{a, c, b, b_0, \ldots, b_n\}$ generates a sublattice of L isomorphic to L_{15}^n, with c/a as a critical quotient (see Figure 5.3).

Using Theorem 0.1.6 it is easy to check that for any $n = 0, 1, \ldots,$ the variety $\{L_{15}^n\}^v$ has at least fifteen join reducible covers $\{L_{15}^n, M_3\}^v$, $\{L_{15}^n, L_1\}^v, \ldots, \{L_{15}^n, L_{14}\}^v$, and at least one join irredicible: the variety $\{L_{15}^{n+1}\}^v$. It turns out that for any natural number n the above list of covers of $\{L_{15}^n\}^v$ is complete. In this section we shall prove this result.

Theorem 5.3.2. For any natural number n, the variety $\{L_{15}^n\}^v$ has only one join irreducible cover, namely the variety $\{L_{15}^{n+1}\}^v$.

The theorem is a corollary of the following proposition.

Proposition 5.3.3. Suppose L is a finite subdirectly irreducible lattice such that $M_3 \notin \{L\}^v$ and $L_i \notin \{L\}^v$ for $i \neq 15$. If $L \neq \mathfrak{2}$, N, then $L \cong L_{15}^k$ for some k.

Proof. By Theorem 5.1.4 $L \cong D[d]$ for some finite distributive lattice D and some $d \in D$. We need to show that:

(i) $(d]$ and $[d)$ are Boolean algebras;

(ii) Each dual atom of $(d]$ has a unique cover in D distinct from d;

(iii) Each atom of $[d)$ covers a unique element of D distinct from d;

(iv) Each element of D that is noncomparable with d covers a dual atom of $(d]$ and is covered by an atom of $[d)$.

The statement (i) is equivalent to the assertion that the meet m of all the elements covered by d is 0, and the join s of all the elements covering d is 1. Suppose $m \neq 0$, and choose $n \in D$ with $n \prec m$. By Theorem 5.1.4, m/n is projective to some quotient x/y with $x = d$ or $y = d$. Thus either $y = d$ or $y \prec d$, and in either case $m \leq y$, which is impossible in view of the distributivity of D. Thus $m = 0$ and, dually, $s = 1$, and (i) therefore holds.

By Theorem 5.1.4 every dual atom x of $(d]$ is meet reducible, and is therefore covered by some element $y \neq d$. On the other hand, x cannot have a third cover z, for y, z and d would then generate an eight element Boolean algebra, and L_{13} would be a sublattice of L. Similarly, each atom of $[d)$ covers precisely one element other than d.

Suppose $z \in D$ is noncomparable with d, and let $x = zd$. If d does not cover x, then there exist distinct dual atoms p and q of $(d]$ with $x < p$ and $x < q$. Choose y with $x \prec y \leq z$. Since $ypq \prec y$, we have

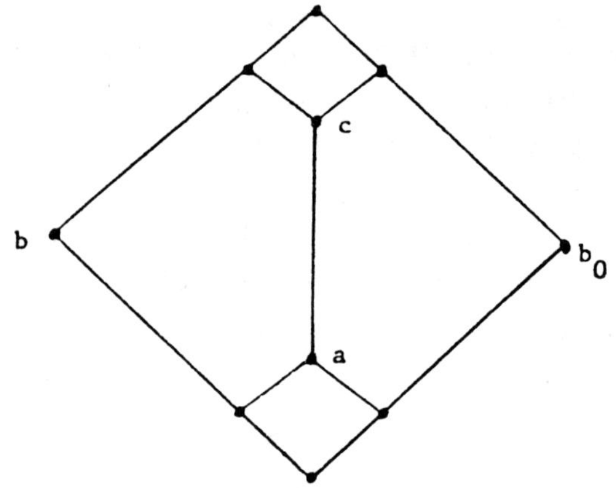

$L^0_{15} = L_{15}$

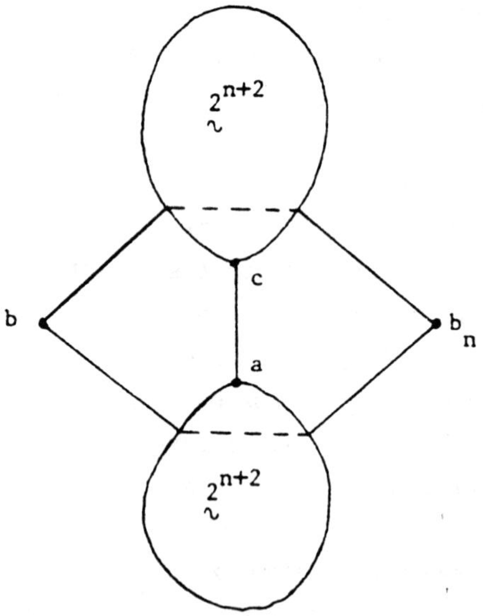

Figure 5.3

$pq \prec y + pq$, and of course p and q also cover pq. Hence p, q and $y + pq$ generate an eight element Boolean algebra, with d as one of the dual atoms, and L therefore contains L_{14} as a sublattice. This is a contradiction, and we infer that $za \prec d$, hence $z \prec z + d$. Dually, $d \prec z + d$ and, therefore, $dz \prec z$. This completes the proof of (iv).

The proof of Theorem 5.3.2 is similar to the proof of Theorem 5.2.2.

CHAPTER 6

RELATED QUESTIONS

6.1. The Varieties $\{L^n_{11}\}^v$ and $\{L^n_{12}\}^v$. Since for any $n = 0,1,\ldots,$ the lattices L^n_{11} and L^n_{12} are mutually dual, we shall consider only the lattices L^n_{12} and the varieties generated by them.

Definition 6.1.1. We say that the quotient c/a_n of a lattice L is an L^n_{12}-quotient if for some $b,d \in L$ the set $\{a_n, b, d\}$ generates a sublattice of L isomorphic to L^n_{12}, with c/a_n as a critical quotient (see Figure 6.1).

Using Theorem 0.1.6 it is easy to check that for any $n = 0,1,\ldots,$ the variety $\{L^{n+}_{12}\}^v$ is a join irreducible cover of $\{L^n_{12}\}^v$. However, the variety $\{L^0_{12}\}^v$ has two join irreducible covers: $\{L^1_{12}\}^v$ and $\{A\}^v$ (for the lattice A see Figure 6.2).

For $n = 0,1,\ldots,$ the lattice L^n_{12} has two critical quotients. Also, $N(b/a_nb,d)$ and $b/a_nb \nearrow (a_n+b)/a_n$. However, the elements a_n, $a_n + b$ and d do not generate a pentagon, and Corollary 1.2.5 is therefore not applicable to L^n_{12}. Further, for n even, the quotient cd/a_nd is critical. However, the sublattice $[a_nd)$ is not distributive and the elements a_nd, cd and d do not generate a pentagon. Similarly, if n is odd, then the quotient cb/a_nb is critical, but the sublattice $[a_nb)$ is not distributive and the elements cb, a_nb and b do not generate a pentagon. Thus Theorem 1.2.7 and Corollaries 1.2.8 and 1.2.9 are not valid for L^n_{12}. All this shows that in order to solve Problem 6.1.2 below we need an approach which will be quite different from the one we developed before.

Problem 6.1.2. How many join irreducible covers does the variety $\{L^0_{12}\}^v$ have? For $n \geq 1$, is the variety $\{L^{n+1}_{12}\}^v$ the unique join irreducible cover of $\{L^n_{12}\}^v$?

6.2. The Ideal I. The main result of this section is Theorem 6.2.10.

In this section we shall consider the collection I of semidistributive lattice varieties which do not have L_{11} and L_{12} as their members. Clearly I is an ideal in the lattice Λ. The following two conjectures are suggested by Professor Bjarni Jónsson.

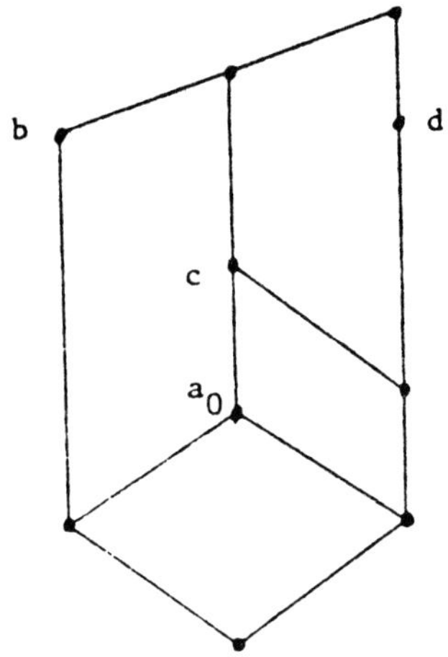

$L_{12} = L_{12}^{0}$

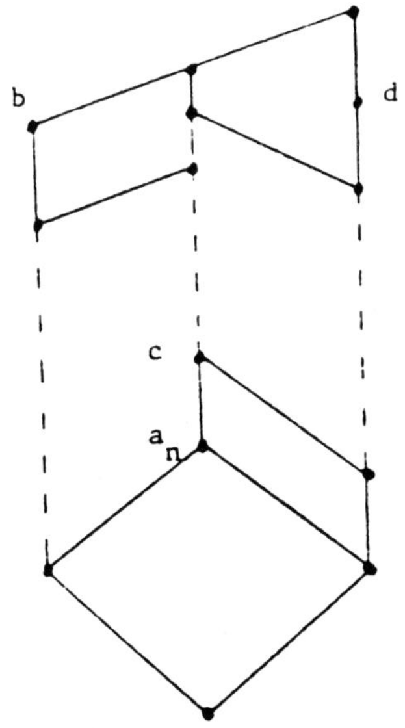

L_{12}^{n} for n even

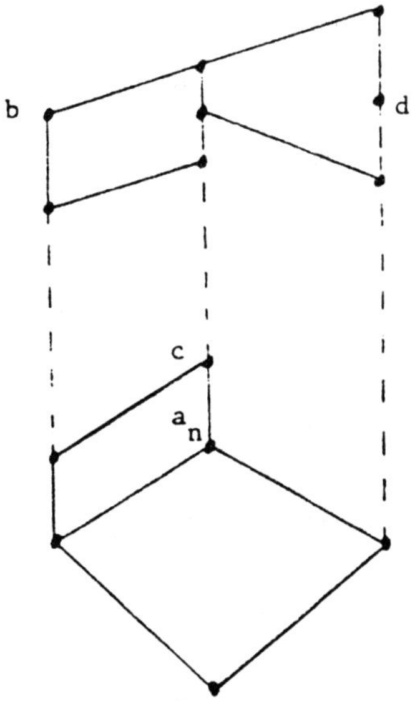

L_{12}^{n} for n odd

Figure 6.1

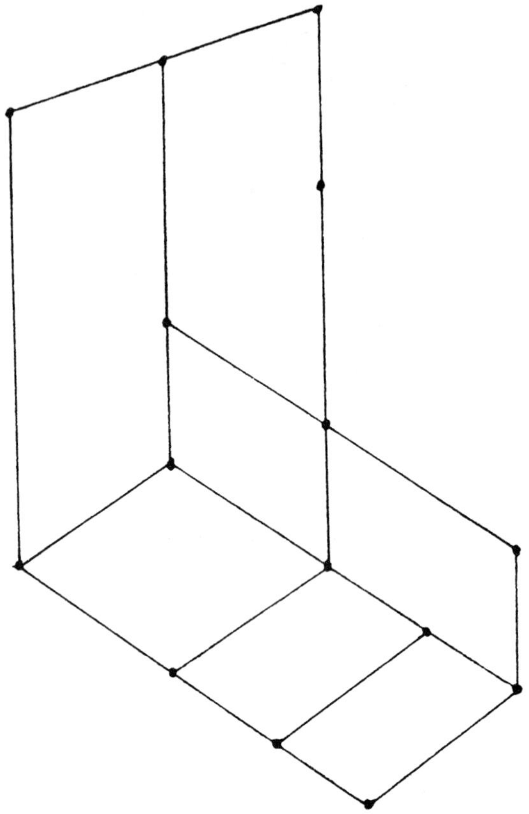

A

Figure 6.2

Conjecture 6.2.1. The ideal I has a largest variety, which is determined by a single identity.

Conjecture 6.2.2. Let $V \in I$, then V is locally finite.

Let L be a subdirectly irreducible lattice such that $\{L\}^V \in I$. By Theorem 1.2.7, L has a unique critical quotient c/a. Also, for any $b \in L$, N(c/a,b) if and only if b is noncomparable with a and c (Corollary 1.2.8), and the sublattices [a) and (c] are distributive (Corollary 1.2.9). If the set $B = \{b \in L: N(c/a,b)\}$ is finite, then by applying Lemma 1.2.9 and its dual we get that the sublattices [a) and (c] are of finite length, and therefore finite. This suggests a weaker version of Conjecture 6.2.2.

Conjecture 6.2.3. If L is finitely generated, then it is finite.

The following three problems can be found in B. Jónsson [17].

Problem 6.2.4. Is it true if the variety V has finitely many subvarieties, then V is generated by a finite lattice? (Equivalently, if V is generated by a finite lattice, so is every variety that covers V).

Problem 6.2.5. Is it true that if the variety V is generated by a finite lattice, it has only finitely many covers?

Problem 6.2.6. Is it true that for any natural number m there are only finitely many varieties having height m?

These problems appear to be very difficult, and there is no prospect of an easy solution. However, the techniques developed in this work give us hope that the problems can be solved for varieties belonging to I.

Let $J(L)$ be the set of all non-zero strictly join irreducible elements of a semidistributive lattice L, and for $u \in J(L)$ let $\overline{u}$ be the unique dual cover of u. For $u,v \in J(L)$ we write $u \sigma v$ if L includes one of the lattices pictured in Figure 6.3.

Definition 6.2.7. (see [5] and [18]). We say that a semidistributive lattice L has a cycle if for some $u_0, u_1, \ldots, u_n \in J(L)$ we have $u_0 \sigma u_1 \ldots \sigma u_n \sigma u_0$. $(0 < n < \omega)$.

Theorem 6.2.8. (See [5] and [18]). A finite semidistributive lattice L is a bounded homomorphic image of a free lattice if and only if L has no cycle. In addition if L satisfies the Whitman condition, then L is a retract of a free lattice and therefore projective.

Lemma 6.2.9. If a semidistributive lattice L has a cycle then L includes at least one of the lattices L_{11} or L_{12}.

Proof. Observe that for $u_0, u_1, \ldots, u_n \in J(L)$ $u_0 \sigma u_1, \ldots \sigma u_n \sigma u_0$ implies that

$$\mathrm{Con}(\overline{u}_0,u_0) \subseteq \mathrm{Con}(\overline{u}_1,u_1) \subseteq \cdots \subseteq (\mathrm{Con}(\overline{u}_n,u_n) \subseteq \mathrm{Con}(\overline{u}_0,u_0)$$

(See Figure 6.3). Suppose that for $j,i \in \{0,1,\ldots,n\}$ we have $u_j \sigma u_i$. Then there exists $x \in L$ such that $N(u_j/\overline{u}_j,x)$ but the elements u_i, $\overline{u}_i$ and x do not generate a pentagon (see Figure 6.3). Since $\mathrm{Con}(\overline{u}_j,u_j) = \mathrm{Con}(\overline{u}_i,u_i)$ and since u_i covers $\overline{u}_i$ the quotient $u_i/\overline{u}_i$ projects weakly onto $u_j/\overline{u}_j$ (Theorem 1.1.3). The lemma follows from Corollary 1.2.5.

Theorem 6.2.10. Let $V \in I$ and suppose that L is a finite lattice of V. Then:

(i) L is a bounded homomorphic image of a free lattice;

(ii) If L satisfies the Whitman condition, then L is a sublattice of a free lattice (= L is projective);

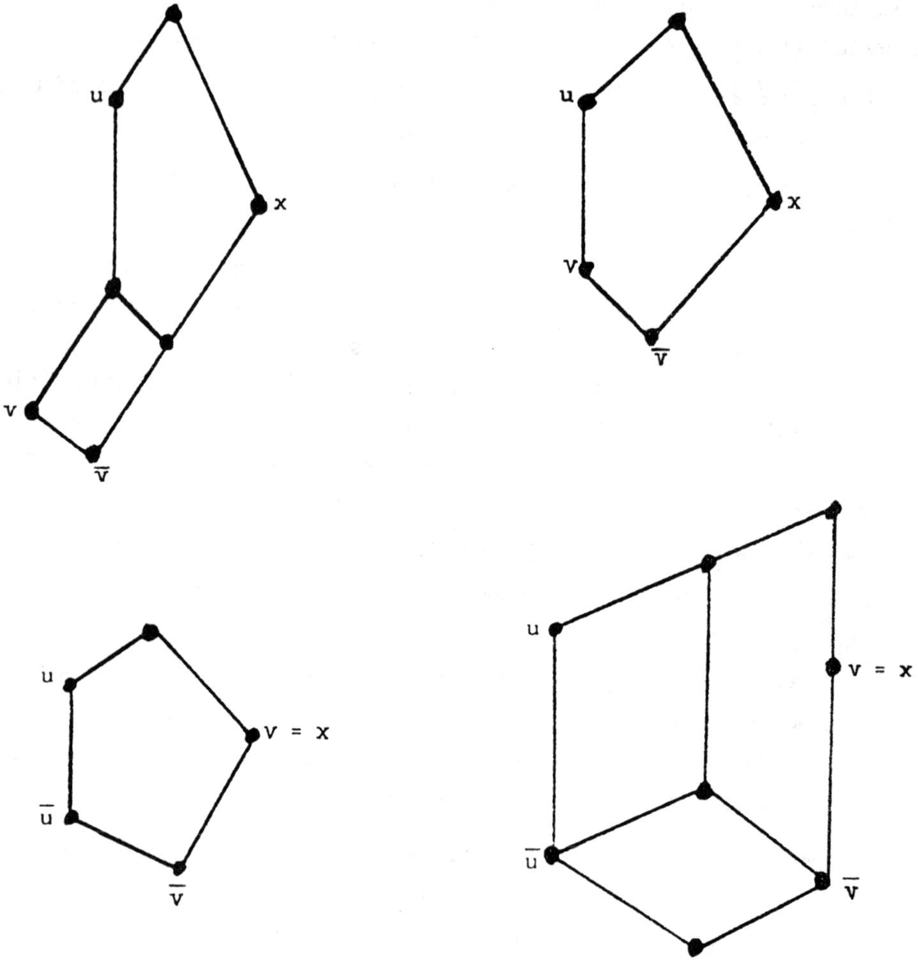

Figure 6.3

(iii) If L is subdirectly irreducible, then L is a splitting lattice.

Proof. (i) and (ii) follow from Theorem 6.2.8 and the preceding lemma. (iii) follows from (i) and Theorem 0.2.5.

6.3. Conjugate Varieties. It is shown in R. Freese [8] that the variety of all modular lattices (the smallest nontrivial conjugate variety) is not generated by its finite members.

Problem 6.3.1. Is there a conjugate variety other than the trivial variety that is generated by its finite members?

It follows from Lemma 1.4.3 that if the variety V is generated by its finite members, then all projective subdirectly irreducible members of V are finite.

Problem 6.3.2. Is there a conjugate variety that has infinite projective subdirectly irreducible members?

Next we turn to the problem of characterization of conjugate varieties determined by self dual identities.

Notation. For a given class A of lattices, we define A_s as follows. $L \in A_s$ if and only if there exists a lattice $L' \in A$ such that $\mathrm{Sub}(L) \cong \mathrm{Sub}(L')$, that is, L and L' have isomorphic lattices of sublattices.

It has been shown in N. D. Filippov [7] and I. Rival [25] that if A is a class of all modular (distributive, complemented) lattices, then $A = A_s$.

Clearly, if $\check{L}$ is a lattice which is dual to L, then $\mathrm{Sub}(L) \cong \mathrm{Sub}(\check{L})$. Thus, if the first order sentence σ is preserved under the map $A \to A_s$, then σ is a self dual. The following simple counterexample shows that the converse is not true.

Counterexample 6.3.3. Let σ be a sentence which determines the elementary class of all lattices having a unique atom and a unique coatom. Then $L \models \sigma$, but $L' \models \sigma$ (see Figure 6.4). However, it is clear that $\mathrm{Sub}(L) \cong \mathrm{Sub}(L')$.

Problem 6.3.4. Let A be an elementary class of lattices which is determined by a self dual first order sentence σ. When is it the case that $A = A_s$?

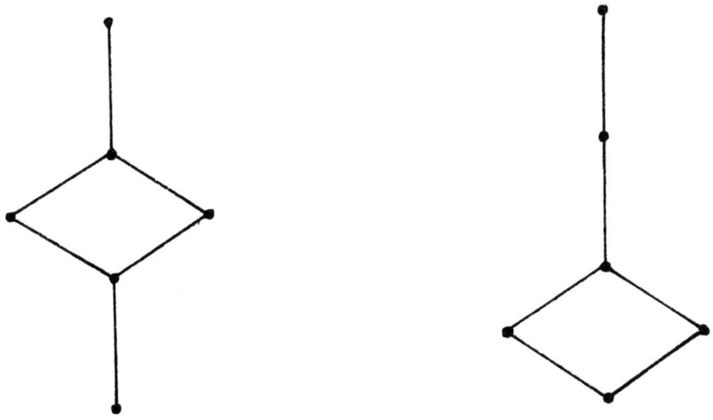

L L'

Figure 6.4

Lattice identities which are preserved under the map $A \to A_s$ appear to be rather rare. However, the conjugate identities of the lattices L_6^n have this property. This follows as a special case of the theorem below.

Theorem 6.3.5. Let P be a self dual projective subdirectly irreducible lattice such that, for any lattice P', $\mathrm{Sub}(P) \cong \mathrm{Sub}(P')$ implies $P \cong P'$. Suppose further that σ is its conjugate identity, and $V = \mathrm{Mod}\ \sigma$. Then $V = V_s$.

Proof. Suppose that for some lattice L we have $L \in V_s$ and $L \notin V$. Then $L \not\models \sigma$, and since $P \in \{L\}^V$, by Corollary 1.4.5 L includes P. Let $L' \in V$ be such that $\mathrm{Sub}(L') \cong \mathrm{Sub}(L)$. Since L includes P, the lattice L' must have a sublattice P' such that $\mathrm{Sub}(P') \cong \mathrm{Sub}(P)$. By assumption, $P \cong P'$, and so $P \in V$ which leads to a contradiction.

REFERENCES

1. Baker, K. "Equational classes of modular lattices." Pacific J. Math. 28 (1969): 9-15.

2. Crawley, P., and Dilworth, R. P. Algebraic Theory of Lattices. Englewood Cliffs, N.J.: Prentice-Hall, 1973.

3. Day, A. "Splitting lattices and congruence modularity." Contributions to Universal Algebra. Proceedings of the Coloquium held in Szeged, 1974. Colloquia Mathematica Societatis János Bolyai, Vol. 17. Amsterdam: North-Holland Publishing Co., 57-71.

4. ________. "Splitting lattices generate all lattices." Algebra Universalis 7 (1977): 163-170.

5. ________. "Characterizations of finite lattices that are bounded - homomorphic images or sublattices of free lattices." Canad. J. Math. 31 (1979): 69-78.

6. Dilworth, R. P. "The structure of relatively complemented lattices." Ann. of Math. 51 (1950): 161-166.

7. Filippov, N. D. "Projectivity of lattices." Mat. Sb. 70 (112) (1966): 36-54. English transl., Amer. Math. Soc. Transl. 96 (1970): 37-58.

8. Freese, R. "The variety of modular lattices is not generated by its finite members." Trans. Amer. Math. Soc. 255 (1979): 277-300.

9. Freese, R. and Nation, J. B. "Projective lattices." Pacific J. Math. 75 (1978): 93-106.

10. Funayama, N. and Nakayama, T. "On the distributivity of a lattice of lattice-congruences." Proc. Imp. Acad. Tokyo 18 (1942): 553-554.

11. Grätzer, G. "Equational classes of lattices." Duke Math. J. 33 (1966): 613-622.

12. ________. General Lattice Theory. Basel and Stuttgart: Birhäuser Verlag, 1978.

13. ________. Universal Algebra. New York: Springer-Verlag, 1979.

14. Jónsson, B. "Sublattices of a free lattice." Canstd. J. Math. 13 (1961): 256-264.

15. ________. "Algebras whose congruence lattices are distributive." Math. Scand. 21 (1967): 110-121.

16. Jónsson, B. "Equational classes of lattices." Math. Scand. 22 (1968): 187-196.

17. ________. "Varieties of lattices: some open problems." Proceedings of the Colloquium held in Estrogem, 1977. Colloquia Mathematica Societatis János Bolyai. To appear.

18. Jónsson, B., and Nation, J. B. "A report on sublattices of a free lattice." Contributions to Universal Algebra. Proceedings of the Colloquium held in Szeged, 1974. Colloquia Mathematica Societatis János Bolyai, Vol. 17. Amsterdam: North-Holland Publishing Co., 223-257.

19. Jónsson, B., and Rival, I. "Critical edges in subdirectly irreducible lattices." Proc. Amer. Math. Soc. 66 (1977): 194-196.

20. ________. "Lattice varieties covering the smallest non-modular variety." Pacific J. Math. 82 (1979): 463-478.

21. Kostinsky, A. "Projective lattices and bounded homomorphisms." Pacific J. Math. 40 (1978): 111-119.

22. McKenzie, R. "Equational bases for lattice theories." Math. Scand. 27 (1970): 24-38.

23. ________. "Equational bases and nonmodular lattice varieties." Trans. Amer. Math. Soc. 174 (1972): 1-43.

24. Neumann, B. H. Universal Algebra. Lecture Notes. Courant Inst. of Math. Sci., New York Univ., 1962.

25. Rival, I. "Projective lattices of modular (distributive, complemented) lattices are modular (distributive, complemented)." Algebra Universalis 2 (1972): 395.

26. Whitman, Ph. "Free Lattices." Ann. of Math. 42 (1941): 325-329.

27. Wille, R. "Primitive subsets of lattices." Algebra Universalis 2 (1972): 95-98.

DEPARTMENT OF MATHEMATICS
UNIVERSITY OF CAPE TOWN
RONDEBOSCH 7700, C.P.
CAPE TOWN
REPUBLIC OF SOUTH AFRICA

General instructions to authors for
PREPARING REPRODUCTION COPY FOR MEMOIRS

For more detailed instructions send for AMS booklet, "A Guide for Authors of Memoirs." Write to Editorial Offices, American Mathematical Society, P. O. Box 6248, Providence, R. I. 02940.

MEMOIRS are printed by photo-offset from camera copy fully prepared by the author. This means that, except for a reduction in size of 20 to 30%, the finished book will look exactly like the copy submitted. Thus the author will want to use a good quality typewriter with a new, medium-inked black ribbon, and submit clean copy on the appropriate model paper.

Model Paper, provided at no cost by the AMS, is paper marked with blue lines that confine the copy to the appropriate size. Author should specify, when ordering, whether typewriter to be used has PICA-size (10 characters to the inch) or ELITE-size type (12 characters to the inch).

Line Spacing – For best appearance, and economy, a typewriter equipped with a half-space ratchet – 12 notches to the inch – should be used. (This may be purchased and attached at small cost.) Three notches make the desired spacing, which is equivalent to 1-1/2 ordinary single spaces. Where copy has a great many subscripts and superscripts, however, double spacing should be used.

Special Characters may be filled in carefully freehand, using dense black ink, or INSTANT ("rub-on") LETTERING may be used. AMS has a sheet of several hundred most-used symbols and letters which may be purchased for $5.

Diagrams may be drawn in black ink either directly on the model sheet, or on a separate sheet and pasted with rubber cement into spaces left for them in the text. Ballpoint pen is *not* acceptable.

Page Headings (Running Heads) should be centered, in CAPITAL LETTERS (preferably), at the top of the page – just above the blue line and touching it.

LEFT-hand, EVEN-numbered pages should be headed with the AUTHOR'S NAME;

RIGHT-hand, ODD-numbered pages should be headed with the TITLE of the paper (in shortened form if necessary).

Exceptions: PAGE 1 and any other page that carries a display title require NO RUNNING HEADS.

Page Numbers should be at the top of the page, on the same line with the running heads.

LEFT-hand, EVEN numbers – flush with left margin;

RIGHT-hand, ODD numbers – flush with right margin.

Exceptions: PAGE 1 and any other page that carries a display title should have page number, centered below the text, on blue line provided.

FRONT MATTER PAGES should be numbered with Roman numerals (lower case), positioned below text in same manner as described above.

MEMOIRS FORMAT

It is suggested that the material be arranged in pages as indicated below.
Note: Starred items (*) are requirements of publication.

Front Matter (first pages in book, preceding main body of text).

Page i – *Title, *Author's name.

Page iii – Table of contents.

Page iv – *Abstract (at least 1 sentence and at most 300 words).

*1980 Mathematics Subject Classifications represent the primary and secondary subjects of the paper. For the classification scheme, see Annual Subject Indexes of MATHEMATICAL REVIEWS beginning in December 1978.

Key words and phrases, if desired. (A list which covers the content of the paper adequately enough to be useful for an information retrieval system.)

Page v, etc. – Preface, introduction, or any other matter not belonging in body of text.

Page 1 – Chapter Title (dropped 1 inch from top line, and centered).

Beginning of Text.

Footnotes: *Received by the editor date.

Support information – grants, credits, etc.

Last Page (at bottom) – Author's affiliation.

ABCDEFGHIJ–AMS–8987654

Number 293

Ronald A. DeVore
and Robert C. Sharpley

Maximal functions measuring smoothness

Memoirs
of the American Mathematical Society

Providence · Rhode Island · USA

January 1984 · Volume 47 · Number 293 (fifth of six numbers) · ISSN 0065-9266

Memoirs of the American Mathematical Society

Number 293

Ronald A. DeVore
and Robert C. Sharpley

Maximal functions measuring smoothness

Published by the
AMERICAN MATHEMATICAL SOCIETY
Providence, Rhode Island, USA

January 1984 · Volume 47 · Number 293 (fifth of six numbers)

MEMOIRS of the American Mathematical Society

This journal is designed particularly for long research papers (and groups of cognate papers) in pure and applied mathematics. It includes, in general, longer papers than those in the TRANSACTIONS.

Mathematical papers intended for publication in the Memoirs should be addressed to one of the editors. Subjects, and the editors associated with them, follow:

MEMOIRS are printed by photo-offset from camera-ready copy fully prepared by the authors. Prospective authors are encouraged to request booklet giving detailed instructions regarding reproduction copy. Write to Editorial Office, American Mathematical Society, P.O. Box 6248, Providence, Rhode Island 02940. For general instructions, see last page of Memoir.

SUBSCRIPTION INFORMATION. The 1984 subscription begins with Number 289 and consists of six mailings, each containing one or more numbers. Subscription prices for 1984 are $148 list; $74 member. A late charge of 10% of the subscription price will be imposed upon orders received from nonmembers after January 1 of the subscription year. Subscribers outside the United States and India must pay a postage surcharge of $10; subscribers in India must pay a postage surcharge of $15. Each number may be ordered separately; *please specify number* when ordering an individual number. For prices and titles of recently released numbers, refer to the New Publications sections of the NOTICES of the American Mathematical Society.

BACK NUMBER INFORMATION. For back issues see the AMS Catalogue of Publications.

TRANSACTIONS of the American Mathematical Society

This journal consists of shorter tracts which are of the same general character as the papers published in the MEMOIRS. The editorial committee is identical with that for the MEMOIRS so that papers intended for publication in this series should be addressed to one of the editors listed above.

Subscriptions and orders for publications of the American Mathematical Society should be addressed to American Mathematical Society, P. O. Box 1571, Annex Station, Providence, R. I. 02901. *All orders must be accompanied by payment.* Other correspondence should be addressed to P. O. Box 6248, Providence, R. I. 02940.

MEMOIRS of the American Mathematical Society (ISSN 0065-9266) is published bimonthly (each volume consisting usually of more than one number) by the American Mathematical Society at 201 Charles Street, Providence, Rhode Island 02904. Second Class postage paid at Providence, Rhode Island 02940. Postmaster: Send address changes to Memoirs of the American Mathematical Society, American Mathematical Society, P. O. Box 6248, Providence, RI 02940.

Table of Contents

Abstract

Maximal functions which measure the smoothness of a function are introduced and studied from the point of view of their relationship to classical smoothness and their use in proving embedding theorems, extension theorems and various results on differentiation. New spaces of functions which generalize Sobolev spaces are introduced.

AMS(MOS) subject classifications (1980).
Primary 26B35, 46E35, 26A15
Secondary 42B25

Keywords and Phrases. Maximal functions, smoothness in several variables, Sobolev embeddings, extension theorems.

Library of Congress Cataloging in Publication Data

DeVore, Ronald A.
Maximal functions measuring smoothness.

(Memoirs of the American Mathematical Society, ISSN 0065-9266 ; no. 293)
"January 1984, volume 47, number 293 (fifth of six numbers)"
Bibliography: p.
1. Functions of several real variables. 2. Smoothness of functions. 3. Maximal functions. 4. Sobolev spaces. I. Sharpley, Robert C., 1946- . II. Title. III. Series.
QA3.A57 no. 293 [QA331.5] 510s [515.8'4] 83-21494
ISBN 0-8218-2293-4

Glossary

Maximal Operators

$f^{\#}_{\alpha}$	maximal function based on $P_{[\alpha]}$	(p. 8)
f^{b}_{α}	maximal function based on $P_{(\alpha)}$	(p. 8)
$f^{\#}_{\alpha,q}$	maximal function based on $\mathcal{P}$	(p. 22)
$f^{b}_{\alpha,q}$	maximal function based on $\mathcal{P}^{b}$	(p. 22)
$N^{\alpha}_{q}(f,x)$	Calderón maximal operator	(p. 28)
M, M_q	Hardy-Littlewood maximal operators	(p. 9, 23)
$\mathcal{M}_Q, \mathcal{M}_q$	variants of Hardy-Littlewood maximal operators	(p. 9, 23)
F^{**}	the averaged rearrangement of F	(p, 63)

Spaces

$\mathbb{P}_k$	polynomials of total degree at most k	(p. 8)
W^k_p	Sobolev spaces of order k	(p. 17)
$B^{\alpha,q}_p$	Besov spaces of order α	(p. 19)
C^{α}_p		(p. 36; p. 104 for $p < 1$)
$\mathcal{C}^{\alpha}_p$		(p. 36; p. 104 for $p < 1$)
$X_{\theta,q}$; $(X_1,X_2)_{\theta,q}$	"real" interpolation spaces	(p. 65)

Projections

P, P_k	projections from L_1 (unit cube) onto $\mathbb{P}_k$	(p. 8)
P_Q	projections from $L_1(Q)$ onto $\mathbb{P}_k$ induced by P	(p. 8)
f_Q	average of f over Q	(p. 8)
$\mathcal{P}_Q$, $\mathcal{P}^{\#}_Q$	best approximation of degree $[\alpha]$ on $L_q(Q)$	(p. 22)
$\mathcal{P}^{b}_Q$	best approximation of degree (α) on $L_q(Q)$	(p. 22)

Glossary

General

$[\alpha]$	greatest integer $\leqq \alpha$	(p. 8)
(α)	greatest integer $< \alpha$	(p. 8)
Q_0	unit cube in $\mathbb{R}^n$	(p. 8)
Ω	open set in $\mathbb{R}^n$	(p. 8)
Δ_h^k	k^{th} difference with step size h	(p. 14)
λQ	dilation of Q by λ	(p. 16)
$\omega_r(f,t)_p$	r^{th} order modulus of smoothness in L_p	(p. 19)
$D_\nu f(x)$	ν^{th} Peano derivative of f at x	(p. 30)
$D^\nu f$	ν^{th} distributional derivative	(p. 33)
P_x	Taylor polynomial	(p. 29, 32)
$K(f,t;X_o,X_1)$	Peetre K-functional	(p. 59)
$K_r(f,t)_p$		(p. 47)
f^*	the decreasing rearrangement of $\|f\|$	(p. 22)
c	generic constant depending at most on α and n unless otherwise specified.	

Acknowledgements

The authors would like to express their thanks to Colin Bennett for early discussions relating to this manuscript. Partial support for this research was provided to the first author by NSF Grant 8101661 and to the second author by NSF Grant 8102194.

We would also like to express our sincere appreciation to Ms. Cleo Washington for her patience and accurate typing of the manscript.

To Jana and Carla

§1. Introduction

Maximal functions play a central role in the study of differentiation, singular integrals and almost everywhere convergence. For example, the classical Lebesgue differentiation theorem follows readily from the mapping properties of the Hardy-Littlewood maximal operator:

(1.1) $$Mf(x) := \sup_{Q \ni x} \frac{1}{|Q|} \int_Q |f|$$

where the sup is taken over all cubes $Q \subset \mathbb{R}^n$ which contain x. The key property of M for differentiation theory is that M is of weak type (1,1), i.e.

(1.2) $$|\{x: Mf(x) > y\}| \leq \frac{c}{y} \int_{\mathbb{R}^n} |f|, \qquad y > 0.$$

It is perhaps less well known that other maximal functions are useful in the study of smoothness of functions and the mapping properties of various operators on smoothness spaces. The main theme of this monograph is to study certain maximal functions of this type and related spaces of functions.

To begin with the simplest example, let $0 \leq \alpha < 1$ and consider the maximal function

(1.3) $$f_\alpha^\#(x) := \sup_{Q \ni x} \frac{1}{|Q|^{1+\alpha/n}} \int_Q |f - f_Q|$$

where

(1.4) $$f_Q := \frac{1}{|Q|} \int_Q f$$

is the average of f over the cube Q. The maximal function $f_\alpha^\#$ was apparently first introduced in a paper of A. P. Calderón and R. Scott [6]. The case $\alpha = 0$ is important in the study of the space BMO - functions of bounded mean oscillation. For example, BMO can be described as the set of functions f such that $f_0^\# \in L_\infty$ and $\|f_0^\#\|_{L_\infty}$ is equivalent to the usual BMO norm. The fact that the L_p spaces are interpolation spaces between L_1 and BMO rests on the fact that $f_0^\# \in L_p$ is "equivalent" to $f \in L_p$ (see §6).

Received by the editors June 1, 1982.

When $0 < \alpha < 1$, the maximal function $f_\alpha^\#$ measures the smoothness of f. For example if $x,y \in \mathbb{R}^n$, we have the simple inequality (cf. (2.16))

$$|f(x) - f(y)| \leqq c\ [f_\alpha^\#(x) + f_\alpha^\#(y)]\ |x-y|^\alpha.$$

Thus, the finiteness of $f_\alpha^\#$ gives a local control for the smoothness of f. In particular, if $f_\alpha^\# \in L_\infty$, then $f \in \mathrm{Lip}\ \alpha$ on $\mathbb{R}^n$. Actually, the converse is also true. Namely, if $f \in \mathrm{Lip}\ \alpha$ on $\mathbb{R}^n$ then $f_\alpha^\# \in L_\infty$ (see Theorem 6.3).

The mappings $f \to f_Q$ are linear projections from $L_1(Q)$ onto the space of constant functions. They arise from the projection P_0: $f \to \int_{Q_0} f$, $Q_0 = [0,1]^n$, by change of scale. To extend the definition of $f_\alpha^\#$ to $\alpha \geqq 1$, we replace P_0 by a projection P_k, $k = [\alpha]$, mapping $L_1(Q_0)$ onto $\mathbb{P}_k$ the space of polynomials of degree at most k. Such a projection P gives rise to projections P_Q: $L_1(Q) \to \mathbb{P}_k$ for each Q by change of scale. This leads to the maximal function

$$(1.5) \qquad f_\alpha^\#(x) := \sup_{Q \ni x} \frac{1}{|Q|^{1+\alpha/n}} \int_Q |f-P_Qf|, \qquad P = P_{[\alpha]}.$$

It turns out that different projections of the same degree give equivalent maximal functions (see §2). In fact, there is an important property which shows that any projection P of degree $\geqq [\alpha]$ when used in (1.5) gives a maximal function equivalent to $f_\alpha^\#$ (cf. Lemma 2.3). This is akin to the Marchaud inequalities for moduli of smoothness.

When α is an integer, there is another important, indeed perhaps more natural, choice for the degree of the projection, namely, (α) - the greatest integer strictly less than α. This choice gives the maximal function

$$(1.6) \qquad f_\alpha^\flat(x) := \sup_{Q \ni x} \frac{1}{|Q|^{1+\alpha/n}} \int_Q |f-P_Qf|, \qquad P = P_{(\alpha)}.$$

Note that $f_\alpha^\flat = f_\alpha^\#$ if α is non-integral. Also it can be shown (Corollary 2.2) that $f_\alpha^\# \leqq c\ f_\alpha^\flat$ if α is an integer.

There are several modifications of the definitions (1.5-6) which lead to equivalent maximal functions. One of the more important is that (§2) the maximal function

$$(1.7) \qquad \sup_{Q \ni x}\ \inf_{\pi \in \mathbb{P}_k} \frac{1}{|Q|^{1+\alpha/n}} \int_Q |f-\pi|$$

is equivalent to $f_\alpha^\#$ if $k = [\alpha]$ and is equivalent to $f_\alpha^\flat$ if $k = (\alpha)$.

Another important variant is the maximal function defined by

$$N_1^\alpha(f,x) := \sup_{Q \ni x} \frac{1}{|Q|^{1+\alpha/n}} \int_Q |f-P_x| \tag{1.8}$$

if there is a polynomial P_x of degree less than α such that (1.8) is finite. Maximal functions of this type were introduced by A. P. Calderón [5] and studied by A. P. Calderón and R. Scott [6]. If there is a P_x which makes (1.8) finite then it is unique. Notice that in (1.8), P_x stays fixed as Q varies, but in (1.6), $P_Q f$ varies with Q. Nevertheless it turns out that the maximal functions $N_1^\alpha(f)$ and $f_\alpha^\flat$ are equivalent (Theorem 5.3). The equivalence of these maximal functions rests on the fact that when $f_\alpha^\flat(x)$ is finite then f has Peano derivatives of order ν at x for each $|\nu| < \alpha$. The polynomial P_x is then the Taylor polynomial of degree (α) formed from these Peano derivatives.

The maximal functions $f_\alpha^\flat$ are related to classical differentiation. For example, it follows from results of Calderón [5] that if $f_k^\flat$ is locally in L_1, then the weak derivatives $D^\nu f$ exist a.e. and satisfy

$$\sum_{|\nu|=k} |D^\nu f(x)| \leqq c\, f_k^\flat(x) , \quad \text{a.e.} \tag{1.9}$$

In the other direction, we have

$$f_k^\flat(x) \leqq c\, M\Big(\sum_{|\nu|=k} |D^\nu f|\Big)(x) \tag{1.10}$$

whenever f has weak derivatives $D^\nu f$ which are locally in L_1. The connections between the finiteness of the maximal functions $f_\alpha^\#$, $f_\alpha^\flat$ with classical differentiation, Peano derivatives and the like are investigated in §5.

The maximal functions $f_\alpha^\#$, $f_\alpha^\flat$ can be used in a natural way to define new spaces of functions. If $1 \leqq p \leqq \infty$ and $\alpha > 0$, let $C_p^\alpha := \{f \in L_p : f_\alpha^\# \in L_p\}$ and $\|f\|_{C_p^\alpha} := \|f\|_{L_p} + \|f_\alpha^\#\|_{L_p}$. The analogous space $\mathcal{C}_p^\alpha$ and norm $\|\ \|_{\mathcal{C}_p^\alpha}$ are defined with $f_\alpha^\flat$ in place of $f_\alpha^\#$. These are spaces of smoothness α. The major theme of this work is to study the properties of these spaces and their use in the study of smoothness properties of functions.

There are several smoothness spaces of fractional order. The most useful are the potential spaces $\mathcal{L}_p^\alpha$ (see [15, Chapter V]) and the Besov spaces $B_p^{\alpha,q}$ (see §3). As we have already noted the spaces C_∞^α are related to Lipschitz spaces. Indeed, we have $C_\infty^\alpha = B_\infty^{\alpha,\infty}$ for all $\alpha > 0$. Recall, $B_\infty^{\alpha,\infty}$ is the space Lip α if α is not an integer and is Lip* α (higher order differences) when α is integral. Also $\mathcal{C}_\infty^\alpha$ = Lip α for all $\alpha > 0$. Moreover, it follows from (1.9-10) that $\mathcal{C}_p^k$ is the Sobolev space W_p^k if $1 < p \leqq \infty$ and k is an integer. It turns out that the spaces C_p^α and $\mathcal{C}_p^\alpha$ are not Besov or potential spaces for any other values of p and α. Rather, they offer an attractive alternative to the Besov and potential spaces for many problems in analysis. One of the main advantages of the spaces C_p^α, $\mathcal{C}_p^\alpha$ lies in the fact that for fractional α the function $f_\alpha^\# = f_\alpha^\flat$ is akin to a fractional derivative of f, or better said, a maximal fractional derivative. Thus, these spaces are similar in nature to the Sobolev spaces.

In §7, we establish embeddings between Besov spaces, potential spaces and C_p^α. If $1 \leqq p \leqq \infty$ and $\alpha > 0$, then we have the continuous embeddings

$$B_p^{\alpha,p} \to C_p^\alpha \to B_p^{\alpha,\infty} .$$

These embeddings cannot be improved within the scale of Besov spaces. For potential spaces, we have the continuous embedding

$$\mathcal{L}_p^\alpha \to C_p^\alpha .$$

Of course, $\mathcal{L}_p^\alpha = \mathcal{C}_p^\alpha$ when α is an integer and $1 < p < \infty$ but they are unequal for all other values of p and α.

For fixed $\alpha > 0$, the spaces C_p^α and $\mathcal{C}_p^\alpha$ form interpolation scales as p ranges over $[1,\infty]$. In fact, we show in §8 the characterization of the K functional

$$K(f,t,C_1^\alpha,C_\infty^\alpha) \approx \int_0^t [f^*(s)+f_\alpha^{\#*}(s)]ds \tag{1.11}$$

where g* denotes the decreasing rearrangement of a function g. A similar result holds for $K(f,t,\mathcal{C}_1^\alpha,\mathcal{C}_\infty^\alpha)$ with $f_\alpha^\#$ replaced by $f_\alpha^\flat$. Of course, (1.11) is a statement about decomposing a function f in C_1^α as $f = f-g + g$ with $g \in C_\infty^\alpha$

and a control on $||f-g||_{C_1^\alpha}$ and $||g||_{C_\infty^\alpha}$. Decompositions of this type were given by A. P. Calderón [5]. For a given $t > 0$, one considers

$$E_t := \{f_\alpha^{\#} > f_\alpha^{\#*}(t)\} \cup \{Mf > (Mf)^*(t)\}.$$

The function f is smooth outside of E_t. The function g is the extension of f from E_t^c to all of $\mathbb{R}^n$. It is also possible to use the techniques developed for (1.11) to the K functional for interpolation between W_1^k and W_∞^k as was done in R. DeVore-K. Scherer [8]. We should mention that for p fixed and α varying, the spaces C_p^α (or $\dot{C}_p^\alpha$) are not interpolation scales with respect to the real method of interpolation since the corresponding interpolation spaces are Besov spaces [see Theorem 8.6].

We prove Sobolev type embedding theorems for the spaces C_p^α (and $\dot{C}_p^\alpha$) in §9. These follow from inequalities for $f_\alpha^{\#}$. For example, the inequality

$$|P_Q f(u)-f(u)| \leqq c \int_0^{|Q|} f_\alpha^{\#*}(s)\, s^{\alpha/n} \frac{ds}{s} \tag{1.12}$$

holds for any Q and f. The right hand side tends to zero as $|Q|\downarrow 0$ whenever $f_\alpha^{\#} \in L_{n,1}$ (the Lorentz space). This gives the embedding $\{f \in L_1 : f_\alpha^{\#} \in L_{n/\alpha,1}\} \to C$. The inequality (1.12) (for $\alpha=1$) can be exploited further to give a straight forward proof of the result of E. Stein [16] which says if $\nabla f \in L_{n,1}$ locally then $|f(x+h)-f(x)-\nabla f(x)\cdot h| = o(|h|)$ a.e. in x.

We also establish continuous embeddings $C_p^\alpha \to C_q^\beta$ if $\alpha - \beta = n(1/p-1/q)$ and $1 \leqq p \leqq q \leqq \infty$. In the case $\beta = 0$, the space C_q^β can be replaced by L_q, $1 \leqq q < \infty$ and BMO, $q = \infty$.

Results in the paper are established for domains in $\mathbb{R}^n$. There are two types of results: those that hold for all domains Ω, and those that hold only with some smoothness conditions on Ω. Whenever a result is of the first type, we prove it in its full generality directly. For results of the second type, we establish them originally only for $\Omega = \mathbb{R}^n$ or Ω a cube in $\mathbb{R}^n$. Later in §11, these results are generalized to domains with minimally smooth boundary in the sense of Stein [15] by using extension theorems for the spaces C_p^α and $\dot{C}_p^\alpha$.

We prove the extension theorems of §10-11 using the ideas of Whitney who first proved such extension theorems for Lip α spaces. The constructon uses a Whitney decomposition of Ω^c into cubes $\{Q_j\}$ whose distance to the boundary is comparable to its sidelength and a related partition of unity $\{\phi_j^*\}_1^\infty$ with ϕ_j^* supported on a cube $Q_j^* \subset \Omega^c$ slightly larger than Q_j. Our extension operator then takes the form

$$Ef(x) := \begin{cases} f(x), & x \in \Omega \\ \sum_1^\infty P_{\tilde{Q}_j} f(x)\phi_j^*(x), & x \in \Omega^c \end{cases}$$

where the cubes $\tilde{Q}_j$ are contained in Ω and dist $(\tilde{Q}_j, Q_j) \leq c$ diam (Q_j). This technique should be compared to the usual approach to extension theorems for Sobolev spaces $W_p^k(\Omega)$ based on potential integrals (see [15, Ch. V]. Since $\mathcal{C}_p^k = W_p^k$, $1 < p \leq \infty$, our results include extension theorems for Sobolev spaces. While preparing this paper, it was pointed out to us by S. Krantz that P. Jones [12] had also used the ideas of Whitney to prove extension theorems for Sobolev spaces although P. Jones' interest is different than ours. Namely he investigates the weakest smoothness on Ω which are sufficient to guarantee extensions for $W_p^k(\Omega)$, $1 \leq p < \infty$.

In §12, we indicate to what extent the results of the previous sections carry over to the case p<1. The spaces C_p^α and $\mathcal{C}_p^\alpha$ for p<1 are not defined in terms of $f_\alpha^\#$ and $f_\alpha^\flat$ but instead use variants $f_{\alpha,p}^\#$ and $f_{\alpha,p}^\flat$ which are defined as in (1.7) but with L_p norms in place of L_1 norms. The maximal functions $f_{\alpha,p}^\#$ and $f_{\alpha,p}^\flat$ are studied in §4. We show among other things that for $1 \leq p \leq \infty$ the space $\{f \in L_p: f_{\alpha,q}^\# \in L_p\}$ is equal to C_p^α provided that $q \leq p$. This equivalence only persists for a certain range of p<1 and in fact the "proper" definition of C_p^α for p<1 is $C_p^\alpha := \{f \in L_p: f_{\alpha,p}^\# \in L_p\}$. With this definition for example, we have that for fixed α, C_p^α $(p_0 \leq p \leq p_1)$ is an interpolation space for the pair $(C_{p_0}^\alpha, C_{p_1}^\alpha)$ whenever $0 < p_0 < p_1 \leq \infty$. Finally, we indicate the proof of the extension theorem for minimally smooth domains where $0 < p \leqq 1$ and use it to get embedding theorems and interpolation theorems for these domains in this case.

As we have already mentioned, the maximal function $f_\alpha^\flat$ is equivalent to the maximal function $N_1^\alpha(f)$ introduced by Calderón. For this reason, there is considerable overlap of this work with the papers [5] and [6], most notably in §5 and §8. Rather than refer the readers back to these papers, we have chosen to integrate their results into our development. We have also included some elementary and for the most part well known results about polynomials and approximation in §3.

We have been encouraged by the referee to make some remarks on homogenous spaces. The results presented in this monograph are for non-homogeneous spaces C_p^α, $\dot{C}_p^\alpha$. The corresponding homogeneous spaces $\mathring{C}_p^\alpha$, $\mathring{\dot{C}}_p^\alpha$ which are defined as equivalence classes of functions with respect to the seminorms $|\cdot|_{C_p^\alpha}$, $|\cdot|_{\dot{C}_p^\alpha}$ are not discussed. These spaces are not merely factor spaces (modulo polynomials of appropriate degree) since the function $f(x) := \phi(x) \log x$ ($\phi \equiv 1$ on (e,∞), $\phi \equiv 0$ on $(-\infty,0)$, smooth otherwise) satisfies $||f_\alpha^\#||_{L_p} < \infty$ for $p > 1/\alpha > 1$, but $f - \pi$ is not in L_p for any polynomial π. On the other hand, it will be clear to the reader that some of the embeddings of §7 and §9 have analogues for homogeneous spaces. For example, Lemma 2.3 can be modified appropriately to give the analogue of Theorem 9.6 for C_p^α: If $0 \leqq \beta \leqq \alpha$; $\alpha - \beta = n(\frac{1}{p} - \frac{1}{q})$; $0 < p,q$, then for each $f \in C_p^\alpha$ there is a polynomial $\pi \in \mathbb{P}_{[\alpha]}$ so that $|f - \pi|_{C_q^\beta} \leqq c\, |f|_{C_p^\alpha}$. Also the proofs in §7 show that $\mathring{B}_p^{\alpha,p} \to \mathring{C}_p^\alpha \to \mathring{B}_p^{\alpha,\infty}$.

We have included a glossary of notation indicating what the notation means and where it is first introduced or defined. Throughout the paper, we use the symbol c for generic constant whose value may be different at each occurence, even on the same line. Most often, the constant c depends at most on n and α. When this is the case, we will not mention that fact. In all other cases, we shall indicate the quantities on which c depends.

§2. Maximal Functions

Let Q_0 be the unit cube in $\mathbb{R}^n$. The space $\mathbb{P}_k$ of polynomials of (total) degree at most k is a Hilbert space with the inner product $(f,g) := \int_{Q_0} fg$. Consider the orthonormal basis $\{\phi_\nu\}$, $|\nu| \leqq k$ which results when the Gram-Schmidt orthogonalization is applied to the power functions $\{x^\nu\}_{|\nu|\leqq k}$ arranged in lexicographic order. The operator P defined by

$$Pf := P_k f := \sum_{|\nu|\leqq k} (f,\phi_\nu)\phi_\nu \tag{2.1}$$

is a projection from $L_1(Q_0)$ onto $\mathbb{P}_k$.

For any cube Q, the projection P induces a projection P_Q from $L_1(Q)$ onto $\mathbb{P}_k$ by change of scale. In particular when $k = 0$, $P_Q f = f_Q := \frac{1}{|Q|}\int_Q f$. Now take any open set $\Omega \subset \mathbb{R}^n$. If f is locally integrable on Ω and $\alpha \geqq 0$, we choose $k := [\alpha]$ and define

$$f_\alpha^{\#}(x) := \sup_{\Omega\supset Q\ni x} \frac{1}{|Q|^{1+\alpha/n}} \int_Q |f - P_Q f|. \tag{2.2}$$

The maximal function $f_\alpha^{\#}$ measures the smoothness of f. When α is an integer, we have made a choice in (2.2) of taking $k = \alpha$. The choice $k = \alpha-1$ is also important and so we introduce

$$f_\alpha^{\flat}(x) := \sup_{\Omega\supset Q\ni x} \frac{1}{|Q|^{1+\alpha/n}} \int_Q |f - P_Q^{\flat} f|$$

where $P^{\flat}$ is the projection of degree (α) (the greatest integer strictly less than α). Then $f_\alpha^{\flat}(x) \equiv f_\alpha^{\#}(x)$ if α is not an integer. The study of $f_\alpha^{\#}$, $f_\alpha^{\flat}$ and certain related maximal functions is the main theme of this paper.

There are many variants which can be incorporated into the definition (2.2) while resulting in equivalent maximal functions. From time to time, these variants are more convenient to use in proofs. Therefore, we wish to study some of these possibilities in this section. To this end, we first make some observations about the projections P_Q. It is simple to see by the construction that

(2.3) $$\|P_Q f\|_{L_\infty(Q)} \leq c \frac{1}{|Q|} \int_Q |f|.$$

Let x_0 be any point in Q, then there are polynomials h_ν (obtained from fixed polynomials on Q_0 by a change of scale) with $\|h_\nu\|_{L_\infty(Q)} \leq c$ for which

(2.4) $$P_Q f(y) = \sum_{|\nu|\leq k} \left(\frac{1}{|Q|} \int_Q f\, h_\nu\right) \left[\frac{y - \tilde{x}_0}{|Q|^{1/n}}\right]^\nu$$

where $\tilde{x}_0$ is the point in Q corresponding to x_0 under the change of scale.

Define a Hardy-Littlewood type maximal function (localized to Q) by

(2.5) $$M_Q f(x) := \begin{cases} \sup_{Q \supset \tilde{Q} \ni x} |P_{\tilde{Q}} f(x)|, & x \in Q \\ 0 \quad , & \text{otherwise} \end{cases}$$

then using (2.3) we see that

(2.6) $$M_Q f(x) \leq cM(f\chi_Q)(x) \qquad \text{if } x \in Q$$

where M is the Hardy-Littlewood maximal operator. In particular M_Q is weak-type (1, 1) and strong type (∞, ∞). Moreover, if $x \in \tilde{Q}$,

$$\begin{aligned} |f(x) - P_{\tilde{Q}} f(x)| &\leq \|f - f_{\tilde{Q}}\|_{L_\infty(\tilde{Q})} + \|P_{\tilde{Q}}(f - f_{\tilde{Q}})\|_{L_\infty(\tilde{Q})} \\ &\leq c\|f - f_{\tilde{Q}}\|_{L_\infty(\tilde{Q})} . \end{aligned}$$

It follows that

(2.7) $$\lim_{\tilde{Q}\downarrow\{x\}} P_{\tilde{Q}} f(x) = f(x)$$

for continuous f. Consequently, the weak type (1, 1) property of the maximal operator M_Q shows that (2.7) holds at each Lebesgue point of f whenever f is in $L_1(Q)$.

Lemma 2.1. If $\alpha \geq 0$ and $k := [\alpha]$, there is a constant $c > 0$ such that

$$c\, f_\alpha^{\#}(x) \leq \sup_{\Omega\supset Q\ni x} \inf_{\pi\in\mathbb{P}_k} \frac{1}{|Q|^{1+\alpha/n}} \int_Q |f - \pi| \leq f_\alpha^{\#}(x) \qquad x \in \Omega .$$

The same result holds for $f_\alpha^{\flat}$ and $k = (\alpha)$.

Proof. The right hand inequality is clear. To prove the left hand estimate, let π be any polynomial of degree at most k. Then $P_Q(\pi) = \pi$

and since P_Q is linear,

$$|f(y) - P_Q f(y)| \leq |f(y) - \pi(y)| + |P_Q(f - \pi)(y)|.$$

Integrating over Q, we obtain from (2.3)

$$\begin{aligned}\int_Q |f - P_Q f| dy &\leq \int_Q |f - \pi| dy + \int_Q |P_Q(f - \pi)| dy \\ &\leq \int_Q |f - \pi| dy + |Q| \, ||P_Q(f - \pi)||_{L_\infty(Q)} \\ &\leq c \int_Q |f - \pi| dy.\end{aligned}$$

The desired result now follows by taking an infinum over π, dividing by $|Q|^{1+\alpha/n}$, and then taking a supremum over all cubes Q containing x. □

The same proof shows that any other projection $\tilde{P}$ from $L_1(Q_0)$ to $\mathbb{P}_k$ would lead to a maximal function which is equivalent to $f_\alpha^{\#}$. The following is an immediate consequence of the last lemma.

Corollary 2.2. If $\alpha > 0$, there is a constant $c > 0$ such that for each $f \in L_1(\text{loc } \Omega)$

$$f_\alpha^{\#}(x) \leq c \, f_\alpha^{b}(x) \quad , \quad x \in \Omega.$$

The next result shows that the projections P_j with $j > [\alpha]$ (cf. (2.1)) give a maximal function equivalent to $f_\alpha^{\#}$.

Lemma 2.3. If $j \geq [\alpha]$, $\alpha \geq 0$, and

$$F_j(x) := \sup_{\Omega \supset Q \ni x} \frac{1}{|Q|^{1+\alpha/n}} \int_Q |f - (P_j)_Q f| \, ,$$

then there are constants c_1, $c_2 > 0$ depending only α, j, and n such that for each $f \in L_1(\Omega) + L_\infty(\Omega)$, $x \in \Omega$

(2.8) $$c_1 F_j(x) \leq f_\alpha^{\#}(x) \leq c_2 F_j(x), \qquad \Omega = \mathbb{R}^n$$

(2.9) $$c_1 F_j(x) \leq f_\alpha^{\#}(x) \leq c_2 [F_j(x) + \int_\Omega |f|], \ \Omega \text{ the unit cube in } \mathbb{R}^n.$$

Remark: Such upper estimates do not hold for f_α^{b} when α is an integer.

Proof. Using Lemma 2.1, the left hand inequalities in (2.8) and (2.9) are clear since $j \geq [\alpha]$.

For the right hand inequality, let $j > [\alpha]$. We will estimate F_{j-1} by F_j for each such j. Begin by choosing cubes $Q = Q_1 \subset Q_2 \subset \cdots \subset Q_N \subset \Omega$ with $|Q_i| = 2^{-n}|Q_{i+1}|$. Further properties of this sequence will be prescribed shortly. If P denotes the projection operator P_j, we can write

(2.10) $$f = [f - P_{Q_1} f] + \sum_{i=1}^{N-1} P_{Q_i}(f - P_{Q_{i+1}} f) + P_{Q_N} f$$

$$=: f - P_{Q_1} f + \sum_{i=1}^{N-1} \pi_i + \pi_N.$$

Now fix x in Ω. According to (2.4), for $1 \leqq i \leqq N-1$, each polynomial π_i can be written

$$\pi_i = \sum_{|\nu|=j} [\frac{1}{|Q_i|} \int_{Q_i} (f - P_{Q_{i+1}} f)\, h_{\nu,i}] \left[\frac{y - x}{|Q_i|^{1/n}}\right]^\nu + \rho_i$$

with ρ_i of degree at most j-1. Similary

$$\pi_N = \sum_{|\nu|=j} [\frac{1}{|Q_N|} \int_{Q_N} f\, h_{\nu,N}] \left(\frac{y - x}{|Q_N|^{1/n}}\right)^\nu + \rho_N .$$

Let $\rho := \sum_1^N \rho_i$ so that ρ has degree at most j - 1. Using (2.10), (2.3), and the fact that the $h_{\nu,i}$'s are uniformly bounded, we find

(2.11) $$\frac{1}{|Q|^{1+\alpha/n}} \int_Q |f-\rho| \leqq \frac{1}{|Q_1|^{1+\alpha/n}} \int_{Q_1} |f-P_{Q_1} f|$$

$$+ \frac{1}{|Q|^{1+\alpha/n}} \sum_{|\nu|=j} \sum_{i=1}^{N-1} [\frac{1}{|Q_i|} \int_{Q_i} |f-P_{Q_{i+1}} f|] \int_Q \left|\left(\frac{y - x}{|Q_i|^{1/n}}\right)^\nu\right| dy$$

$$+ \frac{c}{|Q|^{1+\alpha/n}} \sum_{|\nu|=j} [\frac{1}{|Q_N|} \int_{Q_N} |f|] \int_Q \left|\left(\frac{y - x}{|Q_N|^{1/n}}\right)^\nu\right| dy$$

$$=: I + II + III.$$

We can estimate I trivially

$$I \leqq F_j(x).$$

Using the fact that $x \in Q_i \subset Q_{i+1}$ and $|Q_{i+1}| = 2^n |Q_i|$, we find

$$II \leq \frac{c}{|Q|^{1+\alpha/n}} \sum_{i=1}^{N-1} [\frac{1}{|Q_i|} \int_{Q_i} |f-P_{Q_{i+1}} f|] (\frac{|Q|}{|Q_i|})^{j/n} |Q|$$

$$\leq \frac{c}{|Q|^{\alpha/n}} \sum_{i=1}^{N-1} F_j(x) |Q_i|^{\alpha/n} (\frac{|Q|}{|Q_i|})^{j/n}$$

$$\leq c (\sum_{i=1}^{N-1} 2^{i\alpha} 2^{-ij}) F_j(x) \leq c F_j(x)$$

where the constant c does not depend on N.

The sum III can be estimated by

$$\text{(2.12)} \qquad III \leq \frac{c}{|Q_N|} \int_{Q_N} |f| \quad (\frac{|Q|}{|Q_N|})^{j/n} |Q|^{-\alpha/n} .$$

If $\Omega = \mathbb{R}^n$, the right hand side tends to 0 as $n \to \infty$. Therefore the estimates for I, II, and III in this case give

$$\text{(2.13)} \qquad \frac{1}{|Q|^{1+\alpha/n}} \int_Q |f - \rho| \leq c F_j(x).$$

Since ρ is of degree at most $j - 1$, the argument in Lemma 2.1 then shows

$$F_{j-1}(x) \leq c F_j(x).$$

Repeated application of this inequality establishes (2.8).

When Ω is the unit cube in $\mathbb{R}^n$, we can choose N so that $Q_N \subset \Omega$ and $2^n|Q_N| > |\Omega|$. In this case (2.12) gives

$$III \leq c \frac{1}{|\Omega|^{j/n+1}} \int_\Omega |f| \quad |Q|^{(j-\alpha)/n} \leq c \int_\Omega |f| .$$

Hence

$$F_{j-1}(x) \leq c[F_j(x) + \int_\Omega |f|] .$$

Repeated application of this inequality gives (2.9). □

One other observation will be helpful to us:

(2.14) In the case $\Omega = \mathbb{R}^n$, any maximal function of the type introduced in this section is equivalent to the corresponding maximal function resulting when the supremum over all cubes Q containing the point x is replaced by a supremum over

i) cubes centered at x;

or ii) spheres containing x or centered at x,

or iii) any family of sets $\mathcal{S}_x$ such that for any $S \in \mathcal{S}_x$ there are cubes Q_1, Q_2 containing x with $Q_1 \subset S \subset Q_2$, and $|Q_2| \leqq c_0 |Q_1|$ where c_0 depends at most on n.

For $f^{\#}_{\alpha}$, f^{b}_{α} this follows from the simple fact that when $S_1 \subset S_2$ and $|S_2| \leqq c|S_1|$, then for any $g \geqq 0$

$$\frac{1}{|S_1|^{1+\alpha/n}} \int_{S_1} g \leqq \frac{c}{|S_2|^{1+\alpha/n}} \int_{S_2} g.$$

The maximal functions $f^{\#}_{\alpha}$ and f^{b}_{α} give a control for the smoothness of f as will be shown in our next theorem. First we give the following estimate for $P_Q f$. Henceforth, unless otherwise indicated, if $\alpha \geqq 0$ then P is the projection operator of degree $[\alpha]$.

Lemma 2.4. If $x \in Q^* \subset Q \subset \Omega$,

$$\|D^{\nu}(P_Q f - P_{Q^*} f)\|_{L_\infty(Q^*)} \leqq c\,|Q|^{\frac{\alpha-|\nu|}{n}} \inf_{u\in Q^*} f^{\#}_{\alpha}(u) \tag{2.15}$$

for $0 \leqq |\nu| < \alpha$. This inequality also holds for $|\nu| = \alpha$ provided $|Q| \leqq 2^n |Q^*|$. The same statements hold for P^b replacing P and f^b_α replacing $f^{\#}_{\alpha}$.

Proof. Consider first the case when $|Q| \leqq 2^n |Q^*|$ and $|\nu| \leqq \alpha$, then by Markov's inequality

$$\|D^{\nu}(P_Q f - P_{Q^*} f)\|_{L_\infty(Q^*)} \leqq c|Q^*|^{-|\nu|/n} \|P_Q f - P_{Q^*} f\|_{L_\infty(Q^*)}.$$

Using (2.3) and the fact that P_Q is a projection gives

$$\|P_Q f - P_{Q^*} f\|_{L_\infty(Q^*)} \leqq \|P_{Q^*}(f - P_Q f)\|_{L_\infty(Q^*)} \leqq \frac{c}{|Q^*|} \int_{Q^*} |f - P_Q f|$$

$$\leqq \frac{c}{|Q|} \int_Q |f - P_Q f| \leqq c\,|Q|^{\alpha/n} \inf_{u\in Q^*} f^{\#}_{\alpha}(u)$$

which combines with the preceding inequality to give (2.15) in this case.

For the general case of arbitrary $Q^* \subset Q$ and $|\nu| < \alpha$ choose a sequence of nested cubes $Q^* =: Q_1 \subset Q_2 \subset \ldots \subset Q_m \subset Q =: Q_{m+1}$ with $|Q_{i+1}| = 2^n |Q_i|$, $1 \leqq i \leqq m$, and $|Q_{m+1}| \leqq 2^n |Q_m|$, then using the case we have just established, we have

$$\|D^\nu(P_Q f - P_{Q^*} f)\|_{L_\infty(Q^*)} \leqq \sum_{i=1}^{m} \|D^\nu(P_{Q_{i+1}} f - P_{Q_i} f)\|_{L_\infty(Q_i)}$$

$$\leqq c \sum_{i=1}^{m} |Q_i|^{\frac{\alpha-|\nu|}{n}} \inf_{u \in Q^*} f_\alpha^\#(u)$$

$$\leqq c|Q|^{\frac{\alpha-|\nu|}{n}} \inf_{u \in Q^*} f_\alpha^\#(u)$$

where we have used the fact that $(|Q_i|^{\frac{\alpha-|\nu|}{n}})$ is a geometric sequence. The same proof applies for $P^\flat$ and $f_\alpha^\flat$. □

Let Δ_h denote the difference operator defined by $\Delta_h(f, x) := f(x + h) - f(x)$ and define its powers Δ_h^k inductively as $\Delta_h^k f := \Delta_h(\Delta_h^{k-1} f)$. The difference $\Delta_h^k f$ is defined for each x such that $x, \ldots, x+kh \in \Omega$. Let Ω_h be the set of all points x such that there is a cube $Q_x \subset \Omega$ with $x + ih \in Q_x$, $i = 0, 1, \ldots, k$.

<u>Theorem 2.5</u>. Suppose $k > [\alpha]$ and f is locally integrable on Ω, then for any h,

$$(2.16) \qquad |\Delta_h^k(f, x)| \leqq c \sum_{i=0}^{k} f_\alpha^\#(x + ih)\, |h|^\alpha \quad \text{a.e. } x \in \Omega_h.$$

<u>Proof</u>. Fix h and set $\tilde{\Omega}_h = \{x \in \Omega_h:\ x, \ldots, x + kh$ are Lebesgue points of $f\}$, then $\Omega_h \setminus \tilde{\Omega}_h$ has measure zero. If $x \in \tilde{\Omega}_h$ is fixed, set $y_i := x + ih$ with $i = 0, 1, \ldots, k$. Choose Q as the smallest cube with $\{y_0, y_1, \ldots, y_k\} \subset Q \subset \Omega$. Since each y_i is a Lebesgue point of f, if we choose cubes $Q^* \downarrow \{y_i\}$, then $P_{Q^*} f(y_i) \to f(y_i)$ and so according to Lemma 2.4,

$$|P_Q f(y_i) - f(y_i)| = \lim_{Q^* \downarrow \{y_i\}} |P_Q f(y_i) - P_{Q^*} f(y_i)|$$
$$\leqq c\, f_\alpha^{\#}(y_i)\, |Q|^{\alpha/n} \quad .$$

Since $\Delta_h^k(P_Q f) \equiv 0$, we have

$$|\Delta_h^k(f,x)| = |\Delta_h^k\,(f - P_Q f,\ x)| \leqq c \max_{0 \leqq i \leqq k} |f(y_i) - P_Q f(y_i)|$$
$$\leqq c \max_{0 \leqq i \leqq k} f_\alpha^{\#}(y_i)\, |h|^\alpha$$

which gives (2.16). □

§3. Inequalities for Polynomials

In this section, we give several inequalities for polynomials which will be used in the sequel. We begin by comparing various L_q "norms" of polynomials.

Lemma 3.1. If $k \geqq 0$, $q > 0$, there is a constant $c > 0$ depending at most on q, k and n such that for each $q \leqq p \leqq \infty$, each polynomial $\pi \in \mathbb{P}_k$ and each n-cube Q,

$$(3.1) \qquad \left(\frac{1}{|Q|} \int_Q |\pi|^q\right)^{1/q} \leqq \left(\frac{1}{|Q|} \int_Q |\pi|^p\right)^{1/p} \leqq c \left(\frac{1}{|Q|} \int_Q |\pi|^q\right)^{1/q} .$$

When either q or $p = \infty$ the corresponding expression is replaced by $||\pi||_{L_\infty(Q)}$.

Proof. The left hand inequality is an immediate consequence of Hölder's inequality. It is enough to prove the right hand inequality for $p = \infty$. To this end, choose a point $x_0 \in Q$ such that $|\pi(x_0)| = ||\pi||_{L_\infty(Q)}$. Using Markov's inequality, there is a $c_0 > 0$ depending only on k and n such that

$$|\pi(x) - \pi(x_0)| \leqq |||\nabla\pi|||_{L_\infty(Q)} \; |x-x_0| \leqq c_0 \; ||\pi||_{L_\infty(Q)} \frac{|x-x_0|}{|Q|^{1/n}} .$$

Thus if $S: = \{x \in Q: \; |x-x_0| \leqq \frac{|Q|^{1/n}}{2c_0}\}$, then $|S| \geqq c_1 \, |Q|$ with c_1 depending only on n and c_0 and

$$|\pi(x)| \geqq \frac{1}{2} \, ||\pi||_{L_\infty(Q)} \; , \; x \in S.$$

Integrating we find

$$||\pi||_{L_\infty(Q)} \leqq 2\left(\frac{1}{|S|} \int_S |\pi|^q\right)^{1/q} \leqq c\left(\frac{1}{|Q|} \int_Q |\pi|^q\right)^{1/q}. \quad \square$$

If Q is an n-cube and $\lambda > 0$, we let λQ denote the cube which has the same center as Q and side length $\lambda \ell(Q)$ where $\ell(Q)$ is the side length of Q.

Lemma 3.2. If $k \geqq 0$; $q, \lambda > 0$, then there is a constant c depending only on k, q, λ and n such that for each $\pi \in \mathbb{P}_k$ and each cube Q, we have

(3.2) $$\left(\frac{1}{|\lambda Q|}\int_{\lambda Q}|\pi|^q\right)^{1/q} \leq c\left(\frac{1}{|Q|}\int_Q |\pi|^q\right)^{1/q}.$$

In the case $q = \infty$, the norms in (3.2) are replaced by L_∞ norms over λQ and Q respectively.

Proof. For $Q = Q_0$, the unit cube, (3.2) holds for $1 \leqq q \leqq \infty$ since any two norms on $\mathbb{P}_k$ are equivalent. For any other cube Q and $1 \leqq q \leqq \infty$, (3.2) now follows from the case Q_0 by a change of variables. The case $q < 1$ follows by using (3.1) with $p = 1$. □

Our next lemma estimates the coefficients of a polynomial.

Lemma 3.3. If $k \geqq 0$, $q > 0$, there is a constant c depending only on k, q and n such that for each polynomial $\pi(x) = \sum_{|\nu|\leqq k} c_\nu (y-x_0)^\nu$ and any cube Q with $x_0 \in Q$,

(3.3) $$\sum_{|\nu|\leqq k} |c_\nu||Q|^{|\nu|/n} \leqq c\left(\frac{1}{|Q|}\int_Q |\pi|^q\right)^{1/q}.$$

When $q = \infty$, (3.3) holds if the right hand side is replaced by $c\,||\pi||_{L_\infty(Q)}$.

Proof. By translating the cube if necessary we can assume $x_0 = 0$. Also in view of (3.1), we need only prove (3.3) for $q = \infty$. When $Q = [-1,1]^n$ and $q = \infty$, then (3.3) follows from the fact that any two norms on $\mathbb{P}_k$ are equivalent. The case $Q = [-\lambda,\lambda]^n$ and $q = \infty$ follows from the case $Q = [-1,1]^n$ by a simple change of variables. Finally, for an arbitrary cube Q of side length ℓ with $0 \in Q$, we have $Q \subset [-\ell,\ell]^n =: \bar{Q}$. Hence

$$\sum_{|\nu|\leqq k} |c_\nu|\,\ell^{|\nu|} \leqq c\,||\pi||_{L_\infty(\bar{Q})} \leqq c\,||\pi||_{L_\infty(Q)}$$

where the last inequality uses (3.2) together with the fact that $\bar{Q} \subset 3Q$. □

We now turn briefly to some well known principles (cf [14] or [7]) concerning the approximation of functions by polynomials. Let $W_p^k(\Omega)$, $1 \leqq p \leqq \infty$, $k = 1,2,\ldots$, be the Sobolev spaces and

$$(3.4)\qquad \begin{aligned} |f|_{W_p^k(\Omega)} &:= \sum_{|\nu|=k} \|D^\nu f\|_{L_p(\Omega)} \\ \|f\|_{W_p^k(\Omega)} &:= \|f\|_{L_p(\Omega)} + |f|_{W_p^k(\Omega)} . \end{aligned}$$

<u>Theorem 3.4</u>. Let $1 \leqq p \leqq \infty$ and k be a nonnegative integer. There is a constant $c > 0$ depending at most on p, k, n and Ω such that for each cube Q and any $f \in W_p^k(Q)$, there is a polynominal $\pi \in \mathbb{P}_{k-1}$ with

$$(3.5)\qquad \|f-\pi\|_{L_p(Q)} \leqq c\, |Q|^{k/n}\, |f|_{W_p^k(Q)} .$$

<u>Proof</u>. It is enough to verify (3.5) for the unit cube Q_0 since the case of arbitrary Q then follows from a linear change of variables. Now suppose (3.5) does not hold for Q_0. In this case, there is a sequence of functions (f_m) such that

$$\inf_{\pi \in \mathbb{P}_{k-1}} \|f_m-\pi\|_{L_p(Q_0)} \geqq m\, |f_m|_{W_p^k(Q_0)} .$$

If we let π_m denote best $L_p(Q_0)$ approximant to f_m, $m = 1,2,\ldots$ then by rescaling if necessary, we find functions $g_m = \lambda_m (f_m-\pi_m)$ such that

$$1 = \inf_{\pi \in \mathbb{P}_{k-1}} \|g_m-\pi\|_{L_p(Q_0)} = \|g_m\|_{L_p(Q_0)} \geqq m\, |g_m|_{W_p^k(Q_0)} .$$

Thus $\{g_m\}_1^\infty$ is precompact in $L_p(Q_0)$ [1, p. 143] and for an appropriate subsequence, $g_{m_j} \to g$ with $g \in L_p(Q_0)$. It follows that

$$|g|_{W_p^k(Q_0)} = \lim_{j\to\infty} |g_{m_j}|_{W_p^k(Q_0)} = 0$$

and so $g \in \mathbb{P}_{k-1}$. On the other hand, $\inf_{\pi \in \mathbb{P}_{k-1}} \|g-\pi\|_{L_p(Q_0)} = 1$ and so we have a contradiction. □

Inequalities like (3.5) hold for more general semi-norms on the right hand side. As another example, we consider the Besov spaces. If Ω is domain in $\mathbb{R}^n$, $h > 0$ and r is a positive integer, then define $\Omega_{r,h} := \{x: x, x+h,\ldots,x+rh \in \Omega\}$. When $f \in L_p(\Omega)$, $1 \leqq p < \infty$, ($f \in C(\Omega)$ when $p = \infty$), the r-th order modulus of smoothness in $L_p(\Omega)$ is defined by

$$\omega_r(f,t)_p := \sup_{|h|\leq t} ||\Delta_h^r(f)||_{L_p(\Omega_{r,h})}$$

where Δ_h^r are the usual difference operators (cf. §2).

For any α, $q > 0$, take $r := [\alpha] + 1$ and define

$$(3.6) \qquad |f|_{B_p^{\alpha,q}(\Omega)} := \begin{cases} \{\int_0^\infty [t^{-\alpha}\omega_r(f,t)_p]^q \frac{dt}{t}\}^{1/q} & q < \infty \\ \sup_{0<t} t^{-\alpha}\omega_r(f,t)_p & q = \infty \end{cases}$$

$$||f||_{B_p^{\alpha,q}(\Omega)} := ||f||_{L_p(\Omega)} + |f|_{B_p^{\alpha,q}(\Omega)}.$$

The Besov space $B_p^{\alpha,q}$ is the set of those functions in $L_p(\Omega)$ such that $||f||_{B_p^{\alpha,q}(\Omega)}$ is finite. This is a Banach space if $1 \leq p \leq \infty$.

Theorem 3.5. Let $1 \leq p \leq \infty$ and α, $q > 0$. There is a constant $c > 0$ depending at most on p, α, q, n and Ω such that for each n-cube Q and each $f \in B_p^{\alpha,q}(Q)$, there is a $\pi \in \mathbb{P}_{[\alpha]}$ satisfying

$$(3.7) \qquad ||f-\pi||_{L_p(Q)} \leq c\,|Q|^{\alpha/n}\,|f|_{B_p^{\alpha,q}(Q)}.$$

Remark: The constants in Theorems 3.4 and 3.5 can be chosen independent of p and q but we will not need this.

Proof. Using the fact that the unit ball in $B_p^{\alpha,q}$ is compact in L_p, we can establish (3.7) for $Q = Q_0$ the unit cube in the same way that we have proved (3.6) for the unit cube. For the case of general Q, we note that if f is defined on Q and A is the linear transformation which maps Q_0 onto Q then the function $\tilde{f} = f\circ A$ has a modulus of smoothness which satisfies

$$\omega_r(\tilde{f},t)_p = \ell^{-n/p}\,\omega_r(f,\ell t)_p$$

with ℓ the side length of Q. Thus, $|\tilde{f}|_{B_p^{\alpha,q}(Q_0)} = \ell^{\alpha-n/p}\,|f|_{B_p^{\alpha,q}(Q)}$ and the general case of (3.7) follows easily from the case Q_0. □

We shall need one more technical result which is similar to Theorems 3.4-5 but uses different semi-norms.

<u>Theorem 3.6</u>. Let $0 < k < m$ and $1 \leqq p \leqq \infty$. If Q is a cube in $\mathbb{R}^n$ and $f \in W_p^k(Q)$, then there is a polynomial $\pi \in \mathbb{P}_m$ such that

$$(3.8) \qquad ||f-\pi||_{L_p(Q)} \leqq c\, |Q|^{k/n} \sum_{|\nu|=k} \left(\inf_{\pi_\nu \in \mathbb{P}_{m-k}} ||D^\nu f-\pi_\nu||_{L_p(Q)}\right)$$

with c depending at most on n, m and p.

<u>Proof</u>. As before, it is enough to prove (3.8) for the unit cube Q_0 since then the case of an arbitrary cube Q follows by change of scale. It is also enough to prove (3.8) for functions f which have a zero polynomial as a best $L_p(Q_0)$ approximation from $\mathbb{P}_m$.

Now suppose (3.8) does not hold for Q_0 and such functions f. Then for each $j = 1,2,...$ there is a function f_j such that

$$(3.9) \qquad ||f_j||_{L_p(Q_0)} = \inf_{\pi \in \mathbb{P}_m} ||f_j-\pi||_{L_p(Q_0)}$$

$$\geqq j \sum_{|\nu|=k} \left(\inf_{\pi_\nu \in \mathbb{P}_{m-k}} ||D^\nu f_j-\pi_\nu||_{L_p(Q_0)}\right) .$$

We can also assume that the f_j have been normalized so that

$$(3.10) \qquad ||f_j||_{L_p(Q_0)} + \sum_{|\nu|=k} ||D^\nu f_j||_{L_p(Q_0)} = 1 .$$

It follows that there is a subsequence $(f_{j'})$ of (f_j) such that $f_{j'}$ converges in $L_p(Q_0)$ to a function f in $L_p(Q_0)$.

If $\pi_{\nu,j}$ denotes a best $L_p(Q_0)$ approximation to $D^\nu f_j$ from $\mathbb{P}_{m-k}$, then (3.9) and (3.10) show that for each $|\nu| = k$, $(\pi_{\nu,j})_{j=1}^\infty$ is a bounded sequence. Thus we can assume without loss of generality that the subsequence (j') has the property that $\pi_{\nu,j'}$ converges to a polynomial $\pi_\nu \in \mathbb{P}_{m-k}$ for each $|\nu| = k$. It follows from (3.9) that $D^\nu f_{j'}$ converges to π_ν in $L_p(Q_0)$. Also, for any test function $\phi \in C_0^\infty(Q_0)$

$$\int_{Q_0} D^\nu f\, \phi = (-1)^{|\nu|} \int_{Q_0} f\, D^\nu\phi = \lim_{j'\to\infty} (-1)^{|\nu|} \int_{Q_0} f_{j'} D^\nu\phi$$

$$= \lim_{j'\to\infty} \int_{Q_0} D^\nu f_j'\, \phi = \int_{Q_0} \pi_\nu \phi.$$

Hence $D^\nu f = \pi_\nu$, $|\nu| = k$. This implies that f is a polynomial in $\mathbb{P}_m$. Since a best approximation to each f_j is the zero polynomial, f also has this property and hence $f \equiv 0$ on Q_0. But this implies $D^\nu f \equiv 0$ on Q_0, $|\nu| = k$. This contradicts (3.10) when j' is sufficiently large since $f_{j'} \to f$ and $D^\nu f_{j'} \to D^\nu f$ $(|\nu| = k)$ in $L_p(Q_0)$. □

§4. Additional Estimates

If $0 < q < \infty$, a function f belongs to BMO if and only if

$$\sup_Q \frac{1}{|Q|} \int_Q |f - f_Q|^q < \infty$$

with the supremum taken over all cubes $Q \subset \mathbb{R}^n$. This useful characterization of BMO follows easily from the John-Nirenberg Lemma [10] and is also contained in the inequality [2]

$$(4.1) \qquad [(f - f_Q)\, \chi_Q]^*(t) \leqq c \int_t^{|Q|} (f_Q^{\#})^*(s) \frac{ds}{s}, \qquad 0 < t < \frac{|Q|}{2^n}$$

where $f_Q^{\#}$ denotes the sharp function of f on Q and g^* denotes the decreasing rearrangement of g.

Our interest in this section is to study the analogous situation of taking L_q norms (in place of L_1 norms) in the definition of $f_\alpha^{\#}$ and also to give analogues of (4.1) for $f_\alpha^{\#}$. Such inequalities for $0 < \alpha < 1$ were given in [2]. Throughout this section we assume $\alpha > 0$ unless stated otherwise.

As a starting point, let us introduce some variants of $f_\alpha^{\#}$. If $0 < q < \infty$ and $f \in L_q(Q)$, then f has a set of best approximants from $\mathbb{P}_{[\alpha]}$ in $L_q(Q)$ which we denote by $A(f) := A(f,Q,q)$. Let P_Q be any selection for these best approximants, i.e. $P_Q f \in A(f)$ for each f. Define

$$(4.2) \qquad f_{\alpha,q}^{\#}(x) := \sup_{\Omega \supset Q \ni x} \frac{1}{|Q|^{\alpha/n}} \left(\frac{1}{|Q|} \int_Q |f - P_Q f|^q\right)^{1/q}$$

$$= \sup_{\Omega \supset Q \ni x} \inf_{\pi \in \mathbb{P}_{[\alpha]}} \frac{1}{|Q|^{\alpha/n}} \left(\frac{1}{|Q|} \int_Q |f - \pi|^q\right)^{1/q}.$$

Analogously, define

$$(4.3) \qquad f_{\alpha,q}^{b}(x) := \sup_{\Omega \supset Q \ni x} \frac{1}{|Q|^{\alpha/n}} \left(\frac{1}{|Q|} \int_Q |f - P_Q^b f|^q\right)^{1/q}$$

where P_Q^b is a selection for best approximation in $L_q(Q)$ by polynomials from $\mathbb{P}_{(\alpha)}$. Note that we can take $P_Q^b = P_Q$ when α is not an integer and therefore $f_{\alpha,q}^{\#} = f_{\alpha,q}^{b}$ for such α. For any $\alpha \geqq 0$,

(4.4) $$f^{\#}_{\alpha,q} \leq f^{b}_{\alpha,q} .$$

As we have shown in Lemma 2.1, $f^{\#}_{\alpha,1}$ is equivalent to $f^{\#}_{\alpha}$ and $f^{b}_{\alpha,1}$ is equivalent to f^{b}_{α}. Actually, for any $q \geq 1$, we can replace $\mathcal{P}_Q f$ by $P_Q f$ and get an equivalent maximal function. However for $q < 1$, $P_Q f$ is not necessarily defined since f may not be locally integrable.

Our next task is to give an analogue of the Lebesgue differentiation theorem for $q < 1$. Consider the Hardy-Littlewood type maximal functions

$$\mathcal{M}_q f(x) := \sup_{\substack{\Omega \supset Q \ni x \\ \pi \in A(f,Q,q)}} |\pi(x)|$$

where the supremum is taken not only over all cubes containing x but over all best approximants. It is easy to estimate $\mathcal{M}_q f$ in terms of the Hardy-Littlewood maximal operator M. Indeed, if $\pi \in A(f,Q,q)$, then

$$\begin{aligned}(\textstyle\int_Q |\pi|^q)^{1/q} &\leq c\ [(\textstyle\int_Q |f - \pi|^q)^{1/q} + (\textstyle\int_Q |f|^q)^{1/q}] \\ &\leq c\ (\textstyle\int_Q |f|^q)^{1/q} .\end{aligned}$$

Using Lemma 3.1, we have for $x \in Q$,

(4.5) $$|\pi(x)| \leq ||\pi||_{L_\infty(Q)} \leq c\ (\frac{1}{|Q|} \int_Q |\pi|^q)^{1/q} \leq c\ (\frac{1}{|Q|} \int_Q |f|^q)^{1/q} .$$

Taking now a supremum over all π and Q, we find

(4.6) $$\mathcal{M}_q f \leq c\ M_q f \qquad \text{on } \Omega$$

where $M_q f := [M(|f|^q)]^{1/q}$ and c depends only on q and α.

The inequality (4.6) shows that $\mathcal{M}_q$ is weak type (q,q), i.e. $\mathcal{M}_q$ maps L_q into the Lorentz space $L_{q,\infty}$. Using this, we now prove that $\mathcal{P}_Q f(x) \to f(x)$ a.e. as $Q \downarrow \{x\}$.

<u>Lemma 4.1</u>. If $f \in L_q(\text{loc } \Omega)$, then $\lim_{Q \downarrow \{x\}} \mathcal{P}_Q f(x) = f(x)$ a.e. $x \in \Omega$.

<u>Proof</u>. Since this is a local result, we may assume that $f \in L_q(\Omega)$. Let

$$Af(x) := \overline{\lim_{Q \downarrow \{x\}}}\ (\frac{1}{|Q|} \int_Q |f(y) - f(x)|^q dy)^{1/q}.$$

Since $|f| \leq M_q f$ a.e., we have $Af \leq 2^{1/q} M_q f$ a.e. which shows that A is also weak type (q,q). Therefore

$$|\{x: Af(x) > y\}| \leq c\,(\|f\|_{L_q}/y)^q \;, \qquad y > 0.$$

Now for any continuous function g we have

$$[A(f - g)]^q(x) \leq \overline{\lim_{Q\downarrow\{x\}}}\left(\frac{1}{|Q|}\int_Q |f(y) - f(x)|^q dy\right)$$

$$+ \lim_{Q\downarrow\{x\}}\left(\frac{1}{|Q|}\int_Q |g(y) - g(x)|^q dy\right)$$

$$= Af(x).$$

Hence, $A(f - g) \leq Af$ and it must also follow that $Af \leq A(f - g)$ (use $f - g$ in place of f and $-g$ in place of g). We must therefore have $A(f - g) = A(f)$ whenever g is continuous.

Given $\varepsilon > 0$ and $y > 0$ choose g so that $\|f - g\|_{L_q} \leq \varepsilon y$, then

$$|\{Af > y\}| = |\{A(f - g) > y\}| \leq c\left(\frac{\|f - g\|_{L_q}}{y}\right)^{1/q} \leq c\,\varepsilon^{1/q}.$$

Hence $Af = 0$ a.e. and we have shown

$$\lim_{Q\downarrow\{x\}}\left(\frac{1}{|Q|}\int_Q |f(y) - f(x)|^q dy\right)^{1/q} = 0 \qquad \text{a.e.} \tag{4.7}$$

Return now to $P_Q f$. Fix x_o as any point where (4.7) holds. We have from Lemma 3.1,

$$\|P_Q f - f(x_o)\|_{L_\infty(Q)} \leq c\left(\frac{1}{|Q|}\int_Q |P_Q f(y) - f(x_o)|^q dy\right)^{1/q} \tag{4.8}$$

$$\leq c\left(\frac{1}{|Q|}\int_Q |f(y) - f(x_o)|^q dy\right)^{1/q}$$

where the last inequality uses the fact that $P_q f - f(x_0)$ is a best approximation to $f - f(x_0)$. Taking a limit as $Q\downarrow\{x_0\}$ in (4.8) and using (4.7) shows that $\lim_{Q\downarrow\{x_0\}} P_Q f(x_0) = f(x_o)$. □

Let us now establish our estimates which are similar to (4.1). Notice that if $R^* \subset R$ are cubes with $|R| \leq 2^n\,|R^*|$, then

$$\|P_R f - P_{R^*} f\|_{L_\infty(R^*)} \leq c\left(\frac{1}{|R^*|}\int_{R^*} |P_R f - P_{R^*} f|^q\right)^{1/q}$$

$$\leq c\left[\left(\frac{1}{|R|}\int_R |f - P_R f|^q\right)^{1/q} + \left(\frac{1}{|R^*|}\int_{R^*} |f - P_{R^*} f|^q\right)^{1/q}\right] \tag{4.9}$$

$$\leq c\,|R^*|^{\alpha/n} \inf_{u\in R^*} f^{\#}_{\alpha,q}(u).$$

Suppose $x \in \Omega$ and $\lim_{Q\downarrow\{x\}} P_Q f(x) = f(x)$. If Q is any cube containing x choose $Q =: Q_1 \supset \dots \supset Q_j \supset \dots$ with $x \in Q_j$, $j = 1, 2, \dots$, and $|Q_{j+1}| = 2^{-jn}|Q|$, then using (4.9) we see that

$$(4.10) \qquad |P_Q f(x) - f(x)| \leqq \sum_{j=1}^{\infty} |P_{Q_j} f(x) - P_{Q_{j+1}} f(x)| \leqq c\, f^{\#}_{\alpha,q}(x) \sum_{j=1}^{\infty} |Q_j|^{\alpha/n}$$
$$\leqq c\, |Q|^{\alpha/n} f^{\#}_{\alpha,q}(x)$$

because $x \in Q_j$ for all j. Hence (4.10) holds a.e. on Ω.

The same proofs hold for $f^{b}_{\alpha,q}$ so that

$$(4.9)' \qquad ||P^{b}_R f - P^{b}_{R^*} f||_{L_\infty(R^*)} \leqq c\, |R^*|^{\alpha/n} \inf_{u\in R^*} f^{b}_{\alpha,q}(u)$$

and

$$(4.10)' \qquad |P^{b}_Q f(x) - f(x)| \leqq c|Q|^{\alpha/n} f^{b}_{\alpha,q}(x) \;, \quad \text{a.e. } \Omega$$

are valid.

Now we refine the inequalities (4.10), (4.10)' along the lines of (4.1).

<u>Lemma 4.2</u>. If $f \in L_q(\text{loc }\Omega)$, then for each cube $Q \subset \Omega$

$$(4.11) \qquad [(f - P_Q f)\chi_Q]^*(t) \leqq c[\int_t^{|Q|} F^*(s) s^{\alpha/n} \frac{ds}{s} + t^{\alpha/n} F^*(t)], \quad 0<t\leqq|Q|/2^n$$

with $F := f^{\#}_{\alpha,q,Q}$ where the subscript Q means that $f^{\#}_{\alpha,q}$ is taken as in (4.2) with Q in place of Ω. The inequality (4.11) holds if P_Q is replaced by P^{b}_Q and F is set equal to $f^{b}_{\alpha,q,Q}$.

<u>Proof</u>. Let $E := \{x \in Q: F(x) > F^*(t)\}$ so that $|E| \leqq t$. If $x\in Q\backslash E$ and $\lim_{Q\downarrow\{x\}} P_Q f(x) = f(x)$, then choose cubes $Q =: Q_1 \supset \dots$ with $|Q_{j+1}| = 2^{-nj}|Q|$ and $x \in Q_j$, $j = 1, 2, \dots$. Let m be the integer with $2^{-(m+1)n} \leqq \frac{t}{|Q|} < 2^{-mn}$. Using (4.9), we see that

$$(4.12) \qquad |P_Q f(x) - P_{Q_m} f(x)| \leqq \sum_{2}^{m-1} ||P_{Q_{j-1}} f - P_{Q_j} f||_{L^\infty(Q_j)} \leqq c \sum_{2}^{m-1} |Q_j|^{\alpha/n} \inf_{u\in Q_j} F(u)$$
$$\leqq c \sum_{2}^{m-1} |Q_j|^{\alpha/n} F^*(|Q_j|) \leqq c \int_t^{|Q|} s^{\alpha/n} F^*(s) \frac{ds}{s}.$$

Since $x \in Q\backslash E$ and $\lim_{j\to\infty} P_{Q_j} f(x) = f(x)$, we have by inequality (4.10) that

$$|P_{Q_m} f(x) - f(x)| \leqq c\, F(x)\, |Q_m|^{\alpha/n} \leqq c\, F^*(t) t^{\alpha/n}.$$

This inequality combines with (4.12) to show that

$$|P_Q f(x) - f(x)| \leqq c\, [\int_t^{|Q_0|} F^*(s) s^{\alpha/n} \frac{ds}{s} + t^{\alpha/n} F^*(t)]$$

outside E. Since $|E| \leqq t$, (4.11) follows by the usual properties of decreasing rearrangements. The same proof works for $f^\flat_{\alpha,q}$ by using (4.9)' in place of (4.9). □

Using Lemma 4.2 we can now relate $f^\#_{\alpha,r}$ and $f^\#_{\alpha,q}$. Of course if $q < r$ then it is clear by Hölder's inequality that $f^\#_{\alpha,q} \leqq f^\#_{\alpha,r}$.

<u>Theorem 4.3</u>. If $0 < q < r$ and $f \in L_q(\text{loc } \Omega)$, then

$$f^\#_{\alpha,r}(x) \leqq c\, M_\sigma(f^\#_{\alpha,q})(x) \tag{4.13}$$

with $\sigma := (\frac{1}{r} + \frac{\alpha}{n})^{-1}$ and $M_\sigma(g) := [M(|g|^\sigma)]^{1/\sigma}$ where M is the Hardy-Littlewood maximal operator (for Ω). The inequality (4.13) also holds with # replaced by ♭.

<u>Remark</u>. The critical index σ is the smallest value for which $f^\#_{\alpha,q} \in L^\sigma$ ensures that $f \in L_r(\text{loc})$. See §9.

<u>Proof</u>. The starting point is inequality (4.11). Applying an L_r norm over Q and using Hardy's inequality [17, p. 196], we obtain

$$\int_0^{|Q|/2^n} [t^{1/r}\psi]^r \frac{dt}{t} \leqq c \int_0^{|Q|} [s^{1/\sigma} F^*(s)]^r \frac{ds}{s}$$

where $\psi(t) = [(f - P_Q f)\chi_Q]^*(t)$. But $g = \psi^r$ decreases so $\int_0^{|Q|} g \leqq 2^n \int_0^{|Q|/2^n} g$ and consequently

$$(\int_0^{|Q|} [t^{1/r}\psi]^r \frac{dt}{t})^{1/r} \leqq c (\int_0^{|Q|} [s^{1/\sigma} F^*(s)]^r \frac{ds}{s})^{1/r}.$$

Given an $x \in Q \subset \Omega$, we divide by $|Q|^{1/\sigma}$ and take a supremum over all $Q \ni x$ in our last inequality to find that

$$f^{\#}_{\alpha,r}(x) = \sup_{Q\ni x} \frac{1}{|Q|^{1/\sigma}} ||f - P_Q f||_{L_r(Q)} \leqq \sup_{Q\ni x} \frac{c}{|Q|^{1/\sigma}} ||f^{\#}_{\alpha,q}||_{L^{\sigma,r}(Q)}$$

$$\leqq c \sup_{Q\ni x} [\frac{1}{|Q|} \int_Q (f^{\#}_{\alpha,q})^{\sigma}]^{1/\sigma} = c\, M_{\sigma}(f^{\#}_{\alpha,q})(x)$$

where we have used the notation $L_{\sigma,r}$ for the Lorentz norms and the well known inequality $||.||_{L_{\sigma,r}} \leqq c\, ||.||_{L_{\sigma,\sigma}} = c||.||_{L_{\sigma}}$ when $\sigma < r$ (see [17, p. 192]). The same proof works for b in place of $\#$. □

The following extends Lemma 2.3 to the case $q < 1$.

<u>Lemma 4.4</u>. Let $0 < q < 1$ and $F_j(x) := \sup_{Q\ni x} \frac{1}{|Q|^{\alpha/n}} \inf_{\pi\in \mathbb{P}_j} (\frac{1}{|Q|} \int_Q |f-\pi|^q)^{1/q}$.

If $\alpha \geqq 0$ and $j \geqq [\alpha]$, there is $c_1 > 0$ depending at most on α, j, q and n such that for each $f \in L_q + L_{\infty}$

(4.14)
$$F_j(x) \leqq f^{\#}_{\alpha,q}(x) \leqq c_1 F_j(x) .$$

<u>Proof</u>. The proof is the same as Lemma 2.3 except for certain modifications necessitated by the fact that $q < 1$. The lower inequality in (4.14) follows from the fact that $F_{[\alpha]} = f^{\#}_{\alpha,q}$. The upper inequality follows from the inequality

(4.15)
$$F_{j-1}(x) \leqq c\, F_j(x),$$

which holds for all $j > [\alpha]$.

To prove (4.15), choose cubes $Q = Q_1 \subset Q_2 \subset \ldots \subset Q_N$ as in Lemma 2.3 and write

$$f = f - P_{Q_1} f + \sum_{i=1}^{N-1} [P_{Q_i} f - P_{Q_{i+1}} f] + P_{Q_N} f = f - P_{Q_1} f + \sum_{1}^{N-1} \pi_i + \pi_N$$

where P is the best L_q projection operator of degree j. We write

$$\pi_i = \rho_i + \text{terms of order } j$$

with ρ_i of degree $\leqq j - 1$. If $\rho := \sum_1^N \rho_i$, then

$$\frac{1}{|Q|} \int_Q |f - \rho|^q \leqq I + II + III$$

with the notation corresponding to that in Lemma 2.3.

Each of the terms I, II $\leqq c\,[F_j(x)\ |Q|^{\alpha/n}]^q$. The proof of I is the same as in Lemma 2.3. The proof of II uses Lemma 3.3 and the subadditivity of $\int |\cdot|^q$ with the same basic argument as in Lemma 2.3. Since III $\to 0$ as $N \to \infty$, (4.15) follows. □.

§5. The Calderón Maximal Operator and Peano Derivative

A.P. Calderón [5] and later Calderón and R. Scott [6] have introduced certain maximal operators in conjunction with the study of singular integrals, differentiation and the embeddings of Sobolev spaces. In this section, we shall show that these maximal operators are equivalent to $f^{b}_{\alpha,q}$ and in the process bring out connections between the finiteness of f^{b}_{α} (or $f^{\#}_{\alpha}$) and the differentiability of f.

For $q, \alpha > 0$ and $f \in L_q(\mathrm{loc})$,
define

$$N^{\alpha}_{q}(f,x) := \sup_{\Omega \supset Q \ni x} \frac{1}{|Q|^{\alpha/n}} \left(\frac{1}{|Q|} \int_Q |f - P_x|^q\right)^{1/q} \tag{5.1}$$

if there is a polynomial P_x of degree less than α such that (5.1) is finite, otherwise let $N^{\alpha}_{q}(f,x) := +\infty$. This is in essence the maximal function defined by Calderón although Calderón makes the definition only for $q \geqq 1$ ($q > 1$ in [5] and $q \geqq 1$ in [6]) and takes the sup over balls rather than cubes (which as was noted in §2 leads to an equivalent maximal function). It should be emphasized that in contrast to the definitions of $f^{\#}_{\alpha}$ and f^{b}_{α}, the polynomial in (5.1) does not vary with Q. Nevertheless it turns out that $N^{\alpha}_{q}(f)$ and $f^{b}_{\alpha,q}$ are equivalent.

Much of the material of this section can be found in the paper of Calderón [5]. We begin by showing that $N^{\alpha}_{q}(f,x)$ is well defined for each $0 < q < \infty$ and $0 < \alpha$.

<u>Lemma 5.1</u>. If there is a polynomial P_x of degree less than α such that

$$\sup_{\Omega \supset Q \ni x} \frac{1}{|Q|^{\alpha/n}} \left(\frac{1}{|Q|} \int_Q |f - P_x|^q\right)^{1/q} < \infty,$$

then P_x must be unique.

<u>Proof</u>. Suppose that π_1, π_2 are two polynomials in $P_{(\alpha)}$ which satisfy

$$\sup_{\Omega \supset Q \ni x} \frac{1}{|Q|^{\alpha/n}} \left(\frac{1}{|Q|} \int_Q |f - \pi_j|^q\right)^{1/q} < \infty \qquad j = 1,2,$$

then the polynomial $\rho(y) = \pi_1(y) - \pi_2(y) =: \sum_{|\nu|<\alpha} c_\nu (y-x)^\nu$ satifies

$$\left(\frac{1}{|Q|}\int_Q |\rho|^q\right)^{1/q} \leq c \sum_{j=1}^{2} \left(\frac{1}{|Q|}\int_Q |f-\pi_j|^q\right)^{1/q} \leq c\,|Q|^{\alpha/n}$$

for all Q containing x. Because of Lemma 3.3,

$$\sum_{|\nu|<\alpha} |c_\nu|\,|Q|^{|\nu|/n} \leq c\,|Q|^{\alpha/n}$$

for all Q containing x. Letting $|Q| \to 0$ shows that $c_\nu = 0$ for all ν. □

We start with a definition of the ν-th Peano derivative of f at x_0. Suppose there is a $q > 0$ and an open set $\mathcal{O} \subset \Omega$ with $x_0 \in \mathcal{O}$ such that f is in L_q on $\mathcal{O}$. Suppose further there is a family of polynomials $\{\pi_Q\}_Q$ with $x_0 \in Q$ and $\deg \pi_Q \leq M$, for all $Q \subset \mathcal{O}$, and

$$\left(\frac{1}{|Q|}\int_Q |f-\pi_Q|^q\right)^{1/q} = o(|Q|^{k/n}).$$

Then, if $|\nu| < k$

$$\lim_{Q\downarrow\{x_0\}} D^\nu \pi_Q(x_0) =: D_\nu f(x_0) \tag{5.2}$$

exists and is finite. Indeed, when $Q^* \subset Q$ and $|Q^*| \geq 2^{-n}|Q|$, then using Markov's inequality and Lemma 3.1

$$\begin{aligned} \|D^\nu(\pi_Q - \pi_{Q^*})\|_{L_\infty(Q^*)} &\leq c|Q|^{-|\nu|/n}\|\pi_Q - \pi_{Q^*}\|_{L_\infty(Q)} \\ &\leq c|Q|^{-|\nu|/n}\left(\frac{1}{|Q|}\int_Q |\pi_Q - \pi_{Q^*}|^q\right)^{1/q} \\ &\leq c|Q|^{(k-|\nu|)/n}. \end{aligned}$$

Hence, the same exact telescoping argument as used in the proof of Lemma 2.4 shows that for any $x_0 \in Q^* \subset Q$

$$\|D^\nu(\pi_Q - \pi_{Q^*})\|_{L_\infty(Q^*)} \leq c|Q|^{(k-|\nu|)/n} \tag{5.3}$$

which shows that (5.2) exists.

Whenever such a family of polynomials exist, we call $D_\nu f(x_0)$ as defined by (5.2) the <u>ν-th Peano derivative</u> of f at x_0.

Let us observe that $D_\nu f(x_0)$ does not depend on the neighborhood $\mathcal{O}$, the family π_Q, or on q. If $\{\pi_Q\}$ is a family for $\mathcal{O}$, q, and k, and $\{\tilde{\pi}_Q\}$ a family for $\tilde{\mathcal{O}}$, $\tilde{q}$, and $\tilde{k}$, it follows for a suitably chosen $\mathcal{O}_0$, that whenever $Q \subset \mathcal{O}_0$ and q_0 is the minimum of q and $\tilde{q}$,

$$\|\pi_Q - \tilde{\pi}_Q\|_{L_\infty(Q)} \leq c\left(\frac{1}{|Q|}\int_Q |\pi_Q - \tilde{\pi}_Q|^{q_0}\right)^{\frac{1}{q_0}}$$

$$\leq c\left[\left(\frac{1}{|Q|}\int_Q |\pi_Q - f|^q\right)^{\frac{1}{q}} + \left(\frac{1}{|Q|}\int_Q |\tilde{\pi}_Q - f|^{\tilde{q}}\right)^{\frac{1}{\tilde{q}}}\right]$$

$$\leq c|Q|^{k_0/n}$$

with k_0 the minimum of k and $\tilde{k}$. Since $|\nu| < k_0$

$$|D^\nu(\pi_Q - \tilde{\pi}_Q)(x_0)| \leq c|Q|^{-|\nu|/n}(|Q|^{k_0/n}) = o(1) .$$

This shows that $\lim_{Q\downarrow\{x_0\}} D^\nu\pi_Q(x_0) = \lim_{Q\downarrow\{x_0\}} D^\nu \tilde{\pi}_Q(x_0)$.

Lemma 5.2. If α, $q > 0$; $|\nu| < \alpha$ and f is locally in L_q, then $D_\nu f(x)$ exists at each point where $f^\#_{\alpha,q}(x)$ is finite. In addition, for such x

(5.4) $$|D^\nu(P_Q f)(x) - D_\nu f(x)| \leq c\, f^\#_{\alpha,q}(x)\, |Q|^{\frac{\alpha-|\nu|}{n}} .$$

If $f^\flat_{\alpha,q}(x)$ is finite, then

(5.4)' $$|D^\nu(P^\flat_Q f)(x) - D_\nu f(x)| \leq c\, f^\flat_{\alpha,q}(x)\, |Q|^{\frac{\alpha-|\nu|}{n}} .$$

Proof. If $x \in R_2 \subset R_1$ and $|R_2| \geq 2^{-n}|R_1|$, then from (4.9)

$$\|P_{R_1} f - P_{R_2} f\|_{L_\infty(R_2)} \leq c\, f^\#_{\alpha,q}(x)\, |R_2|^{\alpha/n} .$$

Using the exact same telescoping argument as in Lemma 2.4 shows that

(5.5) $$\|D^\nu(P_Q f - P_{Q^*} f)\|_{L_\infty(Q^*)} \leq c\, f^\#_{\alpha,q}(x)\, |Q|^{(\alpha-|\nu|)/n}$$

for any cubes Q, Q^* with $x \in Q^* \subset Q$. Hence $\{P_Q f\}$ can be used in (5.2), and so $\lim_{Q\downarrow\{x\}} D^\nu P_Q f(x) = D_\nu f(x)$. Using this in (5.5) gives (5.4). To prove (5.4)' use (4.9)' in place of (4.9) and $P^\flat_Q$ in place of P_Q in the above argument. □

Theorem 5.3. If α, $q > 0$, there are constants c_1, $c_2 > 0$ such that for each $f \in L_q(\text{loc})$,

$$c_1 \, f^{\flat}_{\alpha,q}(x) \leqq N^{\alpha}_{q}(f, x) \leqq c_2 \, f^{\flat}_{\alpha,q}(x), \qquad x \in \Omega . \tag{5.6}$$

Proof. The lower estimate in (5.6) is clear from the definitions of these maximal functions. For the upper estimate, suppose $f_{\alpha,q}(x)$ is finite and define $P_x(y) := \sum_{|\nu|<\alpha} D_\nu f(x) \frac{(y-x)^\nu}{\nu!}$ where $D_\nu f(x)$ are the Peano derivatives of f at x which are guaranteed to exist by Lemma 5.2. Using (5.4)', we find for any cube $Q \ni x$

$$\Big(\frac{1}{|Q|} \int_Q |P_x - P^{\flat}_Q f|^q\Big)^{1/q} \leqq c \, \|P_x - P^{\flat}_Q f\|_{L_\infty(Q)}$$

$$\leqq c \sum_{|\nu|<\alpha} |D_\nu f(x) - D^\nu P^{\flat}_Q f(x)| \; \|(\cdot - x)^\nu\|_{L_\infty(Q)}$$

$$\leqq c \sum_{|\nu|<\alpha} f^{\flat}_{\alpha,q}(x) \, |Q|^{\frac{\alpha-|\nu|}{n}} \, |Q|^{\frac{|\nu|}{n}} \leqq c \, f^{\flat}_{\alpha,q}(x) \, |Q|^{\alpha/n}.$$

But $(\int_Q |f - P_x|^q) \leqq c \, (\int_Q |f - P^{\flat}_Q f|^q + \int_Q |P_x - P^{\flat}_Q f|^q)$ which together with the last inequality shows $\big(\frac{1}{|Q|} \int_Q |f - P_x|^q\big)^{1/q} \leqq c \, f^{\flat}_{\alpha,q}(x) \, |Q|^{\alpha/n}$. Dividing by $|Q|^{\alpha/n}$ and taking a supremum over all Q establishes the right hand inequality in (5.6). □

Corollary 5.4. If $\alpha > 0$ there are constants c_1, $c_2 > 0$ such that

$$c_1 \, f^{\flat}_{\alpha}(x) \leqq N^{\alpha}_{1}(f,x) \leqq c_2 \, f^{\flat}_{\alpha}(x).$$

Proof. $f^{\flat}_{\alpha,1}(x)$ is equivalent to $f^{\flat}_{\alpha}$ because of Lemma 2.1. □

Corollary 5.5. If $f^{\flat}_{\alpha,q}(x) < \infty$, then $P_x(y) = \sum_{|\nu|<\alpha} D_\nu f(x) \frac{(y-x)^\nu}{\nu!}$.

Proof. This follows immediately from the proof of Theorem 5.3 and the uniqueness of P_x. □

When α is an integer $f^{\flat}_{\alpha}$ can be estimated in terms of classical derivatives as the following result shows.

Theorem 5.6. There are constants $c_1, c_2 > 0$ such that for any $f \in W_1^k(\text{loc } \Omega)$

$$f_k^b(x) \leqq c_1 M\Big(\sum_{|\nu|=k} |D^\nu f|\chi_\Omega\Big)(x) \tag{5.7}$$

and for any $f \in L_1(\text{loc})$ for which $f_k^b \in L_1(\text{loc})$, the weak derivatives $D^\nu f$, $|\nu| = k$, exist and satisfy

$$\sum_{|\nu|=k} |D^\nu f(x)| \leqq c_2\, f_k^b(x) \qquad \text{a.e. } x \in \Omega. \tag{5.8}$$

Proof. Let $\mathcal{D}f := \sum_{|\nu|=k} |D^\nu f|$. When $f \in W_1^k(\text{loc } \Omega)$ and Q is a cube contained in Ω, then according to Theorem 3.4 there is a polynomial π of degree $< k$ with

$$\int_Q |f - \pi| \leqq c\, |Q|^{k/n} \int_Q |\mathcal{D}f|.$$

Dividing by $|Q|^{k/n+1}$ and taking an inf over π and a sup over all Q containing x gives (5.7).

To prove (5.8), let $f \in L_1(\text{loc})$ and consider any test function $\phi \in C_0^\infty(\Omega)$ with supp $\phi =: K \subset\subset \Omega$. Choose a function $\psi \in C^\infty$ with ψ supported on the unit cube and $\int_{\mathbb{R}^n} \psi = 1$. Set $\psi_\varepsilon(x) := \varepsilon^{-n}\, \psi(\varepsilon^{-1}x)$. If $\varepsilon > 0$ is sufficiently small the functions $F_\varepsilon := f * \psi_\varepsilon$ are defined on K. Also for any $|\nu| = k$, we have for $z \in K$

$$\begin{aligned}|D^\nu F_\varepsilon(z)| &= \Big|\int_{\mathbb{R}^n} f(y) D^\nu \psi_\varepsilon(z-y)\,dy\Big| = \Big|\int_{\mathbb{R}^n} [f(y) - P_z(y)] D^\nu \psi_\varepsilon(z-y)\,dy\Big| \\ &\leqq c\, \varepsilon^{-k-n} \int_{z+Q_\varepsilon} |f(y) - P_z(y)|\,dy \leqq c\, N_1^k(f,z) \leqq c\, f_k^b(z)\end{aligned} \tag{5.9}$$

with Q_ε the cube with side length 2ε centered at 0. The second equality uses the fact that $\int P\, D^\nu g = (-1)^{|\nu|} \int D^\nu P\, g = 0$ if g has compact support and P is a polynomial of degree less than $|\nu|$. We also used the fact that $\|D^\nu \psi_\varepsilon\|_\infty \leqq \varepsilon^{-k-n} \|D^\nu \psi\|_\infty \leqq c\, \varepsilon^{-k-n}$ and ψ_ε is supported on Q_ε. The last inequality is Corollary 5.4.

Using (5.9), we have

$$\Big|\int_{\mathbb{R}^n} D^\nu \phi\, f\Big| = \lim_{\varepsilon \to 0} \Big|\int_K D^\nu \phi\, F_\varepsilon\Big| \leqq \lim_{\varepsilon \to 0} \int_K |\phi|\, |D^\nu F_\varepsilon| \leqq c \int |\phi| f_k^b$$

This estimate shows that the distributional derivative $D^\nu f$ is a distribution of order 0 and hence must be a Radon measure. Moreover, the same estimates show that $D^\nu f$ must be absolutely continuous with respect to Lebesgue measure. Therefore $D^\nu f$ must belong to $L_1(\text{loc})$ and satisfy

$$|D^\nu f| \leqq c\ f_k^b \quad \text{a.e.}$$

as desired. □

Remark. The preceding proof actually shows that the weak derivatives $D^\nu f$ $(|\nu| = k)$ exist and satisfy

(5.10) $$|D^\nu f(z)| \leqq c\ F_k(z) := \sup_{\substack{\Omega\supset Q\ni x\\ |Q|\leqq 1}} \left(\frac{1}{|Q|^{1+k/n}} \int_Q |f(y) - P_z(y)|\right)$$

whenever F_k is locally integrable. This follows since the integration in inequality (5.9) was performed over cubes of measure $(2\varepsilon)^n$ as $\varepsilon \to 0+$.

The following Corollary extends Theorem 5.6 to the case of nonintegral α.

Corollary 5.7. Suppose $\alpha > 0$ and $f_\alpha^b \in L_1(\text{loc}\ \Omega)$, then for each $|\nu| < \alpha$ both the weak derivatives $D^\nu f$ and the Peano derivatives $D_\nu f$ exist a.e., are locally integrable, and coincide a.e. on Ω. Moreover,

(5.11) $$|D^\nu f(x)| \leqq c\ [f_\alpha^b(x) + \int_Q |f| \ / \ |Q|^{1+|\nu|/n}] \quad \text{a.e. } \Omega$$

where Q is any cube satisfying $|Q| \leqq 1$ and $\Omega \supset Q \ni x$.

Proof. Let $k = (\alpha)$ and suppose $|\nu| \leqq k$, then according to Lemma 5.2 the Peano derivative $D_\nu f$ exists a.e. and satisfies for any cube Q with $x \in Q \subset \Omega$

(5.12) $$\begin{aligned} |D_\nu f(x)| &\leqq c\ f_\alpha^b(x)|Q|^{\frac{\alpha-|\nu|}{n}} + |D^\nu(P_Q f)(x)| \\ &\leqq c[|Q|^{\frac{\alpha-|\nu|}{n}} f_\alpha^b(x) + \frac{1}{|Q|^{1+|\nu|/n}} \int_Q |f|] \end{aligned}$$

where the last inequality follows from the representation of $P_Q f$ given in (2.4).

Next we prove that the weak derivaties are locally integrable. Suppose $|\nu| = k$ and let F_k denote the maximal function defined in (5.10). Since the supremum in (5.10) is over all cubes Q with $|Q| \leqq 1$, it follows from Corollary 5.4 that

(5.13) $$F_k(x) \leqq N_1^\alpha(f,x) \leqq c\, f_\alpha^b(x).$$

Since F_k is locally integrable, inequality (5.10) shows that $D^\nu f$ is also locally integrable. Hence, as is well known [1, p. 75], $D^\mu f$ is locally integrable for each $|\mu| < k$.

Finally, in order to complete the proof of the theorem, we must show that $D^\nu f = D_\nu f$ a.e. on Ω for $|\nu| \leqq k$. Define $P_x(y) := \sum_{|\nu|\leqq k} D_\nu f(x) \frac{(y-x)^\nu}{\nu!}$. Let $\psi \in C^\infty$ be supported on the unit cube with $\int\psi = 1$ and set $\psi_\varepsilon(x) := \varepsilon^{-n}\psi(\varepsilon^{-1}x)$, $\varepsilon > 0$. If Q is any closed cube contained in Ω, then $D^\nu f * \psi_\varepsilon$ is defined on Q provided ε is sufficiently small. Moreover (see [15, p. 62]),

(5.14) $$D^\nu f(x) = \lim_{\varepsilon\to0^+} D^\nu f * \psi_\varepsilon(x) = \lim_{\varepsilon\to0^+} f * D^\nu\psi_\varepsilon(x), \quad \text{a.e.} \quad x \in \Omega.$$

Let x be any point in Q where (5.14) holds and where both $D_\nu f(x)$ and $D^\nu f(x)$ exist. Since P_x is a polynomial, $\lim_{\varepsilon\to0^+} D^\nu P_x * \psi_\varepsilon(y) = D^\nu P_x(y)$ holds for each y. But $D^\nu(P_x)(x) = D_\nu f(x)$ by the definition of P_x, so

$$\begin{aligned} |D^\nu f(x) - D_\nu f(x)| &= |D^\nu f(x) - D^\nu P_x(x)| \\ &= \lim_{\varepsilon\to0^+} |(f-P_x) * D^\nu\psi_\varepsilon(x)| \\ &\leqq \overline{\lim_{\varepsilon\to0^+}}\, \varepsilon^{-n-|\nu|} \int_{|y-x|\leqq\varepsilon} |f(y)-P_x(y)|\,dy \\ &\leqq c\, \overline{\lim_{\varepsilon\to0^+}}\, f_\alpha^b(x)\, \varepsilon^{\alpha-|\nu|} = 0. \end{aligned}$$

The last inequality follows since $N_1^\alpha(f,x) \leqq c\, f_\alpha^b(x)$ by Corollary 5.4. □

§6. Smoothness Spaces

We have already pointed out that $f_\alpha^\#$ measures the local smoothness of f. Accordingly for $1 \leqq p \leqq \infty$ [see §12 for the case $0 < p < 1$] and $\alpha > 0$, we define smoothness spaces

$$C_p^\alpha := C_p^\alpha(\Omega): = \{f \in L_p(\Omega): f_\alpha^\# \in L_p(\Omega)\}$$

and

$$\mathcal{C}_p^\alpha := \{f \in L_p(\Omega) : f_\alpha^\flat \in L_p(\Omega)\},$$

then $\mathcal{C}_p^\alpha \subset C_p^\alpha$ and equality holds if α is not an integer. We could also use $f_{\alpha,q}^\#$ $(q \leqq p)$ in place of $f_\alpha^\#$ in the definition of C_p^α. However, in light of the inequalities (Theorem 4.3) $f_\alpha^\# \leqq f_{\alpha,q}^\# \leqq c\, M_\sigma(f_\alpha^\#)$ with $\sigma = (1/q + \alpha/n)^{-1}$ and the fact that M_σ is bounded on L_p, it follows that $f_{\alpha,q}^\# \in L_p$ is equivalent to $f_\alpha^\# \in L_p$ for $1 \leqq q \leqq p$. Also for $0 < q < 1$, we have $f_{\alpha,q}^\# \leqq f_\alpha^\# \leqq c\, M_{\sigma_0} f_{\alpha,q}^\#$ with $\sigma_0: = (1 + \alpha/n)^{-1}$. Since M_{σ_0} is bounded on $L_p(\Omega)$, $f_{\alpha,q}^\# \in L_p(\Omega)$ is equivalent to $f_\alpha^\# \in L_p(\Omega)$ in this case as well. Similar statements hold for $f_\alpha^\flat$ and $f_{\alpha,q}^\flat$.

If $f \in C_p^\alpha$, we define the seminorm

$$|f|_{C_p^\alpha} : = ||f_\alpha^\#||_{L_p(\Omega)}$$

and the norm

$$||f||_{C_p^\alpha} : = ||f||_{L_p(\Omega)} + |f|_{C_p^\alpha} .$$

Similarly, $|f|_{\mathcal{C}_p^\alpha}: = ||f_\alpha^\flat||_{L_p(\Omega)}$ and $||f||_{\mathcal{C}_p^\alpha}: = ||f||_{L_p(\Omega)} + |f|_{\mathcal{C}_p^\alpha}$.

The triangle inequality for the two norms follows from the subadditivity of the $\#$ and $\flat$ maximal operators which is an immediate consequence of the definition (2.2). Another useful inequality which follows from the subadditivity is

$$(6.1) \qquad |f_\alpha^\#(x) - g_\alpha^\#(x)| \leqq (f - g)_\alpha^\#(x) \qquad x \in \Omega$$

which holds whenever $g_\alpha^\#(x)$ is finite.

Lemma 6.1. For $1 \leq p \leq \infty$ and $\alpha > 0$, C_p^α and $\mathcal{C}_p^\alpha$ are Banach spaces under their respective norms.

Proof. We prove that C_p^α is complete with the proof for $\mathcal{C}_p^\alpha$ following in much the same way. Suppose $\{f_m\}$ is Cauchy in C_p^α. Since L_p is complete there exists an $f \in L_p$ such that $f_m \to f$ in L_p. If Q is a cube in $\mathbb{R}^n$, then whenever $h_m \to h$ in L_p there must hold

$$\frac{1}{|Q|^{1+\alpha/n}} \int_Q |h - P_Q h| = \lim_{m\to\infty} \frac{1}{|Q|^{1+\alpha/n}} \int_Q |h_m - P_Q h_m|$$

$$\leq \varliminf_{m\to\infty} (h_m)_\alpha^\#(x) \quad , \qquad x \in Q$$

since the operator P_Q is bounded on $L_1(Q)$. Taking a supremum over all cubes Q containing x gives

$$(6.2) \qquad h_\alpha^\# (x) \leq \varliminf_{m\to\infty} (h_m)_\alpha^\# (x) \qquad\qquad x \in \Omega.$$

Applying this inequality to the sequence $\{f_m\}$, taking p-th powers, and applying Fatou's lemma, we deduce $||f_\alpha^\#||_{L_p} \leq (\int \varliminf_{m\to\infty} |(f_m)_\alpha^\#|^p)^{1/p} \leq \varliminf_{m\to\infty} ||f_m||_{C_p^\alpha}$ and so $f \in C_p^\alpha$. Similar reasoning shows that inequality (6.2) applied to the sequence $\{f_m - f_{m'}\}_{m=1}^\infty$ gives

$$||(f - f_{m'})_\alpha^\#||_{L_p} \leq \varliminf_{m\to\infty} ||(f_m - f_{m'})_\alpha^\#||_{L_p} .$$

But the right hand side converges to zero as $m' \to \infty$ since $\{f_m\}$ is Cauchy in C_p^α. Since $f_m \to f$ in L_p has already been established, $f_m \to f$ in C_p^α. □

The following result of Calderón [5] shows that $\mathcal{C}_p^\alpha$ is the Sobolev space $W_p^\alpha(\Omega)$ when α is an integer and $p > 1$.

Theorem 6.2. (Calderón) If k is a nonnegative integer, then for each $1 < p \leq \infty$, $\mathcal{C}_p^k(\Omega) = W_p^k(\Omega)$ with equivalent norms.

Proof. We have shown in Theorem 5.6 that for $\mathcal{D}f := \sum_{|\nu|=k} |D^\nu f|$,

$$c_2\, \mathcal{D}f \leq f_k^\flat \leq c_1\, M(\mathcal{D}f\chi_\Omega) \qquad\qquad \text{a.e. on } \Omega$$

with M the Hardy Littlewood maximal operator. Since M is bounded on $L_p(\Omega)$, $p > 1$, we have

$$c_2 \, ||f||_{L_p(\Omega)} \leq ||f_k^\flat||_{L_p(\Omega)} \leq c_1 \, ||f||_{L_p(\Omega)}$$

provided $p > 1$. □

The spaces C_∞^α and $\mathfrak{C}_\infty^\alpha$ can also be described in terms of classical smoothness. The following theorem shows that $C_\infty^\alpha = B_\infty^{\alpha,\infty}$ (see §3 for the definition of Besov spaces) when Ω is $\mathbb{R}^n$ or a cube in $\mathbb{R}^n$. More general domains are discussed in §11.

<u>Theorem 6.3</u>. If $\Omega = \mathbb{R}^n$ or a cube in $\mathbb{R}^n$, then $C_\infty^\alpha = B_\infty^{\alpha,\infty}$ with equivalent norms.

<u>Proof</u>. If $f \in C_\infty^\alpha$, then Theorem 2.5 shows that for $k = [\alpha] + 1$

$$\omega_k(f,t)_\infty \leq c \, ||f_\alpha^\#||_{L_\infty(\Omega)} \, t^\alpha , \qquad t > 0 .$$

Hence $f \in B_\infty^{\alpha,\infty}$ and $||f||_{B_\infty^{\alpha,\infty}} \leq c \, ||f||_{C_\infty^\alpha}$.

On the other hand, if $f \in B_\infty^{\alpha,\infty}$, then for each Q there is a polynomial π of degree less or equal $[\alpha]$ (Theorem 3.5) such that

$$||f - \pi||_{L_\infty(Q)} \leq c \, |f|_{B_\infty^{\alpha,\infty}} |Q|^{\alpha/n} .$$

Hence,

$$\frac{1}{|Q|^{1+\alpha/n}} \int_Q |f - \pi| \leq c \, |f|_{B_\infty^{\alpha,\infty}} .$$

Taking a sup over $Q \ni x$ and using Lemma 2.1, we observe that

$$f_\alpha^\#(x) \leq c \, |f|_{B_\infty^{\alpha,\infty}} \qquad x \in \Omega$$

and hence $||f||_{C_\infty^\alpha} \leq c \, ||f||_{B_\infty^{\alpha,\infty}}$. □

When α is not an integer, the space $B_\infty^{\alpha,\infty}$ is the same as the Lipschitz space Lip α. Recall that there are several definitions of the space Lip α. The following theorem shows that these definitions are equivalent when Ω is $\mathbb{R}^n$ or a cube in $\mathbb{R}^n$.

Theorem 6.4. Let Ω be $\mathbb{R}^n$ or a cube in $\mathbb{R}^n$ and $\alpha > 0$. For f locally integrable, the following conditions are equivalent:

i) there exists $M_1 > 0$ and functions $\{f_\nu\}_{|\nu|<\alpha}$ such that $f_0 := f$ and for each

$|\nu| < \alpha$ and for almost every $x \in \Omega$

$$f_\nu(y) = \sum_{|\mu+\nu|<\alpha} f_{\mu+\nu}(x) \frac{(y-x)^\mu}{\mu!} + R_\nu(x,y)$$

with $|R_\nu(x,y)| \leq M_1 \; |y - x|^{\alpha-|\nu|}$ a.e. $y \in \Omega$,

ii) there exists $M_2 > 0$ such that for almost every $x \in \Omega$, there is a polynomial P_x of degree less than α with

$|f(y) - P_x(y)| \leq M_2 \; |x - y|^\alpha$ a.e. $y \in \Omega$,

iii) for k the smallest integer $\geq \alpha$, there is an $M_3 > 0$ such that

$|\Delta_h^k (f,x)| \leq M_3 \; |h|^\alpha$ a.e $x,\ x + kh \in \Omega$,

iv) $f_\alpha^b \in L_\infty(\Omega)$.

In addition, if in i), ii), or iii) M_f denotes the smallest M_i for the corresponding property, then M_f is a seminorm equivalent to $||f_\alpha^b||_{L_\infty(\Omega)}$.

Proof. If i) holds, then ii) holds with $P_x(y) := \sum_{|\nu|<\alpha} f_\nu(x)\frac{(y-x)^\nu}{\nu!}$ and $M_2 = M_1$. If ii) holds and $x,\ x + kh \in \Omega$, then $\Delta_h^k(P_x,x) = 0$ since $\deg(P_x) < k$. Hence

$$|\Delta_h^k(f,x)| = |\Delta_h^k(f - P_x,\ x)| \leq 2^k \max_{0\leq j\leq k} |f(y_j) - P_x(y_j)|$$

$$\leq k^\alpha \; 2^k \; M_2 \; |h|^\alpha$$

with $y_j := x + jh$, $j = 0, \ldots, k$. Hence iii) holds with $M_3 = k^\alpha \; 2^k M_2$.

If iii) holds, then according to Theorem 3.4-5 for each cube $Q \subset \Omega$ there is a polynomial π of degree less than α such that

$$||f - \pi||_{L_\infty(Q)} \leq c \; M_3 |Q|^{\alpha/n}.$$

Hence, if $x \in Q$,

$$\frac{1}{|Q|^{1+\alpha/n}} \int_Q |f - \pi| \leq c \; M_3.$$

Taking a supremum over all such Q and using Lemma 2.1, we see that $||f_\alpha||^b_{L_\infty(\Omega)} \leq c\, M_3$.

Finally, if condition iv) holds, then define $f_\nu := D_\nu f$ with $D_\nu f$ the Peano derivative whose existence is guaranteed by Lemma 5.2. The Peano derivatives satisfy for almost every x, $D_\nu f(x) := \lim_{Q\downarrow\{x\}} D^\nu(P^b_Q f)(x)$, $|\nu| = k$. Fix $x \in \Omega$ for which this holds.

Since

$$D^\nu(P^b_Q f)(y) = \sum_{|\mu+\nu|<\alpha} D^{\mu+\nu}(P^b_Q f)(x) \frac{(y-x)^\mu}{\mu!},$$

if $y \in \Omega$ with $f^b_\alpha(y) < \infty$, then

$$\begin{aligned} |R_\nu(x,y)| &= |f_\nu(y) - \sum_{|\mu+\nu|<\alpha} f_{\mu+\nu}(x) \frac{(y-x)^\mu}{u!}| \\ &\leq |D_\nu f(y) - D^\nu(P_Q f)(y)| \\ &\quad + \sum_{|\mu+\nu|<\alpha} |D^{\mu+\nu}(P_Q f)(x) - D_{\mu+\nu} f(x)| \frac{|(y-x)^\mu|}{\mu!} \end{aligned} \tag{6.5}$$

where Q is chosen as the smallest cube with $x,y \in Q \subset \Omega$. Inequality (5.4)' shows that

$$|D_\nu f(y) - D^\nu(P_Q f)(y)| \leq c\, f^b_\alpha(y)\, |Q|^{\frac{\alpha-|\nu|}{n}}$$

and also

$$\begin{aligned} \sum_{|\mu+\nu|<\alpha} |D^{\mu+\nu}(P_Q f)(x) - D_{\mu+\nu} f(x)| \frac{|(y-x)^\mu|}{\mu!} &\leq c\, f^b_\alpha(x) \sum_{|\mu+\nu|<\alpha} |Q|^{\frac{\alpha-|\mu+\nu|}{n}} |Q|^{\frac{|\mu|}{n}} \\ &\leq c\, f^b_\alpha(x)\, |Q|^{\frac{\alpha-|\nu|}{n}}. \end{aligned}$$

Substituting these estimates into inequality (6.5) gives

$$\begin{aligned} |R_\nu(x,y)| &\leq c\, [f^b_\alpha(y) + f^b_\alpha(x)]\, |x-y|^{\alpha-|\nu|} \\ &\leq c\, ||f^b_\alpha||_{L_\infty} |x-y|^{\alpha-|\nu|} \end{aligned}$$

as desired, since $|Q|^{1/n} \leq c\, |x-y|$. □

Condition i) of Theorem 6.4 is the usual definition of a function in Lip α for Ω closed and is for example the standard hypothesis in the

Whitney extension theorem (cf. [15, p. 176]). Condition ii) is the characterization of Lipschitz functions due to H. Whitney [20]. We choose to adopt i) as the definition of the space Lip α (= Lip(α,Ω)) and define

$$|f|_{\text{Lip }\alpha} := \inf \{M\colon M \text{ satisfies i) of Theorem 6.4}\}$$

and

$$||f||_{\text{Lip }\alpha} := ||f||_{L_\infty} + |f|_{\text{Lip }\alpha} .$$

Corollary 6.5. If Ω is $\mathbb{R}^n$ or a cube in $\mathbb{R}^n$ and $\alpha > 0$, then $\dot{C}^\alpha_\infty$ = Lip α with equivalent norms.

Lemma 6.6. Let $0 < \beta \leqq \alpha$ and $1 \leqq p \leqq \infty$. Then, there is a constant c independent of f such that

$$(6.6)\qquad ||f||_{C^\beta_p} \leqq c\ ||f||_{C^\alpha_p} .$$

Proof. First suppose $p > 1$ and P is the projection operator of degree $[\alpha]$. From Lemma 2.3, we have

$$(6.7)\quad f^\#_\beta(x) \leqq \sup_{Q\ni x} \frac{1}{|Q|^{1+\beta/n}} \int_Q |f-P_Qf| \leqq [\sup_{Q\ni x} \frac{1}{|Q|} \int_Q |f-P_Qf|]^{1-\theta}\ [f^\#_\alpha(x)]^\theta$$

with $\theta := \beta/\alpha$. When $x \in Q$, inequality (2.3) shows that

$$\frac{1}{|Q|} \int_Q |f-P_Qf| \leqq c\ Mf(x)$$

with M the Hardy-Littlewood maximal operator. Using this together with (6.7) gives

$$f^\#_\beta \leqq c\ [Mf]^{1-\theta}\ [f^\#_\alpha]^\theta \leqq c(Mf+f^\#_\alpha).$$

Applying L_p norms and using the fact that M is bounded on L_p readily gives (6.6).

For $p = 1$, we use the techniques of §4 to circumvent the fact that M is not bounded on L_1. Let $q := (1+\beta/n)^{-1}$ and $\mathcal{P}_Qf$ denote a polynomial of best L_q approximation to f from $\mathbb{P}_{[\alpha]}$ on Q. Take $\theta := \beta/\alpha$ and argue as in (6.7) to find

$$f^{\#}_{\beta,q}(x) \leq [\sup_{Q\ni x} (\frac{1}{|Q|} \int_Q |f-P_Qf|^q)^{1/q}]^{1-\theta} [f^{\#}_{\alpha,q}(x)]^{\theta}$$

$$\leq c\ [M_q f(x)]^{1-\theta} [f^{\#}_{\alpha,q}(x)]^{\theta}$$

where we used definition (4.2) and the fact that $\int_Q |f-P_Qf|^q \leq \int_Q |f|^q$. Also we have used Lemma 2.4.

It follows that

$$f^{\#}_{\beta,q} \leq c\ (M_q f + f^{\#}_{\alpha,q}) \leq c\ (M_q f + f^{\#}_{\alpha}),$$

where we used the fact that $f^{\#}_{\alpha,q} \leq f^{\#}_{\alpha}$ for $q \leq 1$. Taking an L_1 norm shows that

$$(6.8) \qquad \|f^{\#}_{\beta,q}\|_{L_1} \leq c\ (\|f\|_{L_1} + \|f^{\#}_{\alpha}\|_{L_1}) = c\ \|f\|_{C^{\alpha}_1}.$$

Finally, recall from Theorem 4.3 that $f^{\#}_{\beta} \leq c\ M_{\sigma}(f^{\#}_{\beta,q})$ with $\sigma := (1+\beta/n)^{-1}$. Since M_{σ} is bounded on L_1, we have $\|f^{\#}_{\beta}\|_{L_1} \leq c\ \|f^{\#}_{\beta,q}\|_{L_1}$. When this is used in (6.8), the inequality (6.6) follows. □

The next result is a "reduction theorem" for the spaces C^{α}_p and $\mathcal{C}^{\alpha}_p$.

<u>Theorem 6.7</u>. Suppose $\alpha > 0$, $1 \leq p \leq \infty$, and $k < \alpha$. The space $\mathcal{C}^{\alpha}_p$ is equal to the space of functions $f \in L_p$ which have weak derivatives $D^{\nu}f \in \mathcal{C}^{\alpha-k}_p$ ($|\nu| = k$) and

$$(6.9) \qquad c_1\ |f|_{\mathcal{C}^{\alpha}_p} \leq \sum_{|\nu|=k} |D^{\nu}f|_{\mathcal{C}^{\alpha-k}_p} \leq c_2\ |f|_{\mathcal{C}^{\alpha}_p}.$$

Similarly, C^{α}_p is equal to the space of functions $f \in L_p$ with weak derivatives $D^{\nu}f$ in $C^{\alpha-k}_p$ ($|\nu| = k$) and

$$(6.10) \qquad c_1\ |f|_{C^{\alpha}_p} \leq \sum_{|\nu|=k} |D^{\nu}f|_{C^{\alpha-k}_p} \leq c_2\ |f|_{C^{\alpha}_p}.$$

<u>Proof</u>. Suppose $f \in \mathcal{C}^{\alpha}_p$. Corollary 5.7 shows that the weak derivatives $D^{\nu}f$ exist and equal the Peano derivatives, $|\nu| = k$. Let $\sigma := (1 + \frac{\alpha-k}{n})^{-1}$ and choose q so that $\sigma < q < 1 \leq p$; then inequality (5.4)' shows that for any cube $Q \subset \Omega$ with $x_0 \in Q$, the polynomial $\pi := D^{\nu}P^{b}_Q$ is of degree less than $\alpha-k$ and satisfies

$$\frac{1}{|Q|^{\frac{\alpha-k}{n}}} \left(\frac{1}{|Q|} \int_Q |D^\nu f - \pi|^q\right)^{1/q} \leq c\left(\frac{1}{|Q|} \int_Q (f_\alpha^b)^q\right)^{1/q} \leq c\, M_q(f_\alpha^b)(x).$$

Taking a supremum over all cubes Q with $x \in Q \subset \Omega$ shows that

$$(D^\nu f)_{\alpha-k,q}(x) \leq c\, M_q(f_\alpha)(x). \tag{6.11}$$

Since M_q is bounded on L_p, this gives

$$||(D^\nu f)_{\alpha-k,q}||_{L_p} \leq c\, |f|_{\mathcal{C}_p^\alpha}.$$

Now it follows from Lemma 2.1 and Theorem 4.3 that for $\alpha' = \alpha - k$

$$(D^\nu f)_{\alpha'}^b \leq c(D^\nu f)_{\alpha',1}^b \leq c\, M_\sigma[(D^\nu f)_{\alpha',q}^b],$$

so since M_σ is bounded on L_p, we have

$$||(D^\nu f)_{\alpha-k}^b||_{L_p} \leq c\, |f|_{\mathcal{C}_p^\alpha}.$$

This gives the right hand inequality in (6.9).

The right hand inequality in (6.10) is proved in the same way. The existence of the weak derivatives $D^\nu f$, $|\nu| = k$ follows from Lemma 6.6, the fact that $C_p^\beta = \mathcal{C}_p^\beta$ if β is not an integer, and Corollary 5.7.

To prove the left hand inequality in (6.9), suppose $f \in L_p$ and $D^\nu f \in \mathcal{C}_p^{\alpha-k}$, $|\nu| = k$. From Theorem 3.6, it follows that for each cube Q

$$\inf_{\pi \in \mathbb{P}_{(\alpha)}} \int_Q |f-\pi| \leq c\, |Q|^{k/n} \sum_{|\nu|=k} \inf_{\pi_\nu \in \mathbb{P}_{(\alpha)-k}} \int_Q |D^\nu f-\pi_\nu|.$$

If we divide both sides by $|Q|^{1+\alpha/n}$, take a supremum over all Q containing x and use Lemma 2.1, we find

$$f_\alpha^b(x) \leq c \sum_{|\nu|=k} (D^\nu f)_{\alpha-k}^b(x). \tag{6.12}$$

Applying L_p norms to (6.12) gives the desired result.

The same argument used in proving (6.12) shows that

$$f_\alpha^\#(x) \leq c \sum_{|\nu|=k} (D^\nu f)_{\alpha-k}^\#(x). \tag{6.13}$$

Hence, the left hand inequality in (6.10) follows by taking L_p norms. □

Up to this point, we have not defined the space C_p^0, $1 \leq p \leq \infty$. The following theorem (see [2]) will motivate our definition.

Theorem 6.8. Suppose $1 < p < \infty$ and f satisfies $\lim_{N\to\infty} (Mf)^*(N) = 0$ where M is the Hardy-Littlewood maximal operator, then

(6.14) $$c_1 \, ||f||_{L_p} \leq ||f_0^{\#}||_{L_p} \leq c_2 \, ||f||_{L_p}$$

with c_1, c_2 independent of f.

Proof. The inequality $||f_0^{\#}||_{L_p} \leq c_2 \, ||f||_{L_p}$ follows immediately from the facts that $f_0^{\#} \leq 2\, Mf$ and that the Hardy-Littlewood maximal operator M is bounded on L_p. To obtain the remaining left hand inequality in (6.9), for each $s > 0$ we define $E := E_s := \{Mf > (Mf)^*(2s)\} \cup \{f_0^{\#} > (f_0^{\#})^*(2s)\}$. Then E is open and $|E| \leq 4s$. Now select for each x a dyadic cube Q(x) containing x which has smallest diameter and satisfies $Q(x) \cap E^c \neq \phi$. Subdividing Q(x) into 2^n congruent dyadic subcubes, we let $\tilde{Q}(x)$ be one of those that contains x, then necessarily $\tilde{Q}(x) \subset E$ and

(6.15) $$|Q(x)| = 2^n |\tilde{Q}(x)| \leq 2^n |Q(x) \cap E|.$$

But dyadic cubes have the property that when any two have intersecting interiors, then one must contain the other; hence we may select from the countable collection $\{Q(x)\}_{x\in E}$ countably many maximal cubes $\{Q_j\}_{j=1}^{\infty}$ whose interiors are pairwise disjoint and so that

(6.16) $$E \subset \bigcup_j Q_j, \qquad Q_j \cap E^c \neq \phi \text{ (each } j), \quad \sum_j |Q_j| \leq 2^n |E|.$$

The last inequality follows from summing inequality (6.15) over all j to get

$$\sum_j |Q_j| \leq 2^n \sum_j |Q_j \cap E| = 2^n \, |E|.$$

Next we decompose f into two functions: $g := \sum_j (f - f_{Q_j})\chi_{Q_j}$ and $h := f - g = \sum_j f_{Q_j} \chi_{Q_j} + f\,\chi_{E^c}$. Since M is weak type (1,1) and strong type (∞,∞), then

(6.17) $$(Mf)^*(s) \leq (Mg)^*(s) + ||Mh||_{L_\infty} \leq \frac{c}{s} \, ||g||_{L_1} + ||h||_{L_\infty} .$$

But $Q_j \cap E^c \neq \phi$, so we observe that

(6.18) $$\frac{1}{|Q_j|} \int_{Q_j} |f - f_{Q_j}| \leq \inf_{u\in Q_j} f_0^{\#}(u) \leq (f_0^{\#})^*(2s)$$

and

$$|f_{Q_j}| \leqq \inf_{u \in Q_j} Mf(u) \leqq (Mf)^*(2s).$$

Moreover, $|f\,\chi_{E^c}| \leqq (Mf)\chi_{E^c} \leqq (Mf)^*(2s)$, so

$$||h||_{L_\infty} \leqq \max\,\{\sup_j |f_{Q_j}|,\ ||f\,\chi_{E^c}||_{L_\infty}\} \leqq (Mf)^*(2s).$$

Estimating the L_1 norm of g we have from (6.18) and (6.16) that

$$||g||_{L_1} \leqq \sum_j \int_{Q_j} |f-f_{Q_j}| \leqq \sum_j |Q_j|\ (f_0^{\#})^*(2s)$$

$$\leqq 2^n\ |E|(f_0^{\#})^*(2s) \leqq c\ s(f_0^{\#})^*(2s).$$

Combining these with (6.17) we obtain

(6.19) $$(Mf)^*(s) \leqq c\ (f_0^{\#})^*(2s) + (Mf)^*(2s)\quad,\quad 0 < s < \infty.$$

Let $N > t > 0$ be arbitrary but fixed real numbers, then integrating (6.19) from $t/2$ to N with weight $1/s$ we obtain

$$\int_{t/2}^N (Mf)^*(s)\,\frac{ds}{s} \leqq c\int_{t/2}^N (f_0^{\#})^*(2s)\frac{ds}{s} + \int_{t/2}^N (Mf)^*(2s)\frac{ds}{s}$$

$$\leqq c\int_t^\infty (f_0^{\#})^*(s)\frac{ds}{s} + \int_t^{2N} (Mf)^*(s)\frac{ds}{s}$$

by changing variables. Subtracting the integral $\int_t^N (Mf)^*(s)\frac{ds}{s}$ from both sides and using the fact that $(Mf)^*$ decreases we see

$$(Mf)^*(t) \leqq c\int_{t/2}^t (Mf)^*(s)\frac{ds}{s} \leqq c\ [\int_t^\infty (f_0^{\#})^*(s)\frac{ds}{s} + \int_N^{2N} (Mf)^*(s)\frac{ds}{s}]$$

$$\leqq c\ [\int_t^\infty (f_0^{\#})^*(s)\frac{ds}{s} + (Mf)^*(N)].$$

By letting $N \to \infty$ and using the hypothesis that $(Mf)^*(N) \to 0$ we find that for $t > 0$,

(6.20) $$(Mf)^*(t) \leqq c\int_t^\infty (f_0^{\#})^*(s)\frac{ds}{s}\ .$$

But now we may use the fact that $|f| \leqq Mf$ a.e. and apply Hardy's inequality to the integral in (6.20) to obtain

$$||f||_{L_p} \leqq ||Mf||_{L_p} \leqq c\ ||f_0^{\#}||_{L_p}$$

as desired. □

For $1 \leqq p < \infty$ we define the space C_p^0 to be L_p and set $||f||_{C_p^0} := ||f||_p$. For $p = \infty$, we define $C_\infty^0 :=$ BMO and $||f||_{C_\infty^0} := ||f||_{BMO} = ||f_0^{\#}||_\infty$. In view Theorem 6.8, these are the natural definitions for $1 < p < \infty$. However, some explanation is needed for the case $p = 1$. As we explain in §12, the proper definition for $p = 1$ is $f_{0,q}^{\#} \in L_1$ for some $q < 1$, which is equivalent to $f \in L_1$ modulo constants. With this definition C_p^0, $1 \leqq p \leqq \infty$, forms an interpolation scale. On the other hand, the space obtained by requiring $f^{\#} \in L_1$ implies $Mf \in L_1(\mathrm{loc})$ and so f belongs to L log L locally. This space does not form an interpolation scale with the L_p spaces $1 < p < \infty$.

§7. Comparison With Besov Spaces

We intend to carry further the study of the relationships of C_p^α and $\mathcal{C}_p^\alpha$ to the classical smoothness spaces. We shall assume that $\Omega = \mathbb{R}^n$ throughout this section. Similar arguments work for cubes in $\mathbb{R}^n$. Other domains are discussed in §11.

We start with some approximation estimates. For $1 \leqq p < \infty$ define

$$E_r(f,\rho,x)_p := \inf_{\pi \in \mathbb{P}_{r-1}} \left(\int_{Q_\rho(x)} |f-\pi|^p\right)^{1/p}$$

where $Q_\rho(x)$ is the cube centered at x with side length ρ and set

$$E_r(f,\rho)_p := \|E_r(f,\rho,\cdot)\|_{L_p}.$$

From Theorem 3.4, it follows that whenever $g \in W_p^r$ then

$$E_r(g,\rho,x)_p \leqq c\, \rho^r \sum_{|\mu|=r} \|D^\mu g\|_{L_p(Q_\rho(x))}.$$

Hence integrating over $x \in \mathbb{R}^n$, we get by Fubini's theorem that

$$E_r(g,\rho)_p \leqq c\, \rho^r \sum_{|\mu|=r} \left(\int_{\mathbb{R}^n} \int_{\mathbb{R}^n} |D^\mu g(y) \chi_{Q_\rho(x)}(y)|^p \, dy\, dx\right)^{1/p} \tag{7.1}$$

$$\leqq c\, \rho^{r+n/p} \|g\|_{W_p^r}.$$

Similarly, when $f \in L_p$

$$E_r(f,\rho)_p \leqq \left[\int_{\mathbb{R}^n} \left(\int_{Q_\rho(x)} |f|^p\right) dx\right]^{1/p} \leqq c\, \rho^{n/p} \|f\|_{L_p}. \tag{7.2}$$

Since E is subadditive, (7.1) and (7.2) give

$$E_r(f,\rho) \leqq E_r(f-g,\rho) + E_r(g,\rho) \leqq c\, \rho^{n/p}\{\|f-g\|_{L_p} + \rho^r \|g\|_{W_p^r}\}.$$

Taking an infinum over all such g gives

$$E_r(f,\rho)_p \leqq c\, \rho^{n/p} K_r(f,\rho^r)_p$$

where $K_r(f,t)_p := K(f,t;L_p,W_p^r)$, $t > 0$, is the K functional for interpolation between L_p and W_p^r. It is known [11] that $K_r(f,t^r)_p \leqq c\, \omega_r(f,t)_p$ for $t > 0$. Thus

$$E_r(f,\rho)_p \leqq c\, \rho^{n/p} \omega_r(f,\rho)_p. \tag{7.3}$$

The same estimate holds when $p = \infty$ with C in place of L_∞.

We are now in a position to prove the following continuous embedding theorem:

Theorem 7.1. If $1 \leqq p \leqq \infty$ and $\alpha > 0$, then we have the embeddings:

$$B_p^{\alpha,p} \to C_p^{\alpha} \to B_p^{\alpha,\infty}. \tag{7.4}$$

Proof. For $r := [\alpha] + 1$ we have from Theorem 2.5,

$$||\Delta_h^r(f,\cdot)||_{L_p} \leqq c\,|h|^{\alpha}||f_{\alpha}^{\#}||_{L_p}$$

which leads immediately to the right hand embedding in (7.4).

To prove the left hand embedding, let $F := f_{\alpha,p}^{\#}$ with $f_{\alpha,p}^{\#}$ as in §4. By the observation (2.14) on the equivalence of maximal operators

$$F(x)^p \leqq c \sup_{\rho>0} \{E_r(f,\rho,x)_p/\rho^{\alpha+n/p}\}^p$$

$$\leqq c \int_0^{\infty} \frac{E_r(f,\rho,x)_p^p}{\rho^{\alpha p+n}} \frac{d\rho}{\rho}$$

because $E_r(f,\rho,x)$ is increasing as a function of ρ. Thus from (7.3)

$$\int_{\mathbb{R}^n} |F|^p \leqq c \int_0^{\infty} \frac{E_r(f,\rho)_p^p}{\rho^{\alpha p+n}} \frac{d\rho}{\rho} \leqq c \int_0^{\infty} \left(\frac{\omega_r(f,\rho)_p}{\rho^{\alpha}}\right)^p \frac{d\rho}{\rho}$$

$$\leqq c\left(|f|_{B_p^{\alpha,p}}\right)^p.$$

Now $f_{\alpha}^{\#} \leqq c\, f_{\alpha,1}^{\#} \leqq c\, f_{\alpha,p}^{\#}$ and hence

$$||f_{\alpha}^{\#}||_{L_p} \leqq c\,|f|_{B_p^{\alpha,p}}$$

as desired. □

Next we show that the embeddings in Theorem 7.1 are best possible within the scale of Besov spaces. We begin with the lower embedding.

Lemma 7.2. If $1 \leqq p < \infty$ and $\alpha > 0$, then there is an f which belongs to $B_p^{\alpha,q}$ for each $p < q \leqq \infty$, but $f \notin C_p^{\alpha}$.

Proof. Consider first the case $0 < \alpha < 1$ and $n = 1$. By the embedding $B_p^{\alpha,q} \subset B_p^{\alpha,\infty}$ it is obvious that we may assume $q < \infty$. Set $\delta := (1 + \frac{1}{p} - \alpha)^{-1}$ and $a := 2^{-\delta} < 1$. Consider the "hat" function

(7.5) $$\psi(x) := \begin{cases} x & 0 \leqq x \leqq 1 \\ 2-x & 1 \leqq x \leqq 2 \\ 0 & \text{otherwise} \end{cases}.$$

We select disjoint intervals $I_j := [a_j, b_j]$ with $\frac{1}{2}(b_j - a_j) = h_j := a^j$. Since $\Sigma\, h_j < \infty$, we can choose the intervals so they are all contained in $[0,A]$ with $A < \infty$. Define

$$f_j(x) := j^{-1/p}\, 2^j\, h_j\, \psi((x-a_j)/h_j).$$

Then f_j is supported on I_j. Further define

$$f := \sum_1^\infty f_j,$$

then

$$||f||_{L_p}^p \leqq \sum_1^\infty (j^{-1/p}\, 2^j\, h_j)^p\, h_j \leqq \sum_1^\infty [a^{\alpha p}]^j < \infty$$

so that $f \in L_p$.

To see that $f \notin C_p^\alpha$ notice that if $x \in I_j$,

(7.6) $$f_\alpha^{\#}(x) \geqq \frac{1}{|I_j|^{1+\alpha}} \int_{I_j} |f - f_{I_j}| = j^{-1/p}\, 2^j\, h_j^{1-\alpha}/2^{2+\alpha}.$$

Hence

$$\int_{\mathbb{R}} [f_\alpha^{\#}]^p \geqq c \sum_1^\infty [j^{-1/p}\, 2^j\, h_j^{1-\alpha}]^p h_j = c \sum_1^\infty j^{-1} = \infty.$$

To estimate the Besov norm we need to estimate $||\Delta_s f||_{L_p}$ for $0 < s < a$. Choose k so that $h_{k+1} \leqq s < h_k$. Then with c depending at most on p and α, we have

$$||\Delta_s f||_{L_p} \leqq \sum_1^k ||\Delta_s f_j||_{L_p} + 2 \sum_{k+1}^\infty ||f_j||_{L_p}$$

$$\leqq c\, [\sum_1^k j^{-1/p}\, 2^j\, s\, h_j^{1/p} + \sum_{k+1}^\infty j^{-1/p}\, 2^j\, h_j^{1+1/p}]$$

(7.7) $$\leqq c\, [s \sum_1^k j^{-1/p}(2a^{1/p})^j + \sum_{k+1}^\infty j^{-1/p}(2a^{1+1/p})^j]$$

$$\leqq c\, [s\, k^{-1/p}\, a^{k(\alpha-1)} + k^{-1/p}\, a^{k\alpha}]$$

$$\leqq c\, s^\alpha\, |\log s|^{-1/p}$$

where we've used the fact that $2a^{1/p} > 1$ and $2a^{1+1/p} < 1$. Inequality (7.7) gives $\omega(f,t)_p \leqq c\, t^\alpha |\log t|^{-1/p}$ for $0 < t < a$ and so

$$\int_0^a \left(\frac{\omega(f,t)_p}{t^\alpha}\right)^q \frac{dt}{t} \leqq c \int_0^a |\log t|^{-q/p} \frac{dt}{t} < \infty.$$

Also $\omega(f,t)_p \leqq 2\, ||f||_{L_p}$, hence

$$\int_a^\infty \left(\frac{\omega(f,t)_p}{t^\alpha}\right)^q \frac{dt}{t} \leqq 2\, ||f||_{L_p}^q \int_a^\infty t^{-\alpha q-1}\, dt < \infty .$$

Thus $f \in B_p^{\alpha,q}$ when $p < q \leqq \infty$.

In the case $\alpha = 1$ and $n = 1$, the construction given above is also valid but it is necessary to make two changes in the estimates. In (7.6) we use the fact that f_j is even on I_j and therefore its best L_1 approximation by a linear function on I_j is the constant $(f_j)_{I_j}$. Hence inequality (7.6) is still valid. In the estimate (7.7) we replace Δ_s by Δ_s^2. The second sum is estimated in the same way with 2 replaced by 4 in the first inequality. For the first sum, we have $||\Delta_s^2 f_j||_{L_p} \leqq c\, j^{-1/p} 2^j s^{1+1/p}$ and therefore the sum is smaller than $c\, k^{-1/p} 2^k s^{1+1/p} \leqq c\, s\, |\log s|^{-1/p}$. This shows as before that $f \in B_p^{1,q}$.

Now consider the case $n > 1$ and $0 < \alpha \leqq 1$. Define $F(x_1,\ldots,x_n) := f(x_1)\, \phi(x_1,\ldots,x_n)$ where ϕ is infinitely differentiable with compact support and $\phi \equiv 1$ on $[0,A]^n$. Clearly $F \in L_p(\mathbb{R}^n)$. To estimate $\Delta_s F$ write

$$\Delta_s(F,x) = \phi(x+s)\, \Delta_{s_1}(f,x_1) + f(x_1)\, \Delta_s(\phi,x).$$

Since ϕ is smooth with compact support, $\phi \equiv 1$ on $[0,A]^n$, this gives

$$\begin{aligned} ||\Delta_s F||_{L_p(\mathbb{R}^n)} &\leqq c\, [\,||\Delta_{s_1} f||_{L_p(\mathbb{R})} + ||f||_{L_p(\mathbb{R})} s] \\ &\leqq c\, |s|^\alpha |\log |s||^{-1/p} \end{aligned}$$

because of inequality (7.7) with c depending at most on p, α, and n. Similarly, for $\alpha = 1$,

$$\begin{aligned} \Delta_s^2(F,x) &= \Delta_{s_1}^2(f,x_1)\phi(x+2s) + f(x_1+s_1)\, \Delta_s^2(\phi,x) \\ &\quad + (f(x_1+s_1) - f(x_1))(\phi(x+2s) - \phi(x)) \end{aligned}$$

from which it follows that

$$||\Delta_s^2 F||_{L_p(\mathbb{R}^n)} \leqq c\ |s|\ |\log|s||^{-1/p}\ .$$

Thus $F \in B_p^{\alpha,q}$ for $q > p$. But for any cube $Q = J_1 \times \ldots \times J_n \quad [0,A]^n$, we have $F_Q = f_{J_1}$ and $F(x) = f(x_1)$, $x \in Q$. Hence for each x with $x_1 \in I_j$, (7.6) gives

$$F_\alpha^{\#}(x) \geqq j^{-1/p}\ 2^j\ h_j^{1-\alpha}/2^{\alpha+2} \qquad x \in [0,A]^n,\ x_1 \in I_j \tag{7.8}$$

from which it follows that $F_\alpha^{\#} \in L_p(\mathbb{R}^n)$ as desired.

Finally, for $\alpha' = k + \alpha$ with $0 < \alpha \leqq 1$, let f_k satisfy $(f_k)^{(k)} = f$ with f as above and set $F_k := f_k\phi$ with ϕ as above. Since ϕ has compact support $F_k \in L_p(\mathbb{R}^n)$. Using Leibnitz's rule of differentiation one finds that $D^\nu F_k \in B_p^{\alpha'-k,q}(\mathbb{R}^n)$ for all $|\nu| = k$. Thus using the reduction theorems for Besov spaces, $F_k \in B_p^{\alpha',q}(\mathbb{R}^n)$ for $q > p$. Since $D^{ke_1}F_k = (f_k)^{(k)} = f$ on $[0,A]^n$, it follows from (7.6) that $D^{ke_1}F_k \notin C_p^{\alpha'-k}$. Hence Theorem 6.7 shows that $F_k \notin C_p^{\alpha'}$. □

<u>Lemma 7.3</u>. If $\alpha > 0$, then there is an f such that for each $1 \leqq p \leqq \infty$ and $1 \leqq q < \infty$, $f \in C_p^\alpha$ but $f \notin B_p^{\alpha,q}$.

<u>Proof</u>. Consider first the case $n = 1$ and $0 < \alpha < 1$. We shall construct a function f in Lip α with compact support such that for sufficiently many x and s

$$|f(x+s) - f(x)| \geqq c\ s^\alpha.$$

This will in turn show that $t^{-\alpha}\omega(f,t)_p \geqq c$ for sufficiently many t and consequently $||f||_{B_p^{\alpha,q}} = \infty$. On the other hand f will be in C_p^α for all $1 \leqq p \leqq \infty$.

Fix a such that $0 < a < \min(5^{1/(\alpha-1)}, 24^{-1/\alpha})$ and set $A := a^{\alpha-1}$ and $\gamma := a^\alpha$. Then $A \geqq 5$ and $0 < \gamma < \frac{1}{24}$. Let $h_j := a^j$, $m_j := A^j$ $(j = 1,2,\ldots)$ and ψ be as in (7.5). The dilated functions $\psi_j(x) := m_j h_j \psi(x/h_j)$ have support on $[0,2h_j]$ and $|(\psi_j)'| = m_j$ a.e. on that interval. With $M_j = [\frac{1}{2h_j}] - 1$ (where the brackets here denotes the greatest integer), define

$$f_j(x) := \sum_{i=0}^{M_j} \psi_j(x-2ih_j).$$

Hence f_j is supported on $[0,1]$. Now define the function f by $f := \sum_j f_j$. Since $\|f_j\|_{L_\infty} \leqq m_j h_j = \gamma^j$, it follows that f is a bounded continuous function.

First we check that $f \in \text{Lip}\,\alpha$. If $a/2 > s > 0$, choose k so that $h_{k+1} \leqq 2s < h_k$, then

$$\|\Delta_s f_j\|_{L_\infty} \leqq \begin{cases} m_j s & \text{if } j \leqq k \\ 2\|f_j\|_{L_\infty} & \text{if } j > k . \end{cases}$$

Hence,

$$\begin{aligned} \|\Delta_s f\|_{L_\infty} &\leqq \sum_1^k m_j s + 2 \sum_{k+1}^{\infty} m_j h_j \\ &\leqq \frac{A}{A-1} m_k s + 2 \frac{\gamma^{k+1}}{1-\gamma} \\ &\leqq 2(a^{\alpha-1})^k s + 4(a^{\alpha})^{k+1} \leqq 10\, s^{\alpha}. \end{aligned}$$

Since f is bounded, this shows that $f_\alpha^{\#} \in L_\infty$ (cf. Theorem 6.3). Observe further that if $\text{dist}(x,[0,1]) =: \delta > 0$, then

$$f_\alpha^{\#}(x) \leqq \sup_{|I|\geqq\delta} \frac{1}{|I|^{\alpha+1}} \int_I |f| \leqq \frac{1}{\delta^{\alpha+1}} \int_0^1 |f| \leqq \frac{c}{\delta^{\alpha+1}}$$

which shows that $f_\alpha^{\#} \in L_p$ for all $1 \leqq p \leqq \infty$.

Next we show that $f \notin B_p^{\alpha,q}$ for any $1 \leqq q < \infty$, $1 \leqq p \leqq \infty$. Fix k and let s satisfy $\frac{1}{3} h_k \leqq s \leqq \frac{1}{2} h_k$. Define the set

$$E_s := \bigcup_{j=0}^{M_k} [2jh_k, 2jh_k + h_k/2]$$

then $|E_s| \geqq \frac{1}{8}$, $E_s \subset [0,1]$, and for $x \in E_s$

$$\begin{aligned} |\Delta_s f(x)| &\geqq |\Delta_s f_k(x)| - |\sum_{j\neq k} \Delta_s f_j(x)| \\ &\geqq m_k s - \{\sum_1^{k-1} m_j s + 2 \sum_{k+1}^{\infty} m_j h_j\}. \end{aligned}$$

But $\sum_{j=1}^{k-1} m_j \leqq \frac{1}{4} m_k$ and $\sum_{k+1}^{\infty} m_j h_j \leqq \frac{1}{4} m_k s$, so

(7.9) $$|\Delta_s f(x)| \geqq \frac{1}{4} m_k s \qquad \text{if } x \in E_s;\ s \in [\tfrac{1}{3}h_k, \tfrac{1}{2}h_k].$$

On the other hand,

$$s^{\alpha-1} \leqq 3m_k$$

and so by (7.9)

$$(7.10) \qquad |\Delta_s f(x)| \geqq \frac{1}{12} s^\alpha \qquad \text{if } x \in E_s.$$

Taking L_p norms we see that

$$\omega(f,s)_p \geqq ||\Delta_s f||_{L_p} \geqq ||(\Delta_s f)\chi_{E_s}||_{L_p} \geqq \frac{s^\alpha}{96}$$

at least if $s \in [\frac{1}{3} h_k, \frac{1}{2} h_k]$, $k = 1,2,\ldots$. But since ω is monotone, $\omega(f,t)_p \geqq c\, t^\alpha$ for all $0 < t \leqq 1$. Hence

$$\int_0^1 [t^{-\alpha} \omega(f,t)_p]^q \frac{dt}{t} = \infty.$$

The same ideas work for $\alpha = 1$, $n = 1$ with the following modifications. We now take $A = 24$ and $a = \frac{1}{24}$. Set

$$\psi(t) := \begin{cases} t^2 & 0 \leqq t \leqq 1 \\ 2-(t-2)^2 & 1 \leqq t \leqq 3 \\ (t-4)^2 & 3 \leqq t \leqq 4 \\ 0 & \text{otherwise} \end{cases}$$

then $\psi_j(t) := m_j h_j^2 \psi(t/h_j)$ is continuously differentiable and $|\psi_j''| \leqq 2\, m_j$ a.e. In the definition of f_j we take $M_j := [\frac{1}{4h_j}] - 1$ and $f_j(x) := \sum_{i=1}^{M_j} \psi_j(x-4ih_j)$, then

$$||\Delta_s^2 f_j||_{L_\infty} \leqq \min(2m_j s^2, 8m_j h_j^2).$$

Hence the same arguments as above show that $||\Delta_s^2 f||_{L_\infty} \leqq c\, s$ and $f_1^\# \in L_p$ for all $1 \leqq p \leqq \infty$. On the other hand, arguing in a similar manner as in (7.9-7.10) will give $\omega_2(f,t) \geqq c\, t$, $0 < t \leqq 1$ and hence $f \notin B_p^{1,q}$ for all $1 \leqq q < \infty$ as desired.

For the case $0 < \alpha \leqq 1$ and $n > 1$, let

$$F(x_1,\ldots,x_n) := f(x_1)\phi(x_1,\ldots,x_n)$$

where f is as above and $\phi \equiv 1$ on $[0,1]^n$, is infinitely differentiable, and is supported on $R := [-1,2]^n$, then for $s = (s_1,\ldots,s_n)$ and $0 < \alpha < 1$

$$||\Delta_s F||_{L_\infty} \leqq ||f||_{L_\infty} ||\Delta_s \phi||_{L_\infty} + ||\phi||_{L_\infty} ||\Delta_{s_1} f||_{L_\infty} \leqq c\, s^\alpha.$$

This shows that $F_\alpha^{\#} \in L_\infty$. Similarly for $\alpha = 1$, $||\Delta_s^2 F||_{L_\infty} \leq c\, s$ and so $F_1^{\#} \in L_\infty$. Also if $\delta(x) := \operatorname{dist}(x,R)$, then $F_\alpha^{\#}(x) \leq c\,\delta(x)^{-\alpha-n}$. Consequently, $F_\alpha^{\#} \in L_p$ for all $1 \leq p \leq \infty$. Since $|\Delta_s(F,x)| = |\Delta_{s_1}(f,x_1)|$, $x, x+s \in [0,1]^n$, it follows from (7.10) that

$$(7.11) \qquad |\Delta_s(F,x)| \geq |\Delta_{s_1}(f,x_1)| \geq \frac{1}{12} s_1^\alpha \quad \text{if } x_1 \in E_{s_1} \text{ and } s_1 \in [\tfrac{1}{3} h_k, \tfrac{1}{2} h_k].$$

This gives

$$\omega(F,t)_p \geq c\, t^\alpha, \quad 0 < t < 1$$

and therefore $F \notin B_p^{\alpha,q}$ for any $1 \leq q < \infty$. A similar argument with second differences shows that this follows for $\alpha = 1$ as well.

Finally, if $\alpha' = k + \alpha$ with $0 < \alpha \leq 1$, let f_k be such that $(f_k)^{(k)} = f$ with f as above and let $F_k := f_k\phi$ with ϕ as above. Then it is readily seen that $F_k \in C_p^{\alpha'}$ for $1 \leq p \leq \infty$ by the reduction theorem for C_p^α spaces (Theorem 6.7). On the other hand $D^{ke_1} F_k = F$ on $[0,1]^n$, therefore (7.11) shows that $D^{ke_1} F_k \notin B_p^{\alpha,q}$ if $q < \infty$. The reduction theorem [3] for Besov spaces then shows that $F_k \notin B_p^{\alpha',q}$ if $q < \infty$. □

<u>Corollary 7.4</u>. If $\alpha > 0$ and $1 \leq p < \infty$, then the space C_p^α is neither a Besov space nor a potential space.

<u>Proof</u>. In view of the embeddings of Theorem 7.1, the only possibility for C_p^α to be a Besov space is for it to equal $B_p^{\alpha,q}$ for some q with $p \leq q \leq \infty$. However, Lemmas 7.2 and 7.3 show that this is not the case.

If C_p^α were a potential space, it would have to be $\mathcal{L}_p^\alpha$ (see Stein [15] for notation). On the other hand [15, p. 155] for $p \geq 2$, $\mathcal{L}_p^\alpha \subset B_p^{\alpha,p}$ which would contradict Lemma 7.3 if $C_p^\alpha = \mathcal{L}_p^\alpha$. For $p \leq 2$, $\mathcal{L}_p^\alpha \subset B_p^{\alpha,2}$ which again would contradict Lemma 7.3 if $C_p^\alpha = \mathcal{L}_p^\alpha$. □

We now want to go a little deeper into the relationship between C_p^α, $\mathcal{C}_p^\alpha$ and the potential spaces $\mathcal{L}_p^\alpha$. If $\alpha = k$ is an integer and $1 < p < \infty$, then as we have shown in Theorem 6.2, $\mathcal{C}_p^k = W_p^k$ and as is well known $\mathcal{L}_p^k = W_p^k$. Hence $\mathcal{C}_p^k = \mathcal{L}_p^k$. Our next theorem gives embeddings when α is non-integral.

Theorem 7.5. If $0 < \alpha$ and $1 < p < \infty$, we have the continuous embeddings

(7.12)
$$\mathcal{L}_p^\alpha \to \mathcal{C}_p^\alpha \to C_p^\alpha .$$

Proof. The right most embedding in (7.12) is well known to us since $f_\alpha^\# \leq c\, f_\alpha^\flat$. As noted above the left embeddings hold for α an integer. We will now use the complex method of interpolation to derive the case of arbitrary α from the case α an integer.

Let m be an integer such that $m < \alpha < m + 1$. Consider the maximal function

(7.13)
$$f_\alpha(x) := \sup_{\rho>0} \rho^{-n-\alpha} \int_{Q_\rho(x)} |f - P_{Q_\rho(x)} f|$$

with Q_ρ the cube with side length ρ and center x and P the projection of degree $m + 1$. It follows from (2.14) i) and Lemma 2.3 that

(7.14)
$$f_\alpha \leq f_\alpha^\# \leq c_1 f_\alpha .$$

It is clear that the supremum in (7.13) can be taken over ρ rational. Let $\{A_k\}_1^\infty$ be a sequence of sets such that A_k contains k positive rationals, $A_k \subset A_{k+1}$, $k = 1,2,\ldots$ and $\bigcup_1^\infty A_k$ is the set of positive rationals.
Define

(7.15)
$$F_k(x) := \max_{\rho\in A_k} \rho^{-n-\alpha} \int_{Q_\rho(x)} |f - P_{Q_\rho(x)} f| ,$$

then $F_k \uparrow f_\alpha$ and hence $\|F_k\|_{L_p} \uparrow \|f_\alpha\|_{L_p}$. It follows from (7.14) that we need only show that

(7.16)
$$\|F_k\|_{L_p} \leq c\, \|f\|_{\mathcal{L}_p^\alpha} , \quad k=1,2,\ldots .$$

Fix $f \in \mathcal{L}_p^\alpha$. Next fix k and let $A_k = \{\rho_1,\ldots,\rho_k\}$. Define

$$\rho(x) := \sum_1^k \rho_j \chi_{S_j}$$

where S_j is the set of x such that the max in (7.15) is taken on for $\rho=\rho_j$ but not for any ρ_i with $i < j$. Since for each j, $\int_{Q_{\rho_j}(x)} |f - P_{Q_{\rho_j}(x)} f|$ is continuous, the function ρ is simple.

Consider now the family of operators S_z, $0 \leq \mathrm{Re}\, z \leq 1$ defined by

$$S_z g(x): = \rho(x)^{-n-m-z} \int_{Q_{\rho(x)}(x)} (g(y)-P_{Q_{\rho(x)}(x)}g(y))\ \phi(x,y)dy$$

$$= \sum_{j=1}^{k} \rho_j^{-n-m-z} \chi_{S_j}(x) \int_{Q_{\rho_j}(x)} [g(y)-P_{Q_{\rho_j}(x)}g(y)]\ \phi(x,y)dy$$

with $\phi(x,y): = \text{sign}[f(y)-P_{Q_{\rho(x)}(x)}f(y)]$. Going further, let $\mathcal{J}_z$ be the Bessel potential operators of order z. Using the form of S_z and the fact that $\mathcal{J}_z$ is operator valued analytic in Re $z > 0$, it follows that

$$T_z: = S_z \circ \mathcal{J}_{z+m}$$

is an analytic family in the sense of Stein [17, p. 205]. Now let us estimate $T_{i\eta}g$ for $g \in L_p$ and $\eta > 0$. From the definition of S_z we have $||S_{i\eta}h||_{L_p} \leqq c\ ||h_m^{\#}||_{L_p} \leqq c\ ||h_m^{\flat}||_{L_p}$ therefore,

(7.17) $$||T_{i\eta}g||_{L_p} \leqq c\ ||(\mathcal{J}_{m+i\eta}g)_m^{\flat}||_{L_p} \leqq c\ ||\mathcal{J}_{m+i\eta}g||_{\mathcal{L}_p^m}$$

$$\leqq c\ ||\mathcal{J}_m g||_{\mathcal{L}_\rho^m} (|\eta|+1)^n \leqq c\ ||g||_{L_p} (|\eta|+1)^n.$$

Here, we used the facts that $\mathcal{J}_{m+i\eta} = \mathcal{J}_{i\eta} \circ \mathcal{J}_m$, $\mathcal{C}_p^m = \mathcal{L}_p^m$, $||\mathcal{J}_{i\eta}|| \leqq c(|\eta|+1)^n$ from L_p to L_p, and $\mathcal{J}_m$ is an isometry from L_p to $\mathcal{L}_p^m$. Similarly, we have

(7.18) $$||T_{1+i\eta}g||_{L_p} \leqq c\ ||g||_{L_p} (|\eta|+1)^n .$$

This shows that T_z satisfies the hypothesis of the Stein interpolation theorem for analytic families. Thus for any $g \in L_p$,

$$||T_{\alpha-m}g||_{L_p} \leqq c\ ||g||_{L_p} .$$

Now since $f \in \mathcal{L}_p^\alpha$, there is a $g \in L_p$ such that $\mathcal{J}_\alpha g = f$ and $||g||_{L_p} = ||f||_{\mathcal{L}_p^\alpha}$. Hence

$$||F_k||_{L_p} = ||T_{\alpha-m}g||_{L_p} \leqq c\ ||g||_{L_p} = c\ ||f||_{\mathcal{L}_p^\alpha}$$

which is (7.16). □

Our final result of this section compares $\mathcal{C}_1^k$ to W_1^k. Although the interpolation spaces for $(\mathcal{C}_1^k, \mathcal{C}_\infty^k)$ and $(W_1^k, W_\infty^k = \mathcal{C}_\infty^k)$ coincide for the real method (see §8), $\mathcal{C}_1^k$ is properly contained in W_1^k.

Lemma 7.6. Suppose Ω is $\mathbb{R}^n$ or a cube in $\mathbb{R}^n$ and k is a positive integer, then there is a function $f \in W_1^k$ which does not belong to C_1^k. Consequently,

$$C_1^k(\Omega) \subsetneq W_1^k(\Omega) \qquad k = 1,2.... .$$

Proof. The containment follows from Theorem 5.6. We will construct f to have compact support within Ω and so $||f||_{W_1^k(\Omega)} = ||f||_{W_1^k(\mathbb{R}^n)}$. Hence by a change of scale we may assume that $\Omega = [-1,1]^n$.

Consider first the case k = 1 and n = 1. Let ψ be an even C^∞ function with $\psi \equiv 1$ on $[-\frac{1}{4},\frac{1}{4}]$, $||\psi||_\infty = 1$, and supp $\psi \subset [-\frac{1}{e},\frac{1}{e}]$. Then define f to be odd with

$$f(x): = \begin{cases} (\log 1/x)^{-1}\ \psi(x), & x > 0 \\ 0, & x = 0 . \end{cases} \tag{7.19}$$

Notice that f is a continuous function which increases on $[-\frac{1}{4},\frac{1}{4}]$. Moreover, $||f||_{L_\infty} \leqq 1$, f is supported in $[-\frac{1}{e},\frac{1}{e}]$, and

$$f'(x) = x^{-1}\ (\log x)^{-2}\ \psi(x) + (\log 1/x)^{-1}\ \psi'(x), \qquad x > 0.$$

Since f is an odd function,

$$||f'||_{L_1} \leqq 2(\int_0^{1/e} (\log x)^{-2}\ \frac{dx}{x} + ||\psi'||_{L_\infty}) < \infty$$

and so $f \in W_1^1(\Omega)$. On the other hand, for $0 < x < 1/12$ (see §5 for notation)

$$\begin{aligned} N_1^1(f,x) &\geqq \sup_{\rho>0} \frac{1}{\rho^2} \int_{x-\rho}^{x+\rho} |f(u)-f(x)|du \\ &\geqq \tfrac{1}{4}x^{-2} \int_{-x}^{3x} |f(u)-f(x)|du \geqq \tfrac{1}{4}x^{-2} \int_{-x}^{x} [f(x)-f(u)]du \\ &= \tfrac{1}{4}x^{-2} \int_{-x}^{x} \int_u^x f'(t)dt\ du \end{aligned} \tag{7.20}$$

where we've used the fact that f is an odd increasing function on $[-\frac{1}{4},\frac{1}{4}]$. But now, by changing the order of integration we see that

$$\begin{aligned} N_1^1(f,x) &\geqq \tfrac{1}{4}x^{-2} \int_{-x}^{x} (x+t)\ f'(t)dt \geqq \frac{1}{4x} \int_0^x f'(t)dt \\ &= \frac{1}{4}\ \frac{f(x)}{x} = \tfrac{1}{4}x^{-1}\ (\log 1/x)^{-1}, \qquad 0 < x < 1/12 . \end{aligned}$$

Hence, from Corollary 5.4 $f_1^\flat \notin L_1(\Omega)$.

In case n > 1, let

$$F(x_1,...,x_n): = f(x_1)\ \phi(x_1,...,x_n)$$

where f is as above and ϕ is an infinitely differentiable function with support in $[-1,1]^n$ and $\phi \equiv 1$ on $[-\frac{1}{4},\frac{1}{4}]^n$. Obviously, $||F||_{L_\infty} \leqq 1$ and

$$\nabla F(x_1,\ldots,x_n) = \phi(x_1,\ldots,x_n)\ f'(x_1)\ e_1 + f(x_1)\ \nabla\phi(x_1,\ldots,x_n).$$

Hence $F \in W_1^1(\Omega)$. However a simple computation shows that $\int_Q F_1^\flat = \infty$, where $Q = [-\frac{1}{4},\frac{1}{4}]^n$.

For $k > 1$, we let f_k satisfy $f_k^{(k-1)} = f$ and $F_k := f_k\phi$ with f and ϕ as above. Using Leibnitz's rule of differentiation we find that $F_k \in W_1^k(\Omega)$. On the other hand, $D_{e_1}^{k-1}F_k = f\phi$ on Q, hence $D_{e_1}^{k-1}F_k \notin \mathcal{C}_1^1(\Omega)$. It follows from the reduction theorem for $\mathcal{C}_p^\alpha$ spaces (Theorem 6.7) that $F_k \in \mathcal{C}_1^k(\Omega)$. □

Actually, our proof could be slightly modified to show that there are constants c_1 and c_2 such that

$$c_1\ Mf'(x) \leqq f_1^\flat(x) \leqq c_2\ Mf'(x) \qquad -\frac{1}{4} \leqq x \leqq \frac{1}{4}$$

if f is any odd function which is continuous, increasing, and concave on [0,1]. The right hand inequality is (5.7).

The embeddings of this section are summarized in Figure I. Spaces connected by line segments indicate that the lower space is embedded in the upper space.

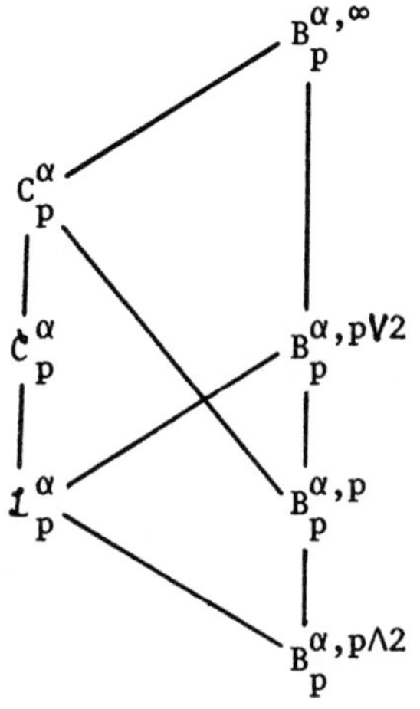

FIGURE I $(\alpha > 0;\ 1 < p < \infty)$

§8. Interpolation

We now examine some interpolation properties of the spaces C_p^α and $\dot{C}_p^\alpha$. It turns out that these spaces form interpolation scales for the real method of interpolation when α is fixed and p varies. We will show this by calculating the K functionals for the pairs $(C_1^\alpha, C_\infty^\alpha)$ and $(\dot{C}_1^\alpha, \dot{C}_\infty^\alpha)$. Recall that for any pair of Banach spaces (X_0,X_1) the K functional is defined for $f \in X_0 + X_1$ by

$$(8.1) \qquad K(f,t,X_0,X_1) := \inf_{f=f_0+f_1} \{||f_0||_{X_0} + t||f_1||_{X_1}\} \qquad t > 0 .$$

A key part of the calculation of these K-functionals is the Whitney extension theorem which extends a function f which is in Lip α on a closed set F to a function in Lip α on all of $\mathbb{R}^n$. We will need only a special case of this theorem for functions f which are defined on all of $\mathbb{R}^n$ to begin with. It will be convenient for us to give a formulation of the extension theorem for this special case in terms of the functions $f_\alpha^\#$ and $f_\alpha^\flat$.

Let f_α denote either of the functions $f_\alpha^\#$ or $f_\alpha^\flat$. Recall that the space $f_\alpha \in L_\infty(\mathbb{R}^n)$ is a Lipschitz space or generalized Lipschitz space (see §6). Suppose f is defined on $\mathbb{R}^n$ with $Mf \leqq m_0$ and $f_\alpha \leqq m_1$ on some closed set $F \subset \mathbb{R}^n$ where M is the Hardy-Littlewood maximal function. Then there is a function g such that g=f on F; $|g| \leqq cm_0$ and $g_\alpha \leqq cm_1$ on $\mathbb{R}^n$ with c a constant depending at most on n. Indeed, g can be constructed as follows.

Let $\{Q_j\}$ be a Whitney decomposition of F^c and ϕ_j^* the corresponding partition of unity (see [15, p. 167-170]). The Q_j have pairwise disjoint interiors, $\bigcup_j Q_j = F^c$ and for each j

$$(8.2) \qquad \operatorname{diam}(Q_j) \leqq \operatorname{dist}(Q_j,F) \leqq 4 \operatorname{diam}(Q_j).$$

The functions ϕ_j^* can be chosen to have support contained in cubes $Q_j^* := \frac{5}{4}Q_j$. Then

$$(8.3) \qquad \operatorname{diam}(Q_j^*) \leqq c \operatorname{dist}(Q_j,F).$$

For each j, let $\tilde{Q}_j$ denote a cube with the same center as Q_j and side length $10\sqrt{n}$ times the side length of Q_j; then $\tilde{Q}_j \cap F \neq \emptyset$. The function g can then be defined as

$$(8.4)\qquad g(x) := \begin{cases} f(x), & x \in F \\ \sum_j P_{\tilde{Q}_j} f(x)\, \phi_j^*(x), & x \in F^c \end{cases}$$

where P is the projection operator $P_{[\alpha]}$ (of degree $[\alpha]$) in case $f_\alpha = f_\alpha^\#$ and P is $P_{(\alpha)}$ (of degree (α)) in case $f_\alpha = f_\alpha^\flat$.

Lemma 8.1. If F is a closed set and f satisfies $Mf \leq m_0$ and $f_\alpha \leq m_1$ on F, then the function g defined by (8.4) satisfies:

i) $g = f$ on F; ii) $|g| \leq c\, m_0$ on $\mathbb{R}^n$; and iii) $g_\alpha \leq c\, m_1$ on $\mathbb{R}^n$.

Proof. From the definition of g, i) holds. To verify ii), first observe that $|g(x)| = |f(x)| \leq m_0$, $x \in F$. Now if $x \in F^c$, then since $\tilde{Q}_j \cap F \neq \emptyset$, it follows from (2.3) and our assumption that $Mf \leq m_0$ on F that $|P_{\tilde{Q}_j} f(x)| \leq c\, m_0$, $x \in \tilde{Q}_j$. Furthermore, $\operatorname{supp} \phi_j^* \subset Q_j^* \subset \tilde{Q}_j$ and so $|P_{\tilde{Q}_j} f(x)\phi_j^*(x)| \leq c\, m_0\, \phi_j^*(x)$. Hence

$$|g(x)| \leq \sum_j c\, m_0\, \phi_j^*(x) = c\, m_0, \quad x \in F^c$$

since $\sum_j \phi_j^*(x) \equiv 1$, $x \in F^c$.

To verify iii), let Q be a cube in $\mathbb{R}^n$. We consider two cases: $Q \cap F \neq \emptyset$; $Q \subset F^c$. Consider first the case $Q \cap F \neq \emptyset$. Observe that if $Q \cap Q_j^* \neq \emptyset$, then $|Q| \geq c|Q_j|$ (because of (8.3)) and hence there is a cube R_j which contains both Q and $\tilde{Q}_j$ with $|R_j| \leq c|Q|$. It follows from (2.15) that

$$\begin{aligned} ||P_{\tilde{Q}_j} f - P_Q f||_{L_\infty(Q \cap Q_j^*)} &\leq ||P_{\tilde{Q}_j} f - P_{R_j} f||_{L_\infty(\tilde{Q}_j)} + ||P_Q f - P_{R_j} f||_{L_\infty(Q)} \\ (8.5)\qquad &\leq c[\inf_{u \in \tilde{Q}_j} f_\alpha(u)\, |R_j|^{\alpha/n} + \inf_{u \in Q} f_\alpha(u)\, |R_j|^{\alpha/n}] \\ &\leq c\, m_1\, |Q|^{\alpha/n} \end{aligned}$$

since both Q and $\tilde{Q}_j$ intersect F. Using (8.4), we can write $g - P_Q f = (f - P_Q f)\chi_F + \sum_j (P_{\tilde{Q}_j} f - P_Q f)\phi_j^*$. Hence from (8.5),

$$\int_Q |g-P_Q f| \leq \int_{Q\cap F} |f-P_Q f| + \sum_j \int_Q \|P_{\tilde{Q}_j} f-P_Q f\|_{L_\infty(Q\cap Q_j^*)} \phi_j^*$$

$$\leq \inf_{u\in Q\cap F} f_\alpha(u)\ |Q|^{1+\alpha/n} + c\ m_1\ |Q|^{\alpha/n} \int_Q (\sum_j \phi_j^*) \tag{8.6}$$

$$\leq c\ m_1\ |Q|^{\alpha/n+1}.$$

Now consider the second case $Q \subset F^c$. We have two possibilities: a) $|Q_{j_o}| > 4^n |Q|$ for some Q_{j_o} which intersects Q; b) $|Q_j| \leq 4^n |Q|$ for all Q_j which intersect Q. In case a), we begin by showing that Q intersects at most $N^2 (N:=12^n)$ cubes Q_j^* and for each such j, $|Q_j| \leq (4^n)^2 |Q_{j_o}|$. To see this we note that any neighbor of Q_{j_o} has measure $\geq 4^{-n} |Q_{j_o}| \geq |Q|$. Therefore Q is contained in the union of Q_{j_o} and its neighbors which number at most N. Now suppose $Q_j^* \cap Q \neq \phi$. Since Q_j^* is contained in the union of Q_j and its neighbors it follows that Q_j and Q_{j_o} have a common neighbor when $Q_j^* \cap Q \neq \phi$. But there are at most N^2 such Q_j and $|Q_j| \leq (4^n)^2 |Q_{j_o}|$ as desired.

Let $k = [\alpha]$ or (α) according to whether f_α is $f_\alpha^{\#}$ or $f_\alpha^{\flat}$ and set m: = k+1. We estimate $D^\nu g$ for any $|\nu| = m$. By Leibnitz's formula, $D^\nu g = \sum_j \sum_{0<\mu\leq\nu} \binom{\nu}{\mu} D^{\nu-\mu} P_{\tilde{Q}_j} f\ D^\mu \phi_j^*$. Note that $D^\nu P_{\tilde{Q}_j} f \equiv 0$, for each j and $\sum D^\mu \phi_j^* \equiv 0$ on F^c for $\mu > 0$. Thus we have

$$D^\nu g(x) = \sum_{Q_j^*\cap Q\neq\emptyset} \sum_{0<\mu\leq\nu} \binom{\nu}{\mu} D^{\nu-\mu}(P_{\tilde{Q}_j} f - P_{\tilde{Q}_{j_o}} f)(x)\ D^\mu \phi_j^*(x). \tag{8.7}$$

Using (2.15), the same argument as (8.5) shows that

$$\|D^{\nu-\mu}(P_{\tilde{Q}_j} f - P_{\tilde{Q}_{j_o}} f)\|_{L_\infty(Q_j^*)} \leq c\ m_1\ |\tilde{Q}_{j_o}|^{(\alpha-|\nu-\mu|)/n}$$

$$\leq c\ m_1\ |Q_{j_o}|^{(\alpha-|\nu|+|\mu|)/n}.$$

Here we used the fact that all the Q_j^* which intersect Q have comparable size to Q_{j_o}. Also, the functions ϕ_j^* satisfy ([15, p. 174])

$$||D^\mu \phi_j^*||_\infty \leqq c\ |Q_j|^{-|\mu|/n} \leqq c\ |Q_{j_o}|^{-|\mu|/n}.$$

Using these last two estimates back in (8.7) gives

$$||D^\nu g||_{L_\infty(Q)} \leqq c\ m_1 \sum_{Q_j^* \cap Q \neq \emptyset} |Q_{j_o}|^{(\alpha-m)/n} \leqq c\ m_1\ |Q|^{(\alpha-m)/n}.$$

Hence from Theorem 3.4, there is a polynomial π of degree k such that

$$||g - \pi||_{L_\infty(Q)} \leqq c\ m_1\ |Q|^{\alpha/n}.$$

Integrating gives

$$\frac{1}{|Q|^{1+\alpha/n}} \int_Q |g - \pi| \leqq c\ m_1\ . \tag{8.8}$$

Finally, we have case b). In this case, we can choose a cube $\tilde{Q}$ of measure $\leqq c\ |Q|$ such that $\tilde{Q}$ contains each $\tilde{Q}_j$ for which Q_j^* intersects Q. Then, using (2.15), $||P_{\tilde{Q}} f - P_{\tilde{Q}_j} f||_{L_\infty(Q_j^*)} \leqq c \inf_{u \in \tilde{Q}_j} f_\alpha(u)\ |\tilde{Q}|^{\alpha/n} \leqq c\ m_1\ |Q|^{\alpha/n}$, and so

$$|(g - P_{\tilde{Q}} f)(x)| \leqq \sum_{Q_j^* \cap Q \neq \emptyset} ||P_{\tilde{Q}_j} f - P_{\tilde{Q}} f\ ||_{L_\infty(Q_j^*)}\ \phi_j^*(x)$$

$$\leqq c\ m_1\ |Q|^{\alpha/n} \sum_j \phi_j^*(x) \leqq c\ m_1\ |Q|^{\alpha/n}\ , \quad x \in Q.$$

Integrating gives

$$\frac{1}{|Q|^{1+\alpha/n}} \int_Q |g - P_{\tilde{Q}} f| \leqq c\ m_1\ , \tag{8.9}$$

hence the three inequalities (8.6), (8.8) and (8.9) show that

$$g_\alpha(x) \leqq c\ m_1$$

as desired. □

The following theorem characterizes the K-functional for the couples $(C_1^\alpha, C_\infty^\alpha)$ and $(\dot{C}_1^\alpha, \dot{C}_\infty^\alpha)$. The decomposition used below can be found in A. P. Calderón [5].

Theorem 8.2. If $\alpha > 0$, there exists constants $c_1, c_2 > 0$ such that

$$(8.10)\qquad c_1 \int_0^t [f^*(s) + (f_\alpha^\#)^*(s)]ds \leq K(f,t;C_1^\alpha,C_\infty^\alpha)$$

$$\leq c_2\int_0^t [f^*(s) + (f_\alpha^\#)^*(s)]ds,\ t > 0$$

and

$$(8.11)\qquad c_1 \int_0^t [f^*(s) + (f_\alpha^\flat)^*(s)]ds \leq K(f,t;\mathcal{C}_1^\alpha,\mathcal{C}_\infty^\alpha)$$

$$\leq c_2\int_0^t [f^*(s) + (f_\alpha^\flat)^*(s)]ds,\ t > 0.$$

Proof. We will only give the proof of (8.10). The proof of (8.11) is the same. First suppose $f = g + h$ with $g \in C_\infty^\alpha$ and $h \in C_1^\alpha$. Since $F \to F_\alpha^\#$ and $F \to F^{**}(t) := \frac{1}{t}\int_0^t F^*(s)ds$ are subadditive

$$\int_0^t [f^*(s) + (f_\alpha^\#)^*(s)]ds \leq \int_0^t [h^*(s) + h_\alpha^{\#*}(s)]ds + \int_0^t [g^*(s) + g_\alpha^{\#*}(s)]ds$$

$$\leq \int_0^\infty (h^*(s) + h_\alpha^{\#*}(s))ds + t\,(||g||_\infty + ||g_\alpha^\#||_\infty)$$

$$= ||h||_{C_1^\alpha} + t||g||_{C_\infty^\alpha}\ .$$

Taking an infimum over such decompositions gives the left hand side of (8.10).

For the right hand inequality in (8.10), let $E := \{x: f_\alpha^\#(x) > (f_\alpha^\#)^*(t)\} \cup \{x: Mf(x) > (Mf)^*(t)\}$ and $F := E^c$; then $|E| \leq 2t$. If g is defined as in (8.4), then according to Lemma 8.1,

$$(8.12)\qquad t\,||g||_{C_\infty^\alpha} = t\,(||g||_{L_\infty} + ||g_\alpha^\#||_{L_\infty}) \leq c\,[t(Mf)^*(t) + tf_\alpha^{\#*}(t)]$$

$$\leq c\,[\int_0^t f^*(s)ds + tf_\alpha^{\#*}(t)] \leq c\int_0^t (f^*(s) + f_\alpha^{\#*}(s))ds$$

where we used the fact that $(Mf)^*(t) \leq c\,f^{**}(t)$, $t > 0$, see [2].

We now want to estimate $h := f-g$ in the C_1^α norm. Let Q_j and $\tilde{Q}_j$ be as in the construction of g and define $\tilde{E} := \bigcup_j \tilde{Q}_j$ and $\tilde{F} = \tilde{E}^c$. Since $h \equiv 0$ on $F := E^c$, we have

$$(8.13)\qquad ||h||_{C_1^\alpha} = ||h||_{L_1} + ||h_\alpha^\#||_{L_1} = \int_E |h| + \int_{\tilde{E}} h_\alpha^\# + \int_{\tilde{F}} h_\alpha^\#.$$

The first two integrals are easy to estimate. Since $|E| \leq 2t$,

$$(8.14)\qquad \int_E |h| \le \int_E |f| + |E|\, \|g\|_{L_\infty} \le c\, [\int_0^{2t} f^*(s)ds + t\,(Mf)^*(t)]$$

$$\le c \int_0^t f^*(s)ds$$

where we used the fact that $\int_0^{at} f^*(s)ds \le a \int_0^t f^*(s)ds$, $a \ge 1$. Similarly, using Lemma 8.1, we obtain

$$(8.15)\qquad \begin{aligned}\int_{\tilde{E}} h_\alpha^\# &\le \int_{\tilde{E}} (f_\alpha^\# + g_\alpha^\#) \le \int_0^{ct} f_\alpha^{\#*}(s)ds + |\tilde{E}|\, \|g_\alpha^\#\|_{L_\infty} \\ &\le c\, [\int_0^t f_\alpha^{\#*}(s)ds + t f_\alpha^{\#*}(t)] \le c \int_0^t f_\alpha^{\#*}(s)ds.\end{aligned}$$

In order to estimate the last integral in (8.13), we estimate $h_\alpha^\#$ on $\tilde{F}$. Suppose $x \in \tilde{F}$ and Q is a cube containing x. Then, since $h \equiv 0$ on $F \supset \tilde{F}$,

$$(8.16)\qquad \begin{aligned}\frac{1}{|Q|^{1+\alpha/n}} \int_Q h &\le \frac{1}{|Q|^{1+\alpha/n}} \sum_j \int_Q |f - P_{\tilde{Q}_j} f| \phi_j^* \\ &\le \sum_j \frac{1}{|Q|^{1+\alpha/n}} \int_{Q\cap Q_j^*} |f - P_{\tilde{Q}_j} f| .\end{aligned}$$

Now, $c\, |Q| \ge [\mathrm{dist}\,(x,Q_j)]^n$ whenever $Q \cap Q_j^* \ne \emptyset$ (recall $\mathrm{dist}(Q_j^*,F)$ is comparable to $\mathrm{diam}\, Q_j$). Also, since $Q_j^* \subset \tilde{Q}_j$,

$$\int_{Q_j^*} |f - P_{\tilde{Q}_j} f| \le f_\alpha^{\#*}(t)\, |\tilde{Q}_j|^{1+\alpha/n} \le c\, f_\alpha^{\#*}(t)\, |Q_j|^{1+\alpha/n} .$$

Using this back in (8.16) and taking a sup over all such Q gives

$$(8.17)\qquad h_\alpha^\#(x) \le c\, f_\alpha^{\#*}(t) \sum_j \frac{|Q_j|^{1+\alpha/n}}{[\mathrm{dist}(x,Q_j)]^{\alpha+n}} \qquad x \in \tilde{F}.$$

Now, since $\mathrm{dist}(x,Q_j) \ge 2\, |Q_j|^{1/n}$ (recall the definition of $\tilde{Q}_j$)

$$\int_{\tilde{F}} [\mathrm{dist}(x,Q_j)]^{-\alpha-n} dx \le c \int_{2|Q_j|^{1/n}}^\infty \rho^{-\alpha-n} \rho^{n-1} d\rho \le c\, |Q_j|^{-\alpha/n}.$$

Hence integrating (8.17) gives

$$(8.18)\qquad \int_{\tilde{F}} h_\alpha^\# \le c\, f_\alpha^{\#*}(t) \sum_j |Q_j| \le c\, t\, f_\alpha^{\#*}(t) \le c \int_0^t f_\alpha^{\#*}(s)\, ds .$$

Therefore, the estimates (8.14), (8.15) and (8.18) used in (8.13) show that

$$\|h\|_{C_1^\alpha} \le c \int_0^t (f^*(s) + f_\alpha^{\#*}(s))ds.$$

This together with (8.12) proves the right hand estimate in (8.10). □

When X_1 and X_2 are Banach spaces with K functional $K(f,\cdot)$, and $0 < \theta < 1$; $0 < q \leqq \infty$, let $X_{\theta,q} := (X_1,X_2)_{\theta,q}$ denote the intermediate space (see [3,p. 167]) with

$$||f||_{X_{\theta,q}} : = (\int_0^\infty [t^{-\theta}K(f,t)]^q \frac{dt}{t})^{1/q}$$

with the appropriate change when $q = \infty$. The spaces $X_{\theta,q}$ are interpolation spaces for (X_1,X_2). It follows from Theorem 8.2 and the Hardy inequality that $(C_1^\alpha, C_\infty^\alpha)_{1-1/p,p} = C_p^\alpha$ with equivalent norms. Similarly, $(\mathcal{C}_1^\alpha, \mathcal{C}_\infty^\alpha)_{1-1/p,p} = \mathcal{C}_p^\alpha$ with equivalent norms. Moreover, from the reiteration theorem for interpolation [3, p. 175], we have the following corollary.

Corollary 8.3. If $\alpha > 0$; $1 \leqq p \leqq q \leqq \infty$ and $\frac{1}{r} = \frac{1-\theta}{p} + \frac{\theta}{q}$ with $0 < \theta < 1$, then

i) $(C_p^\alpha, C_q^\alpha)_{\theta,r} = C_r^\alpha$ with equivalent norms,

ii) $(\mathcal{C}_p^\alpha, \mathcal{C}_q^\alpha)_{\theta,r} = \mathcal{C}_r^\alpha$ with equivalent norms.

As was pointed out to us by Peter Jones, it is also possible to use the decomposition of Theorem 8.2 to prove the interpolation theorem for Sobolev spaces (on $\mathbb{R}^n$) given by R. DeVore and K. Scherer [8]:

Theorem 8.4. If k is a positive integer, there exists constants c_1, $c_2 > 0$ depending at most on k and n such that for all $t > 0$

$$c_1 \int_0^t [f^*(s) + \sum_{|\nu|=k} (D^\nu f)^*(s)]ds \leqq K(f,t,W_1^k,W_\infty^k) \leqq c_2 \int_0^t [f^*(s) + \sum_{|\nu|=k} (D^\nu f)^*(s)]ds . \tag{8.19}$$

Proof. The lower estimate follows in a simple way from the subadditivity of the map $F \to F^{**}$. For the upper estimate, as in the proof of Theorem 8.2, let $E: = \{x: f_k^b(x) > f_k^{b*}(t)\} \cup \{x: Mf(x) > (Mf)^*(t)\}$ and take g as in (8.4) for $\alpha = k$ and $f_k: = f_k^b$. Then using Theorem 6.2, and arguing as in (8.12),

$$||g||_{W_\infty^k} \leqq c||g||_{\mathcal{C}_\infty^k} \leqq c\ [\int_0^t f^*(s)ds + t\ f_k^{b*}(t)]. \tag{8.20}$$

It follows from Theorem 5.6 that $f_k^{b*}(t) \leqq c \sum_{|\nu|=k} (D^\nu f)^{**}(t)$ because $(MF)^* \leqq cF^{**}$ for any $F \in L_1 + L_\infty$. Hence (8.20) gives

(8.21) $$t\, ||g||_{W_\infty^k} \leqq c \int_0^t (f^*(s) + \sum_{|\nu|=k} (D^\nu f)^*(s))ds.$$

Let $h: = f-g$. Then $h \equiv 0$ on E^c and $|E| \leqq 2t$, so

(8.22) $$\begin{aligned} ||h||_{L_1} &= \int_E |h| \leqq \int_E |f| + |E|\, ||g||_{L_\infty} \\ &\leqq c\, [\int_0^t f^*(s)ds + t\, f^{**}(t)] \leqq c \int_0^t f^*(s)ds. \end{aligned}$$

Also, using (8.21), we have for $|\mu| = k$,

(8.23) $$\begin{aligned} ||D^\mu h||_{L_1} &\leqq \int_E |D^\mu h| \leqq \int_E |D^\mu f| + |E|\, ||D^\mu g||_{L_\infty} \\ &\leqq c \int_0^t [f^*(s) + \sum_{|\nu|=k} (D^\nu f)^*(s)]ds. \end{aligned}$$

Hence, (8.22) and (8.23) show that

(8.24) $$||h||_{W_1^k} \leqq c \int_0^t [f^*(s) + \sum_{|\nu|=k} (D^\nu f)^*(s)]ds.$$

The inequalities (8.21) and (8.24) give the right hand inequality in (8.19). □

<u>Corollary 8.5</u>. If $1 \leqq p \leqq q \leqq \infty$ and $\frac{1}{r} = \frac{1-\theta}{p} + \frac{\theta}{q}$ with $0 < \theta < 1$, then

(8.25) $$(W_p^k, W_q^k)_{\theta,r} = W_r^k \text{ with equivalent norms.}$$

Using the results of the previous section we show that the spaces C_p^α do not form an interpolation scale for the real method of interpolation if p is fixed.

<u>Theorem 8.6</u>. Suppose $1 \leqq p \leqq \infty$; $0 < \alpha_0 < \alpha_1$; $0 < \theta < 1$; and $1 \leqq r \leqq \infty$, then

(8.26) $$(C_p^{\alpha_0}, C_p^{\alpha_1})_{\theta,r} = B_p^{\alpha,r}$$

where $\alpha = (1-\theta)\alpha_0 + \theta\alpha_1$. Consequently,

(8.27) $$(C_p^{\alpha_0}, C_p^{\alpha_1})_{\theta,r} \neq C_q^\beta$$

for any values of $1 \leqq p < \infty$; $0 < \theta < 1$; $1 \leqq r \leqq \infty$; $1 \leqq q \leqq \infty$; $0 \leqq \beta$.

Proof. To prove (8.26) we see from Theorem 7.1 that

$$B_p^{\alpha_j,1} \to C_p^{\alpha_j} \to B_p^{\alpha_j,\infty}$$

and then apply the reiteration theorem [3, p. 175] for the real method of interpolation since

$$(L_p,W_p^k)_{\theta_j,1} = B_p^{\alpha_j,1}, \quad (L_p,W_p^k)_{\theta_j,\infty} = B_p^{\alpha_j,\infty} \qquad j = 0,1$$

where $k = [\alpha_1] + 1$ and $\theta_j = \alpha_j/k$, for example.

The fact (8.27) that the spaces C_p^α are not "stable" under the real method follows from (8.26) and Lemma's 7.2 and 7.3 which show that $B_p^{\alpha,r} \neq C_p^\alpha$ if $1 \leqq p < \infty$. □

§9. Embeddings

We shall now discuss Sobolev type embeddings for the spaces C_p^α. Embeddings for $\mathcal{C}_p^\alpha$ follow from these and the classical embeddings for Sobolev spaces. As a starting point, consider embeddings into the space C of continuous functions.

If R and R^* are cubes with $R^* \subset R$ and $|R| \leq 2^n|R^*|$, then (2.15) with $\nu = 0$ in gives

$$||P_R f - P_{R^*} f||_{L_\infty(R^*)} \leq c|R^*|^{\alpha/n} \inf_{u \in R^*} f_\alpha^\#(u) \leq c \int_{|R^*|/2}^{|R^*|} f_\alpha^{\#*}(s)\, s^{\alpha/n} \frac{ds}{s}.$$

More generally, given any two cubes $R^* \subset R$, choose $R_o \supset \ldots \supset R_m$ with $R_o := R$; $R_m := R^*$ and $2^n|R_j| = |R_{j-1}|$, $j=1,2,\ldots,m-1$; $|R_{m-1}| \leq 2^n|R_m|$. Then writing $P_{R^*}f - P_R f = \sum_1^m [P_{R_j} f - P_{R_{j-1}} f]$ gives

$$(9.1) \qquad ||P_R f - P_{R^*} f||_{L_\infty(R^*)} \leq c \int_{|R^*|/2}^{|R|} f_\alpha^{\#*}(s)\, s^{\alpha/n} \frac{ds}{s}.$$

If f is locally in L_1 on Ω, then according to (2.7) $\lim_{Q \downarrow \{x\}} P_Q f(x) = f(x)$, a.e. $x \in \Omega$. In view of (9.1), when $f_\alpha^\#$ is locally in the Lorentz space $L_{n/\alpha,1}$ (see [17, p. 188] for the definition) on Ω, then $\lim_{Q \downarrow \{x\}} P_Q f(x)$ exists for each $x \in \Omega$. Let $g(x) := \lim_{Q \downarrow \{x\}} P_Q f(x)$ so that $g(x) = f(x)$ a.e. Our next result shows that g is a continuous function and in turn gives an embedding of the space $\{f: f_\alpha^\# \in L_{n/\alpha,1}\}$ into C.

Theorem 9.1. If Ω is a domain and $f_\alpha^\#$ is locally in $L_{n/\alpha,1}$ on Ω, then there is a function $g \in C(\Omega)$ with $g = f$ a.e. on Ω. Moreover, if $f_\alpha^\# \in L_{n/\alpha,1}(\Omega)$ and Ω is $\mathbb{R}^n$ or a cube in $\mathbb{R}^n$, then there is a polynomial π of degree at most $[\alpha]$ such that

$$(9.2) \qquad ||g-\pi||_{C(\Omega)} \leq c\, ||f_\alpha^\#||_{L_{n/\alpha,1}(\Omega)}.$$

Proof. Let g be as above, then $g = f$ a.e. on Ω. We show that g is continuous. Let $R_o \subset \Omega$ be any cube and $u \in R_o$. If $Q \subset R_o$ is a cube, then choosing $R := Q$ and $R^* \downarrow \{u\}$ in (9.1) gives

(9.3) $$|P_Q f(u) - g(u)| \leqq c \int_0^{|Q|} F^*(s)\, s^{\alpha/n} \frac{ds}{s}$$

with $F := f^{\#}_{\alpha,R_o}$ where the subscript R_o means that $f^{\#}_{\alpha}$ is defined as in (2.2) with R_o in place of Ω. Hence for any $x,y \in Q$

(9.4) $$|g(x) - g(y)| \leqq c \int_0^{|Q|} F^*(s)\, s^{\alpha/n} \frac{ds}{s} + |P_Q f(x) - P_Q f(y)|.$$

Now $F(x) \leqq f^{\#}_{\alpha}(x)$, $x \in R_o$ and F is supported on R_o. Hence F is in $L_{n/\alpha,1}$. Thus, first choosing Q small, then fixing Q and letting $y \to x$ shows that g is continuous at x.

If $\Omega = R_o$ is a cube in $\mathbb{R}^n$, then (9.3) gives (9.2) with $\pi := P_{R_o} f$. If $\Omega = \mathbb{R}^n$, take a sequence of cubes $\{Q_j\}_1^{\infty}$, with $Q_j \subset Q_{j+1}$ and $|Q_j| = 2^{jn}$, then using (9.1) we have for each $j < k$,

$$||P_{Q_j} f - P_{Q_k} f||_{C(Q_j)} \leqq c \int_{2^{j-1}}^{2^k} f^{\#*}_{\alpha}(s)\, s^{\alpha/n} \frac{ds}{s} \to 0 \quad \text{as } j,k \to \infty .$$

This shows that $\pi := \lim_{j\to\infty} P_{Q_j} f$ exists and is a polynomial of degree at most $[\alpha]$ whenever $f^{\#}_{\alpha} \in L_{n/\alpha,1}(\mathbb{R}^n)$ and

$$||P_{Q_j} f - \pi||_{C(Q_j)} \leqq c \int_{2^{j-1}}^{\infty} f^{\#*}_{\alpha}(s)\, s^{\alpha/n} \frac{ds}{s} .$$

On the other hand, from (9.3)

$$||g - P_{Q_j} f||_{C(Q_j)} \leqq c \int_0^{2^j} f^{\#*}_{\alpha}(s)\, s^{\alpha/n} \frac{ds}{s}$$

and so

$$||g - \pi||_{C(Q_j)} \leqq c \int_0^{\infty} f^{\#*}_{\alpha}(s)\, s^{\alpha/n} \frac{ds}{s} = c||f^{\#}_{\alpha}||_{L_{n/\alpha,1}(\mathbb{R}^n)}.$$

Since j is arbitrary, this gives (9.2). □

The approach above can also be used to study classical differentiability of functions. We illustrate this by giving another proof of the following recent result of E. Stein [16].

Theorem 9.2. Let Ω be a domain in $\mathbb{R}^n$. If ∇f exists in the weak sense and is in $L_{n,1}(\Omega)$, then f can be redefined on a set of measure zero so as to be continuous. Moreover, for this redefined f and for almost all $x \in \Omega$, $\nabla f(x)$ is the classical derivative of f: that is,

(9.5) $$|f(x+h) - f(x) - \nabla f(x)\cdot h| = o(|h|), \quad h \to 0.$$

Proof. We suppose that $n > 1$, since the case $n = 1$ is a classical result (Lebesgue's theorem for f') of real analysis due to the fact that $L_{1,1} = L_1$. Now, Theorem 5.6 and the boundedness of the Hardy Littlewood maximal operator M on $L_{n,1}$ show that the condition $|\nabla f| \in L_{n,1}$ implies $f_1^\flat \in L_{n,1}$. Since $f_1^\# \leq c\, f_1^\flat$, Theorem 9.1 shows that f can be redefined on a set of measure zero so as to be continuous.

In order to prove (9.5), we can work locally and hence we assume for the remainder of the proof that Ω is a cube in $\mathbb{R}^n$ and f is continuous on Ω. Consider the maximal function

$$\Lambda f(x) := \overline{\lim_{h\to 0}} \frac{|f(x+h)-f(x)-h\cdot\nabla f(x)|}{|h|}.$$

We want to give a pointwise estimate between Λf and $T(f_1^\flat)$ where T is defined by

$$Tg(x) := \sup_{\Omega\supset Q\ni x} \frac{\|g\chi_Q\|_{L_{n,1}}}{\|\chi_Q\|_{L_{n,1}}} = \sup_{\Omega\supset Q\ni x} \frac{n}{|Q|^{1/n}} \|g\chi_Q\|_{L_{n,1}}.$$

Let $Q \subset \Omega$ be any cube. If $Q_2 \subset Q_1 \subset Q$ with $|Q_1| \leq 2^n|Q_2|$, then

$$|f_{Q_1} - f_{Q_2}| \leq \frac{c}{|Q_1|}\int_{Q_1}|f-f_{Q_1}| \leq c \inf_{u\in Q_1} f_1^\flat(u)\, |Q_1|^{1/n}$$

$$\leq c \int_{|Q_1|/2}^{|Q_1|} [f_1^\flat\chi_Q]^*(s)\, s^{1/n}\frac{ds}{s}.$$

The same telescoping argument as used in the derivation (9.3) shows that

$$|f(u) - f_Q| \leq c \int_0^{|Q|} [f_1^\flat\chi_Q]^*(s)\, s^{1/n}\frac{ds}{s} = c\, \|f_1^\flat\chi_Q\|_{L_{n,1}}.$$

Hence, given x and h, we choose Q as a cube which contains x and x+h with $|Q| \leq |h|^n$, and find

(9.6) $$|f(x+h) - f(x)| \leq c\, \|f_1^\flat\chi_Q\|_{L_{n,1}} \leq c\, T(f_1)(x)\, |h|.$$

From Theorem 5.6, we have $|\nabla f(x)| \leq c\, f_1^\flat(x)\; c\, T(f_1^\flat)(x)$, a.e. $x \in \Omega$. Combining this with (9.6) shows that

(9.7) $$\Lambda f(x) \leqq c\ T(f_1^\flat)(x), \quad \text{a.e.} \quad x \in \Omega .$$

The sublinear operator T is easily seen to be of restricted weak type (n,n). Indeed,

$$T(\chi_E)(x) = \sup_{\Omega \supset Q \ni x} \frac{|E \cap Q|^{1/n}}{|Q|^{1/n}} = [M(\chi_E)(x)]^{1/n}$$

with M the Hardy-Littlewood maximal operator (for Ω). Recall that M is weak type (1,1). Since $n > 1$, restricted weak type implies weak type [17, p. 195] and so T is of weak type (n,n). In view of (9.7), there is a c such that

$$||\Lambda f||_{L_{n,\infty}(\Omega)} \leqq c\ ||f_1^\flat||_{L_{n,1}(\Omega)}.$$

Hence using Theorem 5.6,

(9.8) $$(\Lambda f)^*(t) \leqq c\ t^{-1/n}\ ||f_1^\flat||_{L_{n,1}(\Omega)} \leqq c\ t^{-1/n} |||\nabla f|||_{L_{n,1}(\Omega)} .$$

To complete the proof, note that $\Lambda(f-\phi) = \Lambda(f)$ when ϕ is smooth and so

$$(\Lambda f)^*(t) \leqq c\ t^{-1/n}\ |||\nabla(f-\phi)|||_{L_{n,1}(\Omega)} .$$

For any $\varepsilon > 0$, there is a smooth function ϕ with

$$|||\nabla(f-\phi)|||_{L_{n,1}(\Omega)} \leqq \varepsilon .$$

Therefore $(\Lambda f)^*(t) = 0$ for all t and so $\Lambda f = 0$ a.e. □

Remark: It is worth pointing out that $f_1^\flat$ in (9.7) can be replaced by $|\nabla f|$ which can be proved directly (using Theorem 3.4) or deduced from (5.7).

To get embeddings of C_p^α into L_q or, more generally, C_q^β, we shall give an inequality between $f_\beta^\#$ and $f_\alpha^\#$ in terms of fractional integrals. Such an inequality for $\beta = 0$, $0 < \alpha < 1$ was given by A. P. Calderón and R. Scott [6] and we follow that idea in the general case. We assume for the remainder of this section that $\Omega = \mathbb{R}^n$ and $p \geqq 1$. More general domains are treated in §11 using extensions while the case $0 < p < 1$ is discussed in §12. Let P be the projection operator (2.1) of degree $[\alpha]$ and assume that $\beta < \alpha$ (and hence $[\beta] \leqq [\alpha]$). From Lemma 2.3, we have

$$(9.9) \qquad f_\beta^\#(x) \le c \sup_{Q \ni x} \frac{1}{|Q|^{1+\beta/n}} \int_Q |f-P_Q f|$$

whenever $f \in L_1 + L_\infty$. On the other hand for any cube $Q \ni x$ and any $0 < r < \frac{n}{\alpha-\beta}$, we have with $\gamma := r(\alpha-\beta) < n$,

$$(9.10) \qquad \frac{1}{|Q|^{1+\beta/n}} \int_Q |f-P_Q f| \le |Q|^{(\alpha-\beta)/n} \inf_{u\in Q} f_\alpha^\#(u) \le \{|Q|^{\gamma/n-1} \int_Q [f_\alpha^\#]^r\}^{1/r}$$

$$\le c\, \{\int_Q [f_\alpha^\#(y)]^r \, |x-y|^{\gamma-n}\, dy\}^{1/r}$$

because $|x-y| \le |Q|^{1/n}$ when $x,y \in Q$. Let I_γ denote the fractional integral operator

$$(9.11) \qquad I_\gamma h(x) := \int_{\mathbb{R}^n} h(y)\, |x-y|^{\gamma-n}\, dy ,$$

then, returning to (9.9-10), we find

$$(9.12) \qquad f_\beta^\#(x) \le c\, \{I_\gamma[(f_\alpha^\#)^r](x)\}^{1/r} , \quad x \in \mathbb{R}^n.$$

Using (9.12) and the mapping properties of I_γ, we prove the following embeddings.

<u>Theorem 9.3</u>. Let $\Omega = \mathbb{R}^n$. If $0 \le \beta \le \alpha < \infty$, $1 \le p \le q < \infty$, and $\frac{1}{p} = \frac{1}{q} + \frac{\alpha-\beta}{n}$, then whenever $f \in L_1 + L_\infty$,

$$(9.13) \qquad \|f_\beta^\#\|_{L_q} \le c\, \|f_\alpha^\#\|_{L_p} .$$

<u>Proof</u>. The case $\beta = \alpha$ requires no proof, so suppose $\beta < \alpha$. The operator I_γ maps $L_{\tilde p}(\mathbb{R}^n)$ boundedly into $L_{\tilde q}(\mathbb{R}^n)$ whenever $1 < \tilde p < \tilde q$ and $1/\tilde p = 1/\tilde q + \gamma/n$ [15, p. 119]. Let $\tilde p := p/r$ and $\tilde q := q/r$ with $r < p$ and $r < n/(\alpha-\beta)$ as above. Then with $g := I_\gamma [(f_\alpha^\#)^r]$, we have from (9.12)

$$\|f_\beta^\#\|_{L_q} \le c\, \|g^{1/r}\|_{L_q} = c\, \|g\|_{L_{\tilde q}}^{1/r} \le c\, \|(f_\alpha^\#)^r\|_{L_{\tilde p}}^{1/r} = c\, \|f_\alpha^\#\|_{L_p} ,$$

which is (9.13). □

We concentrate now on the cases $q = \infty$ and $\beta = 0$.

<u>Corollary 9.4</u>. Let $\Omega = \mathbb{R}^n$, $1 \le p \le \infty$ and $\beta \ge 0$. If $\alpha = \beta + n/p$ and $f \in L_1 + L_\infty$, then

(9.14) $$||f_\beta^{\#}||_{L_\infty} \leqq c\ ||f_\alpha^{\#}||_{L_{p,\infty}} .$$

Proof. Starting with the left most inequality in (9.10), we have

$$\frac{1}{|Q|^{1+\beta/n}} \int_Q |f-P_Q f| \leqq |Q|^{(\alpha-\beta)/n} \inf_{u\in Q} f_\alpha^{\#}(u)$$

$$\leqq |Q|^{(\alpha-\beta)/n} f_\alpha^{\#*}(|Q|) \leqq c\ ||f_\alpha^{\#}||_{L_{p,\infty}} .$$

Taking a supremum over all cubes Q proves (9.14). □

Recall the definition of the space C_p^o, that is $C_p^o: = L_p$, $1 \leqq p < \infty$ and $C_\infty^o: = BMO$.

Corollary 9.5. Let $\Omega = \mathbb{R}^n$, $1 \leqq p \leqq q \leqq \infty$ and $\alpha = n(\frac{1}{p} - \frac{1}{q})$. Then, there is a constant c independent of f such that

(9.15) $$||f||_{C_q^o} \leqq c\ ||f||_{C_p^\alpha} .$$

Proof. For $q < \infty$, (9.13) gives

$$||f_o^{\#}||_{L_q} \leqq c\ ||f_\alpha^{\#}||_{L_p}$$

when $f \in L_1 + L_\infty$. But $f \in C_p^\alpha$ implies $f \in L_p \subset L_1 + L_\infty$. Thus (9.15) holds when $q < \infty$. On the other hand when $q = \infty$, $f \in C_p^\alpha$ implies $f_\alpha^{\#} \in L_p \subset L_{p,\infty}$ and therefore (9.15) follows from (9.14). □

Our next result summarizes the embeddings of C_p^α into C_q^β. These are depicted in Fig. II where for fixed p and α, the shaded region indicates those pairs $(\frac{1}{q},\beta)$ for which $C_p^\alpha \to C_q^\beta$.

Theorem 9.6. Let $\Omega = \mathbb{R}^n$. If $1 \leqq p \leqq q \leqq \infty$ and $0 \leqq \beta \leqq \alpha + n(\frac{1}{q} - \frac{1}{p})$, then

(9.16) $$C_p^\alpha \to C_q^\beta.$$

Proof. In view of Lemma 6.6, it is enough to consider the case $\beta = \alpha + n\ (\frac{1}{q} - \frac{1}{p})$. For this case we want to show $C_p^\alpha \to C_q^\beta$. There are two subcases depending on whether $\frac{1}{q_o} : = \frac{1}{p} - \frac{\alpha}{n}$ is non-negative or negative. In the first case, $C_p^\alpha \to C_{q_o}^o \cap L_p \to L_q$ because of Corollary 9.5 and Theorem 6.8. Also $||f_\beta^\#||_{L_q} \leqq c\ ||f_\alpha^\#||_{L_p}$ because of Theorem 9.3. Hence (9.16) follows in this case.

Consider now the case $\frac{1}{p} - \frac{\alpha}{n}$ negative. Since $n/\alpha < p$ it follows that when $f_\alpha^\# \in L_p$ then $f_{\alpha,Q}^\# \in L_{n/\alpha,1}(Q)$ for each cube Q. Hence Theorem 9.1 gives that f can be redefined on a set of measure zero so as to be continuous and for each cube Q with $|Q| = 1$, the polynomial $P_Q f$ (since P is a projection onto $\mathbb{P}_{[\alpha]}$) satisfies

$$||f- P_Q f||_{C(Q)} \leqq c\ ||f_\alpha^\#||_{L_{n/\alpha,1}(Q)} \leqq c\ ||f_\alpha^\#||_{L_p} .$$

Inequality (2.3) implies that

$$||P_Q f||_{L_\infty(Q)} \leqq c\ ||f||_{L_p(Q)} \leqq c\ ||f||_{L_p} .$$

Hence

$$||f||_{C(Q)} \leqq ||f-P_Q f||_{C(Q)} + ||P_Q f||_{C(Q)} \leqq c\ ||f||_{C_p^\alpha} .$$

Since Q is arbitrary we have

$$||f||_C \leqq c\ ||f||_{C_p^\alpha} .$$

This gives that $f \in C \cap L_p \subset L_q$.

To finish the proof, we note that when $q < \infty$ then (9.16) follows from Theorem 9.3 and when $q = \infty$, (9.16) follows from (9.14) and the fact that

$$||f_\alpha^\#||_{L_{p,\infty}} \leqq ||f_\alpha^\#||_{L_p} \leqq ||f||_{C_p^\alpha} . \quad \square$$

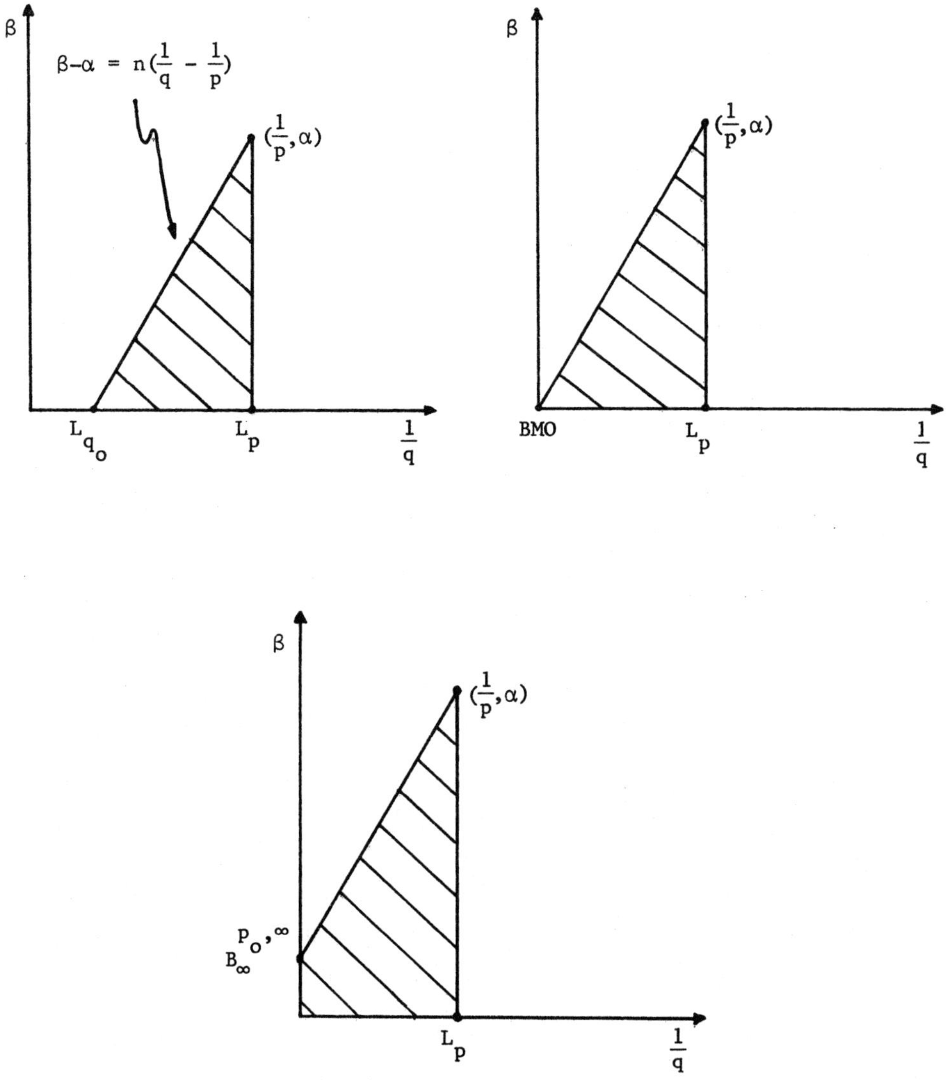

FIGURE II

Embeddings: $C_p^\alpha \to C_q^\beta$

§10. Extension Theorems

In the next section, we shall prove an extension theorems for the spaces $C_p^\alpha(\Omega)$ and $\mathcal{C}_p^\alpha(\Omega)$, $\alpha > 0$, $1 \leqq p \leqq \infty$ when Ω is a domain with a minimally smooth boundary in the sense of Stein [15, p. 189]. This will allow us to generalize various results of the previous sections (proved only for $\mathbb{R}^n$ or a cube in $\mathbb{R}^n$) to Ω. In the process, we show how the seminal ideas of Whitney [20] can be used to prove extension theorems for $1 \leqq p < \infty$. The original theorem of Whitney extends functions in Lip α on a closed set F to all of $\mathbb{R}^n$. Other extension theorems for Sobolev spaces W_p^k, $1 \leqq p < \infty$, are based on potentials as in the early work of Sobolev [14]. We should point out that most of the material in this section is obvious geometrically but rather detailed to prove analytically. The reader may benefit by convincing himself of the statements geometrically in lieu of the analytical arguments given.

We begin in this section by establishing extension theorems for domains $\Omega \subset \mathbb{R}^n$, $n > 1$ of the form $\Omega = \{(u,v):\ u \in \mathbb{R}^{n-1}, v \in \mathbb{R} \text{ and } v > \phi(u)\}$ with ϕ a fixed function in Lip 1. That is, ϕ satisfies $|\phi(u_1) - \phi(u_2)| \leqq M|u_1 - u_2|$ for all $u_1, u_2 \in \mathbb{R}^{n-1}$ and some M which we can take to be larger than 1. Later these extensions are pieced together to get the general case. The case $n = 1$ is discussed separately later in the section.

We need a decomposition of $(\partial\Omega)^c$ into dyadic cubes. In essence, we use the Whitney decompositions as described in [15, p. 167] with certain modification to meet our specific needs. As a starting point, note that the cone $C := \{(u,v): u \in \mathbb{R}^{n-1}, v \in \mathbb{R}; v > M|u|\}$ has the property that $x + C \subset \Omega$ whenever $x \in \Omega \cup \partial\Omega$ and $x - C \subset \Omega^c - \partial\Omega$ whenever $x \in \Omega^c \cup \partial\Omega$.

Let M_k, $k = 0, \pm 1, \ldots$ denote the collection of all dyadic cubes of side length 2^{-k} and $M := \bigcup_{-\infty}^{\infty} M_k$. Each cube $Q \in M_k$ is contained in a cube $Q' \subset M_{k-1}$. We call Q' the parent of Q. For any cube Q and any $\tau > 0$ let τQ denote the cube with the same center as Q and side length $\tau\ell(Q)$ where $\ell(Q)$ is the side length of Q. Define F_o as the set of all cubes $Q \in M$ with center (u,v) such that either $4Q \subset (u,\phi(u)) + C$ or $4Q \subset (u,\phi(u)) - C$ (see Fig. III). Thus when $Q \in F_o$ then either $Q \subset \Omega$ or $Q \subset \Omega^c - \partial\Omega$. Further let F denote all the cubes $Q \in \Omega$ such that $Q \in F_o$ but the parent of Q is not in F_o. Similarly let F_c denote the set of all those cubes $Q \subset \Omega^c - \partial\Omega$ such that $Q \in F_o$ but the parent of Q is not in F_o.

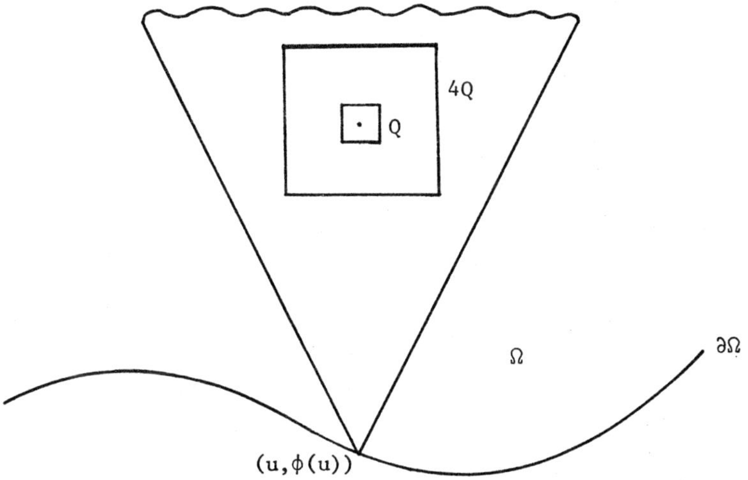

FIGURE III

Suppose now that $x = (u,v) \in \Omega^c\backslash\partial\Omega$, $(u \in \mathbb{R}^{n-1}, v \in \mathbb{R})$. Let x^s be the point in Ω which is "symmetric to x across $\partial\Omega$", i.e. $x^s := (u,\phi(u)+h)$ where $h = \phi(u)-v$. Our next lemma provides a procedure for reflecting cubes $Q \in F_c$ into cubes $Q^s \in F$.

<u>Lemma 10.1</u>. The cubes in F are a cover for Ω with pairwise disjoint interiors and the cubes of F_c are a cover for $\Omega^c - \partial\Omega$ with pairwise disjoint

interiors. Also, there is a constant $c_o > 0$ depending only on n and M such that

(10.1) $\ell(Q) \leqq \mathrm{dist}(Q,\partial\Omega) \leqq c_o\ \ell(Q), \qquad Q \in F \cup F_c$

(10.2) $\sup_{(u,v)\in Q} |v - \phi(u)| \leqq c_o\ \ell(Q), \quad Q \in F \cup F_c$

(10.3) For each Q in F_c, let Q^s be that cube in F which contains (u_o,v_o^s) where (u_o,v_o) is the center of Q; then

i) $c_o^{-1}\ell(Q) \leqq \ell(Q^s) \leqq c_o\ \ell(Q)$,

ii) $\mathrm{dist}(Q,Q^s) \leqq c_o\ \ell(Q)$,

iii) Each cube in F can be the symmetric cube Q^s of at most c_o cubes $Q \in F_c$.

<u>Proof</u>. First we make the observation that for $x: = (u,v) \in \Omega$, if Q is a dyadic cube containing x, then $Q \in F_o$ if Q is small enough (e.g., $\ell(Q) < (v-\phi(u))/(4+4M\sqrt{n})$). On the other hand if Q is too large (e.g., $\ell(Q) > v-\phi(u)$), then $Q \notin F_o$. Since dyadic cubes have the property that when any pair has intersecting interiors, one cube must be contained in the other, we have for each $x \in \Omega$ a maximal cube in F_o containing x. Since F is defined to be the collection of all such maximal cubes, then F is a cover for Ω whose members have pairwise disjoint interiors. The same argument shows that the cubes in F_c are a cover for Ω^c with pairwise disjoint interiors. If $Q \in F \cup F_c$, then $4Q \cap \partial\Omega = \phi$. Hence $\mathrm{dist}(Q,\partial\Omega) \geqq \frac{3}{2}\ \ell(Q) \geqq \ell(Q)$ which is the left hand inequality in (10.1). Suppose now that $Q \in F$ and Q' is the parent of Q. Since $Q' \notin F_o$ there is a point $(u',v') \in 4Q'$ with $v' \leqq \phi(u_o) + M|u'-u_o|$ where (u_o,v_o) is the center of Q'. Hence for any $(u,v) \in Q$

$$\begin{aligned} v-\phi(u) &\leqq v-v' + v'-\phi(u_o) + \phi(u_o)-\phi(u) \\ &\leqq 4\ \ell(Q') + M|u'-u_o| + M|u_o-u| \qquad (10.4) \\ &\leqq 4\ \ell(Q') + 4M\sqrt{n}\ \ell(Q') + M\sqrt{n}\ \ell(Q) \leqq A\ell(Q) \end{aligned}$$

with $A: = (9\ M\sqrt{n} + 8)$. A similar argument holds for $Q \in F_c$. This shows that (10.2) holds for any $c_o \geqq A$. Also, (10.2) implies the right hand side of (10.1).

Finally to see (10.3), let $Q \in F_c$. Since $Q^s \in F$, properties (10.1) and (10.2) imply

$$\ell(Q^s) \leqq \mathrm{dist}(Q^s,\partial\Omega) \leqq v_o^s - \phi(u_o) = \phi(u_o) - v_o \leqq c_o\ \ell(Q)$$

which verifies (10.3) i) if $c_o \geqq A$. The left hand inequality of i) follows similarly. By property (10.2) it is also clear that

$$\mathrm{dist}(Q,Q^s) \leqq c_o\ \ell(Q)$$

if $c_o \geqq 2A$ and so (10.3) ii) follows. Parts i) and ii) then show that iii) holds so long as $c_o \geqq A^2$. Hence if we define $\boxed{c_o := (9M\sqrt{n} + 8)^2}$, then all the conclusions of the lemma follow. □

Let us note some other properties of $F \cup F_c$. If Q_1, Q are two cubes in $F \cup F_c$ which touch, then according to (10.1),

$$\ell(Q_1) \leqq \mathrm{dist}(Q_1,\partial\Omega) \leqq \mathrm{dist}(Q,\partial\Omega) + \sqrt{n}\ \ell(Q) \leqq 2c_o\ \ell(Q) \tag{10.5}$$

so that Q_1 and Q have comparable size. It follows that there is a constant N depending only on n and M such that for each $Q_1 \in F \cup F_c$ at most N cubes Q from $F \cup F_c$ touch Q_1.

Now let $0 < \varepsilon \leqq c_o^{-1}$ and consider the cubes $\tilde{Q} := (1+\varepsilon)Q$ with $Q \in F \cup F_c$. We have the following property for the cubes $\tilde{Q}$:

(10.6) There is an N depending only on n and M such that each x appears in at most N of the cubes $\tilde{Q}$ with $Q \in F \cup F_c$.

Indeed, it follows from (10.5) that $\tilde{Q}$ is contained in the union of Q and all cubes in $F \cup F_c$ which touch Q. If $Q_1 \in F \cup F_c$ and $\tilde{Q}$ intersects Q_1, then Q_1 and Q must touch. As we observed above there are at most N such cubes. Hence (10.6) follows.

Now suppose $Q_1, Q \in F \cup F_c$ and $\mathrm{int}(\tilde{Q}_1) \cap \mathrm{int}(\tilde{Q}) \neq \phi$, then as we observed $\tilde{Q}$ is contained in the union of Q with all cubes in $F \cup F_c$ which touch Q. Similarly $\tilde{Q}_1$ is contained in the union of Q_1 and its neighbors. Therefore Q_1 and Q have a common neighbor and it follows from (10.5) that

(10.7) $$\ell(Q_1) \leqq (2c_o)^2 \ell(Q) \quad \text{whenever } \operatorname{int}(\tilde{Q}_1) \cap \operatorname{int}(\tilde{Q}) \neq \phi.$$

Let $Q_1, Q_2, \ldots$ be an enumeration of the cubes in F_c. Fix $\boxed{\varepsilon_o := (4c_o)^{-1}}$ and set $Q_j^* := (1+\varepsilon_o)Q_j$. Accordingly (see [15, p. 170]), there is a partition of unity $(\phi_j^*)_{j=1}^\infty$ with the properties:

(10.8)
$$\begin{aligned} &\text{i)} \quad 0 \leqq \phi_j^* \leqq 1 \\ &\text{ii)} \quad \Sigma\, \phi_j^* \equiv 1 \quad \text{on} \quad \Omega^c - \partial\Omega \\ &\text{iii)} \quad \phi_j^* \text{ is supported in } \operatorname{int}(Q_j^*) \\ &\text{iv)} \quad \|D^\nu \phi_j^*\|_\infty \leqq c\, [\ell(Q_j)]^{-|\nu|}. \end{aligned}$$

We can now define an extension operator E. Let $\alpha > 0$ be fixed and $P := P_{[\alpha]}$ be the projection in (2.1) of degree $[\alpha]$. If f is locally in $L_1(\Omega)$, define $E := E_\alpha^\#$ by

(10.9) $$Ef(x) := \begin{cases} f(x), & x \in \Omega \\ \sum_{k=1}^\infty P_{Q_k^s} f(x)\, \phi_k^*(x), & x \in \Omega^c - \partial\Omega . \end{cases}$$

We do not define Ef on the set $\partial\Omega$ which has measure 0. The extension operator $E_\alpha^\flat$ is defined in the same manner with $\mathbb{P}_{[\alpha]}$ now replaced by $\mathbb{P}_{(\alpha)}$ and so $E_\alpha^\# = E_\alpha^\flat$ if α is not an integer. In what follows, we will establish the mapping properties of $E_\alpha^\#$. The corresponding estimates for $E_\alpha^\flat$ simplify considerably and we will return this point later in the section.

We want now to estimate $(Ef)_\alpha^\#$. This requires us to estimate

$$\inf_{\pi \in \mathbb{P}_{[\alpha]}} \frac{1}{|R|^{1+\alpha/n}} \int_R |Ef-\pi|$$

for cubes R in $\mathbb{R}^n$. It turns out that the most difficult case is when R is close to the boundary of Ω and therefore we begin with this case.

If $Q \subset \Omega$ is cube in $\mathbb{R}^n$, then

$$\operatorname{Shad}(Q) := \{(u,v): v < \tilde{v},\ (u,\tilde{v}) \in Q\} \cap \Omega$$

is the <u>shadow</u> of Q (see Fig. IV).

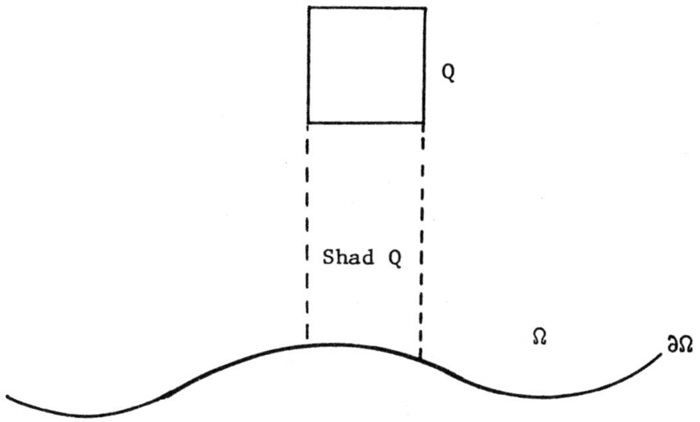

FIGURE IV

Shadow of Q

Lemma 10.2. There is a constant $c_1 > 0$ such that whenever $A \geqq 1$ and R is a cube in $\mathbb{R}^n$ with $\operatorname{dist}(R,\partial\Omega) \leqq A\,\ell(R)$, then there is a corresponding cube R_o with the following properties:

$$\text{i)}\quad \ell(R_o) \leqq c_1\, A\, \ell(R),$$

$$\text{ii)}\quad 4\,R_o \subset \Omega,$$

$$\text{iii)}\quad v-\phi(u) \leqq c_1\, A\,\ell(R),\quad (u,v) \in R_o, \tag{10.10}$$

$$\text{iv)}\quad \text{if } Q \in F \text{ and } Q \cap R \neq \phi, \text{ then } Q \subset \operatorname{Shad}(R_o),$$

$$\text{v)}\quad \text{if } Q_j \in F_c \text{ and } Q_j^* \cap R \neq \phi, \text{ then } Q_j^s \subset \operatorname{Shad}(R_o).$$

Proof. If $Q \in F \cup F_c$ and $Q \cap R \neq \phi$, then according to Lemma 10.1

$$\ell(Q) \leqq \operatorname{dist}(Q,\partial\Omega) \leqq \operatorname{dist}(R,\partial\Omega) + \sqrt{n}\,\ell(R) \leqq (A+\sqrt{n})\,\ell(R) \leqq 2\sqrt{n}\,A\,\ell(R)$$

and so $Q \subset (5\sqrt{n}\,A)R$. Similarly, if $Q_j \in F_c$ and $Q_j^* \cap R \neq \phi$, then a neighbor of Q_j, say $\tilde{Q} \in F_c$, intersects R. Hence (10.5) together with the last inequality shows that

$$(2c_o)^{-1}\,\ell(Q_j) \leqq \ell(\tilde{Q}) \leqq 2\sqrt{n}\,A\,\ell(R).$$

On the other hand, (10.3) ii) gives

$$\begin{aligned}\operatorname{dist}(R,Q_j^s) &\leqq \sqrt{n}\,\ell(Q_j^*) + \operatorname{dist}(Q_j,Q_j^s) \leqq (2c_o)\,\ell(Q_j)\\ &\leqq 8c_0^2\,\sqrt{n}\,A\,\ell(R).\end{aligned}$$

Now define $\boxed{\gamma := 24c_o^2\sqrt{n}}$ and $R_1 := \gamma AR$, then $Q, Q_j^s \subset R_1$ (the second containment use (10.3) i)) whenever Q and Q_j satisfy the assumptions in iv) and v). Next we observe for cubes $\tilde{R}_1 = \lambda e_n + R_1$ $(\lambda>0)$ that $Q, Q_j^s \subset \mathrm{Shad}(\tilde{R}_1)$ since $Q, Q_j^s \subset \Omega$. Define

$$R_o := c_o\, \ell(R_1)\, e_n + R_1.$$

Then R_o satisfies properties i), iv), and v) if $c_1 \geqq \gamma$. Also one easily checks that $4R_o \subset (u_o, \phi(u_o)) + C \subset \Omega$ (where (u_o, v_o) is the center of R). Hence property ii) is also satisfied. Finally, we show inequality iii). If $(u,v) \in R_o$, we can find a $(u,v') \in R_1$ such that $v - v' = c_o\, \ell(R_1)$. Notice $R_1 \cap \partial\Omega \neq \phi$, so there is a point $(u_1, \phi(u_1)) \in R_1 \cap \partial\Omega$ and

$$\begin{aligned} v-\phi(u) &= v - v' + v' - \phi(u_1) + \phi(u_1) - \phi(u) \leqq c_o\, \ell(R_1) + \ell(R_1) + M|u_1-u| \\ &\leqq (c_o+1+M\sqrt{n})\, \ell(R_1) \leqq c_1\, A\, \ell(R) \end{aligned}$$

where $\boxed{c_1 := (c_o+1+\sqrt{n}M)\gamma}$. Here we have used the inequality $|u_1-u| \leqq \sqrt{n}\, \ell(R_1)$ in estimating $|\phi(u_1) - \phi(u)|$. Hence iii) holds. □

Let c_o be the constant of Lemma 10.1. Set $\boxed{A_o := 8c_o^2}$ and apply Lemma 10.2 with $A = A_o$ to obtain for each cube R, with $\mathrm{dist}(R,\partial\Omega) \leqq A_o\, \ell(R)$, a cube R_o with the properties of Lemma 10.2. In particular, $\mathrm{dist}(R_o,\partial\Omega) \leqq c_1 A_o\, \ell(R_o)$ so Lemma 10.2 applies again to R_o with $A = c_1 A_o$. Let $\bar{R}$ be the cube guaranteed by Lemma 10.2 for R_o, then

(10.11)

i) $\mathrm{dist}(\bar{R},\partial\Omega) \leqq c_1^2 A_o\, \ell(R)$

ii) $\ell(\bar{R}) \leqq c_1^2 A_o\, \ell(R)$

iii) $R_o \subset \mathrm{Shad}(\bar{R})$

iv) $Q \subset \mathrm{Shad}(\bar{R})$ if $Q \cap R_o \neq \phi$, $Q \in \mathcal{F}$.

Although the cubes R_o and $\bar{R}$ are not uniquely determined by (10.10) and (10.11), the actual construction in Lemma 10.2 does produce a unique R_o. <u>For the remainder of this paper we take R_o and $\bar{R}$ to be unique cubes generated by the construction in Lemma 10.2.</u>

Lemma 10.3. Let R be a cube in $\mathbb{R}^n$ with $\mathrm{dist}(R,\partial\Omega) \leqq A_o\, \ell(R)$ and let R_o, $\bar{R}$ be the cubes described above; then

$$\int_R |Ef-P_{R_o} f| \leqq c \int_{\mathrm{Shad}(\bar{R})} f_\alpha^{\#}(y)\, \delta(y)^\alpha\, dy$$

where $\delta(y) := v-\phi(u)$ whenever $y = (u,v) \in \Omega$.

Proof. Let $Q \in F$ be any cube with $Q \subset \mathrm{Shad}\, R_o$ and let (u_o,v_o) be its center. Choose a minimal number v_1 with $(u_o,v_1) \in R_o$. The line segment $\{(u_o,v)\colon v_o \leqq v \leqq v_1\}$ intersects a finite number of cubes from F as v ranges from v_1 down to v_o, say $R_1,R_2,\ldots,R_m = Q$. For each $j=2,\ldots,m$, R_j touches R_{j-1} and $\ell(R_j) \leqq \ell(R_{j-1})$. Indeed, the translated cube $R_j' = \ell(R_j)\, e_n + R_j$ is a dyadic cube in F_o and intersects the interior of R_{j-1} nontrivially. Hence one of R_j' or R_{j-1} must contain the other. By the selection criteria for F, $R_j' \subset R_{j-1}$, so $\ell(R_j) \leqq \ell(R_{j-1})$ and in fact

(10.12) $$\mathrm{Shad}(R_j) \subset \mathrm{Shad}(R_{j-1}) \qquad j=2,3,\ldots,m.$$

We need the estimate

(10.13) $$\|P_Q f-P_{R_o} f\|_{L_\infty(Q)} \leqq c \sum_{j=0}^{m} m_{R_j} |R_j|^{\alpha/n}$$

where $m_{R_j} := \inf_{R_j} f_\alpha^{\#}$. To see this define $\tilde{R}_j := 4(R_{j-1})$, $2 \leqq j \leqq m$. Since $\ell(R_{j-1}) \geqq \ell(R_j)$, it follows that $R_j \subset \tilde{R}_j$. For $j=1$, there is a common cube $\tilde{R}_1$ such that $\Omega \supset \tilde{R}_1 \supset R_1 \cup R_o$ and $\ell(\tilde{R}_1) \leqq c\, \ell(R_1)$. Notice that $\tilde{R}_j \subset \Omega$ see (10.10) i)) and $Q \subset (2c_o+1)R_j$, $1 \leqq j \leqq m$, by the selection criteria for F and (10.2) respectively. Now using these facts, together with Lemma 3.2 and inequality (2.15), we see that

$$\|P_Q f - P_{R_o} f\|_{L_\infty(Q)} \leq \sum_{j=1}^{m} \|P_{R_j} f - P_{R_{j-1}} f\|_{L_\infty((2c_o+1)\cdot R_j)}$$

$$\leq c \sum_{j=1}^{m} \|P_{R_j} f - P_{R_{j-1}} f\|_{L_\infty(R_j)}$$

$$(10.14) \qquad \leq c \sum_{j=1}^{m} [\|P_{R_j} f - P_{\tilde{R}_j} f\|_{L_\infty(R_j)} + \|P_{\tilde{R}_j} f - P_{R_{j-1}} f\|_{L_\infty(R_j)}]$$

$$\leq c \sum_{j=0}^{m} m_{R_j} |R_j|^{\alpha/n}$$

which verifies (10.13).

For such cubes Q we define the tower of Q by $T(Q) := \bigcup_{j=0}^{m} R_j$. Now it follows from (10.11) iv) that $T(Q) \subset \text{Shad } \bar{R}$ if $Q \cap R \neq \phi$, $Q \in F$. Hence,

$$\int_Q |f - P_{R_o} f| \leq \int_Q |f - P_Q f| + |Q| \, \|P_Q f - P_{R_o} f\|_{L_\infty(Q)}$$

$$(10.15) \qquad \leq c\,|Q| \sum_{j=0}^{m} m_{R_j} |R_j|^{\alpha/n} \leq c\,|Q| \sum_{j=0}^{m} \int_{R_j} f_\alpha^{\#}(y)\, \delta(y)^{\alpha-n} dy$$

$$= c\,|Q| \int_{T(Q)} f_\alpha^{\#}(y)\, \delta(y)^{\alpha-n} dy$$

since $|R_j|^{1/n}$ is comparable to $\delta(y)$ when $y \in R_j$ (see (10.2)for $j > 0$ and (10.10)iii) for $j = 0$) and $\{R_j\}_{j=1}^{m}$ are disjoint.

First we estimate the integral over $R \cap \Omega$; from (10.15)

$$\int_{R\cap\Omega} |Ef - P_{R_o} f| \leq \sum_{\substack{Q \in F \\ Q\cap R \neq \phi}} \int_Q |f - P_{R_o} f|$$

$$(10.16) \qquad \leq c \sum_{\substack{Q \in F \\ Q\cap R \neq \phi}} |Q| \int_{T(Q)} f_\alpha^{\#}(y)\, \delta(y)^{\alpha-n} dy$$

$$= c \int_{\text{Shad}(\bar{R})} f_\alpha^{\#}(y)\, \delta(y)^{\alpha-n}\, \psi(y)\, dy$$

$$\leq c \int_{\text{Shad}(\bar{R})} f_\alpha^{\#}(y)\, \delta(y)^{\alpha} dy$$

where $\psi(y) = \sum_{\substack{Q \in F \\ Q\cap R \neq \phi}} |Q|\, \chi_{T(Q)}(y)$. In the last inequality we use the fact that if $y = (u',v') \in T(Q)$, then either $y \in Q$ or Q is contained in the "cylinder" $\{(u,v): \phi(u) \leq v \leq v',\ |u-u'| \leq \sqrt{n}\, \delta(y)\}$. Hence, $\psi(y) \leq c\, \delta(y)^n$.

We can estimate $I := \int_{R\cap(\Omega^c\setminus\partial\Omega)} |Ef-P_{R_o} f|$ in much the same way. Namely, if $Q_j^* \cap R \neq \phi$, then Q_j^s is also a cube in F with $Q_j^s \subset \mathrm{Shad}(R_o)$ and so the estimates used in (10.14-16) show that

$$\begin{aligned}
&\sum_{Q_j^*\cap R\neq\phi} |Q_j^s|\ \|P_{Q_j^s}f-P_{R_o}f\|_{L_\infty(Q_j^s)} \\
&\leq c \sum_{Q_j^*\cap R\neq\phi} |Q_j^s| \int_{T(Q_j^s)} f_\alpha^{\#}(y)\ \delta(y)^{\alpha-n}dy \\
&\leq c \int_{\mathrm{Shad}(\bar{R})} f_\alpha^{\#}(y)\ \delta(y)^{\alpha-n}\ \psi(y)dy \\
&\leq c \int_{\mathrm{Shad}(\bar{R})} f_\alpha^{\#}(y)\ \delta(y)^{\alpha}dy
\end{aligned} \tag{10.17}$$

since $Q_j^s \subset \mathrm{Shad}(\bar{R})$. Here we used the fact that Q_j^s arises from at most c_o of the Q_j's because of (10.3) iii). Now since ϕ_j^* is supported on Q_j^* and $0 \leq \phi_j^* \leq 1$,

$$\begin{aligned}
I &\leq \sum_{Q_j^*\cap R\neq\phi} \int_{Q_j^*} |P_{Q_j^s}f-P_{R_o}f|\phi_j^* \leq \sum_{Q_j^*\ R\neq\phi} |Q_j^*|\ \|P_{Q_j^s}f-P_{R_o}f\|_{L_\infty(Q_j^*)} \\
&\leq c \sum_{Q_j^*\cap R\neq\phi} |Q_j^s|\ \|P_{Q_j^s}f-P_{R_o}f\|_{L_\infty((c_o+1)^2Q_j^s)} \\
&\leq c \sum_{Q_j^*\cap R\neq\phi} |Q_j^s|\ \|P_{Q_j^s}-P_{R_o}f\|_{L_\infty(Q_j^s)}
\end{aligned} \tag{10.18}$$

where we've used Lemma 3.2 and the facts that $|Q_j^*| \leq c_o^n\ (1+\varepsilon_o)^n|Q_j^s|$; $Q_j^* \subset (c_o+1)^2Q_j^s$ (by Lemma 10.1). The combination of (10.17-18) gives $I \leq c \int_{\mathrm{Shad}(\bar{R})} f_\alpha^{\#}(y)\ \delta(y)^\alpha\ dy$, which together with (10.16) proves the Lemma. □

Define $\mathcal{Q} := \{Q: \mathrm{dist}(Q,\partial\Omega) \leq A_o\ \ell(Q)\}$ and

$$\mu(f,x) = \sup_{\substack{Q\in\mathcal{Q}\\ Q\ni x}} \frac{1}{|Q|^{1+\alpha/n}} \int_{\mathrm{Shad}(\bar{Q})} f_\alpha^{\#}(y)\ \delta(y)^\alpha\ dy$$

where $\bar{Q}$ is given according to (10.11). The following theorem gives the main estimate of this section.

<u>Theorem 10.4</u>. If f is locally in $L_1(\Omega)$, then

$$(Ef)_\alpha^{\#}\ (x) \leq c\ \mu(f,x) + f_\alpha^{\#}\ (x) \cdot \chi_\Omega(x), \qquad x \in \mathbb{R}^n.$$

Proof. Let R be an cube in $\mathbb{R}^n$. If $\operatorname{dist}(R,\partial\Omega) \leq A_o\, \ell(R)$, then it follows from Lemma 10.3 that for $x \in R$

$$(10.19)\qquad \frac{1}{|R|^{\alpha/n+1}} \int_R |Ef-P_{R_o} f| \leq \frac{c}{|R|^{\alpha/n+1}} \int_{\operatorname{Shad}(\bar{R})} f_\alpha^{\#}(y)\, \delta(y)^\alpha\, dy \leq c\, \mu(f,x).$$

If $\operatorname{dist}(R,\partial\Omega) > A_o\, \ell(R)$, there are two cases depending on whether $R \subset \Omega$ or $R \subset \Omega^c - \partial\Omega$. In the first case, since $Ef = f$ on R, then for each $x \in R$,

$$(10.20)\qquad \frac{1}{|R|^{\alpha/n+1}} \int_R |Ef-P_R f| \leq f_\alpha^{\#}(x)\, \chi_\Omega(x).$$

Consider now the second case $R \subset \Omega^c - \partial\Omega$ and $\operatorname{dist}(R,\partial\Omega) > A_o\, \ell(R)$. We first count how many of the cubes Q_j^* touch R. Let J be the set of all j such that $Q_j \in \mathcal{F}_c$ and $Q_j^* \cap R \neq \phi$, then, for $j \in J$,

$$\ell(R) \leq \frac{1}{A_o} \operatorname{dist}(R,\partial\Omega) \leq \frac{1}{A_o} [\operatorname{dist}(Q_j^*,\partial\Omega) + \sqrt{n}\, \ell(Q_j^*)]$$

$$\leq \frac{1}{A_o} [\operatorname{dist}(Q_j,\Omega) + \frac{9\sqrt{n}}{8}\, \ell(Q_j)]$$

$$\leq \frac{2c_o}{A_o}\, \ell(Q_j) \leq (4c_o)^{-1}\, \ell(Q_j).$$

Hence, the cube $(1+(2c_o)^{-1})Q_j$ contains R. According to (10.6), there are at most N such cubes with N depending only on M and n; that is, $|J| \leq N$.

Now take the largest cube Q_{j_o} with $j_o \in J$. For any other $j \in J$, $|Q_j| \geq c\, |Q_{j_o}|$ because of (10.7). Also, $(1+(c_o)^{-1})Q_{j_o} \cap Q_j^* \neq \phi$ and hence $Q_j^* \subset 4Q_{j_o} =: \tilde{Q}$. We can use Lemma 10.2 for $\tilde{Q}$ because

$$\operatorname{dist}(\tilde{Q},\partial\Omega) \leq \operatorname{dist}(Q_{j_o},\partial\Omega) \leq c_o\, \ell(Q_{j_o}) \leq c_o\, \ell(\tilde{Q}) < A_o\, \ell(\tilde{Q})$$

with c_o the constant of Lemma 10.1. Let $\tilde{Q}_o$ be the cube (for $\tilde{Q}$) guaranteed by Lemma 10.2. If $j \in J$, then $Q_j \subset Q_j^* \subset \tilde{Q}$ and $T(Q_j^s) \subset \operatorname{Shad}(\tilde{Q})^-)$, therefore the estimates in Lemma 10.3 show that for $x \in R \subset \tilde{Q}$,

$$\|P_{Q_j^s} f - P_{\tilde{Q}_o} f\|_{L_\infty(Q_j^s)} \leq c \int_{\operatorname{Shad}((\tilde{Q})^-)} f_\alpha^{\#}(y)\, \delta(y)^{\alpha-n} dy$$

$$\leq c\, |\tilde{Q}|^{\alpha/n}\, \mu(f,x) \leq c\, \ell(Q_j)^\alpha\, \mu(f,x)$$

since $\tilde{Q} \in \mathcal{Q}$, $\delta(y) \geq c\, \ell(\tilde{Q})$ when $y \in T(Q_j^s)$, and $|Q_{j_o}| \leq c\, |Q_j|$ when $j \in J$.

Also since $\operatorname{dist}(Q_j^s,Q_j) \leqq c_o\, \ell(Q_j)$ and $c_o\, \ell(Q_j^s) \geqq \ell(Q_j)$, we have $Q_j^* \subset c(4c_o+1)Q_j^s$. So, using Markov's inequality and Lemma 3.2, we have for any multiindex ν,

$$(10.21) \qquad ||D^\nu(P_{Q_j^s}f-P_{\tilde{Q}_o}f)||_{L_\infty(Q_j^*)} \leqq c\,[\ell(Q_j)]^{\alpha-|\nu|}\,\mu(f,x), \quad j \in J.$$

On the cube R, we have

$$(10.22) \qquad \psi := Ef-P_{\tilde{Q}_o}f = \sum_{j\in J}[P_{Q_j^s}f-P_{\tilde{Q}_o}f]\phi_j^*$$

because each ϕ_j^* is supported on Q_j^*. Differentiating any of the terms in the sum (10.22) and using (10.8) and (10.21) together with Leibnitz' rule gives

$$||D^\nu([P_{Q_j^s}f-P_{\tilde{Q}_o}f]\phi_j^*)||_{L_\infty(R)} \leqq c\,\ell(Q_j)^{\alpha-|\nu|}\,\mu(f,x).$$

Hence

$$(10.23) \qquad ||D^\nu\psi||_{L_\infty(R)} \leqq c\,\ell(Q_{j_o})^{\alpha-|\nu|}\,\mu(f,x)$$

because $|J| \leqq N$. It follows that ψ is in Lip α on R. Indeed, taking $|\mu| = [\alpha] =: k$, and using (10.23) and that $\ell(R) \leqq \ell(Q_{j_o})$ gives

$$|D^\mu\psi(x+h) - D^\mu\psi(x)| \leqq |h| \sum_{|\nu|=k+1} ||D^\nu\psi||_{L_\infty(R)} \leqq c\,|h|\,\ell(Q_{j_o})^{\alpha-k-1}\,\mu(f,x)$$
$$\leqq c\,h^{\alpha-k}\,\mu(f,x)$$

whenever x, x+h $\in$ R. So the Lip α norm of ψ is at most c $\mu(f,x)$. According to Theorem 6.4, there is a polynomial π of degree at most $[\alpha]$ such that

$$||Ef-(\pi+P_{\tilde{Q}_o}f)||_{L_\infty(R)} = ||\psi-\pi||_{L_\infty(R)} \leqq c\,|R|^{\alpha/n}\,\mu(f,x).$$

Integrating over R gives

$$(10.24) \qquad \frac{1}{|R|^{\alpha/n+1}}\int_R |Ef-(\pi+P_{\tilde{Q}_o}f)| \leqq c\,\mu(f,x).$$

Therefore the three estimates (10.19), (10.20), and (10.24) together with Lemma 2.1 prove the theorem. □

Let us now briefly describe the case n=1 and Ω an interval which we take to be (0,1). Unions of intervals are handled in the discussion of extensions for domains with minimally smooth boundary in the following section. Let F_c

be the set of intervals I of the form $[-2^{-\nu}, -2^{-\nu-1}]$ or $[1+2^{-\nu-1}, 1+2^{-\nu}]$ for some $\nu \geq 2$, and associate to such I the interval $I^s := [2^{-\nu-1}, 2^{-\nu}]$ or $I^s := [1-2^{-\nu}, 1-2^{-\nu-1}]$ respectively. Also $I^* := \frac{5}{4}I$. We can enumerate the intervals in $\mathcal{F}_c$ as $\{I_j\}_{j=1}^{\infty}$. This is a covering for $S := (-\frac{1}{4},0) \cup (1,\frac{5}{4})$. Let $\{\phi_j^*\}_{j=1}^{\infty}$ be a partition of unity with the properties (10.8). So, in particular, each ϕ_j^* is supported on I_j^* and $\sum_1^{\infty} \phi_j^* \equiv 1$ on S. The extension operator $E := E_\alpha^{\#}$ is defined by

$$(10.25) \qquad Ef(x) := \begin{cases} f(x), & x \in (0,1) \\ \sum_1^{\infty} P_{I_j^s} f(x)\, \phi_j^*(x), & x \in (-\infty,0) \cup (1,\infty) . \end{cases}$$

It follows that Ef vanishes outside of $(-\frac{1}{4},\frac{5}{4})$.

If I is any interval, then $\mathrm{Shad}(I) := I \cap (0,1)$. Defining $\mu(f,x)$ as before with $A_0 := 2$, then Theorem 10.4 will hold with the same proof. Without going into detail, let us elaborate on a couple of points of the proof. The geometry is much simpler and in particular one does not need Lemma 10.2. Again, there are three cases to consider in estimating

$$\sup_{I \ni x} \frac{1}{|I|^{\alpha+1}} \inf_{\pi \in \mathbb{P}_{[\alpha]}} \int_I |Ef-\pi| .$$

If $I \subset (0,1)$ the estimate is trivial. If $\mathrm{dist}(I,(0,1)) \leq 2\,\ell(I)$ but $I \not\subset (0,1)$, then we select an interval $I_0 \subset (0,1)$ of the form (o,a) or $(x,1)$ with the properties that $|I_0|$ is the same as the largest interval J which hits I and either $J \subset (0,1) \cap I$ or $J \in \mathcal{F}_c$. Then π can be taken as $P_{I} f$. The estimate of $\int_{I_0 \cap (0,1)} |Ef-P_{I_0} f|$ is trival since Ef=f there. The estimate for $P_{I^s} f-P_{I_0} f$ is done as in (10.14). The third case is when $I \subset [0,1]^c$ and $\mathrm{dist}(I,(0,1)) \geq 2\,\ell(I)$. We also need only consider $\ell(I) \leq \frac{1}{8}$ since otherwise $Ef \equiv 0$ on I. It follows that I intersets at most two intervals from $\mathcal{F}_c$ and one can take $\pi := P_{I_0} f$ where I_0 is the largest interval from $\mathcal{F}_c$ which hits I. The proof is then the same as in Theorem 10.4.

The following theorem proves that $Ef \in C_p^\alpha(\mathbb{R}^n)$ whenever $f \in C_p^\alpha(\Omega)$, $1 \leq p \leq \infty$, and $\alpha > 0$.

Theorem 10.5. Let Ω be an interval in the case $n = 1$ or $\Omega := \{(u,v) : u \in \mathbb{R}^{n-1}, v \in \mathbb{R}; v > \phi(u)\}$ in the case $n \geq 2$ with ϕ in Lip 1. The extension operator $E_\alpha^\#$ defined by (10.25), respectively (10.9), is bounded from $C_p^\alpha(\Omega)$ into $C_p^\infty(\mathbb{R}^n)$, $1 \leq p \leq \infty$ with the norm of $E_\alpha^\#$ depending only on α, n, and the Lipschitz constant M. Similiarly, the operators E_k^b are bounded from $\mathcal{C}_p^k(\Omega)$ into $\mathcal{C}_p^k(\mathbb{R}^n)$ with norm depending only on k, n, and M.

Proof. Apply an L_p norm to both sides of the inequality in Theorem 10.4 to find

$$\|(Ef)_\alpha^\#\|_{L_p(\mathbb{R}^n)} \leq c\,[\|\mu(f)\|_{L_p(\mathbb{R}^n)} + \|f_\alpha^\#\|_{L_p(\Omega)}]. \tag{10.26}$$

We now estimate $\|\mu f\|_{L_p(\mathbb{R}^n)}$ by considering the cases $p = 1,\infty$ and then use interpolation.

When $p = \infty$ and $g \in L_\infty$, we have

$$Tg(x) := \sup_{\mathcal{Q}\ni Q\ni x} \left(\frac{1}{|Q|^{\alpha/n+1}} \int_{\mathrm{Shad}(\bar{Q})} |g(y)|\,[\delta(y)]^\alpha dy\right) \leq c\,\|g\|_{L_\infty(\Omega)} \tag{10.27}$$

where we used the facts that $\delta(y) \leq c\,|Q|^{1/n}$, $y \in \mathrm{Shad}(\bar{Q})$, and $|\mathrm{Shad}(\bar{Q})| \leq c\,|Q|$ when $Q \in \mathcal{Q}$. Recall also that $\mathrm{Shad}(\bar{Q}) \subset \Omega$.

For $p = 1$, we note that $c\,|Q|^{1/n} \geq \delta(y) + |x-y|$ whenever $x \in Q$, $y \in \mathrm{Shad}(\bar{Q})$ and $Q \in \mathcal{Q}$. Using these facts shows that for $g \in L_1$,

$$Tg(x) \leq c \int_\Omega |g(y)|\, \frac{[\delta(y)]^\alpha}{[\delta(y)+|x-y|]^{\alpha+n}}\, dy. \tag{10.28}$$

Applying an L_1 norm to both sides of (10.28) gives

$$\begin{aligned} \|Tg\|_{L_1(\mathbb{R}^n)} &\leq c \int_\Omega |g(y)|\, \delta(y)^\alpha \left[\int_{\mathbb{R}^n} (\delta(y)+|x-y|)^{-\alpha-n} dx\right] dy \\ &\leq c \int_\Omega |g(y)|\, \delta(y)^\alpha\, [\delta(y)^{-\alpha}]\, dy = c\,\|g\|_{L_1(\Omega)}. \end{aligned} \tag{10.29}$$

By virtue of (10.27) and (10.29), the sublinear operator T is bounded from $L_\infty(\Omega)$ to $L_\infty(\mathbb{R}^n)$ and $L_1(\Omega)$ to $L_1(\mathbb{R}^n)$. By interpolation T must be bounded from $L_p(\Omega)$ to $L_p(\mathbb{R}^n)$, $1 \leq p \leq \infty$, and so since $\mu f \equiv Tf_\alpha^\#$, we have

$$\|\mu f\|_{L_p(\mathbb{R}^n)} \leq c\,\|f_\alpha^\#\|_{L_p(\Omega)}, \quad 1 \leq p \leq \infty.$$

When this is used back in (10.26), we find

(10.30) $$\|(Ef)^{\#}_{\alpha}\|_{L_p(\mathbb{R}^n)} \le c\,\|f^{\#}_{\alpha}\|_{L_p(\Omega)},\quad 1 \le p \le \infty.$$

Finally, we wish to estimate $\|Ef\|_{L_p(\mathbb{R}^n)}$. It follows from the definition of Ef that

(10.31) $$\|Ef\|^p_{L_p(\mathbb{R}^n)} \le c\,[\|f\|^p_{L_p(\Omega)} + \|\sum_{j=1}^{\infty} P_{Q_j^s} f\,\phi_j^*\|^p_{L_p(\Omega^c)}]\,.$$

Since each $x \in \Omega^c$ appears in at most N cubes Q_j^* with N depending only on n and M, Hölder's inequality gives

$$|\sum_j P_{Q_j^s} f\,\chi_{Q_j^*}|^p \le N^{p-1} \sum_j |P_{Q_j^s} f\,\chi_{Q_j^*}|^p\,.$$

Integrating over Ω^c and using the fact that $\lambda Q_j^s \supset Q_j^*$ $(\lambda=4c_o+1)$, we get by Lemma 3.2

$$\begin{aligned}\|\sum_j P_{Q_j^s} f\,\chi_{Q_j^*}\|^p_{L_p(\Omega^c)} &\le c\sum_j \|P_{Q_j^s} f\|^p_{L_p(Q_j^*)} \le c\sum_j \|P_{Q_j^s} f\|^p_{L_p(\lambda Q_j^s)}\\ &\le c\sum_j \|P_{Q_j^s} f\|^p_{L_p(Q_j^s)} \le c\sum_j \|f\|^p_{L_p(Q_j^s)}\end{aligned}$$

where the last inequality follows from the fact that $P_{Q_j^s}$ is a bounded operator on $L_p(Q_j^s)$ (see inequality (2.3)). Combining this with equality (10.31) shows that

$$\|Ef\|^p_{L_p(\mathbb{R}^n)} \le c\,[\|f\|^p_{L_p(\Omega)} + \sum_{j=1}^{\infty} \|f\|^p_{L_p(Q_j^s)}].$$

But the Q_j^s coincide for different j at most c_o times, hence

$$\|Ef\|_{L_p(\mathbb{R}^n)} \le c\,\|f\|_{L_p(\Omega)},\qquad 1 \le p \le \infty\,.$$

Combining this with (10.30) proves the theorem for $E^{\#}_{\alpha}$. Similar reasoning applies for $E^{\flat}_{\alpha}$. □

Remark. The proof of the extension theorem simplifies considerably for the Sobolev spaces $W^k_p(\Omega)$, $1 \le p \le \infty$. First we do not need the cover constructed in Lemma 10.1 and may use instead the standard Whitney coverings F, F_c of both Ω and $\Omega^c\backslash\partial\Omega$, respectively. We let $\{Q_i\}$ be an enumeration of F_c and let $x_i = (u_i,v_i)$ be the center of Q_i. Defining Q_i^s to be that cube in F containing

$x_i^s := x_i + 2\,\delta(x_i)e_n$ where $\delta(x_i) := |\phi(u_i) - v_i|$, we see immediately that properties (10.1)-(10.3) hold. As before, define the extension operator by

(10.32) $$Ef(x) := \sum_i \pi_i(x)\ \phi_i^*(x) + f(x)\ \chi_\Omega(x)$$

where π_i is a best $\mathbb{P}_{k-1}$ approximation to f on $L_1(Q_i^s)$ and ϕ_i^* is a partition of unity for the open cover $\{\frac{5}{4}Q_i\}$. For each fixed $x \in \Omega^c \setminus \partial\Omega$ there is a neighborhood U of x which intersects at most $N = 12^n$ of the supports of the ϕ_i's. Let i_o be the index such that $x \in Q_{i_o}$ and define $\bar{Q} := A\,Q_{i_o} + \sqrt{n}MAe_n$ with A large (e.g., $A = 3000M^2$), $\bar{Q} \subset \Omega$, each $Q_i^s \subset \mathrm{Shad}(\bar{Q})$ and $\ell(Q_i^s) \approx \ell(\bar{Q})$ if $U \cap \mathrm{supp}\ \phi_i^* \neq \phi$. It is not too difficult to prove that for

$$\mathcal{D}g := \sum_{|\nu|=k} |D^\nu g|$$

(10.33) $$(Ef) \leq c\ T(\mathcal{D}f) + \mathcal{D}f\ \chi_\Omega$$

where the operator $Tg(x) := \sup_{\mathcal{Q}\ni Q\ni x} \frac{1}{|Q|^{k/n+1}} \int_{\mathrm{Shad}\ \bar{Q}} |g(y)|\delta(y)^k dy$ is bounded on L_1 and L_∞ (see (10.27) and (10.29)). Here $\mathcal{Q} := \{Q: \mathrm{dist}(Q,\partial\Omega) \leq \ell(Q)\}$ and $\mathrm{Shad}\ \bar{Q} = \{(u,v) \in \Omega:\ (u, v_o) \in \bar{Q}$ with $v \leq v_o\}$. It follows at once from (10.33) that

$$||Ef||_{W_p^k(\mathbb{R}^n)} \leq c\ ||f||_{W_p^k(\Omega)} .$$

Two main estimates are needed of the proof of (10.33): if $|\nu| = k$, then

(10.34) $$|D^\nu(Ef)(x)| \leq \Big|\sum_{0\leq\mu\leq\nu} \binom{\nu}{\mu} \sum_i D^\mu \pi_i(x)\ D^{\nu-\mu}\phi_i^*(x)\Big|$$
$$\leq c \sum_i ||\pi_i - \bar{\pi}||_{L_\infty(Q_i)} \ell(Q_i)^{-k}\ \chi_{Q_i^*}(x)$$

(where $\bar{\pi} := \mathcal{P}_{\bar{Q}}^b f$, a best $\mathbb{P}_{k-1}$ approximation to f on $L_1(\bar{Q})$) and

(10.35) $$||\mathcal{P}_Q^b f - \mathcal{P}_{Q^*}^b f||_{L_\infty(Q)} \leq c\ \ell(Q)^{k-n} \int_Q \mathcal{D}f(y)dy$$

if $Q^* \subset Q \subset 4Q^*$ with $Q \in \mathcal{F}$.

The first inequality of (10.34) follows by applying Leibnitz' rule while the second follows from the facts that $\bar{\pi} \in \mathbb{P}_{k-1}$ and $D^{\nu-\mu}(\Sigma\phi_i^*) \equiv 0$ if $\mu \neq \nu$, together with Markov's inequality and the estimate $|D^{\nu-\mu}\phi_i^*| \leq c\ \ell(Q_i)^{|\mu|-k}$. Inequality (10.35) follows immediately from Theorem 3.4 with p = 1 and Lemma 3.1. Finally these two estimates are used with the fact that $P^b_{Q_i^s}f - P^b_{\bar{Q}}f$ can be written as a telescoping sum of terms of the type $P^b_Q f - P^b_{Q^*}f$.

§11. Extensions for Domains With Minimally Smooth Boundary

In this section, we piece together the extensions of §10 to give extension operators for more general domains. We first discuss the case n > 1 and leave the case n = 1 to a remark following Theorem 11.4. The domains of §10 were of the form

$$\Omega = \{(u,v): u \in \mathbb{R}^{n-1}, v \in \mathbb{R}; \phi(u) < v\}, \quad |\phi|_{Lip\ 1} \leq M.$$

We call such a domain: a <u>special Lipschitz domain</u>. Any rotation of such a domain is called a <u>special rotated domain</u>.

Suppose, we are given $\varepsilon_o > 0$, an integer $N_o > 0$, a sequence of open sets $\{U_i\}$, and a sequence of special rotated domains $\{\Omega_i\}$ with the properties:

(11.1) i) if $x \in \partial\Omega$, then $B_{\varepsilon_o}(x) \subset U_i$ for some i

ii) $B_{\varepsilon_o}(x)$ intersects at most N_o sets U_i

iii) for each i, $\Omega \cap U_i = \Omega_i \cap U_i$,

then we say Ω is a domain with <u>minimally smooth boundary</u>. This definition is equivalent[a)] to the usual definition [15, p. 189] which replaces ii) by the requirement: ii)' $\Sigma \chi_{U_i} \leq N_o'$. Indeed, if Ω satisfies i), iii), and ii)' for some $(U_i', \varepsilon_o', N_o')$, then the sets $U_i: = (U_i')^{2\varepsilon_o}$ with $\varepsilon_o: = \varepsilon_o'/4$ and $N_o: = N_o'$ satisfy i)-iii) because any sphere $B_{\varepsilon_o}(x_o)$ which intersects U_i satisfies $x_o \in U_i'$.

We now construct a partition of unity as in [15]. For full details of its properties see [15, p. 190-191]. If U is an open set, then $U^\varepsilon: = \{x \in U: B_\varepsilon(x) \subset U\}$. It follows from (11.1) i) that $\{U_i^{\varepsilon_o}\}$ is a cover for $\partial\Omega$. Now, fix $\varepsilon_1: = \varepsilon_o/8$ and define

$$\lambda_i(x): = \chi_{U_i^{2\varepsilon_1}} * \eta_{\varepsilon_1}(x)$$

where η is a C^∞ function supported on the unit ball and $\eta_\varepsilon(x): = \varepsilon^{-n}\eta(x/\varepsilon)$ are the dilates of η. Then λ_i is supported on $U_i^{\varepsilon_1}$ and $\lambda_i \equiv 1$ on $U_i^{3\varepsilon_1}$.

---

a) For the original proof, see R. Sharpley, "Cone conditions and the modulus of continuity", to appear in the Proceedings of the Second Edmonton Conference on Approximation Theory, CMS Conf. Proc., Vol. 3, AMS, 1983.

Going further, let

$$U_o := \{x: \ \text{dist}(x,\Omega) < \varepsilon_1\}$$
$$U_+ := \{x: \ \text{dist}(x,\partial\Omega) < 2\varepsilon_1\}$$
$$U_- := \{x \in \Omega: \ \text{dist}(x,\partial\Omega) > 2\varepsilon_1\}$$

and let λ_o, λ_+ and λ_- be defined as above with $\chi_{\Omega_i^{2\varepsilon_1}}$ replaced by χ_{U_o}, χ_{U_+} and χ_{U_-} respectively. The functions

$$\Lambda_+ := \lambda_o\left(\frac{\lambda_+}{\lambda_+ + \lambda_-}\right) \quad \text{and} \quad \Lambda_- := \lambda_o\left(\frac{\lambda_-}{\lambda_+ + \lambda_-}\right)$$

satisfy: $\Lambda_+ + \Lambda_- = 1$ on $\bar{\Omega}$.

To define our extension operator, set $\phi_i := \Lambda_+\lambda_i/\Sigma\lambda_j^2$. Since $\Sigma\lambda_j^2 \geq 1$ on support of Λ_+, the functions ϕ_i as well as the λ_i, Λ_+ and Λ_- have a uniform bound for their $W_\infty^{[\alpha]+1}$ norms which we denote by L. Finally, define

$$Ef := \Sigma\ \phi_i\ E_i(\lambda_i f) + \Lambda_- f$$

where for each i, E_i is the extension operator for Ω_i guaranteed by Theorem 10.5. We now proceed to show that Ef is in $C_p^\alpha(\mathbb{R}^n)$ whenever $f \in C_p^\alpha(\Omega)$.

Since rotations are involved in the definition of E, we need to examine the effect of replacing the cubes Q in the definition of $f_\alpha^\#$ by rotated cubes or more general collections of sets. We say that a collection $\mathcal{S}$ of measurable subsets of $\mathbb{R}^n$ is admissable if there is a constant $c' > 0$ such that for each standard cube (sides parallel to the axes), there is an $S \in \mathcal{S}$ with $c'S \subset Q \subset S$ ($c'S$ denotes the set S dilated by c' about its center of gravity) and conversely for each $S \in \mathcal{S}$ there is a standard cube Q with $c'Q \subset S \subset Q$. Examples of admissable collections are balls, finite cones with fixed angle, etc. For our purposes the most important admissable collections are the collection of all cubes and the collection of all cubes which are a fixed rotation of standard cubes.

If $\mathcal{S}$ is an admissable collection and Ω is a domain, let

$$\text{(11.2)} \qquad F_\alpha(x) := \sup_{\substack{\Omega\supset S\ni x \\ S\in\mathcal{S}}} \frac{1}{|S|^{1+\alpha/n}} \inf_{\pi\in\mathbb{P}_{[\alpha]}} \int_S |f-\pi|, \qquad x \in \Omega.$$

Lemma 11.1. If Ω is a special rotated domain, $\mathcal{S}$ an admissable collection and $\alpha > 0$, then there are constants $c_1, c_2 > 0$ depending only on α, n, c', and M such that for each $1 \leq p \leq \infty$,

$$(11.3) \qquad c_1 \, |f|_{C_p^\alpha(\Omega)} \leq ||F_\alpha||_{L_p(\Omega)} \leq c_2 \, |f|_{C_p^\alpha(\Omega)} .$$

Proof. Consider first the case $\Omega = \{(u,v): \phi(u) < v\}$. We will use the results of §10 with the following adjustments on the constants appearing there. First, in the definition of the cone C, we increase the value of M so that whenever $Q \in F$ then $\frac{1}{c'} Q \subset \Omega$. This is possible since the effect of increasing M is to push the cubes $Q \in F$ further away from $\partial\Omega$. We also increase the constant A_o so that $A_o \geq 2\sqrt{n}/c'$. The results of §10 hold with A_o arbitrarily large.

Now consider the right hand inequality in (11.3). Suppose $x \in S \subset \Omega$ with $S \in \mathcal{S}$ and let R be a standard cube with $c'R \subset S \subset R$. If $A_o|S|^{1/n} \leq \mathrm{dist}(S,\partial\Omega)$, then $A_o c'|R|^{1/n} \leq \mathrm{dist}(S,\partial\Omega) \leq \mathrm{dist}(c'R,\partial\Omega)$. Since $A_o \geq 2\sqrt{n}/c'$, we have $R \subset \Omega$ and

$$(11.4) \qquad \frac{1}{|S|^{1+\alpha/n}} \inf_{\pi \in \mathbb{P}_{[\alpha]}} \int_S |f - \pi| \leq \frac{c}{|R|^{1+\alpha/n}} \inf_{\pi \in \mathbb{P}_{[\alpha]}} \int_R |f - \pi| \leq c \, f_\alpha^{\#}(x).$$

On the other hand, if $\mathrm{dist}(S,\partial\Omega) \leq A_o \, |S|^{1/n}$ then $\mathrm{dist}(R,\partial\Omega) \leq A_o \ell(R)$ and so by Lemma 10.3

$$(11.5) \qquad \inf_{\pi \in \mathbb{P}_{[\alpha]}} \int_S |f - \pi| \leq \inf_{\pi \in \mathbb{P}_{[\alpha]}} \int_R |E_\Omega f - \pi| \leq c \int_{\mathrm{Shad}(\bar{R})} f_\alpha^{\#}(y)\delta(y)^\alpha dy$$

where E_Ω is the extension operator for Ω. Hence, if T is the operator defined by (10.27) then

$$(11.6) \qquad \frac{1}{|S|^{1+\alpha/n}} \inf_{\pi \in \mathbb{P}_{[\alpha]}} \int_S |f - \pi| \leq c \, Tf_\alpha^{\#}(x)$$

when $\mathrm{dist}(S,\partial\Omega) \leq A_o \, |S|^{1/n}$. Combining (11.4) and (11.6) gives

$$(11.7) \qquad F_\alpha(x) \leq c \, [f_\alpha^{\#}(x) + Tf_\alpha^{\#}(x)] \qquad x \in \Omega.$$

Since T is bounded on L_p, the right hand inequality in (11.3) follows.

The left hand inequality follows from the estimate

$$(11.8) \qquad f_\alpha^{\#} \leq c \, [F_\alpha + TF_\alpha],$$

whose proof is much the same as (11.7). Suppose x is in the standard cube $R \subset \Omega$ and $S \in \mathcal{S}$ satisfies $c'S \subset R \subset S$. If $A_o \ell(R) \leq \operatorname{dist}(R,\partial\Omega)$, then $S \subset \Omega$ and

$$(11.9) \qquad \frac{1}{|R|^{1+\alpha/n}} \inf_{\pi \in \mathbb{P}_{[\alpha]}} \int_R |f - \pi| \leq c\, F_\alpha(x).$$

If $\operatorname{dist}(R, \partial\Omega) \leq A_o\, \ell(R)$, then we proceed as in Lemma 10.3. Let $Q \in F$ with $Q \cap R \neq \phi$ and let $R_m = Q, R_{m-1}, \ldots, R_1, R_o$ be as in Lemma 10.3. For each j, there is a set $S_j \in \mathcal{S}$ with $c'S_j \subset R_j \subset S_j$ and a polynomial $\pi_j \in \mathbb{P}_{[\alpha]}$ which is a best approximation to f in $L_1(S_j)$. Furthermore $S_j \subset \frac{1}{c'} R_j \subset \Omega$, $j = 0,\ldots,m$. Hence the same telescoping argument which was used in deriving (10.13) together with Lemma 3.2 shows that

$$||\pi_m - \pi_o||_{L_\infty(Q)} \leq c \sum_{j=o}^{m} m_j\ |R_j|^{\alpha/n}$$

with $m_j := \inf_{S'_j} F_\alpha$ and $S'_j := c'S_j$. Using the same technique as in the derivation of (10.16) shows that

$$(11.10) \qquad \int_R |f - \pi_o| \leq c \int_{\operatorname{Shad}(\bar{R})} F_\alpha(y)\ \delta(y)^{\alpha-n}\psi(y)dy$$

$$\leq c \int_{\operatorname{Shad}(\bar{R})} F_\alpha(y)\ \delta(y)^{\alpha}dy$$

since $\psi(y) := \sum_{\substack{Q \cap R \neq \phi \\ Q \in F}} |Q|\ \chi_{T(Q)}(y) \leq c\ \delta(y)^n$ with $T(Q) = \bigcup_{j=o}^{m} R_j$.

From (11.10), it follows that

$$\inf_{\pi \in \mathbb{P}_{[\alpha]}} \frac{1}{|R|^{1+\alpha/n}} \int_R |f - \pi| \leq c\ TF_\alpha(x).$$

This together with (11.9) establishes (11.8), and therefore verifies (11.3) for domains $\Omega = \{(u,v)\colon \phi(u) < v\}$.

It follows from what we have proved that given any two admissable collections $\mathcal{S}$ and $\mathcal{S}'$ the corresponding maximal functions F_α and F'_α have comparable L_p norms. Thus given any special rotated domain, (11.3) follows by taking an inverse rotation. □

<u>Remark</u>. In the arguments given above and in §10, we could replace $\mathbb{P}_{[\alpha]}$ by $\mathbb{P}_j$, $j \geq [\alpha]$, and the proofs remain valid for the resulting maximal operators

$$_j f_\alpha(x) := \sup_{\Omega\supset Q\ni x} \{\frac{1}{|Q|^{1+\alpha/n}} \inf_{\pi\in\mathbb{P}_j} \int_Q |f - \pi|\}$$

$$_j F_\alpha(x) := \sup_{\substack{\Omega\supset S\ni x \\ S\in\mathcal{S}}} \{\frac{1}{|S|^{1+\alpha/n}} \inf_{\pi\in\mathbb{P}_j} \int_S |f - \pi|\}.$$

In particular, for $j \geqq [\alpha]$, there are constants $c_1, c_2 > 0$ such that

$$(11.11) \qquad c_1 \, ||_j f_\alpha||_{L_p(\Omega)} \leqq ||_j F_\alpha||_{L_p(\Omega)} \leqq c_2 \, ||_j f_\alpha||_{L_p(\Omega)}.$$

The following lemma is in essence a version of Lemma 2.3 for admissable collections.

Lemma 11.2. If Ω is a special rotated domain, $1 \leqq p \leqq \infty$; $\alpha \geqq 0$ and $j \geqq [\alpha]$ then there are c_1, $c_2 > 0$ such that for $f \in L_1(\Omega) + L_\infty(\Omega)$

$$(11.12) \qquad c_1 \, ||f||_{C_p^\alpha} \leqq ||_j f_\alpha||_{L_p(\Omega)} + ||f||_{L_p(\Omega)} \leqq ||f||_{C_p^\alpha}.$$

Proof. By Lemma 11.1 and the remark following it, we can assume that Ω is a special Lipschitz domain. The right hand inequality is immediate since $\mathbb{P}_{[\alpha]} \subset \mathbb{P}_j$. For the left hand inequality, take $\mathcal{S}$ to be the collection of all finite cones $\{(u,v): v_o + M|u-u_o| < v \leqq v_o + h\}$ of height h and vertex $x_o = (u_o,v_o)$ and let F_α be as in (11.2). If we use cones $S = S_o \subset S_1 \subset \ldots \subset S_N \subset \Omega$, with $|S_i| = 2^{-n} |S_{i+1}|$, in place of the cubes Q_i in the proof Lemma 2.3 then we find

$$F_\alpha \leqq c \; _j F_\alpha.$$

Using (11.3) and (11.11),we have

$$\begin{aligned} ||f||_{C_p^\alpha(\Omega)} &\leqq c \, [||F_\alpha||_{L_p(\Omega)} + ||f||_{L_p(\Omega)}] \\ &\leqq c \, [||_j F_\alpha||_{L_p(\Omega)} + ||f||_{L_p(\Omega)}] \leqq c \, [||_j f_\alpha||_{L_p(\Omega)} + ||f||_{L_p(\Omega)}] \end{aligned}$$

as desired. □

Remark. The estimate (11.12) holds also for the maximal function $_j f_{\alpha,q}$ which is defined in the same manner as $_j f_\alpha$ except with L_q "norms", $0 < q \leqq p$, in place of the L_1 norm. For the proof we make modifications similiar to those made in the proof of Lemma 4.4.

Because of the form of the extension operator E, we will have to estimate $(\lambda g)^{\#}_{\alpha}$ when λ is smooth and g is a general function. Suppose λ is supported in an open set U and $\varepsilon > 0$. Let $N_{\varepsilon} := N_{\varepsilon}(U)$ denote the ε neighborhood of U.

Lemma 11.3. If Ω is a special rotated domain and $1 \leqq p \leqq \infty$, then there is a constant c depending only on ε, M, n, p and $||\lambda||_{W^{[\alpha]+1}_{\infty}}$ such that

$$||\lambda f||_{C^{\alpha}_{p}(\Omega)} \leqq c\, ||f||_{C^{\alpha}_{p}(N_{\varepsilon}\cap\Omega)}$$

Proof. Clearly, $||\lambda f||_{L_p(\Omega)} \leqq c\, ||f||_{L_p(N_{\varepsilon}\cap\Omega)}$. Consider first the case $1 < p \leqq \infty$. According to Lemma 11.2, it suffices to show

$$(11.13) \qquad ||{}_{j}(\lambda f)_{\alpha}||_{L_p(\Omega)} \leqq c\, ||f||_{C^{\alpha}_{p}(N_{\varepsilon}\cap\Omega)}$$

for $j = 2[\alpha]$. Suppose then that $x \in \Omega$ and Q is a cube satisfying $\Omega \supset Q \ni x$.

If $|Q| \geqq \varepsilon^n$, then

$$(11.14) \qquad \inf_{\pi\in\mathbb{P}_j} \frac{1}{|Q|^{1+\alpha/n}} \int_Q |\lambda f - \pi| \leqq c\, M(f\chi_{\Omega\cap U})(x) \leqq c\, M(f\chi_{N_{\varepsilon}\cap\Omega})(x).$$

If $|Q| \leqq \varepsilon^n$, then we may assume $Q \cap U \neq \phi$ since otherwise $\lambda f\chi_Q \equiv 0$. Let π_o and π_{λ} denote best $L_1(Q)$ approximations from $\mathbb{P}_{[\alpha]}$ to f and λ respectively. Writing $\lambda f - \pi_{\lambda}\pi_o = (f - \pi_o)\lambda + \pi_o(\lambda - \pi_{\lambda})$, we have

$$(11.15) \qquad \inf_{\pi\in\mathbb{P}_j} \frac{1}{|Q|^{1+\alpha/n}} \int_Q |\lambda f - \pi| \leqq c\, f^{\#}_{\alpha}(x) + ||\pi_o||_{L_{\infty}(Q)}\lambda^{\#}_{\alpha}(x)$$

$$\leqq c\, [f^{\#}_{\alpha}(x) + M(f\chi_{N_{\varepsilon}\cap\Omega})(x)]$$

where we used the facts that $\lambda \in W^{[\alpha]+1}_{\infty}$, $||\pi_o||_{L_{\infty}(Q)} \leqq \frac{c}{|Q|}\int_Q |f|$ and $Q \subset N_{\varepsilon}$. In this inequality $f^{\#}_{\alpha}$ is taken relative to the domain $N_{\varepsilon} \cap \Omega$. Inequality (11.13) follows easily from (11.14) and (11.15) because M is bounded on L_p.

When $p = 1$, we choose $(1+\frac{\alpha}{n})^{-1} < q < 1$ and use $f^{\#}_{\alpha,q}$ in place of $f^{\#}_{\alpha}$ (see Theorem 4.3) and M_q in place of M to derive an analogous inequality to (11.13) with ${}_{j}f_{\alpha,q}$ in place of ${}_{j}f_{\alpha}$. □

We can now prove the main result of this section.

Theorem 11.4. Suppose Ω is a domain with minimally smooth boundary. For each $\alpha > 0$, and $1 \leqq p \leqq \infty$,

(11.16) $$\|Ef\|_{C_p^\alpha(\mathbb{R}^n)} \leqq c\,\|f\|_{C_p^\alpha(\Omega)}$$

with c depending only on α, n, and Ω.

Proof. Consider first the case $1 < p < \infty$. Let $g_i := \phi_i\, E_i(\lambda_i f)$ and $g_o := \Lambda_- f$. Then,

(11.17) $$\|Ef\|_{C_p^\alpha(\mathbb{R}^n)} \leqq \|\Sigma g_i\|_{C_p^\alpha(\mathbb{R}^n)} + \|g_o\|_{C_p^\alpha(\mathbb{R}^n)}.$$

First, we estimate the term involving g_o. Since Λ_- is supported on Ω^{ε_1}, for any cube Q with $x \in Q$ and $|Q| \geqq (\varepsilon_1/\sqrt{n})^n$ we have

$$\inf_{\pi \in \mathbb{P}_{[\alpha]}} \frac{1}{|Q|^{1+\alpha/n}} \int_Q |g_o - \pi| \leqq c\, M(f\chi_\Omega)(x).$$

On the other hand if $x \in Q$ and $|Q| < (\varepsilon_1/\sqrt{n})^n$, then we can estimate as in (11.15) and obtain

(11.18) $$\begin{aligned}\|g_o\|_{C_p^\alpha(\mathbb{R}^n)} &\leqq c\,[\|f\|_{C_p^\alpha(\Omega)} + \|M(f\chi_\Omega)\|_{L_p(\mathbb{R}^n)}]\\ &\leqq c\,\|f\|_{C_p^\alpha(\Omega)}\end{aligned}$$

because $p > 1$.

To estimate the term involving Σg_i in (11.17), we again consider the case $|Q| \geqq (\varepsilon_1/\sqrt{n})^n$ and find

(11.19) $$\begin{aligned}\inf_{\pi \in \mathbb{P}_{[\alpha]}} \frac{1}{|Q|^{1+\alpha/n}} \int_Q |(\Sigma g_i) - \pi| &\leqq c\, M(Ef - g_o)(x)\\ &\leqq c\,[M(Ef)(x) + M(f\chi_\Omega)(x)].\end{aligned}$$

If $|Q| < (\varepsilon_1/\sqrt{n})^n$ and $x \in Q$, then Q intersects at most N_o of the $U_i^{\varepsilon_1}$. We denote by $I := I(Q)$ the set of such indices i. For $i \in I(Q)$ let π_i denote a best $L_1(Q)$ approximation to g_i from $\mathbb{P}_{[\alpha]}$ and set $\pi := \sum_{i\in I} \pi_i$. Then, $Q \subset U_i$ and so

$$(11.20)\qquad \frac{1}{|Q|^{1+\alpha/n}} \int_Q |(\Sigma g_i) - \pi| \le \frac{1}{|Q|^{1+\alpha/n}} \sum_{i\in I} \int_Q |g_i - \pi_i|$$
$$\le \sum_{i\in I} (g_i)^{\#}_{\alpha}(x)\, \chi_{U_i}(x).$$

This, together with (11.19) gives

$$(11.21)\qquad (\Sigma g_i)^{\#}_{\alpha}(x) \le c\, [M(Ef)(x) + M(f\chi_\Omega)(x) + \sum_{i\in I} (g_i)^{\#}_{\alpha}(x)\chi_{U_i}(x)].$$

Concentrating on the last term, we notice that

$$(11.22)\qquad |\sum_{i\in I}(g_i)^{\#}_{\alpha}(x)\chi_{U_i}(x)|^p \le N_o^{p-1}\, \Sigma(g_i)^{\#}_{\alpha}(x)^p$$

because $\Sigma\chi_{U_i}(x) \le N_o$. Using this in (11.21) gives

$$(11.23)\qquad ||(\Sigma g_i)^{\#}_{\alpha}||^p_{L_p} \le c\, [||M(Ef)||^p_{L_p} + ||M(f\chi_\Omega)||^p_{L_p} + \Sigma\, ||(g_i)^{\#}_{\alpha}||^p_{L_p}].$$

But M is bounded on L_p for $p > 1$ and $E: L_p(\Omega) \to L_p(\mathbb{R}^n)$ and so

$$(11.24)\qquad ||M(Ef)||^p_{L_p} + ||M(f\chi_\Omega)||^p_{L_p} \le c\, ||f||^p_{L_p(\Omega)}$$

For each i, Lemma 11.3 (with $\Omega = \mathbb{R}^n$) and Theorem 10.5 give

$$||(g_i)^{\#}_{\alpha}||_{L_p} \le c\, ||E_i(\lambda_i f)||_{C^\alpha_p} \le c\, ||\lambda_i f||_{C^\alpha_p(\Omega_i)}.$$

This time applying Lemma 11.3 to $\lambda_i f$ with $U = U_i^{\varepsilon_1}$ and using the fact that $N_{\varepsilon_1}(U) \subset U_i$, we have

$$||(g_i)^{\#}_{\alpha}||^p_{L_p} \le c\, ||f||^p_{C^\alpha_p(U_i\cap\Omega_i)} \le c \int_{U_i\cap\Omega} (f^{\#}_{\alpha,\Omega} + |f|)^p$$

because $U_i \cap \Omega_i = U_i \cap \Omega$. Since each x appears in at most N_o U_i's, substituting this and (11.24) back into (11.23), gives

$$||(\Sigma g_i)^{\#}_{\alpha}||_{L_p} \le c\, [||f||_{L_p(\Omega)} + ||f^{\#}_{\alpha}||_{L_p(\Omega)}] \le c\, ||f||_{C^\alpha_p(\Omega)}.$$

Also as noted above

$$||\Sigma g_i||_{L_p} \le ||Ef||_{L_p} + ||f\chi_\Omega||_{L_p} \le c\, ||f||_{L_p(\Omega)}.$$

This completes the proof for $1 < p < \infty$.

For $p = \infty$, we use $\sum_{i\in I} (g_i)^{\#}_{\alpha}(x)\, \chi_{U_i}(x) \le N_o\, \Sigma(g_i)^{\#}_{\alpha}(x)$ in place of (11.22). Then, the same proof with L_∞ norms in place of L_p norms gives the desired result. For $p = 1$, we choose $(1+\frac{\alpha}{n})^{-1} < q < 1$ and use $f^{\#}_{\alpha,q}$ in place of $f^{\#}_{\alpha}$ and $M_q f$ in place of Mf with the same proof and the fact that $||h^{\#}_{\alpha,q}||_{L_1(O)} \leqq c\, ||h^{\#}_{\alpha}||_{L_1(O)}$ for any O with c independent of O (see Theorem (4.3)). □

Remarks.

i) The extension theorem holds for the spaces $\mathcal{C}^{\alpha}_p$, $1 \leqq p \leqq \infty$. When α is not an integer, this follows from the fact that $\mathcal{C}^{\alpha}_p = C^{\alpha}_p$. When α is an integer, it follows from the argument on page 192 of [15] and the Remark on Sobolev spaces at the end of §10. The space $\mathcal{C}^{k}_1$ must be handled separately using the techniques of this section.

ii) The extension operator E can easily be modified so that for a fixed k, E: $C^{\alpha}_p(\Omega) \to C^{\alpha}_p(\mathbb{R}^n)$, for all $\alpha < k$. Notice however that it is not a total extension operator in the sense of [15].

iii) The extension theorem holds for domains $\Omega \subset \mathbb{R}$ such that $\Omega = \bigcup_i I_i$ with the I_i intervals satisfying: $\operatorname{dist}(I_i, I_j) \geqq \varepsilon_o$, $i \neq j$ and $\ell(I_i) \geqq \varepsilon_o$. Here one simply works with a standard partition of unity rather than the more complicated partition used for $n > 1$.

We can now generalize the results of the previous sections which held for special domains to domains with minimally smooth boundary. Maximal functions based on admissable collections rather than cubes can be shown to give equivalent norms for $C^{\alpha}_p(\Omega)$.

The interpolation theorems of §8 hold for domains Ω with minimally smooth boundary. For example, it follows immediately from Theorem 11.4 together with Corollary 8.3 that $C^{\alpha}_p(\Omega)$ is an interpolation space for $C^{\alpha}_{p_o}(\Omega)$ and $C^{\alpha}_{p_1}(\Omega)$, $p_o < p < p_1$. Going further, one can prove in a similar way to Theorem 11.4 and the generalization of Lemma 11.2 that the interpolation results (8.10) and (8.19) hold.

We also have the following embeddings.

Corollary 11.5. If Ω is a domain with minimally smooth boundary, $0 < p \leqq q \leqq \infty$, and $0 \leqq \beta \leqq \alpha + n(\frac{1}{q}-\frac{1}{p})$, then we have the continuous embeddings

$$C_p^\alpha(\Omega) \to C_q^\beta(\Omega).$$

Proof. Let E be an extension operator for α and Ω. For any $\Omega \supset Q \ni x$ and $\pi \in \mathbb{P}_{[\alpha]}$,

$$\frac{1}{|Q|^{1+\beta/n}} \int_Q |f - \pi| \leqq \frac{1}{|Q|^{1+\beta/n}} \int_Q |Ef - \pi|$$

thus,

$$\|f\|_{C_q^\beta(\Omega)} \leqq \|Ef\|_{C_q^\beta(\mathbb{R}^n)}. \tag{11.25}$$

From Theorems 9.6 and 11.4,

$$\|Ef\|_{C_q^\beta(\mathbb{R}^n)} \leqq c\, \|Ef\|_{C_p^\alpha(\mathbb{R}^n)} \leqq c\, \|f\|_{C_p^\alpha(\Omega)}$$

which together with (11.25) proves the Corollary. □

We can also generalize the results of Theorem 7.1. Here, we use the fact that

$$(L_p(\Omega), W_p^k(\Omega))_{\theta/k,q} = B_p^{\theta,q}(\Omega). \tag{11.26}$$

This was proved for domains Ω which satisfy a uniform cone condition in [11].[b)]

Corollary 11.6. If Ω is a domain with minimally smooth boundary, then for $1 < p < \infty$, we have the continuous embeddings

$$B_p^{\alpha,p}(\Omega) \to C_p^\alpha(\Omega) \to B_p^{\alpha,\infty}(\Omega).$$

Proof. Let $k > \alpha$. For the right hand embedding, let E be the extension operator for k and Ω, then using Theorem 7.1 and the Remark ii), we have

$$\|f\|_{B_p^{\alpha,\infty}(\Omega)} \leqq \|Ef\|_{B_p^{\alpha,\infty}(\mathbb{R}^n)} \leqq c\, \|Ef\|_{C_p^\alpha(\mathbb{R}^n)} \leqq c\, \|f\|_{C_p^\alpha(\Omega)}.$$

---

b) Ibid. This condition is actually equivalent to requiring Ω to have a minimally smooth boundary.

For left hand embedding, we use the fact that E: $B_p^{\alpha,p}(\Omega) \to B_p^{\alpha,p}(\mathbb{R}^n)$ because of (11.26). Using Theorem 7.1, we have

$$\|f\|_{C_p^\alpha(\Omega)} \leq \|Ef\|_{C_p^\alpha(\mathbb{R}^n)} \leq c\, \|Ef\|_{B_p^{\alpha,p}(\mathbb{R}^n)} \leq c\, \|f\|_{B_p^{\alpha,p}(\Omega)} . \quad \square$$

§12. The case $0 < p < 1$

We want now to define spaces C_p^α and $\mathcal{C}_p^\alpha$ when $0 < p < 1$. We have purposefully postponed the discussion of this case in order to avoid certain technicalities which would only have obscured the development. As we shall see, many of the results of the previous sections hold for this range of p as well.

If $0 < p < 1$ and $\alpha > 0$, let $C_p^\alpha := C_p^\alpha(\Omega) := \{f \in L_p(\Omega) : f^\#_{\alpha,p} \in L_p(\Omega)\}$ and $\mathcal{C}_p^\alpha := \mathcal{C}_p^\alpha(\Omega) := \{f \in L_p(\Omega) : f^\flat_{\alpha,p} \in L_p(\Omega)\}$ and define

$$|f|_{C_p^\alpha} := \|f^\#_{\alpha,p}\|_{L_p} \qquad |f|_{\mathcal{C}_p^\alpha} := \|f^\flat_{\alpha,p}\|_{L_p}$$

$$\|f\|_{C_p^\alpha} := \|f\|_{L_p} + |f|_{C_p^\alpha} \qquad \|f\|_{\mathcal{C}_p^\alpha} := \|f\|_{L_p} + |f|_{\mathcal{C}_p^\alpha}$$

It follows that $d(f,g)_{C_p^\alpha} := \|f-g\|^p_{C_p^\alpha}$ is a metric on C_p^α and $d(f,g)_{\mathcal{C}_p^\alpha} := \|f-g\|^p_{\mathcal{C}_p^\alpha}$ is a metric on $\mathcal{C}_p^\alpha$.

These spaces are F-spaces with respect to their topologies. For example, the proof of the completeness of C_p^α is the same as in the case $p \geq 1$ described in Lemma 6.1. In this case, the inequality

$$h^\#_{\alpha,p}(x) \leq \varliminf_{m\to\infty} (h_m)^\#_{\alpha,p}(x)$$

whenever $h_m \to h$ in L_p follows from the fact that $P_Q h_m \to P_Q h$, which in turn is a consequence of the continuity of P_Q on L_p.

The definitions of C_p^α and $\mathcal{C}_p^\alpha$ for $0 < p < 1$ are consistent with the case $p \geq 1$. Indeed, as we have observed earlier, when $1 \leq p \leq \infty$, Theorem 4.3 shows that

$$f^\#_\alpha \leq f^\#_{\alpha,p} \leq M_\sigma(f^\#_\alpha) \qquad \sigma := \left(\frac{1}{p} + \frac{\alpha}{n}\right)^{-1} .$$

Since M_σ is bounded on L_p,

$$\|f^\#_\alpha\|_{L_p} \leq \|f^\#_{\alpha,p}\|_{L_p} \leq c\, \|f^\#_\alpha\|_{L_p}$$

and therefore C_p^α could have equivalently been defined as the set of $f \in L_p$ such that $f_{\alpha,p}^{\#} \in L_p$; in addition, $||f_{\alpha,p}^{\#}||_{L_p}$ is equivalent to $|f|_{C_p^\alpha}$.

Suppose now that $\Omega = \mathbb{R}^n$. We want to give embeddings between C_p^α, $0 < p < 1$, and other smoothness spaces. Recall that when $f \in L_p$, $\lim_{Q \downarrow \{x\}} P_Q f(x) = f(x)$, a.e. (Lemma 4.1), and (see (4.10))

(12.1) $$|P_Q f(x) - f(x)| \leqq c\,|Q|^{\alpha/n} f_{\alpha,p}^{\#}(x), \quad \text{a.e. } x \in Q.$$

Here $P_Q f$ a the best $L_p(Q)$ approximation to f from $\mathbb{P}_{[\alpha]}$. It follows from (12.1) that if $r > [\alpha]$,

$$\Delta_h^r\,(f,x) \leqq c\,h^\alpha \sum_{j=1}^{r} f_{\alpha,p}^{\#}(x + jh).$$

Raising both sides to the p-th power and integrating gives the continuous embeddings

(12.2) $$\mathcal{C}_p^\alpha \to C_p^\alpha \to B_p^{\alpha,\infty}$$

with $B_p^{\alpha,q}$ the Besov spaces as defined in §3.

The embeddings

(12.3) $$B_p^{\alpha,p} \to C_p^\alpha \quad , \quad \alpha > 0,$$

also hold for $0 < p < 1$ but their proof requires a litte more care. Let us first consider the case $0 < \alpha < 1$, where there is a simple proof that encompasses the main ideas of the general case. Using Corollary 5.4 and Remark (2.14) i), we have for $Q_\rho := [-\rho,\rho]^n$,

(12.4) $$f_{\alpha,p}^{b}(x) \leqq c \sup_{\rho>0} \frac{1}{\rho^\alpha} \Big(\frac{1}{\rho^n} \int_{Q_\rho} |f(x+s) - f(x)|^p ds\Big)^{1/p}$$
$$\leqq c \int_0^\infty \frac{1}{\rho^\alpha} \Big(\frac{1}{\rho^n} \int_{Q_\rho} |f(x+s) - f(x)|^p ds\Big)^{1/p} \frac{d\rho}{\rho}$$
$$\leqq c \sum_{j=-\infty}^{\infty} 2^{-j\alpha} \Big(2^{-jn} \int_{Q_{2^j}} |f(x+s) - f(x)|^p ds\Big)^{1/p}$$

because $\int_{Q_\rho}$ is increasing with ρ. Recall that for $0 < p < 1$, $(\Sigma\lambda_j)^p \leqq \Sigma(\lambda_j)^p$. Hence (12.4) gives

$$(12.5)\qquad \int_{\mathbb{R}^n} |f^{\flat}_{\alpha,p}|^p \le c \sum_{j=-\infty}^{\infty} 2^{-j\alpha p} \left(2^{-jn} \int_{Q_{2^j}} \int_{\mathbb{R}^n} |f(x+s) - f(x)|^p dx ds\right)$$
$$\le c \int_0^\infty [\rho^{-\alpha}\, \omega(f,\rho)_p]^p \frac{d\rho}{\rho}$$

and (12.3) readily follows since $f^{\flat}_{\alpha,p} = f^{\#}_{\alpha,p}$ for $0 < \alpha < 1$.

The case $\alpha \geqq 1$ is more involved. Let Q be a cube in $\mathbb{R}^n$ with the same notation as above, we define for $\tau > 0$,

$$(12.6)\qquad w_r(f,\tau)_{L_p(Q)} := \left(\tau^{-n} \int_Q \int_{Q_\tau} |\Delta^r_s(f,x)|^p ds dx\right)^{1/p} .$$

For our next lemma, we fix $Q = Q_0$ as the unit cube in $\mathbb{R}^n$ and define S_α as the set of functions in $L_p(\mathbb{R}^n)$ such that

$$||f||_{L_p(a_r Q)} + \sup_{\tau \le 1} \tau^{-\alpha}\, w_r(f,\tau)_{L_p(a_r Q)} \leqq 1$$

where $r := [\alpha] + 1$ and $a_j := 1 + \ldots + j$ for each postive integer j.

<u>Lemma 12.1</u>. For each $\alpha > 0$, S_α is a compact subset of $L_p(Q)$.

<u>Proof</u>. Consider first the case $0 < \alpha < 1$. If m is any postive integer, take $\tau = 1/m$ and subdivide Q into m^n cubes (Q_j) which have pairwise disjoint interiors and each Q_j has side length τ. If $f \in S_\alpha$,

$$\sum_j \int_{Q_j} \int_{Q_\tau} |f(x+s) - f(x)|^p ds dx \leqq \tau^{p\alpha+n}.$$

It follows that for each j there is a constant c_j (for example $c_j = f(x_j)$ with appropriately chosen $x_j \in Q_j$) such that the function $\phi_\tau := \sum c_j \chi_{Q_j}$ satisfies

$$\int_Q |f - \phi_\tau|^p \leqq \tau^{p\alpha+n} .$$

It is clear that the c_j can be chosen as best constants of approximation to f in $L_p(Q_j)$ and therefore we also have

$$\int_Q |\phi_\tau|^p \leqq \int_Q |f - \phi_\tau|^p + \int_Q |f|^p \leqq 2 \int_Q |f|^p.$$

Since the span $\{\chi_{Q_j}\}$ is a finite dimensional space and τ can be made arbitrarily small, the set S_α is compact.

The case $\alpha \geqq 1$ can be reduced to the case just proved. We start with the identity [19, p. 105]

$$\Delta_s^k(f,x) = 2^{-k} [\Delta_{2s}^k(f,x) - \sum_{j=0}^{k-1} \sum_{i=j+1}^{k} \binom{k}{i} \Delta_s^{k+1}(f,x+js)] .$$

With the abbreviated notation $w_j(\tau) := w_j(f,\tau)_{L_p(a_jQ)}$, we have for $\tau < 1$

$$(12.7) \qquad w_k(\tau)^p \leqq 2^{-kp} w_k(2\tau)^p + c\, w_{k+1}(\tau)^p.$$

Since $\tau^n w_k(\tau)^p$ is increasing with τ and $w_k(1) \leqq c\, ||f||_{L_p(a_{k+1}Q)}$, a repeated application of (12.7) gives

$$(12.8) \qquad w_k(\tau)^p \leqq c\, \tau^{kp} [\int_\tau^1 t^{-kp} w_{k+1}(t)^p \frac{dt}{t} + ||f||_{L_p(a_{k+1}Q)}^p]$$

with c depending only on k and p.

Now suppose $f \in S_\alpha$ with $r-1 \leqq \alpha < r$. Let $r-2 \leqq \beta < r-1$ and use (12.8) with $k = r-1$ to find

$$w_k(\tau)^p \leqq c\, [\tau^{\beta p} + \tau^{kp} ||f||_{L_p(a_{k+1}Q)}^p], \qquad \tau \leqq 1.$$

Hence for an appropriate constant λ, we have $\lambda S_\alpha \subset S_\beta$. Repeated application of this result shows that $\lambda S_\alpha \subset S_{1/2}$ for an appropriate λ. Since $S_{1/2}$ is compact and S_α is closed, we have S_α compact. □

Lemma 12.2. Let $\alpha > 0$; $p > 0$, and $r = [\alpha] + 1$. If $f \in L_p(\mathbb{R}^n)$, then for each cube Q of side length ρ there is a polynomial $\pi_Q \in \mathbb{P}_{r-1}$ such that

$$(12.9) \qquad ||f-\pi_Q||_{L_p(Q)} \leqq c\, \rho^\alpha \sup_{\tau \leqq \rho} \tau^{-\alpha} w_r(f,\tau)_{L_p(a_rQ)}$$

with $a_r := \frac{1}{2}r(r+1)$.

Proof. The proof is similar to the proofs of Theorem 3.4 and 3.5. It is enough to prove (12.9) for the unit cube since the case of general cubes then follows by scaling. Now, suppose (12.9) does not hold for $Q = Q_0$. It follows that there is a sequence of functions (f_m) such that

$$(12.10) \qquad \text{i)} \quad \operatorname{dist}(f_m, \mathbb{P}_{r-1})_{L_p(Q)} = ||f_m||_{L_p(Q)}^p = 1$$

$$\text{ii)} \quad \sup_{\tau \leqq 1} \tau^{-\alpha} w_r(f_m,\tau)_{L_p(a_rQ)} \to 0 \qquad m \to \infty.$$

By Lemma 12.1, (f_m) is precompact in $L_p(Q)$. Hence, we can also assume that $f_m \to f$ in $L_p(Q)$ for some f. For each $0 < \tau < 1$, we have from (12.10) ii),

$$(12.11) \qquad \int_{a_rQ} \int_{Q_\tau} |\Delta_s^r(f,x)|^p ds dx \leqq \lim_{m\to\infty} \int_{a_rQ} \int_{Q_\tau} |\Delta_s^r(f_m,x)|^p ds dx = 0.$$

Hence it follows that $f = P$ a.e. for some $P \in \mathbb{P}_{r-1}$. On the other hand, (12.10) i) shows that $\operatorname{dist}(f, \mathbb{P}_{r-1}) = 1$ which is the desired contradition. □

Actually when $p < 1$ in the above proof, it may not be so clear that (12.11) implies that $f = P$ a.e. with $P \in \mathbb{P}_{r-1}$. However, this can be proved by induction on r. The case $r = 1$ is obvious. If $r > 1$ and (12.11) holds, then for all sufficiently small s we have $\Delta_s^r(f,x) = 0$ a.e. x. Now we can write (see [11][c)]) a general difference $\Delta_{t_1} \ldots \Delta_{t_r}$ in terms of pure differences $\{\Delta_{t_i'}^r\}$; hence for all sufficiently small $(t_1,\ldots t_r)$, $\Delta_{t_1} \ldots \Delta_{t_r}(f,x) = 0$ a.e. in x. Our induction hypothesis then gives that for small t, $\Delta_t(f,x)$ is a.e. a polynomial in $\mathbb{P}_{r-2}$, and therefore it is not difficult to see that

$$(12.12) \qquad f(x+t) = f(x) + \sum_{|\nu|\leqq r-2} a_\nu(t)x^\nu \quad \text{a.e. } x$$

with a_ν continuous. Applying now an arbitrary r-th difference Δ_s^r to (12.12) as a function of t gives that each $a_\nu(t)$ is a polynomial of degree at most $r - 1$. Taking finally $x = x_0$ such that both (4.7) and (12.12) hold shows that $f = P$ a.e. with $P \in \mathbb{P}_{r-1}$.

The following are embedding theorems for Besov spaces and C_p^α when $p < 1$.

<u>Theorem 12.3</u>. If $\alpha, p > 0$, we have the continuous embeddings

$$B_p^{\alpha,p}(\mathbb{R}^n) \to C_p^\alpha(\mathbb{R}^n) \to B_p^{\alpha,\infty}(\mathbb{R}^n).$$

---

c) See also Theorem 1 in B. Baishanski, "The asymptotic behavior of the n-th order difference", Enseignement Mathematique <u>15</u> (1969), 29-41.

Proof. We have shown the right hand embedding in (12.2). The left hand embedding has been shown for $0 < \alpha < 1$ and all $p > 0$ and also for all $\alpha > 0$ provided $p \geqq 1$. Consider now the case $\alpha > 0$; $0 < p < 1$. Choose any $r-2 \leqq \beta < r-1$ (recall $r = [\alpha] + 1$) and let

$$\phi(\rho,x) := \sup_{\tau\leq\rho} \tau^{-\beta}\, w_r(f,\tau)_{L_p(x+a_rQ_\rho)}.$$

From Lemma 12.2 and Remark (2.14) i), we have

$$f^{\#}_{\alpha,p}(x) \leqq c \sup_{\rho>0} \rho^{(\beta-\alpha-n/p)}\, \phi(\rho,x) \leqq c \int_0^\infty \rho^{(\beta-\alpha-n/p)}\, \phi(\rho,x)\frac{d\rho}{\rho}.$$

Integrating this inequality gives (cf. (12.4-5))

$$(12.13) \qquad \int_{\mathbb{R}^n} |f^{\#}_{\alpha,p}|^p \leqq c \int_0^\infty \rho^{(\beta-\alpha)p}\, (\rho^{-n} \int_{\mathbb{R}^n} \phi(\rho,x)^p dx)\frac{d\rho}{\rho}.$$

Now,

$$\int_{\mathbb{R}^n} \phi(\rho,x)^p\, \frac{dx}{\rho} = \int_{\mathbb{R}^n} (\sup_{\tau\leq\rho} \tau^{-\beta p-n} \int_{a_rQ_\rho} \int_{Q_\tau} |\Delta^r_s(f,y-x)|^p ds dy) dx$$

$$\leqq c \int_{\mathbb{R}^n} \int_0^\rho (\tau^{-\beta p-n} \int_{a_rQ_\rho} \int_{Q_\tau} |\Delta^r_s(f,y-x)|^p ds dy)\, \frac{d\tau}{\tau} dx$$

$$\leqq c\, \rho^n \int_0^\rho \tau^{-\beta p}\, \omega_r(f,\tau)^p_p\, \frac{d\tau}{\tau}$$

where we used the fact that $\omega_r(f,\sqrt{n}\tau)_p \leqq c\, \omega_r(f,\tau)_p$. Returning to (12.13), we have from Hardy's inequality

$$\int_{\mathbb{R}^n} |f^{\#}_{\alpha,p}|^p \leqq c \int_0^\infty \rho^{(\beta-\alpha)p} \int_0^\rho \tau^{-\beta p}\, \omega_r(f,\tau)^p_p\, \frac{d\tau}{\tau}\, \frac{d\rho}{\rho}$$

$$\leqq c \int_0^\infty \rho^{-\alpha p}\, \omega_r(f,\rho)^p_p\, \frac{d\rho}{\rho}$$

as desired. □

The spaces C^α_p, $0 < p \leqq \infty$, form an interpolation scale as is contained in the following generalization of Theorem 8.2.

Theorem 12.4. If $\alpha > 0$ and $0 < p < \infty$,

$$K(f,t,C^\alpha_p,C^\alpha_\infty) \approx (\int_0^{t^p} [f^* + f^{\#*}_{\alpha,p}]^p)^{1/p}, \qquad t > 0$$

$$K(f,t,\mathcal{C}^\alpha_p,\mathcal{C}^\alpha_\infty) \approx (\int_0^{t^p} [f^* + f^{b*}_{\alpha,p}]^p)^{1/p}, \qquad t > 0.$$

In addition, if $1/r = (1-\theta)/p + \theta/q$ with $0 < \theta < 1$, then

$$(C_p^\alpha, C_q^\alpha)_{\theta,r} = C_r^\alpha \ ; \qquad (\mathcal{C}_p^\alpha, \mathcal{C}_q^\alpha)_{\theta,r} = \mathcal{C}_r^\alpha \ .$$

Proof. The proof of this theorem is much the same as the proof of the case $p = 1$ given in §8. We indicate only the basic changes that have to be made. The projections P_Q are replaced by $\mathcal{P}_Q$ so that $\mathcal{P}_Q f$ is a best $L_p(Q)$ approximant to f of degree $[\alpha]$ in the case of $f^\#_{\alpha,p}$ and of degree (α) in the case of $f^b_{\alpha,p}$. The extension g of Lemma 8.1 is now defined as

$$g(x) := \begin{cases} f(x), & x \in F \\ \sum_j \mathcal{P}_{Q_j} f(x)\phi_j^*(x), & x \in F^c \end{cases} .$$

The role of the Hardy-Littlewood maximal operator M is replaced by M_p and of course f_α is replaced by $f_{\alpha,p}$ which is either $f^\#_{\alpha,p}$ or $f^b_{\alpha,p}$ as appropriate. Lemma 8.1 then reads: If $M_p f \leqq m_0$ and $f_{\alpha,p} \leqq m_1$ on F then i) $g = f$ on F; ii) $g \leqq c\, m_0$ on $\mathbb{R}^n$; and iii) $g_{\alpha,p} \leqq c\, m_1$ on $\mathbb{R}^n$.

The proofs of Lemma 8.1 and Theorem 8.2 require estimates for $\mathcal{P}_Q f - \mathcal{P}_{Q^*} f$ when $Q^* \subset Q$. We have from (5.5)

$$(12.14) \qquad \|D^\nu(\mathcal{P}_Q f - \mathcal{P}_{Q^*} f)\|_{L_\infty(Q^*)} \leqq c\, |Q|^{(\alpha-|\nu|)/n} \inf_{u \in Q^*} f_{\alpha,p}(u).$$

This is used in (8.5) with $\nu = 0$ and in the derivation of (8.8) and (8.9).

In the proof of Theorem 8.2, the set E is now defined by

$$E := \{f^\#_{\alpha,p} > f^{\#*}_{\alpha,p}(t^p)\} \cup \{M_p f > (M_p f)^*(t^p)\}$$

so that $|E| \leqq c\, t^p$. Then, (8.12) becomes

$$t\, \|g\|_{C^\alpha_\infty} \leqq c\, (\textstyle\int_0^{t^p} [f^* + f^{\#*}_{\alpha,p}]^p)^{1/p}.$$

On $\tilde{E}$, the estimate (8.15) becomes

$$\int_{\tilde{E}} [h^\#_{\alpha,p}]^p \leqq c \int_0^{t^p} [f^{\#*}_{\alpha,p}]^p$$

and on $\tilde{F}$ (8.17) becomes,

$$h^\#_{\alpha,p}(x) \leqq c\, f^{\#*}_{\alpha,p}(t^p) \left(\sum_j \frac{|Q_j|^{1+\alpha p/n}}{\operatorname{dist}(x,Q_j)^{n+\alpha p}} \right)^{1/p}, \qquad x \in \tilde{F}$$

and so

$$\int_{\mathbb{R}^n} [h^{\#}_{\alpha,p}]^p \leqq c \sum_j |Q_j| [f^{\#*}_{\alpha,p}(t^p)]^p \leqq c\ t^p\ [f^{\#*}_{\alpha,p}(t^p)]^p \leqq c \int_0^{t^p} [f^{\#*}_{\alpha,p}]^p .$$

This combines with the above inequality for g to give

$$K(f,t,C^{\alpha}_p,C^{\alpha}_{\infty}) \leqq ||h||_{C^{\alpha}_p} + t\ ||g||_{C^{\alpha}_{\infty}}$$

$$\leqq c\ (\int_0^{t^p} [f^* + f^{\#*}_{\alpha,p}]^p)^{1/p}.$$

This inequality can be reversed by using the subadditivity of

$$\int_0^{t^p} [(f^{\#*}_{\alpha,p})^p + (f^*)^p]. \quad \square$$

Remark: One can also characterize the K functional for the pair $(C^0_p,C^0_{\infty}) = (L_p,\mathrm{BMO})$, see [2].

The embedding theorems of §9 also hold when $p < 1$.

Theorem 12.5. If $0 < p \leqq q \leqq \infty$; $0 \leqq \beta \leqq \alpha + n/p - n/q$, then $C^{\alpha}_p \to C^{\beta}_q$.

Proof. This is the extension of Theorem 9.6 to $p < 1$ with essentially the same proof. To begin with, let us note that Lemma 6.6 remains valid for $p < 1$. Indeed the same argument given in the proof of this lemma shows that for any $r > 0$,

$$f^{\#}_{\beta,r}(x) \leqq c\ [M_r f(x)]^{1-\theta}\ [f^{\#}_{\alpha,r}(x)]^{\theta} \leqq c\ [M_r f(x) + f^{\#}_{\alpha,r}(x)]$$

with $\theta := \beta/\alpha$. We take $(\frac{1}{p} + \frac{\beta}{n})^{-1} < r < p$ and use Theorem 4.3 to find

$$||f^{\#}_{\beta,p}||_{L_p} \leqq c\ ||f^{\#}_{\beta,r}||_{L_p} \leqq c\ [||f||_{L_p} + ||f^{\#}_{\alpha,p}||_{L_p}]. \tag{12.15}$$

Now suppose $\beta = \alpha + n/p - n/q$. Let $P_Q f$ denote a best $L_q(Q)$ approximation to f of degree $[\alpha]$. From Lemma 4.4,

$$f^{\#}_{\beta,p}(x) \leqq c \sup_{Q \ni x} \frac{1}{|Q|^{\beta/n}} (\frac{1}{|Q|} \int_Q |f - P_Q f|^p)^{1/p}$$

$$\leqq c \sup_{Q \ni x} (|Q|^{(\alpha-\beta)/n} \inf_{u \in Q} f^{\#}_{\alpha,p}(u))$$

$$\leqq c\ \{I_{\gamma}\ [(f^{\#}_{\alpha,p})^r](x)\}^{1/r}$$

with $\gamma := (\alpha-\beta)r$ and r chosen so that $0 < r < \min\ (n/(\alpha-\beta),p)$.

As in Theorem 9.3, the mapping properties of I_γ and Theorem 4.3 give

(12.16) $$|f|_{C_q^\beta} \leqq c\ \|f^\#_{\beta,p}\|_{L_q} \leqq c\ |f|_{C_p^\alpha}$$

provided $q < \infty$. This inequality also holds for $q = \infty$ as can be seen from the argument in Corollary 9.4 with $f^\#_{\beta,p}$ in place of $f^\#_\beta$ and $f^\#_{\alpha,p}$ in place of $f^\#_\alpha$.

In view of (12.16), to complete the case $\beta = \alpha + n/p - n/q$ we are left with showing that $C_p^\alpha \to L_q$. For this purpose we note that Theorem 6.8 can be extended to the case $p \leqq 1$ by replacing $f^\#_0$ by $f^\#_{0,r}$ with $0 < r < p$. If $1/q_o := 1/p - \alpha/n$ is nonnegative, then it follows from (12.16) that

$$\|f\|_{L_{q_o}} \leqq c\ |f|_{C^o_{q_o}} \leqq c\ \|f\|_{C_p^\alpha}$$

and hence $C_p^\alpha \to L_{q_o} \cap L_p \to L_q$. If $1/p - \alpha/n$ is negative, we use an analogue of Theorem 9.1. Namely, (9.2) holds with $f^\#_\alpha$ replaced by $f^\#_{\alpha,p}$ with the same proof. Arguing as in Theorem 9.6, we find

$$\|f\|_C \leqq c\ \|f\|_{C_p^\alpha}$$

and hence $f \in C \cap L_p \subset L_q$. Thus, we have completed the case $\beta = \alpha + n/p - n/q$.

If $\beta < \alpha + n/p - n/q$, then the embedding $C_p^\alpha \to C_q^\beta$ follows from (12.15) and the case $\beta = \alpha + n/p - n/q$ proved above. □

The extension theorems of §10 and §11 hold for $p < 1$ as well. In the definition of the extension operator E for special Lipschitz domains the polynomial $P_{Q_k^s} f$ is replaced by $\mathcal{P}_{Q_k^s} f$ a polynomial of best L_p approximation to f on Q_k^s. Again let $E^\#_\alpha$ denote the extension operator when polynomials of degree $[\alpha]$ are used and $E^\flat_\alpha$ the operator when polynomials of degree (α) are used. We then have the following analogue of Theorem 10.5.

<u>Theorem 12.6</u>. If Ω is a special Lipschitz domain and $p > 0$ then the extension operator $E^\#_\alpha$ is bounded from $C_p^\alpha(\Omega)$ into $C_p^\alpha(\mathbb{R}^n)$. Similarly $E^\flat_\alpha$ is bounded from $\mathcal{C}_p^\alpha(\Omega)$ into $\mathcal{C}_p^\alpha(\mathbb{R}^n)$.

Proof. In the proof, the obvious changes are made. We replace $f_\alpha^\#$ by $f_{\alpha,p}^\#$ and L_1 estimates by L_p estimates. □

We also have the analogue of Theorem 11.4.

Theorem 12.7. If Ω is a domain with minimally smooth boundary and $\alpha,p > 0$, there is an extension operator E and a constant $c > 0$ such that

$$||Ef||_{C_p^\alpha(\mathbb{R}^n)} \leqq c\, ||f||_{C_p^\alpha(\Omega)} .$$

Proof. Lemmas 11.1 and 11.2 hold for $p < 1$ with no essential change in the proof. In Lemma 11.3, we use $f_{\alpha,q}^\#$ with $(\frac{\alpha}{n} + \frac{1}{p})^{-1} < q < p$ in place of $f_\alpha^\#$ and analogous maximal functions ${}_jf_{\alpha,q}$ in place of ${}_jf_\alpha$. Also the Hardy-Littlewood maximal function M is replaced by M_q. These changes are used then in the proof of Theorem 11.4. □

Using Theorem 12.7, various results for $\mathbb{R}^n$ can be proven for domains Ω with minimally smooth boundaries. Most notably the embeddings of Theorem 12.3 follow for these Ω and it still holds that $C_p^\alpha(\Omega)$ is an interpolation space between $C_{p_o}^\alpha(\Omega)$ and $C_{p_1}^\alpha(\Omega)$ provided $0 < p_o < p < p_1 \leqq \infty$.

References

1. R. A. Adams, Sobolev Spaces, Academic Press, New York, 1975.

2. C. Bennett and R. Sharpley, "Weak type inequalities for H^p and BMO", Proc. Symp. in Pure Math. 35 (I) (1979), 201-229.

3. P. L. Butzer and H. Berens, Semi-Groups of Operators and Approximation, Springer Verlag, New York, 1967.

4. A. P. Calderón, "Lebesgue spaces of differentiable functions and distributions", Proc. Symp. in Pure Math. 4 (1961), 33-49.

5. A. P. Calderón, "Estimates for singular integral operators in terms of maximal functions", Studia Math. 44 (1972), 167-186.

6. A. P. Calderón and R. Scott, "Sobolev type inequalities for $p > 0$", Studia Math. 62 (1978), 75-92.

7. W. Dahmen, R. DeVore, and K. Scherer, "Multidimensional spline approximation", SIAM J. Numer. Anal. 17 (1980), 380-402.

8. R. DeVore and K. Scherer, "Interpolation of linear operators on Sobolev spaces", Ann. of Math. 109 (1979), 583-599.

9. C. Fefferman and E. M. Stein, "H^p spaces of several variables", Acta Math. 129 (1972), 137-193.

10. F. John and L. Nirenberg, "On functions of bounded mean oscillation", Comm. Pure Appl. Math 14 (1961), 415-426.

11. H. Johnen and K. Scherer, "On the equivalance of the K-functional and moduli of continuity and some applications", in Constructive Theory of Functions of Several Variables, Proc. Conf. Oberwolfach 1976, Lecture Notes in Mathematics No. 571, p. 119-140, Spring-Verlag, Berlin/New York, 1976.

12. P. W. Jones, "Quasiconformal mappings and extendability of functions in Sobolev spaces", preprint.

13. P. Krée, "Interpolation d'espaces qui ne sont ni normés, ni complets. Applications", Ann. Inst. Fourier 17 (1967), 137-174.

14. S. L. Sobolev, Applications of Functional Analysis in Mathematical Physics, Transl. Math. Mono. No. 7, American Mathematical Society, Providence, RI, 1963.

15. E. M. Stein, Singular Integrals and Differentiability Properties of Functions, Princeton University Press, Princeton, N.J., 1970.

16. E. M. Stein, "The differentiability of functions in $\mathbb{R}^n$", Ann. of Math. 113 (1981), 383-385.

17. E. M. Stein and G. Weiss, Introduction to Harmonic Analysis on Euclidean Spaces, Princeton University Press, Princeton, N.J., 1971.

18. M. Taibleson and G. Weiss, preprint.

19. A. F. Timan, Theory of Approximation of Functions of a Real Variable, Pergamon Press, Oxford, 1963.

20. H. Whitney, "Analytic extensions of differentiable functions defined in closed sets", Trans. Amer. Math. Soc. 36 (1934), 63-89.

General instructions to authors for
PREPARING REPRODUCTION COPY FOR MEMOIRS

For more detailed instructions send for AMS booklet, "A Guide for Authors of Memoirs." Write to Editorial Offices, American Mathematical Society, P. O. Box 6248, Providence, R. I. 02940.

MEMOIRS are printed by photo-offset from camera copy fully prepared by the author. This means that, except for a reduction in size of 20 to 30%, the finished book will look exactly like the copy submitted. Thus the author will want to use a good quality typewriter with a new, medium-inked black ribbon, and submit clean copy on the appropriate model paper.

Model Paper, provided at no cost by the AMS, is paper marked with blue lines that confine the copy to the appropriate size. Author should specify, when ordering, whether typewriter to be used has PICA-size (10 characters to the inch) or ELITE-size type (12 characters to the inch).

Line Spacing – For best appearance, and economy, a typewriter equipped with a half-space ratchet – 12 notches to the inch – should be used. (This may be purchased and attached at small cost.) Three notches make the desired spacing, which is equivalent to 1-1/2 ordinary single spaces. Where copy has a great many subscripts and superscripts, however, double spacing should be used.

Special Characters may be filled in carefully freehand, using dense black ink, or INSTANT ("rub-on") LETTERING may be used. AMS has a sheet of several hundred most-used symbols and letters which may be purchased for $5.

Diagrams may be drawn in black ink either directly on the model sheet, or on a separate sheet and pasted with rubber cement into spaces left for them in the text. Ballpoint pen is *not* acceptable.

Page Headings (Running Heads) should be centered, in CAPITAL LETTERS (preferably), at the top of the page – just above the blue line and touching it.

LEFT-hand, EVEN-numbered pages should be headed with the AUTHOR'S NAME;
RIGHT-hand, ODD-numbered pages should be headed with the TITLE of the paper (in shortened form if necessary).
Exceptions: PAGE 1 and any other page that carries a display title require NO RUNNING HEADS.

Page Numbers should be at the top of the page, on the same line with the running heads.

LEFT-hand, EVEN numbers – flush with left margin;
RIGHT-hand, ODD numbers – flush with right margin.
Exceptions: PAGE 1 and any other page that carries a display title should have page number, centered below the text, on blue line provided.

FRONT MATTER PAGES should be numbered with Roman numerals (lower case), positioned below text in same manner as described above.

MEMOIRS FORMAT

**It is suggested that the material be arranged in pages as indicated below.
Note: Starred items (*) are requirements of publication.**

Front Matter (first pages in book, preceding main body of text).

Page i – *Title, *Author's name.

Page iii – Table of contents.

Page iv – *Abstract (at least 1 sentence and at most 300 words).

*1980 Mathematics Subject Classifications represent the primary and secondary subjects of the paper. For the classification scheme, see Annual Subject Indexes of MATHEMATICAL REVIEWS beginning in December 1978.

Key words and phrases, if desired. (A list which covers the content of the paper adequately enough to be useful for an information retrieval system.)

Page v, etc. – Preface, introduction, or any other matter not belonging in body of text.

Page 1 – Chapter Title (dropped 1 inch from top line, and centered).
Beginning of Text.
Footnotes: *Received by the editor date.
Support information – grants, credits, etc.

Last Page (at bottom) – Author's affiliation.

ABCDEFGHIJ–AMS–8987654

Number 294

Catherine L. Olsen

Index theory in von Neumann algebras

Memoirs
of the American Mathematical Society

Providence · Rhode Island · USA

January 1984 · Volume 47 · Number 294 (end of volume) · ISSN 0065-9266

Memoirs of the American Mathematical Society
Number 294

Catherine L. Olsen

Index theory in von Neumann algebras

Published by the
AMERICAN MATHEMATICAL SOCIETY
Providence, Rhode Island, USA

January 1984 · Volume 47 · Number 294 (end of volume)

MEMOIRS of the American Mathematical Society

This journal is designed particularly for long research papers (and groups of cognate papers) in pure and applied mathematics. It includes, in general, longer papers than those in the TRANSACTIONS.

MEMOIRS are printed by photo-offset from camera-ready copy fully prepared by the authors. Prospective authors are encouraged to request booklet giving detailed instructions regarding reproduction copy. Write to Editorial Office, American Mathematical Society, P.O. Box 6248, Providence, Rhode Island 02940. For general instructions, see last page of Memoir.

SUBSCRIPTION INFORMATION. The 1984 subscription begins with Number 289 and consists of six mailings, each containing one or more numbers. Subscription prices for 1984 are $148 list; $74 member. A late charge of 10% of the subscription price will be imposed upon orders received from nonmembers after January 1 of the subscription year. Subscribers outside the United States and India must pay a postage surcharge of $10; subscribers in India must pay a postage surcharge of $15. Each number may be ordered separately; *please specify number* when ordering an individual number. For prices and titles of recently released numbers, refer to the New Publications sections of the NOTICES of the American Mathematical Society.

BACK NUMBER INFORMATION. For back issues see the AMS Catalogue of Publications.

TRANSACTIONS of the American Mathematical Society

This journal consists of shorter tracts which are of the same general character as the papers published in the MEMOIRS. The editorial committee is identical with that for the MEMOIRS so that papers intended for publication in this series should be addressed to one of the editors listed above.

Subscriptions and orders for publications of the American Mathematical Society should be addressed to American Mathematical Society, P. O. Box 1571, Annex Station, Providence, R. I. 02901. *All orders must be accompanied by payment.* Other correspondence should be addressed to P. O. Box 6248, Providence, R. I. 02940.

MEMOIRS of the American Mathematical Society (ISSN 0065-9266) is published bimonthly (each volume consisting usually of more than one number) by the American Mathematical Society at 201 Charles Street, Providence, Rhode Island 02904. Second Class postage paid at Providence, Rhode Island 02940. Postmaster: Send address changes to Memoirs of the American Mathematical Society, American Mathematical Society, P. O. Box 6248, Providence, RI 02940.

TABLE OF CONTENTS

ABSTRACT

The object of this paper is to define a natural analytic index function on an arbitrary von Neumann algebra relative to an arbitrary ideal. This index map enables us to develop a complete Fredholm and semi-Fredholm theory in this setting which is parallel to classical Fredholm and semi-Fredholm theory. We obtain a representation of the index group for the algebra and the given ideal as a group of continuous functions on the maximal ideal space of the center, or as a quotient group of such functions. The largest possible domain of continuity for an index map is precisely determined, and the distance from an arbitrary element of the algebra to each semi-Fredholm component is computed. The relevance of our results to the K-theory of C^*-algebras is briefly discussed.

Mathematics subject classification (1980). Primary 46L10, 47D25. Secondary 47C15, 47A53.

Key words and phrases. Fredholm elements, closed ideal in a von Neumann algebra, dimension function, relatively compact, index group, index map, semi-Fredholm component.

Library of Congress Cataloging in Publication Data

Olsen, Catherine L. (Catherine Louise), 1942-
Index theory in von Neumann algebras.

(Memoirs of the American Mathematical Society, ISSN 0065-9266 ; no. 294)
"January 1984, volume 47, number 294."
Bibliography: p.
1. Von Neumann algebras. 2. Analytic functions. 3. Fredholm operators. I. Title. II. Series.
QA3.A57 no. 294 [QA326] 510s [512'.55] 83-22519
ISBN 0-8218-2295-0

INDEX THEORY IN VON NEUMANN ALGEBRAS

1. Introduction.

The object of this paper is to define a natural analytic index function on an arbitrary von Neumann algebra relative to an arbitrary ideal. This index map enables us to develop a complete Fredholm and semi-Fredholm theory in this setting which is parallel to classical Fredholm and semi-Fredholm theory. We obtain a representation of the index group for the algebra and the given ideal as a group of continuous functions on the maximal ideal space of the center, or as a quotient group of such functions. The largest possible domain of continuity for an index map is precisely determined, and the distance from an arbitrary element of the algebra to each semi-Fredholm component is computed. The relevance of our results to the K-theory of C^*-algebras is briefly discussed at the end of this section.

Recall that for a separable Hilbert space $\mathcal{H}$, an operator T belonging to the algebra $\mathcal{B}(\mathcal{H})$ of all bounded linear operators on $\mathcal{H}$ is Fredholm if it has closed range and if the subspaces kernel T and kernel T^* are both finite-dimensional. If $\mathcal{K}$ denotes the ideal of compact operators in $\mathcal{B}(\mathcal{H})$ and $\pi: \mathcal{B}(\mathcal{H}) \to \mathcal{B}(\mathcal{H})/\mathcal{K}$ is the quotient map onto the C^*-quotient (the Calkin algebra) then F. V. Atkinson's theorem asserts that T is Fredholm if and only if $\pi(T)$ is invertible in $\mathcal{B}(\mathcal{H})/\mathcal{K}$ [1]. For a Fredholm operator T, the classical index is the integer $\text{index}(T) = \dim \ker T - \dim \ker T^*$. The index is a homomorphism of the multiplicative semigroup of Fredholm operators onto the additive group $\mathbb{Z}$ of integers. Moreover, the index is invariant under compact perturbations, and two Fredholm operators have the same index if and only if they belong to the same connected component of the open set of Fredholm operators [1]. It follows that the index induces an isomorphism of the group of connected components of the invertible group of $\mathcal{B}(\mathcal{H})/\mathcal{K}$ onto $\mathbb{Z}$.

Note that the compact operators are the unique nontrivial closed two-sided ideal in $\mathcal{B}(\mathcal{H})$, when $\mathcal{H}$ is separable. An arbitrary von Neumann algebra $\mathcal{A}$, acting on a perhaps nonseparable space, however, may have many

Received by the editors March 29, 1979

This research was supported in part by a grant from the National Science Foundation.

nontrivial closed two-sided ideals, and we may seek to define an index relative to each of them. We use the following definition of Fredholm elements of $\mathcal{A}$: for any ideal $\mathcal{J}$ in $\mathcal{A}$ an element A in $\mathcal{A}$ is <u>Fredholm</u> (relative to $\mathcal{J}$) if $\pi(A)$ is invertible in $\mathcal{A}/\mathcal{J}$, where $\pi: \mathcal{A} \to \mathcal{A}/\mathcal{J}$ is the quotient map. Although the range of such a Fredholm element need not be closed, there is a natural analog for the classical theorem of Atkinson described above: A is Fredholm for $\mathcal{J}$ if the orthogonal projections onto ker A and ker A^* both belong to $\mathcal{J}$, and if there is a projection E in $\mathcal{J}$ such that the range of A contains the range of I - F .

To define our analog to the classical index, we need a notion of the dimension of a projection in an arbitrary von Neumann algebra, and such a notion has been provided by J. Tomiyama [32]. If Z is the center of $\mathcal{A}$, then Z is an abelian von Neumann algebra, its maximal ideal space Ω is hyperstonean, and $Z \simeq C(\Omega)$. To each projection E in $\mathcal{A}$, Tomiyama associates a continuous function dim E on Ω. If $\mathcal{A}$ is of type I or III, the function dim E will be cardinal-valued, while if $\mathcal{A}$ is of type II, the values of dim E will be nonnegative reals or infinite cardinal numbers (an arbitrary von Neumann algebra has a central decomposition into these three types). This finitely additive dimension function of Tomiyama generalizes the well-known countably additive dimension function for finite algebras.

By analogy with the classical case, we would like to define the index of a Fredholm element A to be the function $\dim N_A - \dim N_{A^*}$, where N_A and N_{A^*} are the projections onto ker A and ker A^*. However, since these functions are in general infinite-valued, difficulties in cardinal arithmetic arise: this difference will not be a continuous function on Ω. To overcome these difficulties, the subtraction is performed on a suitable dense open subset of Ω, and the resulting function is extended continuously to all of Ω, exploiting the hyperstonean nature of Ω. The function so constructed, we call i(A) .

Let $\mathcal{J}$ be an ideal in $\mathcal{A}$ which is contained in the <u>relatively compact</u> ideal of $\mathcal{A}$ (i.e., the ideal generated by the relatively finite projections in $\mathcal{A}$). Then the map i is invariant under perturbations by elements of $\mathcal{J}$, and is constant on components of the open set of Fredholm elements for $\mathcal{A}/\mathcal{J}$. Moreover, i is a homomorphism of the multiplicative semigroup of Fredholm elements onto a certain subgroup of the continuous, almost everywhere finite functions on Ω. We are able to identify this subgroup quite concretely using a classification of the ideals in a von Neumann algebra due to W. Wils [33]. As in the classical setting, i then induces an isomorphism of this group of functions on Ω, with the <u>index group</u> of connected components of the invertible group of $\mathfrak{A}/\mathfrak{J}$.

If the ideal $\mathfrak{J}$ is not contained in the relatively compact ideal, however, then the function i is not invariant under ideal perturbations, and is not constant on connected components of the set of Fredholm elements for $\mathfrak{J}$. To deal with this, we observe first that there is a central decomposition of $\mathfrak{J}$ into a relatively compact summand, and a completely noncompact summand (no central summand of the latter is relatively compact). The compact summand is taken care of as above; for the remaining completely noncompact part of $\mathfrak{J}$, we show how to modify the map i by taking a quotient, to obtain an index $\bar{i}$ with all the desired properties. As before we obtain a concrete representation of the index group.

In fact, the constructions indicated above are carried out in greater generality. In particular, the functions i(A) and $\bar{i}$(A) are defined for any element A in $\mathfrak{A}$, regardless of whether A is Fredholm for any particular ideal $\mathfrak{J}$. Many of the properties of the classical index are proved in our theory not just for the Fredholm elements, but under more general assumptions. We obtain a complete theory for left and right Fredholm elements in the course of our discussion, by simply proving each property of i and $\bar{i}$ under the most general natural hypotheses. We define A in $\mathfrak{A}$ to be left (right) Fredholm relative to an ideal $\mathfrak{J}$ if $\pi(A)$ is left (right) invertible in $\mathfrak{A}/\mathfrak{J}$. The index i for a relatively compact ideal, or $\bar{i}$ for a completely noncompact ideal is a continuous map of the semigroups of left and right Fredholm elements onto discrete semigroups of continuous functions on Ω . Furthermore i (or $\bar{i}$) provides a concrete representation of the semigroups of connected components of the left or right Fredholm elements (the index semigroup). This generalizes the semi-Fredholm theory in the classical case, done by H. O. Cordes and J. P. Labrousse in [10].

There is a larger natural open domain on which the index is continuous (as a map into a discrete semigroup): this domain includes more than the union of the left and right Fredholm elements for $\mathfrak{J}$, whenever $\mathfrak{A}$ is not a factor. We say an element A in $\mathfrak{A}$ is semi-Fredholm for $\mathfrak{J}$ if there is a central decomposition of $\mathfrak{A}$ and $\mathfrak{J}$ such that in each summand A is left or right Fredholm. The set $\mathcal{S}$ of semi-Fredholm elements is an open partial semigroup in $\mathfrak{A}$ on which the appropriate index map is continuous. We obtain as a corollary to our theory that this set is uniformly dense in $\mathfrak{A}$; in fact, for each A in $\mathfrak{A}$, A is a limit of semi-Fredholm elements for $\mathfrak{J}$ having the same index as A .

We also consider the question of continuously extending an index beyond the domain $\mathcal{S}$. Necessary and sufficient conditions are given for determining when a given index is continuous at a given element of the algebra. The actual distance from any A in $\mathfrak{A}$ to each component of $\mathcal{S}$ is computed in terms of natural parameters, and thus the closure of each component of $\mathcal{S}$ is described. The fact that the index maps are defined at every element of $\mathfrak{A}$, giving information about non-semi-Fredholm elements, is particularly useful here. There may be some elements in the closure of a unique component of $\mathcal{S}$, and others in the closure of every component. Some elements which are in the closure of exactly one component, can nevertheless be approached through an infinite sequence of other components.

M. Breuer has developed a complete abstract Fredholm theory for the relatively compact ideal in a von Neumann algebra [3, 4]. In this case, our index may be regarded as an extension and a representation of Breuer's index. The case considered by Breuer is central, and our development of the properties of the index i for compact ideals uses many of the same ideas. Breuer's theory was elaborated by M. J. O'Neill to define a theory of left and right Fredholm elements [24]. The abstract definition used here becomes quite unwieldy, and our unified presentation of Fredholm and semi-Fredholm theory is a considerable simplification. A left and right Fredholm theory for the case of the relatively compact ideal has also been developed independently by V. Kaftal [19, 20]. Kaftal also studies a more general class called (relatively) almost Fredholm operators [22] and a related notion of relative weak convergence [21].

There have been a number of applications of Breuer's theory, one such being Breuer's own generalization to a theory of Fredholm operators and vector bundles relative to a von Neumann algebra [5]. The case of a type II_∞ factor where the index group is the group of real numbers, has been of particular interest. M. Gartenberg determined the maximal domain of continuity for an index on $\mathcal{L}\mathcal{F} \cup \mathcal{R}\mathcal{F}$, in this case [18]. D. G. Schaeffer has applied Breuer's theory to solve a problem involving finite difference equations [29]. There is a well-known index theorem relating two different $\mathbb{Z}$-valued indices on the C^*-algebra generated by Toeplitz operators with continuous symbol; a real-valued index analog to this result was proved by L. A. Coburn R. G. Douglas, D. G. Schaeffer, and I. M. Singer [9]. Their suggestion for generating an index on a C^*-algebra by representing it in a quotient $\mathfrak{A}/\mathcal{J}$ of a von Neumann algebra was followed up in a theory developed by K. E. Ekmann [16]; he considers the case where $\mathfrak{A}/\mathcal{J}$ is the Calkin algebra. A rather different sort of von Neumann "index of mixed type" was defined by Breuer and R. S. Butcher in [6], in another attempt to generalize von Neumann index theory to a wider class of C^*-algebras.

We have used our index theory in another paper [23] to compute the distance of each element in a von Neumann algebra to the unitary group of the algebra, and to determine which elements have a best unitary approximant in the algebra.

L. A. Coburn and A. Lebow have defined an abstract index group corresponding to each closed ideal $\mathcal{J}$ in a Banach algebra $\mathcal{B}$: it is the group of components of the invertible group of $\mathcal{B}/\mathcal{J}$. They consider index functions, particularly when $\mathcal{B}$ consists of operators on a Banach space and $\mathcal{J}$ is an ideal of compact operators, and determine the closure of each component of the set of Fredholm operators on a separable Hilbert space [8].

B. A. Barnes [2] and M. R. F. Smyth [30] have generalized classical index theory in another direction, namely to Fredholm elements relative to ideals in Banach algebras, where each element of the ideal has finite spectrum. Their results and techniques are quite different from ours. Further discussion of generalizations of Fredholm theory and a bibliography are given by S. Caradus, W. E. Pfaffenburger, and B. Yood in [7].

General notation and basic facts about von Neumann algebras which will be used throughout the paper are given in Section 2. In Section 3 we define the set of semi-Fredholm elements and discuss the topological nature of this partial semigroup, following the definitions of Coburn and Lebow [8]. Here also the index group and semigroup for $\mathcal{J}$ are defined. In Section 4 we prove several equivalent characterizations of the Fredholm and left (right) Fredholm elements for $\mathcal{J}$ which are subsequently useful. In Section 5 we define the index map i, while describing in some detail Tomiyama's dimension function, and the characterization of ideals due to Wils, on which our definition is based. We include a careful discussion of the addition of infinite-valued continuous functions on Ω used in this definition. At the end of Section 5 are several technical results relating Fredholm and semi-Fredholm properties of an element A in $\mathcal{A}$, to the function $i(A)$.

In Section 6 we prove for the index i, analogs to properties of the classical index; the principle theorems being 6.1, which shows when $i(AB) = i(A) + i(B)$ and 6.5, which constructs a semi-Fredholm path from A to B whenever $i(A) = i(B)$. In Section 7 we specialize to relatively compact ideals and show that i is locally constant and invariant under ideal perturbations on the set of semi-Fredholm elements. Theorem 7.5 details the representation of the index group and semigroup as continuous functions on Ω.

Several examples of ideals in a specific type I algebra $\mathcal{A}$ are described in Section 8 to illustrate various aspects of our theory; in each case the index group and semigroup is given. One sees in these examples that the relatively compact ideal $\mathcal{K}$ in $\mathcal{A}$ is central to the theory: the index group of any smaller compact ideal is a subgroup of the index group for $\mathcal{K}$, and the index group for any completely noncompact ideal is a quotient of a subgroup of the group for $\mathcal{K}$. These relationships hold true in general as shown in 7.5 and 10.12. In Section 9 we define the index $\bar{i}$ for completely noncompact ideals, and in Section 10 the index properties of $\bar{i}$ are established, with the representation of the index group and semigroup for these ideals being given in Theorem 10.12. In Section 11, the maximal domain of continuity for index is determined. It is proved that an index for an ideal $\mathcal{J}$ extends continuously to an open maximal domain $\mathcal{D}$ strictly larger than the set of semi-Fredholm elements for $\mathcal{J}$ if and only if $\mathcal{J}$ does not contain the strong radical of $\mathcal{A}$. If $\mathcal{J}$ contains the strong radical, the index does not extend continuously at all. In Section 12, the distance from any A in $\mathcal{A}$ to each semi-Fredholm component is computed, and the nature of the limit points of the domain $\mathcal{S}$ is described.

It is possible to relate our results to the K-theory of C^*-algebras, although K-theory is not discussed in the paper. For a von Neumann $\mathcal{A}$ and an ideal $\mathcal{J}$, the short exact sequence

$$0 \longrightarrow \mathcal{J} \longrightarrow \mathcal{A} \longrightarrow \mathcal{A}/\mathcal{J} \longrightarrow 0$$

gives rise to a six-term exact sequence of K groups

$$K_1(\mathcal{J}) \to K_1(\mathcal{A}) \to K_1(\mathcal{A}/\mathcal{J}) \overset{\delta}{\to} K_0(\mathcal{J}) \to K_0(\mathcal{A}) \to K_0(\mathcal{A}/\mathcal{J})$$

where δ is the connecting homomorphism [31]. Since $\mathcal{A}$ is a von Neumann algebra, the group $K_1(\mathcal{A})$ is easily seen to be trivial, so δ is an injection. If $\mathcal{A}$ is properly infinite, then the group $K_0(\mathcal{A})$ is also trivial, so δ is an isomorphism. It can be shown that the group $K_1(\mathcal{A}/\mathcal{J})$, which is defined [26] to be

$$\underset{\longrightarrow}{\lim}((\mathcal{A}/\mathcal{J}) \otimes M_n)^{-1}/((\mathcal{A}/\mathcal{J}) \otimes Mn)_0^{-1}$$

is in fact isomorphic to the first term in this direct limit, i.e.,

$$K_1(\mathcal{A}/\mathcal{J}) \cong (\mathcal{A}/\mathcal{J})^{-1}/(\mathcal{A}/\mathcal{J})_0^{-1} ,$$

the invertible group of $\mathcal{A}/\mathcal{J}$ modulo its identity component, which we will call the index group $I(\mathcal{A},\mathcal{J})$. Our index function, which represents this group as a concrete group of functions, thus provides a concrete representation of $K_1(\mathcal{A}/\mathcal{J})$. Moreover, using Tomiyama's dimension function [32], the group $K_0(\mathcal{J})$ can be realized as the same concrete group of functions. If we identify $K_0(\mathcal{J})$ with this group of functions and $K_1(\mathfrak{a}/\mathcal{J})$ with $(\mathfrak{a}/\mathcal{J})^{-1}/(\mathfrak{a}/\mathcal{J})_0^{-1}$, then our index map can be shown to provide an explicit realization of the connecting homomorphism δ. For definitions and basic information on K-theory of C^*-algebras, see [15, 26, and 31].

The author wishes to thank William R. Zame for many enlightening discussions during the research for this paper.

2. Basic facts and notation

Let $\mathfrak{A}$ be a von Neumann algebra of operators on a complex Hilbert space $\mathcal{H}$. Denote the center of $\mathfrak{A}$ by $\mathcal{Z}$ and the maximal ideal space of $\mathcal{Z}$ by Ω. Using the Gelfand isomorphism, identify $\mathcal{Z}$ with $C(\Omega)$, the algebra of continuous complex-valued functions on Ω. Thus every projection P in $\mathcal{Z}$ corresponds to the characteristic function of a unique open and closed subset Y of Ω, and we identify P with χ_Y. Let $\overline{X}$ denote the closure of a subset X of Ω.

There is an equivalence relation on the projections of $\mathfrak{A}$, given by $E \sim F$ if and only if there is a partial isometry V in $\mathfrak{A}$ with $V^*V = E$ and $VV^* = F$. Let $A \leq B$ denote the usual ordering on self-adjoint operators. For projections E, F in $\mathfrak{A}$, write $E \precsim F$ if there is a partial isometry V in $\mathfrak{A}$ with $V^*V = E$ and $VV^* \leq F$. For any pair of projections E and F in $\mathfrak{A}$, there is a central projection P such that $PE \succsim PF$ and $(I - P)E \precsim (I - P)F$. We denote the infimum of projections E and F by $E \wedge F$.

If $A \in \mathfrak{A}$, let $A = U|A|$ denote the polar decomposition of A in $\mathcal{B}(\mathcal{H})$, let N_A be the projection onto the null space of A in $\mathcal{B}(\mathcal{H})$, and let R_A be the projection onto the closure of the range of A ($\overline{\text{range } A}$). Then $|A| = (A^*A)^{\frac{1}{2}}$ and U are in $\mathfrak{A}$, and thus $R_A = U^*U$ and $R_{A^*} = UU^* = I - N_A$ are also in $\mathfrak{A}$, with $R_A \sim R_{A^*}$.

A projection E in $\mathfrak{A}$ is called <u>finite</u> relative to $\mathfrak{A}$ if $E \sim F \leq E$ implies $E = F$, for any projection F in $\mathfrak{A}$. An element A in $\mathfrak{A}$ is called <u>finite</u> if R_A is a finite projection. If E and F are equivalent finite projections, then $I - E$ and $I - F$ are also equivalent; thus in particular, $N_A \sim N_{A^*}$ for any finite element A of $\mathfrak{A}$, since $R_{A^*} \sim R_A$. An algebra $\mathfrak{A}$ is <u>finite</u> if every element of $\mathfrak{A}$ is finite, or equivalently, if $I_{\mathfrak{A}}$ is a finite projection; $\mathfrak{A}$ is <u>properly infinite</u> if $\mathfrak{A}$ contains no finite central projections. A projection E is <u>properly infinite</u> if $E\mathfrak{A}$ is properly infinite. In this case there exist projections E_1 and E_2 with $E = E_1 \oplus E_2$ and $E \sim E_1 \sim E_2$. We use $\oplus$ to denote the orthogonal direct sum. In any $\mathfrak{A}$ there is a maximal finite central projection P; then $P\mathfrak{A}$ is finite and $(I - P)\mathfrak{A}$ is properly infinite.

Let $\mathcal{K}$ denote the uniformly closed two-sided ideal of $\mathfrak{A}$ generated by the finite elements of $\mathfrak{A}$; $\mathcal{K}$ will be called the <u>(relatively) compact ideal</u> of $\mathfrak{A}$, and the elements of $\mathcal{K}$ will be called (relatively) compact. Except in the examples of Section 8, we shall have no occasion to refer to the compact operators in $\mathcal{B}(\mathcal{H})$, so no confusion should result if we suppress the word "relatively".

The ideals $\mathcal{J}$ of $\mathcal{A}$ discussed in this paper will always be uniformly closed and two-sided. Let $\mathcal{J}$ be an ideal with $\pi: \mathcal{A} \to \mathcal{A}/\mathcal{J}$ the quotient map. Denote the spectrum of an element A in $\mathcal{A}$ by $\sigma(A)$.

For future reference, we set apart the following:

REMARK 2.1. Let $A \in \mathcal{A}$, where $\mathcal{A} \subseteq \mathcal{B}(\mathcal{H})$. Let $E(\lambda)$ be the spectral resolution for $|A|$ and let $F(\lambda)$ be the spectral resolution for $|A^*|$ in $\mathcal{B}(\mathcal{H})$. Then $E(\lambda)$ and $F(\lambda)$ are in $\mathcal{A}$. If $A = U|A|$ is the polar decomposition for A , then $A^* = U^*|A^*|$ is the polar decomposition for A^* . Thus $|A|$ acting on $U^*U\mathcal{H}$ is unitarily equivalent to $|A^*|$ acting on $UU^*\mathcal{H}$, by $|A^*| = U|A|U^*$. In particular, excluding the null projections $E\{0\}$ and $F\{0\}$, the spectral resolutions $E(\lambda)$ and $F(\lambda)$ are equivalent in $\mathcal{A}$; i.e., $F(0,b] = UE(0,b]U^*$, for every positive number b .

Other definitions and notation will be introduced as needed, primarily at the beginning of each section. The reader is referred to [11] and [27] for basic information about von Neumann algebras and C^*-algebras, and to [14] for a development of the classical index and Fredholm theory.

3. Definition of the semi-Fredholm elements, and of the index group and the index semigroup

DEFINITION 3.1. Let $\mathcal{J}$ be an ideal in $\mathcal{A}$, with $\pi: \mathcal{A} \to \mathcal{A}/\mathcal{J}$. An element A of $\mathcal{A}$ is left Fredholm for $\mathcal{J}$ if $\pi(A)$ is left invertible; A is right Fredholm for $\mathcal{J}$ if $\pi(A)$ is right invertible, and A is Fredholm for $\mathcal{J}$ if $\pi(A)$ is invertible. We say A in $\mathcal{A}$ is semi-Fredholm for $\mathcal{J}$ if there is a central projection P in $\mathcal{A}$ such that $\pi(PA)$ is left invertible in $P\mathcal{A}/P\mathcal{J}$, and $\pi((I - P)A)$ is right invertible in $(I - P)\mathcal{A}/(I - P)\mathcal{J}$. Let $\mathcal{LF}$, $\mathcal{RF}$, $\mathcal{F}$ and $\mathcal{S}$ denote these classes of elements of $\mathcal{A}$ (we may write $\mathcal{F}_{\mathcal{J}}$, $\mathcal{S}_{\mathcal{J}}$, etc.).

Certain topological properties of these classes are evident. Since the semi-groups of left invertible, and right invertible elements in $\mathcal{A}/\mathcal{J}$ are open, and since π is a continuous open map, it is clear that $\mathcal{LF}$, $\mathcal{RF}$, and $\mathcal{F}$ are open sets in $\mathcal{A}$; similarly, $\mathcal{S}$ is open. The algebra $\mathcal{A}$ is locally path-connected so that the components of these open sets are open and path-connected.

For any open semigroup $\mathcal{J}$ in the von Neumann algebra $\mathcal{A}$, or in the quotient C^*-algebra $\mathcal{A}/\mathcal{J}$, a multiplication $\circ$ can be defined on the components of $\mathcal{J}$ (as done by Coburn and Lebow in [8]). For, if a path $\delta(t)$ connects A and A' in a component $\mathcal{C}_1$ and a path $g(t)$ connects B and B' in $\mathcal{C}_2$, then the path $f(t)g(t)$ connects AB and A'B': define $\mathcal{C}_1 \circ \mathcal{C}_2 = \mathcal{C}_3$, where $\mathcal{C}_1\mathcal{C}_2 \subset \mathcal{C}_3$.

For any ideal $\mathcal{J}$ of $\mathcal{A}$ and any open semigroup $\mathcal{J} \subset \mathcal{A}/\mathcal{J}$, Coburn and Lebow show that the semigroup of components of $\mathcal{J}$ and the semigroup of components of $\pi^{-1}(\mathcal{J})$ are isomorphic. Thus in particular, the components of the set $\mathcal{F}$ of Fredholm elements form a group isomorphic to the group of components of the invertible elements in $\mathcal{A}/\mathcal{J}$. This discrete group, which results from taking the quotient of the group of invertible elements in $\mathcal{A}/\mathcal{J}$ by the normal subgroup which is the component containing the identity, will be called the index group of $\mathcal{A}$ for $\mathcal{J}$. Denote this by $I(\mathcal{A},\mathcal{J})$.

Observe that the topological semigroups of left invertible and right invertible elements of $\mathcal{A}/\mathcal{J}$ are isometrically anti-isomorphic: any closed two-sided ideal $\mathcal{J}$ of $\mathcal{A}$ is self-adjoint, and we have $\pi(A)$ is left invertible in $\mathcal{A}/\mathcal{J}$ if and only if $\pi(A^*)$ is right invertible. Therefore, the discrete semigroup of components of $\mathcal{LF}$ is anti-isomorphic to the semi-group of components of $\mathcal{RF}$. This latter discrete semigroup will be called the index semigroup, $J(\mathcal{A},\mathcal{J})$, of $\mathcal{A}$ for $\mathcal{J}$.

Consider the set of components of $\mathcal{S}$, the class of semi-Fredholm elements. We can define a partial multiplication making this set a partial semigroup, as follows: for $\mathcal{C}_1$ and $\mathcal{C}_2$ components, define $\mathcal{C}_1 \circ \mathcal{C}_2 = \mathcal{C}_3$ whenever $\mathcal{C}_1\mathcal{C}_2 \subset \mathcal{C}_3$ and in addition there is a central projection P such that for any $A \in \mathcal{C}_1$ and $B \in \mathcal{C}_2$ both $\pi(AP)$ and $\pi(BP)$ are left invertible in $P\mathcal{A}/P\mathcal{J}$, both $\pi(A(I - P))$ and $\pi(B(I - P))$ are right invertible in $(I - P)\mathcal{A}/(I - P)\mathcal{J}$. The resulting discrete partial semigroup will be called the <u>index partial semigroup</u> $S(\mathcal{A},\mathcal{J})$ of $\mathcal{A}$ for $\mathcal{J}$.

Any homomorphism ψ which maps a partial semigroup $\mathfrak{J}$ in $\mathcal{A}$ continuously onto a discrete partial semigroup will be called an <u>index</u> on $\mathcal{A}$ (note that ψ must be constant on the components of $\mathfrak{J}$). It may provide perspective on these definitions to observe that the group of invertible elements of any von Neumann algebra $\mathcal{A}$ is always connected (this can be shown as in the argument for [4, Lemma 7]). Thus this apparently most natural domain for an index in $\mathcal{A}$ yields only the zero function. As we see above, $\mathcal{L}\mathfrak{F}$, $\mathfrak{F}$ and $\mathcal{S}$ are other natural domains for an index. In this paper we will define an index on $\mathcal{S}$ which is constant on the components of $\mathcal{S}$ and distinguishes between the components. The restriction to $\mathcal{L}\mathfrak{F}$ and $\mathfrak{F}$ will also be an index.

4. Alternative characterizations of the Fredholm and semi-Fredholm elements

In this section we develop several equivalent descriptions for the Fredholm and left and right Fredholm elements for $\mathcal{J}$. First, we define a natural parameter $m_{\mathcal{J}}(A)$ to use in these descriptions (such a parameter is used by D. Rogers in [25]):

DEFINITION 4.1: Let $\mathcal{J}$ be an ideal in $\mathcal{A}$, let $\pi: \mathcal{A} \to \mathcal{A}/\mathcal{J}$, and let $A \in \mathcal{A}$. Define the lower bound $m_{\mathcal{J}}(A)$ of an element A relative to an ideal $\mathcal{J}$ by:

$$m_{\mathcal{J}}(A) = \inf \sigma(\pi(|A|)) .$$

The first two propositions are more or less corollaries to the Spectral Theorem.

PROPOSITION 4.2: Let $\mathcal{J}$ be an ideal of $\mathcal{A}$, and let $A \in \mathcal{A}$. Let $E(\lambda)$ denote the spectral resolution for $|A|$. Then

$$m_{\mathcal{J}}(A) = \inf \{\beta: E[0,\beta + \varepsilon] \notin \mathcal{J} \text{ , for every } \varepsilon > 0\} .$$

PROOF: Let $\alpha = \inf \{\beta: E[0,\beta + \varepsilon] \notin \mathcal{J}$, for every $\varepsilon > 0\}$: we claim $\alpha \in \sigma(\pi(|A|))$. By the choice of α, for any $\varepsilon > 0$, $E[0,\alpha - \varepsilon) \in \mathcal{J}$, and thus $E[\alpha - \varepsilon, \alpha + \varepsilon] \notin \mathcal{J}$. If for some $\varepsilon > 0$, $\pi((|A| - \alpha I)E[\alpha - \varepsilon,\alpha + \varepsilon]) = 0$, then

$$\sigma(\pi(|A|)) \supset \sigma(\pi(|A|E[\alpha - \varepsilon,\alpha + \varepsilon]) = \sigma(\alpha\pi(E[\alpha - \varepsilon,\alpha + \varepsilon])) \supset \{\alpha\} .$$

On the other hand, if for all $\varepsilon > 0$, $0 < \|\pi((|A| - \alpha I)E[\alpha - \varepsilon,\alpha + \varepsilon])\| \le \varepsilon$, then again $\pi(|A| - \alpha I)$ is not invertible, and $\sigma(\pi(|A|))$ contains α.

To finish the proof, we show that if $\beta < \alpha$ then $\beta \notin \sigma(\pi(|A|))$; in particular, if $E[0,\beta + \varepsilon] \in \mathcal{J}$, for some $\varepsilon > 0$, then $\beta \notin \sigma(\pi(|A|))$. Let

$$E = E(\beta + \varepsilon, \|A\|] = I - E[0, \beta + \varepsilon] .$$

Then computing the spectrum of $E|A|$ in $E\mathcal{A}$, we have $\sigma(E|A|) \subset [\beta + \varepsilon, \|A\|]$, so that $A|E| = \beta E$ is invertible in $E\mathcal{A}$ with inverse B, so

$$(|A| - \beta E)B = B(|A| - \beta E) = E .$$

Hence

$$\pi((|A| - \beta E)B) = \pi(B(|A| - \beta E)) = \pi(I) ,$$

so $\beta \notin \sigma(\pi|A|)$.

PROPOSITION 4.3. _Let_ $A \in \mathcal{A}$. _If_ $m_{\mathcal{J}}(A)$ _and_ $m_{\mathcal{J}}(A^*)$ _are both nonzero, they are equal._

PROOF. Observe that for any element B of a C*-algebra $\mathcal{B}$, $\sigma(|B|) \cup \{0\} = \sigma(|B^*|) \cup \{0\}$: consider $\mathcal{B} \subset \mathcal{B}(\mathcal{H})$, for some Hilbert space $\mathcal{H}$. Then as in Remark 2.1, $|B|$ on $R_{|B|}\mathcal{H}$ is unitarily equivalent to $|B^*|$ on $R_{|B^*|}\mathcal{H}$. For the case at hand, we have

$$\sigma(\pi(|A|)) \cup \{0\} = \sigma(\pi(|A^*|)) \cup \{0\} ,$$

from which the result follows.

The next lemma is well-known; we include a proof for the sake of completeness.

LEMMA 4.4. _If_ A _is an element of_ $\mathcal{A}$ _such that the range of_ A _is closed, then there is a_ B _in_ $\mathcal{A}$ _with_ $AB = R_A$, $BA = R_{A^*}$.

PROOF. Let $A^* = U^*|A^*|$ be the polar decomposition for A^* , so $A = |A^*|U$, and the range of A equals the range of $|A^*|$. Hence $\sigma(|A^*|) \subset \{0\} \cup [\varepsilon, \|A\|]$ for some $\varepsilon > 0$. Using the continuous functional calculus, $R_A = R_{|A^*|}$ is a limit of polynomials in $|A^*|$, having no constant term. Hence there is an element $C = \lim p_n(|A^*|)$ such that $C|A^*| = |A^*|C = R_A$. Set $B = U^*C$ to get

$$AB = |A^*|UU^*C = |A^*|C = R_A$$

$$BA = U^*C|A^*|U = U^*U = R_{A^*} .$$

THEOREM 4.5. _Let_ $\mathcal{J}$ _be an ideal of_ $\mathcal{A}$, _with_ $\pi: \mathcal{A} \to \mathcal{A}/\mathcal{J}$, _and let_ $A \in \mathcal{A}$. _Then the following are equivalent:_

i) A _is left Fredholm for_ $\mathcal{J}$;

ii) $\pi(A)$ _is left invertible;_

iii) $\pi(|A|)$ _is invertible;_

(iv) $m_{\mathcal{J}}(A) > 0$;

(v) *the range of* A^* *contains the range of* $I - E$ *for some projection* E *in* $\mathcal{J}$ *(then also* $N_A \in \mathcal{J}$*)* .

PROOF. By definition, i) $\Leftrightarrow$ ii) and (iii) $\Leftrightarrow$ (iv) . Also ii) $\Leftrightarrow$ iii) since $\pi(|A|) = |\pi(A)|$ is positive in $\mathcal{A}/\mathcal{J}$.
That iv) $\Rightarrow$ v): if $m_{\mathcal{J}}(A) > 0$, then by 4.2, $E[0,\delta] \in \mathcal{J}$, for some $\delta > 0$, where $E(\lambda)$ is the spectral resolution for $|A|$. Then

$$I - E[0,\delta] = E(\delta, \|A\|] \leq E(0, \|A\|] = R_{|A|} = R_{A^*} ,$$

so range $(I - E[0,\delta]) \subset$ range A^* .
That v) $\Rightarrow$ i): Suppose the range of $(I - E)A^*$ equals the range of $I - E$, for some projection $E \in \mathcal{J}$. Then there is some B in $\mathcal{A}$ with $(I - E)A^*B = I - E$, by 4.4.
Hence $B^*A = I - E + B^*AE$, so A is left invertible modulo $\mathcal{J}$.

By a similar proof we have the analogous result for right Fredholm elements:

THEOREM 4.6. *Let* $\mathcal{J}$ *be an ideal of* $\mathcal{A}$, *with* $\pi: \mathcal{A} \to \mathcal{A}/\mathcal{J}$, *and let* $A \in \mathcal{A}$. *These are equivalent*:

i) A *is right Fredholm for* $\mathcal{J}$;

ii) $\pi(A)$ *is right invertible*;

iii) $\pi(|A^*|)$ *is invertible*;

iv) $m_{\mathcal{J}}(A^*) > 0$;

v) *the range of* A *contains the range of* $I - E$ *for some projection* E *in* $\mathcal{J}$ *(then also* $N_{A^*} \in \mathcal{J}$*)* .

Combining these we have alternative characterizations of the Fredholm elements for $\mathcal{J}$.

THEOREM 4.7. *Let* $\mathcal{J}$ *be an ideal of* $\mathcal{A}$ *with* $\pi: \mathcal{A} \to \mathcal{A}/\mathcal{J}$, *let* $A \in \mathcal{A}$. *These are equivalent*:

i) A *is Fredholm for* $\mathcal{J}$;

ii) $\pi(A)$ *is invertible*;

iii) $m_{\mathcal{J}}(A) = m_{\mathcal{J}}(A^*) > 0$;

iv) *the range of* A *contains the range of* $I - E$ *for some projection* E *in* $\mathcal{J}$, *and* $N_A \in \mathcal{J}$;

v) A *is right Fredholm and* $N_A \in \mathcal{J}$;

vi) A *is left Fredholm and* $N_{A^*} \in \mathcal{J}$.

PROOF. By applying 4.3, 4.5, and 4.6, we need only show that iv) implies iii). From iv) and 4.6 we have $m(A^*) > 0$. Hence there is some $\varepsilon > 0$ with $F[0,\varepsilon] \in \mathcal{J}$, where F is the spectral resolution for $|A^*|$. Since $F[0,\varepsilon] = N_{A^*} + F(0,\varepsilon]$, we have $F(0,\varepsilon] \in \mathcal{J}$. But $E(0,\varepsilon] = U^*F(0,\varepsilon]U$, where $E(\lambda)$ is the spectral resolution for $|A|$, and $A = U|A|$ is the polar decomposition. Since $E[0,\varepsilon] = N_A + E(0,\varepsilon]$, then $E[0,\varepsilon] \in \mathcal{J}$, so $m_{\mathcal{J}}(A) > 0$. Then 4.3 implies $m_{\mathcal{J}}(A) = m_{\mathcal{J}}(A^*)$, so iv) $\Rightarrow$ iii) is proved.

In the classical case for the algebra $\mathcal{B}(\mathcal{H})$, and the ideal of compact operators, F. V. Atkinson proved that condition (ii) was equivalent to: N_A and N_{A^*} are finite rank projections and the range of A is closed [1]. Condition iv) was conceived by M. Breuer as the appropriate generalization of this for the ideal $\mathcal{K}$ of relatively compact elements [3]. Breuer proved the equivalence of ii) and iv). In this setting, as in general, the range of a Fredholm element is usually not closed. In his left and right Fredholm theory for the ideal $\mathcal{K}$, V. Kaftal proves the equivalence of i), ii), and v) of 4.5 and 4.6 [19].

5. Definition of the map i

In this section we define an index map i on the von Neumann algebra $\mathcal{A}$, based on the relative dimension function of J. Tomiyama [32]. This definition will use the characterization of the ideals of $\mathcal{A}$ given by W. Wils [33].

Let $\mathcal{K}$ be the compact ideal of $\mathcal{A}$. The function i will be constant on the components of the semi-Fredholm elements $\mathcal{S}_{\mathcal{J}}$ for $\mathcal{J}$ where $\mathcal{J}$ is any ideal contained in $\mathcal{K}$, and will distinguish the components of $\mathcal{S}_{\mathcal{J}}$. Generalizations of the properties of the classical index will be proved for i. Then in Section 9, the function i will be modified to accomodate non-compact ideals.

We begin by describing Wils' characterization of the closed two-sided ideals of $\mathcal{A}$. Let $\mathcal{Z}$ be the center of $\mathcal{A}$, with maximal ideal space Ω; identify $\mathcal{Z}$ with $C(\Omega)$. The compact set Ω is partitioned into open and closed subsets Ω_j, with characteristic functions χ_{Ω_j}, such that $\mathcal{A}_{\chi_{\Omega_j}}$ is of type j, $j = I, II, III$. Specify three sets:

$V_I = \{0\} \cup \mathbb{N} \cup \{\aleph : \aleph$ an infinite cardinal, $\aleph \le \dim \mathcal{H}\}$
(where $\mathbb{N}$ is the positive integers);

$V_{II} = [0,\infty) \cup \{\aleph : \aleph$ an infinite cardinal, $\aleph \le \dim \mathcal{H}\}$;

$V_{III} = \{0\} \cup \{\aleph : \aleph$ an infinite cardinal, $\aleph \le \dim \mathcal{H}\}$.

We endow each V_j with the order topology; each V_j is compact. Let $\mathcal{D}$ be the lattice of all continuous functions from Ω into the disjoint union V of the V_j such that $f(\Omega_j) \subset V_j$ for each j [30].

The following result of J. Tomiyama establishes the existence of a finitely-additive relative dimension function defined on the projections of $\mathcal{A}$; in particular it extends previous definitions for finite algebras.

THEOREM 5.1 (Tomiyama). *Let $\mathcal{A}$ be a von Neumann algebra on a Hilbert space $\mathcal{H}$. There exists a function dim mapping the projections in $\mathcal{A}$ to the functions in $\mathcal{D}$ with the following properties:*

(i) $0 \le \dim E \le$ *dimension of* $\mathcal{H}$ *for each projection* E, *and* $\dim E = 0$ *if and only if* $E = 0$;

(ii) $\dim E \le \dim F$ *if and only if* $E \precsim F$;

(iii) *if* E *and* F *are mutually orthogonal projections then* $\dim(E + F) = \dim E + \dim F$;

(iv) *if* P *is a central projection then* $\dim(PE) = P \dim E$.

DEFINITION 5.2 (Tomiyama). The function dim described above is called a dimension function on the von Neumann algebra $\mathfrak{A}$.

THEOREM 5.3 (Wils). For any von Neumann algebra $\mathfrak{A}$, the range of the dimension function dim is precisely

$$\dim \mathfrak{A} = \{f \in \mathfrak{D}: f \le \dim I_{\mathfrak{A}}\}$$

Wils obtains an extremely useful system of invariants for the ideals of $\mathfrak{A}$ in terms of ideal bases (a classification of closed two-sided ideals in a von Neumann algebra was first given by F. B. Wright [34]).

DEFINITION 5.4 (Wils). By an ideal base in $\dim \mathfrak{A}$ is meant a subset $\Gamma \subseteq \dim \mathfrak{A}$ which satisfies:

(i) f, g in Γ implies $f \vee g$ in Γ ;

(ii) $h \le f$ and f in Γ implies h in Γ ;

(iii) f in Γ implies $2f \wedge \dim I_{\mathfrak{A}}$ in Γ ;

where $f \vee g = \sup\{f,g\}$ and $f \wedge g = \inf\{f,g\}$.

For any ideal $\mathcal{J}$ of $\mathfrak{A}$, let the dimension set of $\mathcal{J}$ be

$$\dim \mathcal{J} = \{f \in \dim \mathfrak{A}: \dim E = f \text{ , some } E \text{ in } \mathcal{J}\} .$$

THEOREM 5.5 (Wils). For each ideal $\mathcal{J}$, $\dim \mathcal{J}$ is an ideal base. There is a lattice isomorphism between the lattice of closed two-sided ideals of $\mathfrak{A}$, and the lattice of ideal bases in $\dim \mathfrak{A}$, given by $\mathcal{J} \mapsto \dim \mathcal{J}$; moreover

$$\mathcal{J} = \overline{\text{span}}\ \{A \text{ in } \mathfrak{A}: R_A \in \dim \mathcal{J}\} .$$

REMARK 5.6. We note some properties of the topological space Ω . Recall that a compact Hausdorff space is Stonean if the closure of every open set is open. The maximal ideal space Ω of $\mathcal{Z}$ is Stonean; in fact, Ω is hyperstonean in that it admits the structure of a perfect Borel measure [12]. In particular, for this measure, no open and closed set has measure zero, and every measurable set is the symmetric difference of an open and closed set and a set of measure zero. It is also the case that the closure of every set of measure zero is a set of measure zero.

Thus every set whose complement is of measure zero contains a dense open set whose complement is of measure zero. In particular, to say that a property holds on a dense open subset of Ω is equivalent to saying that it holds almost everywhere (a.e.). It will often be convenient to use the notation a.e. for this notion. We will also have occasion to use the fact that every bounded measurable complex-valued function on Ω differs from a continuous function on a set of measure zero.

For any open set $X \subset \Omega$, the closure $\overline{X}$ of X in Ω is the Stone-Čech compactification βX of X (this is true in any Stonean space) [28, page 109].

We now define the set of values for our proposed index function.

DEFINITION 5.7. Using the notation in the introductory paragraph to this section, let

$$-V_j = \{-a: a \in V_j\} \text{ with } -a \leq -b \text{ if } a \geq b ,$$

for $j = I, II, III$. Identify -0 and 0 and give the set $-V_j \cup V_j$ the obvious linear order and the order topology. Note that this space is compact. For a in V_j, let $|a| = |-a| = a$.

Let $C_c(\Omega)$ denote the set of continuous functions f such that

$$f(\Omega_j) \subset -V_j \cup V_j \text{ , each } j = I, II, III$$

and

$$|f| \leq \dim I_{\mathcal{G}} .$$

Let $C_c^+(\Omega)$ be the nonnegative functions in $C_c(\Omega)$.

The next result was observed without proof by Tomiyama in [32], and we include a proof.

PROPOSITION 5.8. <u>A projection</u> E <u>in</u> $\mathcal{G}$ <u>is relatively finite if and only if</u> $\dim E$ <u>is finite on a dense open subset of</u> Ω.

PROOF. Assume F is a projection in $\mathcal{G}$, where $f = \dim F$ is finite on a dense open subset $Y \subset \Omega$. If $F \sim E \leq F$, then

$$\dim (F - E) + \dim E = \dim F$$

where for any t in Y, $\dim (E)(t) = \dim (F)(t)$ is a real number. Thus $\dim (F - E) \equiv 0$ on Y, and hence on all Ω; so, $F - E = 0$.

Conversely, assume $\dim F = f \geq \aleph_0$ on some open subset $X \subset \Omega$. Then $\overline{X}$ is open and closed, so $\chi_{\overline{X}}$ is in $C_c(\Omega)$. By Theorem 5.3 there is a projection E in $\mathcal{G}$ with $\dim E = \chi_{\overline{X}}$. Then $\dim E < \dim F \neq \dim E$, so for some nonzero projection $F_0 \neq F$, we have $E \sim F_0 < F$. Then

$$\dim F = \dim F_0 + \dim (F - F_0) .$$

Now $\dim F_0 \equiv 0$ on $\Omega \backslash \overline{X}$; whereas on $\overline{X}$, $\dim F_0 \equiv 1$ and $\dim F \geq \aleph_0$. We conclude that $\dim F = \dim (F - F_0)$, so that $F \sim (F - F_0)$ and F is not finite.

COROLLARY 5.9. <u>Let</u> $\mathcal{K}$ <u>be the compact ideal of</u> $\mathcal{G}$. <u>Then</u>

$$\dim \mathcal{K} = \{f \text{ in } \dim \mathcal{G}\colon f \text{ is finite a.e.}\} .$$

COROLLARY 5.10. <u>A projection</u> E <u>in</u> $\mathcal{G}$ <u>is properly infinite if and only if values taken by</u> $\dim E$ <u>are infinite or zero</u>.

REMARK 5.11. If $\mathcal{G}$ is a properly infinite von Neumann algebra, then the ideal bases in $\dim \mathcal{G}$ are precisely the order ideals in $\dim \mathcal{G}$. For, in this case, $\dim I_{\mathcal{G}} \geq \aleph_0$. Thus condition 5.4 iii) defining an ideal base in $\dim_{\mathcal{G}}$ can be replaced by either of:

iii)' f in Γ implies $2f$ in Γ;

iii)" f and g in Γ implies $f + g$ in Γ.

Because of the disconnected topology of Ω, an addition of functions in $C_c(\Omega)$ can be defined, which agrees with pointwise addition on dense open subsets of Ω.

DEFINITION 5.12. Let f and g be functions in $C_c(\Omega)$. Let X be the open set,

$$X = \{t \text{ in } \Omega\colon f(t) \neq -g(t)\} .$$

Let $h(t) = f(t) + g(t)$ for t in X: the function h is a well-defined, continuous function on X, taking values in a compact Hausdorff space ($|h| \leq \dim I_{\mathcal{G}}$). By the functorial property of the Stone-Čech compactification, h has a continuous extension k to $\beta X = \overline{X}$. Furthermore, $\overline{X}$ is open and closed, so we define the <u>sum</u> of f and g to be the continuous function $f + g$ where

$$(f+g)(t) = \begin{cases} h(t), & t \in \overline{X} \\ 0, & t \in \Omega \setminus \overline{X} . \end{cases}$$

REMARK 5.13. This operation on $C_c(\Omega)$ is commutative, and has an identity and inverses; it is not in general associative. However, it is associative on the subset of functions which are finite a.e. Thus the set of finite a.e. functions in $C_c(\Omega)$ is an abelian group.

We can single out a maximal restriction of this operation which is associative: for f, g in $C_c(\Omega)$, define $f \dot{+} g = f + g$ whenever the sets

$$\{t: f(t) \geq \aleph_0\} \cap \{t: g(t) \leq -\aleph_0\}$$

$$\{t: f(t) \leq -\aleph_0\} \cap \{t: g(t) \geq \aleph_0\}$$

are nowhere dense in Ω. It is straightforward to check that $f \dot{+} (g \dot{+} h)$ is defined if and only if $(f \dot{+} g) \dot{+} h$ is defined, and that they are equal. The set $C_c(\Omega)$ with this restricted operation is a partial semigroup.

DEFINITION 5.14. Let $\mathcal{A}$ be a von Neumann algebra. Define the map i of $\mathcal{A}$ into $C_c(\Omega)$ by

$$i(A) = \dim N_A - \dim N_{A^*} ,$$

for each A in $\mathcal{A}$. It is immediate that $i(A^*) = -i(A)$, and this obviously reduces to the classical index when $\mathcal{A} = \mathcal{B}(\mathcal{H})$.

Note that in a finite algebra $\mathcal{A}$, the map i is identically zero, and the notions of Fredholm and semi-Fredholm coincide. In fact, any finite element of any von Neumann algebra must have zero index: for, let $E(\lambda)$ and $F(\lambda)$ be spectral resolutions for $|A|$ and $|A^*|$. Then $E(0,\|A\|]$ and $F(0,\|A\|]$ are finite projections equivalent in $\mathcal{A}$, and hence their orthogonal complements N_A and N_{A^*} are equivalent.

We now include several propositions relating the function $i(A)$ and the Fredholm or semi-Fredholm properties of A.

PROPOSITION 5.15. *Let* $A \in \mathcal{A}$. *Then*

i) $i(A) \geq 0$ implies $\dim N_A = \dim N_A{}^* + i(A)$;

ii) $i(A) \leq 0$ implies $\dim N_A{}^* = \dim N_A - i(A)$.

PROOF. We prove i), the proof of ii) is similar. Since $i(A) \geq 0$, $\dim N_A \geq \dim N_A{}^*$. Thus

$$\dim N_A{}^* + (\dim N_A - \dim N_A{}^*) = \dim N_A$$

regardless of whether these functions are finite or infinite-valued.

PROPOSITION 5.16. Let A in $\mathcal{A}$ be semi-Fredholm for $\mathcal{J}$. There is a central projection P in $\mathcal{A}$ such that

$i(PA) \leq 0$ and PA is left Fredholm for $P\mathcal{J}$ in $P\mathcal{A}$

$i(I - P)A) \geq 0$ and $(I - P)A$ is right Fredholm for $(I - P)\mathcal{J}$ in $(I - P)\mathcal{A}$.

PROOF. Let X be the closure of the open subset of Ω on which $i(A) < 0$. Then $P = \chi_X$ is a central projection satisfying the conclusion: observe that any right Fredholm element with negative index must also be left Fredholm.

PROPOSITION 5.17. Let A and B be semi-Fredholm for $\mathcal{J}$, and suppose $i(A) = i(B)$. Then

i) A left (right) Fredholm implies B is left (right) Fredholm;

ii) A Fredholm implies B is Fredholm.

PROOF. Part ii) follows from i). By taking adjoints, it suffices to prove i) when A is left Fredholm. In this case, $N_A \in \mathcal{J}$. We may assume $\mathcal{A}$ is properly infinite by 5.14.

By the preceding proposition, there is a central projection P such that $i(PB) \leq 0$ and PB is left Fredholm for $P\mathcal{J}$ in $P\mathcal{A}$; and, $i((I - P)B) \geq 0$ and $(I - P)B$ is right Fredholm for $(I - P)\mathcal{J}$ in $(I - P)\mathcal{A}$. Hence it obviously suffices to show $(I - P)B$ is also left Fredholm. By passing to this summand, we assume $i(B) \geq 0$, and B is right Fredholm. Then $N_B{}^* \in \mathcal{J}$, and by 4.7 we need only show $N_B \in \mathcal{J}$. However,

$$\dim N_A + \dim N_B^* \geq (\dim N_A - \dim N_A^*) + \dim N_B^*$$

$$= (\dim N_B - \dim N_B^*) + \dim N_B^*$$

$$= \dim N_B ,$$

since $N_B \gtrsim N_B^*$, and $i(A) = i(B)$. Thus $\dim N_B \in \dim \mathcal{J}$, by 5.11 so $N_B \in \mathcal{J}$.

PROPOSITION 5.18. <u>Let</u> A <u>be semi-Fredholm for</u> $\mathcal{J}$, <u>and let</u> $|\text{ind } A| \in \dim \mathcal{J}$. <u>Then</u> A <u>is Fredholm</u>.

PROOF. Assume first that A is left Fredholm and $i(A) \leq 0$. It suffices to show $N_A^* \in \mathcal{J}$, by 4.7. However, by 5.15

$$\dim N_A^* = \dim N_A - i(A) = \dim N_A + |i(A)| ,$$

so $\dim N_A^* \in \dim \mathcal{J}$, using 5.11 and 5.14.

If A is right Fredholm and $i(A) \geq 0$ the proof is similar. Using 5.16, the general result reduces to these two cases.

REMARK 5.19. M. Breuer has developed abstract Fredholm theory in the important case of the relatively compact ideal $\mathcal{K}$ of $\mathfrak{A}$ [3,4]. He defines an index α on the set $\mathfrak{F}$ of Fredholm elements for $\mathfrak{A}/\mathcal{K}$, mapping $\mathfrak{F}$ onto a discrete group G. The group G is the quotient of the free group generated by the equivalence classes $[E]$ of relatively finite projections E in $\mathfrak{A}$, by the relation $[E + F] = [E] + [F]$ whenever E and F are orthogonal.

It is obvious there is an isomorphism $\phi: G \to i(\mathfrak{F})$, where $i(\mathfrak{F})$ is the image of $\mathfrak{F}$ under the map i defined in 5.14, such that $i = \phi \circ \alpha$. We will see that $i(\mathfrak{F})$ is the abelian group

$$i(\mathfrak{F}) = \{f \text{ in } C_c(\Omega): f \text{ is finite a.e.}\} .$$

Thus our theory is an extension of Breuer's in this case, and provides a natural representation of his theory.

6. Properties of the map i

In this section we obtain properties of the map i which are analogous to properties of the classical index. Such properties are usually proved under the assumption that the operators involved are Fredholm or semi-Fredholm. However, for many of these results left or right invertibility conditions are not relevant; all that matters are certain assumptions on the kernels and co-kernels of the operators involved. For some other analogs of the classical results, such as 6.3 and 6.5, even these assumptions are unnecessary.

THEOREM 6.1. *Let* A *and* B *be elements of a von Neumann algebra* $\mathcal{A}$. *Then*

$$i(AB) = i(A) + i(B)$$

whenever any one of the following holds:

i) N_A *and* N_B *are both finite;*

ii) N_A *and* N_{A^*} *are both finite, and* $i(A) = 0$;

iii) N_{AB} *is finite and* $i(AB) = 0$.

PROOF. The proof uses properties of equivalence of projections to rewrite the desired conclusion as an equation involving six independent functions in $C_c(\Omega)$; then one checks the cardinal arithmetic to see that this equation holds under the various hypotheses. The argument is based in part on the proof by M. Breuer for the corresponding result in his theory [4, Theorem 2]. We will use notation $E_\perp$ for $I - E$, where E is a projection.

Consider the projections $E = N_{B^*} = (R_B)_\perp$ and $F = N_A = (R_{A^*})_\perp$; they can be decomposed in $\mathcal{A}$ as follows:

$$E = E' \oplus E'' \oplus E''', \quad E_\perp = E'_\perp \oplus E''_\perp \oplus E'''_\perp$$

$$F = F' \oplus F'' \oplus F''', \quad F_\perp = F'_\perp \oplus F''_\perp \oplus F'''_\perp ,$$

such that $E' = F'$, $E'' = F''_\perp$, $E''_\perp = F''$, and $E''' \sim F''' \sim E'''_\perp \sim F'''_\perp$, [11, page 18, Lemme 1, 3].

Letting $A = U|A|$ and $B = V|B|$ be the polar decompositions (so $B^* = V^*|B^*|$) , we have

$$N_{AB} = N_B \oplus V^*(N_A \wedge R_B)V = N_B \oplus V^*(F \wedge E_\perp)V = N_B \oplus V^*F''V .$$

Similarly,

$$N_{(AB)*} = N_{B*A*} = N_{A*} \oplus UE''U^* .$$

Thus

(1) $i(AB) = \dim N_{AB} - \dim N_{(AB)*} = (\dim N_B + \dim F'') - (\dim N_{A*} + \dim E'')$,

and,

(2) $$i(A) + i(B) = (\dim N_A - \dim N_{A*}) - (\dim N_B - \dim N_{B*}) ,$$

$$= [(\dim F' + \dim F'' + \dim F''') - \dim N_{A*}]$$

$$+ [\dim N_B - (\dim E' + \dim E'' + \dim E''')]$$

$$= [(\dim F' + \dim F'' + \dim F''') - \dim N_{A*}]$$

$$+ [\dim N_B - (\dim F' + \dim E'' + \dim F''')] .$$

Thus the only obstruction to the equality of $i(AB)$ and $i(A) + i(B)$ is the nonassociativity of the addition in $C_c(\Omega)$. In particular, if all six functions in the final expression in (2) are finite a.e. on Ω then (1) = (2) . To finish the proof one checks that (1) and (2) are equal under hypotheses (i), (ii) or (iii).

Assume i): that N_A and N_B are both finite. Then there is a dense open subset $X \subset \Omega$ such that $\dim F'$, $\dim F''$, $\dim F'''$, and $\dim N_B$ are finite on X . Clearly, whether or not $\dim E''$ and $\dim N_{A^*}$ are finite-valued, we have $i(AB) = i(A) + i(B)$ on X , and hence on Ω .

Assume ii): that N_A and N_{A^*} are both finite and $i(A) = 0$. There is a dense open subset $X \subset \Omega$ such that $\dim F'$, $\dim F''$, $\dim F'''$, and $\dim N_{A^*}$ are finite on X . Let Y be the largest subset of X on which both $\dim N_B$ and $\dim E''$ are finite. Then (1) and (2) are equal on Y . On $X\backslash\overline{Y}$ at least one of $\dim N_B$ and $\dim E''$ is infinite. Thus since $i(A)$ is zero, on $X\backslash\overline{Y}$ we have

$$i(AB) = \dim N_B - \dim E'' = i(A) + i(B) .$$

The proof under hypothesis iii) proceeds similarly, and we are done.

COROLLARY 6.2. *One has* $i(AB) = i(A) + i(B)$ *whenever either of the following holds:*

i) *both* N_{A^*} *and* N_{B^*} *are finite;*

ii) *both* N_B *and* N_{B^*} *are finite, and* $i(B) = 0$.

PROOF. This follows from 6.1 by symmetry and by taking adjoints.

As remarked in the proof of 6.1, the only obstruction to proving that $i(AB) = i(A) + i(B)$ for every A and B, is the nonassociativity of the addition in $C_c(\Omega)$. It is easy to see, even for the classical index, that this index equation does not always hold; thus we see that this non-associativity is intrinsic and that the image $i(\mathfrak{A})$ cannot be a (nontrivial) group.

COROLLARY 6.3. *Let* $A \in \mathfrak{A}$, *and let* $C \in \mathfrak{A}$ *be finite. Then* $i(A + C) = i(A)$.

PROOF. Set $N_C = B$ as in 6.2 ii); since C is finite, $R_{C^*} = I - N_C = N_B = N_{B^*}$ is finite, and $i(N_C) = 0$. Thus

$$i(A + C) + i(N_C) = i((A + C)N_C) = i(AN_C) = i(A) + i(N_C) ,$$

so $i(A + C) = i(A)$.

LEMMA 6.4. *Let* $A \in \mathfrak{A}$, *with* $i(A) \leq 0$. *Then*

i) *there is an isometry* V *in* $\mathfrak{A}$, *with* $A = V|A|$;

ii) *there is a path* A_t *in* $\mathfrak{A}$ *with* $A_0 = A, A_1 = V$; $i(A_t) = i(A)$, *all* t ; *and* A_t *is left-invertible, each* $t \neq 0$.

PROOF. Let $A = U|A|$ be the polar decomposition. Let $P = \chi_{\overline{X}}$ where X is the open set on which $i(A) < 0$; so, on $\Omega \setminus \overline{X}$, $i(A) \equiv 0$. Then there is a partial isometry W in $\mathfrak{A}$ such that $W^*W = N_A$, $WW^* \leq N_{A^*}$, and $(I - P)WW^* = (I - P)N_{A^*}$. Set $V = W + U$. Then on $\overline{X}$,

$$i(A) = \dim N_A - (\dim N_A + \dim (N_{A^*} - WW^*)) = i(V) ,$$

and on $\Omega \setminus \overline{X}$, $i(A) \equiv 0 \equiv i(V)$; so $i(V) = i(A)$.

Since $|A|$ is positive, there is a path joining $|A|$ to I: in $C(\sigma(|T|))$ there is a path $f_t(\lambda) = (1 - t)\lambda + t$ joining $f_0(\lambda) = \lambda$ to $f_1(\lambda) = 1$. Using the continuous functional calculus, $f_t(|A|)$ is a path from $|A|$ to I, and note that $f_t(|A|)$ is invertible for $t > 0$. Therefore $A_t = Vf_t(|A|)$ is a path from A to V, where A_t is left invertible and $i(A_t) = i(V) = i(A)$, for $t > 0$.

THEOREM 6.5. *Let A and B be elements of $\mathfrak{A}$ such that $i(A) = i(B)$. There is a path A_t in $\mathfrak{A}$ such that $A_0 = A$, $A_1 = B$, and $i(A_t) = i(A)$, for each t. Furthermore this path can be chosen so that A_t is semi-Fredholm for every ideal $\mathcal{J}$ of $\mathfrak{A}$, for each $t \neq 0,1$. If A is (left or right) Fredholm, then A_t is also (left or right) Fredholm, for each $t \neq 1$.*

PROOF. Assume first that $i(A) = i(B) \leq 0$. By Lemma 6.4, there are paths connecting A to an isometry U, and connecting B to an isometry V; where each element of the paths is left invertible and has the desired index. It remains to show that any two isometries U and V in $\mathfrak{A}$ with $i(V) = i(U)$, are joined by a left invertible path having the same index.

Since $i(UV^*) = \dim N_{V^*} - \dim N_{U^*} = 0$, then in the polar decomposition $UV^* = W|UV^*|$, we can assume W is a unitary in $\mathfrak{A}$. From the proof of Lemma 6.4, there is a path from UV^* to W such that every element but UV^* is invertible. Then, since the invertible group of $\mathfrak{A}$ is open and connected, there is a path from W to $I_{\mathfrak{A}}$. This gives an invertible path T_t from UV^* to I, so T_tV is a left invertible path from U to V, with $i(T_tV) = i(V)$, each t, by Theorem 6.1.

In case $i(A) = i(B) \geq 0$, we obtain the desired result by taking adjoints. In general, let $X = \{t \in \Omega: i(A)(t) > 0\}$. Then $\chi_{\overline{X}}$ provides a central decomposition of $\mathfrak{A}$, that reduces the theorem to the two cases already considered.

The final statement of the theorem follows by 5.17.

COROLLARY 6.6. *If $\mathcal{J}$ is any ideal in a finite von Neumann algebra $\mathfrak{A}$, then the sets of Fredholm elements and semi-Fredholm elements for $\mathcal{J}$ coincide, and this set is connected. Thus, $I(\mathfrak{A},\mathcal{J}) = \{0\} = J(\mathfrak{A},\mathcal{J})$.*

PROOF. For any A in $\mathfrak{A}$, $N_A \sim N_{A^*}$, so $i(A) = 0$ (see 5.14).

COROLLARY 6.7. *For any ideal $\mathcal{J}$ of $\mathfrak{A}$, the set of semi-Fredholm elements for $\mathcal{J}$ is dense in $\mathfrak{A}$. In fact, for any A in $\mathfrak{A}$, $A = \text{limit } S_n$, where S_n is semi-Fredholm for $\mathcal{J}$ with $i(S_n) = i(A)$, each n.*

7. A representation of the index group and the index semigroup for relatively compact ideals

In this section we consider (relatively) compact ideals of $\mathcal{A}$, that is, those $\mathcal{J} \subseteq \mathcal{K}$, where $\mathcal{K}$ is the closed ideal generated by the relatively finite elements of $\mathcal{A}$. For a compact ideal $\mathcal{J}$, with Fredholm elements $\mathcal{F}$ and right Fredholm elements $\mathcal{RF}$, we will show that i is an index, that $i(\mathcal{F})$ is naturally isomorphic to the index group $I(\mathcal{A}, \mathcal{J})$, and that $i(\mathcal{RF})$ is naturally isomorphic to the index semigroup $J(\mathcal{A},\mathcal{J})$. However, this is not true for ideals not contained in $\mathcal{K}$. In Section 9, we will modify the definition of i to represent the index group and semigroup for these larger ideals.

Results 7.3 and 7.4 were obtained by M. Breuer [4] for the ideal $\mathcal{J} = \mathcal{K}$, for components of Fredholm elements. Also, for $\mathcal{J} = \mathcal{K}$, V. Kaftal has independently shown the stability of left and right Fredholm elements under ideal perturbations and that these classes are open semigroups [19, 2.13, 2.14].

The next result is proved in the classical case by Rogers [25]. When we investigate the closures of the components of $\mathcal{F}$ and $\mathcal{S}$ for general ideals, more precise refinements of this result are obtained in 11.8 and 12.13.

THEOREM 7.1. *Let $\mathcal{J}$ be a compact ideal in a von Neumann algebra $\mathcal{A}$, and let A and B belong to $\mathcal{A}$. If*

$$\|A - B\| < m_{\mathcal{J}}(A) ,$$

then $i(A) = i(B)$ *and* A *and* B *are left Fredholm for* $\mathcal{J}$.

PROOF. Since $m_{\mathcal{J}}(A) > 0$, A is left Fredholm by 4.5. We will prove the theorem in the case $i(A) \le 0$, and in the case $i(A) \ge 0$. Then the general case follows by a central decomposition.

Assume that $i(A) \le 0$. Let $E(\lambda)$ be the spectral resolution for $|A|$. Choose η so that $\|A - B\| < \eta < m_{\mathcal{J}}(A)$. Then for $E = E[0,\eta]$, $E \in \mathcal{J}$ by 4.2. We can write $A = V|A|$, where V is an isometry in $\mathcal{A}$, by 6.4. Define C by

$$A + C = A(I - E) + \eta VE ;$$

then $C \in \mathcal{J}$. Using the continuous functional calculus for $|A|(I - E)$, there is an element $T = (I - E)T(I - E)$ in $\mathcal{A}$ with $\|T\| \le 1/\eta$, and

$T|A| = I - E$. Then for

$$D = TV^* + 1/\eta EV^*$$

$D \in \mathcal{G}$, $\|D\| \leq 1/\eta$, and $D(A + C) = I$. Thus

$$\|I - D(B + C)\| = \|D(A + C) - D(B + C)\| < 1 ,$$

so $D(B + C)$ is invertible, and thus B is left Fredholm. Furthermore, using 6.1 iii) and 6.3:

$$i(D) + i(B + C) = i(D(B + C)) = 0 ;$$

$$i(D) + i(A + C) = i(D(A + C)) = 0 ;$$

$$i(B) = i(B + C) = -i(D) = i(A + C) = i(A) .$$

Thus the result follows in the case $\text{ind } A \leq 0$.

Assume now that $\text{ind } A \geq 0$. Then $N_A \gtrsim N_{A^*}$; but A is left Fredholm, so N_A and also N_{A^*} are in $\mathcal{J}$. Therefore A is actually Fredholm, so $m_{\mathcal{J}}(A^*) = m_{\mathcal{J}}(A)$, by 4.7. The above argument can now be applied to A^* and B^* , to conclude $i(A) = i(B)$ and B is right Fredholm. Then B is also left Fredholm by 5.17. The theorem is proved.

COROLLARY 7.2. <u>Let</u> A <u>and</u> B <u>belong to</u> $\mathcal{G}$. <u>If</u>

$$\|A - B\| < m_{\mathcal{J}}(A^*) ,$$

<u>then</u> $i(A) = i(B)$ <u>and</u> A <u>and</u> B <u>are right Fredholm for</u> $\mathcal{J}$.

COROLLARY 7.3. <u>The map</u> i <u>is constant on the connected components of</u> $S_{\mathcal{J}}$, <u>for any compact ideal</u> $\mathcal{J}$.

PROOF. Let A be semi-Fredholm for $\mathcal{J}$. There is a central projection P such that AP is left Fredholm for $P\mathcal{J}$, and $A(I - P)$ is right Fredholm for $(I - P)\mathcal{J}$. Then $m_{P\mathcal{J}}(PA)$ in $P\mathcal{G}$ and $m_{(I-P)\mathcal{J}}((I - P)A^*)$ in $(I - P)\mathcal{G}$ are both positive: let ε be the minimum. For any B in $\mathcal{G}$ with $\|A - B\| < \varepsilon$, we have $i(B) = i(A)$ and $B \in S_{\mathcal{J}}$.

THEOREM 7.4. *Let* $\mathcal{J}$ *be a compact ideal in a von Neumann algebra* $\mathfrak{A}$. *Let* $K \in \mathcal{J}$, *and let* A *in* $\mathfrak{A}$ *be semi-Fredholm for* $\mathcal{J}$. *Then* $A + K$ *is also semi-Fredholm, and*

$$i(A + K) = i(A) .$$

PROOF. That $A + K$ is semi-Fredholm follows from the definition. By passing to a central summand, assume without loss of generality that A is left Fredholm; then $m_{\mathcal{J}}(A) > 0$. There is a finite C in $\mathcal{J}$ with $\|K - C\| < m_{\mathcal{J}}(A)$, by 5.5. Then

$$\|(A + K) - (A + C)\| < m_{\mathcal{J}}(A) ,$$

so

$$i(A + K) = i(A + C) = i(A) ,$$

by 6.3.

For the next theorem, we split off the finite central summand of $\mathfrak{A}$, on which any index is trivial.

THEOREM 7.5. *Let* $\mathfrak{A}$ *be a properly infinite von Neumann algebra, and let* $\mathcal{J}$ *be a compact ideal in* $\mathfrak{A}$. *The map* $i: \mathfrak{A} \to C_c(\Omega)$ *is an index on* $\mathfrak{A}$, *continuous on* $\mathcal{S}_{\mathcal{J}}$, *which induces the following correspondences:*

i) *the index group* $I(\mathfrak{A},\mathcal{K})$ *is isomorphic to the group of finite a.e. functions in* $C_c(\Omega)$,

ii) *the index group* $I(\mathfrak{A},\mathcal{J})$ *is a subgroup of* $I(\mathfrak{A},\mathcal{K})$ *which is isomorphic to the subgroup of the finite a.e. functions consisting of* $\{f \in C_c(\Omega): \ |f| \in \dim \mathcal{J}\}$,

iii) *the index semigroup* $J(\mathfrak{A},\mathcal{J})$ *is isomorphic to* $C_c^+(\Omega) + I(\mathfrak{A},\mathcal{J})$,

iv) *the index partial semigroup* $S(\mathfrak{A},\mathcal{J})$ *is isomorphic to the partial semigroup* $C_c(\Omega)$ *with the restricted operation (see 5.13),*

v) *the components of the set* $\mathcal{F}_{\mathcal{J}}$ *of Fredholm elements for* $\mathcal{J}$ *consist of the intersections with* $\mathcal{F}_{\mathcal{J}}$ *of components of the set* $\mathcal{F}_{\mathcal{K}}$ *of Fredholm elements for* $\mathfrak{A}/\mathcal{K}$,

vi) *the components of* $\mathfrak{L}\mathcal{F}_{\mathcal{J}}$ *and* $\mathfrak{R}\mathcal{F}_{\mathcal{J}}$ *are a subset of the components of* $\mathcal{S}_{\mathcal{J}}$; *the components of* $\mathcal{F}_{\mathcal{J}}$ *are those components of* $\mathcal{S}_{\mathcal{J}}$ *which are subsets of* $\mathfrak{L}\mathcal{F}_{\mathcal{J}}$ *and of* $\mathfrak{R}\mathcal{F}_{\mathcal{J}}$.

PROOF: Combining the results 6.1, 6.2, 6.5, and 7.3, we see that i is a homomorphism on the open semigroups of left and right Fredholm elements, and on the open group of Fredholm elements for $\mathcal{J}$; i is constant on the components of $\mathcal{S}$, and distinguishes between components of $\mathcal{S}$. Thus i induces one-to-one onto homomorphisms

$$i: I(\mathcal{A},\mathcal{J}) \to i(\mathcal{F})$$

$$i: J(\mathcal{A},\mathcal{J}) \to i(\mathcal{R}\mathcal{F})$$

$$i: S(\mathcal{A},\mathcal{J}) \to i(\mathcal{S}) .$$

Clearly each of these three images is contained in the indicated subset of $C_c(\Omega)$. To show the reverse containment, we observe that for each $f \geq 0$ in $C_c(\Omega)$, there is a coisometry U in $\mathcal{A}$ with $i(U) = f$: for, $\mathcal{A}$ is properly infinite, so there is a projection E in $\mathcal{A}$ with $E \sim (I - E) \sim I$. Therefore there is an $F \leq E$ with $\dim F = f$; and, $I \geq I - F \geq I - E \sim I$ implies $I - F \sim I$. Hence there is a coisometry U in $\mathcal{A}$ with $U^*U = I - F$, and $UU^* = I$: so, $i(A) = f$. For $f \leq 0$, take adjoints; for the general f , a central decomposition reduces to the positive or negative cases. Furthermore, if f is finite a.e., and $|f| \in \dim \mathcal{J}$ then the A here constructed with $i(A) = f$, is Fredholm for $\mathcal{J}$ by 5.18. Hence we have proved i), ii), and iii), and iv) follows from these; $i(\mathcal{S}) = C_c(\Omega)$.

Statement v) follows from 6.5, and statement vi) follows from 5.17.

COROLLARY 7.6. *Let $\mathcal{A}$ be a properly infinite von Neumann algebra. Let Γ be an order ideal of $\dim \mathcal{A}$ such that each function in Γ is finite a.e. There is a unique compact ideal $\mathcal{J}$ in $\mathcal{A}$ such that*

$$I(\mathcal{A},\mathcal{J}) \simeq \{f \in C_c(\Omega): |f| \in \Gamma\} .$$

COROLLARY 7.7. *Let $\mathcal{J}$ be a compact ideal in a properly infinite von Neumann algebra $\mathcal{A}$. For any index α mapping $\mathcal{F}$ continuously onto a discrete group G , we have G is a quotient group of $i(\mathcal{F})$ and $\alpha = \nu \circ i$, where ν is the quotient map.*

REMARK 7.8. As was shown 7.4, $i(A) = i(A + K)$ for any A in $\mathcal{A}$, K in $\mathcal{K}$. Hence for any compact ideal $\mathcal{J}$, we can unambiguously define the function i on $\mathcal{A}/\mathcal{J}$ by setting $i(\pi(A)) = i(A)$, where $\pi: \mathcal{A} \to \mathcal{A}/\mathcal{J}$ is the quotient map. Moreover, the map π establishes a correspondence between the components of $\mathfrak{F}_{\mathfrak{J}}$ and of the invertible group of $\mathfrak{A}/\mathfrak{J}$ [8]. Hence i is also an index on $\mathfrak{A}/\mathfrak{J}$.

8. Examples

We now consider several examples to illustrate the theorems of the previous sections and motivate the results to be proved in the following sections.

Let $\mathcal{A}$ be the (von Neumann) direct sum of a countable number of copies of $\mathcal{B}(\mathcal{H})$, where the dimension of $\mathcal{H}$ is $\aleph_1$:

$$\mathcal{A} = \Sigma \oplus \mathcal{B}(\mathcal{H}_n) .$$

The elements of $\mathcal{A}$ are the uniformly bounded sequences $T = \{T_n\}$, T_n in $\mathcal{B}(\mathcal{H}_n)$. The center Z of $\mathcal{A}$ is all $Z = \{\lambda_n I_n\}$, where I_n is the identity in $\mathcal{B}(\mathcal{H}_n)$, and $\{\lambda_n\}$ is a bounded sequence of complex numbers. Thus $Z \simeq \ell^\infty \simeq C(\beta\mathbb{N})$; the maximal ideal space of Z is $\beta\mathbb{N}$, the Stone-Čech compactification of the positive integers.

This type I von Neumann algebra is certainly accessible, and it provides illuminating examples of most of the phenomena considered in this paper. We will exhibit the index group and semigroup for several natural ideals of $\mathcal{A}$: including the compact ideal $\mathcal{K}$, an ideal $\mathcal{J} \subsetneqq \mathcal{K}$, an ideal $\mathcal{J} \not\subseteq \mathcal{K}$, the strong radical $\mathcal{R}$ of $\mathcal{A}$, and a maximal ideal $\mathfrak{M}$ of $\mathcal{A}$.

We will see that the index group $I(\mathcal{A},\mathcal{K})$ occupies a central place in the theory: the index groups for other ideals are subgroups or quotients of subgroups of $I(\mathcal{A},\mathcal{K})$.

Let V be the set $\{-\aleph_1,-\aleph_o\} \cup \mathbb{Z} \cup \{\aleph_o,\aleph_1\}$ with the order topology. Then

$$C_c(\beta\mathbb{N}) = C(\beta\mathbb{N}, V) = V^{\mathbb{N}} ,$$

$$\dim \mathcal{A} = C_c^+(\beta\mathbb{N}) = \{0,1,2,3,\ldots,\aleph_o,\aleph_1\}^{\mathbb{N}} .$$

Let $\{A_n\} \in \mathcal{A}$. Then $N_A = \{N_{A_n}\}$, $\dim N_A = \{\dim N_{A_n}\}$, and $i(A) = \{\dim N_{A_n} - \dim N_{A_n^*}\}$.

EXAMPLE 8.1. Let $\mathcal{K}$ be the relatively compact ideal of $\mathcal{A}$. A projection E in $\mathcal{A}$ is relatively finite if $E = \{E_n\}$, where each E_n is a finite rank projection. Thus each $\{K_n\}$ in $\mathcal{K}$ is a bounded sequence of compact operators.

An element $A = \{A_n\}$ of $\mathcal{A}$ is Fredholm for $\mathcal{K}$ if each A_n is a (classical) Fredholm operator in $\mathcal{B}(\mathcal{H}_n)$ and if

$$m_{\mathcal{K}}(A) = \inf m_{\mathcal{K}_n}(A_n) > 0 .$$

Then A is semi-Fredholm for $\mathcal{K}$ if there is a set $\Lambda \subset \mathbb{N}$ such that

$$\inf_{\Lambda} m_{\mathcal{K}_n}(A_n) > 0 \quad \text{and} \quad \inf_{\mathbb{N}\setminus\Lambda} m_{\mathcal{K}_n}(A_n^*) > 0 ,$$

and A_n is a left (right) Fredholm operator in $\mathcal{B}(\mathcal{H}_n)$ for $n \in \Lambda$ $(n \in \mathbb{N}\setminus\Lambda)$. If $\Lambda = \mathbb{N}$ $(\Lambda = \phi)$ then A is left (right) Fredholm for $\mathfrak{A}/\mathcal{K}$.

If $E = \{E_n\}$ is a relatively finite projection, then $\dim E = \{\dim E_n\}$ is a (not necessarily bounded) sequence of positive integers. Thus

$$\dim \mathcal{K} \simeq \mathbb{N}^{\mathbb{N}} \quad \text{and} \quad I(\mathfrak{A},\mathcal{K}) \simeq \mathbb{Z}^{\mathbb{N}} .$$

Alternatively,

$$I(\mathfrak{A},\mathcal{K}) \simeq \{f \text{ in } C_c(\beta\mathbb{N}): f \text{ is finite on } \mathbb{N}\} .$$

This is the group of finite a.e. functions: $\mathbb{N}$ is the minimal dense open set in $\beta\mathbb{N}$, and a perfect measure on $\beta\mathbb{N}$ is provided by assigning point mass at each n in $\mathbb{N}$. The index semigroup is

$$J(\mathfrak{A},\mathcal{K}) \simeq \{\mathbb{Z} \cup \{\aleph_0,\aleph_1\}\}^{\mathbb{N}} .$$

EXAMPLE 8.2. Let $\mathcal{J}$ be the ideal of $\mathfrak{A}$ generated by the set of all projections $E = \{E_n\}$, such that $\dim E$ is a bounded sequence of positive integers. Then $\mathcal{J} \subseteq \mathcal{K}$, and the index group of $\mathcal{J}$ is

$$I(\mathfrak{A},\mathcal{J}) \simeq C(\beta\mathbb{N},\mathbb{Z}) .$$

The index semigroup is

$$J(\mathfrak{A},\mathcal{J}) \simeq C(\beta\mathbb{N},\mathbb{Z}) + C^+(\beta\mathbb{N},V) .$$

An element $A = \{A_n\}$ of $\mathfrak{A}$ is Fredholm for $\mathfrak{A}/\mathcal{J}$ if each A_n is a Fredholm operator, and $\{\dim N_{A_n}\}$ and $\{\dim N_{A_n^*}\}$ are bounded sequences.

EXAMPLE 8.3. Let $\mathcal{R} = \{A$ in $\mathfrak{A}$: range of A is separable$\}$; $\mathcal{R}$ is the strong radical of $\mathfrak{A}$ (the intersection of the maximal ideals). Then $\{A_n\}$ is Fredholm for $\mathcal{R}$ if for some $\varepsilon > 0$, the spectral projections $E_n[0,\varepsilon]$ and $F_n[0,\varepsilon]$ for $|A_n|$ and $|A_n^*|$ respectively, have separable range for each n .

We now show that the set $\mathfrak{F}$ of Fredholm elements for $\mathcal{C}/\mathcal{R}$ is connected, so that $I(\mathcal{C},\mathcal{R}) = \{0\}$: let $A \in \mathfrak{F}$; we construct a path in $\mathfrak{F}$ from A to I . By passing to a central summand, assume $i(A) \leq 0$, so $A = U|A|$, where U is an isometry in $\mathcal{C}$, and $i(U) = i(A)$. By 6.4, there is a path in $\mathfrak{F}$ from A to U . There is also a path in $\mathfrak{F}$ from U to I: let $N = \{N_n\}$ where $\dim N_n = \aleph_o$ for each n , and let $U_t = U(I - tN)$. For each t , U_t is Fredholm, with $U_0 = U$ and $U_1 = U(I - N)$. Note further, that $i(U(I - N)) = 0$: for, $U_1 = \{U_n(I - N_n)\}$ where the kernel and cokernel of $U_n(I - N_n)$ are both countably infinite in $\mathcal{B}(\mathcal{H}_n)$. Hence 6.5 ensures a path through $\mathfrak{F}$ from U_1 to I .

In Section 10, we will see that if $\mathcal{J}$ is any ideal such that $\dim \mathcal{J}$ contains a function f with $f \geq \aleph_o$, then $I(\mathcal{C},\mathcal{J}) = \{0\}$. However, $J(\mathcal{C},\mathcal{J})$ is always nontrivial in a properly infinite algebra. For the ideal $\mathcal{R}$ of this example, we will see that

$$J(\mathcal{C},\mathcal{R}) \simeq \{0,\aleph_1\}^{\mathbb{N}} \simeq C(\beta\mathbb{N}, \{0,\aleph_1\}) .$$

EXAMPLE 8.4. Let $\mathcal{J}$ be the ideal in $\mathcal{C}$ consisting of all sequences $\{K_n\}$ such that the range of each K_n is separable and K_n is compact for large n . Thus $\dim \mathcal{J}$ is the eventually finite sequences in $(\mathbb{N} \cup \{\aleph_0\})^{\mathbb{N}} \subseteq C_c^+(\beta\mathbb{N})$.

Note that for each n in $\mathbb{N}$, $f(n) = \aleph_o$ for some f in $\dim \mathcal{J}$, and note that the singleton $\{n\}$ is open in $\beta\mathbb{N}$. On the other hand, if $t \in \beta\mathbb{N}\setminus\mathbb{N}$, there is no f in $\dim \mathcal{J}$ with f infinite on a neighborhood of t . We will see that $I(\mathcal{C},\mathcal{J})$ is isomorphic to the group of germs at $\beta\mathbb{N}\setminus\mathbb{N}$ of the finite a.e. functions in $C_c(\beta\mathbb{N})$. Restating this in a way that highlights the relationship between $I(\mathcal{C},\mathcal{J})$ and $J(\mathcal{C},\mathcal{J})$: we will see that

$$I(\mathcal{C},\mathcal{J}) \simeq G/H \quad \text{and} \quad J(\mathcal{C},\mathcal{J}) \simeq [C_c^+(\beta\mathbb{N}) + G]/[\mathbf{J}^+ + H] ,$$

where G is the finite a.e. group,

$$H = \{f \text{ in } G\colon\ f \text{ vanishes on a neighborhood of } \beta\mathbb{N}\setminus\mathbb{N}\} ,$$

$$\mathbf{J}^+ = \{f \text{ in } C_c^+(\beta\mathbb{N})\colon\ f \text{ vanishes on a neighborhood of } \beta\mathbb{N}\setminus\mathbb{N}\} ,$$

noting that $\mathbf{J}^+$ defines a congruence in $C_c^+(\beta\mathbb{N})$.

EXAMPLE 8.5. Let $\mathcal{L}$ be the ideal of $\mathfrak{a}$, consisting of all sequences of operators $\{T_n\}$ such that $\|T_n\| \to 0$. Thus $\dim \mathcal{L}$ is all finitely nonzero sequences in $\{\mathbb{N}, \aleph_0, \aleph_1\}^{\mathbb{N}}$. In this case we will see

$$I(\mathfrak{a},\mathcal{L}) \simeq \{0\} ,$$

$$J(\mathfrak{a},\mathcal{L}) \simeq \text{semigroup of germs at } \beta\mathbb{N}\backslash\mathbb{N} \text{ of the functions in } C_c^+(\beta\mathbb{N}) .$$

EXAMPLE 8.6. Let $\mathfrak{m}$ be a maximal ideal of $\mathfrak{a}$; then $\mathfrak{m} \cap Z$ is a maximal ideal in Z associated with some point t in $\beta\mathbb{N}$, and $\mathfrak{m} = \mathfrak{m}_t$ is the ideal in $\mathfrak{a}$ generated by $\mathfrak{m} \cap Z$. Or, in terms of Wils' characterization: for this fixed t in $\beta\mathbb{N}$, $\mathfrak{m}_t$ is generated by all the projections E in $\mathfrak{a}$ such that $\dim(E)(t) \le \aleph_0$. Then we will be able to calculate that $I(\mathfrak{a},\mathfrak{m}_t) \simeq \{0\}$ and $J(\mathfrak{a},\mathfrak{m}_t)$ is isomorphic to the semigroup $\{0,\aleph_1\}$, consisting of two elements. Note that these do not vary with t , although the quotient $\mathfrak{a}/\mathfrak{m}_t$ most certainly varies as $t \in \mathbb{N}$ or $t \in \beta\mathbb{N}\backslash\mathbb{N}$, or as t is associated with different sorts of ultrafilters in $\beta\mathbb{N}$.

9. Definition of an index for noncompact ideals

We have seen that if an ideal $\mathcal{J}$ is not relatively compact, then the function i may not be constant on the components of $\mathfrak{F}$ (for example, the ideal $\mathfrak{R}$ of $\mathcal{A}$ in 8.3). In this section we define a modified map $\bar{i}$ sending $\mathcal{A}$ into a quotient of $C_c(\Omega)$ which will give a representation of $I(\mathcal{A},\mathcal{J})$ and $J(\mathcal{A},\mathcal{J})$ for noncompact ideals.

Observe first that the relatively compact part of any ideal can be split off.

~~DEFINITION 9.1. Let $\mathcal{J}$ be an ideal in a von Neumann algebra $\mathcal{A}$. Let~~ Δ denote the open subset of the maximal ideal space Ω of Z:

$$\Delta = \{t \in \Omega : \exists f \text{ in } \dim \mathcal{J} \text{ with } f \geq \aleph_0 \text{ on a neighborhood of } t\}$$

DEFINITION 9.2. If Δ is dense in Ω for an ideal $\mathcal{J}$ of $\mathcal{A}$, we say $\mathcal{J}$ is <u>completely noncompact</u> (relative to $\mathcal{A}$). Equivalently, $\mathcal{J}$ is completely noncompact if there is no nonzero central projection Q such that the elements of $Q\mathcal{J}$ are relatively compact in $Q\mathcal{A}$.

Note that the existence of a completely noncompact ideal of $\mathcal{A}$ implies $\mathcal{A}$ must be properly infinite.

Examples 8.3 - 8.6 are completely noncompact ideals. Note that $\Omega \backslash \Delta$ may be a single point, or it might be empty.

PROPOSITION 9.3. <u>For any ideal $\mathcal{J}$ of $\mathcal{A}$, there is a unique central projection P such that $P\mathcal{J}$ is completely noncompact in $P\mathcal{A}$, and $(I - P)\mathcal{J}$ is relatively compact in $(I - P)\mathcal{A}$.</u>

PROOF. The set Δ is open; let $P = \chi_{\bar{\Delta}}$. If $f \in \dim \mathcal{J}$, then f is finite a.e. on $\Omega \backslash \bar{\Delta}$; so $(I - P)\mathcal{J}$ is relatively compact in $(I - P)\mathcal{A}$.

In view of 9.3, we see that Fredholm theory and index theory for any ideal $\mathcal{J}$ of $\mathcal{A}$ splits into consideration of the (relatively) compact part and the completely noncompact part of $\mathcal{J}$. Thus we may consider these two summands of $\mathcal{A}$ and $\mathcal{J}$ separately; we have developed the theory for compact ideals and we turn now to completely noncompact ideals.

DEFINITION 9.4. Let $\mathcal{J}$ be a completely noncompact ideal in $\mathcal{A}$. Consider the subset $\mathbf{I}$ of $C_c(\Omega)$:

$\mathbf{J} = \{f$ in $C_c(\Omega)$: $|f| \in \dim \mathcal{J}$ and f is zero in a neighborhood of $\Omega\backslash\Delta\}$

We say f is equivalent to g modulo $\mathbf{J}$ and write $f \equiv g \pmod{\mathbf{J}}$ if $f - g \in \mathbf{J}$.

PROPOSITION 9.5. <u>The relation of equivalence</u> mod $\mathbf{J}$ <u>is a congruence in</u> $C_c(\Omega)$ <u>for the operation of addition defined in</u> 5.12.

PROOF. Let f_1, f_2, g_1, g_2 in $C_c(\Omega)$ be such that $f_1 \equiv f_2 \pmod{\mathbf{J}}$, and $g_1 \equiv g_2 \pmod{\mathbf{J}}$. We first show $(f_1 + g_1) \equiv (f_2 + g_2) \pmod{\mathbf{J}}$.

We have that $|f_1 - f_2|$ and $|g_1 - g_2|$ are in $\dim \mathcal{J}$, and that both are zero on some open and closed set Y with $\Omega\backslash\Delta \subset Y \subset \Omega$. If the operation on $C_c(\Omega)$ were associative, this proof would be a trivial matter; as it is not, we will restrict to various subsets of Ω and check the cardinal arithmetic with the restricted functions, to show $|(f_1 + g_1) - (f_2 + g_2)|$ is in $\dim \mathcal{J}$, and to show this function is zero on Y.

i) Let $X_1 \subset \Omega$ be the open set where not both f_1 and f_2 are infinite and not both g_1 and g_2 are infinite: then on X_1 (and hence on $\overline{X}_1$),

$$(f_1 + g_1) - (f_2 + g_2) = (f_1 - f_2) + (g_1 - g_2) ;$$

except possibly where $f \equiv -g_j$ and both are infinite. However, it is still true that

$$\chi_{\overline{X}_1} |(f_1 + g_1) - (f_2 + g_2)| \in \dim \mathcal{J} ,$$

and this function is zero on $Y \cap \overline{X}_1$.

ii) Let X_2 be the open subset of $\Omega\backslash\overline{X}_1$ where f_1 and f_2 are finite, or g_1 and g_2 are finite. Then on X_2,

$$|(f_1 + g_1) - (f_2 + g_2)| \leq |g_1 - g_2| \vee |f_1 - f_2| ,$$

so if we restrict to $\chi_{\overline{X}_2}\mathfrak{G}$, the desired result follows.

iii) Let X_3 be the open subset of $\Omega\backslash(\overline{X}_1 \cup \overline{X}_2)$ where $f_1 \neq f_2$, and $g_1 \neq g_2$. Then $\overline{X}_3 \cap Y = X_3 \cap Y = \phi$. Note that in this and remaining cases, at most one function is finite. Thus on X_3,

$$|g_1 - g_2| = |g_1| \vee |g_2| , \quad |f_1 - f_2| = |f_1| \vee |f_2| ,$$

so that on $\overline{X}_3$ all four functions are in $\dim \mathcal{J}$; the desired result follows on $\overline{X}_3$.

iv) Let X_4 be the open subset of $\Omega \setminus \bigcup_{i\le 3}\overline{X}_i$ where $f_1 \ne f_2$, but $g_1 = g_2 < f_2$ or $g_1 = g_2 < f_1$. As in iii), $\overline{X}_4 \cap Y = \phi$ and $|f_i| \in \dim \mathcal{J}$ on $\overline{X}_4$. Furthermore here $|g_i| \le |f_2|$ so these also are in $\dim \mathcal{J}$ on $\overline{X}_4$.

v) Let X_5 be the open subset of $\Omega \setminus \bigcup_{i\le 4}\overline{X}_i$ where $f_1 \ne f_2$, and $g_1 = g_2 \ge f_i$. Here $\overline{X}_5 \cap Y = \phi$, and

$$(f_1 + g_1) - (f_2 + g_2) = g_1 - g_2 = 0 .$$

vi) The open subset X_6 of $\Omega \setminus \bigcup_{i\le 5}\overline{X}_i$ where $f_1 = f_2$ and $g_1 \ne g_2$ is taken care of as were X_4 , and X_5 .

vii) Finally, on $X_7 = \Omega \setminus \bigcup_{i\le 6}\overline{X}_i$ we have $f_1 \equiv f_2$, $g_1 \equiv g_2$, so $(f_1 + g_1) - (f_2 + g_2) \equiv 0$.

It remains to show that this is an equivalence relation; it is obviously reflexive and symmetric. To see that it is transitive, suppose $f_1 \equiv f_2$ (mod $\mathbf{J}$) and $f_2 \equiv f_3$ (mod $\mathbf{J}$) . Then $-f_3 \equiv -f_2$ (mod $\mathbf{J}$) and therefore by the above

$$(f_1 - f_3) \equiv (f_2 - f_2) \equiv 0 \pmod{\mathbf{J}} .$$

The proof is complete.

REMARK 9.6. Since $\mathbf{J}$ defines a congruence, the addition on $C_c(\Omega)$ induces a commutative (not a priori associative) addition with inverses on the quotient set $C_c(\Omega)/\mathbf{J}$. For f in $C_c(\Omega)$, let $\overline{f}$ denote the coset $f + \mathbf{J}$.

We now define what will prove to be the index map corresponding to the ideal $\mathcal{J}$:

DEFINITION 9.7. Let $\mathcal{J}$ be a completely noncompact ideal of $\mathfrak{A}$, and let $\mathbf{J}$ be as above, determined by $\mathcal{J}$. Define $\overline{i}\colon \mathfrak{A} \to C_c(\Omega)/\mathbf{J}$ to be the function given by

$$\overline{i}(A) = i(A) + \mathbf{J}$$

for each A in $\mathfrak{A}$.

The next result shows that any coset containing functions in $\dim \mathcal{J}$

also contains a finite a.e. function; thus these cosets (and their negatives) will be a group under the induced operation.

PROPOSITION 9.8. *Let* $f \in C_c(\Omega)$ *with* $|f|$ *in* $\dim \mathcal{J}$. *Then there is a function* g *in* J *such that* $f + g$ *is finite a.e. Furthermore, if* $f \geq 0$, *we can choose* $f + g \geq 0$.

PROOF. Let X be the open subset of Ω where $|f| < \aleph_0$. Then on the open and closed set $\Omega \backslash \overline{X}$, we have $|f| \geq \aleph_0$; so $\Omega \backslash \overline{X} \subset \Delta$. Thus $g \in J$ where $g = -(\chi_{\Omega \backslash \overline{X}})f$, and $f + g = \chi_{\overline{X}} f$, which is finite off the nowhere dense boundary $\overline{X} \backslash X$.

10. Properties of the map $\bar{i}$.

We obtain analogs for the properties of i , and of the classical index. In this section, $\mathcal{J}$ is a completely noncompact ideal in a properly infinite von Neumann algebra $\mathfrak{A}$.

PROPOSITION 10.1. *Let A and B belong to $\mathfrak{A}$. Assume both are semi-Fredholm for $\mathcal{J}$, and that $\bar{i}(A) = \bar{i}(B)$. Then*

i) *if A is left (right) Fredholm, then B is left (right) Fredholm;*

ii) *if A is Fredholm then B is Fredholm.*

PROOF. The argument is verbatim the same as the proof of 5.17, except to show $N_B \in \mathcal{J}$:

We have $i(A) = i(B) + g$, some g in $\mathfrak{J}$, and $N_B \gtrsim N_{B^*}$. On the open set $Y \subset \Omega$ where $\dim N_B > |g|$, we have

$$\dim N_A + \dim N_{B^*} \geq (\dim N_A - \dim N_{A^*}) + \dim N_{B^*}$$

$$= [(\dim N_B - \dim N_{B^*}) + g] + \dim N_{B^*}$$

$$= \dim N_B + g .$$

Thus on Y , $\dim N_A + \dim N_{B^*} + |g| \geq \dim N_B$. Hence both $\chi_{\bar{Y}} \dim N_B$ and $\chi_{\Omega \setminus \bar{Y}} \dim N_B$ are in $\dim \mathcal{J}$, so $N_B \in \mathcal{J}$, and the proof is complete.

THEOREM 10.2. *Let A and B belong to $\mathfrak{A}$, and let $\bar{i}$ be defined for a completely noncompact ideal $\mathcal{J}$. Then*

$$\bar{i}(AB) = \bar{i}(A) + \bar{i}(B)$$

whenever any one of the following holds:

i) *both N_A and N_B are in $\mathcal{J}$;*

ii) *both N_A and N_{A^*} are in $\mathcal{J}$, and $\bar{i}(A) = 0$;*

iii) *$N_{AB} \in \mathcal{J}$, and $\bar{i}(AB) = 0$.*

PROOF. We know from the proof of Theorem 6.1 that the projections $E = N_{B^*}$ and $F = N_A$ can be decomposed in $\mathfrak{A}$ as:

$$E = E' \oplus E'' \oplus E''' , \quad E_\perp = E'_\perp \oplus E''_\perp \oplus E'''_\perp$$

$$F = F' \oplus F'' \oplus F''' , \quad F_\perp = F'_\perp \oplus F''_\perp \oplus F'''_\perp$$

with $E' = F'$, $E'' = F''_\perp$, $F'' = E''_\perp$ and $E''' \sim E'''_\perp \sim F''' \sim F'''_\perp$. And for $A = U|A|$, $B = V|B|$ polar decompositions,

$$N_{AB} = N_B \oplus V^*F''V , \quad N_{(AB)^*} = N_A + UE''U^* .$$

And, we have

$$i(AB) = (\dim N_B + \dim F'') - (\dim N_{A^*} + \dim E'') ,$$

$$i(A) + i(B) = [(\dim F' + \dim F'' + \dim F''') - \dim N_{A^*}]$$

$$+ [\dim N_B - (\dim F' + \dim E'' + \dim F''')] .$$

Assume i): then N_B, F', F'' and F''' are all in $\mathcal{J}$. By 9.8 we can choose nonnegative functions n_B, f', f'', f''' in $C_c(\Omega)$, all finite on some dense open set $X \subset \Omega$, such that $n_B - \dim N_B$, $f' - \dim F'$, $f'' - \dim F''$, and $f''' - \dim F'''$ are all in $\mathbf{J}$. Thus,

$$\bar{i}(AB) = (n_B + f'') - (\dim N_{A^*} + \dim E'') + \mathbf{J}$$

$$\bar{i}(A) + \bar{i}(B) = [(f' + f'' + f''') - \dim N_{A^*}] + [n_B - (f' + \dim E'' + f''')] + \mathbf{J} .$$

On the set X, the two functions which define these two cosets are equal; so the cosets are equal, and i) is proved.

The proof for ii) is analogous to the proof of 6.1 ii) in a similar fashion. The argument under hypothesis iii) is similar.

COROLLARY 10.3. <u>One has</u> $\bar{i}(AB) = \bar{i}(A) + \bar{i}(B)$ <u>whenever</u>

i) <u>both</u> N_{A^*} <u>and</u> N_{B^*} <u>are in</u> $\mathcal{J}$;

<u>or</u> ii) <u>both</u> N_B <u>and</u> N_{B^*} <u>are in</u> $\mathcal{J}$, <u>and</u> $\bar{i}(B) = 0$.

COROLLARY 10.4. <u>Let</u> $A \in \mathfrak{G}$, <u>and let</u> $C \in \mathfrak{G}$ <u>with</u> $R_C \in \mathcal{J}$. <u>Then</u> $\bar{i}(A + C) = \bar{i}(A)$.

PROOF: The proof is analogous to the proof of 6.3.

THEOREM 10.5. *Let $\mathcal{J}$ be a completely noncompact ideal of $\mathcal{G}$. Let A and B be elements of $\mathcal{G}$ such that $\overline{i}(A) = \overline{i}(B)$. There is a path A_t in $\mathcal{G}$ such that $A_0 = A$, $A_1 = B$ and $\overline{i}(A_t) = \overline{i}(A)$, for each t. Furthermore A_t is semi-Fredholm for $\mathcal{J}$ for each $t \neq 0,1$. If A is (left or right) Fredholm then A_t is (left or right) Fredholm for $\mathcal{J}$ for each $t \neq 0,1$.*

PROOF. We prove this first under several special hypotheses, and then show how the general result reduces to these cases.

Case (i): assume first that $f \geq \aleph_0$, for some f in $\dim \mathcal{J}$. Then $\Delta = \Omega$, so

$$J = \{f \in C_c(\Omega): |f| \in \dim \mathcal{J}\} .$$

Assume also that $i(B) \leq i(A) \leq 0$. Applying Lemma 6.4, there exist paths A_t from A to an isometry U, and B_t from B to an isometry V such that for all t, $i(A_t) = i(A)$ and $i(B_t) = i(B)$, and such that A_t and B_t are left invertible for $t \neq 0$. Hence to prove the theorem in this case, it suffices to exhibit a path from U to V of left Fredholm elements U_t, such that $\overline{i}(U_t) = \overline{i}(U)$, all t.

Since $\overline{i}(U) = \overline{i}(V)$, there is a projection E in $\mathcal{J}$ with

$$\dim E = |\dim N_{U^*} - \dim N_{V^*}| .$$

Let F be a projection in $\mathcal{J}$ with $f \geq \aleph_0$ on Ω, and let $G = E \vee F$. Then $G \in \mathcal{J}$, and G is properly infinite, by 5.9. Thus UGU^* is also properly infinite, so we can write

$$UGU^* = H_1 \oplus H_2 , \quad H_1 \sim H_2 \sim UGU^* .$$

For some projection H in $\mathcal{G}$, $E \sim H \leq H_1$, and

$$\dim G = \dim UGU^* \geq \dim (UGU^* - H) \geq \dim H_2 = \dim G ,$$

so $G \sim (UGU^* - H)$. There is a partial isometry W in $\mathcal{G}$ with $W^*W = G$ and $WW^* = UGU^* - H$. Let

$T_t = U(I - tG)$ be a path from U to $U(I - G)$,

$S_t = U(I - G) + tW$ be a path from $U(I - G)$ to $U(I - G) + W$.

The composition of these is a path from U to $U(I - G) + W$ such that $\bar{i}(T_t) = \bar{i}(U) = \bar{i}(S_t)$ for each t, and such that each T_t and S_t is left Fredholm, by 10.4. Furthermore S_1 is an isometry with $R_{S_1} = UU^* - H$. Thus $N_{S_1^*} = N_{U^*} + H$, so

$$\dim N_{S_1^*} = \dim N_{U^*} + (\dim N_{V^*} - \dim N_{U^*}) = \dim N_{V^*} ,$$

since $i(V) \leq i(U)$ implies $\dim N_{V^*} \geq \dim N_{U^*}$. Therefore $i(S_1) = i(V)$, so there is a path M_t from S_1 to V of left Fredholm elements such that $i(M_t) = i(V)$ for each t, by 6.5. This completes the proof for case i).

Case (ii): again, assume $f \geq \aleph_0$ for some f in $\dim \mathcal{J}$, and assume $i(A) \leq -i(B) \leq 0$. Then

$$|i(A)| \leq |i(A) - i(B)| ,$$

so that $i(A)$ is in $\mathbf{J}$ and $\bar{i}(A) = 0 = \bar{i}(B)$. As in case (i) there is a path from A to U through Fredholm elements (5.18) at which $\bar{i} = 0$, where U is an isometry. We wish now to connect U to I by a path on which $\bar{i} = 0$; this is done by imitating the proof above where we connect U to V (only now $V = I$). That is, with $V = I$ so that we take $E = N_{U^*}$, we follow the argument above to get a path T_t from U to $U(I - G)$. Then

$$i(U(I - G)) = \dim G - \dim (UGU^* + N_{U^*}) = \dim G - (\dim G + \dim E) = 0 ,$$

since $\dim G$ is infinite and $\dim G \geq \dim E$. This means there is a path from $U(I - G)$ to I through Fredholm elements on which $i = 0$, by 6.5. Similarly we can join B^* to I, and take adjoints to complete the proof in case (ii).

Case (iii): assume $f \geq \aleph_0$ for some f in $\dim \mathcal{J}$; we can dispense with the remaining possible relationships between $i(A)$ and $i(B)$. There is a partition of Ω into open and closed subsets such that on each subset one of the conditions for case i) or case ii) or $i(B) \geq i(A) \geq 0$, or $i(A) \geq -i(B) \geq 0$, or one of these with A and B switched, holds. The theorem follows in each of these summands as in i) and ii), or by taking adjoints.

Case (iv): finally, assume $\dim \mathcal{J}$ contains no such $f \geq \aleph_0$, so that $\Omega\backslash\Delta \neq \phi$. Since $i(A) - i(B) \in \mathbf{J}$, the zero set of $i(A) - i(B)$ contains an open and closed neighborhood Y of $\Omega\backslash\Delta$. Therefore $\Omega\backslash Y$ is a compact subset of Δ , so there is some $f \in \dim \mathcal{J}$ with $f \geq \aleph_0$ on $\Omega \setminus Y$. Let $P = \chi_{\Omega\setminus Y}$. In $P\mathcal{A}$ we have f in $\dim P\mathcal{J}$ with $f \geq \aleph_0$, so the theorem follows in this summand as above. In $(I - P)\mathcal{A}$, $i(I - P)A \equiv i(I - P)B$; in this summand the theorem follows by 6.5.

The final statement of the theorem follows by 10.1.

COROLLARY 10.6. *If* $\dim \mathcal{J}$ *contains some* f *with* $f \geq \aleph_0$, *then the index group* $I(\mathcal{A},\mathcal{J})$ *is zero*.

PROOF. The hypothesis implies $\Delta = \Omega$. Let $A \in \mathcal{A}$, with A Fredholm for $\mathcal{J}$. Then $\dim N_A$ and $\dim N_{A^*}$ belong to J , so $\bar{i}(A) = 0$. Then by 10.5, the set of Fredholm elements is path connected.

COROLLARY 10.7. *Let* $\mathcal{A}$ *be a type III von Neumann algebra. The index group* $I(\mathcal{A},\mathcal{J})$ *is zero for any ideal* $\mathcal{J}$ *in* $\mathcal{A}$.

THEOREM 10.8. *Let* $\mathcal{J}$ *be a completely noncompact ideal in* $\mathcal{A}$, *and let* A *and* B *belong to* $\mathcal{A}$. *If*

$$\|A - B\| < m_{\mathcal{J}}(A) ,$$

then $\bar{i}(A) = \bar{i}(B)$, *and* A *and* B *are left Fredholm for* $\mathcal{J}$.

PROOF. This proof is verbatim the same as the proof of the analogous result 7.1 for compact ideals, to the point where 6.1 iii) and 6.3 are invoked. Here in place of those results we use 10.2 iii) and 10.4 to obtain the analogous equations for $\bar{i}$. The rest of the proof is similar to the proof of 7.1; using 10.1 instead of 5.17.

The next three results follow exactly as do their compact analogs 7.2 - 7.4.

COROLLARY 10.9. *Let* A *and* B *belong to* $\mathcal{A}$. *If*

$$\|A - B\| < m_{\mathcal{J}}(A^*)$$

then $\bar{i}(A) = \bar{i}(B)$ *and* A *and* B *are right Fredholm for* $\mathcal{J}$.

COROLLARY 10.10. *Let* $\bar{i}$ *be defined for* $\mathcal{J}$. *Then* $\bar{i}$ *is constant on the connected components of* $\mathcal{S}_{\mathcal{J}}$.

THEOREM 10.11. *Let* K *belong to a completely noncompact ideal* $\mathcal{J}$ *, and let* A *in* $\mathfrak{A}$ *be semi-Fredholm for* $\mathcal{J}$ *. Then* $A + K$ *is also semi-Fredholm, and*

$$\bar{i}(A + K) = \bar{i}(A) .$$

The next theorem gives the desired representation of $I(\mathfrak{A},\mathcal{J})$, $J(\mathfrak{A},\mathcal{J})$ and $S(\mathfrak{A},\mathcal{J})$. Let G and H be the following subgroups of the group of finite a.e. functions in $C_c(\Omega)$:

$$G = \{f \text{ in } C_c(\Omega): |f| \in \dim \mathcal{J} \text{ and } f \text{ is finite a.e.}\}$$

$$H = \{f \text{ in } G: f \text{ vanishes on a neighborhood of } \Omega\backslash\Delta \}.$$

Recall that $\{f \in C_c(\Omega): f \text{ is finite a.e.}\}$ is isomorphic to $I(\mathfrak{A},\mathcal{K})$, so that G and H are isomorphic to subgroups of $I(\mathfrak{A},\mathcal{K})$. Let $\mathbf{J}^+$ denote the semigroup of nonnegative functions in $\mathbf{J}$. Then $\mathbf{J}^+ + H$ defines a congruence in the semigroup $C_c^+(\Omega) + G$.

THEOREM 10.12. *Let* $\mathcal{J}$ *be a completely noncompact ideal in a properly infinite von Neumann algebra* $\mathfrak{A}$ *. The function*

$$\bar{i}: \mathfrak{A} \to C_c(\Omega)/\mathbf{J}$$

is an index on $\mathfrak{A}$ *, continuous on* $\mathfrak{S}_{\mathcal{J}}$ *, which induces the following correspondences:*

i) *the index group* $I(\mathfrak{A},\mathcal{J})$ *is isomorphic to* G/H *, for* G *and* H *as defined above, and where* $G \simeq I(\mathfrak{A}, \mathcal{J} \cap \mathcal{K})$ *,*

ii) $I(\mathfrak{A},\mathcal{J})$ *is isomorphic to the group of germs at* $\Omega\backslash\Delta$ *of the functions in* G *,*

iii) *the index semigroup* $J(\mathfrak{A},\mathcal{J})$ *is isomorphic to* $[C_c^+(\Omega) + G]/[\mathbf{J}^+ + H]$ *,*

iv) *the index partial semigroup* $\mathfrak{S}(\mathfrak{A},\mathcal{J})$ *is isomorphic to the partial semigroup* $C_c(\Omega)/\mathbf{J}$ *,*

v) *the components of* $\mathfrak{L}\mathfrak{F}$ *and* $\mathfrak{R}\mathfrak{F}$ *are a subset of the components of* $\mathfrak{S}$ *; the components of* $\mathfrak{F}$ *are those components of* $\mathfrak{S}$ *which are subsets of* $\mathfrak{L}\mathfrak{F}$ *and of* $\mathfrak{R}\mathfrak{F}$.

PROOF: As in Theorem 7.5, it follows from 10.2, 10.3, 10.5, and 10.10, that $\bar{i}$ is a homomorphism on the semigroups of left and right Fredholm elements for $\mathcal{J}$; $\bar{i}$ is constant on the components of $\mathfrak{S}$, and distinguishes between components of $\mathfrak{S}$. Thus $\bar{i}$ induces onto isomorphisms

$$\bar{i}: I(\mathfrak{a},\mathcal{J}) \to i(\mathfrak{F})/\mathbf{J}$$

$$\bar{i}: J(\mathfrak{a},\mathcal{J}) \to i(\mathfrak{R}\mathfrak{F})/\mathbf{J}$$

$$\bar{i}: S(\mathfrak{a},\mathcal{J}) \to i(\mathfrak{S})/\mathbf{J} .$$

To prove i), observe that there is a group structure on $i(\mathfrak{F})/\mathbf{J}$ induced by the isomorphism with $I(\mathfrak{a},\mathcal{J})$. For each g in $i(\mathfrak{F})$, $|g| \in \dim \mathcal{J}$, so there is a finite a.e. function g_o with $|g_o| \in \dim \mathcal{J}$, and $g - g_o \in \mathbf{J}$, by 9.8. Define

$$\psi: i(\mathfrak{F})/\mathbf{J} \to G/H \quad \text{by} \quad \psi(g + \mathbf{J}) = g_o + H .$$

It is straightforward to show ψ is a well-defined injective map of $i(\mathfrak{F})/\mathbf{J}$ onto G/H which preserves the induced group structure on $i(\mathfrak{F})/\mathbf{J}$. That $G \simeq I(\mathfrak{a}, \mathcal{J} \cap \mathcal{K})$ follows from 7.5, so i) is proved.

Assertion ii) is immediate from i).

To prove iii) observe that $i(\mathfrak{R}\mathfrak{F})/\mathbf{J}$ has a semigroup structure induced by the isomorphism with $\mathbf{J}(\mathfrak{a},\mathcal{J})$.

For each A in $\mathfrak{R}\mathfrak{F}$, there is a $P = \chi_Y$ such that $i(PA) \le 0$ and PA is Fredholm for $P\mathcal{J}$, and $i(I - P) \ge 0$ and $(I - P)A$ right Fredholm for $(I - P)\mathcal{J}$, by 5.16. Therefore, $|g| \in \dim \mathcal{J}$ for $g = \chi_Y i(A)$. Hence there is a finite a.e. function g_o with $|g_o| \in \dim \mathcal{J}$ and $g - g_o \in \mathbf{J}$ (9.8). Define

$$\phi: i(\mathfrak{R}\mathfrak{F})\mathbf{J} \longrightarrow [C_c^+(\Omega) + G]/[\mathbf{J}^+ + H] ,$$

$$\phi(i(A) + \mathbf{J}) = \chi_{\Omega/Y} i(A) + g_o + \mathbf{J}^+ + H .$$

Then ϕ is a well-defined isomorphism of semigroups, so iii) holds.

The proof of (iv) is similar; $i(S) = C_c(\Omega)$.

Finally, assertion v) follows from 10.1. The proof is complete.

COROLLARY 10.13. <u>Let</u> $\mathfrak{a}$, $\mathcal{J}$, G <u>and</u> H <u>be as in the theorem. For any index</u> α <u>mapping the set of Fredholm elements for</u> $\mathcal{J}$ <u>continuously onto a discrete group</u> G_o , <u>we have</u> G_o <u>is a quotient group of</u> G/H , <u>and</u> $\alpha = \nu \circ \bar{i}$, <u>where</u> ν <u>is the quotient map</u>.

Corollary 7.6 identifies those groups which arise as index groups $I(\mathfrak{A},\mathcal{J})$ for some compact ideal $\mathcal{J}$; the following result does the same thing for completely noncompact ideals.

COROLLARY 10.14. *Let* $\mathfrak{A}$ *be a properly infinite von Neumann algebra. Let* Γ *be an order ideal of* $\dim \mathfrak{A}$ *such that each function in* Γ *is finite a.e., and let* Λ *be a closed nowhere dense subset of* Ω , *the maximal ideal space of the center of* $\mathfrak{A}$. *Then there is a completely noncompact ideal* $\mathcal{J}$ *of* $\mathfrak{A}$ *such that the index group* $I(\mathfrak{A},\mathcal{J})$ *is isomorphic to the group of germs at* Λ *of the functions* f *in* $C_c(\Omega)$ *such that* $|f| \in \Gamma$.

PROOF: Let $\mathcal{J}$ be the ideal associated with the order ideal $\dim \mathcal{J}$ in $C_c(\Omega)$, where

$$\dim \mathcal{J} = \{f \in C_c(\Omega)\colon \text{for some } g \text{ in } \Gamma ,\ f = g \text{ on a neighborhood of } \Lambda\} .$$

REMARK 10.15. Let $\mathfrak{A}$ be an algebra with no type I summand, and let $\mathcal{J}$ be an ideal of $\mathfrak{A}$. There is a central decomposition of $\mathcal{J} = P\mathcal{J} \oplus Q\mathcal{J}$ into compact and completely noncompact summands, and a corresponding decomposition of the Fredholm elements $\mathfrak{F}$ for $\mathfrak{A}/\mathcal{J}$. Let α be any index on $\mathfrak{A}$ which maps $\mathfrak{F}$ continuously onto a discrete group G . Observe that for each f in $\dim \mathcal{J}$, $(1/n)f$ is also in $\dim \mathcal{J}$; thus the groups $i(P\mathfrak{F})$ and $\bar{i}(Q\mathfrak{F})$ are each divisible. Then from 7.7 and 10.13, we see that $\alpha(P\mathfrak{F})$ and $\alpha(Q\mathfrak{F})$ are divisible groups; hence G is a divisible group.

11. The maximal domain of continuity for the index.

In this section $\mathcal{A}$ is a properly infinite von Neumann algebra. The index map for an ideal $\mathcal{J}$ is continuous on the set of semi-Fredholm elements for $\mathcal{J}$, but is in fact defined on all of $\mathcal{A}$. We turn now to the natural question of whether such an index may be continuous on a larger domain. We speak here (as throughout the paper) of continuity as a map into a discrete space.

It is well known that the classical index defined for the set of semi-Fredholm operators on a separable Hilbert space, does not extend continuously beyond this set. However, in the general situation, the maximal domain of continuity of an index for $\mathcal{J}$ may well include more than the semi-Fredholm elements for $\mathcal{J}$. This is trivially true if $\mathcal{J}$ is a compact ideal of $\mathcal{A}$ with $\mathcal{J} \neq \mathcal{K}$. The map i serves as an index for $\mathcal{J}$ and for $\mathcal{K}$; obviously i extends continuously beyond the semi-Fredholm elements for $\mathcal{J}$ at least to the semi-Fredholm elements for $\mathcal{K}$. In fact, the index for any ideal $\mathcal{J}$ extends continuously to an open maximal domain $\mathcal{D}$ strictly larger than the semi-Fredholm elements for $\mathcal{J}$ if and only if $\mathcal{J}$ does not contain the <u>strong radical</u> of $\mathcal{A}$ (the intersection of the maximal ideals of $\mathcal{A}$). In this case, the index is a homomorphism on the group of Fredholm components of $\mathcal{D}$, and on the semi-groups of left Fredholm components and of right Fredholm components. If $\mathcal{J}$ contains the strong radical the index does not extend continuously beyond the semi-Fredholm elements for $\mathcal{J}$.

NOTATION 11.1. The index for any compact ideal of the properly infinite algebra $\mathcal{A}$ is given by i; the index relative to a completely noncompact ideal is denoted by $\bar{i}$. For an arbitrary ideal $\mathcal{J}$, we denote the index for $\mathcal{J}$ by $\tilde{i}$; thus, $\mathcal{J} = \mathcal{J}_0 \oplus \mathcal{J}_1$ where $\mathcal{J}_0$ is compact and $\mathcal{J}_1$ is completely noncompact, and $\tilde{i} = i \oplus \bar{i}$ where $\bar{i}$ is the index for $\mathcal{J}_1$. Let the coset values for $\tilde{i}$ be denoted by $\tilde{f}, \tilde{g}$, etc. where f, g are in $C_c(\Omega)$.

If P is some central projection, write $m_{\mathcal{J}}(A;P)$ to mean $m_{P\mathcal{J}}(PA)$ computed in $P\mathcal{A}$: that is, $P\pi\colon P\mathcal{A} \to P\mathcal{A}/P\mathcal{J}$, and $m_{\mathcal{J}}(A;P)$ is the minimum of the spectrum of $P\pi(P|A|)$ in $P\mathcal{A}$.

A few observations about the variation of this nonnegative real parameter as P and $\mathcal{J}$ vary will be helpful. Verification of the following is straightforward:

PROPOSITION 11.2. <u>Let $\mathcal{J}$ and $\mathcal{I}$ be ideals in $\mathcal{A}$ and let P and Q be central projections. Let $A \in \mathcal{A}$. Then</u>

(i) $m_{\mathcal{J}}(A;P) = 0$ if $P \in \mathcal{J}$;

(ii) if $Q \leq P$ and $Q \notin \mathcal{J}$ then

$$m_{\mathcal{J}}(A;Q) \geq m_{\mathcal{J}}(A;P)$$

(iii) if $P\mathcal{J} \subseteq P\mathcal{J}'$ and $P \notin \mathcal{J}'$ then

$$m_{\mathcal{J}}(A;P) \leq m_{\mathcal{J}'}(A;P) .$$

DEFINITION 11.3. For any ideal $\mathcal{J}$ in $\mathcal{A}$, and any f in $C_c(\Omega)$, define an ideal $\mathcal{J}(f)$ as follows: the set

$$\dim \mathcal{J} \cup \dim \mathcal{K} \cup \{g \in C_c^+(\Omega): g < |f| \text{ a.e.}\}$$

generates an order ideal in $C_c^+(\Omega)$. Let $\mathcal{J}(f)$ be the corresponding ideal in $\mathcal{A}$. Observe that the set

$$\{h: h \leq g_1 + \ldots + g_n + h_1 + h_2\}$$

where $h_1 \in \dim \mathcal{J}$, h_2 is finite a.e., and $g_j < |f|$ a.e. each j ; is an order ideal in $C_c^+(\Omega)$ which contains the generators of $\dim \mathcal{J}(f)$, and which is in fact equal to $\dim \mathcal{J}(f)$.

Note that $\mathcal{J} \subseteq \mathcal{J}(f)$, and if $\mathcal{J}$ is compact $\mathcal{J}(f) = \mathcal{K}(f)$.

We now establish some useful properties of $\mathcal{J}(f)$ by exploiting the structure of $C_c(\Omega)$.

LEMMA 11.4. <u>For any ideal $\mathcal{J}$ in $\mathcal{A}$, and any f in $C_c(\Omega)$, $\mathcal{J}$ and $\mathcal{J}(f)$ contain the same central projections.</u>

PROOF. Let $P = \chi_X$ be a central projection belonging to $\mathcal{J}(f)$. Thus $\dim P = \chi_X \dim I$ belongs to $\mathcal{J}(f)$, so there exist functions r_1 in $\dim \mathcal{J}$, r_2 finite a.e., and $g_j < |f|$ a.e. $j = 1,2,\ldots,n$, such that

$$\chi_X \dim I \leq g_1 + \ldots + g_n + h_1 + h_2 .$$

Since $\dim I$ maximizes every function in $C_c^+(\Omega)$, then

$$\chi_X \dim I \geq \chi_X(|f| \vee \aleph_o)$$

so that

$$\chi_X \dim I > \chi_X(g_1 + \ldots + g_n + h_2) \quad \text{a.e.},$$

and therefore $\chi_X \dim I \leq \chi_X h_1$. Hence $\dim P \in \dim \mathcal{I}$, so $P \in \mathcal{I}$.

LEMMA 11.5. <u>Let</u> $\mathcal{I}$ <u>be a completely noncompact ideal in</u> $\mathcal{C}$, <u>and let</u> $f \in C_c(\Omega)$. <u>Let</u> Δ <u>be defined for</u> $\mathcal{I}(f)$ <u>(as in 9.1) and assume</u> $\Delta = \Omega$. <u>Then</u> $|f| \in \dim \mathcal{I}(f)$ <u>implies</u> $\mathcal{I} = \mathcal{I}(f)$.

PROOF. Assume that $|f| \in \dim \mathcal{I}(f)$. Write

$$|f| \leq g_1 + \ldots + g_n + h_1 + h_2 ,$$

where $h_1 \in \dim \mathcal{I}$, h_2 finite a.e., and $g_j < |f|$ a.e. each j . Partition $\Omega = X \cup Y$ into open and closed sets with f finite a.e. on X and $f \geq \aleph_o$ on Y . Then $|f| \leq h_1$ on Y , so $\chi_Y |f| \in \dim \mathcal{I}$.

Since Ω is compact and $\Delta = \Omega$, there is some h in $\dim \mathcal{I}(f)$ with $h \geq \aleph_o$; in particular $\chi_X h \geq \chi_X |f|$. We can write

$$\chi_X h \leq k_1 + k_2 + \ell_1 + \ldots + \ell_m$$

where $k_1 \in \dim \mathcal{I}$, k_2 finite a.e., and $\ell_j < |f|$ a.e. each j . This means ℓ_j is finite a.e. each j , so therefore $\chi_X h \leq k_1$; thus $\chi_X h \in \dim \mathcal{I}$. We conclude from this that $|f| \in \dim \mathcal{I}$, and that $\dim \mathcal{I}$ contains $\chi_X h + \chi_Y |f|$. This $\dim \mathcal{I} = \dim \mathcal{I}(f)$.

LEMMA 11.6. <u>Let</u> $\mathcal{I}$ <u>be an ideal with index</u> $\tilde{i}$. <u>If</u> $\tilde{f} = \tilde{g}$ <u>for some</u> f <u>and</u> g <u>in</u> $C_c(\Omega)$ <u>then</u> $\mathcal{I}(f) = \mathcal{I}(g)$.

PROOF. Since $\tilde{f} = \tilde{g}$, then $g = f + h$ where $h \in \dim \mathcal{I}$. If $k \in \dim \mathcal{I}(f)$, then

$$k < \ell_1 + \ldots + \ell_n + m_1 + m_2$$

where $\ell_j < |f|$ each j , $m_1 \in \dim \mathcal{I}$ and m_2 is finite a.e. Then

$$k < ((\ell_1 - |h|) \vee 0) + \ldots + ((\ell_n - |h|) \vee 0) + (m_1 + n|h|) + m_2 ,$$

where $(\ell_j - |h|) \vee 0 < |f + h|$ each j , and $m_1 + n|h| \in \dim \mathcal{I}$, so

$k \in \dim \mathcal{J}(g)$. Thus $\dim \mathcal{J}(f) \subseteq \dim \mathcal{J}(g)$, and the same trick will show $\dim \mathcal{J}(g) \subseteq \dim \mathcal{J}(f)$. So $\mathcal{J}(g) = \mathcal{J}(f)$ by Wils' Theorem.

LEMMA 11.7. *The strong radical* $\mathfrak{R}$ *of a properly infinite von Neumann algebra* $\mathfrak{A}$ *can be characterized by:*

$$\dim \mathfrak{R} = \{f \in C_c(\Omega) : 0 \quad f < \dim I \quad \text{a.e.}\}$$

PROOF. By definition, $\mathfrak{R}$ is the intersection of the maximal ideals $\mathfrak{M}$ of $\mathfrak{A}$. By Theorem 5.5, if $\mathfrak{M}$ is maximal in $\mathfrak{A}$, then $\dim \mathfrak{M}$ is a maximal order ideal in $C_c^+(\Omega)$. It is not hard to see that this means $\mathfrak{M} = \mathfrak{M}_\lambda$ for some fixed $\lambda \in \Omega$ where:

$$\dim \mathfrak{M}_\lambda = \{f \in C_c^+(\Omega) : \text{ each neighborhood of } \lambda \text{ contains some } \mu \text{ with } f(\mu) < \dim I(\mu)\} .$$

Thus $\dim \mathfrak{R} = \cap \dim \mathfrak{M}_\lambda$.

The next result is a crucial refinement of 7.1 and 10.8. Note that $m_{\mathcal{J}(h)}(A)$ may be larger than $m_{\mathcal{J}}(A)$, as decomented in Theorem 11.12. In fact an even more delicate result will be obtained in 12.13, when we have introduced pointwise measurement of $m_{\mathcal{J}(h)}(A)$.

THEOREM 11.8. *Suppose* A *and* B *are elements of* $\mathfrak{A}$ *with* $i(A) = f$ *and* $i(B) = g$ *where* $f \neq g$ *a.e. Set* $h = |f| \vee |g|$. *Then for* $\mathcal{J}$ *an ideal in* $\mathfrak{A}$ *with index* $\tilde{i}$ *such that* $\tilde{i}(A) \neq \tilde{i}(B)$, *we have*

$$\|A - B\| \geq m_{\mathcal{J}(h)}(A) .$$

PROOF. There is a central decomposition into cases where $|f| > |g|$ a.e. or $|f| < |g|$ a.e. or $f = -g$ a.e.; and where $\mathcal{J}(h) \subset \mathcal{K}$ or $\mathcal{J}(h)$ is completely noncompact. If $I = \Sigma P_j$ is such a decomposition, then $\|A - B\|$ is the maximum of $\|P_j(A - B)\|$ over all j , and $m_{\mathcal{J}(h)}$ is the minimum of $m_{\mathcal{J}(h)}(A;P_j)$ over those j for which $P_j \notin \mathcal{J}$. Thus it suffices to consider each summand separately. Observe that if $\mathcal{J}(h) \subset \mathcal{K}$, the result is immediate from 7.1. Furthermore the cases where $|f| < |g|$ a.e. or $f = -g$ a.e. follow in virtually identical fashion to that where $|f| > |g|$ a.e. So we assume that $|f| > |g|$ a.e. (so that $h = |f|$); and $\mathcal{J}(h)$ is completely noncompact.

Let Δ, $\mathbf{J}$ and $\bar{i}$ be defined for $\mathcal{J}(h)$ as in 9.1 - 9.4. When

$\Omega\backslash\Delta \neq \phi$ we have $i(A) \neq i(B)$ on any neighborhood of $\Omega\backslash\Delta$, so $\bar{i}(A) \neq \bar{i}(B)$.

Suppose $\Omega = \Delta$. Since $|g| \in \mathcal{J}(h)$, we have $\bar{i}(B) = 0$; thus if $f \in \dim \mathcal{J}(h)$ we again have $\bar{i}(A) \neq \bar{i}(B)$. On the other hand, suppose that $\Omega = \Delta$, but that $|f| \in \dim \mathcal{J}(h)$. Since $h = |f|$, Lemma 11.5 implies $\mathcal{J}(h) = \mathcal{J}$. But then $\bar{i}$ is the index for $\mathcal{J}$, where $\bar{i}(A) = \bar{i}(B) = 0$, contradicting the hypotheses: we conclude that if $\Omega = \Delta$ then $\bar{i}(A) \neq 0$, and $\bar{i}(A) \neq \bar{i}(B)$.

Thus if $|f| > |g|$ a.e. and $\mathcal{J}(h)$ is completely noncompact, then $\bar{i}(A) \neq \bar{i}(B)$ and the result follows by 10.8.

COROLLARY 11.9. *With the hypotheses of 11.8,*

$$\|A - B\| \geq m_{\mathcal{J}(h)}(A^*) .$$

PROOF. Take adjoints.

THEOREM 11.10. *Let $\mathcal{J}$ be an ideal with index $\tilde{i}$. The set*

$$\mathcal{S} = \{A \in \mathcal{A}: A \text{ is semi-Fredholm for } \mathcal{J}(i(A))\}$$

is open, and $\tilde{i}$ is locally constant on $\mathcal{S}$.

PROOF. Let $A \in \mathcal{S}$. We will exhibit a neighborhood of A which is contained in $\mathcal{S}$, and on which $\tilde{i}$ is constant.

Using 5.16, pass to a central summand and assume without loss of generality that A is left-Fredholm for $\mathcal{J}(i(A))$, and that $i(A) \leq 0$. Denote $i(A) = f$; so, $m_{\mathcal{J}(f)}(A) = \varepsilon > 0$.

Let $B \in \mathcal{A}$ with $i(B) = g$, where $\tilde{g} \neq \tilde{f}$. We show this implies $\|A - B\| \geq \varepsilon$. Let Y be the closure of the open set where f and g differ differ, and set $P = \chi_Y$. Now $P \notin \mathcal{J}$, since $\tilde{g} \neq \tilde{f}$, and hence $P \notin \mathcal{J}(f)$ by Lemma 11.4; thus, by 11.2

$$m_{\mathcal{J}(f)}(A;P) \geq m_{\mathcal{J}(f)}(A) = \varepsilon .$$

Also, if we set $h = |f| \vee |g|$, then $P\mathcal{J}(h) \supseteq P\mathcal{J}(f)$, and $P \notin \mathcal{J}(h)$ either, so again by 11.2,

$$m_{\mathcal{J}(h)}(A;P) \geq m_{\mathcal{J}(f)}(A;P) .$$

Since $f \nmid g$ a.e. on Y, we can apply Theorem 11.8 on $P\mathfrak{A}$ to conclude

$$\|PA - PB\| \geq m_{\mathcal{J}(h)}(A;P) = \varepsilon .$$

Thus $\tilde{i}(B) = \tilde{i}(A)$ for any B with $\|A - B\| < \varepsilon = m_{\mathcal{J}(f)}(A)$.

To show this ε neighborhood of A is contained in $\mathfrak{D}$: for B with $\|A - B\| < \varepsilon$ we show B is semi-Fredholm for $\mathcal{J}(g)$. Theorems 7.1 and 10.8 imply that B is semi-Fredholm for $\mathcal{J}(f)$. Since $\tilde{g} = \tilde{f}$, then $\mathcal{J}(f) = \mathcal{J}(g)$ by 11.6, so the proof is complete.

LEMMA 11.11. *Let* $A \in \mathfrak{A}$ *such that* $i(A) \leq 0$, *and let* $E(\lambda)$ *and* $F(\lambda)$ *be the spectral resolutions for* $|A|$ *and* $|A^*|$ *respectively. For any* $\alpha > 0$, *if* $\dim E[0,\alpha] \geq |i(A)| + \aleph_0$, *then* $E[0,\alpha] \sim F[0,\alpha]$.

PROOF. Note that

$$\dim E[0,\alpha] = \dim N_A + \dim E(0,\alpha]$$

$$\dim F[0,\alpha] = \dim N_{A^*} + \dim F(0,\alpha] ,$$

where $E(0,\alpha] \sim F(0,\alpha]$, and $N_A \precsim N_{A^*}$; so, $E[0,\alpha] \precsim F[0,\alpha]$. Also, for some g in $C_c^+(\Omega)$, $\dim N_{A^*} \equiv \dim N_A + g$.

Since $\dim E\ 0,\alpha] \geq |i(A)| + \aleph_0$, we get:

$$\dim E[0,\alpha] = |i(A)| + \aleph_0 + \dim N_A + \dim E(0,\alpha]$$

$$= [(\dim N_A + g) - \dim N_A] + \aleph_0 + \dim N_A + \dim F(0,\alpha] .$$

On the open set where $\dim N_A < g$, we have

$$[(\dim N_A + g) - \dim N_A] = g ,$$

so $\dim E[0,\alpha] \geq \dim F[0,\alpha]$ on the closure of this set. On the remaining set where $\dim N_A \geq g$, we have

$$\aleph_0 + \dim N_A = \aleph_0 + \dim N_{A^*} ,$$

so also we get $\dim E[0,\alpha] \geq \dim F[0,\alpha]$ on this set, and the lemma is proved.

There is an obvious analog to this lemma which is true when $i(A) \geq 0$.

THEOREM 11.12. <u>Let $\mathcal{J}$ be an ideal with index $\tilde{i}$. The maximal domain of continuity for $\tilde{i}$ which contains the semi-Fredholm elements for $\mathcal{J}$ is the open set</u>

$$\mathcal{D} = \{A \in \mathcal{G} : A \text{ is semi-Fredholm for } \mathcal{J}(i(A))\}$$

PROOF. In view of 11.10, we need only show that if A is not semi-Fredholm for $\mathcal{J}(i(A)))$ then A is a limit of a sequence in $\mathcal{S}_{\mathcal{J}}$ on which $\tilde{i}$ differs from $\tilde{i}(A)$.

By passing to a central summand, we can assume that $f \leq 0$ (for $f \geq 0$, argue for A^* , and take adjoints). Also, there is a central decomposition of $\mathcal{J}$ into compact and completely noncompact summands; we pass to the summands which will be considered simultaneously. If $\mathcal{J}$ is completely noncompact, let $\mathbf{J}$ and $\bar{i}$ denote the corresponding congruence and index.

For an arbitrary $\varepsilon > 0$, we will define B in $\mathcal{G}$ with $i(B) \not\equiv i(A)$ (or $\bar{i}(A) \not\equiv \bar{i}(B)$ if $\mathcal{J}$ is completely noncompact), and with $\|A - B\| < 2\varepsilon$. By 6.7, B is a limit of semi-Fredholm elements for $\mathcal{J}$ having the same index as B , so the result will follow from this.

Let $E(\lambda)$ and $F(\lambda)$ denote the spectral resulutions for $|A|$ and $|A^*|$. Then $F[0,\varepsilon] \gtrsim E[0,\varepsilon]$, for any $\varepsilon > 0$, and $E[0,\varepsilon] \notin \mathcal{J}(i(A))$ since we have assumed A is not semi-Fredholm for $\mathcal{J}(i(A))$, and using 4.2 and 4.5.

Denote $f = i(A)$. Let X be the closure of the open set in Ω where $\dim E[0,\varepsilon] \geq |f| + \aleph_o$; set $P = \chi_X$. Note that $(I - P)E[0,\varepsilon] \in \mathcal{J}(f)$, so that $PE[0,\varepsilon] \notin \mathcal{J}(f)$. Apply the preceding lemma in $P\mathcal{G}$ to see that $\dim E[0,\varepsilon] = \dim F[0,\varepsilon]$ on X .

To define B , two cases are considered: assume first that f is not identically zero on X (or, that $\chi_X f \notin \mathbf{J}$) . In this case, set $B = A(I - E[0,\varepsilon])$. Then

$$i(B) = \dim N_B - \dim N_{B^*} = \dim E[0,\varepsilon] - \dim F[0,\varepsilon] ,$$

so that $i(B) = 0$ on X . Hence $i(B) \not\equiv f$ (and $i(B) \not\equiv f)$, where $\|A - B\| \leq \varepsilon$.

For the second case, assume that $f \equiv 0$ on X (or, if $\mathcal{J}$ is completely noncompact assume that $\chi_X f \in \mathbf{J})$. By the choice of X , $\dim E[0,\varepsilon]$ and $\dim F[0,\varepsilon]$ are infinite on X , and hence PE and PF are properly infinite.

Thus there are projections F_1 and F_2 in $\mathcal{A}$ with $F_1 \sim F_2 \sim PF[0,\varepsilon]$ and $PF[0,\varepsilon] = F_1 \oplus F_2$; and there is a partial isometry V in $\mathcal{A}$ with $V^*V = PE[0,\varepsilon]$ and $VV^* = F_2$. Now, set $B = A(I - E[0,\varepsilon]) + \varepsilon V$. Then on X ,

$$i(B) = \dim N_B - \dim N_{B^*} = \dim 0 - \dim F_2 = -\dim E[0,\varepsilon] .$$

Since $PE[0,\varepsilon] \notin \mathcal{J}(f)$, then $\chi_X \dim E[0,\varepsilon] \not\leq 0$, (or, in the noncompact case, $\chi_X \dim E[0,\varepsilon] \notin \mathbf{J}$) . Thus $i(B) \not\leq f$ (respectively $\overline{i}(B) \not\leq \overline{f}$) , where

$$\|A - B\| \leq \|A\, E[0,\varepsilon] + \varepsilon V\| \leq 2\varepsilon ,$$

so the theorem is proved.

THEOREM 11.13. <u>Let $\mathcal{J}$ be an ideal in $\mathcal{A}$. For any f in $C_c(\Omega)$ such that $\mathcal{J} \not\leq \mathcal{J}(f)$, there is some A in $\mathcal{A}$ which is not semi-Fredholm for $\mathcal{J}$, but which is semi-Fredholm for $\mathcal{J}(f)$ (so that the index for $\mathcal{J}$ is continuous at A).</u>

PROOF. Let $f \in C_c(\Omega)$ be such that $\mathcal{J}(f) \not\leq \mathcal{J}$. By passing to a central summand, assume without loss of generality that $f \leq 0$.

We directly construct the desired element A . There is an isometry V in $\mathcal{A}$ with $i(V) = f$ (as constructed in the proof of 7.5). The set $\mathcal{J}(f)\backslash\mathcal{J}$ must contain projections. If it contains a properly infinite projection E , proceed as follows: $E \in \mathcal{J}(f)$, so $I - E \notin \mathcal{J}(f)$ by 11.4. Write $E = \Sigma_{n=1}^{\infty} E_n$ as a sum of pairwise orthogonal projections in $\mathcal{A}$, each equivalent to E . Set

$$A = \sum_{n=1}^{\infty} \frac{1}{n} V E_n + V(I - E) .$$

Clearly $i(A) = i(V) = f$, and $m_{\mathcal{J}}(A) = 0 = m_{\mathcal{J}}(A^*)$. Thus A is not left Fredholm for $\mathcal{J}$, so A is not semi-Fredholm for $\mathcal{J}$ by 5.16 and 5.17. However, $(I - E)V^*$ is a left inverse for A modulo $\mathcal{J}(f)$.

On the other hand, suppose $\mathcal{J}(f)\backslash\mathcal{J}$ contains a relatively finite projection E . Then set $A = V(I - E)$. Then $N_A = E$ and $N_{A^*} = I - VV^* \oplus VEV^*$,

$$i(A) = \dim E - (\dim(I - VV^*) + \dim E) ,$$

where $-\dim(I - VV^*) = f$, and $\dim E$ is finite a.e. Thus on the dense open

set where dim E is finite we have $i(A) = f$, so $i(A) \equiv f$. Since both
dim N_A and dim N_{A^*} majorize dim E where $E \notin \mathcal{I}$, then A is not semi-
Fredholm for $\mathcal{I}$. But $(I - E)V^*$ is a left inverse for A modulo $\mathcal{I}(f)$.
Thus a suitable A exists in either case.

The continuity at A of the index for $\mathcal{I}$ follows by the preceding
theorem.

THEOREM 11.14. If $\mathcal{I}$ is any ideal which does not contain the strong radical
of $\mathcal{G}$, then the open maximal domain of continuity $\mathcal{D}$ for the index is
strictly larger than the set of semi-Fredholm elements for $\mathcal{I}$.

If $\mathcal{I}$ contains the strong radical then the index for $\mathcal{I}$ does not
extend continuously beyond the semi-Fredholm elements for $\mathcal{I}$.

PROOF. Suppose $\mathcal{I}$ does not contain the strong radical $\mathcal{R}$. Then let
$f = \dim I_{\mathcal{G}}$: from 11.3 and 11.7 we see $\dim \mathcal{I}(f)$ contains $\dim \mathcal{R}$, so
$\mathcal{I}(f) \supseteq \mathcal{R}$. Thus $\mathcal{I} \neq \mathcal{I}(f)$, and the result follows from 11.12 and 11.13.

On the other hand, if $\mathcal{I} \supseteq \mathcal{R}$ we can show $\mathcal{I} = \mathcal{I}(f)$ for any f in
$C_c(\Omega)$. Observe that

$$\dim \mathcal{I} \supseteq \dim \mathcal{R} = \{g \in C_c(\Omega): 0 \leq g \leq \dim I_{\mathcal{G}}\} ,$$

and $f \leq \dim I_{\mathcal{G}}$. Hence if $g < f$ a.e. then $g \in \dim \mathcal{I}$. Also, since $\mathcal{G}$ is
properly infinite, $\dim \mathcal{R}$ contains the finite a.e. functions. Then clearly
$\mathcal{I} = \mathcal{I}(f)$. It follows by 11.12, that $\mathcal{D}$ equals set of semi-Fredholm
elements for $\mathcal{I}$.

REMARK 11.15. Properties of the domain $\mathcal{D}$. Considerable information about
the maximal domain $\mathcal{D}$ corresponding to $\mathcal{I}$ and $\tilde{i}$ can be deduced from our
results. Note first that the open set $\mathcal{S}$ of semi-Fredholm elements for $\mathcal{I}$
is dense in the open set $\mathcal{D}$. In fact each component of $\mathcal{S}$ is dense in a
corresponding component of $\mathcal{D}$: the open connected component
$\mathcal{D}_{\tilde{f}} = \{A \in \mathcal{D}: \tilde{i}(A) = \tilde{f}\}$ of $\mathcal{D}$ consists of limit points of the corresponding
component $\mathcal{S}_{\tilde{f}} = \{A \in \mathcal{S}: \tilde{i}(A) = \tilde{f}\}$ of $\mathcal{S}$, by 6.5 and 6.7.

If $\mathcal{S}_{\tilde{f}}$ is a left Fredholm (right Fredholm, Fredholm) component of $\mathcal{S}$,
we refer to $\mathcal{D}_{\tilde{f}}$ as a left Fredholm (etc.) component of $\mathcal{D}$. Also it is
easy to see that if A is in a left Fredholm component for $\mathcal{D}$ then A is
actually left Fredholm for $\mathcal{I}(i(A))$.

The Fredholm components of $\mathcal{D}$ are precisely those $\mathcal{D}_{\tilde{f}}$ for which

$|f| \in \dim \mathcal{J}$ (5.18). If $\mathcal{J}$ is completely noncompact, then for such f, $\mathcal{J}(f) = \mathcal{J}$, so $\mathcal{D}_{\tilde{f}} = \mathcal{S}_{\tilde{f}}$, and thus the Fredholm components of $\mathcal{D}$ are identical to those of $\mathcal{S}$. If $\mathcal{J}$ is compact so that $\tilde{i} = i$ and $\tilde{f} = f$, then whenever $|f| \in \dim \mathcal{J}$, $\mathcal{J}(f) = \mathcal{K}$. Thus in this case the Fredholm components of $\mathcal{D}$ are sets $\mathcal{D}_f = \{A\colon A$ is Fredholm for $\mathcal{K}$, $i(A) = f\}$. In any case then it is only the nonFredholm components of $\mathcal{D}$ which may be larger in an interesting fashion than those of $\mathcal{S}$.

The left Fredholm components of $\mathcal{D}$ form a semigroup: if A and B are left Fredholm in $\mathcal{D}$ with indices $\tilde{f}$ and $\tilde{g}$, this means A and B are left Fredholm for $\mathcal{J}(f)$ and $\mathcal{J}(g)$ respectively, and we wish to see that AB is left Fredholm for $\mathcal{J}(f+g)$. On the open set X where $f \neq -g$ or both are finite, cardinality agruments of the sort repeatedly used in this section show $\mathcal{J}(f)$ and $\mathcal{J}(g)$ are contained in $\mathcal{J}(f+g)$. Thus A, B and AB are all left Fredholm for the larger ideal, when we restrict to $\overline{X}$. On the remaining set $f = -g$, $\mathcal{J}(f) = \mathcal{J}(g)$ and $\mathcal{J}(f+g) = \mathcal{J}$. Here since both A and B are left Fredholm for $\mathcal{J}(f)$ with indices of opposite sign, one must actually be Fredholm for $\mathcal{J}(f)$. As observed above this one is Fredholm for $\mathcal{J}$, but then both are Fredholm for $\mathcal{J}$. So AB is Fredholm for $\mathcal{J}$. Of course the right Fredholm elements of $\mathcal{D}$ also form a semigroup, and the Fredholm elements a group.

It follows also from the preceding discussion and additivity of $\tilde{i}$ on $\mathcal{S}$ that if we approximate $\mathcal{D}$ by $\mathcal{S}$ and use the continuity of $\tilde{i}$, we see that $\tilde{i}$ is a homomorphism on $\mathcal{D}$.

12. The closure of the semi-Fredholm components; the distance to each component.

Let $\mathcal{A}$ be a properly infinite von Neumann algebra with ideal $\mathcal{J}$. In this section we discuss the limit points of the connected components of the open set $\mathcal{S}$ of semi-Fredholm elements for $\mathcal{J}$. We measure the distance from each A in $\mathcal{A}$ to the group of invertible elements of $\mathcal{A}$. More generally, the distance from A to each component of $\mathcal{S}$ is determined. J. Feldman and R. V. Kadison found the closure of the invertible group in [17]. In the classical case where $\mathcal{J}$ is the ideal of compact operators in $\mathcal{B}(\mathcal{H})$, $\mathcal{H}$ separable, then each operator which is not semi-Fredholm is a limit point of every component of the semi-Fredholm operators [8]. The previous section shows this certainly does not always happen for other ideals in other algebras.

An element A is always in the closure of that connected component of $\mathcal{S}$ on which the index is constantly equal to its value at A. An element of the open maximal domain of continuity $\mathcal{D}$ (see 11.10) for the index for $\mathcal{J}$ must be a limit point of this single component, and not a limit point of the complement in $\mathcal{S}$ of this component. Other elements, while being in the closure of only one single component, may nevertheless be a limit point of the union of other components. Those elements which are in the closure of every component of $\mathcal{S}$ are determined. The nature of the limit points of $\mathcal{S}$ is discussed further.

In view of the results of the preceding section, where the open maximal domain $\mathcal{D}$ of continuity for an index is described, it might seem more appropriate to here discuss the limit points of the components of $\mathcal{D}$. However, $\mathcal{S}$ is dense in $\mathcal{D}$, and each connected component of $\mathcal{S}$ is dense in the corresponding component of $\mathcal{D}$. Thus our results in this section also apply to $\mathcal{D}$.

NOTATION 12.1. In this section $\mathcal{A}$ is properly infinite, $\mathcal{J}$ is an ideal in $\mathcal{A}$ with index $\tilde{i}$, and $\mathbb{J}$ is the congruence for the completely noncompact summand of $\mathcal{J}$. In the open set $\mathcal{S}$ of semi-Fredholm elements for $\mathcal{J}$, let $\mathcal{S}_{\tilde{f}}$ denote the connected component such that $B \in \mathcal{S}_{\tilde{f}}$ means $\tilde{i}(B) = \tilde{f}$. By the distance between A in $\mathcal{A}$ and $\mathcal{S}_{\tilde{f}}$ we mean

$$\text{dist } (A,\mathcal{S}_{\tilde{f}}) = \inf_{B\in\mathcal{S}_{\tilde{f}}} \|A - B\| .$$

We shall continue to use previously introduced notation, in particular, the parameter $m_{\mathcal{J}}(A;P)$ from Section 11 will be important here.

DEFINITION 12.2. Given an ideal $\mathcal{J}$, we can associate with each element A of $\mathfrak{A}$ a positive function $\mu_{\mathcal{J}}(A)$ defined on Ω (the maximal ideal space of the center of $\mathfrak{A}$). Intuitively, one can think of this function as measuring the lower bound of $\pi(A)$ in $\mathfrak{A}/\mathcal{J}$ at each point of Ω. Define:

$$\mu_{\mathcal{J}}(A)(t) = \limsup_{t \in P} m_{\mathcal{J}}(A;P)$$

where the limit is over the net of all central projections P such that t is in the open and closed support X of $P = \chi_X$ (write $t \in P$).

Write Λ to denote the open subset of Ω given by

$$\Lambda = \{t \in \Omega : t \in P \text{ , for some central projection } P \in \mathcal{J}\} .$$

Note that Λ may not be closed, and in fact may be dense as in Example 8.5.

The function $\mu_{\mathcal{J}}(A)$ will be used to measure the distance from A to each component of $\mathcal{S}$. In general these functions are not continuous, as the example below demonstrates. We will see that all the $\mu_{\mathcal{J}}(A)$ are lower semicontinuous when restricted to a distinguished closed subset of Ω, and for certain important ideals, they are all continuous.

EXAMPLE 12.3. *Let* $\mathfrak{A} = \Sigma \oplus \mathcal{B}(\mathcal{H}_n)$ *each* $\mathcal{H}_n$ *separable, and let* $\mathcal{J}$ *be the ideal generated by the finitely nonzero sequences of finite rank projections. So* $\mathcal{J}$ *is all* $K = \{K_n\}_n$ *sequences of compact operators which tend to zero in norm. Let* $U = \{U_n\}_n$ *be a sequence of backward unilateral shifts of multiplicity* 1. *Then* $\mu_{\mathcal{J}}(U)(n) = 1$, *for each* $n \in \mathbb{N}$, *but* $\mu_{\mathcal{J}}(U)(t) = 0$, *each* $t \in \beta\mathbb{N} \setminus \mathbb{N}$.

PROPOSITION 12.4. *Let* $\mathcal{J}$ *be an ideal with associated set* Λ *as in* 12.2. *Then*

$$\mu_{\mathcal{J}}(A)(t) \equiv 0 \quad \text{on} \quad \Lambda$$

$$\mu_{\mathcal{J}}(A)(t) = \sup_{t \in P} m_{\mathcal{J}}(A;P) \quad \text{on} \quad \Omega \setminus \Lambda .$$

Furthermore, $\mu_{\mathcal{J}}(A)$ *is lower semicontinuous on* $\Omega \setminus \Lambda$.

PROOF. The value of $\mu_{\mathcal{J}}(A)$ on Λ follows from the definitions and 11.2. For $t \in \Omega \setminus \Lambda$, if $t \in Q$ for some central projection Q, then $Q \notin \mathcal{J}$, and if $Q \le P$ then $m_{\mathcal{J}}(A;Q) \ge m_{\mathcal{J}}(A;P)$ by 11.2, so we get the second equality.

It is easy to see that for each positive a,

$$\{t \in \Omega\backslash\Lambda : \mu_{\mathcal{J}}(A)(t) > a\}$$

is open in $\Omega\backslash\Lambda$: for, if $\mu_{\mathcal{J}}(A)(t_0) > a$ for some $t_0 \in \Omega\backslash\Lambda$, then there is some central projection Q with $t_0 \in Q$ and with $m_{\mathcal{J}}(A;Q) > a$. Then for each $t \in Q \cap (\Omega\backslash\Lambda)$,

$$\mu_{\mathcal{J}}(A)(t) > m_{\mathcal{J}}(A;Q) > a .$$

COROLLARY 12.5. <u>If</u> $\mathcal{J}$ <u>contains no central projections, then for each</u> A <u>in</u> $\mathfrak{A}$, $\mu_{\mathcal{J}}(A)$ <u>is lower semicontinuous.</u>

By relating the function $\mu_{\mathcal{J}}(A)$ to $m_{\mathcal{J}}(A)$, it can be used to determine whether A is semi-Fredholm for $\mathcal{J}$. The following elementary lemma will be useful.

LEMMA 12.6. <u>Let</u> μ_1 <u>and</u> μ_2 <u>be nonnegative lower semicontinuous functions on a compact totally disconnected space</u> X <u>such that</u> $\mu_1 + \mu_2 > 0$. <u>Then there is an</u> $\varepsilon > 0$ <u>and a partition on</u> X <u>into disjoint open sets</u> X_1 <u>and</u> X_2 <u>such that</u> $\mu_i > \varepsilon$ <u>on</u> X_i.

PROOF. If $\lim(\mu_1 + \mu_2)(t_n) = 0$ then there is a limit point $t \in X$ for t_n, and $(\mu_1 + \mu_2)(t) = 0$ by lower semicontinuity. Hence $\mu_1 + \mu_2 > \delta$ for some $\delta > 0$. Then for

$$Y = \{t : \mu_1(t) > \tfrac{\delta}{2}\}, \quad Z = \{t : \mu_2(t) \leq \tfrac{\delta}{4}\},$$

Y is open and Z is compact, and $Z \subset Y$. Hence there is some open and closed X_1 with $Z \subset X_1 \subset Y$. Set $\varepsilon = \frac{\delta}{4}$ and $X_2 = X\backslash X_1$.

PROPOSITION 12.7. <u>Let</u> $\mathcal{J}$ <u>be an ideal, and let</u> $A \in \mathfrak{A}$. <u>Then</u>

$$m_{\mathcal{J}}(A) = \inf_{t\in \Omega\backslash\Lambda} \mu_{\mathcal{J}}(A)(t) .$$

PROOF. If $t \in \Omega\backslash\Lambda$, and $t \in P$ then

$$\mu_{\mathcal{J}}(A)(t) \geq m_{\mathcal{J}}(A;P) \geq m_{\mathcal{J}}(A) ,$$

using 12.2 and 12.4; so $\inf_{\Omega\backslash\Lambda}\mu_{\mathcal{J}}(A) \geq m_{\mathcal{J}}(A)$.

Suppose $\inf_{t\in\Omega\setminus\Lambda}\mu_{\mathcal{J}}(A)(t) > a$. Then for every t in $\Omega\setminus\Lambda$ there is some central projection P_t with $t \in P_t$ and $m_{\mathcal{J}}(A;P_t) > a$. Observe that $\sigma(\pi(|A|))$ in $\mathcal{A}/\mathcal{J}$ is the closure of the union of $\sigma(\pi(P_t|A|))$ in $P_t\mathcal{A}/P_t\mathcal{J}$. Hence

$$m_{\mathcal{J}}(A) = \inf m_{\mathcal{J}}(A;P_t) > a .$$

THEOREM 12.8. <u>An element</u> $A \in \mathcal{A}$ <u>is semi-Fredholm for</u> $\mathcal{J}$ <u>if and only if at each</u> $t \in \Omega\setminus\Lambda$, <u>one of</u> $\mu_{\mathcal{J}}(A)$ <u>or</u> $\mu_{\mathcal{J}}(A^*)$ <u>is nonzero.</u>

PROOF. Assume A is semi-Fredholm for $\mathcal{J}$. Then there is a central projection P such that PA is left-Fredholm in $P\mathcal{A}$ for $P\mathcal{J}$, and $(I - P)A$ is right-Fredholm in $(I - P)\mathcal{A}$ for $(I - P)\mathcal{J}$. Hence $m_{\mathcal{J}}(A;P) > 0$, so for every central projection $Q \leq P$ such that $Q \notin \mathcal{J}$,

$$m_{\mathcal{J}}(A;Q) > m_{\mathcal{J}}(A;P) = \varepsilon > 0 .$$

Thus $\mu_{\mathcal{J}}(A) > \varepsilon$ on $(\Omega\setminus\Lambda) \cap P$. Analogously, there is a $\delta > 0$ with $\mu_{\mathcal{J}}(A^*) > \delta$ on $(\Omega\setminus\Lambda) \cap (I - P)$.

Assume conversely that $\mu_{\mathcal{J}}(A) + \mu_{\mathcal{J}}(A^*) > 0$. Both these functions are lower semicontinuous when restricted to $\Omega\setminus\Lambda$, so Lemma 12.7 gives a partition of $\Omega\setminus\Lambda$ which can obviously be extended to an open and closed partition $\Omega = X_1 \cup X_2$ such that $\mu_{\mathcal{J}}(A) > \varepsilon$ on $X_1 \cap (\Omega\setminus\Lambda)$ and $\mu_{\mathcal{J}}(A^*) > \varepsilon$ on $X_2 \cap (\Omega\setminus\Lambda)$. For $P_i = \chi_{X_i}$ we have $m_{\mathcal{J}}(A;P_1) > \varepsilon$ and $m_{\mathcal{J}}(A^*;P_2) > \varepsilon$ by the previous result, so A is semi-Fredholm for $\mathcal{J}$.

PROPOSITION 12.9. <u>If</u> $\mathcal{J}$ <u>is an ideal such that for some fixed</u> f <u>in</u> $C_c(\Omega)$,

$$\dim \mathcal{J} = \{g \in C_c(\Omega): 0 \leq g < f \quad \text{a.e.}\}$$

<u>then</u> $\mu_{\mathcal{J}}(A)$ <u>is continuous for every</u> A <u>in</u> $\mathcal{A}$.

PROOF. There is a largest function in $C_c(\Omega)$, namely, $\dim I_{\mathcal{A}}$. If $P = \chi_X$ is some central projection in $\mathcal{A}$, then $\dim P = \dim I_{\mathcal{A}}$ on X . Thus under our hypothesis, $\mathcal{J}$ contains no central projections, so $\mu_{\mathcal{J}}(A)$ is lower semicontinuous by 12.5.

We show for each $a > 0$, that

$$\{t \in \Omega: \mu_{\mathcal{J}}(A)(t) < a\}$$

is open.

Assume that $\mu_{\mathcal{J}}(A)(t_o) < b < a$ and suppose that every neighborhood of t_o contains some s with $\mu_{\mathcal{J}}(A)(s) \geq a$. Then t_o is in the closure of the open set $G = \{S: \mu_{\mathcal{J}}(A)(s) > b\}$.

For each $s \in G$, there is some open and closed neighborhood of s and associated central projection P such that $m_{\mathcal{J}}(A;P) > b$. Let $E(\lambda)$ be the spectral resolution for $|A|$. Then $PE(\lambda)$ is the spectral resolution for $P|A|$, and $m_{\mathcal{J}}(A;P) > b$ implies $PE[0,b] \in \mathcal{J}$. Therefore

$$P \dim E[0,b] = \dim PE[0,b] < f \text{ a.e.},$$

so $\dim E[0,b] < f$ a.e. on the closure $\overline{G}$ of G. Let $Q = \chi_{\overline{G}}$; we have $QE[0,b] \in \mathcal{J}$, which means $m_{\mathcal{J}}(A;Q) \geq b$. But $t_0 \in Q$, and $\mathcal{J}$ contains no central projections, so

$$\mu_{\mathcal{J}}(t_o) = \sup_{t_o \in P} m_{\mathcal{J}}(A;P) \geq b .$$

a contradiction. Thus $\mu_{\mathcal{J}}(A) < a$ on some neighborhood of t_o, and the proof is complete.

COROLLARY 12.10. <u>If $\mathcal{J}$ is the zero ideal, the ideal of all compact elements, or the strong radical, then $\mu_{\mathcal{J}}(A)$ is continuous, for each A in $\mathfrak{a}$.</u>

PROOF. Note that the preceding proposition is still true for $\dim \mathcal{J} = \{g: 0 \leq g \leq f\}$ as long as $\mathcal{J}$ contains no central projection, so take $f \equiv 0$ to get the result for the zero ideal. For the rest, apply characterizations 5.8 and 11.7.

DEFINITION 12.11. Let $\mathcal{J}$ be an ideal in $\mathfrak{a}$ with index $\tilde{i}$ and with corresponding Δ and $\mathbf{J}$. For $\tilde{f}$ in $C(\Omega)/\mathbf{J}$ and $t \in \Omega$, define the <u>germ</u> of $\tilde{f}$ at t to be

$$\tilde{f}_t = \{\tilde{g} \in C(\Omega)/\mathbf{J}: \tilde{g} = \tilde{f} \text{ on some neighborhood of } t\}.$$

Equivalently, $\tilde{g} \in \tilde{f}_t$ means: there is an open and closed Y containing t with $\chi_Y|f - g|$ in $\dim \mathcal{J}$ and $\chi_Y(f - g) \equiv 0$ on a neighborhood of $\Omega \setminus \Delta$.

The next result is a further refinement of 7.1, 10.8, and 11.8.

PROPOSITION 12.12. <u>Let $\mathcal{J}$ be an ideal with index $\tilde{i}$. Let A, B in $\mathfrak{a}$</u>

and set

$$X = \{t \in \Omega: \tilde{i}(A)_t \neq \tilde{i}(B)_t\} .$$

Then

$$\|A - B\| \geq \sup_X \mu_{\mathcal{J}(h)}(A)$$

where $h = |i(A)| \vee |i(B)|$.

PROOF. Let $t_o \in X$ with $\mu_{\mathcal{J}(h)}(A)(t_o) = m$. Since $\mu = \limsup_{t_o \in P} m_{\mathcal{J}(h)}(P;A)$ we can choose P with $t_o \in P$ and $m_{\mathcal{J}(h)}(P;A) > m - \varepsilon$. Let Q be the projection corresponding to the closure of the set where $i(A)$ and $i(B)$ differ. We must have $t_o \in Q$. Assume $Q \leq P$, by passing to QP . Clearly, $Q \notin \mathcal{J}$ or we would have $\tilde{i}(A)_{t_o} = \tilde{i}(B)_{t_o}$; this implies $Q \notin \mathcal{J}(h)$ by 11.4. Hence

$$m_{\mathcal{J}(h)}(Q;A) \geq m_{\mathcal{J}(h)}(P;A)$$

by 11.2. Now applying 11.8 and 11.9 in the algebra $Q\mathfrak{A}$, we get

$$\|Q(A - B)\| \geq m_{\mathcal{J}(h)}(Q;A) ,$$

so $\|A - B\| \geq m - \varepsilon$. The result follows.

REMARK 12.13. Under the hypotheses of the theorem we can take adjoints to get

$$\|A^* - B^*\| \geq \sup_X \mu_{\mathcal{J}(h)}(A)$$

and hence

$$\|A - B\| \geq \sup_X \mu_{\mathcal{J}(h)}(A^*) .$$

THEOREM 12.14. *Let* $\mathcal{J}$ *be an ideal with index* $\tilde{i}$. *Let* $A \in \mathfrak{A}$ *and* $g \in C_c(\Omega)$, *and let* $h = |i(A)| \vee |g|$. *Set*

$$X = \{t \in \Omega: \tilde{i}(A)_t \neq \tilde{g}_t\} .$$

<u>Then the distance from</u> A <u>to</u> $\mathcal{S}_{\tilde{g}}$ <u>is the larger of</u> $\sup_X \mu_{\mathcal{J}(h)}(A)$ <u>and</u> $\sup_X \mu_{\mathcal{J}(h)}(A^*)$.

PROOF. Let m denote this larger supremum. In view of the preceding results, it remains to show $\mathrm{dist}(A,\mathcal{S}_{\tilde{g}}) \le m$. For a given ε , we construct $B \in \mathcal{A}$ with $\tilde{i}(B) = \tilde{g}$ and $\|A - B\| < m + 2\varepsilon$. Since B is a limit point of $\mathcal{S}_{\tilde{g}}$ by 6.5 and 10.5, this suffices to prove the theorem.

Set $f = i(A)$, and pass to a central summand where $f \le 0$ a.e. (an analogous argument works on the other summand).

Let $E(\lambda)$ and $F(\lambda)$ be the spectral resolutions for $|A|$ and $|A^*|$ respectively. Set $E = E[0,m + \varepsilon]$, $F = F[0,m + \varepsilon]$, and $h = |i(A)| \vee |g|$. We first isolate a neighborhood of X on which dim E is infinite and dim E $\ge$ h . Let

$$Y = \{t \in \Omega\colon (\dim E)(\lambda) < h(t)\} .$$

Then dim E < h a.e. on $\overline{Y}$; hence for $P = \chi_{\overline{Y}}$, $P \dim E \in \mathcal{J}(h)$. Note that PE is the spectral projection for $P|A|$ in $P\mathcal{A}$ corresponding to the interval $[0,m + \varepsilon]$. Thus $m_{\mathcal{J}(h)}(A;P) \ge m + \varepsilon$, provided $P \notin \mathcal{J}(h)$.

Suppose that $\overline{Y} \cap X$ contains some point t: since $t \in X$ and $t \in P$, then $P \notin \mathcal{J}(h)$, so

$$\mu_{\mathcal{J}(h)}(A)(t) = \sup_{t \in Q} m_{\mathcal{J}(h)}(A;Q) \ge m_{\mathcal{J}(h)}(A;P) \ge m + \varepsilon ,$$

which contradicts the choice of m .

We conclude that the complement of $\overline{Y}$ is an open and closed neighborhood of X on which dim E $\ge$ h . By a similar argument using the set where dim E $< \aleph_0$, we obtain an open and closed neighborhood Z of X on which dim E $\ge$ h and dim E $\ge \aleph_0$. Furthermore, on $\Omega \setminus Z$, $\tilde{i}(A) = \tilde{g}$. By 11.11, we have for $Q = \chi_Z$, that $Q \dim E = Q \dim F$.

Now to define B: by passing to a central summand, we can assume $g \le 0$ (in the other summand just reverse the roles of E and F in the following construction). Now, QE is properly infinite, and on Z we have that

$$|g| \le h \le \dim E = \dim F .$$

Hence there is a partial isometry W in $\mathcal{A}$ with $W^*W = QE$, $WW^* \le QF$, and with

$$\dim (QF - WW^*) = \chi_Z |g|$$

(W is constructed as is the coisometry in the proof of 7.5). Set

$$B = (I - Q)A + QA(I - E) + \varepsilon W .$$

The ranges of these three summands are orthogonal, as are the initial spaces. On $\Omega\setminus Z$, $\tilde{i}(B) = \tilde{i}(A) = \tilde{g}$. On the range of Q, $QA(I - E)$ maps the range of $Q(I - E)$ one-to-one and onto the range of $Q(I - F)$, and εW maps the range of QE one-to-one onto the range of WW^*. Thus on Z,

$$i(B) = -\dim (QF - WW^*) = g .$$

Thus $\tilde{i}(B) = \tilde{g}$, and

$$\|A - B\| \le \|QAE - \varepsilon W\| \le m + 2\varepsilon .$$

The proof is complete.

COROLLARY 12.15. *Let* $A \in \mathfrak{A}$. *The distance from* A *to the group of invertible elements of* $\mathfrak{A}$ *is the larger of*

$$\sup_X \mu_{\mathcal{K}(i(A))}(A) \quad \text{and} \quad \sup_X \mu_{\mathcal{K}(i(A))}(A^*)$$

with X *being the closure of the set where* $i(A) \neq 0$.

PROOF. Apply the theorem for $\mathcal{J} = \{0\}$.

THEOREM 12.16. *An element* A *of* $\mathfrak{A}$ *is in the closure of every component of the semi-Fredholm elements for* $\mathcal{J}$ *if and only if*

$$\mu_{\mathcal{J}+\mathcal{R}}(A) = 0 = \mu_{\mathcal{J}+\mathcal{R}}(A^*)$$

where $\mathcal{R}$ *is the strong radical of* $\mathfrak{A}$.

PROOF. Observe first that $\mathcal{J} + \mathcal{R} = \mathcal{J}(k)$ where $k = \dim I_{\mathfrak{A}}$: by 11.7,

$$\dim \mathcal{R} = \{f \in C_c(\Omega) : 0 \le f < k \ \text{ a.e.}\} .$$

Hence $\mathcal{R} \subset \mathcal{J}(k)$, and $\mathcal{J} \subset \mathcal{J}(k)$, so $\mathcal{J} + \mathcal{R} \subset \mathcal{J}(k)$. It is easy to see that if F is a projection in $\mathcal{J}(k)$, then $F \in \mathcal{J} + \mathcal{R}$: write $\dim F = f_1 + f_2$, $f_1 f_2 = 0$, where $f_1 < k$ a.e., and $f_2 = k$ on some open and closed set.

There is a corresponding central decomposition of $F = F_1 \oplus F_2$ where $F_1 \in \mathcal{R}$, and F_2 is a central projection in $\mathcal{J}(k)$ and hence in $\mathcal{J}$: thus $\mathcal{J}(k) \subset \mathcal{J} + \mathcal{R}$.

Suppose $\mu_{\mathcal{J}(k)}(A) = 0 = \mu_{\mathcal{J}(k)}(A^*)$. For $g \in C_c(\Omega)$, set $h = |i(A)| \vee |g|$. Then for any central projection P , $P\mathcal{J}(k) \supseteq P\mathcal{J}(h)$, and $P \in \mathcal{J}(k)$ implies $P \in \mathcal{J}$, so we can conclude

$$m_{\mathcal{J}(k)}(P;A) \geq m_{\mathcal{J}(h)}(P;A) ,$$

thus $\mu_{\mathcal{J}(k)}(A) \geq \mu_{\mathcal{J}(h)}(A)$, and similarly for A^* . So $\operatorname{dist}(A, \mathcal{S}_{\tilde{g}}) = 0$ by the Theorem 12.14.

Conversely, suppose A is a limit point of every semi-Fredholm component for $\mathcal{J}$. We can choose $g \in C_c(\Omega)$ with $g \neq i(A)$ a.e. and such that $|g| = \dim I_{\mathfrak{a}}$: thus $|i(A)| \vee |g| = \dim I_{\mathfrak{a}} = k$. Let

$$X = \{\lambda \in \Omega: \tilde{i}(A)_\lambda \neq \tilde{g}_\lambda\} ,$$

where $\tilde{i}$ is the index for $\mathcal{J}$. Since $\operatorname{dist}(A, \mathcal{S}_{\tilde{g}}) = 0$, then 12.14 implies

$$\mu_{\mathcal{J}(k)}(A) = 0 = \mu_{\mathcal{J}(k)}(A^*)$$

on the set X . If $t \notin X$, then there is a central projection $P = \chi_Y$ with $t \in Y$ and with $\tilde{i}(A) = \tilde{g}$ on Y . Thus $\chi_Y(g - i(A)) \in \mathbb{J}$ and

$$\dim P = \chi_Y \dim I_{\mathfrak{a}} = \chi_Y |g| = \chi_Y |g - i(A)|$$

which implies $P \in \mathcal{J}$. Then $P \in \mathcal{J}(k)$, and so $\mu_{\mathcal{J}(k)}(A)(t) = 0 = \mu_{\mathcal{J}(k)}(A^*)(t)$ by 12.4. The proof is complete.

REMARK 12.17. Note that if $\mathcal{J}$ contains no central projections, then $\mathcal{J} + \mathcal{R} = \mathcal{R}$: for, if $f \in \dim \mathcal{J}$ with $f = \dim I_{\mathfrak{a}}$ on some open and closed, $X \subset \Omega$, then χ_X is a central projection in $\mathcal{J}$.

THEOREM 12.18. <u>Let</u> $\mathcal{J}$ <u>be a compact ideal and let</u> $A \in \mathfrak{a}$. <u>The following are equivalent</u>:

(i) A <u>is in the closure of at least two semi-Fredholm components</u>,

(ii) <u>there is a central projection</u> P <u>on which</u>

$$\mu_{\mathcal{J}(i(A))}(A) = 0 = \mu_{\mathcal{J}(i(A))}(A^*) .$$

PROOF. Denote $i(A)$ by f: we know A is a limit point of $\mathcal{S}_f$.

To show (ii) implies (i), assume that $P = \chi_X$ satisfies (ii). If $\chi_X f \notin \dim \mathcal{J}$, set $g = \chi_{\Omega\setminus X} f$. If $\chi_X f \in \dim \mathcal{J}$, then set $g = \chi_{\Omega\setminus X} f + \chi_X \aleph_o$. Either way, $\mathcal{J}(f) = \mathcal{J}(|f| \vee |g|)$, and $f \neq g$, with $f = g$ on $\Omega\setminus X$. Thus A is a limit point of $\mathcal{S}_g$ by 12.14, with $\mathcal{S}_g \neq \mathcal{S}_f$.

That (i) implies (ii): suppose A is a limit point of $\mathcal{S}_g$, with $g \neq f$, and let X be the open set where g and f differ. By 12.14, $\mu_{\mathcal{J}(h)}(A) = 0 = \mu_{\mathcal{J}(h)}(A^*)$ on all of X, where $h = |f| \vee |g|$. Now, $\mathcal{J}$ contains no central projections, and hence neither do $\mathcal{J}(f)$ nor $\mathcal{J}(h)$. For $t \in X$, if $t \in Q$, for Q a central projection, then

$$m_{\mathcal{J}(h)}(A;Q) \geq m_{\mathcal{J}(f)}(A;Q) ,$$

and similarly for A^* by 11.2. It follows that $\mu_{\mathcal{J}(f)}(A) = 0 = \mu_{\mathcal{J}(f)}(A^*)$ on X. There is a central projection P whose support is contained in X, so the result follows.

EXAMPLE 12.19. The following example shows that the result above is not true in general for other ideals (even if one makes an obviously indicated change in (ii) to require $P \notin \mathcal{J}$).

Let $\mathcal{A}$ and $\mathcal{J}$ be as in Example 8.4. Define $\{A_n\}_n = A$ in $\mathcal{A}$ by

$$A_n = \frac{1}{n} U \oplus (I - U^*U) ,$$

where U is a unilateral shift of multiplicity 1 on a separable subspace of $\mathcal{H}_n$, for each n. Then $i(U) = -1$ on all of $\beta\mathbb{N}$, and $\mathcal{J}(-1) = \mathcal{J}$. Furthermore, for each integer n,

$$\mu_{\mathcal{J}}(A)(n) = m_{\mathcal{J}}(A;\chi_{\{n\}}) = 1 .$$

For any central projection $P = \chi_X$, X must contain some integer, so (ii) cannot hold. However, (i) does hold: note that

$$-\tilde{1} = \{g \in C_c(\beta\mathbb{N}): |-1 - g| \leq \aleph_o \text{, and } g = -1 \text{ except for finitely many } n\}$$

$$\tilde{0} = \{g \in C_c(\beta\mathbb{N}): |g| \leq \aleph_o \text{, and } g = 0 \text{ except for finitely many } n\} .$$

Thus $\mathcal{S}_{-\tilde{1}} \neq \mathcal{S}_{\tilde{0}}$, and A is a limit point of $\mathcal{S}_{-\tilde{1}}$. But A is also a limit point of $\mathcal{S}_{\tilde{0}}$: $A = \lim V_M$ where V_M equals A, except that for all $n > M$, the summand $1/n\, U$ is replaced by a zero summand. It is clear that

$\tilde{i}(V_M) = \tilde{0}$, for all M .

It seems likely that (ii) implies (i) is also false in general; this is suggested by such examples as 8.5.

For compact ideals, our results on limit points on $\mathcal{S}$ can be coherently summarized:

THEOREM 12.20. *Let* $\mathcal{J}$ *be a compact ideal. If* $A \in \mathcal{A}$ *with* $i(A) = f$, *then* A *is a limit point of* $\mathcal{S}_f$ *and*

(i) A *is not a limit point of* $\mathcal{S}\backslash\mathcal{S}_f$ *if and only if for every* $\lambda \in \Omega$ *one of* $\mu_{\mathcal{J}(f)}(A)$ *and* $\mu_{\mathcal{J}(f)}(A^*)$ *is nonzero.*

(ii) A *is a limit point of* $\mathcal{S}_g$ *for some* $g \neq f$ *if and only if* $\mu_{\mathcal{J}(f)}(A) = 0 = \mu_{\mathcal{J}(f)}(A^*)$ *on some open subset of* Ω .

(iii) A *is a limit point of every* $\mathcal{S}_g$, $g \in C_c(\Omega)$, *if and only if*

$$\mu_{\mathcal{R}}(A) = 0 = \mu_{\mathcal{R}}(A^*) .$$

PROOF. Part (i) describes the situation in which A is a point of continuity for the index i : this occurs precisely when A is semi-Fredholm for $\mathcal{J}(f)$ by 11.10. Thus (i) follows from 12.8. Parts (ii) and (iii) are 12.16, 12.17, and 12.18.

EXAMPLE 12.21. This theorem implies that if the zeros of $\mu_{\mathcal{J}(f)}(A) + \mu_{\mathcal{J}(f)}(A^*)$ form a nonempty nowhere dense subset of Ω then A will not be a limit point of any component $\mathcal{S}_g$ with $g \neq i(A)$; but on the other hand then A must be a limit point of some infinite union of components.

It is easy to construct a natrual example which indicates that this is a common occurrence. Let $\mathcal{A}$ and $\mathcal{K}$ be as in Example 8.1. Define $\{A_n\}_n = A$ in $\mathcal{A}$ by

$$A_n = \frac{1}{n} U^n \oplus (I - U^*U) ,$$

where U is a unilateral shift of multiplicity 1 on a separable subspace of $\mathcal{H}_n$, for each n . Here $i(A) = \{-n\}_n$ is finite a.e. on $\beta\mathbb{N}$, so $\mathcal{K}(i(A)) = \mathcal{K}$. And, for $n \in \mathbb{N}$,

$$\mu_{\mathcal{K}}(A)(n) = m_{\mathcal{K}}(A;\chi_{\{n\}}) = \frac{1}{n} .$$

Thus A is not a limit point of any $\mathcal{S}_g$ for $g \neq i(A)$. However, $A = \lim B_M$

for B_M semi-Fredholm each $M = 1,2,\ldots$ where $B_M = \{B_{M_n}\}_n$,

$$B_{M_n} = \begin{cases} A_n & n \le M \\ \frac{1}{n} U^*U \oplus (I - U^*U) & n > M , \end{cases}$$

(U as in definition of A_n) so

$$i(B_M) = \{-1,\ldots,-M,0,0,\ldots\} .$$

REFERENCES

1. F. V. Atkinson, "The normal solubility of linear equations in normal spaces." Math. Sbornik N. S. 28 (70), (1951), 3-14 (Russian).

2. B. A. Barnes, "The Fredholm elements of a ring," Canadian J. Math. 21 (1969), 84-95.

3. M. Breuer, "Fredholm theories in von Neumann algebras I," Math. Ann. 178 (1968), 243-254.

4. ________, "Fredholm theories in von Neumann algebras II," Math. Ann. 180 (1969), 313-325.

5. ________, "Theory of Fredholm operators and vector bundles relative to a von Neumann algebra," Rocky Mountain J. Math., 3 (1973), 383-429.

6. ________, and R. S. Butcher, "Fredholm theories of mixed type with analytic index functions," Math. Ann., 209 (1974), 31-42.

7. S. R. Caradus, W. E. Pfaffenburger, and B. Yood, Calkin algebras and algebras of operators on Banach spaces, Marcel Dekker, New York: 1974.

8. L. A. Coburn and A. Lebow, "Algebraic theory of Fredholm operators," J. Math. and Mech., 15 (1966), 577-583.

9. ___________, R. G. Douglas, D. G. Schaeffer, and I. M. Singer, "C^*-algebras of operators on a half-space II: index theory," Inst. Haut Etude Sci. Publ. Math., 40 (1971), 69-79.

10. H. O. Cordes and J. P. Labrousse, "The invariance of the index in the metric space of closed operators," J. Math. and Mech., 12 (1963), 693-720.

11. J. Dixmier, "Etude sur les varietes et les operateurs de Julia, avec quelques applications," Bull. Soc. Math. France 77 (1949), 11-101.

12. _________, "Sur certains espaces considérés par M. H. Stone," Summa Brasil Math., 2 (11), (1951), 151-182.

13. _________, Les C^*-algèbres et leur représentations, Gauthier-Villars, Paris: 1969.

14. R. G. Douglas, Banach Algebra Techniques in Operator Theory, Academic Press, New York: 1972.

15. E. G. Effros, Dimensions and C^*-algebras, C.B.M.S. Regional Conf. Series in Mathematics, to appear.

16. K. E. Ekman, "Indices on C^*-algebras through representations in the Calkin algebra," Duke J. Math., 41 (1974), 413-432.

17. J. Feldman and R. V. Kadison, "The closure of the regular operators in a ring of operators," Proc. Amer. Math. Soc., 5 (1954), 909-916.

18. M. Gartenberg, "Extensions of the index in factors of type II_∞," Proc. Amer. Math. Soc., 43 (1974), 163-168.

19. V. Kaftal, "On the theory of compact operators in von Neumann algebras I," Indiana U. Math. J., 26 (1977), 447-457.

20. ________, "On the theory of compact operators in von Neumann algebras II," Pacific J. Math., 79 (1978), 129-137.

21. ________, "Relative weak convergence in W^*-algebras," preprint.

22. ________, "Classes of almost Fredholm operators in von Neumann algebras," preprint.

23. C. L. Olsen, "Approximation by unitary elements in a von Neumann algebra," preprint.

24. M. J. O'Neill, "Semi-Fredholm operators in von Neumann algebras," University of Kansas Technical Report No. 21 (New Series).

25. D. D. Rogers, "Approximation by unitary and essentially unitary operators," Acta Sci. Math. (Szeged), 39 (1977), 141-151.

26. J. Rosenberg, "Homological invariants of extensions of C^*-algebras," to appear in the Proceedings of the Amer. Math. Soc. Summer Institute on Operator Algebras and Applications, Kingston 1980.

27. S. Sakai, C^*-algebras and W^*-algebras, Springer-Verlag, New York: 1971.

28. Helmut H. Schaefer, Banach lattices and positive operators, Springer-Verlag, New York: 1974.

29. D. G. Schaeffer, "An application of von Neumann algebras to finite difference equations," Ann. Math., 95 (1972), 116-129.

30. M. R. F. Smyth, "Fredholm theory in Banach algebras," Trinity College Dublin preprint, 1975.

31. J. L. Taylor, "Banach algebras and topology," Algebras in Analysis, J. H. Williamson, ed., Academic Press, London-New York, 1975, 118-186.

32. J. Tomiyama, "Generalized dimension function for W^*-algebras of infinite type," Tokoku Math. J., 10 (1958), 121-129.

33. W. Wils, "Two-sided ideals in W^*-algebras," J. fur die Reine und Angewandte Math., 242-4 (1970), 55-68.

34. F. B. Wright, "A reduction for algebras of finite type," Ann. Math., 60 (1954) 560-570.

State University of New York at Buffalo

General instructions to authors for
PREPARING REPRODUCTION COPY FOR MEMOIRS

For more detailed instructions send for AMS booklet, "A Guide for Authors of Memoirs." Write to Editorial Offices, American Mathematical Society, P. O. Box 6248, Providence, R. I. 02940.

MEMOIRS are printed by photo-offset from camera copy fully prepared by the author. This means that, except for a reduction in size of 20 to 30%, the finished book will look exactly like the copy submitted. Thus the author will want to use a good quality typewriter with a new, medium-inked black ribbon, and submit clean copy on the appropriate model paper.

Model Paper, provided at no cost by the AMS, is paper marked with blue lines that confine the copy to the appropriate size. Author should specify, when ordering, whether typewriter to be used has PICA-size (10 characters to the inch) or ELITE-size type (12 characters to the inch).

Line Spacing – For best appearance, and economy, a typewriter equipped with a half-space ratchet – 12 notches to the inch – should be used. (This may be purchased and attached at small cost.) Three notches make the desired spacing, which is equivalent to 1-1/2 ordinary single spaces. Where copy has a great many subscripts and superscripts, however, double spacing should be used.

Special Characters may be filled in carefully freehand, using dense black ink, or INSTANT ("rub-on") LETTERING may be used. AMS has a sheet of several hundred most-used symbols and letters which may be purchased for $5.

Diagrams may be drawn in black ink either directly on the model sheet, or on a separate sheet and pasted with rubber cement into spaces left for them in the text. Ballpoint pen is *not* acceptable.

Page Headings (Running Heads) should be centered, in CAPITAL LETTERS (preferably), at the top of the page – just above the blue line and touching it.

LEFT-hand, EVEN-numbered pages should be headed with the AUTHOR'S NAME;

RIGHT-hand, ODD-numbered pages should be headed with the TITLE of the paper (in shortened form if necessary).

Exceptions: PAGE 1 and any other page that carries a display title require NO RUNNING HEADS.

Page Numbers should be at the top of the page, on the same line with the running heads.

LEFT-hand, EVEN numbers – flush with left margin;

RIGHT-hand, ODD numbers – flush with right margin.

Exceptions: PAGE 1 and any other page that carries a display title should have page number, centered below the text, on blue line provided.

FRONT MATTER PAGES should be numbered with Roman numerals (lower case), positioned below text in same manner as described above.

MEMOIRS FORMAT

It is suggested that the material be arranged in pages as indicated below.
Note: <u>Starred items</u> (*) <u>are requirements of publication.</u>

Front Matter (first pages in book, preceding main body of text).

Page i – *Title, *Author's name.

Page iii – Table of contents.

Page iv – *Abstract (at least 1 sentence and at most 300 words).

*1980 Mathematics Subject Classifications represent the primary and secondary subjects of the paper. For the classification scheme, see Annual Subject Indexes of MATHEMATICAL REVIEWS beginning in December 1978.

Key words and phrases, if desired. (A list which covers the content of the paper adequately enough to be useful for an information retrieval system.)

Page v, etc. – Preface, introduction, or any other matter not belonging in body of text.

Page 1 – Chapter Title (dropped 1 inch from top line, and centered).

Beginning of Text.

Footnotes: *Received by the editor date.
Support information – grants, credits, etc.

Last Page (at bottom) – Author's affiliation.

ABCDEFGHIJ–AMS–8987654